SCHOEN

THE
ESSENTIALS OF
RISK
MANAGEMENT

THE
ESSENTIALS OF
RISK
MANAGEMENT

SECOND EDITION

MICHEL CROUHY, DAN GALAI, ROBERT MARK

New York   Chicago   San Francisco   Athens
London   Madrid   Mexico City   Milan
New Delhi   Singapore   Sydney   Toronto

2 3 4 5 6 7 8 9 0   DOC/DOC   1 9 8 7 6 5 4

ISBN   978-0-07-181851-3
MHID   0-07-181851-0

e-ISBN   978-0-07-182115-5
e-MHID   0-07-182115-5

This publication is designed to provide accurate and authoritative information in regard to the subject matter covered. It is sold with the understanding that neither the author nor the publisher is engaged in rendering legal, accounting, securities trading, or other professional services. If legal advice or other expert assistance is required, the services of a competent professional person should be sought.
> —From a Declaration of Principles Jointly Adopted by a Committee of the American Bar Association and a Committee of Publishers and Associations

Library of Congress Cataloging-in-Publication Data

Crouhy, Michel, 1944-
    The essentials of risk management / Michel Crouhy, Dan Galai, and Robert Mark. — Second edition.
        pages   cm
    ISBN 978-0-07-181851-3 (hardback) — ISBN 0-07-181851-0 (hardback)
1. Risk management.   I. Galai, Dan.   II. Mark, Robert (Robert M.)   III. Title.
    HD61.C773 2013
    658.15'5—dc23   2013034208

CONTENTS

FOREWORD

The world changed after the global financial crisis of 2007–2009, and the change was especially dramatic for banks. The second edition of this book is therefore very welcome and helps to clarify both the implications of the crisis for risk management and the far-reaching process of regulatory change that will come into full force over the next few years.

Banks are reforming their risk management processes, but the challenge goes much deeper. Banks must rethink their business models and even question the reason for their existence. Do they exist to take proprietary risks (on or off their balance sheet) or to provide a focused set of services and skills to their customers and business partners?

At Natixis, our business adopts the latter model. We have recently completed an aggressive push to adapt to post-crisis regulatory constraints, end our proprietary activities, reduce our risk profile, and refocus on our three core businesses: wholesale banking, investment solutions, and specialized financial services.

The far higher capital costs under Basel III are likely to shift many other banks toward a more service-based business model with less risk retained. The new regulations are also obliging banks to change their funding strategies—e.g., by making use of new funding tools in addition to reformed approaches to securitization and traditional funding avenues.

This change of philosophy may mean developing trusted partnerships with different kinds of financial institutions, such as insurance companies and pension funds, that can absorb the risks that banks no longer wish to carry on their balance sheets—a process that Natixis has already begun.

As banks change their approach, they must also take a fresh look at their corporate governance. The crisis showed that banks had been driven by too simplistic a notion of growth and short-term profitability. Going forward, firms must build a wider and longer-term view of stakeholder interests—e.g., by defining long-term risk appetites explicitly and connecting these securely to strategic and operational decisions. Ensuring the right kind of growth will require many of the best-practice mechanisms of corporate governance discussed in this book.

The crisis also showed that banks need to pay more than lip service to the concept of enterprise risk management. They must improve their understanding of how a wide range of risks—credit, market, liquidity, operational, reputation, and more—can interact with and exacerbate each other in a bank's portfolios and business models when the financial system is under strain.

In turn, this requires the development of new risk management methodologies and bankwide infrastructures—for example, in the area of macroeconomic stress testing. One of the accomplishments of this book is that it helps set out these new methodologies and explains their strengths and also their limitations. The authors believe that financial institutions must not rely on any single risk measure, new or old. Risk measurement and management methodologies are there to help decision makers, not to supply simplistic answers.

It is critical that institutions (as well as regulators) develop a better understanding of the interconnected nature of the global financial system. As this book explains in its various chapters, systemic risks, counterparty interconnections, liquidity risks, credit risks, and market risks all feed on one another in a crisis. Understanding how risks concentrate during good times and then spread through systemic interconnections during bad times needs to become part of the philosophy of bank risk management. Without this understanding, it is difficult for financial institutions to resist activities that boost growth and profitability in the short term, but that may create unsustainable levels of risk in the longer term.

The global economy is trying to find a path toward sustainable growth at the same time that developed nations have begun to unwind the unprecedented support given to economies and banking systems during the crisis years. This will give rise to many challenges as well as opportunities. Natixis plays a frontline role in financing the real economy, but we know that this must be built on solid risk-managed foundations.

In this sense, the book supports the business philosophy we are developing at Natixis. We believe that long-term success comes to institutions and economies that can deliver growth while managing downside risks through *both* improved risk management and the careful selection of fundamental business models.

Laurent Mignon
Chief Executive Officer of Natixis
September 13, 2013

FOREWORD

I think that the concept of the Crouhy, Galai, and Mark book, *The Essentials of Risk Management*, Second Edition, is brilliant. In my career as an academic and in investment management, I found that there is too large a separation between the technocrats who build risk-management models and systems and those who should be using them. In addition, the model builders seem to me to be too far from economics, understanding what risk management can and cannot do and how to structure the risk management problem. Crouhy, Galai, and Mark bridge that gap. They bring the academic research together with applications and implementation. If risk-management model builders come to appreciate the economics underlying the models, they would be better prepared to build risk-management tools that have real value for banks and other entities. And, as the authors bring up time and again, board members of corporations must also become as familiar with the models and their underlying economics to ask the correct follow-up questions.

Risk management is often described as being an independent activity of the firm, different from generating returns. Most macro and micro models in economics start from a framework of certainty and add an error term, a risk term to represent uncertainty. When describing predicted actions that arise from these models, the error or uncertainty term disappears because the modelers assume that it's best to take expectations as their best guess as to future outcomes.

In both cases, however, this is incorrect. Risk management is part of an optimization program, the tradeoffs between risk and return. As described in the book, the three tools of risk management are (a) reserves, (b) diversification, and (c) insurance. With greater reserves against adverse outcomes, the risk of the firm or the bank is reduced. Greater reserves, however, imply lower returns. And, the dynamics of the reserve need to be known. For example, if a bank needs capital or liquidity reserves to shield it against shock, is the reserve static or can it be used, and how is it to be used at time of shock? If it is a reserve that must always be at a static level, it is not a reserve at all. These are important optimization and planning questions under uncertainty. With more diversification, the bank reduces idiosyncratic risks and retains systematic risks, which it might also transfer to the market.

Diversification has benefits. But, if a bank earns profits because its clients want particular services such as mortgages, it might want to concentrate and make money by taking on additional idiosyncratic risk, for it is not possible to diversify away all risks and still earn abnormal profits. The bank must respond to its client's demands and, as a result, take on idiosyncratic risks. The same is true of insurance. Unlike car insurance, wherein, say, the value of the car is knowable over the year, and the amount of the insurance is easy to ascertain, as the book describes, the bank might not know how much insurance is necessary and when it might need the insurance. Nor does it know the dynamics of the insurance plan as prices change in the market.

That is why risk management is integrated into an optimization system where there always are tradeoffs between risk and return. To ignore risk considerations is inappropriate; to concentrate on risk is inappropriate. The boards of banks or corporations are responsible to understand and challenge the optimization problem. Likewise, modelers must also understand the economic tradeoffs. Prior to the financial crisis of 2008, many banks organized their risk management activities in line and not circle form. That is, the risk department was separate and below the production department. The risk management systems of the future must be designed such that the optimization problem is the center focus. This involves deciding on the level of capital employed not only for working capital, or physical investment capital, or human capital but also the amount of risk capital in deciding on the profitability of various business lines and how they coordinate with each other.

Risk management involves measurement and model building. This book provides us with a description of many of the problems in building models and in providing the inputs to the models. But, once the senior management and the modelers understand the issues, they will change their focus and address the modeling and measurement issues. For example, there are three major problems in the model building/data provision or calibration of the model framework: (1) using historical data to calibrate the model, (2) assuming the spatial relationships will remain unchanged, such as how particular assets are grouped together into clusters or how clusters move together, and, (3) assuming that once the model is built and calibrated that others don't reverse engineer the model and its calibration and game against those using the model. There are myriad examples and applications of each of these, or these in combination with each other in this book. For example, the rating agencies used historical data to calibrate the likelihood of declines in housing price such that homeowners would default on their mortgages. Unfortunately they used too short a time period and assumed incorrectly that the best prediction of the future would be provided from these short-period data inputs. They also assumed that homeowners default on their mortgages randomly, while ignoring the possibility that the independent clusters of possible mortgage defaults that they assumed existed would become one cluster during a crisis such as the 2008 financial crisis. Moreover, once they provided their ratings on complicated mortgage structured products, market participants reverse engineered how they rated mortgage products and gamed against them by putting lower and lower quality mortgages into structures to pass just the ratings level that they wanted to attain. These three lessons are pervasive in risk management and are illustrated brilliantly in one form or the other over and over again in this book.

There are decisions that should be made, in part, proactively and decisions that should be made, in part, reactively. Risk management includes an understanding of how to plan to respond to changes in the opportunity set and to changes in the costs of adjusting assets and to financing activities. There is a value in planning for uncertainty. Ignoring risk might supply large short-term profits but at the expense of survivorship of the business, for not setting aside sufficient risk capital threatens survivorship of the business. And understanding includes evaluating the returns and risks of embedded and explicit options.

All risk management systems require a careful combination of academic modeling and research with practical applications. Academic research highlighted in this book has made a major contribution to risk management techniques. Practice must be aware of the underlying assumptions of these models and in what situations they apply or don't apply and adjust them accordingly. Practical applications include understanding data issues in providing inputs to these risk models and in calibrating them consistent with underlying economics. The 2008 crisis highlighted once again the importance of risk management. I believe that all board members must become as conversant in risk management as in return generation. That will become a prerequisite for board participation. This book highlights the importance of these issues.

Myron S. Scholes, Frank E. Buck Professor of Finance, Emeritus, Stanford University Graduate School of Business; 1997 recipient of the Nobel Prize in Economics
November, 2013

INTRODUCTION TO THE SECOND EDITION: REFORMING RISK MANAGEMENT FOR THE POST-CRISIS ERA

Half a dozen years and more have passed since the start of the global financial crisis of 2007–2009,[1] and even the European sovereign debt crisis of 2010 is fading into history. In neither case can we be sure that the crises are fully resolved, and their aftershocks and ramifications continue to shape our world. However, enough time may have elapsed for us to absorb the main lessons of the crisis years and to begin to understand the implications of the still unfolding reforms of the world's financial industries.

In this new edition of *The Essentials of Risk Management*, we have revisited each chapter in light of what has been learned from risk management failures during the crisis years, and in this Introduction we pick out key trends in risk management since we published the first edition in 2006.

However, we have also tried to prevent the book as a whole from becoming too dominated by the extraordinary events of 2007–2009 and the immediate succeeding years. Some of the lessons learned in those years were lessons that earlier crises had already taught risk managers, and that

---

[1]Throughout this book, we've used the phrase "financial crisis of 2007–2009" to define, reasonably precisely, the banking and financial system crisis of that period. Others choose to use the term "global financial crisis," or GFC.

were covered in some detail in the first edition of the book—even if some firms found it hard to put them into practice. The crisis years also spawned a series of fundamental reforms of the regulation of financial institutions, and one thing we can be sure of in risk management is that major structural change creates new business environments, which in turn transform business behavior and risk.

One of the curses of risk management is that it perennially tries to micromanage the last crisis rather than applying the first principles of risk management to forestall the next—a trap we have tried to avoid.

We hope this book contributes to the attempt to strengthen the overall framework of risk management by encouraging the right mix of theoretical expertise, knowledge of recent and past events, and curiosity about what might be driving risk trends *today*.

***

The financial crisis that started in the summer of 2007 was the culmination of an exceptional boom in credit growth and leverage in the financial system that had been building since the previous credit crisis in 2001–2002, stimulated by an accommodative monetary policy. The boom was fed by an extended period of benign economic and financial conditions, including low real interest rates and abundant liquidity, which encouraged borrowers, investors, and intermediaries to increase their exposure in terms of risk and leverage. The boom years were also marked by a wave of financial innovations related to securitization, which expanded the capacity of the financial system to generate credit assets but outpaced its capacity to manage the associated risks.[2]

The crisis uncovered major fault lines in business practices and market dynamics: failures of risk management and poorly aligned compensation systems in financial institutions, failures of transparency and disclosure, and many more. In the years following the crisis, many areas of weakness have begun to be addressed through regulation and from the very top of financial institutions (the board of directors and the management committee) down to business line practices, including the misalignment of incentives between the business and its shareholders, bondholders, and investors. Below, we

---

[2]Securitization and structured credit products are discussed in Chapter 12.

summarize some of the major problem areas uncovered by the global financial crisis; the rest of the book addresses these issues in more detail.

Governance and Risk Culture

Risk management has many different components, but the essence of what went wrong in the run-up to the 2007–2009 financial crisis had more to do with the lack of solid corporate governance structures for risk management than with the technical deficiencies of risk measurement and stress testing. In the boom period, risk management was marginalized in many financial institutions. The focus on deal flow, business volume, earnings, and compensation schemes drove firms increasingly to treat risk management as a source of information, not as an integral part of business decision making. Decisions were taken on risk positions without the debate that needed to happen. To some degree, this is a matter of risk culture, but it also has to do with governance structures inside organizations:

- *The role of the board must be strengthened.* Strengthening board oversight of risk does not diminish the fundamental responsibility of management for the risk management process. Instead, it should make sure that risk management receives some enhanced attention in terms of oversight and, hopefully, a longer-term and wider perspective. Chapter 4 on corporate governance elaborates on the role and obligations of the board.
- *Risk officers must be re-empowered.* Some firms distinguish between a "risk control" function, responsible for quantitative measures, and a "risk management" function, which has a more strategic focus. Either way, it is no longer appropriate for risk management to be only an "after the fact" monitoring function. It needs to be included in the development of the firm's strategy and business model. Chief risk officers (CROs) should not be just risk managers but also proactive risk strategists. With the strength of regulators and an angry public behind them, risk managers presently wield some clout. The trick will be to make sure this lasts in periods of recovery (or growing corporate frustration with unexciting returns). Chapter 4 elaborates on the role of the CRO in a best-practice institution.

Inadequate Execution of the Originate-to-Distribute Business Model

One common view is that the crisis was caused by the originate-to-distribute (OTD) model of securitization, through which lower quality loans were transformed into highly rated securities. To some extent, this characterization is unfortunately true.

The OTD model of securitization reduced incentives for the originator of the loan to monitor the creditworthiness of the borrower, because the originator had little or no skin in the game. In the securitization food chain for U.S. mortgages, intermediaries in the chain made fees while transferring credit into an investment product with such an opaque structure that even the most sophisticated investors had no real idea what they were holding.

Although the pre-crisis OTD model of securitization, and its lack of checks and balances, was clearly an important factor, the huge losses that affected banks, especially investment banks, mainly occurred because financial institutions *did not follow the business model of securitization*. Rather than acting as intermediaries by transferring the risk from mortgage lenders to capital market investors, these institutions themselves took on the role of investors. Chapter 12 elaborates on this issue.

Poor Underwriting Standards

The OTD model generated a huge demand for loans to feed the securitization machine, and this in itself contributed to a lowering of underwriting standards. But benign macroeconomic conditions and low default rates also gave rise to complacency and an erosion of sound practices in the world's financial industries. Across a range of credit segments, business volumes grew much more quickly than investment in the supporting infrastructure of controls and documentation. The demand for high-yielding assets encouraged a loosening of credit standards and, particularly in the U.S. subprime mortgage market, not just lax but fraudulent practices proliferated from late 2004. Chapter 9 elaborates further on the issue of retail risk management.

Shortcomings in Firms' Risk Management Practices

The crisis highlighted the risk of model error when making risk assessments. The risk control/risk management function must become more transparent about the limitations of risk metrics and models used to make important decisions in the firm. Models are powerful tools, but they necessarily involve simplifications and assumptions; they must be approached critically and with a heavy dash of expert judgment. When risk metrics, models, and ratings become ends in themselves, they become obstacles to true risk identification. This applies also to the post-crisis rash of new models and risk assessment procedures. Chapter 15 analyzes the problems associated with model risk.

- *Stress testing and scenario analysis.* Stress testing, discussed in Chapter 16, is now a formal requirement of Basel III and the Dodd-Frank Act and has become a much more prominent part of the risk manager's toolkit. Properly applied, stress testing is a critical diagnostic and risk identification tool, but it can be counterproductive if it becomes too mechanical or consumes resources unproductively. It is important to approach stress testing as one aspect of a multifaceted risk analysis program. In particular, stress testing must be carefully designed to gauge the business strengths and weaknesses of each individual firm; it cannot follow a "one size fits all" approach. Firms need to ensure that stress testing methodologies and policies are consistently applied throughout the firm, take into account multiple risk factors, and adequately deal with correlations between risk factors. Results must have a meaningful impact on business decisions.
- *Concentration risk.* Firms need to improve their firmwide management of concentration risks, embracing not only large risks from individual borrowers but also concentrations in sectors, geographic regions, economic factors, counterparties, and financial guarantors. For example, a concentrated exposure to one (exotic) product can give rise to major losses during a market shock if liquidity dries up and it becomes impossible to rebalance a hedging position in a timely fashion.

- *Counterparty credit risk.* The subprime crisis highlighted several shortcomings of over-the-counter (OTC) trading in credit derivatives, most notably the treatment of counterparty credit risk. The primary issue is that collateral and margin requirements are set bilaterally in OTC trading and do not take account of the risk imposed on the rest of the system (e.g., as experienced following the failures of Lehman Brothers and the quasi-bankruptcies of Bear Stearns, AIG, and others). Counterparty credit risk is discussed in Chapter 13.

Overreliance on Misleading Ratings from Rating Agencies

Credit rating agencies were at the center of the 2007–2009 crisis, as many investors had relied on their ratings to assess the risk of mortgage bonds, asset-backed commercial paper issued by structured investment vehicles, and the monolines that insured municipal bonds and structured credit products.

Money market funds are restricted to investing in AAA-rated assets, while pension funds and municipalities are restricted to investing in investment-grade assets.[3] In the low interest rate environment of the period before the crisis, many of these conservative investors invested in assets that were complex and contained exposure to subprime assets, mainly because these instruments were given an investment-grade rating or higher while promising a yield above that of traditional assets, such as corporate and Treasury bonds, with an equivalent rating. Chapter 10 discusses ratings and the controversial role of the rating agencies.

Poor Investor Due Diligence

Many investors placed excessive reliance on credit ratings, neither questioning the methodologies of the credit rating agencies nor fully understanding the risk characteristics of rated products. Also, many investors

---

[3]Most of the US$2.5 trillion sitting in money market funds is traditionally invested in such assets as U.S. Treasury bills, certificates of deposit, and short-term commercial debt.

erroneously took comfort from the belief that insurance companies conducted a thorough investigation into the assets they insured.[4]

Going forward, institutional investors will have to upgrade their risk infrastructure in order to assess risk independently of external rating agencies. If institutions are not willing or able to do this, they should probably refrain from investing in complex structured products.

For U.S. retail investors who lack the knowledge and the tools to evaluate and make decisions about financial products, the Dodd-Frank Act creates the Bureau of Consumer Financial Protection (BCFP) as an independent bureau within the Federal Reserve System. However, it is by no means certain that more vigilant consumer protection would have prevented the speculative frenzy in the housing market in the run-up to the financial crisis. In Chapter 3, we discuss the Dodd-Frank Act in more detail.

Incentive Compensation Distortions

Incentive compensation should align compensation with long-term shareholder interests and risk-adjusted return on capital. Over the two decades before the 2007–2009 financial crisis, bankers and traders had increasingly been rewarded with bonuses tied to short-term profits, giving them an incentive to take excessive risks, leverage up their investments, and sometimes bet the entire bank on astonishingly reckless investment strategies. More on this topic in Chapter 4 and Chapter 17, where we discuss the RAROC (risk-adjusted return on capital) approach.

Weaknesses in Disclosure

Weaknesses in public disclosures by financial institutions, particularly concerning the type and magnitude of risks associated with on- and off-balance-sheet exposures, damaged market confidence during the 2007–2009 financial crisis. This remains a significant challenge to the world's

---

[4]Floyd Norris, "Insurer's Maneuver Wins a Pass in Court," *New York Times*, Business Section, March 8, 2013.

xxii • *Introduction to the Second Edition*

financial industries. The need to disclose more information is a requirement of Basel II/III, discussed in Chapter 3.

Valuation Problems in a Mark-to-Market World

Fair value/mark-to-market accounting has generally proven highly valuable in promoting transparency and market discipline and is an effective and reliable accounting method for securities in liquid markets. However, in secondary markets that may have no or severely limited liquidity, it can create serious valuation problems and can also increase the uncertainties around any valuations. Chapter 3 and the appendix to Chapter 1 elaborate further on this issue.

Liquidity Risk Management

During the boom years, many banks and other financial institutions allowed themselves to become vulnerable to any prolonged disruption in their funding markets. However, the 2007–2009 financial crisis demonstrated, once and for all, how extraordinarily dysfunctional the interbank funding market can become in times of uncertainty.

Liquidity risk is not a new threat: it lay behind the failure of LTCM (Long Term Capital Management) in August 1998, discussed in Chapter 15, and a number of historical bank failures. In the post-crisis era, however, risk managers will need to be wary of overdependence on any single form of funding, including access to securities markets, in their day-to-day liquidity risk management, stress testing, and contingency planning. As we discuss in Chapter 3, Basel III has introduced a new liquidity framework to address liquidity risk. Banks will have to satisfy two liquidity ratios—i.e., a liquidity coverage ratio (LCR) and a net stable funding ratio (NSFR). Chapter 8 discusses funding risk more broadly.

Systemic Risk

Of the many regulatory issues at stake in the post-crisis era, one is of primary importance: systemic risk. How can we construct a system that prevents decisions made in a single institution, or a small group of institutions, from plunging the world's economies into deep recession? Somehow, the system must be engineered to prevent one failure's causing a chain reaction or domino effect on other institutions that threatens the stability of the financial markets. Systemic risk and the regulators' efforts to prevent it is a recurring theme in the chapters of this book, especially Chapters 3 and 13.

Procyclicality

Banks are said to behave in a procyclical fashion when their actions amplify the momentum of the underlying economic cycle—e.g., by intensifying lending during economic booms or imposing more stringent restrictions or risk assessments on loans during a downturn. Procyclicality partly explains the correlations between asset prices that we see in the financial sector. The forces that contribute to procyclicality are the regulatory capital regime, risk measurement techniques such as value-at-risk, loan-loss provisioning practices, interaction between valuation and leverage, and compensation-based incentives. Basel III includes several mechanisms for mitigating procyclicality, such as a countercyclical capital cushion and reduced reliance on cyclical VaR-based capital requirements (e.g., by expanding the role of stress testing). Procyclicality is discussed in Chapter 3.

RISK MANAGEMENT:
A HELICOPTER VIEW[1]

The future cannot be predicted. It is uncertain, and no one has ever been successful in consistently forecasting the stock market, interest rates, exchange rates, or commodity prices—or credit, operational, and systemic events with major financial implications. However, the financial risk that arises from uncertainty can be managed. Indeed, much of what distinguishes modern economies from those of the past is the new ability to identify risk, to measure it, to appreciate its consequences, and then to take action accordingly, such as transferring or mitigating the risk. One of the most important aspects of modern risk management is the ability, in many instances, to price risks and ensure that risks undertaken in business activities are correctly rewarded.

This simple sequence of activities, shown in more detail in Figure 1-1, is often used to define risk management as a formal discipline. But it's a sequence that rarely runs smoothly in practice. Sometimes simply identifying a risk is the critical problem; at other times arranging an efficient economic transfer of the risk is the skill that makes one risk manager stand out from another. (In Chapter 2 we discuss the risk management process from the perspective of a corporation.)

To the unwary, Figure 1-1 might suggest that risk management is a continual process of corporate risk reduction. But we mustn't think of the modern attempt to master risk in defensive terms alone. Risk management is really about how firms actively select the type and level of risk that it is appropriate for them

---

[1]We acknowledge the coauthorship of Rob Jameson in this chapter.

FIGURE 1-1 The Risk Management Process

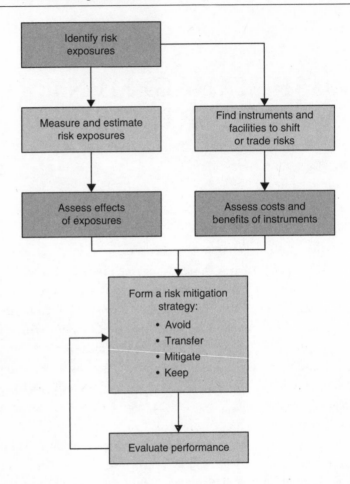

to assume. Most business decisions are about sacrificing current resources for future uncertain returns.

In this sense, *risk management* and *risk taking* aren't opposites, but two sides of the same coin. Together they drive all our modern economies. The capacity to make forward-looking choices about risk in relation to reward, and to evaluate performance, lies at the heart of the management process of all enduringly successful corporations.

Yet the rise of financial risk management as a formal discipline has been a bumpy affair, especially over the last 15 years. On the one hand, we have had some extraordinary successes in risk management mechanisms (e.g., the lack of financial institution bankruptcies in the downturn in credit quality in 2001–2002) and we have seen an extraordinary growth in new institutions that earn their keep by taking and managing risk (e.g., hedge funds). On the other hand, the spectacular failure to control risk in the run-up to the 2007–2009 financial crisis revealed fundamental weaknesses in the risk management process of many banks and the banking system as a whole.

As a result, risk management is now widely acknowledged as one of the most powerful forces in the world's financial markets, in both a positive and a negative sense. A striking example is the development of a huge market for credit derivatives, which allows institutions to obtain insurance to protect themselves against credit default and the widening of credit spreads (or, alternatively, to get paid for assuming credit risk as an investment). Credit derivatives can be used to redistribute part or all of an institution's credit risk exposures to banks, hedge funds, or other institutional investors. However, the misuse of credit derivatives also helped to destabilize institutions during the 2007–2009 crisis and to fuel fears of a systemic meltdown.

Back in 2002, Alan Greenspan, then chairman of the U.S. Federal Reserve Board, made some optimistic remarks about the power of risk management to improve the world, but the conditionality attached to his observations proved to be rather important:

> *The development of our paradigms for containing risk has emphasized dispersion of risk to those willing, and presumably able, to bear it. If risk is properly dispersed, shocks to the overall economic system will be better absorbed and less likely to create cascading failures that could threaten financial stability.*[2]

In the financial crisis of 2007–2009, risk turned out to have been concentrated rather than dispersed, and this is far from the only embarrassing failure of risk management in recent decades. Other catastrophes range from the near failure of the giant hedge fund Long-Term Capital Management (LTCM) in 1998 to the string of financial scandals associated with the millennial boom in the equity and technology markets (from Enron, WorldCom, Global Crossing, and Qwest in the United States to Parmalat in Europe and Satyam in Asia).

---

[2]Remarks by Chairman Alan Greenspan before the Council on Foreign Relations, Washington, D.C., November 19, 2002.

Unfortunately, risk management has not consistently been able to prevent market disruptions or to prevent business accounting scandals resulting from breakdowns in corporate governance. In the case of the former problem, there are serious concerns that derivative markets make it easier to take on large amounts of risk, and that the "herd behavior" of risk managers after a crisis gets underway (e.g., selling risky asset classes when risk measures reach a certain level) actually increases market volatility.

Sophisticated financial engineering played a significant role in obscuring the true economic condition and risk-taking of financial companies in the run-up to the 2007–2009 crisis, and also helped to cover up the condition of many nonfinancial corporations during the equity markets' millennial boom and bust. Alongside simpler accounting mistakes and ruses, financial engineering can lead to the violent implosion of firms (and industries) after years of false success, rather than the firms' simply fading away or being taken over at an earlier point.

Part of the reason for risk management's mixed record here lies with the double-edged nature of risk management technologies. Every financial instrument that allows a company to transfer risk also allows other corporations to assume that risk as a counterparty in the same market—wisely or not. Most important, every risk management mechanism that allows us to change the shape of cash flows, such as deferring a negative outcome into the future, may work to the short-term benefit of one group of stakeholders in a firm (e.g., managers) at the same time that it is destroying long-term value for another group (e.g., shareholders or pensioners). In a world that is increasingly driven by risk management concepts and technologies, we need to look more carefully at the increasingly fluid and complex nature of risk itself, and at how to determine whether any change in a corporation's risk profile serves the interests of stakeholders. We need to make sure we are at least as literate in the language of risk as we are in the language of reward.

The nature of risk forms the topic of our next section, and it will lead us to the reason we've tried to make this book accessible to everyone, from shareholders, board members, and top executives to line managers, legal and back-office staff, and administrative assistants. We've removed from this book many of the complexities of mathematics that act as a barrier to understanding the essential principles of risk management, in the belief that, just as war is too important to be left to the generals, risk management has become too important to be left to the "rocket scientists" of the world of financial derivatives. This book is made suitable to students at colleges and universities who are interested in the emerging and expanding field of risk management in financial as well as nonfinancial corporations.

What Is Risk?

We're all faced with risk in our everyday lives. And although risk is an abstract term, our natural human understanding of the trade-offs between risk and reward is pretty sophisticated. For example, in our personal lives, we intuitively understand the difference between a cost that's already been budgeted for (in risk parlance, a predictable or expected loss) and an unexpected cost (at its worst, a catastrophic loss of a magnitude well beyond losses seen in the course of normal daily life).

In particular, we understand that risk is not synonymous with the *size* of a cost or of a loss. After all, some of the costs we expect in daily life are very large indeed if we think in terms of our annual budgets: food, fixed mortgage payments, college fees, and so on. These costs are big, but they are not a threat to our ambitions because they are reasonably predictable and are already allowed for in our plans.

The real *risk* is that these costs will suddenly rise in an entirely unexpected way, or that some other cost will appear from nowhere and steal the money we've set aside for our expected outlays. The risk lies in how *variable* our costs and revenues really are. In particular, we care about how likely it is that we'll encounter a loss big enough to upset our plans (one that we have not defused through some piece of personal risk management such as taking out a fixed-rate mortgage, setting aside savings for a rainy day, and so on).

This day-to-day analogy makes it easier to understand the difference between the risk management concepts of *expected loss* (or expected costs) and *unexpected loss* (or unexpected cost). Understanding this difference is the key to understanding modern risk management concepts such as economic capital attribution and risk-adjusted pricing. (However, this is not the only way to define risk, as we'll see in Chapter 5, which discusses various academic theories that shed more light on the definition and measurement of risk.)

One of the key differences between our intuitive conception of risk and a more formal treatment of it is the use of statistics to define the extent and potential cost of any exposure. To develop a number for unexpected loss, a bank risk manager first identifies the risk factors that seem to drive volatility in any outcome (Box 1-1) and then uses statistical analysis to calculate the probabilities of various outcomes for the position or portfolio under consideration. This probability distribution can be used in various ways. For example, the risk manager might pinpoint the area of the distribution (i.e., the extent of loss) that the institution would find worrying, given the probability of this loss occurring (e.g., is it a 1 in 10 or a 1 in 10,000 chance?).

BOX 1-1   RISK FACTORS AND THE MODELING OF RISK

In order to measure risk, the risk analyst first seeks to identify the key factors that seem likely to cause volatility in the returns from the position or portfolio under consideration. For example, in the case of an equity investment, the risk factor will be the volatility of the stock price (categorized in the appendix to this chapter as a market risk), which can be estimated in various ways.

In this case, we identified a single risk factor. But the number of risk factors that are considered in a risk analysis—and included in any risk modeling—varies considerably depending on both the problem and the sophistication of the approach. For example, in the recent past, bank risk analysts might have analyzed the risk of an interest-rate position in terms of the effect of a single risk factor—e.g., the yield to maturity of government bonds, assuming that the yields for all maturities are perfectly correlated. But this one-factor model approach ignored the risk that the dynamic of the term structure of interest rates is driven by more factors—e.g., the forward rates. Nowadays, leading banks analyze their interest-rate exposures using at least two or three factors, as we describe in Chapter 6.

Further, the risk manager must also measure the influence of the risk factors on each other, the statistical measure of which is the "covariance." Disentangling the effects of multiple risk factors and quantifying the influence of each is a fairly complicated undertaking, especially when covariance alters over time (i.e., is *stochastic*, in the modeler's terminology). There is often a distinct difference in the behavior and relationship of risk factors during normal business conditions and during stressful conditions such as financial crises.

Under ordinary market conditions, the behavior of risk factors is relatively less difficult to predict because it does not change significantly in the short and medium term: future behavior can be extrapolated, to some extent, from past performance. However, during stressful conditions, the behavior of risk factors becomes far more unpredictable, and past behavior may offer little help in predicting future behavior. It's at this point that statistically measurable risk threatens to turn into the kind of unmeasurable uncertainty that we discuss in Box 1-2.

The distribution can also be related to the institution's stated "risk appetite" for its various activities. For example, as we discuss in Chapter 4, the senior risk committee at the bank might have set boundaries on the amount of risk that the institution is willing to take by specifying the maximum loss it is willing to tolerate at a given level of confidence, such as, "We are willing to countenance a 1 percent chance of a $50 million loss from our trading desks on any given day." (At this point we should explain that while some chapters of this book focus on aspects of bank risk management—e.g., in Chapter 3 we elaborate on the regulation of risk management in banks—the risk management issues and concepts we cover are encountered in some form by many other industries and organizations, as we highlight in Chapter 2.)

Since the 2007–2009 financial crisis, risk managers have tried to move away from an overdependence on historical-statistical treatments of risk. For example, they have laid more emphasis on scenario analysis and stress testing, which examine the impact or outcomes of a given adverse scenario or stress on a firm (or portfolio). The scenario may be chosen not on the basis of statistical analysis, but instead simply because it is both plausible and suitably severe—essentially, a judgment call. However, it can be difficult and perhaps unwise to remove statistical approaches from the picture entirely. For example, in the more sophisticated forms of scenario analysis, the firm will need to examine how a change in a given macroeconomic factor (e.g., unemployment rate) leads to a change in a given risk factor (e.g., the probability of default of a corporation). Making this link almost inevitably means looking back to the past to examine the nature of the statistical relationship between macroeconomic factors and risk factors, though a degree of judgment must also be factored into the analysis.

The use of statistical, economic, and stress testing concepts can make risk management sound pretty technical. But the risk manager is simply doing more formally what we all do when we ask ourselves in our personal lives, "How bad, within reason, might this problem get?" The statistical models can also help in pricing risk, or pricing the instruments that help to eliminate or mitigate the risks.

What does our distinction between expected loss and unexpected loss mean in terms of running a financial business, such as a specific banking business line? Well, the *expected* credit loss for a credit card portfolio, for example, refers to how much the bank expects to lose, on average, as a result of fraud and defaults by cardholders over a period of time, say one year. In the case of large and well-diversified portfolios (i.e., most consumer credit portfolios), expected loss accounts for almost all the losses that are incurred in normal times. Because it is, by definition, predictable, expected loss is generally viewed as one of the costs of doing business, and ideally it is priced into the products and services offered to the customer. For credit cards, the expected loss is recovered by charging the businesses a certain commission (2 to 4 percent) and by charging a spread to the customer on any borrowed money, over and above the bank's funding cost (i.e., the rate the bank pays to raise funds in the money markets and elsewhere). The bank recovers mundane operating costs, such as the salaries it pays tellers, in much the same way.

The level of loss associated with a large standard credit card portfolio is relatively predictable because the portfolio is made up of numerous bite-sized exposures and the fortunes of most customers, most of the time, are not closely tied to one another. On the whole, you are not much more likely to lose your job today because your neighbor lost hers last week. There are some important exceptions to this, of course. During a prolonged and severe recession, your fortunes may become much more correlated with those of your neighbor, particularly if you work in the same industry and live in a particularly vulnerable region. Even in the relatively good times, the fortunes of small local banks, as well as their card portfolios, are somewhat driven by socioeconomic characteristics, as we discuss in Chapter 9.

A corporate loan portfolio, however, tends to be much "lumpier" than a retail portfolio (i.e., there are more big loans). Furthermore, if we look at industry data on commercial loan losses over a period of decades, it's much more apparent that in some years losses spike upward to *unexpected* loss levels, driven by risk factors that suddenly begin to act together. For example, the default rate for a bank that lends too heavily to the technology sector will be driven not just by the health of individual borrowers, but by the business cycle of the technology sector as a whole. When the technology sector shines, making loans will look risk-free for an extended period; when the economic rain comes, it will soak any banker that has allowed lending to become too concentrated among similar or interrelated borrowers. So, correlation risk—the tendency for things to go wrong together—is a major factor when evaluating the risk of this kind of portfolio.

The tendency for things to go wrong together isn't confined to the clustering of defaults among a portfolio of commercial borrowers. Whole classes of risk factors can begin to move together, too. In the world of credit risk, real estate–linked loans are a famous example of this: they are often secured with real estate collateral, which tends to lose value at exactly the same time that the default rate for property developers and owners rises. In this case, the "recovery-rate risk" on any defaulted loan is itself closely correlated with the "default-rate risk." The two risk factors acting together can sometimes force losses abruptly skyward.

In fact, anywhere in the world that we see risks (and not just credit risks) that are lumpy (i.e., in large blocks, such as very large loans) and that are driven by risk factors that under certain circumstances can become linked together (i.e., that are correlated), we can predict that at certain times high "unexpected losses" will be realized. We can try to estimate how bad this problem is by looking at the historical severity of these events in relation to any risk factors that we define and then examining the prevalence of these risk factors (e.g., the type and concentration of real estate collateral) in the particular portfolio under examination.

A detailed discussion of the problem of assessing and measuring the credit risk associated with commercial loans, and with whole portfolios of loans, takes up most of Chapters 10 and 11 of this book. But our general point immediately explains why bankers became so excited about new credit risk transfer technologies such as credit derivatives, described in detail in Chapter 12. These bankers weren't looking to reduce predictable levels of loss. Instead, the new instruments seemed to offer ways to put a cap on the problem of high unexpected losses and all the capital costs and uncertainty that these bring.

The conception of risk as unexpected loss underpins two key concepts that we'll deal with in more detail later in this book: value-at-risk (VaR) and economic capital. VaR, described and analyzed in Chapter 7, is a statistical measure that defines a particular level of loss in terms of its chances of occurrence (the "confidence level" of the analysis, in risk management jargon). For example, we might say that our options position has a one-day VaR of $1 million at the 99 percent confidence level, meaning that our risk analysis shows that there is only a 1 percent probability of a loss that is greater than $1 million on any given trading day.

In effect, we're saying that if we have $1 million in liquid reserves, there's little chance that the options position will lead to insolvency. Furthermore, because we can estimate the cost of holding liquid reserves, our risk analysis gives us a pretty good idea of the cost of taking this risk.

Under the risk paradigm we've just described, risk management becomes not the process of controlling and reducing expected losses (which is essentially a budgeting, pricing, and business efficiency concern), but the process of understanding, costing, and efficiently managing unexpected levels of variability in the financial outcomes for a business. Under this paradigm, even a conservative business can take on a significant amount of risk quite rationally, in light of

- Its confidence in the way it assesses and measures the unexpected loss levels associated with its various activities
- The accumulation of sufficient capital or the deployment of other risk management techniques to protect against potential unexpected loss levels
- Appropriate returns from the risky activities, once the costs of risk capital and risk management are taken into account
- Clear communication with stakeholders about the company's target risk profile (i.e., its solvency standard once risk-taking and risk mitigation are accounted for)

This takes us back to our assertion that risk management is not just a defensive activity. The more accurately a business understands and can measure its risks against potential rewards, its business goals, and its ability to withstand unexpected but plausible scenarios, the more risk-adjusted reward the business can aggressively capture in the marketplace without driving itself to destruction.

As Box 1-2 discusses, it's important in any risk analysis to acknowledge that some factors that might create volatility in outcomes simply can't be measured—even though they may be very important. The presence of this kind of risk factor introduces an uncertainty that needs to be made transparent, and perhaps explored using the kind of worst-case scenario analysis we describe in Chapter 16. Furthermore, even when statistical analysis of risk *can* be conducted, it's vital to make explicit the robustness of the underlying model, data, and risk parameter estimation—a topic that we treat in detail in Chapter 15, "Model Risk."

The Conflict of Risk and Reward

In financial markets, as well as in many commercial activities, if one wants to achieve a higher rate of return on average, one often has to assume more risk. But the transparency of the trade-off between risk and return is highly variable.

BOX 1-2   RISK, UNCERTAINTY . . . AND TRANSPARENCY ABOUT THE DIFFERENCE

In this chapter, we discuss risk as if it were synonymous with uncertainty. In fact, since the 1920s and a famous dissertation by Chicago economist Frank Knight,[1] thinkers about risk have made an important distinction between the two: variability that can be quantified in terms of probabilities is best thought of as "risk," while variability that cannot be quantified at all is best thought of simply as "uncertainty."

In a speech some years ago,[2] Mervyn King, then governor of the Bank of England, usefully pointed up the distinction using the example of the pensions and insurance industries. Over the last century, these industries have used statistical analysis to develop products (life insurance, pensions, annuities, and so on) that are important to us all in looking after the financial well-being of our families. These products act to "collectivize" the financial effects of any one individual's life events among any given generation.

Robust statistical tools have been vital in this collectivization of risk within a generation, but the insurance and investment industries have not found a way to put a robust number on key risks that arise *between* generations, such as how much longer future generations might live and what this might mean for life insurance, pensions, and so on. Some aspects of the future remain not just risky, but uncertain. Statistical science can help us to only a limited degree in understanding how sudden advances in medical science or the onset of a new disease such as AIDS might drive longevity up or down.

As King pointed out in his speech, "No amount of complex demographic modeling can substitute for good judgment about those unknowns."

---

[1]Frank H. Knight, *Risk, Uncertainty and Profit*, Boston, MA: Hart, Schaffner & Marx; Houghton Mifflin Company, 1921.

[2]Mervyn King, "What Fates Impose: Facing Up to Uncertainty," Eighth British Academy Annual Lecture, December 2004.

Indeed, attempts to forecast changes in longevity over the last 20 years have all fallen wide of the mark (usually proving too conservative).[3]

As this example helps make clear, one of the most important things that a risk manager can do when communicating a risk analysis is to be clear about the degree to which the results depend on statistically measurable risk, and the degree to which they depend on factors that are entirely uncertain at the time of the analysis—a distinction that may not be obvious to the reader of a complex risk report at first glance.

In his speech, King set out two principles of risk communication for public policy makers that could equally well apply to senior risk committees at corporations looking at the results of complex risk calculations:

> *First, information must be provided objectively and placed in context so that risks can be assessed and understood. Second, experts and policy makers must be open about the extent of our knowledge and our ignorance. Transparency about what we know and what we don't know, far from undermining credibility, helps to build trust and confidence.*

---

[3]We can't measure uncertainties, but we can still assess and manage them through worst-case scenarios, risk transfer, and so on. Indeed, a market is emerging that may help institutions to manage the financial risks of increased longevity. In 2003, reinsurance companies and banks began to issue financial instruments with returns linked to the aggregate longevity of specified populations, though the market for instruments that can help to manage longevity risk is still relatively immature.

In some cases, relatively efficient markets for risky assets help to make clear the returns that investors demand for assuming risk. For example, Figure 6-1, in Chapter 6, illustrates the risk/return relationship in the U.S. bond markets, showing the spreads for government bonds and corporate bonds of different ratings and maturities since 2007.

Even in the bond markets, the "price" of credit risk implied by these numbers for a particular counterparty is not quite transparent. Though bond prices are a pretty good guide to relative risk, various additional factors, such as liquidity risk and tax effects, confuse the price signal (as we discuss in Chapter 11). Moreover, investors' appetite for assuming certain kinds of risk varies over time. Sometimes the differential in yield between a risky and a risk-free bond narrows to such an extent that commentators talk of an "irrational" price of credit. That was the case during the period from early 2005 to mid-2007, until the eruption of the subprime crisis. With the eruption of the crisis, credit spreads moved up dramatically, and reached a peak following the collapse of Lehman Brothers in September 2008.

However, in the case of risks that are not associated with any kind of market-traded financial instrument, the problem of making transparent the relationship between risk and reward is even more profound. A key objective of risk management is to tackle this issue and make clear the potential for large losses in the future arising from activities that generate an apparently attractive stream of profits in the short run.

Ideally, discussions about this kind of trade-off between future profits and opaque risks would be undertaken within corporations on a basis that is rational for the firm as a whole. But organizations with a poor risk management and risk governance culture sometimes allow powerful business leaders to exaggerate the potential returns while diminishing the perceived potential risks. When rewards are not properly adjusted for economic risk, it's tempting for the self-interested to play down the potential for unexpected losses to spike somewhere in the economic cycle and to willfully misunderstand how risk factors sometimes come together to give rise to severe correlation risks. Management itself might be tempted to leave gaps in risk measurement that, if mended, would disturb the reported profitability of a business franchise. (The run-up to the 2007–2009 financial crisis provided many examples of such behavior.)

This kind of risk management failure can be hugely exacerbated by the compensation incentive schemes of the companies involved. In many firms across a broad swathe of industries, bonuses are paid today on profits that may later turn out to be illusory, while the cost of any associated risks is pushed, largely unacknowledged, into the future.

We can see this general process in the banking industry in every credit cycle as banks loosen rules about the granting of credit in the favorable part of the cycle, only to stamp on the credit brakes as things turn sour. The same dynamic happens whenever firms lack the discipline or means to adjust their present performance measures for an activity to take account of any risks incurred. For example, it is particularly easy for trading institutions to move revenues forward through either a "mark-to-market" or a "market-to-model" process. This process employs estimates of the value the market puts on an asset to record profits on the income statement before cash is actually generated; meanwhile, the implied cost of any risk can be artificially reduced by applying poor or deliberately distorted risk measurement techniques.

This collision between conflicts of interest and the opaque nature of risk is not limited solely to risk measurement and management at the level of the individual firm. Decisions about risk and return can become seriously distorted across whole financial industries when poor industry practices and regulatory rules allow this to happen—famous examples being the U.S. savings and loan crisis in the 1980s and early 1990s (see Box 8-1) and the more recent subprime crisis. History shows that industry regulators can also be drawn into the deception. When the stakes are high enough, regulators all around the world have colluded with local banking industries to allow firms to misrecord and misvalue risky assets on their balance sheets, out of fear that forcing firms to state their true condition will prompt mass insolvencies and a financial crisis.

Perhaps, in these cases, regulators think they are doing the right thing in safeguarding the financial system, or perhaps they are just desperate to postpone any pain beyond their term of office (or that of their political masters). For our purposes, it's enough to point out that the *combination* of poor standards of risk measurement with a conflict of interest is extraordinarily potent at many levels—both inside the company and outside.

The Danger of Names

So far, we've been discussing risk in terms of its expected and unexpected nature. We can also divide up our risk portfolio according to the *type* of risk that we are running. In this book, we follow the latest regulatory approach in the global banking industry to highlight three major broad risk categories that are controllable and manageable:

> *Market risk* is the risk of losses arising from changes in market risk factors. Market risk can arise from changes in interest rates, foreign exchange rates, or equity and commodity price factors.[3]
> *Credit risk* is the risk of loss following a change in the factors that drive the credit quality of an asset. These include adverse effects arising from credit grade migration, including default, and the dynamics of recovery rates.

---

[3]The definition and breakdown of market risk into these four broad categories is consistent with the accounting standards of IFRS and GAPP in the United States.

Operational risk refers to financial loss resulting from a host of potential operational breakdowns that we can think in terms of risk of loss resulting from inadequate or failed internal processes, people, and systems, or from external events (e.g., frauds, inadequate computer systems, a failure in controls, a mistake in operations, a guideline that has been circumvented, or a natural disaster).

Understanding the various types of risk is important, beyond the banking industry, because each category demands a different (but related) set of risk management skills. The categories are often used to define and organize the risk management functions and risk management activities of a corporation. We've added an appendix to this chapter that offers a longer and more detailed family tree of the various types of risks faced by corporations, including key additional risks such as liquidity risk and strategic risk. This risk taxonomy can be applied to any corporation engaged in major financial transactions, project financing, and providing customers with credit facilities.

The history of science, as well as the history of management, tells us that classification schemes like this are as *valuable* as they are *dangerous*. Giving a name to something allows us to talk about it, control it, and assign responsibility for it. Classification is an important part of the effort to make an otherwise ill-defined risk measurable, manageable, and transferable. Yet the classification of risk is also fraught with danger because as soon as we define risk in terms of categories, we create the potential for missed risks and gaps in responsibilities—for being blindsided by risk as it flows across our arbitrary dividing lines.

For example, a sharp peak in market prices will create a market risk for an institution. Yet the real threat might be that a counterparty to the bank that is also affected by the spike in market prices will default (credit risk), or that some weakness in the bank's systems will be exposed by high trading volumes (operational risk). If we think of price volatility in terms of market risk alone, we are missing an important factor.

We can see the same thing happening from an organizational perspective. While categorizing risks helps us to organize risk management, it fosters the creation of "silos" of expertise that are separated from one another in terms of personnel, risk terminology, risk measures, reporting lines, systems and data, and so on. The management of risk within these silos may be quite efficient in terms of a particular risk, such as market or credit risk, or the risks run by a particular business unit. But if executives and risk managers can't communicate with one another across risk silos, they probably won't be able to work together efficiently to manage the risks that are most important to the institution as a whole.

Some of the most exciting recent advances in risk management are really attempts to break down this natural organizational tendency toward silo risk management. In the past, risk measurement tools such as VaR and economic capital have evolved, in part, to facilitate integrated measurement and management of the various risks (market, credit, and operational) and business lines. More recently, the trend toward worst-case scenario analysis is really an attempt to look at the effect of macroeconomic scenarios on a firm across its business lines and, often, across various types of risk (market, credit, and so on).

We can also see in many industries a much more broadly framed trend toward what consultants have labeled *enterprisewide risk management*, or ERM. ERM is a concept with many definitions. Basically, though, ERM is a deliberate attempt to break through the tendency of firms to operate in risk management silos and to ignore enterprisewide risks, and an attempt to take risk into consideration in business decisions much more explicitly than has been done in the past. There are many potential ERM tools, including conceptual tools that facilitate enterprisewide risk measurement (such as economic capital and enterprisewide stress testing), monitoring tools that facilitate enterprisewide risk identification, and organizational tools such as senior risk committees with a mandate to look at all enterprisewide risks. Through an ERM program, a firm limits its exposures to a risk level agreed upon by the board and provides its management and board of directors with reasonable assurances regarding the achievement of the organization's objectives.

As a trend, ERM is clearly in tune with a parallel drive toward the unification of risk, capital, and balance sheet management in financial institutions. Over the last 10 years, it has become increasingly difficult to distinguish risk management tools from capital management tools, since risk, according to the unexpected loss risk paradigm we outlined earlier, increasingly drives the allocation of capital in risk-intensive businesses such as banking and insurance.

Similarly, it has become difficult to distinguish capital management tools from balance sheet management tools, since risk/reward relationships increasingly drive the structure of the balance sheet.

A survey in 2011 by management consultant Deloitte found that the adoption of ERM has increased sharply over the last few years: "Fifty-two percent of institutions reported having an ERM program (or equivalent), up from 36 percent in 2008. Large institutions are more likely to face complex and interconnected risks, and among institutions with total assets of $100 billion or more, 91 percent reported either having an ERM program in place or [being] in the process of implementing one."[4] But we shouldn't get too carried away here. ERM is a goal, but most institutions are a long way from fully achieving the goal.

Numbers Are Dangerous, Too

Once we've put boundaries around our risks by naming and classifying them, we can also try to attach meaningful *numbers* to them. A lot of this book is about this problem. Even if our numbers are only judgmental rankings of risks within a risk class (Risk No. 1, Risk Rating 3, and so on), they can help us make more rational in-class comparative decisions. More ambitiously, if we can assign absolute numbers to some risk factor (a 0.02 percent chance of default versus a 0.002 percent chance of default), then we can weigh one decision against another with some precision. And if we can put an absolute cost or price on a risk (ideally using data from markets where risks are traded or from some internal "cost of risk" calculation based on economic capital), then we can make truly rational economic decisions about assuming, managing, and transferring risks. At this point, risk management decisions become fungible with many other kinds of management decision in the running of an enterprise.

But while assigning numbers to risk is incredibly useful for risk management and risk transfer, it's also potentially dangerous. Only some kinds of numbers are truly comparable, but all kinds of numbers tempt us to make comparisons. For example, using the face value or "notional amount" of a bond

---

[4]Deloitte, *Global Risk Management Survey*, seventh edition, 2011, p. 14.

to indicate the risk of a bond is a flawed approach. As we explain in Chapter 7, a million-dollar position in a par value 10-year Treasury bond does not represent at all the same amount of risk as a million-dollar position in a 4-year par value Treasury bond.

Introducing sophisticated models to describe risk is one way to defuse this problem, but this has its own dangers. Professionals in the financial markets invented the VaR framework as a way of measuring and comparing risk across many different markets. But as we discuss in Chapter 7, the VaR measure works well as a risk measure only for markets operating under normal conditions and only over a short period, such as one trading day. Potentially, it's a very poor and misleading measure of risk in abnormal markets, over longer time periods, or for illiquid portfolios.

Also, VaR, like all risk measures, depends for its integrity on a robust control environment. In recent rogue-trading cases, hundreds of millions of dollars of losses have been suffered by trading desks that had orders not to assume VaR exposures of more than a few million dollars. The reason for the discrepancy is nearly always that the trading desks have found some way of circumventing trading controls and suppressing risk measures. For example, a trader might falsify transaction details entered into the trade reporting system and use fictitious trades to (supposedly) balance out the risk of real trades, or tamper with the inputs to risk models, such as the volatility estimates that determine the valuation and risk estimation for an options portfolio.

The likelihood of this kind of problem increases sharply when those around the trader (back-office staff, business line managers, even risk managers) don't properly understand the critical significance of routine tasks, such as an independent check on volatility estimates, for the integrity of key risk measures. Meanwhile, those reading the risk reports (senior executives, board members) often don't seem to realize that unless they've asked key questions about the integrity of controls, they might as well tear up the risk report.

As we try to base our risk evaluations on past data and experience, we should recall that all statistical estimation is subject to estimation errors, and these can be substantial when the economic environment changes. In addition we must remember that human psychology interferes with risk assessment. Professor Daniel Kahneman, the Nobel laureate in Economics, warns us that people tend to misassess extreme probabilities (very small ones as well as very large ones). Kahneman also points out that people tend to be risk-averse in the domain of gains and risk-seeking in the domain of losses.[5]

While the specialist risk manager's job is an increasingly important one, a broad understanding of risk management must also become part of the wider culture of the firm.

The Risk Manager's Job

There are many aspects of the risk manager's role that are open to confusion. First and foremost, a risk manager is not a prophet! The role of the risk manager is not to try to read a crystal ball, but to uncover the sources of risk and make them visible to key decision makers and stakeholders in terms of probability. For example, the risk manager's role is not to produce a point estimate of the U.S. dollar/euro exchange rate at the end of the year; but to produce a distribution estimate of the potential exchange rate at year-end and explain what this might mean for the firm (given its financial positions). These distribution estimates can then be used to help make risk management decisions, and also to produce risk-adjusted metrics such as risk-adjusted return on capital (RAROC).

As this suggests, the risk manager's role is not just defensive—firms need to generate and apply information about balancing risk and reward if they are to compete effectively in the longer term (see Chapter 17). Implementing the appropriate policies, methodologies, and infrastructure to risk-adjust numbers and improve forward-looking business decisions is an increasingly important element of the modern risk manager's job.

But the risk manager's role in this regard is rarely easy—these risk and profitability analyses aren't always accepted or welcomed in the wider firm when they deliver bad news. Sometimes the difficulty is political (business leaders want growth, not caution), sometimes it is technical (no one has found a best-practice way to measure certain types of risk, such as reputation or franchise risk), and sometimes it is systemic (it's hard not to jump over a cliff on a business idea if all your competitors are doing that too).

---

[5]Daniel Kahneman, *Thinking, Fast and Slow*, Farrar, Straus and Giroux, 2011.

This is why defining the role and reporting lines of risk managers within the wider organization is so critical. It's all very well for the risk manager to identify a risk and measure its potential impact—but if risk is not made transparent to key stakeholders, or those charged with oversight on their behalf, then the risk manager has failed. We discuss these corporate governance issues in more detail in Chapter 4.

Perhaps the trickiest balancing act over the last few years has been trying to find the right relationship between business leaders and the specialist risk management functions within an institution. The relationship should be close, but not too close. There should be extensive interaction, but not dominance. There should be understanding, but not collusion. We can still see the tensions in this relationship across any number of activities in risk-taking organizations—between the credit analyst and those charged with business development in commercial loans, between the trader on the desk and the market risk management team, and so on. Where the balance of power lies will depend significantly on the attitude of senior managers and on the tone set by the board. It will also depend on whether the institution has invested in the analytical and organizational tools that support balanced, risk-adjusted decisions.

As the risk manager's role is extended, we must increasingly ask difficult questions: "What are the risk management standards of practice?" and "Who is checking up on the risk managers?" Out in the financial markets, the answer is hopefully the regulators. Inside a corporation, the answer includes the institution's audit function, which is charged with reviewing risk management's actions and its compliance with an agreed-upon set of policies and procedures (Chapter 4). But the more general answer is that risk managers will find it difficult to make the right kind of impact if the firm as a whole lacks a healthy risk culture, including a good understanding of risk management practices, concepts, and tools.

The Past, the Future—and This Book's Mission

We can now understand better why the discipline of risk management has had such a bumpy ride across many industries over the last decade (see Box 1-3). The reasons lie partly in the fundamentally elusive and opaque nature of risk—if it's not unexpected or uncertain, it's not risk! As we've seen, "risk" changes shape according to perspective, market circumstances, risk appetite, and even the classification schemes that we use.

BOX 1-3   UPS AND DOWNS IN RISK MANAGEMENT

Ups

- Dramatic explosion in the adoption of sophisticated risk management processes, driven by an expanding skill base and falling cost of risk technologies
- Increase in the skill levels and associated compensation of risk management personnel as sophisticated risk techniques have been adopted to measure risk exposures
- Birth of new risk management markets in credit, commodities, weather derivatives, and so on, representing some of the most innovative and potentially lucrative financial markets in the world
- Birth of global risk management industry associations as well as a dramatic rise in the number of global risk management personnel
- Extension of the risk measurement frontier out from traditional measured risks such as market risk toward credit and operational risks
- Cross fertilization of risk management techniques across diverse industries from banking to insurance, energy, chemicals, and aerospace
- Ascent of risk managers in the corporate hierarchy to become chief risk officers, to become members of the top executive team (e.g., part of the management committee), and to report to both the CEO and the board of the company

Downs

- The financial crisis of 2007–2009 revealed significant weaknesses in managing systemic and cyclical risks.
- Firms have been tempted to over-rely on historical-statistical measures of risk—a weakness that improved stress testing seeks to address.
- Risk managers continue to find it a challenge to balance their fiduciary responsibilities against the cost of offending powerful business heads.

- Risk managers do not generate revenue and therefore have not yet achieved the same status as the heads of successful revenue-generating businesses.
- It's proving difficult to make truly unified measurements of different kinds of risk and to understand the destructive power of risk interactions (e.g., credit and liquidity risk).
- Quantifying risk exposure for the whole organization can be hugely complicated and may descend into a "box ticking" exercise.
- The growing power of risk managers could be a negative force in business if risk management is interpreted as risk avoidance; it's possible to be too risk-averse.

The reasons also lie partly in the relative immaturity of financial risk management. Practices, personnel, markets, and instruments have been evolving and interacting with one another continually over the last couple of decades to set the stage for the next risk management triumph—and disaster. Rather than being a set of specific activities, computer systems, rules, or policies, risk management is better thought of as a set of concepts that allow us to see and manage risk in a particular and dynamic way.

Perhaps the biggest task in risk management is no longer to build specialized mathematical measures of risk (although this endeavor certainly continues). Perhaps it is to put down deeper risk management roots in each organization. We need to build a wider risk culture and risk literacy, in which all the key staff members engaged in a risky enterprise understand how they can affect the risk profile of the organization—from the back office to the boardroom, and from the bottom to the top of the house. That's really what this book is about. We hope it offers both nonmathematicians as well as mathematicians an understanding of the latest concepts in risk management so that they can see the strengths and question the weaknesses of a given decision.

Nonmathematicians must feel able to contribute to the ongoing evolution of risk management practice. Along the way, we can also hope to give those of our readers who are risk analysts and mathematicians a broader sense of how their analytics fit into an overall risk program, and a stronger sense that their role is to convey not just the results of any risk analysis, but also its meaning (and any broader lessons from an enterprisewide risk management perspective).

Appendix 1.1

TYPOLOGY OF RISK EXPOSURES

In Chapter 1 we defined risk as the volatility of returns leading to "unexpected losses," with higher volatility indicating higher risk. The volatility of returns is directly or indirectly influenced by numerous variables, which we called risk factors, and by the interaction between these risk factors. But how do we consider the universe of risk factors in a systematic way?

Risk factors can be broadly grouped together into the following major categories: market risk, credit risk, liquidity risk, operational risk, legal and regulatory risk, business risk, strategic risk, and reputation risk (Figure 1A-1).[1] These categories can then be further decomposed into more specific categories, as we show in Figure 1A-2 for market risk and credit risk. Market risk and credit risk are referred to as financial risks.

In this figure, we've subdivided market risk into equity price risk, interest rate risk, foreign exchange risk, and commodity price risk in a manner that is in line with our detailed discussion in this appendix. Then we've divided interest rate risk into trading risk and the special case of gap risk; the latter relates to the risk that arises in the balance sheet of an institution as a result of the different sensitivities of assets and liabilities to changes of interest rates (see Chapter 8).

In theory, the more all-encompassing the categorization and the more detailed the decomposition, the more closely the company's risk will be captured.

---

[1] Board of Governors of the Federal Reserve System, Trading and Capital Markets Activities Manual, Washington D.C., April 2007.

FIGURE 1A-1 Typology of Risks

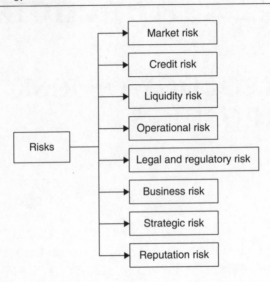

In practice, this process is limited by the level of model complexity that can be handled by the available technology and by the cost and availability of internal and market data.

Let's take a closer look at the risk categories in Figure 1A-1.

FIGURE 1A-2 Schematic Presentation, by Categories, of Financial Risks

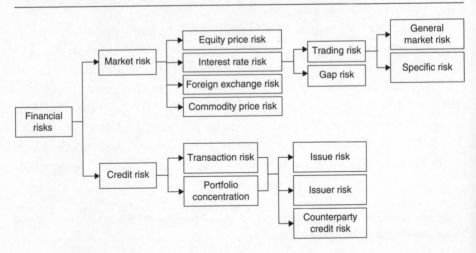

Market Risk

Market risk is the risk that changes in financial market prices and rates will reduce the value of a security or a portfolio. Price risk can be decomposed into a general market risk component (the risk that the market as a whole will fall in value) and a specific market risk component, unique to the particular financial transaction under consideration. In trading activities, risk arises both from open (unhedged) positions and from imperfect correlations between market positions that are intended to offset one another.

Market risk is given many different names in different contexts. For example, in the case of a fund, the fund may be marketed as tracking the performance of a certain benchmark. In this case, market risk is important to the extent that it creates a risk of tracking error. *Basis risk* is a term used in the risk management industry to describe the chance of a breakdown in the relationship between the price of a product, on the one hand, and the price of the instrument used to hedge that price exposure, on the other. Again, it is really just a context-specific form of market risk.

There are four major types of market risk: interest rate risk, equity price risk, foreign exchange risk, and commodity price risk.[2]

Interest Rate Risk

The simplest form of interest rate risk is the risk that the value of a fixed-income security will fall as a result of an increase in market interest rates. But in complex portfolios of interest-rate-sensitive assets, many different kinds of exposure can arise from differences in the maturities and reset dates of instruments and cash flows that are asset-like (i.e., "longs") and those that are liability-like (i.e., "shorts").

In particular, as we explain in more detail in Chapter 6, "curve" risk can arise in portfolios in which long and short positions of different maturities are effectively hedged against a *parallel shift* in yields, but not against a change in the *shape of the yield curve*. Meanwhile, even when offsetting positions have the same maturity, basis risk can arise if the rates of the positions are imperfectly correlated. For example, three-month Eurodollar instruments and three-month Treasury bills both naturally pay three-month interest rates. However,

---

[2]These four categories of market risk are, in general, consistent with accounting standards.

these rates are not perfectly correlated with each other, and spreads between their yields may vary over time. As a result, a three-month Treasury bill funded by three-month Eurodollar deposits represents an imperfect offset or hedged position (often referred to as *basis risk*).

Equity Price Risk

This is the risk associated with volatility in stock prices. The general market risk of equity refers to the sensitivity of an instrument or portfolio value to a change in the level of broad stock market indices. The specific or idiosyncratic risk of equity refers to that portion of a stock's price volatility determined by characteristics specific to the firm, such as its line of business, the quality of its management, or a breakdown in its production process. According to portfolio theory, general market risk cannot be eliminated through portfolio diversification, while specific risk can be diversified away. In Chapter 5 we discuss models for measuring equity risk.

Foreign Exchange Risk

Foreign exchange risk arises from open or imperfectly hedged positions in particular foreign currency denominated assets and liabilities leading to fluctuations in profits or values as measured in a local currency. These positions may arise as a natural consequence of business operations, rather than from any conscious desire to take a trading position in a currency. Foreign exchange volatility can sweep away the return from expensive cross-border investments and at the same time place a firm at a competitive disadvantage in relation to its foreign competitors.[3] It may also generate huge operating losses and, through the uncertainty it causes, inhibit investment. The major drivers of foreign exchange risk are imperfect correlations in the movement of currency prices and fluctuations in international interest rates. Although it is important to acknowledge exchange rates as a distinct market risk factor, the valuation of foreign exchange transac-

---

[3]A famous example is Caterpillar, a U.S. heavy equipment firm, which in 1987 began a $2 billion capital investment program. A full cost reduction of 19 percent was eventually expected in 1993. During the same period the Japanese yen weakened against the U.S. dollar by 30 percent, which placed Caterpillar at a competitive disadvantage vis-à-vis its major competitor, Komatsu of Japan, even after adjusting for productivity gains.

tions requires knowledge of the behavior of domestic and foreign interest rates, as well as of spot exchange rates.[4]

Commodity Price Risk

The price risk of commodities differs considerably from interest rate and foreign exchange risk, since most commodities are traded in markets in which the concentration of supply is in the hands of a few suppliers who can magnify price volatility. For most commodities, the number of market players having direct exposure to the particular commodity is quite limited, hence affecting trading liquidity which in turn can generate high levels of price volatility. Other fundamentals affecting a commodity price include the ease and cost of storage, which varies considerably across the commodity markets (e.g., from gold to electricity to wheat). As a result of these factors, commodity prices generally have higher volatilities and larger price discontinuities (i.e., moments when prices leap from one level to another) than most traded financial securities. Commodities can be classified according to their characteristics as follows: hard commodities, or nonperishable commodities, the markets for which are further divided into precious metals (e.g., gold, silver, and platinum), which have a high price/weight value, and base metals (e.g., copper, zinc, and tin); soft commodities, or commodities with a short shelf life that are hard to store, mainly agricultural products (e.g., grains, coffee, and sugar); and energy commodities, which consist of oil, gas, electricity, and other energy products.

Credit Risk

Credit risk is the risk of an economic loss from the failure of a counterparty to fulfill its contractual obligations, or from the *increased risk* of default during the term of the transaction.[5] For example, credit risk in the loan portfolio

---

[4]This is because of the interest rate parity condition, which describes the price of a futures contract on a foreign currency as equal to the spot exchange rate adjusted by the difference between the local interest rate and the foreign interest rate.

[5]In the following we use indifferently the term "borrower" or "counterparty" for a debtor. In practice, we refer to issuer risk, or borrower risk, when credit risk involves a funded transaction such as a bond or a bank loan. In derivatives markets, counterparty credit risk is the credit risk of a counterparty for an unfunded derivatives transaction such as a swap or an option.

of a bank materializes when a borrower fails to make a payment, either of the periodic interest charge or the periodic reimbursement of principal on the loan as contracted with the bank. Credit risk can be further decomposed into four main types: default risk, bankruptcy risk, downgrade risk, and settlement risk. Box 1A-1 gives ISDA's definition of a credit event that may trigger a payout under a credit derivatives contract.[6]

BOX 1A-1   CREDIT DERIVATIVES AND THE ISDA DEFINITION OF A CREDIT EVENT

The spectacular growth of the market for credit default swaps (CDS) and similar instruments since the millennium has obliged the financial markets to become a lot more specific about what they regard as a credit event—i.e., the event that triggers the payment on a CDS. This event, usually a default, needs to be clearly defined to avoid any litigation when the contract is settled. CDSs normally contain a "materiality clause" requiring that the change in credit status be validated by third-party evidence.

The CDS market has struggled somewhat to define the kind of credit event that should trigger a payout under a credit derivatives contract. Major credit events, as stipulated in CDS documentation and formalized by the International Swaps and Derivatives Association (ISDA), are:

- Bankruptcy, insolvency, or payment default
- Obligation/cross default, which means the occurrence of a default (other than failure to make a payment) on any other similar obligation
- Obligation acceleration, which refers to the situation in which debt becomes due and repayable prior to maturity (subject to a materiality threshold of $10 million, unless otherwise stated)
- Stipulated fall in the price of the underlying asset
- Downgrade in the rating of the issuer of the underlying asset
- Restructuring (this is probably the most controversial credit event)

---

[6]ISDA is the International Swap and Derivatives Association.

- Repudiation/moratorium, which can occur in two situations: First, the reference entity (the obligor of the underlying bond or loan issue) refuses to honor its obligations. Second, a company could be prevented from making a payment because of a sovereign debt moratorium (e.g., City of Moscow in 1998).

One of the most controversial aspects of the debate is whether the restructuring of a loan—which can include changes such as an agreed reduction in interest and principal, postponement of payments, or change in the currencies of payment—should count as a credit event. The Conseco case famously highlighted the problems that restructuring can cause. Back in October 2000, a group of banks led by Bank of America and Chase granted to Conseco a three-month extension of the maturity of a short-term loan for approximately $2.8 billion while simultaneously increasing the coupon and enhancing the covenant protection. The extension of credit might have helped prevent an immediate bankruptcy, but as a significant credit event it also triggered potential payouts on as much as $2 billion of CDS.[1]

In May 2001, following this episode, ISDA issued a Restructuring Supplement to its 1999 definitions concerning credit derivative contractual terminology. Among other things, this document requires that to qualify as a credit event, a restructuring event must occur to an obligation that has at least three holders, and at least two-thirds of the holders must agree to the restructuring. The ISDA document also imposes a maturity limitation on deliverables—the protection buyer can only deliver securities with a maturity of less than 30 months following the restructuring date or the extended maturity of the restructured loan—and it requires that the delivered security be fully transferable. Some key players in the market dropped restructuring from their list of credit events. See also discussion in Chapter 12.

---

[1] The original sellers of the CDS were not happy, and were annoyed further when the CDS buyers seemed to play the "cheapest to deliver" game by delivering long-dated bonds instead of the restructured loans; at the time, these bonds were trading significantly lower than the restructured bank loans. (The restructured loans traded at a higher price in the secondary market due to the new credit mitigation features.)

Default risk corresponds to the debtor's incapacity or refusal to meet his/her debt obligations, whether interest or principal payments on the loan contracted, by more than a reasonable relief period from the due date, which is usually 60 days in the banking industry.

Bankruptcy risk is the risk of actually taking over the collateralized, or escrowed, assets of a defaulted borrower or counterparty. In the case of a bankrupt company, debt holders are taking over the control of the company from the shareholders.

Downgrade risk is the risk that the perceived creditworthiness of the borrower or counterparty might deteriorate. In general, deteriorated creditworthiness translates into a downgrade action by the rating agencies, such as Standard and Poor's (S&P), Moody's, or Fitch in the United States, and an increase in the risk premium, or credit spread of the borrower. A major deterioration in the creditworthiness of a borrower might be the precursor of default.

Settlement risk is the risk due to the exchange of cash flows when a transaction is settled. Failure to perform on settlement can be caused by a counterparty default, liquidity constraints, or operational issues. This risk is greatest when payments occur in different time zones, especially for foreign exchange transactions, such as currency swaps, where notional amounts are exchanged in different currencies.[7]

Credit risk is an issue only when the position is an asset—i.e., when it exhibits a positive replacement value. In that situation, if the counterparty

---

[7]Settlement failures due to operational problems result only in payment delays and have only minor economic consequences. In some cases, however, the loss can be quite substantial and amount to the full amount of the payment due. A famous example of settlement risk is the 1974 failure of Herstatt Bank, a small regional German bank. The day it went bankrupt, Herstatt had received payments in Deutsche marks from a number of counterparties but defaulted before payments were made in U.S. dollars on the other legs of maturing spot and forward transactions.

Bilateral netting is one of the mechanisms that reduce settlement risk. In a netting agreement, only the net balance outstanding in each currency is paid instead of making payments on the gross amounts to each other. Currently, around 55 percent of FX transactions are settled through the CLS bank, which provides a payment-versus-payment (PVP) service that virtually eliminates the principal risk associated with settling FX trades (Basel Committee on Payment and Settlement Systems, *Progress in Reducing Foreign Exchange Settlement Risk*, Bank for International Settlements, Basel, Switzerland, May 2008).

defaults, the firm loses either all of the market value of the position or, more commonly, the part of the value that it cannot recover following the credit event. The value it is likely to recover is called the *recovery value*, or *recovery rate* when expressed as a percentage; the amount it is expected to lose is called the *loss given default (LGD)*.

Unlike the potential loss given default on coupon bonds or loans, the LGD on derivative positions is usually much lower than the nominal amount of the deal, and in many cases is only a fraction of this amount. This is because the economic value of a derivative instrument is related to its replacement or market value rather than its nominal or face value. However, the credit exposures induced by the replacement values of derivative instruments are dynamic: they can be negative at one point in time, and yet become positive at a later point in time after market conditions have changed. Therefore, firms must examine not only the current exposure, measured by the current replacement value, but also the distribution of potential future exposures up to the termination of the deal (see Chapter 13).

Credit Risk at the Portfolio Level

The first factor affecting the amount of credit risk in a portfolio is clearly the credit standing of specific obligors. The critical issue, then, is to charge the appropriate interest rate, or spread, to each borrower so that the lender is compensated for the risk it undertakes, and to set aside the right amount of risk capital.

The second factor is "concentration risk," or the extent to which the obligors are diversified in terms of exposures, geography, and industry. This leads us to the third important factor that affects the risk of the portfolio: the state of the economy. During the good times of economic growth, the frequency of default falls sharply compared to periods of recession. Conversely, the default rate rises again as the economy enters a downturn. Downturns in the credit cycle often uncover the hidden tendency of customers to default together, with banks being affected to the degree that they have allowed their portfolios to become concentrated in various ways (e.g., customer, region, and industry concentrations). Credit portfolio models are an attempt to discover the degree of correlation/concentration risk in a bank portfolio

The quality of the portfolio can also be affected by the maturities of the loans, as longer loans are generally considered riskier than short-term loans.

Banks that build portfolios that are not concentrated in particular maturities—"time diversification"—can reduce this kind of portfolio maturity risk. This also helps reduce liquidity risk, or the risk that the bank will run into difficulties when it tries to refinance large amounts of its assets at the same time.

Liquidity Risk

Liquidity risk comprises both "funding liquidity risk" and "trading liquidity risk" (see Figure 1A-3). Funding liquidity risk relates to a firm's ability to raise the necessary cash to roll over its debt; to meet the cash, margin, and collateral requirements of counterparties; and to satisfy capital withdrawals. Funding liquidity risk can be managed through holding cash and cash equivalents, setting credit lines in place, and monitoring buying power. (Buying power refers to the amount a trading counterparty can borrow against assets under stressed market conditions.) Chapter 8 looks at funding liquidity risk in more detail, and Chapter 15 discusses the liquidity aspects of the Long-Term Capital Management crisis of August 1998, after Russia defaulted on its debt obligations.

Trading liquidity risk, often simply called liquidity risk, is the risk that an institution will not be able to execute a transaction at the prevailing market price because there is, temporarily, no appetite for the deal on the other side of the market. If the transaction cannot be postponed, its execution may lead to a substantial loss on the position. Funding liquidity risk is also related to the size of the transaction and its immediacy. The faster and/or larger the transaction, the greater the potential for loss. This risk is generally very hard to quantify. (In current implementations of the market value-at-risk, or VaR, approach,

FIGURE 1A-3 The Dimensions of Liquidity Risk

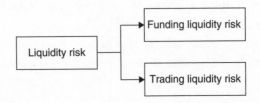

liquidity risk is accounted for only in the sense that one of the parameters of a VaR model is the period of time, or holding period, thought necessary to liquidate the relevant positions.) Trading liquidity risk may reduce an institution's ability to manage and hedge market risk as well as its capacity to satisfy any shortfall in funding by liquidating its assets. Box 1A-2 discusses valuation problems faced in a marked-to-market world in times of low asset liquidity.

BOX 1A-2   VALUATION PROBLEMS IN A MARKED-TO-MARKET WORLD IN TIMES OF LOW LIQUIDITY

Financial instruments are held in the:

- "trading book," where they are measured at fair value through profit and loss, or
- "banking book," as assets available for sale (AFS), where they are subject to amortized cost accounting (also referred to as accrual accounting).

Any change in the fair value of a trading book instrument has a direct impact on a firm's income statement in the period in which the change occurs. Changes in the fair value of financial assets classified as AFS are recorded directly in equity without affecting profit and loss until the financial assets are sold, at which point the cumulative change in fair value is charged or credited to the income statement.

In contrast, unless held for sale, loans are typically measured at amortized cost using the effective interest method, less "allowance" or "provision" for impairment losses. Loans held for sale may be reported in trading or AFS portfolios or, in the United States, in held-for-sale portfolios at the lower of cost or fair value.

Instruments subject to fair value accounting are valued with reference to prices obtained from active markets, when these are available for identical or similar instruments. When market liquidity dries up—e.g., during a market crisis—price discovery based on market prices becomes much more difficult. Other valuation techniques may become necessary, such as applying a model to estimate a value.[1] Where liquid market prices are unavailable, other approaches inevitably carry with them a range of uncertainties and can give a false impression of precision.

Fair value/mark-to-market accounting has generally proven highly valuable in promoting transparency and market discipline and is an effective and reliable accounting method for securities in liquid markets. However, it can create serious, self-reinforcing challenges that make valuation more difficult and increase uncertainties around those valuations when there is no or severely limited liquidity in secondary markets. Three main criticisms of fair value accounting have been expressed:[2]

- First, unrealized losses recognized under fair value accounting may reverse over time. Market prices may deviate from fundamental values because of market illiquidity or because prices are bubble prices.

---

[1]The accounting standard for fair value (FAS 157) creates a hierarchy of inputs into fair value measurements, from most to least reliable:

- Level 1 inputs are unadjusted quoted market prices in active liquid markets for identical products.

- Level 2 inputs are other directly or indirectly observable market data. There are two broad subclasses of these inputs. The first and generally preferable subclass is quoted market prices in active markets for similar instruments. The second subclass is other observable market inputs such as yield curves, exchange rates, empirical correlations, and so on. These inputs yield mark-to-model measurements that are disciplined by market information, but that can only be as reliable as the models and the inputs that have been employed.

- Level 3 inputs are unobservable, firm-supplied estimates, such as forecasts of home price depreciation and the resulting severity of credit losses on mortgage-related positions.

[2]Looking at the pros and cons of fair value accounting, fair value accounting still seems better than the alternative of accrual accounting. Accrual accounting suppresses the reporting of losses and reduces the incentives for voluntary disclosure. This means that it can discourage the actions that may be necessary to resolve a crisis. The savings and loan crisis in the United States provides the best illustration. The crisis began when interest rates rose during the first oil crisis/recession in 1973–1975, causing thrifts' fixed mortgage assets to experience large economic losses that were not recognized under amortized cost accounting. This nonrecognition of economic losses allowed bank regulators and policy makers to permit the crisis to continue for 15 years, effectively encouraging thrifts to invest in risky assets, exploit deposit insurance, and in some cases even commit fraud—activities that significantly worsened the ultimate cost of the crisis.

- Second, market illiquidity may render fair values difficult to measure, yielding overstated and unreliable reported losses.
- Third, firms reporting unrealized losses under fair value accounting may trigger unhelpful feedback effects—i.e., trigger further deterioration of market prices through the destabilizing downward spiral of forced liquidations, write-downs, and higher risk and liquidity premiums.

Operational Risk

Operational risk refers to potential losses resulting from a range of operational weaknesses including inadequate systems, management failure, faulty controls, fraud, and human errors; in the banking industry, operational risk is also often taken to include the risk of natural and man-made catastrophes (e.g., earthquakes, terrorism) and other nonfinancial risks. As we discuss in Chapters 14 and 15, many of the large losses from derivative trading over the last decade are the direct consequence of operational failures. Derivative trading is more prone to operational risk than cash transactions because derivatives, by their nature, are leveraged transactions. The valuation process required for complex derivatives also creates considerable operational risk. Very tight controls are an absolute necessity if a firm is to avoid large losses.

Human factor risk is a special form of operational risk. It relates to the losses that may result from human errors such as pushing the wrong button on a computer, inadvertently destroying a file, or entering the wrong value for the parameter input of a model. Operational risk also includes fraud—for example, when a trader or other employee intentionally falsifies and misrepresents the risks incurred in a transaction. *Technology risk*, principally computer systems risk, also falls into the operational risk category.

Legal and Regulatory Risk

Legal and regulatory risk arises for a whole variety of reasons; it is closely related to operational risk as well as to reputation risk (discussed below). For example, a counterparty might lack the legal or regulatory authority to engage in a risky transaction. Legal and regulatory risks are classified as operational risks under Basel II Capital Accord.

In the derivative markets, legal risks often only become apparent when a counterparty, or an investor, loses money on a transaction and decides to sue the provider firm to avoid meeting its obligations (for an example, see Box 6-4 in Chapter 6).

Another aspect of regulatory risk is the potential impact of a change in tax law on the market value of a position. For example, when the British government changed the tax code to remove a particular tax benefit during the summer of 1997, one major investment bank suffered huge losses.

Business Risk

Business risk refers to the classic risks of the world of business, such as uncertainty about the demand for products, or the price that can be charged for those products, or the cost of producing and delivering products. We offer a recent example of business risk in Box 1A-3.

BOX 1A-3 NONBANKING EXAMPLE OF BUSINESS RISK: HOW PALM TUMBLED FROM HIGH-TECH STARDOM

Palm was a pioneer in "handheld computers" in the early 1990s. In December 2000 annual sales were up 165 percent from the previous year. In March 2001 the first sign of slowing sales hit the firm. The top management of Palm decided that the appropriate response was to quickly launch their newest model of handheld computers, the m500 line.

The CEO, Carl Yankowski, received assurances from his management that the m500 line could be out in two weeks. Palm unveiled the m500 line on March 19. Sales of Palm's existing devices slowed further as customers decided to wait for the new model. The problem was that the waiting time wasn't two weeks. Palm didn't leave enough time for the testing of the m500 before sending the design to be manufactured. Production of the m500 line kept hitting snags. Palm wasn't able to ship the new model in volume until May, more than six weeks after the announcement.

Inventory of the older product began to pile up, leading to a huge $300 million write-off of excess inventory and a net loss of $392 million for the fiscal quarter that ended June 1, compared with a profit of $12.4 million a year earlier. The firm's stock price plummeted and, as a consequence, an acquisition that was key to Palm's strategy collapsed—the deal was for $264 million in Palm's stock. The company cut 250 workers, lost key employees, and halted the construction of new headquarters.

Palm's rivals such as RIM (BlackBerry) and Microsoft increased their efforts to capitalize on Palm's mistakes.

In the world of manufacturing, business risk is largely managed through core tasks of management, including strategic decisions—e.g., choices about channel, products, suppliers, how products are marketed, inventory policies, and so on. There is, of course, a very large, general business literature that deals with these issues, so for the most part we skirt around the problem of business risk in this book.

However, there remains the question of how business risk should be addressed within formal risk management frameworks of the kind that we describe in this book and that have become prevalent in the financial industries. Although business risks should surely be assessed and monitored, it is not obvious how to do this in a way that complements the banking industry's treatment of classic credit and market risks. There is also room for debate over whether business risks need to be supported by capital in the same explicit way. In the Basel II Capital Accord, "business risk" was excluded from the regulators' definition of operational risk, even though some researchers believe it to be a greater source of volatility in bank revenue than the operational event/failure risk that the regulators *have* included within bank minimum capital requirements.

Business risk is affected by such factors as the quality of the firm's strategy and/or its reputation, as well as other factors. Therefore, it is common practice to view strategic and reputation risks as components of business risk, and the risk literature sometimes refers to a complex of business/strategic/reputation risk. In this typology we differentiate these three components. In Chapter 2 we further discuss business risk management issues in nonbank corporations.

Strategic Risk

Strategic risk refers to the risk of significant investments for which there is a high uncertainty about success and profitability. It can also be related to a change in the strategy of a company vis-à-vis its competitors. If the venture is not successful, then the firm will usually suffer a major write-off and its reputation among investors will be damaged. Box 1A-4 gives an example of strategic risk.

Banks, for example, suffer from a range of business and strategic risks (see Box 1A-5). Some of these risks are very similar to the kind of risk seen in nonfinancial companies, while others are driven by market or credit variables, even though they are not conventionally thought of as market risks or credit risks.

BOX 1A-4   NONBANKING EXAMPLE OF STRATEGIC RISK: HOW NOKIA, CHASING THE TOP END OF THE MARKET, GOT HIT IN THE MIDDLE TWICE

Part 1: First Strategic Mistake

In 1999 Nokia launched a huge and costly effort to explore the new market for cell phones that allowed users to get on the Internet, watch movies, and play video games. Nokia spent hundreds of millions of dollars launching a string of "smartphones," allocating 80 percent of its research and development budget ($3.6 billion a year) to software, much of it designed to give phones computer-like capabilities. Nokia was also racing to thwart the threat of Microsoft's coming "first to market" with similar software for smartphones (which would set the standards for this new market).

Retrospectively, it appears that Nokia focused on the wrong battle and picked the wrong competitor to worry about. Smartphones proved too bulky and too expensive for many consumers, and remained (at the time) a tiny presence in the market.

Moreover, in concentrating on smartphones, Nokia neglected one of the hottest growth sectors in cell phones—i.e., cheaper midrange models with sharp color screens and cameras—giving competitors, such as Samsung Electronics and archrival Motorola, a rare opportunity to steal market share. The bet that phones would one day converge with computers was premature.

Nokia's global market share plunged to 29 percent from 35 percent by mid-2003. In 2003 Nokia sold 5.5 million smartphones, far short of Nokia's target of 10 million. In the first quarter of 2004, Nokia's sales fell 2 percent in a global cell phone market that grew 40 percent from the year before, as measured by the number of units sold.

Part 2: Second Strategic Mistake

In the half-dozen years leading up to 2013, Nokia failed to successfully adjust its strategy to capitalize on the smartphone revolution. The firm faces significant competition in the smartphone market, including Apple and competitors that have adopted Google's Android. Ironically, given Nokia's earlier concern that Microsoft would introduce first-to-market software for smartphones, Nokia's strategy in early 2013 was to deploy Microsoft Windows (in lieu of their own Symbian operating system) in order to make their product more attractive. Nokia might succeed in its strategy, or Nokia could be acquired; the company has extensive cash holdings, significant strategic value (say, for Microsoft), and patents that could potentially be worth billions.[1] However, Nokia has destroyed significant shareholder value: its share price has dropped by a factor of 10 and is less than its cash holding per share, while its credit rating has been downgraded to junk status.

---

[1]As this book went to press in September 2013 Microsoft announced that it had purchased Nokia's devices and services business and licenced Nokia's patents.

BOX 1A-5   EXAMPLES OF BUSINESS AND STRATEGIC RISK IN BANKING

Retail Banking

- The advent of new business models puts pressure on existing business strategies.
- A major acquisition turns out to be much less profitable than forecasted.

Mortgage Banking

- A sharp rise in interest rates triggers a sharp fall in mortgage origination volume.
- A decline in demand for new housing in a certain location leads to a decline in mortgage origination volume.

Wealth Management

- Falling or uncertain stock markets lead to lower investment fund sales.

Capital Markets Activities

- Relative size of the bank may limit its ability to win large loan underwritings.
- Higher exposure to capital markets creates earnings volatility.

Credit Cards

- Increased competition can lead banks to offer credit cards to new market segments (e.g., subprime customers whose payment behavior is not well understood).
- Competitors with sophisticated credit risk management systems may begin to steal genuinely profitable market share, leaving competitors that cannot differentiate between customers unwittingly offering business to relatively risky customers.

Reputation Risk

From a risk management perspective, reputation risk can be divided into two main classes: the belief that an enterprise can and will fulfill its promises to counterparties and creditors; and the belief that the enterprise is a fair dealer and follows ethical practices.

The importance of the first form of reputation risk is apparent throughout the history of banking and was a dramatic feature of the 2007–2009 crisis. In particular, the trust that is so important in the banking sector was shattered after the Lehman Brothers collapse in September 2008. At a time of crisis, when rumors spread fast, the belief in a bank's soundness can be everything.

The second main form of reputation risk, for fair dealing, is also vitally important and took on a new dimension around the turn of the millennium following accounting scandals that defrauded the shareholders, bondholders, and employees of many major corporations during the late 1990s boom in the equity markets. Investigations into the mutual funds and insurance industry by New York Attorney General Eliot Spitzer made clear just how important a reputation for fair dealing is, with both customers and regulators.

In a survey released in August 2004 by PricewaterhouseCoopers (PwC) and the Economist Intelligence Unit (EIU), 34 percent of the 134 international bank respondents believed that reputation risk is the biggest risk to corporate market value and shareholder value faced by banks, while market and credit risk scored only 25 percent each.

No doubt this was partly because, at the time, corporate scandals like Enron, Worldcom, and others were still fresh in bankers' minds. However, more recently, concern about reputation risk has become prominent again with the rapid growth of public and social networks. Anybody can spread a rumor over the Internet, and the viral spread of news, the use of talkbacks on digital news pages, and the growth of blogs can all create headaches for corporations trying to maintain their reputation.

Reputation risk poses a special threat to financial institutions because the nature of their business requires the confidence of customers, creditors, regulators, and the general market place. The development of a wide array of structured finance products, including financial derivatives for market and credit risk, asset-backed securities with customized cash flows, and specialized financial conduits that manage pools of purchased assets, has put pressure on the interpretation of accounting and tax rules and, in turn, has given rise to significant concerns about the legality and appropriateness of certain transactions. Involvement in such transactions may damage an institution's reputation and franchise value.

Financial institutions are also under increasing pressure to demonstrate their ethical, social, and environmental responsibility. As a defensive mechanism, 10 international banks from seven countries announced in June 2003 the adoption of the "Equator Principles," a voluntary set of guidelines developed by the banks for managing social and environmental issues related to the financing of projects in emerging countries. The Equator Principles are based on the policy and guidelines of the World Bank and International Finance Corporation (IFC) and require the borrower to conduct an environmental assessment for high-risk projects to address issues such as sustainable development and use of renewable natural resources, protection of human health, pollution prevention and waste minimization, socioeconomic impact, and so on.

Systemic Risk

Systemic risk, in financial terms, concerns the potential for the failure of one institution to create a chain reaction or domino effect on other institutions and consequently threaten the stability of financial markets and even the global economy.

Systemic risk may be triggered by losses at an institution. However, simply the perception of increased risk may lead to panic about the soundness of an institution, or to a more general "flight to quality" away from risky assets and toward assets perceived to be less risky. This may cause serious market disruptions to propagate across otherwise healthy segments of the market. In turn, these disruptions may trigger panicked "margin call" requests, obliging counterparties to put up more cash or collateral to compensate for falling prices. As a consequence, borrowers may have to sell some of their assets at fire-sale prices, pushing prices further down, and creating further rounds of margin calls and forced sales.

One proposal for addressing this kind of systemic risk is to make the firms that create the systemic exposure pay a fair price for having created it and for imposing costs on other market participants.[8] However, this would mean measuring, pricing, and then taxing the creation of systemic risk—a potentially complex undertaking.

The many interconnections and dependencies among financial firms, in both the regulated and unregulated sectors, exacerbate systemic risk under crisis conditions. The failures and near-failures of Bear Stearns, Lehman Brothers, and AIG during the financial crisis of 2007–2009 all contributed to systemic risk by creating massive uncertainty about which of the key interconnections would transmit default risk.

The size of an institution that is in trouble can lead to panic about the scale of the default, but this is not the only concern. Market participants may fear that large-scale liquidations will disrupt markets, break the usual market interconnections, and lead to a loss of intermediation functions that then may take months, or years, to rebuild.

---

[8]See V. V. Acharya, T. F. Cooley, M. P. Richardson, and I. Walter, eds., *Regulating Wall Street: The Dodd-Frank Act and the New Architecture of Global Finance*, Wiley, 2010.

The Dodd-Frank Act (see Chapter 3) focuses on systemic risk. It establishes a Financial Stability Oversight Council (FSOC) whose role is to identify systemic risks wherever they arise and recommend policies to regulatory bodies. A very important feature of the Dodd-Frank Act is the decision to move the market for a wide range of OTC derivatives onto centralized clearing and/or exchange trading platforms. As a consequence, the counterparty risk inherent in OTC derivative transactions will be transformed into an exposure to a central counterparty. The central clearinghouse will set margins so that risk positions will be marked-to-market. Even so, the remaining central clearinghouse risk is potentially itself a threat to the financial system and must be carefully regulated and monitored. However, this should be easier than regulating private OTC markets because clearinghouses are supervised public utilities.

2

CORPORATE RISK
MANAGEMENT: A PRIMER

Nonfinancial companies are exposed to many traditional business risks: earnings fluctuate due to changes in the business environment, new competitors, new production technologies, and weaknesses in supply chains. Firms react in various ways: holding inventories of raw materials (in case of unexpected interruption in supply or an increase in raw material prices), storing finished products (to accommodate unexpected increases in demand), signing long-term supply contracts at a fixed price, or even conducting horizontal and vertical mergers with competitors, distributors, and suppliers.[1] This is classic business decision making but it is also, often, a form of risk management. In this chapter, we'll look at a more specific, and relatively novel, aspect of enterprise risk management: why and how should a firm choose to hedge the financial risks that might affect its business by means of financial contracts such as derivatives?

This issue has received attention from corporate management in recent years as financial risk management has become a critical corporate activity and as regulators, such as the Securities & Exchange Commission (SEC) in the

---

[1] For example, Delta Air Lines bought a ConocoPhillips refinery to gain more control over its fuel costs (*The New York Times*, May 1, 2012).

United States, have insisted on increased disclosures around risk management policies and financial exposures.[2]

In this chapter, we'll focus on the practical decisions a firm must make if it decides to engage in active risk management. These include the problem of how the board sets the risk appetite of a firm, the specific procedure for mapping out a firm's individual risk exposures, and the selection of risk management tactics. We'll also sketch out how exposures can be tackled using a variety of risk management instruments such as swaps and forwards—and take a look at how this kind of reasoning has been applied by a major pharmaceutical company (Box 2-1). We'll use manufacturing corporations as our examples, since the arguments in this chapter apply generally to enterprise risk management (ERM).

But before we launch into the practicalities of hedging strategies, we must first confront a theoretical problem: according to the most fundamental understanding of the interests of shareholders, executives should not actively manage the risks of their corporation at all!

Why *Not* to Manage Risk in Theory . . .

Among economists and academic researchers, the starting point to this discussion is a famous analysis by two professors, Franco Modigliani and Merton Miller (M&M), laid out in 1958, which shows that the value of a firm cannot be changed merely by means of financial transactions.[3] The M&M analysis is based on an important assumption: that the capital markets are perfect, in the sense that they are taken to be highly competitive and that participants are not subject to transaction costs, commissions, contracting and information costs, or taxes.

---

[2]In the United States, the Sarbanes-Oxley (SOX) legislation enacted by the U.S. Congress in the summer of 2002 requires internal control certifications by chief executive officers (CEOs) and chief financial officers (CFOs). This legislation was prompted by a rash of extraordinary corporate governance scandals that emerged during 2001 to 2003 as a result of the 1990s equity boom. While some firms had been using risk management instruments overenthusiastically to "cook the books," others had not involved themselves sufficiently in analyzing, managing, and disclosing the fundamental risks of their business.

[3]F. Modigliani and M. H. Miller, "The Cost of Capital, Corporation Finance, and the Theory of Investment," *American Economic Review* 48 (1958), pp. 261–297.

Under this assumption, M&M reasoned that whatever the firm can accomplish in the financial markets, the individual investor in the firm can also accomplish or unwind on the same terms and conditions.

This line of reasoning also lies behind the seminal work of William Sharpe, who in 1964 developed a way of pricing assets that underlies much of modern financial theory and practice: the capital asset pricing model (CAPM).[4] In his work, Sharpe establishes that in a world with perfect capital markets, firms should not worry about the risks that are specific to them, known as their idiosyncratic risks, and should base their investment decisions only on the risks they hold in common with other companies (known as their systematic or beta risks). This is because all specific risks are diversified away in a large investment portfolio and, under the perfect capital markets assumption, this diversification is assumed to be costless. (See Chapter 5 for an elaboration of these models.) Firms should therefore not engage in any risk reduction activity that individual investors can execute on their own without any disadvantage (due to economies of scale, for example).

Those opposed to active corporate risk management often argue that hedging is a zero-sum game and cannot increase earnings or cash flows. Some years ago, for example, a senior manager at a U.K. retailer pointed out, "Reducing volatility through hedging simply moves earnings and cash flows from one year to another."[5] This line of argument is implicitly based on the perfect capital markets assumption that the prices of derivatives fully reflect their risk characteristics; therefore, using such instruments cannot increase the value of the firm in any lasting way. It implies that self-insurance is a more efficient strategy, particularly because trading in derivatives incurs transaction costs.

We've listed some theoretical arguments against using derivatives for risk management, but there are also some important practical objections. Active hedging may distract management from its core business. Risk management requires specialized skills, knowledge, and infrastructure, and also entails significant data acquisition and processing effort. Especially in small and medium-sized corporations, management often lacks the skills and time necessary to

---

[4]W. Sharpe, "Capital Asset Prices: A Theory of Market Equilibrium under Conditions of Risk," *Journal of Finance* 19 (1964), pp. 425–442.

[5]J. Ralfe, "Reasons to Be Hedging—1,2,3," *Risk* 9(7), 1996, pp. 20–21.

engage effectively in such activity.[6] Furthermore, a risk management strategy that is not carefully structured and monitored can drag a firm down even more quickly than the underlying risk (see Box 2-2 later in this chapter).

As a final point, even a well-developed risk management strategy has compliance costs, including disclosure, accounting, and management requirements. Firms may avoid trading in derivatives in order to reduce such costs or to protect the confidential information that might be revealed by their forward transactions (for example, the scale of sales they envisage in certain currencies). In some cases, hedging that reduces volatility in the true economic value of the firm could *increase* the firm's earnings variability as transmitted to the equity markets through the firm's accounting disclosures, due to the gap between accounting earnings and economic cash flows.

... And Some Reasons *for* Managing Risk in Practice

Such arguments against hedging seem powerful, but there are strong objections and counterarguments. The assumption that capital markets operate with perfect efficiency does not reflect market realities. Also, corporations that manage financial risks often claim that firms hedge in order to reduce the chance of default, for none of the theories we described above take account of one crucial and undeniable market imperfection: the high fixed costs associated with financial distress and bankruptcy.

A related argument is that managers act in their own self-interest, rather than in the interests of shareholders (referred to as "agency risk"). Since managers may not be able to diversify the personal wealth that they have accumulated (directly and indirectly) in their company, they have an incentive to reduce volatility. It can be further argued that managers have an interest in reducing risks, whether or not they have a large personal stake in the firm, because the results of a firm provide signals to boards and investors concerning the skills

---

[6]In an empirical research project using data on 7,139 firms from 50 countries, Bartram, Brown and Fehle found evidence that large, profitable companies with low market-to-book ratios tend to hedge more of their financial risks than smaller, less profitable firms with greater growth opportunities. (S. Bartram, G. Brown, and F. Fehle, "International Evidence on Financial Derivatives Usage," unpublished working paper, University of North Carolina, 2004.)

of its management. Since it is not easy for shareholders to differentiate volatility that is healthy from volatility that is caused by management incompetence, managers may prefer to manage their key personal performance indicator (the equity price of their firm) directly, rather than risk the confusion of managing their firm according to the long-term economic interests of a fully diversified shareholder.

Another argument for hedging rests on the collateral effects of taxation. First, there is the effect of progressive tax rates, under which volatile earnings induce higher taxation than stable earnings.[7] The empirical evidence for this as a general argument is not very strong. There is also the claim that hedging increases the debt capacity of companies, which in turn increases interest tax deductions.[8] Certainly, many firms use derivatives for tax avoidance rather than risk management purposes, but this represents a rather separate issue.

More important, perhaps, is that risk management activities allow management better control over the firm's natural economic performance. Each firm may legitimately communicate to investors a different "risk appetite," confirmed by the board. By employing risk management tools, management can better achieve the board's objectives.

Furthermore, the theoretical arguments do not condemn risk reduction activity that offers synergies with the operations of the firm. For example, by hedging the price of a commodity that is an input to its production process, a firm can stabilize its costs and hence also its pricing policy. This stabilization of prices may in itself offer a competitive advantage in the marketplace that could not be replicated by any outside investor.

As a side argument, it's worth pointing out that individuals and firms regularly take out traditional insurance policies to insure property and other assets at a price that is higher than the expected value of the potential damage (as assessed

---

[7]See Rene Stulz, "Rethinking Risk Management," *Journal of Applied Corporate Finance* 9(3), Fall 1996, pp. 8–24. The argument relates to the convexity of the tax code with increasing marginal tax rates, limits on the use of tax-loss carry forward, and minimum tax rate. Maintaining taxable income in a range so that it is neither too high nor too low can produce tax benefits.

[8]See J. Graham and D. Rogers, "Do Firms Hedge in Response to Tax Incentives?" *Journal of Finance* 57, 2002, pp. 815–839. Available at SSRN: http//ssrn.com/abstract=279959. They perform empirical testing for 442 firms and find that the statistical benefit from increased debt capacity is 1.1% of firm value. They also find that firms hedge to reduce the expected cost of financial distress.

in actuarial terms). Yet very few researchers have questioned the rationale of purchasing insurance with the same vigor as they have questioned the purchase of newer risk management products such as swaps and options.

Perhaps the most important argument in favor of hedging, however, is its potential to reduce the cost of capital and enhance the ability to finance growth. High cash flow volatility adversely affects a firm's debt capacity and the costs of its activities—no one is happy to lend money to a firm likely to suffer a liquidity crisis. This becomes particularly expensive if the firm is forced to forego profitable investment opportunities related to its comparative advantages or private information.

Campello et al. (2011) sampled more than 1,000 firms and found that hedging reduces the cost of external financing and eases the firms' investment process. They focused on the use of interest rate and foreign currency derivatives for the period 1996–2002. They found that hedging reduces the incidence of investment restrictions in loan agreements. They also showed that hedgers were able to invest more than nonhedgers, controlling for many other factors.[9]

An earlier empirical study in the late 1990s investigated why firms use currency derivatives.[10] Rather than analyze questionnaires, the researchers looked at the characteristics of Fortune 500 nonfinancial corporations that in 1990 seemed potentially exposed to foreign currency risk (from foreign operations or from foreign-currency-denominated debt). They found that approximately 41 percent of the firms in the sample (of 372 companies) had used currency swaps, forwards, futures, options, or combinations of these instruments. The major conclusion of the study was "that firms with greater growth opportunities and tighter financial constraints are more likely to use currency derivatives." They explain this as an attempt to reduce fluctuations in cash flows so as to be able to raise capital for growth opportunities.

However, McKinsey has pointed out that boards of nonfinancial firms are often unimpressed when looking inside their firm for insight into how the firm should manage risk. Many nonfinancial companies possess only poorly structured

---

[9]M. Campello, C. Lin, Y. Ma, and H. Zou, "The Real and Financial Implications of Corporate Hedging," *Journal of Finance* 66(5), October 2011, pp. 1615–1647.

[10]C. Geczy, B. A. Minton, and C. Schrand, "Why Firms Use Currency Derivatives," *Journal of Finance* 82(4), 1997, pp. 1323–1354.

information on the key risks facing their company, which in turn complicates decisions on the best approach to hedging their risks.[11]

The theoretical argument about why firms might legitimately want to hedge may never produce a single answer; there are a great many imperfections in the capital markets and a great many reasons why managers might want to gain more control over their firm's results. But the theoretical argument against hedging has one important practical implication. It tells us that we should not take it for granted that risk management strategies are a "good thing," but instead should examine the logic of the argument in relation to the specific circumstances and aims of the firm (and its stakeholders). Meanwhile, we can be pretty sure that firms should not enter derivatives markets to *increase* exposure to a risk type unless they can demonstrate that understanding, managing, and arbitraging this risk is one of their principal areas of expertise.

Hedging Operations Versus Hedging Financial Positions

When discussing whether a particular corporation should hedge its risks, it is important to look at how the risk arises. Here we should make a clear distinction between hedging activities related to the operations of the firm and hedging related to the balance sheet.

If a company chooses to hedge activities related to its operations, such as hedging the cost of raw materials (e.g., gold for a jewelry manufacturer), this clearly has implications for its ability to compete in the marketplace. The hedge has both a size and a price effect—i.e., it might affect both the price and the amount of products sold. Again, when an American manufacturing company buys components from a French company, it can choose whether to fix the price in euros or in U.S. dollars. If the French company insists on fixing the price in euros, the American company can opt to avoid the foreign currency risk by hedging the exposure. This is basically an operational consideration and, as we outlined above, lies outside the scope of the CAPM model, or the perfect capital markets assumption.

---

[11]"Top-down ERM: A Pragmatic Approach to Managing Risk from the C-Suite," McKinsey working paper on Risk 22, August 2010.

In a similar way, if a company exports its products to foreign countries, then the pricing policy for each market is an operational issue. For example, suppose that an Israeli high-tech company in the infrastructure business is submitting a bid to supply equipment in Germany over a period of three years, at predetermined prices in euros. If most of the high-tech firm's costs are in dollars, then it is natural for the company to hedge the future euro revenues. Why should the company retain a risky position in the currency markets? Uncertainty requires management attention and makes planning and the optimization of operations and processes more complicated. It is generally accepted that companies should concentrate on business areas in which they have comparative advantages and avoid areas where they cannot add value. It follows that reducing risk in the production process and in selling activities is usually advisable.

The story is quite different when we turn to the problem of the balance sheet of the firm. Why should a firm try to hedge the interest rate risk on a bank loan? Why should it swap a fixed rate for a variable rate, for example? In this case, the theoretical arguments we outlined above, based on the assumption that capital markets are perfect, suggest that the firm should not hedge.

Equally, however, if we believe financial markets are in some sense perfect, we might argue that investors' interests are also unlikely to be much harmed by appropriate derivatives trading. The trading, in such a case, is a "fair game." Nobody will lose from the activity, provided it is properly controlled and the firm's policy is fully transparent and disclosed to all investors.

If one argues that financial markets are not perfect, then the firm may gain some advantage from hedging its balance sheet. It may have a tax advantage, benefit from economies of scale, or have access to better information about a market than investors.

This all suggests a twofold conclusion to our discussion:

- Firms should risk-manage their operations.
- Firms may also hedge their assets and liabilities, so long as they disclose their hedging policy.

In any case, whether or not it makes use of derivative instruments, the firm must make risk management decisions. The decision not to hedge is also, in effect, a risk management decision that may harm the firm if the risk exposure turns into a financial loss.

In most cases, the relevant question is not whether corporations should engage in risk management but, rather, how they can manage and communicate their particular risks in a rational way. In Box 2-1 we can see one example of how Merck, a major pharmaceutical company, chose to describe one part of its hedging policy to investors in a particular financial year. We can see that the firm has adopted a particular line of reasoning to justify its hedging activities, and that it has tried to link some of the specific aims of its hedging activities to information about specific programs. As this example illustrates, each firm has to consider which risks to accept and which to hedge, as well as the price that it is willing to pay to manage those risks. The firm should take into account how efficiently it will be able to explain its aims to investors and other stakeholders.

BOX 2-1   HOW MERCK MANAGES FOREIGN EXCHANGE AND INTEREST RISK EXPOSURES[1]

The Company [Merck] operates in multiple jurisdictions and, as such, virtually all sales are denominated in currencies of the local jurisdiction. Additionally, the Company has entered and will enter into acquisition, licensing, borrowings or other financial transactions that may give rise to currency and interest rate exposure.

Since the Company cannot, with certainty, foresee and mitigate against such adverse fluctuations, fluctuations in currency exchange rates and interest rates could negatively affect the Company's results of operations, financial position and cash flows.

In order to mitigate against the adverse impact of these market fluctuations, the Company will from time to time enter into hedging agreements. While hedging agreements, such as currency options and interest rate swaps, may limit some of the exposure to exchange rate and interest rate fluctuations, such attempts to mitigate these risks may be costly and not always successful.

---

[1]Extracted from Merck's Form 10-K filing with the Securities & Exchange Commission, February 28, 2013.

Foreign Currency Risk Management

The Company has established revenue hedging, balance sheet risk management, and net investment hedging programs to protect against volatility of future foreign currency cash flows and changes in fair value caused by volatility in foreign exchange rates.

The objective of the revenue hedging program is to reduce the potential for longer-term unfavorable changes in foreign exchange rates to decrease the U.S. dollar value of future cash flows derived from foreign currency denominated sales, primarily the euro and Japanese yen. To achieve this objective, the Company will hedge a portion of its forecasted foreign currency denominated third-party and intercompany distributor entity sales that are expected to occur over its planning cycle, typically no more than three years into the future. The Company will layer in hedges over time, increasing the portion of third-party and intercompany distributor entity sales hedged as it gets closer to the expected date of the forecasted foreign currency denominated sales. The portion of sales hedged is based on assessments of cost-benefit profiles that consider natural offsetting exposures, revenue and exchange rate volatilities and correlations, and the cost of hedging instruments. . . . The Company manages its anticipated transaction exposure principally with purchased local currency put options. . . . In connection with the Company's revenue hedging program, a purchased collar option strategy may be utilized. . . . The Company may also utilize forward contracts in its revenue hedging program.

The primary objective of the balance sheet risk management program is to mitigate the exposure of foreign currency denominated net monetary assets of foreign subsidiaries where the U.S. dollar is the functional currency from the effects of volatility in foreign exchange. In these instances, Merck principally utilizes forward exchange contracts, which enable the Company to buy and sell foreign currencies in the future at fixed exchange rates and economically offset the consequences of changes in foreign exchange from the monetary assets. Merck routinely enters into contracts to offset the effects of exchange on exposures denominated in developed country currencies, primarily the euro and Japanese yen. For exposures in developing country currencies, the Company will enter into forward contracts to partially offset the effects of exchange on exposures when it is deemed economical to do so based on a cost-benefit analysis that considers the magnitude of the exposure, the volatility of the exchange rate and the cost of the hedging instrument. . . .

A sensitivity analysis to changes in the value of the U.S. dollar on foreign currency denominated derivatives, investments and monetary assets and liabilities indicated that if the U.S. dollar uniformly weakened by 10% against all currency exposures of the Company at December 31, 2012, *Income before taxes* would have declined by approximately $20 million in 2012.

Foreign exchange risk is also managed through the use of foreign currency debt. The Company's senior unsecured euro-denominated notes have been designated as, and are effective as, economic hedges of the net investment in a foreign operation.

Interest Rate Risk Management
The Company may use interest rate swap contracts on certain investing and borrowing transactions to manage its net exposure to interest rate changes and to reduce its overall cost of borrowing. The Company does not use leveraged swaps and, in general, does not leverage any of its investment activities that would put principal capital at risk.

Putting Risk Management into Practice

Determining the Objective

A corporation should not engage in risk management before deciding clearly on its objectives in terms of risk and return. Without clear goals, determined and accepted by the board of directors, management is likely to engage in inconsistent, costly activities to hedge an arbitrary set of risks. Some of these goals will be specific to the firm, but others represent important general issues.

The first step is to determine the "risk appetite" of the firm as the board defines it. Risk appetites can be expressed in a number of ways, including quantitative and qualitative statements.[12] For example, the risk appetite might set out the types of risk that the firm is willing to tolerate and, therefore, which risks should be hedged and which risks the company should assume as part of its business strategy. The risk appetite might also indicate the maximum losses the organization is willing to incur at a given confidence limit during a given time period, where such statistical calculations can be made in a way that is practical and robust. Many firms nowadays use stress testing to help articulate their risk appetite; that is, the firm analyzes the likely level of losses in a range of plausible but severely adverse scenarios and the board says clearly which losses are tolerable and which are not. The board can then direct management to mitigate or insure against extreme losses that offend against the corporate risk appetite, and the firm can budget for this activity. Chapter 4 discusses the issue of aligning the risk appetite of the firm to its strategy. One point is clear: accepting projects with positive risk-adjusted net present value (NPV) can enhance the welfare of all stakeholders.

Boards face a key dilemma when setting the risk appetite for a firm: whose interests is the firm trying to capture in its risk appetite statement? For example, debt holders are relatively conservative in the risks they would like the firm to adopt and may worry about downside risks that threaten the firm's solvency even if these risks seem to be on the borderline of plausibility. A shareholder with a large portfolio of investments, on the other hand, may find it more acceptable for a firm to remain exposed to a large but unlikely risk, so long as the returns for assuming the risk are large enough.

The objectives that the board sets out should not take the form of slogans, such as "maximum profit at minimal risk." The board should also consider which of the corporation's many risks should be hedged, and which risks the company should assume as part of its business strategy. The objectives should be set in clear, executable directives. In addition, the criteria for examining whether the objectives are attained should be set in advance. A jewelry company may decide to fully hedge its gold inventory, or it may insure the price of gold below a certain

---

[12]"Quantitative measures may include financial targets, e.g., capital adequacy, target debt rating, earnings volatility, credit or other external ratings. Qualitative measures may refer to reputational impact, management effort and regulatory compliance," KPMG, *Understanding and Articulating Risk Appetite*, 2008, p. 4.

level. By following such a policy the company can remove all or some of the risk stemming from raw material prices for a given period.

The board should declare whether the aim is to hedge accounting profits or economic profits, and short-term profits or long-term profits. With regard to the former issue, the two measures of profit do not necessarily coincide, and at times their risk exposure is vastly different. Imagine a U.S. firm that purchases a plant in the United Kingdom that will serve U.K. clients, for a sum of £1 million. The investment is financed with a £1 million loan from a British bank. From an economic point of view, the sterling loan backed by a plant in the United Kingdom is fully hedged. However, if the plant is owned and managed by the U.S. company (that is, if it fails the "long arm test" that determines whether a subsidiary should be considered as an independent unit), its value is immediately translated into U.S. dollars, while the loan is kept in pounds. Hence, the company's accounting profits are exposed to foreign exchange risk: if the pound is more expensive, in terms of the dollar, at the end of the year, the accounts will be adjusted for these financial costs and will show a reduction in profits.

Should the U.S. company hedge this kind of accounting risk? If it buys a futures contract on the pound, its accounting exposure will be hedged, but the company will be exposed to economic risk! In this case, no strategy can protect both the accounting and economic risks simultaneously. (As we hinted earlier, while most managers claim that they are concerned with economic risk only, in practice many corporations, especially publicly traded corporations, hedge their accounting risks in order to avoid fluctuations in their reported earnings.)

It is the board's prerogative, subject to local regulatory provisions, to decide whether to smooth out the ups and downs of accounting profits, even at significant economic cost. Such a decision should be conveyed to management as a guiding policy for management actions. If the board is concerned with economic risk instead, this policy should also be made clear, and a budget should be allocated for this purpose.

Another important factor that the board should make clear is the time horizon for any of the risk management objectives set for management. Should hedging be planned to the end of the quarter or the end of the accounting year? Should it be set three years into the future? Hedging a future expected transaction with a long-term option or futures contract has liquidity, accounting, and tax implications. For example, should the U.S. firm hedge a sales order from a French customer that will be delivered two years from now? Remember that the income will be allowed to enter the firm's books only upon delivery, while the futures contract will be marked-to-market at the end of each quarter (see also Box 2-2). The derivatives contract may also incur a tax liability if, at the end of the tax year, it shows a profit.

It may make sense for the board to make clear certain "risk limits"—i.e., to allow management to operate within a given zone of prices and rates, and be exposed to the risk within the zone, but to disallow risk exposure beyond those limits. In such a case, the limits should be set clearly. For example, a British company might decide to avoid dollar exposures of more than $5 million. It might also decide to tolerate fluctuations of the dollar rate within the exchange rate zone of $1.45 to $1.60 to the pound, but to hedge currency risks that fall outside these limits.

Defining an objective in terms of a simple formula that can be immediately translated into clear practical instructions is rarely feasible. The objective should be broken down into clear rules that can be implemented in line with the major policy principles (such as the time horizon, and whether the hedging aims are those of bondholders or shareholders).

Mapping the Risks

After the objectives have been set and the general nature of the risks to be managed is decided upon, it is essential to map the relevant risks and to estimate their current and future magnitudes.

For example, let us assume that the board has decided to hedge *currency risks* arising from current positions and expected transactions in the next year. Now the office of the chief financial officer of the firm will have to map the specific risks likely to arise from exchange rate fluctuations. It should make a record of all assets and liabilities with values that are sensitive to exchange rate changes, and should classify all these positions in terms of the relevant currency. In addition, information should be collected from the sales or marketing division on firm orders from foreign clients for each currency that are due over the coming year, as well as on expected orders from foreign clients that will need to be fulfilled during this period. (A decision must be made about whether to hedge unconfirmed sales. It might be decided, for example, to base the hedge on expected revenues.) Then, all expected expenses over the coming year that are denominated in foreign currencies should be traced (with the help of the production division). Again, the firm will have to decide how it is going to distinguish between firm purchasing commitments and uncertain purchase orders. The timing of cash inflows and outflows for each foreign currency can then be matched.

The same sort of mapping can be applied to other risk factors and risky positions, starting with the business risk of the firm and moving to its market risks and credit risks. Operational risk elements should also be identified.

The firm should prepare a list (a "hit parade") of the 10 most significant risk exposures of the firm. The process leading to such a list can be very rewarding to the firm in understanding the most threatening risks it faces. Each risk on the list should be characterized in terms of its potential damage and the probability of its occurrence, say, during the next 12 months.

In the United States, the SEC has since 1998 required publicly traded companies to assess and quantify their exposure to financial instruments that are linked to changes in interest rates, exchange rates, commodity prices, and equity prices. However, the SEC does not require firms to assess their underlying or "natural" exposure to changes in the same risk factors. Management, needless to say, cannot ignore these natural positions, whether they are matched to derivative positions or not.

When mapping a firm's risks, it is important to differentiate between risks that can be insured against, risks that can be hedged, and risks that are noninsurable and nonhedgeable. This classification is important because the next step is to look for instruments that might help to minimize the risk exposure of the firm.

Instruments for Risk Management

After mapping the risks, the next step is to identify instruments that can be used to risk-manage the exposures. Some of the instruments can be devised internally. For example, a U.S. firm with many assets denominated in British pounds can borrow money in pounds, in a loan transaction with the same time-to-maturity as the assets, and thus achieve a natural hedge (at least, an economic hedge, though not necessarily an accounting hedge). Similarly, a division with a euro liability may be hedged internally against another division with euro-denominated assets. Internal or "natural" hedging opportunities like this sidestep the transaction costs and many of the operational risks associated with purchasing risk management contracts and so should be considered first.

Next, the company should compare competing ways to manage the risks that have been identified as transferable or insurable in the risk-mapping process, and evaluate the likely costs and benefits. The firm might decide to fully insure or offset some risks, partially insure others, and refrain from insuring some insurable risks. With regard to traditional insurance products, many large and well-diversified companies, operating in a variety of geographical areas, nowadays opt to self-insure their property (including cars, plants, and equipment). The same logic can sometimes be applied to financial risks.

Plenty of financial instruments for hedging risks have been developed over the last few decades, as we can see in Figure 2-1 (we describe some of them in more detail in Chapter 6). The most fundamental distinction is between instruments traded on public exchanges versus over-the-counter (OTC) instruments that represent private contracts between two parties (often a corporation and a bank). Exchange-traded instruments are based on a limited number of underlying assets and are much more standardized than OTC contracts. For example, the strike prices and maturities of exchange-traded options are defined and set in advance by the exchanges in order to "commoditize" the risk management product and promote a thriving and liquid market.

Conversely, OTC products are issued by commercial and investment banks and thus can be tailored to customers' needs. For example, an OTC option on the British pound can be customized to a size and maturity that fits the needs of the customer and to a strike price that suits the client's strategy. OTC instruments can be made to "fit" a customer's risk exposure quite closely, but they tend to lack the price transparency and liquidity advantages of exchange products. Another concern in the OTC market is the credit risk associated with the counterparty to each contract. During the financial crisis of 2007–2009, many OTC contracts collapsed or endured an extended period of uncertainty about the ability of counterparties to honor them, while all exchange-based products were honored.[13]

The active markets for exchange-traded instruments in the United States are mainly the Chicago Board Options Exchange (CBOE), which offers active markets in equity and index options; the Philadelphia Options Exchange, which

---

[13]Prior to the financial crisis of 2007–2009, counterparty credit risk was not considered to be a particularly key area and the concept of Credit Value Adjustment (CVA), discussed in Chapter 13, was largely ignored in practice.

FIGURE 2-1 The Evolution of Financial Instruments for Hedging Risks

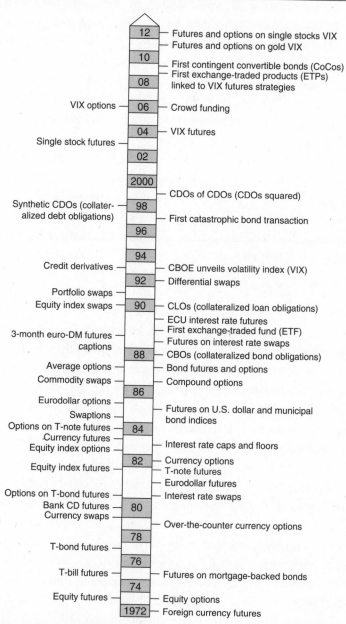

is the leader in foreign exchange options; the International Securities Exchange (ISE), which is the leader in electronic trading of derivatives; the Chicago Board of Trade (CBOT), which runs huge markets in futures on stock indexes, bonds, and major commodities; the Chicago Mercantile Exchange (CME), with major markets in currency futures; and the International Monetary Market (IMM), with options trading on futures on foreign currencies and on bonds and interest rates. There are also active markets for options and futures in London (LIFFE), Paris, Brussels, Amsterdam (Euronext), Frankfurt, and Zurich (Eurex) and in most major countries and financial centers.

The variety of exchange-traded and, especially, OTC instruments is huge. In fact, investment bankers are willing to price almost any possible derivative based on known, traded underlying financial instruments. This leaves the corporate hedger with the considerable problem of identifying the most suitable instruments to hedge the specific risky positions of his or her firm, taking into consideration cost and liquidity.

Constructing and Implementing a Strategy

The office of the CFO must have access to all the relevant corporate information, market data, and statistical tools and models before attempting to devise a hedging strategy. The firm will need to select certain pricing and hedging models to help in the formation of the strategy. A firm can opt to purchase statistical estimates and/or models from external vendors. However, the officers in charge of risk management must have a deep understanding of the tools they are about to employ to reach decisions.

A key tactical decision is whether to hedge risks by means of "static" strategies or to plan more "dynamic" strategies. In a static strategy, a hedging instrument is purchased to match the risky position as exactly as possible and is maintained for as long as the risky position exists (or for a set horizon). This kind of strategy is relatively easy to implement and monitor. Dynamic strategies involve an ongoing series of trades that are used to calibrate the combined exposure and the derivative position. This strategy calls for much greater managerial effort in implementing and monitoring the positions, and may incur higher transaction costs.

For example, suppose that a U.S. company exporting to England is expecting to receive 5 million British pounds three months from today and wishes to hedge the downside risk—i.e., the risk that the pound will devalue against the

U.S. dollar. It could simply follow the static strategy of buying a put option for the full quantity and term of the exposure. Alternatively, to hedge dynamically, the firm might buy a longer-term put option than the three-month maturity of the exposure (longer maturity options often trade at a lower implied volatility and thus cost less per unit of risk) and adjust the quantity of the put so that it simulates the three-month put option in the static strategy. The dynamic strategy may require the hedger to adjust the put position on a daily or weekly basis and to increase or reduce the quantities of options, and possibly switch to other options with still lower relative risk premiums (maintaining the relevant hedge ratio through time). To follow a dynamic approach, the firm must possess sophisticated and reliable models with which to trade in the markets and monitor its positions—and the staff and skills to put these tools to use. But even this will not necessarily save the firm from making significant errors in communicating and implementing its risk management strategy. In Box 2-2 we take a look at a dynamic corporate risk management strategy put in place by a major U.S. energy trading company, Metallgesellschaft Refining & Marketing, Inc. (MGRM)—a strategy that went badly wrong. It's worth noting that in this case there has never been any suggestion of fraud or malpractice; problems arose purely through the nature, implementation, and communication of the corporate risk management strategy.

BOX 2-2   DYNAMIC RISK MANAGEMENT STRATEGIES CAN GO BADLY WRONG: THE MGRM EXAMPLE

In 1993 MGRM (MG Refining & Marketing), the U.S. subsidiary of Metallgesellschaft (MG), entered into contracts to supply end-user customers with 150 million barrels of oil products (gasoline and heating oil) over a period of 10 years, at fixed prices.

MGRM's fixed-price forward delivery contracts exposed it to the risk of rising energy prices. In the absence of a liquid market for long-term futures contracts, MGRM hedged this risk with both short-dated energy futures contracts on the New York Mercantile Exchange (NYMEX) and over-the-counter (OTC) swaps. The derivative positions were concentrated in short-dated futures and swaps, which had to be rolled forward monthly as they matured. Each month, the size of the derivatives position was reduced by the amount of product delivered that month, with the intention of preserving a one-to-one hedge. According to Culp and Miller (1995), "such a strategy is neither inherently unprofitable nor fatally flawed, provided top management understands the program and the long-term funding commitments necessary to make it work."[1]

This rolling hedge strategy can be profitable when markets are in a state known as "backwardation" (oil for immediate delivery commands a higher price than does oil for future delivery), but when markets are in contango (the reverse relationship) it can result in losses. This is because when a company is rolling the hedge position in a backwardated market, the contract near expiration is sold at a higher price than the replacement contract, which has a longer delivery date, resulting in a rollover profit. The contrary applies when the market is in contango.

This meant that MGRM was exposed to curve risk (backwardation versus contango) and to basis risk, which is the risk that short-term oil prices might temporarily deviate from long-term prices. During 1993, cash prices fell from close to $20 a barrel in June to less than $15 a barrel in December, leading to $1.3 billion of margin calls that MGRM had to meet in cash. The problem was further compounded by the change in the shape of the price curve, which moved from backwardation to contango. MGRM's German parent reacted in December 1993 by liquidating the hedge, thus turning paper losses into realized losses.

Whether or not the cash drain from the negative marked-to-market of the futures positions was sustainable, the decision by the supervisory board to liquidate the hedge might not have been the optimal one. According to Culp and Miller, at least three viable alternatives should have been contemplated to avoid the price impact of unwinding the hedges in the marketplace: securing additional financing and continuing the program intact; selling the program to another firm; or unwinding the contracts with the original customers.

---

[1] C. Culp and M. Miller, "Blame Mismanagement, Not Speculation, for Metall's Woes," *European Wall Street Journal*, April 25, 1995.

Another fundamental consideration in the hedging strategy is the planning horizon. The horizon can be fixed at the end of a quarter or the end of the tax year, or it might be a rolling horizon. Investment horizons should be made consistent with performance evaluations.

Other important considerations are accounting issues and potential tax effects. Accounting rules for derivatives are quite complex and are constantly being revised. Under the current rules, derivatives used for hedging must be perfectly matched to an underlying position (e.g., with regard to quantities and dates). They can then be reported together with the underlying risky positions, and no accounting profit or loss needs to be reported. If the positions are not perfectly matched, the marked-to-market profit or loss in the hedge must be recorded in the firm's accounts, even though changes in the value of the underlying exposure are not. Accounting rules affect how derivatives are presented in quarterly or year-end financial reports and how they affect the profit-and-loss statement. The MGRM case highlights the discrepancy between economic and accounting hedging. While MGRM was about fully hedged in economic terms, it was fully exposed in accounting terms, and was also not prepared to absorb liquidity risk.

Tax considerations can be very important because they affect the cash flows of the firm. Different derivative instruments with different maturities may incur very different tax liabilities; tax treatment is also inconsistent from country to country. This means that a multinational corporation might find it advantageous to use derivatives in one country to hedge positions that are related to its business in another country. Professional advice on tax matters is a key factor when devising hedging strategies.

A strategy is only as good as its implementation, but however skillful the implementation, some deviation from the plan can be expected. Prices in the marketplace can change and make some hedges unattractive. Since different people within the firm are often responsible for establishing risky positions and hedging positions, special care should be taken to monitor the positions. For example, if the British client in our earlier example pays the firm after two, rather than three, months, then the three-month put must be liquidated before it matures.

Performance Evaluation

The corporate risk management system must be evaluated periodically. Crucially, the evaluation should assess the extent to which the overall goals have been achieved—not whether specific transactions made a profit or loss. Whenever a risk is hedged, the party on one side of the hedge transaction inevitably shows a profit while the counterparty inevitably shows a loss. The corporation can never know in advance which side will increase in value and which side will lose value—after all, that's why it is managing the risk in the first place. So if the goal is to eliminate risk, and risk is eliminated, then the risk manager has done the job well even if the hedged position has generated an economic or accounting loss (compared to the original, unhedged position).

Reducing earnings volatility may not be the only criterion, however. Risk managers can legitimately be evaluated in terms of how well they manage the transaction costs of hedging, including the tax payments that can arise out of employing derivatives. He or she should also act within a given budget; major deviations from the budget should be explored and explained.

When evaluating the performance of risk management, the board of directors should also decide whether or not to change the policy of the company. There is nothing wrong with a firm's changing its objectives, so long as the changes are based on thorough analysis and are consistent with the other activities and aims of the firm. Local regulatory requirements for the disclosure of risks may mean that policy changes in market risk management should be made public if the changes are material.

3

BANKS AND THEIR REGULATORS: THE POST-CRISIS REGULATORY FRAMEWORK

In this chapter we move on from our earlier discussion of corporate risk management to look at the special case of bank risk management and regulation, partly because it is so important in itself, especially after the near collapse of the world financial system following the 2007–2009 financial crisis and subsequent sovereign debt crises, and partly because bank risk management techniques have had a huge influence on the more general world of financial risk management in all sectors of the economy.

There is little disagreement over the fact that banks are special entities and require tight risk management standards and regulation. Box 3-1 describes why in more detail. How this should be achieved is another story, and the recent history of bank regulation is complex. In this chapter we take a global perspective and focus on the successive waves of international banking standards devised by the Basel Committee (Basel I, II, and III) as well as important new legislation in the United States (the Dodd-Frank Act). However, readers must bear in mind three real-world complications:

- First, it takes time for countries to adopt and implement international banking standards within their local legislative and regulatory frameworks—usually several years.

- Second, some countries may decide not to adopt a standard for the whole of their banking sector. For example, large banks may be obliged to follow a certain set of Basel standards, while small banks might not.
- Third, once adopted, international standards are implemented using a considerable degree of interpretation by national regulators (and, indeed, individual banks). For example, the European CRD 4 (Capital Requirements Directive 4), which transposes Basel III into European law, takes into account the fact that European banks often own insurance companies and exempts them from deducting investments in insurance entities from their common equity tier 1 capital.

BOX 3-1 BANK REGULATION AND RISK MANAGEMENT

Regulators try to carefully watch over bank activities, closely monitor their risk management standards, and impose on them a unique set of minimum required regulatory capital rules. Why do they do so? There are two key reasons: banks collect deposits from ordinary savers, and they play a key role in the payment and credit system.

Although bank deposits are often insured by specialized institutions (such as the Federal Deposit Insurance Corporation [FDIC] in the United States, the Canadian Deposit Insurance Corporation [CDIC] in Canada and the Deposit Insurance Corporation [DIC] in Japan), in effect national governments act as the final guarantor. Some also act as a lender of last resort—e.g., the Federal Reserve in the United States during the 2007–2009 financial crisis and the European Central Bank's rescue of the Spanish banking system in 2012. National governments therefore have a very direct interest in ensuring that banks remain capable of meeting their obligations: they wish to limit the cost of the government "safety net" in the case of a bank failure. By acting as a buffer against unanticipated losses, regulatory capital helps to privatize a burden otherwise borne by national governments.

Furthermore, fixed-rate deposit insurance itself creates the need for capital regulation. As deposits are insured up to a given limit, there is no incentive for depositors who stay within the insured limits to select their bank cautiously. Instead, depositors may be tempted to look for the highest deposit rates, without paying enough attention to a bank's creditworthiness.

Regulators also try to make sure that banks are well-enough capitalized to avoid a systemic "domino effect," whereby an individual bank failure, or the fear of such a failure leading to a run on a bank, propagates to the rest of the financial system. Such "domino effects" can cause other banks and financial companies to fail, disrupting world economies and incurring heavy social costs. The panic during the financial crisis of 2007–2009 is far from the only example. It was the fear of such a failure that led regulators in the United States to intervene to help Continental Illinois. Continental Illinois was the largest bank ever rescued by the FDIC in 1984, until Washington Mutual failed in 2008, which ended up being over several times larger than the failure of Continental Illinois. As another example, a series of bank runs in Russia in the summer of 2004 led to significant fears of a domino effect in the Russian banking system, though this was averted.

The underlying threat is that banks will transmit failures in the financial sector through to the wider economy. The years of recession and slow growth in many developed economies following the 2007–2009 financial crisis are simply the latest example of this, albeit on a massive, global scale.

Meanwhile, the world does not stay still. While the complex process of adoption and implementation for Basel II was still in process around the world, the 2007–2009 financial crisis and subsequent sovereign debt crises began to unfold. As a result, Basel II had to be reformed (not replaced) with various additions and supplements that came to be known as Basel III, which will itself be phased in over many years around the world—and augmented at the local level by additional national legislation and regulatory rules.

For all these reasons, the global map of implemented banking regulation looks more like a complex, continually evolving geological map than the sleek, finished design of some carefully crafted jet engine.

In this chapter, we first introduce and define Basel I, II, and III to help readers build a historical perspective on the regulatory evolution. Then we look in more detail at the principles (or three "pillars" in banking jargon) that underpin Basel II, because these continue to drive much of the implemented banking regulation around the world today and will also underpin Basel III. We then look at how Basel III attempts to improve post-crisis bank regulation and, finally, survey the most important piece of local post-crisis legislation—the Dodd-Frank Act in the United States.[1]

Basel I, II, and III: A Quick Introduction

Figure 3-1 summarizes the last 30 years of bank capital and risk management regulation devised by the Basel Committee. The journey began back in the 1980s, when structural changes in the global financial markets prompted national regulators to consider how they might create a more "level playing field" in terms of bank soundness and regulation. These structural changes included the internationalization of banking and the rise of the Japanese banks, as well as the dramatic growth of derivatives markets in the 1980s.

The organizational point of articulation for national regulators was the Basel Committee on Banking Supervision (BCBS), or "Basel Committee," initially composed of officials from the G10 plus Switzerland and Luxembourg.[2] Countries are represented by their central bank and also by the authority with formal responsibility for the prudential supervision of the banking industry, where this is not the central bank. The Basel Committee does not have any formal supranational supervisory authority; however, it encourages convergence toward common approaches and common standards.

Over the years, the work of the Committee has fallen into three broad stages: Basel I, II, and III, with various supplements.

---

[1]Dodd-Frank Wall Street Reform and Consumer Protection Act, 111th Congress of the United States, Public law 11-203, July 21, 2010.

[2]Created in 1974, the Basel Committee was initially composed of the officials from the G10 (Belgium, Canada, France, Germany, Italy, Japan, the Netherlands, Sweden, the United Kingdom, and the United States) plus Switzerland and Luxembourg. In 2009, the Basel Committee was enlarged to include the G20 countries with the addition of Argentina, Australia, Brazil, China, Hong Kong, India, Indonesia, Mexico, Russia, Saudi Arabia, Singapore, South Africa, South Korea, Spain, and Turkey. There are now 27 country members of the Basel Committee (including nine from the European Union).

The Basel Committee reports to the central bank governors and heads of supervision of its member countries. It meets four times a year, usually in Basel, Switzerland, under the patronage of the Bank for International Settlements (BIS).

FIGURE 3-1 Twenty Five Years of Capital Regulation

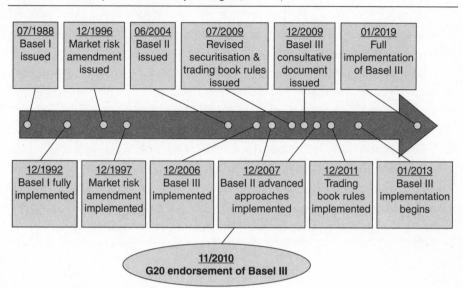

Source: Bank for International Settlements

Basel I

The 1988 Basel Accord,[3] now referred to as the Accord or Basel I, represented the first internationally agreed capital standard for banks. The Accord was intended to raise capital ratios, which were generally perceived to be too low, and to harmonize minimum capital ratios for banks in all major jurisdictions across the world.

To begin with, the Accord addressed only credit risk, taken to be the predominant risk of the banking industry. Importantly, the Accord established the principle that the amount of capital required to protect against losses from an asset should vary depending upon the riskiness of the asset. At the time, the Accord set 8 percent as the minimum level of capital to be held against the sum of all risk-weighted assets (RWA). It also set out how different types of assets could

---

[3]Basel Committee on Banking Supervision, *International Convergence of Capital Measurement and Capital Standards.* Basel, Switzerland: Basel Committee on Banking Supervision, 1988.

be divided into broad classes (e.g., OECD banks versus corporate borrowers), each of which was then linked to a specific capital requirement. (Appendix 3.1 provides the details.) The increasing importance of market risk for some banks led to the Market Risk Amendment of 1996 (Appendix 3.2).[4]

As a standard, the 1988 Accord was strikingly successful and has now been adopted in some form in more than 100 countries. Although the banking industry has designed new regulatory frameworks, Basel II and now Basel III, that will supersede the 1988 Accord, the 1988 Accord is a long way from being "old hat." Around the world, the Basel II regulations have often not yet replaced the 1988 Accord: although Europe adopted Basel II in 2008, the United States will largely bypass Basel II and move larger banks directly to Basel III over the next few years. Many banks around the world will be allowed to continue to conform to the 1988 Accord standards for some years, and perhaps indefinitely.

Basel II

The Basel II regulatory reforms were a long time coming. The Basel Committee worked on the new standards from at least 1998, issuing a stream of working papers, consultative papers, and conducting-intensive quantitative impact studies (QIS), until publishing the main Basel II Accord in June 2004[5] with revisions in June 2006. The Basel Committee said that the Accord's key objectives were to focus on large, internationally active banks and the stability of the banking system, and to enhance competitive equality (i.e., two banks with the same

---

[4]Basel Committee on Banking Supervision, *Amendment to the Capital Accord to Incorporate Market Risk Capital Requirements*. Basel, Switzerland: Basel Committee on Banking Supervision, 1996.

[5]Basel Committee on Banking Supervision, *International Convergence of Capital Measurement and Capital Standards*. Basel, Switzerland: Basel Committee on Banking Supervision, June 2004.

    Basel II is generally taken to include the June 2004 Accord, revisions to the Accord published in June 2006, elements of the 1988 Accord that were not revised during the Basel II process, the 1996 Market Risk Amendment, and the July 2005 paper on the treatment of double default effects, i.e., Basel Committee on Banking Supervision, *The Application of Basel II to Trading Activities and the Treatment of Double Default Effects*. Basel, Switzerland: Basel Committee on Banking Supervision, June 2005.

portfolios should hold the same capital wherever they were located).[6] The reforms were intended to promote safety and soundness in the financial system by maintaining at least the same level of capital in the system as banks maintained under Basel I.[7]

The reforms had three organizing principles or "pillars": capital adequacy; supervisory review; and market discipline. The main innovations, compared to Basel I, included:

- A relatively more risk-sensitive Standardized Approach to calculating capital for credit risk (to replace the risk weightings under Basel I)
- The opportunity—sometimes the obligation—for banks to shift to more sophisticated internal ratings based on IRB approaches to calculating minimum required credit risk capital, which allowed banks to apply their own internal risk ratings methodologies
- A more comprehensive approach to risks—in particular, requiring banks to include bank operational risk, covering a whole range of event risks such as computer failures and fraud by staff, in their capital calculations

We describe the three pillars of Basel II in the next section of this chapter and provide further details of the Accord, including descriptions of the Foundation and Advanced IRB approaches to credit risk calculation, in Appendix 3.3.

Although Basel II influenced regulatory reform in other financial industries (Box 3.2), it is often thought that the crisis of 2007–2009 and the failure of

---

[6]The scope of application of the Basel II Accord was also extended to include, on a fully consolidated basis, any holding company that is the parent entity within a banking group (to ensure that it captures the risk of the whole banking group). Banking groups are groups that engage predominantly in banking activities; in some countries, a banking group may be registered as a bank. Majority-owned or -controlled banking entities, securities entities (where subject to broadly similar regulation or where securities activities are deemed banking activities), and other financial entities should generally be fully consolidated.

[7]In the case of Basel II, unlike Basel III, the Basel Committee had no desire to change the capital requirements for the banking system as a whole: it calibrated its new capital adequacy regime to make sure that, overall, capital levels would remain unchanged. However, among individual banks the Committee intended there to be a redistribution of capital according to each bank's risk profiles and business activities.

BOX 3-2   BASEL II: A MODEL FOR NONBANK FINANCIAL INSTITUTIONS?

The succession of Basel regulatory reforms has stimulated the thinking of nonbank financial institution regulators.

For example, the Securities and Exchange Commission (SEC) in the United States has adopted Basel II, allowing securities firms to opt into the new regulatory capital regime. The insurance industry is also currently looking to apply more sophisticated regulatory capital standards, most notably through Europe's Solvency II initiative.

Solvency II is a European initiative that will apply to European insurance companies a regulatory framework similar to Basel II. Solvency II has three pillars, just like Basel II. However, the application of Solvency II keeps being postponed, the latest estimate being January 2016, as there is strong opposition from the European insurance industry, which is worried that it will be left at a competitive disadvantage relative to the rest of the world.

Under Solvency II, both assets and liabilities will be marked-to-market, or estimated at their "fair value" if markets are not liquid enough to generate prices. Capital requirements are risk based.

According to the industry's quantitative impact study (QIS5), the new capital requirements would not only lead to a massive increase in equity capital (solvency capital requirement, or SCR) and technical reserves, but would also force insurance companies to exit, or at least substantially reduce their investment in, the equity markets, securitized products such as RMBS, and long-term corporate bonds, which are strongly penalized in terms of capital charge relative to sovereign bonds, short-term corporate bonds, and real estate assets.

---

many banks proved that Basel II is a failed piece of bank regulation. However, this may not be entirely fair. While Basel II was being implemented in Europe at about the time of the crisis, it had not yet been implemented in the United States, where the crisis started.[8] Furthermore, Basel II regulations were imposed

---

[8]U.S. banks continue to report risk-weighted assets (RWAs) according to Basel I standards. According to the Basel Committee, this reduces the capital requirements for U.S. banks by 20 percent relative to Basel II requirements.

on commercial banks, and not on the investment banking sector, where many of the earliest and worst problems appeared.[9] Certainly, however, the crisis revealed many potential inadequacies in Basel II, and the Basel III reforms are an explicit attempt to map out and remedy these weaknesses.

Basel III

The subprime crisis that erupted in July 2007, and which nearly led to a total collapse of the financial system in the United States and other countries after the bankruptcy of Lehman Brothers in September 2008, prompted a major revision of bank regulation.

First, as something of an emergency measure, the Basel II market risk framework was revised in July 2009—a set of reforms known as Basel 2.5, set out in more detail in Appendix 3.4.[10] The basic aim of Basel 2.5 was to offset deficiencies in the existing value-at-risk approaches to calculating market risk capital by introducing stressed value-at-risk calculations and an incremental capital charge to cover losses in value due to credit migration and loss of liquidity, as well as more stringent capital ratios for securitization tranches.[11] Basel 2.5 is regarded as something of an interim measure, and a more fundamental review

---

[9]Following the failure of Lehman Brothers, the last two investment banks in the United States, i.e., Goldman Sachs and Morgan Stanley, were forced to become bank holding companies regulated by the Fed. Going forward, they will have to comply with Basel regulations, especially with regard to capital requirements.

[10]The Basel 2.5 Accord is described in three documents:

Basel Committee on Banking Supervision, *Revision to the Basel II Market Risk Framework*. Basel, Switzerland: Basel Committee on Banking Supervision, June 2009

Basel Committee on Banking Supervision, *Enhancement to the Basel II Framework*. Basel, Switzerland: Basel Committee on Banking Supervision, June 2009

Basel Committee on Banking Supervision, *Guidelines for Computing Capital for Incremental Risk in the Trading Book*. Basel, Switzerland: Basel Committee on Banking Supervision, July 2009

[11]Basel Committee on Banking Supervision, *Revisions to the Basel Securitization Framework*, Consultative Document, December 2012.

of the treatment of bank trading books is under way (e.g., a consultative paper on the fundamental review of the trading book was published in May 2012[12]).

Second, a series of fundamental reforms to Basel II were introduced, collectively known as Basel III.[13] These included, most prominently:

- A new and tighter definition of capital, placing the emphasis firmly on equity capital
- Increased capital requirements and new liquidity requirements
- The coverage of additional risks in the minimum capital requirement calculations (e.g., counterparty credit risk for OTC derivatives and repo transactions)
- The introduction of a backstop leverage ratio in case the risk-weighted calculations failed to capture bank risk
- Additional requirements for institutions deemed to be systemically important
- A series of measures intended to make sure bank capital requirements did not act to heighten economic cycles, including a new countercyclical capital buffer

A detailed analysis of these reforms takes up much of the rest of this chapter. However, first we must introduce readers to the fundamental "three pillars" approach to bank regulation introduced in Basel II. These three pillars remain important organizing principles under Basel III.

The Pre-Crisis Regulatory Framework: Basel II's Enduring Three Pillars

The Basel Committee developed its Basel II comprehensive framework for capital regulation around what the regulators called their "three pillars": minimum capital requirements, supervisory review, and market discipline. In this section

---

[12]Basel Committee on Banking Supervision, *Fundamental Review of the Trading Book*, Consultative document. Basel, Switzerland: Basel Committee on Banking Supervision, May 2012.

[13]Basel Committee on Banking Supervision, *Basel III: A Global Regulatory Framework for More Resilient Banks and Banking Systems*. Basel, Switzerland: Basel Committee on Banking Supervision, December 2010 (revised June 2011).

we will look at what the three pillars try to achieve under Basel II, before examining in the next section how they are modified by the Basel III reforms.

Pillar I: Capital Adequacy

The objective of Pillar I was to revise the 1988 Basel I Accord's capital ratios by aligning minimum capital requirements more closely to each bank's actual risk profile. The new minimum capital requirement framework encompassed three areas of risk: (1) credit risk (included in the 1988 Accord); (2) the market risk of trading activities (introduced in the 1996 Market Risk Amendment); and (3) operational risk (new).

In particular, Pillar I was designed to do a better job than the 1988 Accord in obligating banks to hold more capital for high-risk borrowers relative to low-risk borrowers. To make the regulations sensitive to the varying degrees of sophistication among banking institutions, the regulators laid out three options for the calculation of the minimum required capital for credit risk.

Under the Standardized Approach, risk weights are based on available external credit ratings—for example, from rating agencies such as Standard & Poor's, Moody's, and Fitch. This option was really designed for banks engaged in less complex forms of lending and credit underwriting.

More sophisticated banks are allowed to use one of two Internal Ratings Based (IRB) approaches to credit risk. Under an IRB approach, banks are allowed to rely partly on their own assessment of their borrowers' credit risk to determine their minimum capital requirement, provided they can satisfy the regulators on a number of topics such as the quality of the internal credit data available to them, the processes they use to set and validate the parameters used in the calculation, and the soundness of various control processes. The result is that implementing Basel II around the world has brought about many significant changes in bank systems, processes, and data gathering. (We describe the Standardized Approach and the Foundation and Advanced IRB Approaches in detail in Appendix 3.3.)

Similar to the range of options available for assessing credit risk exposures, Basel II allows banks to choose one of three approaches for measuring operational risk exposures: (1) the Basic Indicator Approach, (2) the Standardized Approach, or (3) the Advanced Measurement Approach (AMA). The first two approaches don't really try to measure operational risk accurately; instead, they apply regulator-defined proxy measurements that, under the Standardized Approach, are broadly tailored to the kind of business lines that constitute the bank.

The AMA offers a more radical approach to the problem. Under the AMA, banks are permitted to choose their own methodology for assessing operational risk, so long as it is sufficiently comprehensive and systematic. The regulators deliberately did not set out standards and criteria for use of the AMA in great detail, in an effort to spur the development of innovative operational risk approaches by the banking industry. The regulators said that any operational risk measurement system must have certain "key features," including the use of "internal data, relevant external data, scenario analysis and factors reflecting the business environment and internal control systems." They also insisted that banks develop a "credible, transparent, well-documented and verifiable approach for weighting these fundamental elements" in any operational risk calculations. (We discuss approaches to measuring operational risk in much more detail in Chapter 14.)

The inclusion of operational risk in the Basel II capital requirements, together with the 1996 Market Risk Amendment to the 1988 Accord that extended the initial Accord to include risk-based capital requirements for market risks incurred in bank trading books, meant that Basel II covered a much wider spectrum of risks than Basel I. The 1996 Amendment encompassed debt and equity positions in bank trading books, and foreign exchange and commodity positions in both the trading and banking books, and included all financial instruments that are marked-to-market, whether they are plain vanilla products such as bonds or stocks, or complex derivative instruments such as options, swaps, or credit derivatives. The authorities recognized the complexity of correctly assessing market risk exposure, especially for derivative products. The Basel Committee therefore allowed institutions that met certain risk management standards to choose between employing their own internal value-at-risk (VaR) model,[14] known as the "internal models

---

[14]It's worth noting that bank regulators in the United Kingdom had implemented model-based market risk capital charges some years earlier under the Amsterdam Accord.

approach," and a standard model proposed by the Basel Committee, known as the "standardized approach." (We explain the concept behind value-at-risk modeling in Chapter 7 and look at the 1996 Amendment more closely in Appendix 3.2.)

Under Basel II, banks are encouraged by their local regulators to move along the spectrum of available approaches for both credit and operational risks as they develop more sophisticated controls and validation techniques and build ever more comprehensive databases. But the rate of adoption of Basel II and its variant methodologies has varied considerably from regulator to regulator around the world.[15]

When developing Basel II, the Basel Committee recognized the need to provide tangible incentives for banks to adopt the more advanced approaches to capital measurement. Banks that invested in enhanced risk management, and could therefore adopt the most advanced methodologies for calculating minimum capital requirements, believed they might gain some reductions in minimum regulatory capital; in any case, risk-sensitive minimum capital requirements should allow bank capital to be used more efficiently to protect against risk.

Retail exposures, such as credit card receivables, do not attract as much capital as corporate exposures because, under Basel II, they were considered to be part of large, stable, diversified portfolios composed of many small transactions.

In addition, small and medium-sized enterprises (SMEs) which, under Basel II, are considered as retail exposures, benefit from a size adjustment that can lead to a reduction in required capital of up to 20 percent compared to similar large corporate exposures that exhibit the same default rate. This favorable treatment was a response to the fear, voiced by a number of influential commentators, that the new capital regime would reduce the supply of credit to SMEs and make borrowing more expensive for them. Since SMEs are an important component of the economy, that would have adversely affected economic growth, innovation, and employment.

---

[15]So far, no U.S. bank has formally complied with Basel II.

Pillar II: The Supervisory Review Process

The supervisory review process of capital adequacy is intended to ensure that a bank's capital position and strategy are consistent with its overall risk profile. Early supervisory intervention will be encouraged if the capital amount is thought not to provide a sufficient buffer against risk.

The objective here is to ensure that banks follow rigorous processes, measure their risk exposures correctly, and have enough capital to cover their risks. This pillar allows regulators to scrutinize bank practices that look like attempts at regulatory arbitrage. Pillar II is also the route for supervisors to make sure banks have considered risks that are not explicitly covered under Pillar I. For example, under Basel II, interest rate risk in the banking book, a significant form of bank risk, is treated under Pillar II and is not part of the Pillar I capital requirement calculations. Interest risk capital charges are applied to banks only when interest rate risks in an individual institution's banking book are significantly above average.

Under Pillar II, supervisors can require banks to hold capital in excess of minimum required regulatory ratios depending on a variety of factors such as the experience and quality of its management and control process, its track record in managing risks, the nature of markets in which the bank operates, and the volatility of its earnings. In assessing capital adequacy, the regulators have to consider the effects of business cycles and the overall macroeconomic environment, as well as the systemic impact on the banking system should the bank fail.

The danger of the Basel II supervisory approach is that determinations of capital adequacy on a bank-by-bank basis can prove to be arbitrary and inconsistent. Soundness, in our view, should be defined as the probability of insolvency over a one-year horizon. Minimum soundness then becomes the insolvency probability consistent with an investment grade rating for the bank—i.e., BBB or better. Most banks currently target an insolvency probability of four to five basis points (i.e., 0.04–0.05%), which is consistent with a AA rating.

Under Basel II, all internationally active banks are expected to develop internal processes and techniques to carry out a self-assessment of their capital adequacy in relation to objective and quantifiable measures of risks. Banks should perform comprehensive and rigorous stress tests to identify possible events or changes in market conditions that could have an adverse effect on the bank.

Pillar III: Market Discipline

Basel II's Pillar III introduced a radical new requirement on banks to disclose risk information to the equity and credit markets, in the hope that investors would be better able to exert discipline on bank behavior (i.e., discourage them from taking inappropriate risks).

The Basel Committee's intention was to foster market transparency so that market participants could better assess bank capital adequacy.[16] The disclosure requirements pushed banks to publish detailed qualitative and quantitative information about capital levels, including details of capital structure and reserves for credit and other potential losses, risk exposures, and capital adequacy. These requirements cover not only the way in which a bank calculates its capital adequacy, but also the techniques it employs in its risk assessment.

The requirements of Pillar III of Basel II should be viewed against the backdrop of the long-term changes under way in the financial system. Bank operations have increasingly become more complex and sophisticated. Banks have considerable exposure to financial markets and are increasingly active in markets for complex financial products such as derivatives. These products can be used to hedge existing risks on banks' balance sheets or to take on new risks. During the 2007–2009 crisis, for instance, it became apparent that the growth of the credit derivatives market and the increased use of securitization were having a profound impact on the structure of bank risk profiles. In addition, large banks tend to operate internationally, in some cases with a majority of their operations taking place outside their home country.

---

[16]The disclosure requirements built on guidelines published in September 1998 by the Basel Committee on "Enhancing Bank Transparency." The Committee recommended that banks provide timely information across six broad areas: financial performance; financial position (including capital, solvency, and liquidity); risk management strategies and practices; risk exposures (including credit risk, market risk, liquidity risk, and operational, legal, and other risks); accounting policies; and basic business, management, and corporate governance information. These disclosures should be made at least annually, and more frequently if necessary. These recommendations have also been adopted by the G-10.

The Post-Crisis Regulatory Framework: Basel III and the Dodd-Frank Act

With the benefit of hindsight, capital standards were too weak for the type of risks that were building up in the world's financial system in the run-up to the financial crisis of 2007–2009.[17] In particular, the scale and nature of funding and market liquidity risks were not properly anticipated or managed in financial institutions, and both financial institutions and their regulators largely ignored the buildup of systemic risk concentrations such as those posed by the investment bank Lehman Brothers before it went bankrupt in 2008.

We turn now to the deficiencies in bank regulation and risk management in financial institutions that led to the 2007–2009 crisis and to the post-crisis regulatory framework that is being devised to avoid a repeat of these failures.

The events of September 2008 and their immediate aftermath were very dramatic. Lehman Brothers declared bankruptcy; the last two large U.S. investment banks, Goldman Sachs and Morgan Stanley, converted to bank holding companies (BHCs); Fannie Mae and Freddie Mac were nationalized; AIG was brought back from the brink of collapse; Fortis, the Dutch financial conglomerate, was broken up and sold; Iceland's largest commercial bank, and subsequently the Icelandic banking system, collapsed; and many countries had to step in to provide massive support to their banks.

This represented the height of the "subprime" crisis; however, it triggered huge public costs in both the short and medium term. Many government budgets, especially in Europe, were stretched by the need to offer massive amounts of official support to their banking systems. This contributed to the European sovereign debt crisis, which unfolded during 2010 as rescue packages were extended to Greece, Portugal, and Ireland and market participants realized that European sovereign debt could indeed default. For an extended period, other major economies in southern Europe came under severe pressure and looked as if they, too, might require external financial support. The spillover from the financial crisis to the real economy resulted in a massive loss of

---

[17]However, five days before its bankruptcy Lehman Brothers boasted a tier 1 capital ratio of 11 percent, almost three times the regulatory minimum. The immediate collapse of the bank was due to its lack of liquidity (including a refusal of the Treasury and the Fed to provide any relief).

wealth and significant unemployment in most European countries and the United States.

The deficiencies leading to the crisis were numerous and are attributable to bankers, investors, rating agencies, and regulators—among others. Here we briefly summarize the key deficiencies as background for our discussion of Basel III and other regulatory actions.

- *Capital:* The level and quality of capital held by banks proved to be inadequate. In particular, tier 1 hybrid capital did not play its intended loss-absorbing role.[18]
- *Leverage:* There was too much leverage in the banking system, particularly when this was combined with weak credit underwriting. Losses were made worse by a procyclical deleveraging process.
- *Conflict of interest:* This was a particular problem with regard to the "issuer pays" model of ratings for securitized products. This led to inflated ratings from rating agencies. The rated securitized products carried yields that were higher than usual for bonds in that rating category, indicating that the bond market understood that these bonds were riskier than the rating suggested.
- *Capital rules governing the trading book:* Banks had built up massive illiquid credit exposures in their portfolios. The VaR-based capital regime, with its ten-day liquidity horizon, was not designed to measure this kind of risk.[19] Banks abused this regime and warehoused highly illiquid, structured credit assets in the trading book while holding far too little capital against these assets. The assets proved impossible to value when liquidity disappeared.
- *Poor funding liquidity risk management and insufficient liquidity buffers:* Many banks relied excessively on wholesale short-term funding to finance long-term illiquid assets and securitized products. In particular, banks used asset-backed commercial paper (ABCP) conduits to increase their reported return on equity. They did this by moving loans,

---

[18]Hybrid capital is junior debt, usually subordinated long term, issued by commercial banks. In terms of seniority, the payment of principal and interest is behind other liabilities and before equity capital.

[19]Value-at-risk (VaR) is discussed in Chapter 7.

mortgages, and securitized products off balance sheet into a conduit or special investment vehicle (SIV), for which only a capital charge for the backup liquidity line was required (as opposed to the higher capital required if the assets had been held in the bank portfolios). In reality, the banks retained exposure to their assets in the off-balance-sheet vehicle. In the second half of 2007, when it became difficult to roll short-term funding, banks were obliged to bring the assets held in conduits and SIVs back onto their balance sheets.[20]

- *Poor incentives and governance:* There were many shortcomings in compensation practices, risk management, and the quality of supervision from boards and management, along with a lack of transparency that made it nearly impossible to understand a bank's exposures or the quality of the capital backing these exposures.

- *Insufficient understanding of systemic risk:* Systemic risk arises when firms or markets have the potential to propagate shocks or credit events and to inflict significant damage on the financial system and broader economy. In the crisis, major losses were incurred by systemically important and interconnected institutions that were considered too big to fail.

The crisis obliged the banking industry and its regulators to address these shortcomings and put in place longer-term reforms that they hope will make the financial system more resilient during future periods of stress. The Basel Committee has again been at the core of this reforming agenda, which crystallized at the G20 Leaders' Summit in Pittsburgh in 2009.[21] On November 12, 2010, the Basel III framework was endorsed by the G20 leaders in South Korea.

---

[20]Chapter 12 describes structured credit products and off-balance-sheet vehicles, and their applications.

[21]The G20 also required the two international accounting associations—i.e., IASB at the world level and FASB at the U.S. level—to work on the convergence of their accounting norms. The U.S. accounting system (U.S. GAAP), based on "fair value," is different from the IASB approach (IFRS and IAS), which is a mixed model of fair value and accrual accounting. The latter has been applied in the European Union since January 2005.

FIGURE 3-2 The Basel III Reform of Bank Capital Regulation

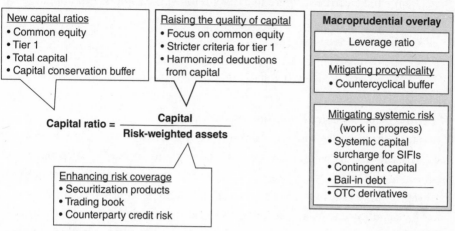

Source: Bank for International Settlements

Basel III is both a firm-specific, risk-based framework and a systemwide, systemic-risk-based framework.[22] That is, it seeks to make sure that individual firms hold enough capital and are adequately risk-managed, given their risk profile, while also trying to make sure that the system as a whole contains enough capital and is managed in a way that minimizes systemic risk. Figure 3-2 summarizes the new features of Basel III compared to Basel II.

Let's look first at the key firm-specific reforms before turning to the systemic-risk-based framework.

Basel III: The Key Firm-Specific Reforms

The main firm-specific reforms in Basel III attempt to increase the amount and quality of capital available to firms, and to improve each firm's funding and liquidity strategies.

---

[22]H. Hannoun, *The Basel III Capital Framework: A Decisive Breakthrough*, Bank for International Settlements, 2010.

One way to think through the Basel III capital reforms is to look at how they change the treatment of the three elements in the capital equation:

- The numerator—i.e., capital
- The denominator—i.e., risk-weighted assets
- The capital ratio itself

The Numerator: A Strict Definition of Capital

First and foremost, the Basel III framework raises the quality of capital. Prior to the crisis, the amount of tangible common equity at many banks, when measured against risk-weighted assets, had fallen as low as 1 to 3 percent, net of deductions. That represents a risk-based leverage of 100 to 1 and 33 to 1, respectively.

It was allowed to fall so low only because the definition of acceptable capital had been drawn much more broadly than tangible common equity. Under the old definition, capital comprised various elements with a complex set of minimums and maximums for each element. Banks had to keep track of tier 1 capital, innovative hybrid tier 1 instruments with debt-like features, such as the trust preferred securities (TruPSs), upper and lower tier 2, and tier 3 capital. Each type of capital had its own ceiling, in terms of its permitted contribution to regulatory capital, and these ceilings were sometimes a function of other capital elements. The complexity in the definition of capital made it difficult to determine how much capital would be available should losses arise.

The industry learned from the crisis that only common equity, including retained earnings, provided loss absorption. That is, while shareholders in banks suffered losses through a fall in bank share prices, investors in hybrid instruments hardly suffered any losses even when banks were in severe trouble because banks continued to pay interest on their hybrid debt to avoid being shut out of the market in the future.

As a result, hybrid tier 1 instrument is not included in the new Basel III definition of capital, and those currently in existence will be phased out over a ten-year horizon beginning in 2013. Tier 1 capital instead includes only tangible common equity and retained earnings—the highest-quality component of a bank's capital—and certain other instruments that have a loss absorbing capacity on a "going concern" basis—e.g., certain kinds of contingent convertible (CoCo) bonds. CoCo bonds are an important new type of instrument, discussed in some detail in Appendix 3.5, which can be eligible for both tier 1 and tier 2 capital depending on their characteristics.

The point is that all tier 1 capital must be able to absorb losses while the financial institution remains solvent and viable as a firm.

Furthermore, a number of deductions are made from common equity in order to allow it to qualify as tier 1 capital, including goodwill and intangibles, deferred tax assets, shortfall of provisions over expected loss, defined benefit pension assets, investment in core equity tier 1 instruments of banking, financial, and insurance entities (beyond 10 percent of capital), certain securitization exposures, and significant investments in commercial entities.[23]

Tier 2 capital will continue to provide loss absorption on a "gone concern" basis—i.e., following insolvency and upon liquidation. Tier 2 capital will typically consist of subordinated debt and contingent convertible capital, such as CoCo bonds.

Tier 3 capital, which was used to cover a portion of a bank's market risk capital charge, will be eliminated.

With respect to transparency, banks will be required to provide full disclosure and reconciliation of all capital elements.

The Denominator: Enhanced Risk Coverage

In the period leading up to the 2007–2009 crisis, banks reported a significant increase in their total assets. Yet, under the Basel II rules, the amount of risk-weighted assets showed only a modest increase. This was because some assets and activities that were risky were not properly captured, or were underestimated, in the calculation of risk-weighted assets.

Basel III substantially improves the coverage of the risks, especially those related to capital market activities: trading book, securitization products, and counterparty credit risk on OTC derivatives and repos. This enhanced risk coverage is expected to cause risk-weighted assets to increase substantially.

The challenge of improving risk weightings   One way to improve bank capital adequacy rules is to make sure that higher risk weights are attached to relatively riskier assets. The risk weightings, and the methodology behind them,

---

[23]This is a particular issue for German and French banks, which often own insurance companies. They have already asked for exemptions.

were significantly enhanced in the transition from Basel I to Basel II, and they have now been further refined under Basel III, especially for some asset classes such as securitization tranches and counterparty credit risk.

Nonetheless, the crisis made clear one fundamental problem when defining risk weights: assets that are not very risky in normal times may suddenly become very risky during a systemic crisis. For example, apparently risk-free assets, such as highly rated sovereign bonds, tranches of AAA structured products, and collateralized repos, to name just a few, turned out to exhibit a rather large tail risk. That is, in the rare instances when these assets show a large deterioration in value, the deterioration can turn out to be very serious indeed.

Let us illustrate some of the most challenging issues when setting risk weights, not all of which are fully addressed by Basel III:

- *Sovereigns:* The sovereign debt crisis of 2010 has shown that the zero risk weights given to AAA- and AA-rated sovereigns under the Standardized Approach of Basel II are unrealistic. They do not reflect the chance of a dramatic deterioration in the fiscal and debt positions of a country—e.g., as experienced by some European countries.
- *OTC derivatives (falling under ISDA's CSA, or Credit Support Annex) and repos:* The Lehman and Bear Stearns failures demonstrated that the very low capital charge on OTC derivatives and repos did not capture the systemic risk associated with the interconnectedness of key counterparties and the fact that the failure of a major counterparty may seriously damage other market participants (even if they have no direct exposure to the failing institution).
- *Senior tranches of securitization exposures:* AAA-rated tranches of structured products, such as super-senior tranches of ABS CDOs, proved to be much riskier than their high ratings suggested. The risk weight of 7 percent for super-senior tranches was too low and has now been raised to 20 percent.

Conversely, the financial crisis revealed that some assets with high risk weights, such as equity stakes in hedge funds, corporate bonds, and some retail exposures, experienced only modest losses during the crisis.

These examples show that there can be a rather weak correlation between risk weights and losses during periods of systemwide stress. Moreover, low risk weights may themselves encourage the buildup of systemwide risks.

In recognition of this general problem, the Basel Committee has introduced a simple leverage ratio as a backstop on bank risk taking. This requires a minimum ratio of bank capital to total assets, without any reference to risk weights (see discussion below).

The trading book and securitizations Basel II focused primarily on the banking book. But many of the major losses during the financial crisis of 2007–2009 came from the trading book, especially from complex structured products such as tranches of CDOs. The revised framework now requires:

- Introduction of a "stressed VaR" capital charge intended to capture the risk of a 12-month period of financial stress (see Appendix 3.3)
- Application of an incremental risk capital (IRC) charge to measure specific, or idiosyncratic, risk in credit sensitive positions when using VaR (see Appendix 3.3)
- Similar treatments for both trading and banking book securitizations
- Assignment of higher risk weights for resecuritizations (20 percent instead of 7 percent for AAA-rated tranches)
- Assignment of higher credit conversion factors (bond equivalents) for short-term liquidity facilities such as off-balance-sheet conduits and SIVs (the shadow banking system)
- Reliance more on internal rather than on external ratings for securitized exposures

As a result of this enhanced risk coverage, banks will now hold capital for trading book assets that, on average, is about four times greater than required under the old capital requirements.[24]

---

[24]The Basel Committee is also conducting a fundamental review of the market risk framework rules, including the rationale for the distinction between the banking book and trading book, in order to eliminate the possibility of regulatory arbitrage between the banking book and the trading book (Appendix 3.3).

Counterparty credit risk on derivatives and repos The Basel Committee is strengthening the capital requirements for counterparty credit risk on OTC derivatives and repos by requiring that these exposures be measured using stressed inputs.

Basel II addressed counterparty credit risk only in terms of defaults and credit migrations. But during the crisis, mark-to-market losses due to credit valuation adjustments (CVA) represented two-thirds of the losses from counterparty credit risk. Banks must now hold capital for the mark-to-market losses associated with the deterioration of counterparty credit quality (see Chapter 13 for a detailed discussion of this risk).

Capital Ratios: Calibration of the New Requirements

The new Basel III capital ratios are calibrated to absorb losses during times of economic stress as well as in normal times. To this end, banks will now be required to hold a minimum of 4.5 percent of risk-weighted assets, versus 2 percent under Basel II, and a capital conservation buffer of 2.5 percent, both in tangible common equity. Taken together, this means that banks will need to maintain a 7 percent common equity ratio.[25] However, during bad times this buffer can be reduced so that the minimum level will be above 4.5 percent.

As a bank's capital levels move closer to minimum requirements, the conservation buffer will impose a constraint on the bank's discretionary distributions, including dividend payments, share buybacks, and bonuses. Retaining a bigger proportion of earnings during a downturn will help ensure that capital remains available to support the bank's ongoing business operations and lending during the period of stress. Figure 3-3 compares the capital requirements under Basel II versus Basel III.

The new capital standards were initially scheduled to begin to take effect in all of the G20 countries on January 1, 2013, with a relatively long transition period. However, only 11 countries met this deadline.[26] The other jurisdictions, including the United States and the European Union, postponed complying with Basel III for at least one year. More delays in the implementation of the rest of

---

[25]Given the tighter definition of capital and enhanced coverage, this translates into roughly a sevenfold increase in the common equity requirements for internationally active banks.

[26]Australia, Canada, China, India, Japan, Hong Kong, Mexico, Saudi Arabia, Singapore, South Africa, and Switzerland.

FIGURE 3-3 Capital Requirements under Basel II vs. Basel III

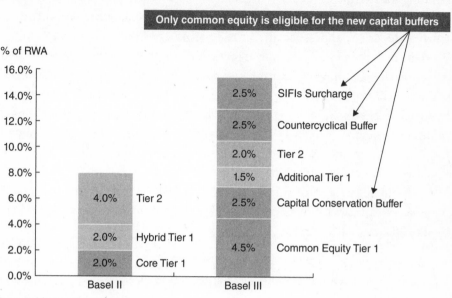

Source: Bank for International Settlements

Basel III can be expected, including delays in implementing the capital conservation buffer (initially scheduled to be fully phased in by the end of 2018).[27]

Large international banks have been steadily raising their capital ratios since 2008. The shortfall in common equity capital relative to the minimum of 7 percent, including the conservation buffer, was estimated by the Basel Committee at 374 billion euros in 2012, down from 577 billion euros at the end of 2009.

---

[27]According to the Basel Committee in December 2010, the estimated common equity tier 1 capital shortfall for participating banks under the new Basel III regime is €165 billion and €577 billion if they are to reach a common equity tier 1 capital ratio target of 4.5 percent and 7 percent as required by 2015 and 2019, respectively. The analysis was based on data as of December 31, 2009.

The European Banking Authority (EBA) in January 2012, produced a report that requires 31 European banks to raise €115 billion in tier 1 capital to reach a 9 percent ratio by July 1, 2012, under the Basel II definition of tier 1 capital that allows for hybrid securities and convertible bonds. The shortfall in tier 1 capital will increase with the implementation of Basel III in 2013, given its stricter definition of core tier 1 capital.

Liquidity Ratios: The Liquidity Coverage Ratio (LCR) and the Net Stable Funding Ratio (NSFR)

Basel III introduces an entirely new framework for managing liquidity risk. During the crisis, and especially in the period after the collapse of Lehman Brothers in September 2008, funding remained in short supply for an extended period of time. Ultimately, central banks assumed the role of the money market in providing liquidity, in a bid to overcome the effect of mistrust between financial institutions. In response, the Basel Committee has proposed global minimum liquidity standards to make banks more resilient to potential short-term disruptions in access to funding and to address longer-term structural liquidity mismatches in their balance sheets.[28]

The liquidity coverage ratio (LCR) requires that banks maintain high-quality liquid assets sufficient to withstand a 30-day stressed funding scenario specified by supervisors

$$LCR = \frac{\text{Stock of high-quality liquid assets}}{\text{Net cash outflows over the next 30 calendar days}} \geq 100\%$$

where net cash outflows over the next 30 calendar days = outflows − Min[inflows; 75% of outflows].

The stress scenario for the LCR entails a combination of idiosyncratic (institution-specific) and marketwide shocks that result in:

- The runoff of a proportion of retail deposits
- A partial loss of unsecured, short-term financing with certain collateral and counterparties
- Contractual outflows, including requirements to post collateral, that would arise from a downgrade in the bank's public credit rating by up to, and including, three notches

---

[28]Federal Reserve Chairman Ben S. Bernanke said "the Fed plans to avert strains in the banking system by pushing financial companies to better manage liquidity risk and reduce reliance on wholesale funding. Regulators will continue to press banks to reduce further their dependence on wholesale funding, which proved highly unreliable during the crisis." Speech given on April 8, 2013, in Stone Mountain, Georgia.

- An increase in market volatilities that, in turn, affects the quality of collateral and the potential future exposure of derivatives positions
- Unscheduled drawdowns of committed, but unsecured, credit and liquidity facilities
- The potential need to buy back debt or honor noncontractual obligations in the interest of mitigating reputational risk

The stock of high-quality liquid assets is subject to quantitative and qualitative eligibility criteria.[29] The net cash outflows are calculated according to strict parameters specified by supervisors.

This is complemented by the net stable funding ratio (NSFR), which is a longer-term (one year) structural ratio designed to address liquidity mismatches and reduce reliance on the wholesale funding that proved so unreliable during the crisis.

$$\text{NSFR} = \frac{\text{Available amount of stable funding}}{\text{Required amount of stable funding}} \geq 100\%$$

With respect to implementing the new liquidity framework, the Basel Committee decided to take a deliberate but cautious approach. Initially the LCR was scheduled to be implemented in 2015 and the NSFR in 2018, with an observation period that will enable supervisors to address any unintended

---

[29]The stock of high-quality liquid assets is composed of Level 1 assets and Level 2 assets.

Level 1 assets: cash, central bank reserves, sovereign and supranational bonds assigned a zero percent risk weight under the Basel II Standardized Approach.

Level 2 assets: sovereign and supranational bonds assigned a 20 percent risk weight under the Basel II Standardized Approach, corporate and covered bonds rated AA by a recognized rating agency (or internally rated with a corresponding PD) with a minimum 15 percent haircut (for all assets, the maximum price decline over a 30-day period in the relevant period of stress should not exceed 10 percent). In January 2013 more instruments, such as equities, corporate debt, and covered bonds, were made eligible.

consequences across business models and funding structures before finalizing and introducing the revised liquidity ratios.[30]

One problem was that the new liquidity standards will affect the profitability of banks and reduce their capacity to finance the economy. To mitigate this, the Basel Committee decided in January 2013 to revise the LCR by expanding the range of assets that can be classified as high-quality liquid assets—e.g., allowing banks to use equities, corporate debt, and securities backed by mortgages. The Committee also modified the calculation of net cash outflows and the timetable for the phase-in of the new standard.[31] Specifically, the LCR will be introduced as planned on January 1, 2015, but the minimum requirement will begin at 60 percent, rising in equal steps of 10 percentage points to reach 100 percent on January 1, 2019.[32]

The next priority of the Basel Committee is to reexamine the NSFR before it is applied in 2018. The NSFR will put European banks at a disadvantage relative to U.S. banks. In the United States, most corporations make use of the capital markets for their long-term financing needs—the banks have been disintermediated for quite some time. This is not the case in Europe, where most corporations continue to rely on bank funding. As a consequence, in 2012 European banks were providing close to 20 billion euros of long-term funding based on only 9 billion euros of long-term resources. European banks are clearly more engaged in maturity intermediation than their U.S. counterparts. Closing the gap to meet the NSFR rule will increase funding costs for European banks and oblige them to reduce the maturity and size of loans they offer to

---

[30]To meet these new liquidity constraints, banks and insurance companies have begun to engage in "liquidity swap" transactions. Insurance companies hold in their portfolios huge amount of government bonds, the only securities recognized as liquid by the regulator. They can therefore offer to exchange government bonds for other securities, held by banks, that are not eligible to count in the calculation of liquidity ratios. Liquidity swaps have developed in the period since 2008, a year in which banks faced great difficulties in refinancing their short-term debt. However, the FSA and the other European regulators are working on new recommendations to limit the development of this market. The FSA has already blocked several transactions of this type.

[31]These new eligible assets are subject to different haircuts depending on their credit ratings.

[32]At the end of 2010, a $1.5 trillion shortfall in liquid assets was identified in the U.S. banking industry with regard to complying with the LCR.

customers—with a predictable knock-on effect for long-term investments in Europe.

Basel III: A Systemwide, Systemic-Risk-Based Framework

The Basel III regulators have also devised a "macroprudential overlay" intended to reduce systemic risk and lessen procyclicality—the tendency for bank lending to rise when times are good and tighten when times are worse, thus exacerbating the economic cycle. The macroprudential overlay consists of five elements, which we will discuss in turn.

Leverage Ratio

The leverage ratio is a simple measure of capital that supplements Basel III's risk-based ratios and constrains the build-up of leverage in the system. Before the crisis, many banks reported strong tier 1 risk-based ratios while, at the same time, building up unsustainably high levels of leverage, both on and off balance sheet.

The leverage ratio is a measure of a bank's tier 1 capital as a percentage of its assets plus the bank's off-balance-sheet exposures and derivative exposures (calculated as an average over the quarter).

Banks will not be allowed to lower their leverage ratio below 3 percent:

$$\frac{\text{Tier1 Capital}}{\text{Exposure}} \geq 3\%$$

For derivatives, regulatory net exposure will be used plus an add-on for potential future exposure. Netting of all derivatives will be permitted. The leverage ratio will include off-balance-sheet items in the measure of total assets (e.g., commitments and letters of credit, unless they are unconditionally cancelable), and these will be converted using a flat 100 percent credit conversion factor.

Supervisory monitoring of bank leverage ratios started on January 1, 2011. The ratio is to be tested until January 2017, and some final adjustments will be made in the first half of 2017. Banks will be required to disclose publicly their leverage ratio in January 2015, and the leverage ratio will migrate to Pillar I in 2018.

Countercyclical Capital Buffer

In addition to the capital conservation buffer, the Basel Committee has introduced a countercyclical capital buffer to further mitigate procyclicality. [33]

The countercyclical capital buffer is designed to protect the banking sector from the losses resulting from a period of excess credit growth followed by a period of stress, and also to help make sure that credit remains available during this period of stress. In addition, during periods of credit growth, the countercyclical capital buffer may cause the cost of credit to increase, acting as a brake on bank lending.

The countercyclical capital buffer will range between 0 and 2.5 percent and should be held in tangible common equity. Its level will vary across jurisdictions, depending on the degree to which local regulators think they can observe a rise in systemwide risk. Later in the cycle, local regulators will allow banks to release capital from the buffer to help absorb losses in the banking system that might otherwise pose a risk to financial stability.

For banks operating in several jurisdictions, the countercyclical buffer is calculated as the weighted average of buffers deployed across all jurisdictions where a firm has credit exposure.

Additional Loss-Absorbing Capital for Systemically Important Financial Institutions (SIFIs)

One result of the 2007–2009 crisis is that it is now broadly recognized that SIFIs should have loss-absorbing capacity beyond the basic regulatory standards. Under Basel III, a 1 percent to 2.5 percent capital surcharge will be imposed on SIFIs, in tangible common equity, and this will kick in gradually between 2016 and 2019.[34]

On November 4, 2011, the Basel Committee and the Financial Stability Board (FSB) released a list of the 29 institutions that had been designated as SIFIs based on five criteria: size, complexity, interconnectivity, international activities, and product substitutability, with each criterion having a 20 percent weight in the final calculation. This list, which presently includes 17 European

---

[33] The next section details the factors that contribute to procyclicality—in particular, risk-sensitive capital regulation.

[34] This surcharge would require U.S. banks, collectively, to raise an additional $200 billion in common equity above and beyond the increases generally required under Basel III.

banks, will be revised every year, and the methodology will be revised every three to five years to reflect structural changes in the banking sector and new ways of measuring systemic risk.[35]

It is interesting to note that this list of SIFIs matches pretty closely the Systemic Risk Ranking of the "vlab" of NYU Stern.[36] The "vlab" systemic risk measure, SRISK, is defined as the expected capital shortfall of a firm in a crisis. This single measure captures many of the features used by the FSB such as size, leverage, interconnectedness, and risk. The measure provides a natural cost/benefit calculation, as it represents the dollars that would need to be invested in a firm in order to prevent its failure in a crisis. This is consistent with the Dodd-Frank Act, which requires banks to conduct stress tests on a regular basis to assess their potential capital shortfall in a stress scenario.[37]

The Financial Stability Board was established in 2010 at the request of the G20 to make recommendations for global financial reforms and monitor progress in the development and implementation of the G20 recommendations. The FSB is an independent organization hosted by the Bank for International Settlements. The FSB's current list of priority areas includes implementation of the Basel II, 2.5, and III framework, OTC derivatives market reforms, compensation practices, policy measures for SIFIs, resolution frameworks, and the shadow banking system. The FSB includes central bankers, regulators, and financial ministry officials from the G20 countries.

Systemically Important Markets and Infrastructures (SIMIs): The Case of OTC Derivatives

Just as there are systemically important financial institutions, there are also systemically important markets and infrastructures. To address the problem of interconnectedness as it relates to derivatives, the Basel Committee and Financial Stability Board are pushing the market to move as many trades as possible through centralized clearing and trade reporting. Derivative counterparty credit exposures to central counterparty clearing houses (CCPs) will continue to have

---

[35]This list was revisited in November 2012 and now contains 28 international banks. Three banks were deleted from the initial list, and two others were added.

[36]www.vlab.stern.nyu.edu/welcome/risk or www.systemicriskranking.stern.nyu.edu.

[37]See C. T. Brownlees and R. Engle, "Volatility, Correlation and Tails for Systemic Risk Measurement," working paper, June 2011.

preferential capital treatment, recognizing that such an exposure is low risk compared to an OTC deal with a single counterparty. However, trades through a CCP will require a low risk weight (in the range of 1% to 3%) rather than the current zero capital requirement. The higher capital requirement for bilateral OTC transactions increases the incentive to use CCPs and exchanges. However, regulators are working to ensure that the CCPs are appropriately managed and capitalized to avoid a new concentration of systemic risk.

Capture of Systemic Risk/Tail Events in Stress Testing and Risk Modeling

For some time now, banks have attempted to capture market risk by means of value-at-risk (VaR) models that transform complex and multifaceted risk positions into a single risk figure. During the crisis these models severely underestimated the tail events and the high loss correlations under systemic stress.

VaR is a reliable measure of risk in normal market conditions. VaR models rely on historical data for the calibration of their parameters and as such are somewhat backward looking—they expect future market conditions to be similar to past market conditions. It is not surprising, therefore, that they do not fare well when markets behave in an unexpected, extreme, or unprecedented manner. The rate and extent of failure of VaR models, however, is more surprising. Over the past few decades, systemic events have occurred far more frequently than expected and the losses incurred during such events have been far heavier than VaR estimates have implied.[38] (In Chapter 7 we explain how VaR is defined, estimated, and used in practice. Appendix 3.4 discusses how VaR is used for regulatory capital purposes.)

Hence, there is a need to complement traditional VaR measures with a strong forward-looking stress testing program that can better capture tail events and incorporate the systemic risk dimension in bank risk management (see Chapter 16 for a discussion of stress testing methodologies).[39] The Basel III framework provides a bigger role for stress testing in the determination of capital buffers under Pillar II.

---

[38]Assuming a normally distributed loss function, the maximum loss at the 99 percent confidence level is 2.33 standard deviations (or sigma). The probability of a "4-sigma" event is one in every 125 years. In the recent past we have experienced a series of events with more than 10-sigma losses!

[39]See also Basel Committee for Banking Supervision, *Principles for Sound Stress Testing Practices and Supervision.* Basel, Switzerland: Basel Committee on Banking Supervision, 2009.

Procyclicality

Banks tend to reinforce the momentum of underlying economic cycles. They lend more during economic booms and then restrict lending during economic downturns. The years leading up to and then following the 2007–2009 financial crisis provide a vivid illustration of the disruptive effects of this kind of "procyclicality" and how it exacerbates financial instability. In this section, we look at the root causes of bank procyclicality and explain how these relate to some of the key Basel III reforms we mentioned earlier.

During an economic boom, banks tend to be excessively optimistic about the economy and their customers' financial health. Their lending, credit rating policies, risk measurement, and provisioning practices begin to move in correlation with the economy's short-term business cycle. Specifically, they make loans against poorer collateral, reduce loan covenants, reduce risk premiums, and allocate fewer loan reserves to cover expected losses. At the same time, there is usually an increase in bank profitability during an economic upturn that contributes to rapid credit growth, the rise of collateral values, and artificially low lending spreads. This is exactly what happened in the years preceding the 2007–2009 financial crisis.

The opposite is true during an economic downturn. After 2008, institutions that experienced extensive losses found it difficult to replenish capital. This, in turn, induced them to reduce lending and dispose of assets in illiquid markets at fire-sale prices. Their retrenchment precipitated a weakening of economic activity, thereby raising the risk of a further deterioration in the strength of financial institutions.

Financial regulation that relies on risk-based capital charges also tends to exacerbate procyclicality, for reasons we discuss below. However, risk sensitivity is a very valuable attribute in itself in terms of dissuading banks from taking on too much risk: risk sensitivity needs to be retained despite its association with procyclicality. This means that a key challenge for policy makers is countering procyclicality while continuing to encourage banks to develop risk-based decision-making processes. We can see the Basel III regulators trying to achieve the right balance in a number of a key areas, discussed below.[40]

---

[40]Financial Stability Forum, *Report of the Financial Stability Forum on Addressing Procyclicality in the Financial System*, April 2009.

Limitations in Risk Measurement

VaR models have several widely recognized shortcomings. While banks have developed many variants of VaR models, all of them still rely on a relatively short period of historical data to estimate the volatilities and correlations of market factors and the probability distribution of future outcomes. The risk sensitivity of VaR, therefore, is cyclical, rising and falling with market volatility. For example, a bank employing VaR in late 2008 would have seen a sharp increase in its VaR numbers compared to earlier periods, everything else equal, simply because of a revision upward of the volatility and correlation parameters in the risk model. This would have sent the bank a signal to reduce its trading positions.

From the perspective of a bank, this reduction in trading positions during a period of high volatility is sensible: it will reduce risk. However, if many market participants react to an increase of volatility in the same way, herd behavior can lead to less benign results. Falling asset prices will cause VaR to increase, which will lead to breaches of VaR-based risk limits, obliging the bank to close out risky positions in an increasingly illiquid market. This will lead to further sharp price falls and a further increase in volatility. The use of risk-sensitive measures can create more risk in the system as a whole.

Basel 2.5, the revised framework for the trading book, proposes various changes to mitigate procyclicality in VaR-based capital requirements. First, the role of stress testing was expanded to reduce the reliance on cyclical VaR-based capital estimates. "Stress VaR" should prevent measures of risk—and therefore risk capital—from falling too much in periods of low market volatility. Second, the new incremental risk charge (IRC) covers default and migration risk on credit products in the trading book, and should reduce incentives for derivatives for the specific purpose of reducing capital requirements. (See Appendix 3.4 for a detailed description of Basel 2.5.)

Basel III has introduced a 2.5 percent countercyclical capital buffer of tier 1 equity capital that should be built up during calm market environments and then be allowed to deplete during turbulent market environments. This counter-cyclical buffer should play the role of a risk absorber across the economic cycle.

Regulatory Risk-Sensitive Capital Charges

Any regulatory risk-sensitive capital charge is somewhat procyclical. A recent example is the credit value adjustment (CVA) charge imposed by Basel III. (See Chapter 13.) It uses CDS spreads to calculate counterparty exposure in derivatives trades and requires banks to hold capital against that number. It also allows banks to mitigate the capital requirement by buying CDS protection. The result is procyclical: when the CVA charge increases, banks are incentivized to buy protection; if they buy protection, spreads rise and the capital charge increases further.

When one bank needs to buy more protection, they all do. This rise in demand for protection creates a rise in the spreads that is driven by the liquidity (or absence of liquidity) in the market, and not by an increase in default probabilities.

Provisioning

The contribution of provisioning to procyclicality of capital depends on the timing of provisions relative to the economic cycle and the impact of provisioning on capital.

The International Accounting Standards Board (IASB) recommends "dynamic provisioning" in which provisions are based on the recognition of the one-year forward expected losses inherent in a loan at its origination. Expected losses are, in turn, a function of the probability of default and loss-given-default and should be revised periodically (in anticipation of a change in the business cycle). If there is a "material" degradation in the credit quality of the loan, then the provision should be a function of default probability over the residual life of the loan.

To permit forward-looking provisioning in the held-to-maturity part of the banking book, provisions on loans should reflect through-the-cycle expected losses.

For the trading book, banks should allocate "valuation reserves" while maintaining fair value accounting, to allow for circumstances in which market prices deviate from the perception of the underlying value. This buffer should be built up during upswings so that it can be drawn down in the event of a downturn.

Margin Requirements

Banks require clients to post collateral as protection against counterparty credit risk for specific credit exposures (Chapter 13). The initial margin requirement is the amount of collateral required to open a position. Thereafter, "margin calls," which can be as frequent as daily, adjust the collateral amount to the exposure: when the credit exposure increases, more collateral is required (and less is required when the exposure declines). The initial margin requirement acts as a buffer to mitigate an increase in counterparty credit risk between margin calls. Margin rules that stipulate lower margin requirements during boom times (liquid markets and low volatility) and higher margin requirements during down times (illiquid markets and high volatility) induce procyclical behavior.

One way to mitigate the procyclicality of margin rules is to make them less dependent on near-term market conditions. This involves determining price volatility and margin rates using long-term historical data sets and making sure that past extreme events are captured in these data. If there are no extreme events in the data, then stress tests can be used to simulate such outcomes. This should lead to less variability in required minimum margin rates. It may, however, lead to higher margins on average.

Leverage and Liquidity

A combination of high leverage and maturity mismatches lay at the root of the fragility of financial institutions during the 2007–2009 crisis. Some large financial institutions funded a growing amount of illiquid long-term assets using short-term liabilities in wholesale markets.

We described above Basel III's key mechanisms for combating this. Banks must report their leverage ratio—a kind of systemic vulnerability indicator—and Basel III also imposes new short-term and long-term liquidity ratios—i.e., the 30-day LCR and the NSFR. The NSFR, in particular, should help to counter procyclicality because it is designed to ensure that banks reduce their reliance on wholesale short-term funding. (When this funding evaporates during a credit crisis, it forces banks to shed assets at depressed prices to meet liquidity requirements.)

Compensation

Compensation schemes that focus on short-term returns and do not adequately adjust for risk are likely to exacerbate the development of asset price bubbles and encourage firms to take on too much risk.

The Financial Stability Forum (FSF) has made a series of recommendations to more effectively align compensation with prudent risk taking. In particular, compensation must be adjusted for all types of risk; compensation payout schedules must be sensitive to the time horizon of risks; and the mix of cash, equity, and other forms of compensation must be consistent with risk alignment.[41]

Work in Progress

Basel III is still, to some degree, a work in progress. In particular, there is more work to be done on drafting new market risk rules, protecting systemically important banks,[42] reducing the reliance on external ratings, and large counterparty exposures. The Basel Committee is conducting a fundamental review of the trading book. The review is addressing basic questions such as: Should the distinction between the trading book and the banking book be maintained? Is VaR the best method for calculating capital requirements? How should trading activities be defined?

More generally, the regulators will take a closer look at how banks arrive at their measures of exposure, how they risk-weight their assets, and how they engage in risk mitigation activities.

Figure 3-4 shows the implementation calendar as of June 2011. As of spring 2013, some important details have already changed since this calendar was first set out. For example, the LCR will now be phased in and reach 90 percent of its target by 2018, as opposed to being fully introduced in 2018. Furthermore, as discussed earlier, this calendar won't be respected by all countries, in particular the United States and the European Union, and it is likely to be subject to revisions in the future.

However, many of the principles agreed in Basel III will be applied, in effect, well before formal implementation in the banking systems of developed economies. For example, in the United States the Federal Reserve has maintained pressure on the largest U.S. banks by asking them to run macroeconomic stress tests that are consistent with the Basel III rules, and linking this to the bank's capital plans and capital planning processes.

---

[41]Financial Stability Forum (FSF), *Principles for Sound Compensation Practices*, 2009.

[42]This includes developing a methodology with indicators, both quantitative and qualitative, to identify systemically important banks at the global level.

FIGURE 3-4 Phase-in Arrangement for Basel III Implementation (2011 initial schedule)

Phase-in arrangements
(shading indicates transition periods—all dates are as of 1 January)

	2011	2012	2013	2014	2015	2016	2017	2018	As of 1 January 2019
Leverage Ratio	Supervisory monitoring		Parallel run 1 Jan 2013 – 1 Jan 2017 Disclosure starts 1 Jan 2015					Migration to Pillar 1	
Minimum Common Equity Capital Ratio			3.5%	4.0%	4.5%	4.5%	4.5%	4.5%	4.5%
Capital Conservation Buffer						0.625%	1.25%	1.875%	2.50%
Minimum Common Equity Plus Capital Conservation Buffer			3.5%	4.0%	4.5%	5.125%	5.75%	6.375%	7.0%
Phase-in of deductions from CET1 (including amounts exceeding the limit for DTAs, MSRs and financials)				20%	40%	60%	80%	100%	100%
Minimum tier 1 capital			4.5%	5.5%	6.0%	6.0%	6.0%	6.0%	6.0%
Minimum total capital			8.0%	8.0%	8.0%	8.0%	8.0%	8.0%	8.0%
Minimum total capital plus conservation buffer			8.0%	8.0%	8.0%	8.625%	9.25%	9.875%	10.5%
Capital instruments that no longer qualify as non-core tier 1 capital or tier 2 capital			Phased out over 10-year horizon beginning 2013						
Liquidity coverage ratio	Observation period begins				Introduce minimum standard				
Net stable funding ratio	Observation period begins							Introduce minimum standard	

Source: Bank for International Settlements

The Dodd-Frank Wall Street Reform and Consumer Protection Act of 2010 (Dodd-Frank Act)

On July 21, 2010, the United States Congress and the Obama administration enacted the Dodd-Frank Act in an attempt to convince a skeptical public that the stability of the U.S. financial system would not remain vulnerable to bad decisions by a handful of executives at major financial institutions—institutions that had been effectively guaranteed against failure by the U.S. government and, more pertinently, its taxpayers.

On its own, the Act runs to 848 pages—more than 20 times the size of the Glass-Steagall Act. This is just a starting point. For implementation, Dodd-Frank requires an additional close to 400 pieces of detailed rule making by a variety of U.S. regulatory agencies. This is a complex undertaking—the Act is widely described as the most ambitious and far-reaching overhaul of financial regulation since the 1930s, following the Great Depression—and it has become clear that implementing Dodd-Frank will take considerable time.

Dodd-Frank is specific to the United States and has no equivalent in the rest of the world. In Europe, new bank regulation might adopt some rules similar in intent to the Dodd-Frank proposals, though these will be different in detail and often structure—e.g., the U.K. proposal to ring-fence risky bank activities to protect deposits.

The Dodd-Frank Act attempts to address a vast variety of issues: regulatory powers, too big to fail, derivatives clearing and transparency, consumer protection, proprietary trading, rating agencies, executive pay, corporate governance, and more. Here, we will focus on half a dozen key themes.

Strengthening the Fed While Restricting Intervention

The Dodd-Frank Act strengthens the supervisory authorities and responsibilities of the Federal Reserve in three areas dealing with systemic risk:

- It expands the population of firms subject to Fed supervision to include all "systemically important financial institutions" (SIFIs)—i.e., BHCs with more than $50 billion in total consolidated worldwide assets, savings and loan holding companies, any nonbank financial firms (shadow institutions) and financial market utilities designated as systemically important by a new body headed by the Treasury, the Financial Stability Oversight Council (FSOC).[43]
- It extends the Fed's mandate to include macroprudential supervision. The Act does not set specific prudential requirements, but it identifies areas where the FSOC can recommend higher prudential standards and where the Fed must impose them. These higher standards include heightened capital requirements, rigorous leverage and liquidity requirements,

---

[43]The role of the Financial Stability Oversight Council is to "identify risks to the financial stability of the United States that could arise from the material financial distress or failure, or ongoing activities, of large interconnected bank holding companies or nonbank financial companies or that could arise outside the financial services market place." A support organization, the Office of Financial Research (OFR), attached to the FSOC within the Treasury, supports the work of the FSOC with data and research. This setup is a response to discussions in the United States about the safe level of capital in the event of major market shocks and to a growing dissatisfaction with the Basel III risk weights approach, as well as an increasing preference for measures that assess the systemic risk of financial institutions using market data or through regulatory stress tests.

risk management requirements, concentration limits, resolution plans (so-called "living wills"), and stress tests.[44]
- It allows the Fed to obtain information from, and impose prudential standards on, the subsidiaries of BHCs.[45]

However, the Act also prevents or limits emergency federal assistance to individual institutions. Restricting the Fed's ability to perform a lender-of-last-resort function during the orderly resolution of SIFIs may prove to be damaging and even devastating if the new resolution mechanisms prove ineffective.[46]

On balance, therefore, the Dodd-Frank Act better equips the Fed to prevent a crisis by limiting systemic risk, while potentially leaving the Fed less well equipped to manage a crisis should one occur.

Ending Too Big to Fail

The Act proposes an end to "too big to fail" through (1) the creation of an "orderly liquidation authority" (OLA) that will replace the bankruptcy code and

---

[44]While the Dodd-Frank Act provides its own capital guidelines, it is generally assumed that implementation of the Act will, to the extent possible, coincide closely with Basel III. However, the Act requires that whatever capital and leverage standards are arrived at, these will eventually constitute a floor with respect to the standards proposed in any future Basel Accords.

[45]The Graham-Leach-Bliley Act passed in 1999 largely abolished the restrictions embodied in the Glass-Steagall Act of 1933. It enabled bank holding companies to convert to financial service holding companies (FSHCs) that could combine commercial banking, securities broker-dealer activities, investment banking and insurance activities under one corporate holding company umbrella, thereby encouraging the growth of universal banking in the United States. It is not clear that this deregulation contributed in any meaningful way to the buildup of credit risks in the run-up to the 2007–2009 financial crisis, as securitization and loan syndication were already permitted for U.S. banks under the Glass-Steagall Act. However, the Graham-Leach-Bliley Act included so-called "Fed-lite" restrictions that limited the ability of the Fed to examine, collect information from, and impose prudential standards on subsidiary banks and other functionally regulated subsidiaries of BHCs.

[46]For example, the restriction on emergency liquidity assistance from the Fed when a clearinghouse is in trouble might prove disastrous, as an orderly liquidation may take several weeks, if not months. The natural response in such a case would be to provide temporary federal assistance and require the participants in the clearinghouse to bear the losses, encouraging its private recapitalization through capital contributions from participants.

other applicable insolvency laws for liquidating financial companies and certain of their subsidiaries under certain circumstances, and (2) a requirement for certain financial institutions to conduct stress testing.

Resolution Plan

Under the Dodd-Frank Act, bankruptcy is the preferred resolution process in the event that a large institution fails. With the new liquidation authority (OLA), the Treasury secretary would have the authority to appoint the FDIC as receiver of any financial company if certain conditions are met.

A requirement for a "dissolution insurance fund," to be financed by annual premiums paid by SIFIs, was ultimately dropped from the legislation. Instead, the costs of remediation, beyond the direct losses of the failed institution, are to be borne by surviving firms—i.e., firms that turned out to be better managed and less risky. This burden will fall at a time when these firms are likely to be facing the risk of contagion from failing institutions, and it may have the perverse effect of encouraging systemic risk taking and a race to the bottom.

SIFIs are required to submit to the Fed and the FDIC a "living will" that specifies the corporate governance structure for resolution planning. These "living wills" demonstrate, should the institution fail, how the institution would be resolved quickly and in an orderly fashion under the U.S. bankruptcy system. SIFIs are expected to file their revised "living wills" annually, or more frequently if a major event has a material effect on the resolution plan.

Stress Testing

The Dodd-Frank Act requires banks with total consolidated assets of more than $10 billion to conduct annual stress tests. The banks must report their test results to the FDIC (Federal Deposit Insurance Corporation) and the Federal Reserve Board, and summaries of these results are disclosed in a public document.

The purpose of these stress tests is to require BHCs to develop and maintain robust and forward-looking capital and funding liquidity plans. Following the 2007–2009 financial crisis, regulators and market participants need to be convinced that large institutions have sufficient capital and liquid assets to operate through periods of economic and financial market stress. (More on this topic in Chapter 16.)

Derivatives Markets

The Act also proposes a complete overhaul of the regulation and transparency of derivatives markets, with the aim of helping market participants to deal better with counterparty risk.[47, 48] In particular, the Act provides for the central clearing of standard derivatives, such as interest rate swaps and credit default swaps; the regulation of complex derivatives that remain traded OTC (i.e., outside of central clearing platforms); increased transparency for all derivatives trading in terms of prices, volumes, and exposures (information must be supplied to regulators and, in aggregated form, to the public);[49] and separation of "nonvanilla" positions (i.e., more complex trades) into well-capitalized subsidiaries—all with exceptions for derivatives used for commercial hedging.

A great deal of uncertainty regarding these new requirements will remain until the various regulators—i.e., the Fed, the SEC, and the CFTC—spell out the details of implementation.

The Volcker Rule

The Act intends to reduce complexity in banking and help simplify the resolution of failed institutions. The Act reinstates a limited form of the Glass-Steagall Act through the Volcker rule. This rule prevents BHCs from conducting proprietary

---

[47]The European Commission is currently conducting a similar initiative: the European Market Infrastructure Regulation initiative, also known as EMIR.

[48]Mandatory use of central counterparties (CCPs) for derivatives transactions that are sufficiently standardized and liquid could substantially reduce, although not eliminate, systemic risk posed by OTC derivatives by diminishing counterparty and trade replacement risks. Banks clearing derivatives transactions through a CCP will be exposed to two types of risks—i.e., risk related to the transaction itself (margin calls and collateral deposited with the CCP), and risk related to the "default fund" that that acts to mutualize the losses arising from any default. The Basel Committee decided to impose on banks a capital charge of 2 percent of their exposure.

[49]In Europe, the European Commission will address public transparency requirements in the Market in Financial Instrument Directive (MiFID) reform.

trading activities and from making large investments in hedge funds and private equity (or from bailing out investments made through these channels).[50]

The Volcker rule was initially supposed to become effective on July 21, 2012. This has been delayed several times, as it has taken more time than expected for the regulatory agencies to produce the formal rules; it is presently scheduled to become effective in July 2014.[51] The Volcker rule has been criticized for its potential impact on market liquidity. Issuers could see their annual borrowing costs rise, and investors may experience an increase in transaction costs and a fall in the value of their portfolio as corporate bond yields increase.[52]

Protecting Consumers

The Act creates a Bureau of Consumer Financial Protection (BCFP) that will write rules governing the consumer financial services and products offered by banks and nonbanks. The BCFP is commonly referred to as the Consumer Financial Protection Bureau (CFPB). It will have the mandate to ensure that consumers can obtain the clear, accurate information they need to shop for mortgages, credit cards, and other financial products, and to protect them from hidden fees, abusive terms, and deceptive practices.

---

[50]Contrary to the Vickers Report in the United Kingdom (Independent Commission on Banking, Final Report, Recommendations, http://bankingcommission.independent.gov.uk, September 2011), to be implemented in 2019, the Dodd-Frank Act together with the Volcker Rule does not recommend the separation of retail and investment banking activities. The Act only limits BHCs to *de minimis* investment in proprietary trading activities, such as hedge funds and private equity, and prohibits them from bailing out these investments.

[51]Financial products excluded from the scope of the Volcker Rule are loans, spot commodities, spot FX, U.S. government and agency obligations, repos/reverse repos, and positions taken in connection with bona fide liquidity management. Activities permitted under the Volcker Rule are securities and underwriting activities, "bona fide" market-making activities, and risk-mitigating hedging and trading in U.S. government obligations but not foreign government bonds. Foreign governments such as Japan, Canada, and the United Kingdom have already filed complaints that the exclusion of non-U.S. sovereign bonds will create an unlevel playing field for government bond markets, increase borrowing costs for non-U.S. governments, and dramatically affect the liquidity of these markets as well as make them more volatile.

[52]Oliver Wyman reports that a 5 percent reduction in liquidity would result in corporate bond yields' rising by an average of 16 bps.

Other Key Issues

In addition, the Act introduces a range of reforms concerning mortgage lending practices, hedge fund disclosure, conflict resolution at rating agencies, a requirement for securitizing institutions to retain a 5 percent interest in the underlying assets, risk control for money market funds, shareholders' "say on pay,"[53] and governance. Also, the Dodd-Frank Act requires financial institutions to include off-balance-sheet activities when computing their capital requirements.[54]

The Dodd-Frank Act may also have quite an impact on foreign banks operating in the United States, as these institutions may have to place their U.S. activities within an intermediate holding company (IHC). The capital and liquidity requirements of this structure would be the same as for a bank holding company (BHC), without regard to the financial strength of the foreign bank itself.

Dodd-Frank Concluding Remarks

The Dodd-Frank Act poses a challenge for the U.S adoption of Basel 2.5 because it prohibits the use of external credit ratings in financial rules. The biggest problems here are the standardized rules for debt, securitization, and resecuritizations, which are largely based on ratings.

Because the U.S. version of Basel 2.5 would not include higher risk weights for debt, securitization, and resecuritization positions, there are growing concerns about potential regulatory arbitrage between the United States and Europe. Apparently, U.S. banks are already snapping up portfolios of structured credit products from their European counterparts as a result of this discrepancy.

A more fundamental problem is that Dodd-Frank does not fully address the main problem it set out to solve. This is that "too-big-to-fail" and "too-systemic-to-fail" financial firms are currently not paying for the costs they impose on others when they run into trouble. Perhaps the greatest failure of Dodd-Frank is that it lacks a clear and coherent set of policies for dealing with the shadow banking

---

[53] Among the proposed reforms is the need to expose executives to downside risk through compensation deferral and clawbacks—i.e., maluses to operate in tandem with bonuses.

[54] The term "off-balance-sheet activities" is defined by the Dodd-Frank Act to mean an existing liability that is not on the balance sheet but may move on balance sheet upon the occurrence of some future event. The definition explicitly includes standby letters of credit, repos, interest rate swaps, and credit swaps, among others.

system and bringing it under the regulatory umbrella in a systematic fashion. Much of the instability of the shadow banking system stems from its use of short-term funding—e.g., the repo market—to support longer-term investment.[55] However, within Dodd-Frank there is no serious consideration of how to define banking for regulatory purposes (i.e., what is, and what is not, a bank) or how to cope with the maturity mismatching that makes the shadow banking system so fragile.

European Banking Law(s)

European countries are still debating whether to break up universal banks. In the United Kingdom, the Vickers Report asks for a clear separation of retail and investment banking activities; it is due to be implemented in 2019. In continental Europe, the High-Level Expert Group on reforming the structure of the European Union banking sector, chaired by Erkki Liikanen in 2012, proposed

---

[55]The shadow banking system consists of the following: money market funds collecting uninsured short-term deposits and funding financial firms, which effectively reintroduces the fragile maturity mismatch of traditional banking that the Banking Act of 1933 had attempted to avoid; investment banks performing many functions of commercial banks and vice versa; and a range of derivatives and securitization markets providing tremendous liquidity for otherwise illiquid loans but operating unregulated (or at least weakly regulated) in the shadow of regulated banks. The result has been a parallel or "shadow" banking sector that is both opaque and highly leveraged. These institutions look like banks, act like banks, and borrow and lend like banks, but have never been regulated like banks.

According to the FSB, the size of the shadow banking system is US$67 trillion in 2011 compared to US$26 trillion in 2002. The share of the euro zone and the United Kingdom increased from 40 to 46 percent, while the share of the United States declined from 44 to 35 percent. The shadow banking system accounts for almost half the assets in the regulated banking system.

The Dodd-Frank Act does not fully resolve the issue of dealing with a full-scale run on money market funds, as witnessed following the collapse of Lehman Brothers. The repo market represents another glaring omission, even though the repo run on Bear Stearns was among the most salient failure mechanisms of the crisis. (Viral V. Acharya, Thomas F. Cooley, Matthew P. Richardson, and Ingo Walter, *Regulating Wall Street*, Wiley, 2011, ch. 10, 11.)

Also, the Act does nothing to address the worst-performing shadow banks: Fannie Mae and Freddie Mac. Fannie Mae and Freddie Mac were at the center of the housing expansion and had to be taken into government conservatorship in the early fall of 2008. They have already cost U.S. taxpayers $150 billion in capital contributions from the Treasury, and there is at least another $50 billion, and possibly as much as $250 billion, still to come.

separating proprietary trading and other significant trading activities and placing them in a trading entity aside from insured deposit-taking operations. The new independent legal entities would have their own capital and funding and be independently subject to regulatory standards.

The Liikanen separation proposal is similar in intention to the U.K. and U.S. ring-fencing proposals. The U.K. Vickers proposal creates a retail ring-fence isolating deposits and other activities from risky wholesale activities. The U.S. Volcker rule imposes restrictions on proprietary trading. However, it is legitimate to ask the question: to what problem are these separation proposals the solution? The banks that defaulted or had to be rescued earliest in the crisis were specialized banks, not universal banks: Northern Rock was a mortgage bank; Lehman, Bear Stearns, and Merrill Lynch were investment banks. Meanwhile, when the universal banks did run into trouble, it was often as much to do with their lending and other "traditional" banking activities as their fondness for proprietary trading. If separation and ring fencing are a solution at all, they are likely to be only a partial solution.

Europe has a bigger problem than ring fencing or the lack of it. The fragmentation of the continent into national financial systems has led investors to identify banking system risk with sovereign risk. As a consequence, the yields on government bonds showed a wide dispersal as confidence sagged in the post-crisis years. In early 2010, all European government bond yields were closely aligned to the German treasury bond market. By early 2013, the yield on ten-year German bonds was around 1.2 percent while it was close to 6 percent for Greece.

This is important because a sound bank in a high-risk nation will be penalized by high spreads, driven by the country spread, forcing the bank to charge higher interest rates to customers (e.g., corporations) and reducing investment into a nation that desperately needs to invest.

In order to break the link between sovereign and banking system risk, the European Community decided in 2012 to propose a Banking Union built on three pillars:

- A single supervisor for all the banks in the euro zone—i.e., around 6,000 institutions
- A single system of deposit insurance
- A resolution mechanism to deal with bank failures in an orderly fashion, with a common dedicated fund

It is also expected that such a Banking Union, when put in place, will facilitate the transmission of monetary policy to the real economy, which flows essentially through the banking system.

Conclusion: If Basel III Is Good, Is It Good Enough?

Basel III is a response to the U.S. subprime and European sovereign debt crises, which together showed that the financial system was not sufficiently resilient. The amount and quality of capital in financial institutions was too low, the risk posed by complex structured products was not well measured, liquidity risk was not properly taken into account, and risk control was weak in many financial institutions.

These weaknesses helped both precipitate and worsen the consequences of the crisis, and have had a strong negative impact on the short-term and long-term financing of the world's economies, especially in Europe. Many banks are still alive thanks to costly government interventions, but many countries, such as Portugal, Ireland, Greece, and Spain (PIGS) cannot afford to further bail out their banks.

The purpose of Basel III is to prevent this happening again in the future by imposing:

- More, and better quality, loss-absorbing capital
- Better protection against some risks, such as market risk in general, securitization, counterparty credit risk, and liquidity risk
- Better treatment of cyclicality in the economy and financial markets
- Better risk governance in financial institutions

Some have criticized the new regulatory framework as too costly. The cost of implementing Basel III in the G20 countries has been estimated by the IIF at US$1.3 trillion, compared with the cost of the crisis, estimated by the IMF in 2009 at US$4 trillion. The same people argue that Basel III is too complex and should be replaced by a simple leverage ratio, calculated as tangible equity to non-risk-weighted assets.[56]

---

[56]Andrew G. Haldane, "The Dog and the Frisbee," Bank of England. Speech given at the Federal Reserve Bank of Kansas City's 36th economic symposium, "The Changing Policy Landscape," Jackson Hole, Wyoming, August 2012. Haldane argues that the complexity of the regulatory system did not serve its purpose during the financial crisis of 2007–2009. He advocates the use of simple rules of thumb that may be more useful than sophisticated models.

But we should not underestimate how much Basel III strengthens the rules surrounding bank capital adequacy. A fundamental feature of the new regulatory framework is the significant increase in required capital levels. All banks must hold common equity capital of at least 7 percent of their risk-weighted assets, compared with only 2 percent previously. In the event of a credit boom, banks would potentially need to hold a further 2.5 percent in common equity, bringing the total to 9.5 percent. Finally, the most systemically important banks must hold up to 2.5 percent in additional common equity. That is a total of 12 percent, a sixfold increase from the pre-crisis levels for these institutions.

Another important step has been the introduction of a non-risk-based leverage ratio as a supplement to the risk-based requirements. On its own, a non-risk-based leverage ratio creates incentives to shed safe assets and increase the riskiness of asset portfolios, to forego risk-reducing hedging strategies that result in higher capital requirements, and to engage in off-balance-sheet activities and other sophisticated structures that expose banks to contingent risks. Together with the risk-based capital requirements, however, the leverage ratio will help contain excessive leverage in the banking system, serving as a backstop to the risk-based regime and safeguarding, somewhat, against attempts to game the risk-based requirements.

Regulatory complexity is a by-product of the desire, among regulators and banks, for risk sensitivity. Still, voices have started to question the efficiency of complex regulations. Some call for much more capital and much less debt in the banking system, and the argument is a strong one. More capital—e.g., 50 percent or more—would be far more effective than the thousands of pages of Dodd-Frank regulations and armies of regulators trying to keep highly leveraged and subsidized too-big-to-fail banks from taking too much risk.

One myth must be slain if this argument is to gather force: requiring more capital does not reduce the funds available for lending. Capital is not the same as reserves. Instead, we should think of capital as a source of money, not a use of money. Raising more capital does not require a bank to raise more money to make a loan because for every dollar of stock that the bank must issue, it needs to borrow one dollar less. Also, capital is not an inherently more expensive source of funds than debt. Banks have to promise stockholders high returns because bank stock is presently risky. If banks issued more stock, bank stock would be less risky, and the cost of capital would be lower. Stocks with bond-like risks need to pay only bond-like returns.[57]

The debate on more capital versus more complex regulation is likely to heat up in the coming years.

---

[57]See Anat Admati and Martin Hellwig, *The Bankers' New Clothes*, Princeton University Press, 2013. The authors also claim that because bank debt is highly subsidized, leverage increases the value of the subsidies to management and shareholders. Equity is expensive to banks only because it dilutes the subsidies they get from the government. That is why increasing bank equity would be cheap for taxpayers and the economy, to say nothing of removing the cost of occasional crises.

Appendix 3.1

BASEL I

The 1988 Basel Accord, also referred to as the Accord or Basel I, established international minimum capital guidelines for the world's banking systems. Its principal reform was to use a simple scheme to link each bank's capital requirements to the bank's specific credit exposures. To do so, the regulators divided bank exposures into broad classes that grouped together similar types of borrowers such as OECD banks, non-OECD banks, and corporate borrowers. Each borrower type was then linked to specific capital requirements.

What Exactly Did the 1988 Accord Require of Banks?

The 1988 Accord is laid out in a document called "International Convergence of Capital Measurement and Capital Standards," published in July 1988. It defines two minimum standards for meeting acceptable capital adequacy requirements: an assets-to-capital multiple and a risk-based capital ratio.

The assets-to-capital multiple is an overall measure of the bank's capital adequacy. The second and more critical measure focuses on the credit risk associated with specific on- and off-balance-sheet asset categories. It takes the form of a solvency ratio, known as the Cooke ratio, defined as the ratio of capital to risk-weighted on-balance-sheet assets plus off-balance-sheet exposures (the risk weights being assigned on the basis of the broad classes of counterparty credit risk mentioned above).

Below, we review the main features of the 1988 Basel Accord as it stands today after several modifications.

The Assets-to-Capital Multiple

The assets-to-capital multiple is calculated by dividing the bank's total assets, including specified off-balance-sheet items, by its total capital. The off-balance-sheet items included in this test are direct credit substitutes (including letters of credit and guarantees), transaction-related contingencies, trade-related contingencies, and sale and repurchase agreements. All of these items are included at their notional principal amount.

The maximum multiple allowed under Basel I is 20. It is conceivable that a bank with large off-balance-sheet activities might trigger this multiple as the minimum capital requirement, but in general the assets-to-capital multiple is not the binding constraint on a bank's activities.

The Risk-Weighted Amount Used to Compute the Cooke Ratio

The second and more critical measure takes the form of a solvency ratio, known as the Cooke ratio.[1] This is defined as the ratio of capital to risk-weighted on-balance-sheet assets plus off-balance-sheet exposures, where the weights are assigned on the basis of credit risk.

In effect, the Cooke ratio requires banks to calculate the sum of their risk-weighted assets of various kinds (e.g., 100 percent for corporate loans, 50 percent for uninsured residential mortgages) and then set aside a flat fixed percentage (i.e., 8 percent or more under Basel I) of the total as regulatory capital against default.

To work out the sum of their risk-weighted assets, banks have to consider both the on-balance-sheet and specific off-balance-sheet items. On-balance-sheet items have risk weightings from zero percent for cash, revolving credit agreements with a term of less than one year, and OECD government securities, to 100 percent for corporate bonds and others. Off-balance-sheet items are first expressed as a credit equivalent and then appropriately risk-weighted by counterparty. The risk-weighted amount is then the sum of the two components: the risk-weighted assets for on-balance-sheet instruments and the risk-weighted credit equivalent for off-balance-sheet items.

---

[1]After W. P. Cooke, Bank of England, who chaired the Cooke Committee, a forerunner of the present Basel Committee.

TABLE 3A-1 Risk Capital Weights by Broad On-Balance-Sheet Asset Category (WA)

Risk Weights (%)	Asset Category
0	Cash and gold bullion, claims on OECD governments such as Treasury bonds, or insured residential mortgages
20	Claims on OECD banks and OECD public-sector entities such as securities issued by U.S. government agencies or claims on municipalities
50	Uninsured residential mortgages
100	All other claims, such as corporate bonds, less developed country debt, claims on non-OECD banks, equity, real estate, premises, plant and equipment

Table 3A-1 gives the full list of risk capital weights (WA) by asset categories, and Table 3A-2 shows the weights that apply to credit equivalents by type of counterparty (WCE).

There is an apparent inconsistency between Table 3A-1 and Table 3A-2, because the risk weight for corporate assets as they relate to off-balance-sheet instruments is half that required for on-balance-sheet assets. The original rationale for this asymmetry was the superior quality of the corporations that participated in the market for off-balance-sheet products. However, this quickly became an outdated assumption.

Calculation of the Credit Equivalent for Off-Balance-Sheet Exposures
For nonderivative off-balance-sheet exposures, a conversion factor applies. This is because the notional or "face value" amount of these instruments is rarely representative of the true credit risk that is being assumed; the value of the

TABLE 3A-2 Risk Capital Weights for Off-Balance-Sheet Credit Equivalents by Type of Counterparty (WCE)

Risk Weights (%)	Type of Counterparty
0	OECD governments
20	OECD banks and public-sector entities
50	Corporations and other counterparties

TABLE 3A-3 Credit Conversion Factors for Nonderivative Off-Balance-Sheet Exposures

Conversion Factor (%)	Off-Balance-Sheet Exposure Factor
100	Direct credit substitutes, bankers' acceptances, standby letters of credit, sale and repurchase agreements, forward purchase of assets
50	Transaction-related contingencies such as performance bonds, revolving underwriting facilities (RUFs), and note issuance facilities (NIFs)
20	Short-term self-liquidating trade-related contingencies such as letters of credit
0	Commitments with an original maturity of one year or less

conversion factor is set by the regulators at somewhere between zero and one, depending on the nature of the instrument (Table 3A-3). The resulting credit equivalents are then treated exactly as if they were on-balance-sheet instruments.

The Accord also recognizes that the credit risk exposure of long-dated financial derivatives fluctuates in value. The Accord methodology estimates this exposure by supplementing the current marked-to-market value with a simple measure of the projected future risk exposure.

Calculation of the Accord risk-weighted amount for derivatives proceeds in two steps, as shown in Figure 3A-1. The first step involves computing a credit equivalent amount, which is the sum of the current replacement cost when it is positive (and zero otherwise), and an add-on amount that approximates future

FIGURE 3A-1 Calculation of the Risk-Weighted Amount for Derivatives

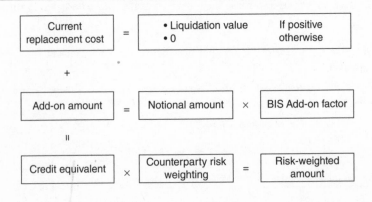

projected replacement costs. The current replacement value of a derivative is its marked-to-market or liquidation value. (When the value is negative, the institution is not exposed to default risk as the replacement cost of the contract is zero.)

The add-on amount is computed by multiplying the notional amount of the transaction by the Accord-required add-on factor.

Capital and the Cooke Ratio

Banks are required to maintain a capital amount equal to at least 8 percent of their total risk-weighted assets (as calculated in the previous section). Capital, as defined by the Cooke ratio, is much broader than equity capital. It has three components:

> Tier 1, or core capital, which includes common stockholders' equity, noncumulative perpetual preferred stock, and minority equity interests in consolidated subsidiaries, less goodwill and other deductions.
>
> Tier 2, or supplementary capital, which includes hybrid capital instruments, such as cumulative perpetual preferred shares and qualifying 99-year debentures. These instruments are essentially permanent in nature and have some of the characteristics of both equity and debt. Tier 2 capital also includes instruments with more limited lives, such as subordinated debt with an original average maturity of at least five years.

According to the original Accord, tier 1 and tier 2 capital should represent at least 8 percent of the risk-weighted assets, to protect the bank against credit risk. At least 50 percent of this amount must take the form of tier 1 capital.

In practice, the capital levels of regulated banks tend to exceed minimum requirements. There are various reasons why banks might want to retain capital in excess of the minimum required by regulators, but research suggests the most important is to create a buffer that prevents their accidentally transgressing the regulatory rules. Other powerful reasons are peer pressure and the need for banks to maintain credit ratings and credit standings that allow them to access wholesale markets cheaply. The rating agencies take their own view of how well capitalized a bank is, and this may not be directly related to the bank's minimum capital requirement. This does not mean that minimum capital requirements are unimportant: they are very important drivers of overall capital levels, even if they don't determine those levels exactly.

Under the 1996 Amendment to the original Basel Accord, now itself superseded by Basel 2.5 (see Appendix 3.4), banks were allowed to use a third tier of capital to cover market risk in the trading book (but not credit risk in the banking book). Tier 3, or sub-supplementary capital, consisted of short-term subordinated debt with an original maturity of at least two years. It had to be unsecured and fully paid up. It was also subject to lock-in clauses that prevented the issuer from repaying the debt before maturity, or even at maturity if the issuer's capital ratio threatened to fall below 8 percent after repayment.

What Are the Key Weaknesses of Basel I?

The rules of the original 1988 Accord are generally acknowledged to be flawed for five main reasons.

First, the risk-weighted ratios in the rules don't differentiate adequately between the riskiness of bank assets—and are in some ways nonsensical. For example, they assume that a loan to a corporate counterparty generates five times the amount of credit risk as does a loan to an OECD bank, regardless of their respective creditworthiness. That means a loan to a highly creditworthy corporate counterparty (e.g., rated AA+) has to be supported by five times as much regulatory capital as a similar loan to a Mexican (BBB) or Turkish bank (BBB−), and that the loan is also considered to be considerably more risky than the sovereign debt of Turkey or Mexico. Clearly, this is the opposite of what one might think appropriate.

Second, regulatory rules assume that all corporate borrowers pose an equal credit risk. For example, a loan to an AA-rated corporation requires the same amount of capital as a loan to a B-rated credit. This is also clearly inappropriate.

Third, the 1988 Accord does not appropriately take maturity factors into effect. For example, revolving credit agreements with a term of less than one year do not require any regulatory capital, while a short-term facility with 366 days to maturity bears the same capital charge as any long-term facility. (A revolver is a facility that allows a corporation to borrow and repay the loan at will within a certain period of time.) The bank is clearly at risk from offering short-term revolver facilities, yet so long as the term is less than one year no regulatory capital is required. This led to the creation by many banks of a 364-day facility, in which banks commit to lend for 364 days only but then continuously roll over the facility into the next year—a clear example of how banks alter their behavior to circumvent regulatory rules. (Such a facility attracts no capital under Basel I, even if the terms of the facility are such that if the commitment is canceled, the obligor then has the right to pay back the drawn amount over a number of years.)

Fourth, the Accord does not provide any incentive for credit risk mitigation techniques such as the use of credit derivatives.

Fifth, the Accord does not address complex issues such as portfolio effects, even though credit risk in any large portfolio is bound to be partially offset by diversification across issuers, industries, and geographical locations. For example, a bank is required to set aside the same amount of regulatory capital for a single $100 million corporate loan as for a portfolio of 100 different and unrelated (independent) $1 million corporate loans. While a single $100 million loan might go sour, it's extremely unlikely that 100 loans of a similar standing in a fully diversified portfolio will all go wrong at once.

Under Basel I, these shortcomings produced a distorted assessment of actual risks and led to a misallocation of capital. The problem is a general one: as the definition of regulatory capital drifts further away from the bank's understanding of the true amount of risk capital necessary to support a position (i.e., economic capital), the bank faces a strong incentive to play a game of "regulatory arbitrage."

Regulatory arbitrage describes a bank's attempt to modify its behavior so it incurs lower capital charges while still incurring the same amount of actual risk—a bit like tax avoidance, only with regard to regulatory risk capital. Banks often do this by using financial engineering constructs such as, for example, securitization through various types of collateralized debt obligations (CDOs) and the use of credit derivatives.

In the process, banks sometimes end up transferring high-grade exposures from their banking book to their trading book, or outside the banking system, so that these high-grade exposures do not attract regulatory capital. But that means that the quality of the assets remaining in the bank's books deteriorates— exactly the reverse of the outcome sought by regulators.

The elimination of regulatory arbitrage can be achieved by a better alignment of regulatory and economic capital—that is, by making sure regulatory capital truly reflects the amount of economic risk a bank is taking. That way, banks have little incentive to bend the rules in their favor. However, it is very challenging to craft rules that truly capture economic risk.

Even if the 1988 Accord measured risk more accurately, it would still be inadequate for modern banks because of the rate of change and innovation in the banking industry. Improvements in internal risk management processes, the adoption of more advanced risk measurement techniques, and the increasing use of credit risk mitigation techniques have changed banks' monitoring and management of exposures and activities to an extraordinary extent over the last couple of decades.

These problems with the 1988 Accord led larger banks to argue that banks should be allowed to develop their own internal credit portfolio models to determine VaR for credit in lieu of the overly simplistic standards set by the 1988 Accord. These credit VaR models would be approved by regulators and used by the industry to calculate the minimum required regulatory credit risk capital associated with the traditional loan products in the banking book (see Chapter 11). However, in working out the new rules for Basel II, regulators refused to go quite that far. Instead, they created a menu of increasingly advanced approaches to calculating credit risk that attempted to incorporate some of the sophistication of a true portfolio credit model (see Appendix 3.3).

Appendix 3.2

THE 1996 MARKET RISK AMENDMENT

Background: The Explosion of Bank Market Risk

When devising the 1988 Accord, regulators focused primarily on the credit risks that banks were exposed to, and ignored market risk and other risks. But this hardly reflected the reality of many bank risk exposures, even during the 1980s.

Modern banks are engaged in a range of activities that extend well beyond lending and the credit risk this generates. They trade all types of cash instruments, as well as derivatives such as swaps, forward contracts, and options—either for their own account or to facilitate customer transactions.

This kind of bank trading activity grew exponentially in the 1980s and 1990s, so that by the time the Basel Committee published its important 1996 Market Risk Amendment the Federal Reserve Bank estimated that U.S. banks possessed more than $37 trillion of off-balance-sheet assets and liabilities, compared to approximately $1 trillion only 10 years earlier. According to a more recent BIS publication, as of November 2011, banks worldwide had a total exposure to derivatives of approximately $708 trillion.

The rise in importance of risk management instruments over the last few decades has been driven by a rise in volatility in many of the principal financial markets, which has led banks to become both users and providers of risk management instruments.

The prime example of this change is the foreign currency market. From 1944, with the signing of the Bretton Woods Agreement, international foreign exchange rates were artificially fixed. Central banks intervened in their foreign currency markets whenever necessary to maintain stability. Exchange rates were changed only infrequently, with the permission of the World Bank and the International Monetary Fund (IMF). These bodies usually required a country that devalued its currency to adopt tough economic measures in order to ensure the stability of the currency in the future.

The regime of fixed exchange rates broke down during the late 1960s due to global economic forces. These included a vast expansion of international trading and inflationary pressure in the major economies. The shift to flexible foreign exchange rates introduced daily (and intra-day) volatility to exchange rates. As the hitherto obscured volatility surfaced in traded foreign currencies, the financial market began to offer currency traders special tools for insuring against these "new" risks.

Figure 3A-2 depicts the percentage change in the value of the German Deutsche mark relative to the U.S. dollar up to the early 1990s.[1] The shift in the levels of volatility is very noticeable in the early 1970s, as the currency market moved to floating exchange rates. As indicated in the figure, the shift precipitated a string of novel financial contracts based on the exchange rates of leading currencies.

The first contracts tended to be various kinds of futures and forwards, though these were soon followed by foreign currency options. In 1972, the Mercantile Exchange in Chicago (CME) created the International Monetary Market (IMM), which specialized in foreign currency futures and options on futures on the major currencies. In 1982, the Chicago Board Option Exchange (CBOE) and the Philadelphia Stock Exchange introduced options on spot exchange rates. Banks joined the trend by offering over-the-counter (OTC) forward contracts and options on exchange rates to their customers.

The development of interest rate volatility and derivative instruments followed a similar story from the early 1970s, as we describe in Chapter 6. The equity and commodity markets also came to support significant derivatives markets, often actively developed by banking institutions. The end result of bank activity in these new derivatives markets was that banks naturally became ever

---

[1]On January 1, 1999, the euro was launched and became the official currency of the eurozone, which consists of 17 of the 27 member states of the European Union. The euro replaced former national currencies such as the German Deutsche mark and the French franc.

FIGURE 3A-2 Month-End German Deutsche Mark/U.S. Dollar Exchange Rates

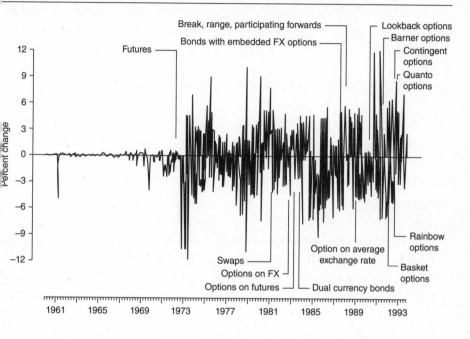

more exposed to volatile derivative instruments—and these exposures had to be carefully risk-managed.

Group of Thirty (G30) Policy Recommendations

The 1996 Amendment to the Basel Accord had a notable precursor. In 1993, the Group of Thirty (G30) published a report that described best-practice price risk management recommendations for dealers and end users of derivatives (as well as for legislators, regulators, and supervisors). The report was based in part on a detailed survey of industry practice among dealers and end users around the world.

The G30 focused on providing practical guidance in terms of managing derivatives businesses, offering an important benchmark against which participants could measure their own price risk management practices. Its recommendations covered sound market risk policies (e.g., the establishment of a market risk function independent from trading decisions), credit risk policies, enforceability policies, infrastructure policies, accounting and disclosure policies, and so on. They continue to act as the cornerstones of any modern bank risk management framework.

The 1996 Market Risk Amendment ("1996 Amendment")

The recommendations in the G30 report helped establish qualitative standards for bank risk management of derivative market risk. But the explosion in bank trading of derivatives and more mundane securities clearly had implications for how regulators calculated the amount of regulatory capital a bank should set aside to cover risk.

The 1996 Amendment to the 1988 Accord, implemented in 1998, extended the initial Accord to include risk-based capital requirements for the market risks that banks incur in their trading accounts. The fundamental innovation of the 1996 Amendment was to allow sophisticated banks to use their own internal VaR model (see Chapter 7) to calculate regulatory capital for market risk in their trading book.

Market risk is not the only risk arising from instruments such as derivatives: they give rise to credit risk as well. Under the 1996 Amendment, off-balance-sheet derivatives, such as swaps and options, are subject to both the market risk charge and the credit risk capital charges stipulated in the original 1988 Accord.

By contrast, on-balance-sheet assets in the trading portfolio are subject to the market risk capital charge only—a feature that helped offset the aggregate effect of the new rules on the amount of capital banks had to set aside.

Also, banks adopting the internal models approach tended to realize substantial capital savings, on the order of 20 to 50 percent, depending on the size of their trading operations and the type of instruments they traded. This is because internal models can be designed to capture diversification effects by modeling the correlations between positions.

In addition to the market risk capital adequacy requirements, the Basel Committee set limits on concentration risks. Under the Amendment, risks that exceed 10 percent of the bank's capital must be reported, and banks are forbidden to take positions that are greater than 25 percent of the bank's capital. As a historical footnote, had these rules been in effect in 1994, Barings Bank would have been prohibited from building up such huge exchange-traded futures positions, and the world's most famous example of rogue trading might have been avoided. (At the time the bank collapsed in February 1995, Barings' exposures on the SIMEX and OSE were 40 percent and 73 percent of its capital, respectively.)

1996 Amendment Qualitative Requirements

Before an institution became eligible to use its own internal VaR model to assess the regulatory capital related to market risk, the regulators insisted it must put sound risk management practices in place—largely in accord with the G30 recommendations we described earlier.

In particular, the institution needed to demonstrate that it had a strong risk management group, independent of the business units that the group monitored and reporting directly to the senior executive management of the institution.

Implementing a VaR model is a significant endeavor, as we describe in more detail in Chapter 7. An important part of setting up any VAR model for regulatory purposes is ensuring that the risk factor model inputs are reliable and accurate:

- A formal vetting system is needed to approve the models, any modifications to them, their assumptions, and their calibration.
- Model parameters should be estimated independently of the trading desks to avoid the temptation by the traders to "fudge" volatility numbers and other key parameters.

Appendix 3.3

BASEL II AND MINIMUM CAPITAL REQUIREMENTS FOR CREDIT RISK

The Basel II framework maintained both the wide definition of capital employed by Basel I and the minimum capital requirement of 8 percent of risk-weighted assets (though these decisions were undermined by the 2007–2009 financial crisis and have been altered in Basel III). However, Basel II made two key changes with regard to minimum capital requirements.

First, the regulators extended the risk calculation to include both market risk (i.e., incorporation of the 1996 Amendment on market risk) and operational risk:

$$\frac{Total\ Capital}{Credit\ Risk + Market\ Risk + Operational\ Risk} = Capital\ Ratio\ (Minimum\ 8\%) \quad (1)$$

where risk-weighted assets are the sum of the assets subject to market, credit, and operational risk. Tier 2 capital cannot exceed 50 percent of total regulatory capital, which is the sum of tier 1 and tier 2 capital.

The second key change concerns the way that credit risk is to be calculated. Basel II set out an improved standard approach for calculating credit risk (known as the Standardized Approach), as well as two more advanced approaches based on a bank's own internal ratings: the IRB (internal-ratings-based) Foundation and Advanced approaches to calculating minimum required capital for credit risk.

There is a significant wrinkle in how the three approaches treat expected and unexpected losses. Under the Standardized Approach, Basel II incorporates both expected and unexpected losses (see Chapter 1 for their definition) into the calculation of credit risk capital requirements (in contrast to the 1996 Market Risk Amendment, which is only concerned with *unexpected loss* for market risk in the trading book).[1] Under both the IRB approaches, the above treatment of the 1988 Accord to include general loan loss reserves in tier 2 capital is withdrawn. Instead, banks need to compare the expected loss to the total eligible provisions. When expected loss is greater than the eligible provisions, banks have to deduct the difference from capital, with the deduction being on the basis of 50 percent from tier 1 and 50 percent from tier 2 capital. In the other instance, when expected loss is less than the eligible provisions, banks may recognize the difference in tier 2 capital up to a maximum of 0.6 percent of credit-risk-weighted assets.

Now let's look in more detail at the Standardized, IRB Foundation, and IRB Advanced approaches to calculating minimum required capital for credit risk.

The Standardized Approach

The Standardized Approach is conceptually the same as the 1988 Accord, but was designed to be more risk sensitive. The bank allocates a risk weight to each of its assets and off-balance-sheet positions and produces a sum of risk-weighted asset values.

For example, a risk weight of 50 percent means that an exposure is included in the calculation of risk-weighted assets at 50 percent of its full value, which then translates into a capital charge equal to 8 percent of that value or, equivalently, to 4% (= 8% × 50%) of the exposure.

Individual risk weights depend both on the broad category of borrower—that is, whether the borrower is a sovereign, a bank, or a corporation—and on the rating provided by an external rating agency (Table 3A-4). For banks' exposures

---

[1] The justification for including expected losses in the capital requirement is that loan loss reserves are already counted as tier 2 capital and are constituted to protect the bank against credit losses. However, loan loss reserves are only eligible for tier 2 capital up to a maximum of 1.25 percent of risk-weighted assets.

TABLE 3A-4 Standardized Approach: New Risk Weights

			Credit Assessment			
Claim	AAA to AA⁻	A+ to A⁻	BBB+ to BBB⁻	BB+ to BB⁻ (B⁻)ᵃ	Below BB⁻ (B⁻)ᵃ	Unrated
Sovereigns	0%	20%	50%	100%	150%	100%
Banks Option 1ᵇ	20%	50%	100%	100%	150%	100%
Banks Option 2ᶜ	20%	50%	50%	100%	150%	50%
Short-term claimsᵈ	20%	20%	20%	50%	150%	20%
Corporates	20%	50%	100%	100%	150%	100%
Securitization tranchesᵉ	20%	50%	100%	350%	Deduction from capital	

ᵃB⁻ is the cutoff rating for sovereigns and banks. It is BB⁻ for corporates and securitization exposures.

ᵇRisk weighting based on risk weighting of sovereign in which the bank is incorporated. Banks incorporated in a given country will be assigned a risk weight one category less favorable than that assigned to claims on the sovereign, with a cap of 100% for claims to banks in sovereigns rated BB+ to B⁻.

ᶜRisk weighting based on the assessment of the individual bank.

ᵈShort-term claims in option 2 are defined as having an original maturity of three months or less.

ᵉThe risk weights for short-term ratings are 20% for A-1/P-1, 50% for A-2/P-2, and 100% for A-3/P-3; for all other ratings or unrated, there is capital deduction.

Source: Basel Committee on Banking Supervision, 2004.

to sovereigns, the Basel Committee applies the published credit scores of export credit agencies.

For claims on corporations, Basel II retains a risk weight of 100 percent except for highly rated companies (those rated AAA to A⁻) and non-investment-grade borrowers rated below BB⁻. Highly rated companies benefit from a lower risk weight of 20 to 50 percent. Non-investment-grade companies rated below BB⁻ are attributed a risk weight of 150 percent. Short-term revolvers, with a term less than a year, are subject to a capital charge of 20 percent instead of zero under Basel I. Therefore, Basel II puts highly rated corporate claims on the same footing as the obligations of banks and government-sponsored enterprises.

Shortcomings of the Standardized Approach

How successful is the Standardized Approach at mending the gaps in the original 1988 Accord? Our view is that the Standardized Approach is an improvement, but presents flaws rather similar in kind to those of the 1988 Accord. Banks have the same incentive to play the regulatory arbitrage game for the following reasons:

- There is not enough differentiation among credit categories: six credit categories (including unrated) are not sufficient. For example, the same risk weight (100 percent) is attributed to a corporate investment-grade facility rated BBB and a non-investment-grade facility rated BB⁻.
- The unrated category receives a risk weight of 100 percent, which is less than that attributed to non-investment-grade facilities rated below BB⁻. This does not make much sense since it removes any incentive for high-risk institutions to pay for a rating. So long as they remain unrated, they will be treated as if they were investment grade. Clearly, the highest risk weight should apply to any firms that elect to remain unrated.
- The Standardized Approach attributes too much capital—more than is required for economic protection—to investment-grade facilities (e.g., 1.6 percent for AA facilities) and not enough to non-investment-grade debt (e.g., 12 percent to B facilities).

For example, if we look at the period 1981–1999, there was not a single default on bonds rated AAA to AA⁻ (corresponding to the first bucket of the Standardized Approach) within one year of an entity holding that rating (though a few exceptions did occur in subsequent years). Yet the Standardized Approach attributes 1.6 percent of capital to such assets held by a bank.

The IRB Approach

Under the IRB (internal-ratings-based) approach to assess risk capital requirements, banks have to categorize banking book exposures into at least five broad classes of assets with different underlying credit risk characteristics: corporations, banks, sovereigns, retail, and equity. This classification is broadly consistent with established bank practices. Within the corporate and retail asset classes, subclasses are separately identified. The IRB proposes a specific treatment for securitization exposures.

The IRB approach provides for distinct analytical frameworks for different types of loan exposures—e.g., corporate and retail lending. Here, we'll focus on corporate loans and bonds.

Banks adopting the IRB approach are allowed to use their own internal risk ratings methodology to assess credit risk, subject to the approval by the regulator of the bank's internal rating system and validation of the way the bank produces the key risk parameters for calculating credit risk.

These key risk parameters include the probability of default (PD) for each rating category, the loss given default (LGD), and exposure at default (EAD) for loan commitments.

Under the IRB, the calculation of the potential future loss amount, which forms the basis of the minimum capital requirement, encompasses unexpected losses. It is derived from a formula whose key inputs are the PD, LGD, EAD, and maturity, M, of the facility.

In the Foundation approach, banks estimate the PD associated with each borrower, and the supervisors supply the other inputs, as follows:

- LGD = 45 percent for senior unsecured facilities and 75 percent for subordinated claims; the existence of collateral will lower the estimated LGD
- EAD = 75 percent for irrevocable undrawn commitments[2]
- M = 2.5 years, except for repo-style transactions where the effective maturity will be six months

In the Advanced IRB approach, banks that meet rigorous standards in terms of their internal ratings system and capital allocation process are permitted to set the values of all the necessary inputs. That is, they won't be restricted to estimating the PD of their assets but can also estimate the LGD, EAD, and M risk parameters.

Still, the Basel Committee stopped short of permitting banks to calculate their capital requirements on the basis of their own internal credit risk portfolio models, which would have allowed each bank to capture unique portfolio effects that tend to reduce total bank risk exposure. Instead, the IRB approach allocates

---

The credit conversion factor is zero percent only for unconditionally and immediately cancelable commitments.

capital facility by facility (though some portfolio effects are indirectly captured in the formula through the average asset correlation embedded in the calculation of the risk weights). However, the Basel Committee does encourage banks to use more sophisticated approaches and models to assess credit risk under Pillar II of the new rules.

Appendix 3.4

BASEL 2.5: ENHANCEMENTS TO THE BASEL II FRAMEWORK

During the 2007–2009 crisis a number of banks experienced large losses in their trading books, the risk of which had not been captured in the banks' VaR models. This pointed to a number of deficiencies in the VaR-based capital methodology, which is typically based on a 99 percent one-day VaR, scaled up to 10 days. The following additional capital charges were therefore imposed:[1]

- *Stressed value-at-risk.* Banks using internal models in the trading book must calculate a stressed value-at-risk based on a 12-month period of significant financial stress. The calculation should be portfolio-specific. This additional capital charge recognizes that traditional VaR calculations capture the risk of normal markets and are not calibrated to period of stress.
- *Incremental capital charge* (IRC). Many of the losses during the credit crisis were not caused by defaults, but rather by a loss of liquidity and a decline in values due to credit migration and a widening of credit spreads. The IRC represents an estimate of the default and migration risks of unsecuritized credit products over a one-year horizon at the

---

[1]Banks were originally expected to comply with the revised requirements by December 31, 2010; however, by 2012, only Australian, European, and several Asian banks had implemented Basel 2.5.

99.9 percent confidence level, taking into account the liquidity horizons of individual positions, or sets of positions.[2]

The IRC encompasses all positions subject to a capital charge for specific interest rate risk according to the internal models approach, except securitization positions which have a different treatment as discussed below.

The IRC model should also capture the impact of rebalancing positions at the end of their liquidity horizons so as to achieve a constant level of risk over a one-year horizon; that is, existing exposures are rebalanced at the end of the liquidity horizon or rolled over when they mature so as to maintain the initial risk level as indicated by a risk metric such as VaR or the profile of exposures by credit rating and concentration.

The IRC charge includes the impact of clustering of default and migration events during stressed markets.

The impact of diversification between default or migration events and other market factors is not taken into account. Therefore, the IRC capital charge is simply added to the VaR-based capital charge for market risk.

For securitized products in the trading book, the capital charges of the banking book apply, with the exception of so-called "correlation trading portfolios." So-called "resecuritizations"—e.g., collateralized debt obligations of asset-backed securities (CDOs of ABSs)—also receive a specific rating-based charge, reflecting their prominent role in the credit crisis.

Correlation trading books[3] are exempt from the full treatment for securitization positions and qualify for a revised standardized charge or a capital

---

[2]The liquidity horizon represents the time required to sell the position or hedge all material risks covered by the IRC model in a stressed market. The liquidity horizon has a minimum term of three months.

[3]Correlation trading portfolios may include simple securitization exposures and n-to-default credit derivatives that meet the following criteria:

- The position is not a resecuritization, an option on a securitization tranche, or a synthetically leveraged super-senior tranche.
- All reference entities are single-name products, including single-name credit derivatives, CDS Index tranches, and bespoke tranches for which a two-way market exists.

Even so, these desks are exposed to "basis risk"—e.g., between the bespoke and index tranches. At sophisticated firms, these risks are measured through VaR, which typically includes base correlation VaR and specific VaR.

charge based on a "comprehensive risk measure" (CRM) that captures not only incremental default and migration risks, but all price risks, including basis risk. But capital charges for these portfolios remain subject to a floor of 8 percent of the standardized charge.

In addition, banks using the internal models approach for market risk should have in place a rigorous and comprehensive stress testing program. Banks' stress scenarios should cover a range of factors that can create extraordinary losses or gains in trading portfolios. These factors include low-probability events in all major types of risks (market, credit, operational, and liquidity risks).

Scenarios should include past periods of significant disturbances, such as the 1987 equity market crash, the exchange rate mechanism crises of 1992 and 1993, the fall in bond markets in the first quarter of 1994, the 1998 Russian financial crisis and subsequent LTCM failure, the bursting of the technology stock bubble at the turn of the millennium, and the 2007–2009 financial crisis. The scenarios should include both the large price movements and the sharp reduction in liquidity associated with these events. Furthermore, the bank should also develop a second type of scenario to evaluate the sensitivity of the bank's market risk exposure to shocks in risk factors such as volatilities and correlations. Regulators say that banks must develop bank-specific scenarios, selecting the most challenging scenarios given the unique characteristics of each bank's portfolios.

Taken as a whole, the result of the Basel 2.5 reforms is that each bank must meet, on a daily basis, a capital requirement expressed as the sum of:

$$\text{Capital} = \max \{\text{VaR}, k \times (\text{average VaR over 60 days})\} +$$
$$\max \{\text{Stress VaR}, k \times (\text{average Stress VaR over 60 days})\} + \text{IRC}$$

where

- $k \geq 3$
- VaR is measured at the 99 percent confidence level over a ten-day period and combines both "general market risk" and "specific risk."
- Stress VaR is computed using data from a stressful period, such as 2007–2009.
- IRC (incremental risk charge) is a credit VaR calculated over a one-year period at the 99.9 percent confidence level that should capture both default risk and migration risk and should be calibrated to the bank's own "through the cycle" historical loss experience. All positions that generate a potential credit risk should be included in the IRC. Note that

all sovereign bonds are subject to the IRC, which poses the thorny question of the probability of default of a country—e.g., the United States.[4]

Discussion of Basel 2.5

Trading book capital used to be predominantly driven by one risk measure, VaR. Under Basel 2.5 it is driven by VaR, stressed VaR, the IRC, the CRM, and the standardized charges for securitization, plus a standardized floor for the CRM.

The main problem with this additional complexity is that it has many internal inconsistencies. Basel 2.5 is a patchwork of overconservative, overlapping rules that, added together, generate a punitive level of capital for the trading book. For some trades, the amount of capital may even exceed the face value of the position—i.e., be more than the bank can possibly lose.[5] According to the

---

[4]Even if certain sovereign bonds are subject to a zero percent risk weight under the Standardized Approach, they will attract a capital charge under the IRC.

[5]Assume for illustrative purposes that

- volatility under stressed market conditions is three times the volatility of a normal market environment and
- returns are normally distributed

so that stress VaR is three times normal VaR, neglecting IRC for the purpose of the exercise.

Now suppose that the portfolio has an annualized volatility in normal market conditions of 10 percent.

Then, over ten days, the standard deviation is 2 percent.

The ten-day standard deviation in stress conditions is thus 6 percent, according to our (not unreasonable) assumption.

The sum of these—i.e., 8 percent—must be multiplied by the 99 percent standard normal critical value of 2.33, and then by a multiplier of at least 3.

Assuming a "green zone" model—i.e., a multiplier of 3—regulatory capital under the new rules (and ignoring the IRC) is $2.33 \times 3 \times 8\% = 56\%$ of the portfolio exposure.

Now, given a well-diversified and partially hedged portfolio with an annualized volatility of 5 percent and an "old" regulatory capital of 7 percent of the exposure, the new charge will be 28 percent.

But with a partially diversified and lightly hedged portfolio, with a normal volatility 15 percent and a stress volatility of 60 percent, the new rules lead to a capital charge of 105 percent of the size of the portfolio, which, if the positions are long, is higher than the maximum loss that could be incurred on this portfolio.

Note that under our simple but illustrative assumptions, the new regulatory capital charge will always be four times the capital charge without the stressed component.

Basel Committee's own calculations, as a result of the Basel 2.5 revisions, market risk capital requirements will increase by an estimated average of three to four times for large internationally active banks. The banking industry is therefore hoping that a forthcoming fundamental review of trading book capital (see below) will propose a more consistent capital charge for market risk.

However, the rules themselves are not the only problem. Prompted by growing complaints from banks and analysts that the ratio of RWAs to assets can be inexplicably different from one institution to the next, the Basel Committee conducted a study in 2012 to review the calculation of the RWAs for the trading book. The Basel Committee handed the same hypothetical trading portfolio to 15 large banks in nine countries and asked them to calculate the total capital to support it. The results, published in January 2013, ranged from 13 to 35 million euros. This was worrying enough; however, the variation within individual asset classes, such as credit risk or interest rate portfolios, reached as much as eight times (from bank to bank).

The Basel Committee discovered that the variance in the results was driven as much by the decisions of different supervisors as by bank modeling decisions. In some countries, supervisors routinely instruct individual banks, or banks of a certain class, to hold extra capital against particular kinds of assets. Similarly, some supervisors restrict the kind of risk model that can be used by banks, while others allow banks more freedom. Whatever the cause, the results are clearly somewhat alarming and indicate the need for an overall revision of industry practices when computing trading book RWAs.

Fundamental Review of the Trading Book

Basel 2.5 was something of an emergency response to the undercapitalization of banks' trading books revealed during the subprime crisis. However, it suffers a number of recognized shortcomings. Regulators are preparing for a more fundamental review that is likely to address the following areas:

- *Lack of coherence:* The current framework is characterized by a layer of overlapping capital charges that can lead, as we discussed above, to a capital charge that is higher than the actual maximum loss.
- *Boundary between the trading book and the banking book:* Large differences in the capital requirements for similar types of risk in the trading

book and the banking book (e.g., treatment of interest rate risk) may lead to regulatory arbitrage.

- *Market liquidity risk:* The industry needs to develop a comprehensive framework that captures the risk of market illiquidity during stressed periods.
- *Internal-models-based approach and risk measure:* A number of weaknesses have been identified with regard to the use of value-at-risk (VaR) for determining regulatory requirements, including its inability to capture "tail risk." The Basel Committee is contemplating adopting an alternative: the expected shortfall (ES) approach. This measures the expected loss beyond a given confidence level, as we discuss in more detail in Chapter 7. In addition, risk models would be calibrated to a period of significant financial stress.
- *Standardized approach:* The current standardized approach to market risk would be revamped to improve risk sensitivity, in order to reduce the risk sensitivity gap between the standardized and the models-based approaches. The revised standardized approach would also become a more credible fallback in case a bank's internal risk model is deemed inadequate.
- *Credit value adjustments (CVA):* The relationship between counterparty credit risk and the trading book regime needs to be clarified.

Appendix 3.5

CONTINGENT CONVERTIBLE BONDS

Contingent convertible bonds, known as "CoCos" or "CoCo bonds," are bonds issued by a bank or an insurance company that convert into common equity, or are subject to a write-down, at prespecified trigger levels as soon as the bank enters a life-threatening situation. Conversion, or the write-down, happens via a predefined trigger mechanism—e.g., when core tier 1 capital (CT1) falls below 5 percent.

Contingent capital can be viewed as a form of catastrophe insurance. When the bank is in a stressed situation, with a high risk of default, investors provide automatic loss-absorbing capital, with the debt being partially canceled or converted into common equity.

Conversion into common equity creates dilution for existing shareholders but helps to protect taxpayers from a costly bailout if a conversion event occurs. From a bank perspective, these securities can help fulfill post-crisis capital requirements without diluting common equity holders, as long as conversion does not occur.

CoCos and Regulation

The primary function of capital is to absorb losses as they arise and help preserve the bank as a going concern. However, bank hybrid tier 1 capital, such as trust preferreds, was found to be ineffective in practice during the 2007–2009 financial crisis. Banks continued to pay interest on their hybrid debt to avoid being shut out of the market in the future. Tier 2 capital instruments also failed to perform their loss-absorbing function, beyond occasional coupon deferrals and voluntary exchanges, because institutions were often not permitted to fail.

Basel III specifically mentions the potential role for CoCos in meeting capital requirements.[1] According to Basel III, the new capital requirements are a minimum CT1 of 4.5 percent, with a minimum tier 1 capital ratio of 6 percent and a minimum total capital ratio of 8 percent. Since September 2010, Basel III requires banks to constitute, in addition to these minimums, a capital conservation buffer (CCB) of 2.5 percent over the period 2016–2019. It follows that banks are permitted under Basel III to hold 1.5 percent of their risk-weighted assets in noncore tier 1 (6% tier 1 – 4.5% CT1) and 2 percent in tier 2 capital. This 3.5 percent bucket of noncore tier 1 and tier 2 capital could be met by using CoCos.

In addition, banks may use CoCos to meet capital requirements imposed by national regulators that are above the minimum tier 1 set by Basel III. In October 2010, the Swiss government asked Swiss banks to hold 19 percent of their risk-weighted assets as tier 1 capital, of which 9 percent could be held in the form of CoCos; of the 9 percent, 3 percent must trigger if CT1 falls below 7 percent, and the other 6 percent must trigger if CT1 falls below 5 percent. Swedish and Danish regulators have said banks may be able to use CoCos to meet additional capital requirements.

The European Commission's new Basel III directive (CRD 4) explicitly refers to CoCos as a way of meeting additional tier 1 capital, with a trigger event occurring when CT1 falls below 5.125 percent (or at a higher level set by the institution).[2]

Tax laws in Europe allow banks to deduct the coupon on CoCos from their taxable income, whether the CoCos are of the convertible or write-down variety. However, the U.S. Internal Revenue Service treats CoCos as equity so issuers' interest payments are not tax deductible—making CoCos much less attractive for U.S. banks. This wrinkle probably explains why the Basel Committee decided

---

[1] But the Basel Committee ruled against the use of CoCos to meet the capital surcharge for SIFIs. Only common equity will be eligible for that purpose.

[2] European Directive CRD, European Commission 2011, pp. 74–77. The European Directive CRD 4 translates the Basel III rules into law for European banks.

not to allow the use of CoCos to meet the additional capital surcharge for systemically important financial institutions.

Features of CoCos

There are various kinds of CoCo, differentiated by the timing of the cash infusion (funded versus unfunded), the type of trigger, and the conversion amount.

Funded vs. Unfunded CoCos

So far, we've mainly discussed funded CoCos, which allow an institution to raise capital in the good times and, potentially, to meet regulatory capital requirements.

By contrast, unfunded CoCos provide cash only when the conversion is triggered, offering loss-absorbing capital and liquidity during times of crisis. The institution pays a premium for this option: a commitment fee. Typically, the commitment is of finite duration.[3] Unfunded CoCos create counterparty risk because the bank only receives the cash when conversion is triggered, typically at a time of systemic stress that may also affect the counterparty.

Trigger Events

Trigger events can be either accounting-based or market-based, although so far only accounting-based triggers have been proposed.

Accounting-Based Triggers

Accounting triggers are in the form of tier 1 capital or equity capital thresholds—e.g., when tier 1 capital falls below 5 percent. One problem here is that tier 1 ratios are not directly observable by market participants. They are reported on a quarterly basis by most banks, or at the discretion of the banks, though regulators and supervisors have access to this information and can require the bank to make it public.

A second problem is that in the run-up to the 2007–2009 financial crisis, there was little difference between the tier 1 ratios of "crisis banks"—i.e., those

---

[3]Unfunded CoCos are somewhat similar to a CDS except that when triggered new equity is exchanged for cash.

that eventually failed or were bailed out by their governments—and banks that survived.[4] On a related note, regulators have become concerned about variations in the risk weights assigned to similar assets by different banks, which may reflect an intention by some banks to underplay risk.[5] This kind of variation means that capital ratios may not be easy to compare.

The worry that capital triggers lack transparency, can be manipulated, and may be triggered far too late explains why regulators often retain the option to force conversion if they judge that the bank is close to default.

Market-Based Triggers

Potentially, market-based triggers can be used to circumvent the limitations of accounting-based triggers. They could take various forms—for example:

- Pre-agreed minimum price level for bank shares
- Ratio of market capitalization to book value of assets
- Credit default swap spread on the debt issued by the bank

Market-based triggers are relatively objective and transparent and can be verified in real time by regulators and market participants. They could also help in enhancing supervisory discretion and market discipline.

There are some potential issues to overcome. For example, during the "Flash Crash" of May 6, 2010, almost all the stocks traded in the United States suffered a huge downward price correction, only to recover minutes later. A share price trigger might have forced a CoCo conversion for no good reason. However, most of these practical concerns, including manipulation by short sellers, can be overcome quite easily—e.g., by basing the trigger on a rolling average of stock prices over the preceding 20 or 30 days.

---

[4]Indeed, many banks that failed in 2008 were better capitalized before the crisis than those that did not fail. Five U.S. financial institutions that either failed or were forced into government-assisted mergers in 2008—Bear Stearns, Washington Mutual, Lehman Brothers, Wachovia, and Merrill Lynch—had regulatory capital ratios 50 to 100 percent above the regulatory minimum of 8 percent. Citibank had a tier 1 capital ratio that never fell below 7 percent during the course of the financial crisis and stood at 11.8 percent in December 2008 when the bank's stock market capitalization reached its lowest level. (A. Kuritzkes and H. Scott, "Markets Are the Best Judge of Bank Capital," *Financial Times*, September 23, 2009)

[5]"A Weight on Their Minds," *Risk Magazine*, July 2011, pp. 36–39.

Conversion Amount

Most CoCo issues are converted into shares of common equity either according to a predetermined number of shares (or, equivalently, at a predetermined share price), which affects the extent of the dilution to existing shareholders, or at a share price defined in reference to the share price prevailing when conversion is triggered.

CoCos that have the conversion strike set at the spot level prevailing at issuance imply a significant risk for the CoCo holders, potentially increasing the risk premium to potentially uneconomical levels for the issuer. By contrast, if the new shares are issued at the share price prevailing when conversion is triggered, then there is no dilution and no loss of value for the CoCo holders. It is expected that the regulator will oblige the holders of CoCos to participate in losses, so the trigger will be probably set at around 50 percent of the stock price at issuance.

An alternative to conversion into shares of common equity is a partial or total write-down of the nominal of the CoCos. This is more natural than conversion into new shares for a nonpublic institution.

Pros and Cons of CoCos

CoCos provide leverage in good times and a buffer to absorb losses and relief from debt-servicing obligations in bad times. They can help to reduce the risk to the taxpayer from implicit "too-big-to-fail" government guarantees. Both the funded and unfunded versions incentivize financial institutions to engage in conservative and prudent risk management because the cost of diluting incumbent shareholders and management (through their holding of company shares) is substantial.

However, the triggering of a CoCo might itself trigger a wider stress scenario if it signals to investors that other banks might also be in a stressed situation. There is also the risk of contagion if the bank's CoCos have been mainly invested in by other financial institutions, which are forced to absorb large losses. Also, as the trigger point comes closer, some investors may protect their investment by short-selling shares against their long position in the CoCos—potentially setting off a "death spiral" for the bank. Furthermore, as the trigger comes closer, banks might be tempted to take additional excessive risks to force conversion—wiping out their outstanding CoCo debt. Finally, it is possible that contingent capital will introduce market inefficiencies because conversion will eliminate or postpone a default event, which is often the moment that inefficient businesses are restructured and poor managers replaced.[6]

CoCo Issuers

As of early 2013, five banks (Lloyds in November 2009, Rabobank in March 2010, Credit Suisse in February 2011, Bank of Cyprus in April 2011, and KBC in January 2013), one insurance company (Allianz, the German insurer, in July 2011), and one reinsurance company (Swiss Re in March 2013) have issued CoCos.[7]

While CoCo issuance has gotten off to a relatively slow start, other international institutions are now contemplating CoCos—e.g., the Spanish and Portuguese governments plan to use CoCos to help support their banks.

Other CoCo and CoCo-Related Issues

An example of an unfunded CoCo is the contingent capital solution provided in 2009 by the U.K. government to the Royal Bank of Scotland (RBS). The U.K. government is committed to providing RBS with £8 billion of capital if its CT1 falls below 5 percent.

Another example of an unfunded guarantee akin to a CoCo is the deal brokered by Royal Bank of Canada (RBC) in 2001 with Swiss Re. Swiss Re will inject C$200 million into RBC in exchange for preferred shares if a high loss/low probability event happens to lower a large portion of RBC's reserves.

In the same insurance context, in 2010, SCOR, a Paris-based insurance and reinsurance company, entered into a three-year contingent capital deal with UBS. If the amount of net catastrophe losses experienced by SCOR reaches a certain trigger, UBS is committed to inject €150 million into SCOR in exchange for shares of common equity at a preset price.

---

[6]O. Hart and L. Zingales, "A New Capital Regulation for Large Financial Institutions," working paper, April 2009.

[7]For a detailed analysis of these CoCo bonds, consult J. De Spiegeleer and W. Schoutens, *Contingent Convertible (CoCo) Notes: Structure and Pricing*, Euromoney Books, 2011.

CoCo Bonuses

The bonus culture in investment banks has been blamed for encouraging disproportionately risky behavior, which in turn helped lead to the financial crisis. New compensation schemes are needed that better align compensation with long-term shareholder interests,[8] and perhaps also with the interests of other bank stakeholders.

So far, the schemes that have been suggested are largely based on equity. However, the trouble with equity incentives is that equity is the equivalent of a call option on the assets of the bank—the holder enjoys all of the upside of a share price rise, but only a limited amount of the downside. Given this limited liability, executives paid in equity have a powerful incentive to take excessive risks. And when the bank is in trouble, they may be tempted to bet the bank, in the knowledge that they can only lose their residual near-valueless equity; bondholders and creditors have much more at stake if the bank fails.

The G20 meeting of September 2009 recommended that bankers should be exposed to downside risk by deferring compensation and through mechanisms that could claw back bonuses.

CoCos offer an interesting way to achieve this. Bonuses paid in the form of a CoCo bond have a value that is closely tied to the health and actual performance of banks. They increase exposure to downside risk, and they do not incentivize strategies that would ramp up the share price in the short term (as equity can).[9] With CoCo bonuses, there should be no risk of a "death spiral," as banks and regulators can enforce rules against employee short-selling and hedging CoCo exposures.[10]

---

[8]However, a substantial portion of the equity at both Lehman Brothers and Bear Stearns was in the hands of the CEOs and top executives, who probably believed that their interests were aligned with those of outside shareholders. This suggests that shareholder alignment may offer only a partial solution to the problem.

[9]There is "unlimited" upside only after conversion, when the bank becomes closely monitored by the regulator.

[10]There may still be a "perception" problem here. CoCos usually pay a high coupon to compensate for the conversion risk. Public opinion may regard this as a "double bonus"—i.e., a high coupon plus a cash payment at maturity. Therefore, CoCo bonuses should be structured so that they don't pay any coupon or pay very low interest.

In 2010, the European Parliament gave banks the green light to use CoCos as part of their compensation packages, as follows:

- Upfront cash bonuses will be capped at 30 percent of the total bonus and at 20 percent for particularly high bonuses.
- Between 40 and 60 percent of any bonus must be deferred for at least three years.
- At least 50 percent of the total bonus will be paid as contingent capital and shares.

Barclays Capital was the first bank to say publicly, in January 2011, that it will issue CoCos and use them as bonus payments to employees (as part of their deferred compensation). These CoCo bonds would become worthless should Barclays' CT1 fall below 7 percent. Barclays' preferred version of CoCos takes the form of a loss-absorbing bond—e.g., possibly one that loses its coupons or has a haircut in value—rather than a bond that converts into equity.

4

CORPORATE GOVERNANCE AND RISK MANAGEMENT

The first decade of the millennium saw two major waves of corporate failures, first in the nonfinancial sector (2001–2003) and then in the financial sector (2007–2009), both of which were attributed in part to failures of corporate governance. As a result, corporate governance[1] and its relationship to risk oversight is a continuing concern around the world, and especially in the United States and Europe.

The first wave of failures included, most notoriously, the bankruptcy of energy giant Enron in 2001, a wave of "new technology" and telecom industry accounting scandals at companies such as WorldCom and Global Crossing, and, to prove that the problem wasn't confined to the United States, the collapse of the Italian dairy products giant Parmalat in late 2003. In many cases, boards were provided with misleading information or there was a breakdown in the process by which information was transmitted to the board and shareholders. The breakdowns often involved financial engineering and the nondisclosure of economic risks—as well as outright fraud.

---

[1]"Corporate governance involves a set of relationships between a company's management, its board, its shareholders and other stakeholders. Corporate governance also provides the structure through which the objectives of the company are set, and the means of attaining those objectives and monitoring performance are determined." Preamble, OECD Principles of Corporate Governance, 2004, p. 11.

This first wave of scandals led to a wave of reforms, including legislation in the United States and reforms of corporate codes in Europe, designed to mend perceived failures in corporate governance practices and, especially, to improve financial controls and financial reporting. A striking feature of these reforms was that they sought to penalize inattention and incompetence as much as deliberate malfeasance. In the United States, the main mechanisms of reform were the Sarbanes-Oxley Act (SOX) of 2002 and associated changes in stock exchange rules, as described in Boxes 4-1 and 4-2.

BOX 4-1 SARBANES-OXLEY (SOX)

In response to the series of accounting and management scandals that surfaced soon after the millennium, the U.S. Congress passed the Sarbanes-Oxley Act of 2002 (SOX). The act has created a more rigorous legal environment for the board, the management committee, internal and external auditors, and the CRO (chief risk officer).

SOX places primary responsibility on the chief executive officer and the chief financial officer of a publicly traded corporation for ensuring the accuracy of company reports filed with the Securities and Exchange Commission. SOX requires these senior corporate officers to report on the completeness and accuracy of the information contained in the reports, as well as on the effectiveness of the underlying controls.

Specifically, SOX calls for the CEO and CFO to certify quarterly and annually that the report filed with the Securities and Exchange Commission does not contain any untrue statements or omit any material facts. Senior officers must certify that the financial statements fairly present (in all material respects) the results of the corporation's operations and cash flows. They also must take responsibility for designing, establishing, and maintaining disclosure controls and procedures.

The CEO and CFO must also disclose to the audit committee and to the company's external auditors any deficiencies and material weaknesses in internal controls, as well as any fraud (material or not) involving anyone with a significant role in internal control. The act requires that senior management annually assess the effectiveness of the corporation's internal control structure and procedures for financial reporting.

The act also seeks to make sure that the board of the company includes some members who are experts in understanding financial reports. Companies are compelled to disclose the number and names of persons serving on the critical audit committee whom the board has determined to be "financial experts." A financial expert is someone with an understanding of generally accepted accounting principles and financial statements, and should also have experience with internal accounting controls and an understanding of the function of the audit committee.

BOX 4-2   U.S. EXCHANGES TIGHTEN UP THE RULES

In January 2003 the U.S. Securities and Exchange Commission issued a rule—as directed by the Sarbanes-Oxley Act—that requires U.S. national securities exchanges and national securities associations (i.e., the NYSE, Amex, and Nasdaq) to make sure that their securities listing standards conform to the existing and evolving SEC rules.

These standards cover a number of areas that are critical to corporate governance and risk management, such as

- Composition of the board of directors—e.g., the board must have a majority of independent directors
- Establishment of a corporate governance committee with duties such as the development of broad corporate governance principles and oversight of the evaluation of the board and management
- Duties of the compensation committee—e.g., it should make sure that CEO compensation is aligned with corporate objectives
- Activities of the audit committee—e.g., to review external auditors' reports describing the quality of internal control procedures, and to adopt and disclose corporate governance guidelines and codes of business conduct

However, the reforms proved insufficient[2] to avert the subprime crisis in the United States and the subsequent global financial crisis. Following a series of failures and near-failures of large financial institutions between 2007 and 2009, boards professed ignorance of the risks that had been assumed in the pursuit of profit—and sometimes senior management offered the same excuse. In particular, the risk management function at many firms failed to attract the attention of senior management, or the boards, to the risk accumulated in structured financial products. One reason may have been a process of marginalization of the role of risk management in financial institutions during the boom years in the run-up to the crisis.

A note of frustration characterized the debate about corporate governance following the 2007–2009 crisis. Would it do any good to reform corporate governance once again with detailed legislation and new rules, when the enormous effort expended on the Sarbanes-Oxley reforms had proved inadequate to prevent a second wave of disaster?[3] Others have argued that a principles-based approach might work better, given that the regulators of the banking industry have already set out some of the key principles of improved risk governance in Pillar II of Basel II. Table 4-1 sets out some of the key areas of debate on financial institution corporate governance following the crisis; we return to many of these themes throughout this chapter.

Together with the Basel III reforms that we described in Chapter 3, these concerns and their remedies in various jurisdictions are shaping the broader corporate governance and risk management environment. More generally, the dramatic collapse in public confidence in the corporate and financial world caused by the two waves of scandals continues to put pressure on boards and

---

[2]Perhaps because the first wave of reforms focused on internal controls and financial reporting rather than risk management in its wider sense including the risk of pursuing fundamentally flawed business models. Following the 2007–2009 crisis, a new emphasis on stress testing programs and "recovery and resolution" style regulatory approaches should help to guard against the danger of a firm's pursuing a flawed business model.

[3]Some of the key legislative reforms can be seen as ways to force bank boards to do what they should have been doing all along—e.g., in the United States, the Dodd-Frank Act forces larger banks to run worst-case macroeconomic scenarios and to take the results into account in their capital planning and dividend payouts (see Chapter 16).

TABLE 4.1 Key Post-Crisis Corporate Governance Concerns: The Banking Industry

Stakeholder priority	Inquiries into the 2007–2009 financial crisis found that there was little focus in some firms on controlling tail risks and considering truly worst-case outcomes. This has led to debate about the uniquely complicated set of stakeholders in banking institutions and how this should affect corporate governance structures. In addition to equity, banks have very large amounts of deposits, debt, and implicit guarantees from governments. Depositors, debt holders, and taxpayers have a much stronger interest in minimizing the risk of bank failure than do most shareholders, who often seem to press for short-term results. The usual solution to corporate governance issues (empowering shareholders) may therefore not be the complete solution in banking.[1]
Board composition	The crisis reignited a long-term debate about how to ensure that bank boards contain the right balance of independence, engagement, and financial industry expertise. However, analyses of failed banks do not show any clear correlation between a predominance of "expert insiders" or "independents" and either failure or success. The first large failure of the crisis, the U.K.'s Northern Rock in 2007, had a number of banking experts on its board.
Board risk oversight	One key post-crisis trend has been a realization that boards need to become much more actively involved in risk oversight. This means educating boards on risk and making sure they maintain a direct link to the risk management infrastructure (e.g., giving CROs direct reporting responsibilities to the board, and more generally re-empowering risk managers).
Risk appetite	Regulators have pushed banks to set out a formal board-approved risk appetite that defines the firm's willingness to take risk and to tolerate threats to solvency. This can then be translated into an enterprisewide set of risk limits. Engaging the board in the limit-setting process helps to make sure that the board thinks clearly about the firm's risk-taking and what this means for day-to-day risk decisions. However, defining risk appetites and translating them successfully into limit frameworks remains a work in progress.
Compensation	One of the key levers of the board in determining bank behavior on risk is its control over compensation schemes. Some banks have begun to institute reforms such as making bonuses a smaller part of the compensation package, introducing bonus clawbacks and deferred payments to capture longer-terms risks, and similar measures. Boards have a particular duty to examine how pay structures might exacerbate risk-taking and whether risk adjustment mechanisms capture all the key long-term risks.

[1]See discussion in Hamid Mehran et al., "Corporate Governance and Banks: What Have We Learned from the Financial Crisis?" Federal Reserve Bank of New York, Staff Report no. 502, June 2011.

their committees to carry out corporate governance risk oversight responsibilities in a more effective manner.

In this chapter we'll use the example of an archetypal bank to try to answer three critical questions:

- How does best-practice corporate governance relate to best-practice risk management?
- How do boards and senior executives organize the delegation of risk management authority through key committees and risk executives?
- How can agreed risk limits be transmitted down the line to business managers in a way that can be monitored and that makes sense in terms of day-to-day business decisions?

Our aim is to give an idea of how risk management should be articulated from the top of an organization to the bottom. We focus on banks, since this topic is particularly critical in banking, but the concepts usually apply equally to other financial institutions as well as to nonbank corporations.

Setting the Scene: Corporate Governance and Risk Management

From a corporate governance perspective, a primary responsibility of the board is to look after the interests of shareholders. For example, does it make sense for the corporation to assume a particular risk, given the projected returns of the business activity and the potential threat to the corporation if the risk is realized? The board also needs to be sensitive to the concerns of other stakeholders such as debt holders. Debt holders are most interested in the extreme downside of risk—how likely is it that a risk will damage a corporation so badly that it will become insolvent?

In particular, the board needs to be on the alert for any conflict that may arise between the interests of management in boosting returns while assuming risks, and the interests of the company's longer-term stakeholders. (This kind of conflict of interest is often referred to in the academic literature as an "agency risk.")

Conflicts of interest can easily happen if, for example, executives are rewarded with options that they can cash in if the share price of the company rises above a certain level. Such an arrangement gives management an incentive to push the share price up, but not necessarily in a sustainable way. For example, management might encourage business lines to earn short-term rewards in exchange for assuming long-term risks. By the time the chickens come home to roost, managers, including CEOs, may well have picked up their bonuses or even changed jobs.

The tension between the interests of the CEO and the interests of longer-term stakeholders helps to explain why boards of directors need to maintain their independence from executive teams, and why there is a global push to separate the role of the CEO and the chairman of the board. The bankruptcy of MF Global, a brokerage firm, in October of 2011—one of the 10 largest U.S. bankruptcies ever—offers an example of poor governance. Many commentators have pointed out the danger of the board of a company falling under the spell of a charismatic CEO.[4]

This all explains why it is becoming difficult to draw a line between corporate governance and risk management, and we can see some clear effects of this at an organizational level. For example, over the last few years, many corporations have created the role of chief risk officer (CRO). A key duty of the CRO is often to act as a senior member of the management committee and to attend board meetings regularly. The board and the management committee increasingly look to the CRO to integrate corporate governance responsibilities with the risk function's existing market, credit, operational, and business risk responsibilities. Following the financial crisis of 2007–2009, many CROs were given a direct reporting line to the board or its risk committees in addition to reporting to the executive team and CEO.[5]

---

[4]Jon Corzine, the CEO of MF Global, took huge bets on European sovereign debt, eventually leading to an increase in required capital, increased margin calls as positions soured, a ratings downgrade, and a loss of confidence in the firm. MF Global was left without the cash to support its operations and was faced with a classic run on the bank. Bankruptcy followed.

[5]The Basel Committee says that a bank CRO should "report and have direct access to the board and its risk committee without impediment. . . . Interaction between the CRO and the board should occur regularly. . . . Non-executive board members should have the right to meet regularly—in the absence of senior management—with the CRO." Basel Committee, *Principles for Enhancing Corporate Governance*, October 2010.

True Risk Governance

The primary responsibility of the board is to ensure that it develops a clear understanding of the bank's business strategy and the fundamental risks and rewards that this implies. The board also needs to make sure that risks are made transparent to managers and to stakeholders through adequate internal and external disclosure.

Although the board is not there to manage the business, it is responsible for overseeing management and holding it accountable. It must also contribute to the development of the overall strategic plan for the firm, taking into consideration how any changes might affect business opportunities and the strategy of the firm. This necessarily includes the extent and types of risks that are acceptable for the firm—i.e., the board must characterize an appropriate "risk appetite" for the firm, as we discussed in Chapter 2.[6]

The firm's risk appetite should clearly be connected to its overall business strategy and capital plan. Some business activities may simply be wrong for a given firm, given the risks they entail and the size of the activity in relation to the firm's balance sheet. Business planning, which tends to be driven by earnings goals in a competitive environment, needs to involve risk management from the beginning of the planning process, in order to test how targets fit with the firm's risk appetite and to assess potential downsides. Equally important is clear communication throughout the firm of the firm's risk appetite and risk position.

To fulfill its risk governance responsibilities, the board must ensure that the bank has put in place an effective risk management program that is consistent with these fundamental strategic and risk appetite choices. And it must make sure that there are effective procedures in place for identifying, assessing, and managing all types of risk—e.g., business risk, operational risk, market risk, liquidity risk, and credit risk. For every business disaster where a firm has knowingly taken on too much risk, there is another where the firm has failed to identify a risk, such as an underlying liquidity risk, or ignored the risk because it was thought so unlikely that it did not deserve active risk management.

---

[6]See also risk appetite discussion in Senior Supervisors Group, *Risk Management Lessons from the Global Banking Crisis of 2008*, October 2009, pp. 23–24; and in KPMG, *Understanding and Articulating Risk Appetite*, 2008.

The board may be challenged by the complexity of the risk management process, but the principles at a strategic level are quite simple. There are only four basic choices in risk management:

- Avoid risk by choosing not to undertake some activities.
- Transfer risk to third parties through insurance, hedging, and outsourcing.
- Mitigate risk, such as operational risk, through preventive and detective control measures.
- Accept risk, recognizing that undertaking certain risky activities should generate shareholder value.

In particular, the board should ensure that business and risk management strategies are directed at economic rather than accounting performance, contrary to what happened at Enron and some of the other firms involved in highly publicized corporate governance scandals around the turn of the millennium.

This includes making sure that all the appropriate policies, methodologies, and infrastructure are in place across the enterprise.[7] The infrastructure includes both operating elements (e.g., sophisticated software, hardware, data, and operational processes) and personnel.

This might sound like an onerous task, but there are various levers that the board can pull. For example, one way to gauge how seriously a company takes its risk management process is to look at the human capital that is employed:

- What kind of a career path does the risk management function offer?
- Whom do risk managers report to?
- What salaries are paid to risk managers in comparison to "reward-oriented" personnel such as traders?
- Is there a strong ethical culture in evidence?

An effective board will also establish strong ethical standards and work to ensure that it understands the degree to which management follows them. Some banks have set up ethics committees within their business divisions to try to

---

The OECD's paper on *Corporate Governance and the Financial Crisis: Conclusions and Emerging Good Practices to Enhance Implementation of the Principles*, February 2010, p. 4, says that "an important conclusion is that the board's responsibility for defining strategy and risk appetite needs to be extended to establishing and overseeing enterprisewide risk management systems."

make sure that "soft" risks such as unethical business practices don't slip through the mesh of their "hard" risk-reporting framework.

Another important lever available to the board is the firm's performance metrics and compensation strategy. The board has a critical responsibility to make sure that the way staff are rewarded and compensated is based on risk-adjusted performance (see Chapter 17) and is aligned with shareholders' interests. The increase in misreporting after the millennial stock market boom paralleled the rise of equity-based compensation for CEOs, which arguably provided a perverse incentive to executives to manipulate financial results to boost the share price in the short term.

A related responsibility is to ensure that any major transactions the bank enters into are consistent with the risk authorized and the associated strategies of the bank.

The board should ensure that the information it obtains about risk management is accurate and reliable. Directors should demonstrate healthy skepticism and require information from a cross section of knowledgeable and reliable sources, such as the CEO, senior management, and internal and external auditors. Directors should be prepared to ask tough questions, and they should make themselves able to understand the answers.

The duty of the board is not, however, to undertake risk management on a day-to-day basis, but to make sure that all the mechanisms used to delegate and drive risk management decisions are functioning properly. As we discussed above, the 2007–2009 financial crisis highlighted the need to strengthen the role of the board, and therefore:[8]

- Board members need to be educated on risk issues and be given the means to explore and determine the risk appetite of the organization. They should be able to assess the risk of loss that the firm is willing to accept over a specified time horizon, taking into account its business

---

[8]In October 2010, the Basel Committee issued principles for enhancing corporate governance that addressed such issues as the role of the board of directors, the qualification of board members, and the importance of an independent risk management function. (Basel Committee, *Principles for Enhancing Corporate Governance*, October 2010.) In the United States, the Dodd-Frank Act requires a dedicated risk committee of the board of directors for publicly traded bank holding companies with total assets of $10 billion or more, as well as for systemically important publicly traded nonbank financial companies.

mix and strategy, earnings goals, and competitive position. This involves understanding the firm's current risk profile and its business culture vis-à-vis the firm's risk appetite, and monitoring the firm's ongoing performance against its risk appetite.

- Board members of the risk committee need some technical sophistication with regard to the key risk disciplines as well as solid business experience so that they can build clear perspectives on risk issues.
- The risk committee of the board should remain separate from the audit committee, as different skills are required for each fiduciary responsibility.

Committees and Risk Limits: Overview

We've set out some of the goals of best-practice risk governance. Now we'll take a look at some of the mechanisms that financial institutions and other nonfinancial risk-taking corporations use to translate these goals into reality.

In the following we'll focus on corporate governance in the banking industry. However, many of the same principles and structures could be applied in other industries.

At most banks, the board charges its main committees—e.g., the audit and risk management committees—with ratifying the key policies and associated procedures of the bank's risk management activities. These committees also make sure that the implementation of these key policies is effective.

The committees help to translate the overall risk appetite of the bank, approved by the board, into a set of limits that flow down through the bank's executive officers and business divisions. All banks, for example, should have in place a credit risk management committee to keep an eye on credit risk reporting, as well as a system of credit risk limits.

The exact name for each committee tends to vary quite a lot across the industry, as do the specific duties of each committee. For our purposes, we'll imagine an archetypal bank with a senior risk committee to oversee risk management practices and detailed reporting. Junior risk committees that look after specific types of risk, such as the credit risk committee, often report to this senior risk committee.

Let's now look at two specific mechanisms for risk governance, before examining how risk committees use risk metrics and limit frameworks to delegate risk authority down through the bank.

A Key Traditional Mechanism: The Special Role of the Audit Committee of the Board

The role of the audit committee of the board is critical to the board's oversight of the bank. The audit committee is responsible not only for the accuracy of the bank's financial and regulatory reporting, but also for ensuring that the bank complies with minimum or best-practice standards in other key activities, such as regulatory, legal, compliance, and risk management activities. Audit committee members are now required to be financially literate so that they can carry out their duties.

We can think of auditing as providing independent verification for the board on whether the bank is actually doing what it says it is doing. Although some of the audit committee's functions can sound quite close to risk management, it is this key verification function that separates the audit committee's work from the work of other risk committees.

The audit committee's duties involve not just checking for infringements, but also overseeing the quality of the processes that underpin financial reporting, regulatory compliance, internal controls, and risk management.

In a later section, we look specifically at how the audit function, which often has a direct reporting relationship with the audit committee, acts as an independent check on the bank's risk management process.

To function properly, an audit committee needs members with the right mix of knowledge, judgment, independence, integrity, inquisitiveness, and commitment. In most banks, a nonexecutive director leads the audit committee, and most members are nonexecutives. The audit committee also needs to establish an appropriate interaction with management—independent but productive, and with all the necessary lines of communication kept open.

The audit committee needs to ask itself several key questions with respect to each of its principal duties. For example, with respect to financial statements, the audit committee needs to be satisfied not only that the financial statements are correct, but also that the company adequately addresses the risk that the financial statements may be materially misstated (intentionally or unintentionally).

The audit committee also needs to be clear about the reporting and risk management elements of governance that it oversees on behalf of the board. These might include financial reporting, operational effectiveness and efficiency, as well as compliance with laws and regulations. Again, the recent financial crisis revealed the weaknesses of the audit committees in many banks and financial institutions—e.g., they did not uncover the excess risk assumed by traders or the risk of building up large portfolios of structured credit products.

A Key New Mechanism: The Evolving Role of a Risk Advisory Director

Not all board members will have the skills to determine the financial condition of a complex risk-taking corporation such as a bank (or an insurance company, or an energy company).

This is especially likely if the selection of nonexecutives on the board is designed to include nonexecutives who come from outside the firm's industry and are truly independent of the corporation. This is a problem because many of the recent corporate governance scandals have shown that it is easy for executives to bamboozle nonexecutives who lack the skills to ask probing questions, or to understand the answers to these questions in a rigorous manner.

There are various ways to square this circle, including training programs for board members and establishing some kind of independent support for interpreting information about risk and risk processes (i.e., independent of the senior executive team).

One approach is for the board to gain the support of a specialist risk advisory director—that is, a member of the board (not necessarily a voting member) who specializes in risk matters. An advisory director works to improve the overall efficiency and effectiveness of the senior risk committees and the audit committee, as well as the independence and quality of risk oversight by the main board. The concerns of such a director are listed in Box 4-3, which in effect is also a checklist of some of the key duties of the board with regard to risk management.

In terms of specific activities, the advisory director might:

- Participate in audit committee meetings to support members.
- Participate periodically in key risk committee meetings to provide independent commentary on executive risk reporting.
- Meet regularly with key members of management.
- Observe the conduct of business.

- Share insights on best-practice corporate governance and risk management with respect to best-in-class policies, methodologies, and infrastructure.
- Provide a high-level educational perspective on the risk profiles of key business areas and on the risks associated with the business model.

A key goal of the advisory director would be an ongoing examination of the interface between corporate governance and risk management in terms of risk policies, methodologies, and infrastructure.

BOX 4-3 WHAT MIGHT A RISK ADVISORY DIRECTOR DO?

In the main text, we describe a new mechanism of corporate governance, the risk advisory director. Such a director should review, analyze, and become familiar with

- Risk management policies, methodologies, and infrastructure
- Daily and weekly risk management reports
- The overall business portfolio and how it drives risk
- Business strategies and changes that shape risk
- Internal controls to mitigate key market, credit, operational, and business risks
- Financial statements, critical accounting principles, significant accounting judgments, material accounting estimates, and off-balance-sheet financings
- Financial information and disclosures that are provided in support of securities filings
- Internal audit and external audit reports and associated management letters
- Interplay between the company and its affiliates, including intercompany pricing issues, related-party transactions, and interrelationship of the external auditors selected for each of the enterprises
- Relevant regulatory, accounting profession, industry, rating agency, and stock exchange–based requirements and best practices
- Practices of external competitors and industry trends in risk management
- Industry corporate governance and risk-related forums

The Special Role of the Risk Management Committee of the Board

At a bank, the risk management committee of the board is responsible for independently reviewing the identification, measurement, monitoring, and controlling of credit, market, and liquidity risks, including the adequacy of policy guidelines and systems. If the committee identifies any issues concerning operational risk, it typically refers these to the audit committee for review.

The board of directors also typically delegates to the risk management committee the responsibility for approving individual credits (e.g., loans) above a certain amount, as well as for reviewing individual credits within limits delegated to the chairman and chief executive officer by the board, but above certain reporting thresholds. These aspects are usually set out in a formal document—e.g., the "investment and lending delegation of authority resolution"—approved by the board.

The risk management committee reports back to the board on a variety of items, such as all loans and/or credits over a specified dollar limit that are special, or being made to related parties (e.g., bank officers). The risk management committee also monitors credit and securities portfolios, including major trends in credit, market, and liquidity risk levels, portfolio composition, and industry breakdowns.

The risk management committee also typically provides opportunities for separate, direct, and private communication with the chief inspector (head of internal audit), the external auditors, and the management committee.

The Special Role of the Compensation Committee of the Board

One of the main lessons of the 2007–2009 financial crisis was that compensation schemes in financial institutions encouraged disproportionate risk-taking with insufficient regard to long-term risks. Over the previous two decades, bankers and traders had increasingly been rewarded with bonuses tied to short-term profits or to business volume, incentivizing them to front-load fees and income and back-load the risks. Also, the compensation schemes were structured like a call option (see Chapter 5 for the definition of a call) in that compensation increased with the upside, but there were no real penalties in the case of losses. With the help of excessive leverage, this sometimes led bank personnel to bet the entire bank on astonishingly reckless investment strategies.

In many countries, securities authorities now require public companies to set up a special board compensation committee to determine the compensation of top executives. This was driven by concerns over corporate governance, particularly the ability of CEOs to convince board members to compensate the CEO and other officers at the expense of shareholders, who had virtually no say in such decisions.

It is now widely recognized that incentive compensation should be aligned with the long-term interests of shareholders and other stakeholders, and with risk-adjusted return on capital. To the extent that this is not the case, it is important for banks to address any potential distortions. Incorporating risk management considerations into performance goals and compensation decisions has become a leading practice, and compensation planning is viewed as a key tool in enterprisewide risk management.

However, it will always be tempting for firms to offer attractive compensation packages to revenue-generating talent. International cooperation may be necessary to prevent financial firms from arbitraging the market for human capital through their choice of jurisdiction. In September 2009, the G20 endorsed the notion that excessive compensation in the financial sector encouraged excessive risk-taking and contributed to the financial crisis. Among the G20 recommendations was the removal of guaranteed bonuses, with executives being exposed to downside risk through compensation deferral and clawbacks in the event that a strategy incurs losses in the longer term.[9] Moreover, EU regulators have adopted a rule, taking effect in 2014, which caps bankers' bonuses at one times their salary, or twice their salary if shareholders explicitly agree by a two-thirds majority. Also, in 2013 the European Parliament voted to cap bonuses in the asset management industry. Bonuses should not exceed base salaries for managers of mutual funds regulated by the European Union.

Stock-based compensation helps to align the interests of executives with those of shareholders, but it is not a panacea. Before Lehman's bankruptcy, about a third of the firm was owned by the employees, and many employees lost a large chunk of their life savings. Stock ownership can also encourage risk-taking, as shareholders' gains are not limited on the upside, while their losses are capped on the downside.

One solution could be to make employees creditors of the company by including restricted notes or bonds as part of their compensation package. Such

---

[9] The Financial Stability Board's implementation standards list specific propositions and time periods for deferral, such as 40 percent to 60 percent lockup of compensation for three years. The Board also recommended that firms prohibit employees from hedging to undermine the intended risk incentive alignment. The Board also suggests that at least 50 percent of pay be based on shares along with a share retention policy, as opposed to the use of guaranteed bonuses.

a solution has been adopted by UBS, which will pay part of the bonuses of its most highly compensated employees with "bonus bonds"—i.e., bonds that will be forfeited if the bank's regulatory capital ratio falls below 7.5 percent.

Furthermore, UBS's use of contingent debt (see Appendix 3.5) is structured to complement this compensation strategy. The contingent debt converts into equity if the capital ratio falls below 5 percent, a trigger set deliberately lower than the trigger for forfeiture of deferred compensation. The reason is that bond investors are expected to pay more for contingent debt if they expect management to recapitalize the distressed firm before it crosses the threshold for conversion of debt to equity.

Compensation policies such as these should improve social welfare more generally by reducing both the likelihood and expected costs of future bailouts.[10, 11]

Roles and Responsibilities in Practice

We've described the basic structures and mechanisms for risk governance at the board level. But how do these structures and mechanisms work together to make sure that the day-to-day activities of the bank conform to the board-agreed general risk appetite and the limits set by the board and management committees?

The senior risk committee of the bank recommends to the risk committee of the board an amount at risk that it is prudent for the risk committee of the board to approve. In particular, the senior risk committee of the bank determines the amount of financial risk (i.e., market risk and credit risk) and nonfinancial risk (i.e., operational risk and business risk) to be assumed by the bank as a whole, in

---

[10]Compensation schemes similar to this have been advocated by *The Squam Lake Report* (French et al., 2010), which recommends: "Systemically important financial institutions should be required to hold back a substantial share—perhaps 20%—of the compensation of employees who can have a meaningful impact on the survival of the firm. This holdback should be forfeited if the firm's capital ratio falls below a specified threshold. The deferral period—perhaps 5 years—should be long enough to allow much of the uncertainty about managers' activities to be resolved before the bonds mature. Except for forfeiture, the payoff on the bonds should not depend on the firm's performance, nor should managers be permitted to hedge the risk of forfeiture. The threshold for forfeiture should be crossed well before a firm violates its regulatory capital requirements and well before its contingent convertible securities convert to equity."

[11]In 2008, Credit Suisse paid a portion of senior management's bonuses in bonds linked to a pool of toxic assets, helping the firm to dispose of risky assets and free up capital.

line with the bank's business strategies. At the top of the tree, the risk committee of the board approves the bank's risk appetite each year, based on a well-defined and broad set of risk measures (such as the amount of overall interest rate risk). The risk committee of the board delegates authority to the senior risk committee of the bank, chaired by the CEO of the firm, whose membership includes, among others, the chief risk officer (CRO), the head of compliance, the heads of the business units, the CFO, and the treasurer.

The senior risk committee of the bank is also responsible for establishing, documenting, and enforcing all policies that involve risk, and for delegating specific business-level risk limits to the CRO of the bank. The CRO is typically a member of the management committee and is responsible, among other things, for designing the bank's risk management strategy. Specifically, the CRO is responsible for the risk policies, risk methodologies, and risk infrastructure as well as for corporate risk governance.

The senior risk committee of the bank delegates to the CRO the authority to make day-to-day decisions on its behalf, including the authority to approve risks in excess of the limits provided to the bank's various businesses as long as these limits do not breach the overall risk limits approved by the board.

At many banks, the CRO plays a pivotal role in informing the board, as well as the senior risk committee of the bank, about the appetite for risk across the bank. The CRO also communicates the views of the board and senior management down through the organization. Each business unit, for example, may be given a mandate to assume risk on behalf of the bank up to a specific risk limit. The senior risk committee of the bank must satisfy itself that the bank's infrastructure can support the bank's risk management objectives. The senior risk committee of the bank also reviews in detail and approves (say, annually) each business unit mandate in terms of their risk limits, and delegates the monitoring of these limits to the CRO.

In large banks, the process for developing and renewing this authority is explicit. For example, business unit risk authority typically expires one year after the senior risk committee of the bank approves it. The CRO may approve an extension of an authority beyond one year to accommodate the senior risk committee's schedule.

A balance needs to be struck between ensuring that a business can meet its business goals and maintaining its overall risk standards (including ensuring that limits can be properly monitored). Key infrastructure and corporate governance groups are normally consulted when preparing a business unit's mandate

The CRO is responsible for independently monitoring the limits throughout the year. The CRO may order business units to reduce their positions or close them out because of concerns about risk such as market, credit, or operational risks.

The CRO also delegates some responsibilities to the heads of the various business units. For example, at an investment bank, the head of global trading is likely to be made responsible for the risk management and performance of all trading activities, and he or she in turn delegates the management of limits to the business managers. The business managers are responsible for the risk management and performance of the business, and they in turn delegate limits to the bank's traders.

This delegation process is summarized in Figure 4-1 with reference to market risk authorities.

At the level of each major business, there may also be a business risk committee. The business risk committee is typically made up of both business and risk personnel. The focus of the business risk committee is to make sure that business decisions are in line with the corporation's desired risk/reward trade-offs and that risks are managed appropriately at the business line level (see Box 4-4).

BOX 4-4 FORMAT FOR OBTAINING APPROVAL OF A BUSINESS UNIT MANDATE

The format for obtaining approval of a business unit mandate can be quite standardized, as follows:

- First, the business unit seeking approval provides an overview and points out the key decisions that need to be taken.
- Second, the business unit brings everyone up to date about the business—e.g., key achievements, risk profile, and a description of any new products (or activities) that may affect the risk profile.
- Third, the business unit outlines future initiatives.
- Fourth, the business unit proposes financial (i.e., market and credit) risk limits in line with the business strategy and the limit standards that we discuss in the main text.
- Fifth, the business unit describes all the nonfinancial risks that it is exposed to. This might include the impact of any finance, legal, compliance, business conduct, and tax issues.

FIGURE 4-1 Delegation Process for Market Risk Authorities

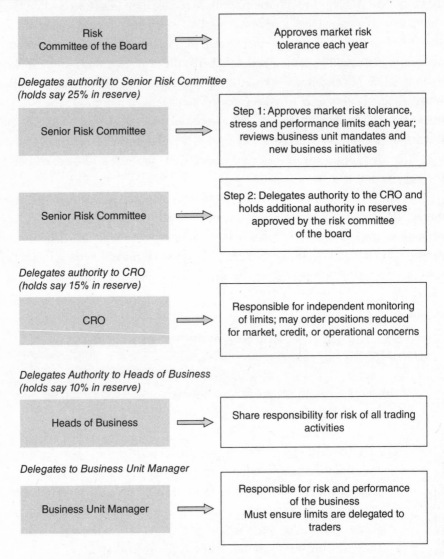

The business risk committee might be responsible for managing business-level design issues that set out exactly how a particular risk will be managed, reflecting the agreed-upon relationship between the business and the bank's risk management function. The business risk committee also approves policies that define the appropriate measurement and management of risk, and provides a detailed review of risk limits and risk authorities within the business unit.

Below the board committee level, executives and business managers are necessarily dependent upon each other when they try to manage and report on risk in a bank (Figure 4-2). Business managers also ensure timely, accurate, and complete deal capture and sign-off on the official profit and loss (P&L) statement.

The bank's operations function is particularly critical to risk oversight. In the case of an investment bank, for example, it is this function that independently books trades, settles trades, and reconciles front- and back-office positions—which should provide the core record of all the bank's dealings. Operations staff also prepare the P&L report and independent valuations (e.g., mark to market of the bank's positions) and support the operational needs of the various businesses.

Meanwhile, the bank's finance function develops valuation and finance policy and ensures the integrity of the P&L, including reviews of any independent valuation processes. Finance also manages the business planning process and supports the financial needs of the various businesses.

FIGURE 4-2 Interdependence for Managing Risk

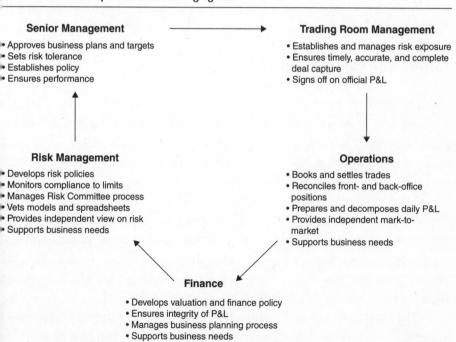

Senior Management
- Approves business plans and targets
- Sets risk tolerance
- Establishes policy
- Ensures performance

Trading Room Management
- Establishes and manages risk exposure
- Ensures timely, accurate, and complete deal capture
- Signs off on official P&L

Risk Management
- Develops risk policies
- Monitors compliance to limits
- Manages Risk Committee process
- Vets models and spreadsheets
- Provides independent view on risk
- Supports business needs

Operations
- Books and settles trades
- Reconciles front- and back-office positions
- Prepares and decomposes daily P&L
- Provides independent mark-to-market
- Supports business needs

Finance
- Develops valuation and finance policy
- Ensures integrity of P&L
- Manages business planning process
- Supports business needs

The financial crisis highlighted the need to re-empower risk officers in financial institutions, particularly at a senior level. The key lessons are:

- CROs should not just be after-the-fact risk managers but also risk strategists; that is, they should play a significant role in determining the risks that the bank assumes as well as helping to manage those risks. To ensure there is a strategic focus on risk management at a high level, the CRO in a bank or other financial institution should report to the chief executive officer (CEO) and have a seat on the risk management committee of the board.
- The CRO should engage directly, on a regular basis, with the risk committee of the board. The CRO should also report regularly to the full board to review risk issues and exposures. A strong independent voice will mean that the CRO will have a mandate to bring to the attention of both line and senior management, or the board, any situation that could materially violate risk appetite guidelines.
- The CRO should be independent of line business management and have a strong enough voice to make a meaningful impact on decisions.
- The CRO must evaluate all new financial products to verify that the expected return is consistent with the risks undertaken, and that the risks are consistent with the business strategy of the institution.

Limits and Limit Standards Policies

To achieve best-practice corporate governance, a corporation must be able to tie its board-approved risk appetite and risk tolerances to particular business strategies. This means, in turn, that an appropriate set of limits and authorities must be developed for each portfolio of business and for each type of risk (within each portfolio of business), as well as for the entire portfolio.

Market risk limits serve to control the risk that arises from changes in the absolute price (or rate) of an asset. Credit risk limits serve to control and limit the number of defaults as well as limit a downward migration in the quality of the credit portfolio (e.g., the loan book). The bank will also want to set tight policies regarding exposure to both asset/liability management risk and market liquidity risk, especially in the case of illiquid products.

The exact nature of each limit varies quite widely, depending on the bank's activities, size, and sophistication. It is best practice for institutions to set down on paper the process by which they establish risk limits, review risk exposures, approve limit exceptions, and develop the analytic methodologies used to calculate the bank's risk exposures.

At many banks, best-practice risk governance will call for the development and implementation of sophisticated risk metrics, such as value-at-risk (VaR) measures for market risk and credit risk or potential exposure limits by risk grade for credit risk.

As we discuss further in Chapter 7, risk-sensitive measures such as VaR are useful for expressing risk in normal market conditions and for most kinds of portfolios, but less good in extreme circumstances or for specialized portfolios (e.g., certain kinds of option portfolios). So limits should also be related to scenario and stress testing measures to make sure the bank can survive worst-case scenarios—e.g., extreme volatility in the markets.

Most institutions employ two types of limits—let's call them limit type A and limit type B. Type A (often referred to as tier 1) limits might include a single overall limit for each asset class (e.g., a single limit for interest rate products), as well as a single overall stress test limit and a cumulative loss from peak limit. Type B (often referred to as tier 2) limits are more general and cover authorized business and concentration limits (e.g., by credit class, industry, maturity, region, and so on).

The setting of the risk limit level in terms of a particular metric should be consistent with certain underlying standards for risk limits (proposed by the risk management function and approved by the senior risk committee).

It's not realistic on practical grounds to set limits so that they are likely to be fully utilized in the normal course of events—that would be bound to lead to limit transgressions. Instead, limit setting needs to take into account an assessment of the business unit's historical usage of limits. For example, type A limits for market risk might be set at a level such that the business, in the normal course of its activities and in normal markets, has exposures of about 40 percent to 60 percent of its limit. Peak usage of limits, in normal markets, should generate exposures of perhaps 85 percent of the limit.

A consistent limit structure helps a bank to consolidate its approach to risk across many businesses and activities. Additionally, if the limits are expressed in a common language of risk, such as economic capital, then type B limits can be made fungible across business lines. Nevertheless, such transfers would require the joint approval of the head of a business and the CRO.

If banks had followed the above principles and procedures, many of the troubles revealed during the financial crisis of 2007–2009 could have been prevented.

Standards for Monitoring Risk

Once a bank has set out its risk limits in a way that is meaningful to its business lines, how should it monitor those limits to make sure they are followed? Let's take the example of market risk, which is perhaps the most time-sensitive of limits.

First, all market risk positions should be valued daily. Units that are independent of traders should prepare daily profit and loss statements and provide them to (nontrading) senior management. All the assumptions used in the models to price transactions and to value positions should be independently verified.

There should be timely and meaningful reports to measure the compliance of the trading team with risk policy and risk limits. There should be a timely escalation procedure for any limit exceptions or transgressions—i.e., it should be clear what a manager must do if his or her subordinates breach the limits.

The variance between the actual volatility of the value of a portfolio and that predicted by means of the bank's risk methodology should be evaluated. Stress simulations should be executed to determine the impact of major market or credit risk changes on the P&L.

The bank must distinguish between data used for monitoring type A limits (where data must be independent of risk-takers) and data used to supply other kinds of management information. For other types of analysis, where timeliness is the key requirement, risk managers may be forced to use front-office systems as the most appropriate sources. For example, real-time risk measurement, such as that used to monitor intraday trading exposures, may simply have to be derived from front-office systems.

But data used in limit monitoring must be:

- Independent of the front office
- Reconciled with the official books of the bank in order to ensure their integrity
- Derived from consolidated data feeds
- In a data format that allows risk to be properly measured—e.g., it might employ the market risk VaR or credit risk VaR methodology

Business units should be under strict orders to advise the risk management function that they might exceed a limit well before the limit excess happens. For example, there might be an alert when an exposure is at, say, 85 percent of the type A or type B limit. The CRO, jointly with the head of the business line, might then petition the senior risk committee of the bank for a temporary increase in limits. The business risk committee should also approve the need for an increase in limits prior to the request being passed to the senior risk committee of the bank.

If risk management is advised of a planned excess, then it should be more likely that the excess will be approved—this gives the business unit a necessary incentive to provide early warnings.

What happens if the limit is breached? The risk management function, as illustrated in Figure 4-3, should immediately put any excess on a daily "limit type A or limit type B exception report," with an appropriate explanation and a plan of action to cope with the excess. The head of risk management may authorize the use of a reserve.

Limit type A excesses must be cleared or corrected immediately. Limit type B excesses should be cleared or approved within a relatively short time

FIGURE 4-3 Limit Excess Escalation Procedure

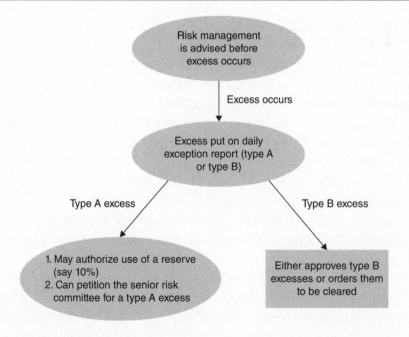

frame—say, a week. The risk managers should then report all limit excesses across the bank in an exception report, which may be discussed at a daily risk meeting and which should distinguish between limit type A and type B excesses. No manager should have the power to exclude excesses from the daily excess report.

It should be noted that when limits become effective, they impose a hidden cost: the bank cannot assume additional risk and thus may have to give up profitable opportunities. As a limit is approached, the opportunity cost of the limit should be evaluated so that the bank can decide in good order whether or not the limit should be relaxed.

What Is the Role of the Audit Function?

We've set out, in general terms, a risk management process that should be able to support best-practice risk governance. But how does the board know that the executives and business managers are living up to the board's stated intentions (and to minimum legal and regulatory requirements)?

The answer lies in the bank's audit function and the periodic investigations it carries out across the bank. A key role of the audit function is to provide an independent assessment of the design and implementation of the bank's risk management.

For example, regulatory guidelines typically call for internal audit groups to review the overall risk management process. This means addressing the adequacy of documentation, the effectiveness of the process, the integrity of the risk management system, the organization of the risk control unit, the integration of risk measures into daily risk management, and so on.

Let's again take the example of market risk. Regulatory guidelines typically call for auditors to address the approval process for vetting derivatives pricing models and valuation systems used by front- and back-office personnel, the validation of any significant change in the risk measurement process, and the scope of risks captured by the risk measurement model.

Regulators also require that internal auditors examine the integrity of the management information system and the independence, accuracy, and completeness of position data.

Above and beyond any local regulatory requirements, a key audit objective should be to evaluate the design and conceptual soundness of the risk measures (including the methodologies associated with stress testing). Internal auditors should verify the accuracy of models through an examination of the back-testing process.

Audit should also evaluate the soundness of elements of the risk management information system (the "risk MIS"), such as the processes used for coding and implementation of internal models. This should include examining controls over market position data capture, as well as controls over the parameter estimation processes (e.g., volatility and correlation assumptions).

Audit responsibilities often include providing assurance as to the design and conceptual soundness of the financial rates database that is used to generate parameters entered into the market VaR and credit VaR analytic engines. Audit also reviews the adequacy and effectiveness of the procedures for monitoring risk, the progress of plans to upgrade risk management systems, the adequacy and effectiveness of application controls within the risk MIS, and the reliability of the vetting processes.

Audit should also examine the documentation relating to compliance with the qualitative/quantitative criteria outlined in any regulatory guidelines. Audit should comment on the reliability of any value-at-risk reporting framework.

Box 4-5 sets out in general terms what a statement of audit's findings on the risk management function might look like. It also helps to make clear the dangers that might arise from any confusion between the role of risk management and that of audit. Box 4-6, in contrast, looks at an approach to scoring the risk management function that might be adopted by third parties (such as rating agencies, which need to compare the risk management structures of many different organizations).

BOX 4-5   EXAMPLE: STATEMENT OF AUDIT FINDINGS

If all is well from a risk management perspective, then audit should state that adequate processes exist for providing reliable risk control and ensuring compliance with regulatory criteria.

For example, in short form, the audit group's conclusion regarding risk control in a bank trading business might be:

- The risk control unit is independent of the business units.
- The internal risk models are utilized by business management.
- The bank's risk measurement model captures all material risks.

Furthermore, if all is well, then the audit group should state that adequate and effective processes exist for

- Risk-pricing models and valuation systems used by front- and back-office personnel
- Documenting the risk management systems and processes
- Validating any significant change in the risk measurement process
- Ensuring the integrity of the risk management information system
- Capturing position data (and ensuring that any positions that are not captured do not materially affect risk reporting)
- Verifying the consistency, timeliness, and reliability of data sources used to run internal models, and that the data sources are independent
- Ensuring the accuracy and appropriateness of volatility and correlation assumptions
- Ensuring the accuracy of the valuation and risk transformation calculations
- Verifying the model's accuracy through frequent back-testing

---

BOX 4-6   IS IT POSSIBLE TO SCORE THE QUALITY OF AN INSTITUTION'S RISK MANAGEMENT?

In much of this chapter, we talk about establishing the right structures for best-practice risk governance. But is there any way to score risk management practice across an institution so that both the institution itself and external observers can gain some objective idea of the institution's risk management culture and standards?

One of the authors has worked with a credit rating agency to construct such a score.

Under this approach, the risks underlying each aspect of the enterprise risk management function within institutions are assessed using a questionnaire tailored along three key dimensions:

- Policies—e.g., is the tolerance for risk consistent with the business strategy? Is risk properly communicated internally and externally?

- Methodologies—e.g., are the risk methodologies tied into performance measurement? Are risk stress testing methodologies performed? Are the mathematical models properly vetted? Does senior management understand the risks in the models?
- Infrastructure—e.g., are the appropriate people and operational processes (such as data, software, systems, and quality of personnel) in place to control and report on the risks?

The basic PMI (policies, methodologies, infrastructure) framework can be used for most industries; within each of the three key dimensions, more detailed questions can be developed that tackle aspects relevant to a particular industry.

For example, for trading financial institutions, we might require a description of the process around limits delegation for market risk and credit risk (as it pertains to the trading book).

Gathering this information involves supplying questionnaires and also scheduling the time of senior management at the trading institution for review sessions. The completed assessments would be presented to an internal committee at the rating agency, where the primary credit analyst will take them into consideration in the rating agency's overall review of the institution.

A negative assessment could affect the credit rating of the institution—a clear indicator of how important the nexus between risk management, corporate governance, and risk disclosure has become.

Internal auditors have devised international standards to provide objective assurance about control, governance, and risk management. The Institute of Internal Auditors (IIA) provides guidance that has been organized into an International Professional Practices Framework (IPPF), offering both mandatory and strongly recommended guidance. The IPPF has performance standards that encompass a variety of activities.[12]

---

[12]See the Professional Guidance section of the IIA's website. These IIA standards include Managing the Internal Audit Activity, Nature of Work, Engagement Planning, Performing the Engagement, Communicating Results, Monitoring Progress, and Resolution of Senior Management's Acceptance of Risk. The Governance and Risk Management Standards are a subset of the Nature of Work standard. The Risk Management standards cover topics such as evaluating an organization's risk exposure, evaluating fraud risks, reviewing risk during consulting, and risk knowledge gained during consultancy.

There has been some discussion in the banking industry about whether the audit function should control the operational risk management function at the bank—after all, audit has a natural interest in the quality of internal controls.

Unfortunately, allowing the audit function to develop a bank's operational risk management function is an error. Audit's independence from the risk management function is a prerequisite for the value of any assurances it gives to the board. Unless this independence is preserved, there is a danger that audit will end up trying to give an independent opinion about the quality of risk management activities that audit itself has designed or helped administer. This would imply a classic conflict of interest right at the heart of bank risk governance.

Conclusion: Steps to Success

In complex risk-taking organizations, it's not possible to separate best-practice risk management from best-practice corporate governance.

Boards can't monitor and control the financial condition of a risk-taking institution without excellent risk management and risk metrics. Meanwhile, the risk management function depends on sponsors at the senior executive and board level to gain the investment it requires—and the influence it needs to balance out powerful business leaders.

It's worth stressing an important lesson of business history: Many fatal risks in a corporation are associated with business strategies that at first look like runaway successes. It's only later on that the overlooked or discounted risks come home to roost.

Recent history provides us with ample evidence. Subprime loans, and the structured products backed by such loans, looked very lucrative due to the high promised yield. But investors and institutions failed to correctly assess the risks, including the possible effect of a drop in the price of houses across the whole United States together with an economic recession.

At a best-practice institution, everything flows from a clear and agreed-upon risk management policy at the top. For example, senior management and the board must approve a clear notion of the institution's risk appetite and set out how this is to be linked to an enforceable system of limits and risk metrics.

Without this kind of platform, it's very difficult for risk managers further down the management chain to make key decisions on how they approach and measure risk. For example, without a clearly communicated concept of an institution's risk appetite, how would risk managers define a "worst-case risk" in any extreme risk scenario analysis? How would they decide whether the institution could live with the small chance of a worst-case outcome or, alternatively, avoid any risk to solvency by severely limiting business volumes or even closing down a business line (in the face of attractive profits)?

The risk committees of the institution also need to be involved, to some degree, in setting the basic risk measurement methodologies employed by the institution. Most banks know that they have to be able to define their risk in terms of market risk and credit risk, but banks have also now extended their risk measurement framework to include more sophisticated approaches to liquidity risk and operational risk, as well as a whole new class of enterprise stress tests. It's important that risk committees understand the strengths and weaknesses of any new metrics if they are to make sense of risk reports.

There are also unavoidable strategic, political, and investment reasons why the board and top executive management must be closely involved in determining an institution's risk management strategy. Without their involvement, how can the managers of the institution agree on a credible organizational infrastructure that avoids both gaps and duplications in risk oversight? The key to designing an efficient organization is to ensure that the roles and responsibilities of each risk mechanism and unit are carefully spelled out and remain complementary to one another. Meanwhile, data for risk analysis, including enterprisewide macroeconomic stress testing, has to be drawn from many business lines and bank functions. An enterprisewide perspective is increasingly essential.

We should not think of board and top management time spent on risk management as time spent purely on the defensive "risk control" aspects of the business. A best-practice risk system can be applied to gain offensive advantages. A board with a sound understanding of the risk profile of its key existing or anticipated business lines can support aggressive strategic decisions with much more confidence. Sophisticated risk measures such as VaR, stress testing, and economic capital offer a way of setting risk limits, but they are also vital in helping the institution decide which business lines are profitable (once risk is taken into account).

Ideally, businesses would use the risk infrastructure as a tactical management tool in deal analysis and pricing, and also take account of its results in incentive compensation schemes, to help make sure that risk management and business decisions are aligned.

A joint approach to corporate governance and risk management has become a critical component of a globally integrated best-practice institution—from board level to business line.

5

A USER-FRIENDLY GUIDE TO THE THEORY OF RISK AND RETURN

While risk management is a practical activity, it cannot be understood independently of a body of academic research about risk and reward. It's difficult to work out the trade-off between retaining and avoiding risk without reference to the theory of risk valuation; after all, risk management does not mean the complete elimination of risk.

In this chapter, we review five key theoretical models and demonstrate how they relate both to one another and to the practice of risk management. We'll look at modern portfolio theory (MPT), the capital asset pricing model (CAPM), arbitrage pricing theory (APT), the classic Black-Scholes (BS) approach to pricing an option, and the Modigliani-Miller (M&M) theory of corporate finance. We'll also take a brief look at the fast-developing field of behavioral finance.

Like all theories of risk management, the key theoretical models are based on simplifying assumptions. Real life is complicated and includes many details that models cannot, and maybe should not, accommodate. The role of models is to highlight the most important factors and the relationships among these factors. A "good" financial model is one that helps the analyst separate the wheat from the chaff—that is, the major explanatory variables from a noisy background.

As Milton Friedman made clear in his 1953 seminal article "The Methodology of Positive Economics," a model should be evaluated only in terms of its predictive power.[1] It can be simple and yet be judged successful if it helps predict the future and improves the efficiency of the decision-making process. Despite criticism of the use of models in risk management following the 2007–2009 financial crisis—mainly issues of model selection, implementation, and overinterpretation—we strongly believe that models and theories are essential to modern risk management.

Harry Markowitz and Portfolio Selection

The foundations of modern risk analysis are to be found in a seminal paper by Harry Markowitz written in 1952, based on his Ph.D. dissertation at the University of Chicago, concerning the principles of portfolio selection.[2] (Markowitz was awarded the Nobel Prize in Economics for this research in 1990.)

Markowitz showed that rational investors select their investment portfolio using two basic parameters: expected profit and risk. While "profit" is measured in terms of the average (mean) rate of return, "risk" is measured in terms of how much returns vary around this average rate of return. The greater the variance of the returns, the riskier the portfolio.

When building a portfolio, investors like to reduce variance as much as possible by diversifying their investments. To put it simply, they avoid putting all their eggs in one basket. Even better, by investing in assets that fluctuate in different directions, investors can actively offset the specific risks inherent in individual stocks. (We can see the same behavior in individual firms. Following such a business strategy, for example, Head Corp., which focused initially on ski equipment, diversified into supplying tennis equipment. This strategic move helped to reduce the impact of weather and season on its periodic profits.)

As a result, according to Markowitz, investors select financial assets, such as stocks and bonds, for their portfolio based on each asset's contribution to the portfolio's *overall* mean and variance. It follows that we must think of the risk of

---

[1]M. Friedman, "The Methodology of Positive Economics," in *Essays in Positive Economics* (Chicago: University of Chicago Press, 1953).

[2]H. M. Markowitz, "Portfolio Selection," *Journal of Finance* 7, 1952, pp. 77–91.

a single investment not in terms of its own variance, but in terms of its interaction with other assets in the portfolio.

Through the power of portfolio diversification, investors can dilute (i.e., reduce) the risk that is specific to an individual stock at virtually no cost. While it is true that the mitigation of risk may also lead to the lowering of expected profits, if assets are selected carefully, then diversification can allow investors to achieve a higher rate of return for a given level of risk.

To the extent that investors succeed in achieving this state, they arrive at the *efficient frontier*, represented by the curved solid line in Figure 5-1. Put formally, this efficient frontier contains all portfolios of assets such that there are no other portfolios (or assets) that for a given amount of risk (in terms of standard deviation of rates of return) offer a higher expected rate of return.

For example, portfolio P in Figure 5-1 has the same amount of risk as portfolio A, but P has a higher expected rate of return. There is no portfolio in Figure 5-1 with the same amount of risk as P that also exhibits a higher expected rate of return than P.

Once a portfolio contains only assets that are on the efficient frontier, it can be seen that a higher expected rate of return can be achieved *only* by increasing the riskiness of the portfolio. Conversely, a less risky portfolio can be achieved *only* by reducing the expected return on the portfolio. The lower part of the frontier, which contains all the inefficient assets and portfolios, is represented by a dotted line. It indicates the most inefficient combinations of assets with the lowest possible expected return for a given level of risk.

FIGURE 5-1 The Efficient Frontier of Markowitz

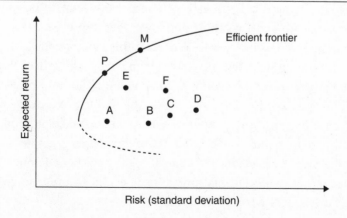

We can extend this concept to consider the whole investment market. In this framework, if the market is in equilibrium, then portfolio M, the "market portfolio," will include all risky assets in the economy, each entering the portfolio in a proportion equal to its relative market value. For example, an imperfect but often useful proxy for all the risky equity assets in the economy of the United States is the S&P 500 index, or a wider-based index such as the Russell 2000. In Europe, the Euro Stoxx 50 index of blue-chip stocks can be used.

In this kind of market portfolio, the power of diversification means that the specific, or idiosyncratic, risk of a security is not much taken into account by the market in its pricing of a security. However, in recent years, the role of diversification "à la Markowitz" has been challenged as the average correlation of stock returns has increased dramatically from around 25 percent in the 1970s to nearly 75–80 percent during the financial crisis of 2007–2009. Correlations across asset classes have also increased substantially, even in normal market conditions. One reason invoked for this increase in the covariations of asset prices is the huge development in basket trading and exchange-traded funds (ETFs). Large baskets of assets that compose benchmark indices are traded simultaneously, independently of analyst recommendations concerning the relative performance of these assets.

To adapt to this new environment, quantitative asset management techniques have been proposed that consist of identifying risk regimes and optimizing portfolio allocations for each risk regime. For example, there may be periods in which market participants are very worried and uncertain about the future. Markets adjust quickly to these situations, giving rise to higher market volatility—e.g., higher level of the VIX (the volatility index for the S&P 500)—and also higher credit spreads. These periods tend to be followed by quieter periods, with lower volatility and lower credit spreads. Asset managers have been developing techniques to anticipate this kind of change in a market regime. When they anticipate a high-risk regime, they switch their portfolio to a very conservative asset allocation, such as investing only in money market funds; in anticipation of a low-risk regime, they switch to a more aggressive asset allocation (e.g., including equities, emerging markets, commodities, and high yield bonds). Each asset allocation is optimized to generate the highest return for the regime it is associated with. These approaches combine risk management techniques with optimal portfolio selection in order to control the volatility of investment portfolio returns.

The Capital Asset Pricing Model (CAPM)

In the mid-1960s, William Sharpe and John Lintner took the portfolio approach to risk management one step further by introducing a model based on overall capital market equilibrium.[3] For this breakthrough, Sharpe was awarded the Nobel Prize in 1990. (Lintner, a finance professor at Harvard Business School, had passed away many years earlier.) Building on Markowitz, the two professors showed that the risk of an individual asset could be decomposed into two portions:

1. Risk that can indeed be neutralized through diversification (called diversifiable or specific risk)
2. Risk that cannot be eliminated through diversification (called systematic risk)

To build their CAPM, Sharpe and Lintner made the assumption that investors can choose to invest in any combination of a risk-free asset and a "market portfolio" that includes all the risky assets in an economy. Investors therefore weight their personal portfolios as a combination of these two investment vehicles, in various proportions based on their "risk appetite."

This conception allowed Sharpe and Lintner to define the premium that investors demand for taking on the risk of the market portfolio, as opposed to investing in the risk-free asset. This "market risk premium" is simply the difference between the expected rate of return on the risky market portfolio and the risk-free rate.

For example, we might determine the market risk premium by subtracting the interest rate on an asset that is free of default risk, such as a certificate of deposit or U.S. Treasury bill, from the expected return on a market index such as the Dow Jones or S&P 500. (Agreeing on the exact market risk premium evident in real-world data has proved to be a lively area of debate among financial economists, but we won't allow these technicalities to detain us here.)[4]

---

[3]W. F. Sharpe, "Capital Asset Prices: A Theory of Market Equilibrium under Conditions of Risk," *Journal of Finance* 19, 1964, pp. 425–442; J. Lintner, "Security Prices, Risk and Maximal Gains from Diversification," *Journal of Finance* 20, 1965, pp. 587–615.

[4]For an updated empirical estimation of the market risk premiums of different countries, see the website of Professor Aswath Damodaran: http://pages.stern.nyu.edu/~adamodar/New_Home_Page/datafile/ctryprem.html

Estimates of the market risk premium tell us how much investors have to be paid to take on some notional "average" amount of market risk generated by the complete market portfolio. But how can we estimate the risk, and the risk premium, for an individual asset?

Well, according to the CAPM, if the market is in equilibrium, the price (and, hence, the expected return) of a given asset will reflect the relative contribution of that asset to the total risk of the market portfolio. In the CAPM, this contribution is accounted for by means of a factor called beta (β). (Beta is often referred to as "systematic risk" in the wider literature.)

More formally, an asset's beta is a measure of the covariance between that asset's return and the return on the market index, divided by the market's variance. So, it is a relative measure of the risk of an asset normalized by the total market risk.

From an investor's perspective, beta represents the portion of an asset's total risk that cannot be neutralized by diversification in a portfolio of risky assets and for which some compensation must be demanded. Put another way, the more beta risk a portfolio manager assumes by investing in higher-beta securities, the higher the risk and also the higher the expected future rate of return of the portfolio.

Beta is the key to working out the expected return on an individual asset. We can think of this expected return as consisting of the interest on the riskless asset (invested over the same time period as the holding period of the asset), plus the market risk premium adjusted by beta. This can be represented more formally as

Expected rate of return on security = risk-free interest rate + beta risk × (expected rate of return on the market portfolio − risk-free interest rate)

Figure 5-2 is based on Sharpe's work. It shows the *market line*, which depicts the linear relationship between the expected rate of return on any asset and its systematic risk as measured in relation to assets that are beta-efficient.

In Figure 5-2, the intersection with the vertical axis yields the risk-free interest rate, R_F. This rate of return reflects the yield on an asset with zero beta. Assets B and C are beta-efficient, since they lie on the market line; C is riskier than B, and therefore is expected to yield a higher return. M, the market portfolio,

FIGURE 5-2 The Market Line Connecting the Beta Risk and Individual Assets and Their Expected Rates of Return

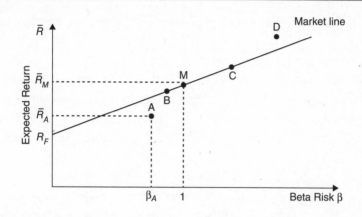

is also beta-efficient, and its beta is 1, by definition. Asset A is inferior, since it lies under the line, meaning that another asset (or a portfolio of assets) can be found with the same amount of beta risk but a higher expected rate of return. Asset D is a "winner," since it is expected to yield more in relation to its risk than assets on the market line. But if participants in the financial market realize that D is superior, they will increase the demand for D, putting pressure on its price. As the price of this asset rises, its rate of return can be expected to fall until D lies on the market line.

So how does beta vary across different kinds of securities? Well, as a baseline, we can think of the beta factor for a risk-free asset as zero, since the returns of that asset are indifferent to fluctuations in the capital market. Likewise, the beta of the complete market portfolio is 1, since by definition the market portfolio expresses the average beta risk for the whole market and thus requires no adjustment to take into account the specific risk of the portfolio. The beta of an individual stock (or other financial asset) can have any positive or negative value, depending on its characteristics.

Let us illustrate this last point with a numerical example based on U.S. historical data. The average rate of return on the New York Stock Exchange CRSP (Center for Research in Security Prices) index over 70 years is approximately 10 percent. The average risk-free rate on risk-free U.S. government bonds is approximately 4 percent. Hence the market risk premium, on average, is 6 percent.

Now, if a given stock has a beta estimated at 0.8, its expected rate of return is:

4 percent + 0.8(6 percent) = 8.8 percent

If the past is prologue (i.e., predicts the future), then we can expect the average rate of return on the market index to be 10 percent and the average rate of return on the specific stock to be 8.8 percent.

In this example, beta is positive but rather lower than the market average of 1. If the beta of a stock is higher than 1, the stock is considered "aggressive," or riskier than the market portfolio. Conversely, if the beta is lower than 1, the stock is considered "defensive," as it will have a mitigating effect on the total risk of the portfolio.

Figure 5-3, taken from Bloomberg L.P., shows the estimate of beta for IBM stock, based on weekly rates of return, for the period January 12, 2007, to August 23, 2013. The beta is estimated as the slope of a regression line of the rates of return for IBM on the rates of return for the market index. The regression line points to a raw, unadjusted beta of 0.83.

An interesting class of assets is that defined as having a negative beta. Negative beta denotes an asset, such as gold, that consistently moves counter to

FIGURE 5-3 Raw Beta Computation for IBM

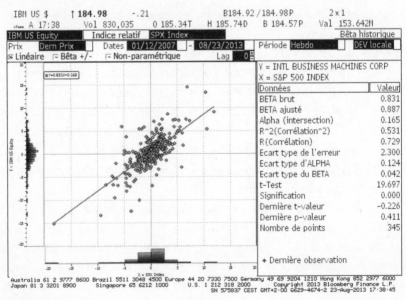

Source: Bloomberg.

market trends—when prices in the market tend to move up, this asset tends to lose value, and vice versa. Investment in such an asset serves to lower the risk of a portfolio without necessarily reducing its expected return.

If the market is in equilibrium, then the chances of finding such a jewel are virtually nil. Market forces will naturally work to drive the price of this kind of asset up, bringing down its future expected rate of return. In other words, to reduce the riskiness of their portfolios, investors will have to sacrifice some reward.

The CAPM has become a key tool of financial economists in understanding the behavior that can be seen in the capital markets every day. But the beta of a stock is not simply a concern of investors; it's important to the managers of any company who are concerned about share price and the creation of shareholder value. Beta has numerous day-to-day implications for managers. For example, many firms employ a hurdle rate of return to assess whether a new investment is worthwhile in terms of building shareholder value. This hurdle rate is based on the unique rate of return that the firm thinks investors demand; that is, it is based more or less explicitly on assumptions the firm makes about its beta factor (or about the beta factor of any new project it is considering for an investment). If the firm misunderstands the demands of investors, it is likely to set the wrong hurdle rate. If it sets its target rate of return too high, it will turn down worthwhile investments; if it sets the target too low, it will make investments that offer too low a return. Either way, it will drive down its beta-adjusted returns and make its stock less attractive to investors on a risk-adjusted basis.

As we discuss in Chapter 17, corporations use a range of related new risk-adjusted measures to better understand the real rate of return they offer to investors. Banks increasingly use a measure called risk-adjusted return on capital (RAROC), and nonfinancial corporations often use a related measure called economic value added (EVA). The implementation of these performance measures necessitates the estimation of the beta factor for a given activity or division of the corporation.

The Arbitrage Pricing Theory

The CAPM is a normative theory of how the expected rate of return on a financial asset is determined. It describes the expected rate of return as a linear function of the market's risk premium, and beta risk is the coefficient, or slope, of the relationship. The arbitrage pricing theory (APT) is an extension of the logic behind the CAPM, explaining the expected rate of return on an asset as a linear function of several market factors. The APT suggests adding more factors that can contribute to the explanation of the expected rate of return, though it does not say which factors to add. It only suggests that there may be factors, such as macroeconomic factors or some stock, bond, or commodity indices, that add to the explanatory power of the relationship. The model is referred to as a multifactor or a multi-index pricing model.

This model was initially proposed in 1976 by Professor Steve Ross. It was later tested by Roll and Ross (1980) and Chen, Roll, and Ross (1986).[5] Chen, Roll, and Ross found that the following macroeconomic factors were important in explaining the realized average rates of return on the stocks traded on the New York Stock Exchange (NYSE): the surprise in the inflation rate, the unexpected trends in GNP, changes in the default premium of bonds, and drifts in the slopes of the yield curves.

Many empirical works prefer to use the APT approach rather than the CAPM as the latter is a special case of the former (though the CAPM has more fundamental theoretical foundations). The CAPM is a one-factor model: the market index is the only variable used to explain the expected return for any security. The APT is a multifactor model, whereby a number of different indices can be used to explain the variation in expected rates of return. Therefore, the APT is often used to decompose the factors' contributions to the expected return of stocks so that we can see the contribution of any fundamental index used to explain the stock's expected rate of return.

How to Price an Option

The next important development in the analysis of risk arrived in 1973 with the publication of two papers on the pricing of options by Fischer Black and Myron

[5]S. Ross, "The Arbitrage Theory of Capital Asset Pricing," *Journal of Economic Theory* 13(3), 1976, pp. 341–360; R. Roll and S. Ross, "An Empirical Investigation of the Arbitrage Pricing Theory," *Journal of Finance* 35(5), 1980, pp. 1073–1103; Nai-Fu Chen, R. Roll, and S. Ross, "Economic Forces and the Stock Market," *Journal of Business* 59(3), 1986, pp. 383–403.

Scholes and by Robert Merton.[6] At the time of the publication of their seminal paper, Black and Scholes were professors at the University of Chicago, while Merton was a professor at MIT. In 1998, Merton and Scholes received the Nobel Prize. (Black had passed away in 1995.)

Options are financial assets that entitle their holders to purchase or sell another asset by or on a predetermined day, at a predetermined price called the striking price. An option to buy the asset is referred to as a *call*, while an option to sell the asset is called a *put*. (See also Chapter 6.)

The price paid up front for the call option is generally a fraction of the current price of the underlying asset on which the option (contract) is written. The remainder is paid at the time of execution, or exercise, at some point in the future. Hence, one advantage of purchasing a call option is the ability to buy an asset on credit.

At the time of exercise, the purchaser retains the right to renege on his or her intention to complete the contract. So if the asset price at the time of exercise is lower than the price set in the call option contract, the purchaser of the call can opt to let the contract expire. In effect, the call option offers a form of price insurance.

Figure 5-4 describes the cash flow from a call option at maturity (i.e., when it expires). The option has zero cash flow at maturity so long as the price of the underlying instrument is below the striking price (exercise price) K. For prices above the striking price, the owner of the call is entitled to the difference between the price of the underlying instrument and the striking price. This latter cash flow is described by the sloping line, increasing from point K to the right as the price of the underlying asset rises.

For a put option, the reverse is true. The buyer pays for the right to sell a stock in the future at a preset price. That exercise price constitutes a guaranteed minimum price. On the other hand, if the market price of the asset is higher than the price the put purchaser would receive from exercising the put, he or she can choose to ignore the option contract and opt instead to sell the asset on the open market for its full price. Figure 5-4b shows the payoff of a put option at maturity, which is positive when the underlying asset price falls below the exercise price. So a put option, held with the underlying asset, provides insurance against a reduction in value of the underlying asset to below the exercise price.

---

[6] F. Black and M. Scholes, "The Pricing of Options and Corporate Liabilities," *Journal of Political Economy* 81, 1973, pp. 637–654; R. C. Merton, "Theory of Rational Option Pricing," *Bell Journal of Economics and Management Science* 4(1), 1973, pp. 141–183.

FIGURE 5-4a The Payoff for a Call Option at Maturity

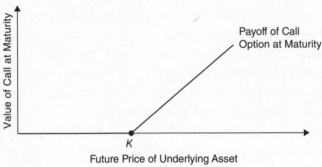

In their publications in 1973, Black and Scholes (frequently referred to as B&S in the literature) developed a classic model for pricing options. Merton, who collaborated with B&S, also published an important paper in 1973, offering an alternative way to prove the valuation model and many additional extensions. Moreover, in addition to calculating equilibrium market prices for publicly traded options, this model specified the various components of an option and their interrelationships.

For example, as we've discussed already, a call option can be characterized as a "package deal" that includes:

- Buying a stock (or other asset)
- Taking out a loan
- Buying insurance

FIGURE 5-4b The Payoff for a Put Option at Maturity

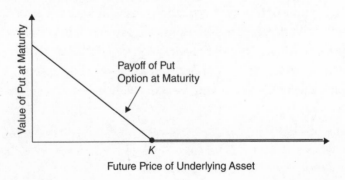

It can be shown that over a very short time interval, a call option can be decomposed into buying a certain ratio of the underlying instrument (this ratio is referred to as the "delta" of the option) and taking out a loan (with the amount of the loan being proportional to the probability that the option will be exercised). Options theory has proved invaluable to portfolio and risk management. Using these ideas, portfolio managers can dynamically tailor investment positions to reflect changing expectations, market conditions, and client needs. Purchasing puts against the assets held in a portfolio is synonymous with taking out insurance on those assets. Purchasing and selling combinations of calls and puts can help investors maneuver in volatile or uncertain markets. (See a discussion of options as risk mitigators in Chapter 6.)

The detailed mathematics that lie behind the B&S model is somewhat complex and is not readily calculated without the aid of computer technology. But the functions that govern an option's price are quite intuitive. Simply stated, the price of an option is a function of:

- The price of the underlying asset
- The exercise (or striking) price set in the contract
- The prevailing risk-free rate of interest
- The volatility of the underlying asset
- The time remaining until the predetermined exercise date

If the stock price increases and we hold all the other parameters constant, then the value of the call option increases. Similarly, if the option is sold with a lower exercise price or a longer maturity, its value will be higher.

As the underlying asset becomes more volatile, the value of the call increases. This is because a call option has no downside risk—that is, no matter how far the call is out of the money at expiration, its value is still zero—while increasing volatility increases the probability that the option will end up in the money at maturity (i.e., the stock price is more likely to reach a higher value). Furthermore, as the interest rate increases, the value of the call increases (because the present value of the exercise payment in the event of exercise declines as interest rates increase). Similar arguments hold for put options, although the sensitivity of the put options to some of the factors is reversed; it is a declining function of the price of the underlying asset and the risk-free interest rate and an increasing function of the exercise price and volatility.

Of all these factors, the most crucial to the valuation and risk management of an option is the volatility of the underlying asset. It's often said that options are "risk-friendly": an increase in the volatility (i.e., an increase in the risk) of the underlying asset, assuming that all other parameters remain constant, leads to an increase in the price of the option, both for calls and for puts. As you may recall, volatility is measured in terms of the standard deviation (the square root of the variance) of the rate of return for the underlying asset during some selected historical period.

In applying historical data to the calculation of future volatilities, we are making a problematic assumption: that volatility remains constant over time. Where there are liquid options markets, however, the B&S model offers one way of working around this problem. Remember that the B&S model offers a way to price options provided that we have access to the inputs, listed earlier. On the other hand, if we already have the price of an option from a liquid options market, then we can use this "output" as one of the inputs. The formula can then be used to calculate a missing input, such as volatility. In effect, using the B&S formula in this way is computing the volatilities *implied* by the prices of options in the market. That's why this number is often simply called "implied volatility."

Implied volatilities are of tremendous practical importance to those who regularly trade options in the market, and they are often re-input into the B&S model to calculate the price of a slightly different option series with different exercise prices or maturities. But because implied volatility cannot be directly observed and is dependent on the model, it has in the past been a weak link in the operational risk management of option desks. A trader who prices option positions for risk management purposes using an implied volatility number that he or she computes from the market can be faced with some severe temptations. In the past, traders at certain investment banks have deliberately input wrong implied volatility numbers to transform the apparent value of their under-the-water options portfolio. Implied volatility is a particular worry because it's the one input into the B&S model that cannot be checked by an auditor without some degree of specialized knowledge. This is one example of how issues surrounding the principles of risk modeling affect the operational practice of risk management, a theme we'll return to in Chapter 15.

Since 1993, the Chicago Board Options Exchange (CBOE) has calculated an implied volatility index for the S&P 500 Index. Known as the VIX, this volatility index is calculated using the prices of synthetic 30-day, at-the-money traded

FIGURE 5-5 Evolution of the VIX and Major Market Events During the Period 2007–2013

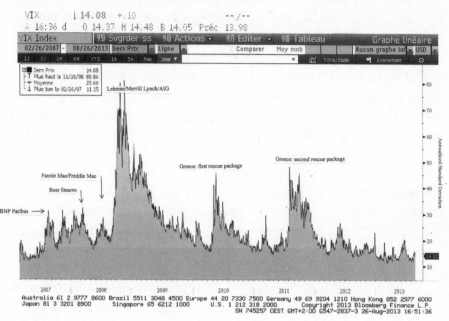

Source: Bloomberg.

options on the stock index, an approach initially proposed in 1986 by Professors Menachem Brenner and Dan Galai of the Hebrew University.[7] Futures on the VIX started trading in 2004, and options started trading in 2006. Since then many other volatility indices have been published, and options and futures contracts are often traded on them (Figure 2-1). Figure 5-5 shows the evolution of the VIX and the S&P 500 from the beginning of the subprime crisis in July 2007 until March 2013.

The VIX is often referred to as a fear indicator because it spikes during crises and market crashes and, more generally, in reaction to unanticipated events. As such, VIX-based strategies can be used to protect equity portfolios against "gap risk"—i.e., a significant unexpected drop in the equity markets. The short-term VIX responds quickly and strongly to negative events, jumping upward,

---

[7]M. Brenner and D. Galai, "New Financial Instruments for Hedging Changes in Volatility," *Financial Analysts Journal*, July/August 1989, pp. 61–65; M. Brenner and D. Galai, "Options on Volatility," *Option Embedded Bonds*, I. Nelken (ed.), Irwin Professional Publishing, 1997, pp. 273–286.

sometimes quite dramatically, as shown in Figure 5-5. So, one way to buy protection against "gap risk" is to go long futures contracts on the VIX.

The B&S model also provides insights into how options introduced into a portfolio of financial assets interact with those assets and affect the overall risk of the portfolio. The systematic risk (beta) of a call or put option is a function of the beta of the underlying asset multiplied by the *elasticity* of the call or put. By elasticity, we mean the percentage change in the value of the option for a 1 percent change in the price of the underlying security. The model determines that the elasticity of a call is positive and greater or equal to 1, while the elasticity of a put is less than or equal to −1. Hence, adding call options to a portfolio will tend to increase the overall risk of the portfolio (assuming a positive beta), while adding puts will have a mitigating effect on a portfolio's risk. Shorting calls—i.e., writing call options—can also have a mitigating effect on the portfolio risk, since such a position has a negative beta.

The B&S model can also be used to compute the *hedge ratio* of an option position, also known as the *delta*. This ratio describes the change in value of an option resulting from a small change in the price of the underlying asset. The hedge ratio indicates how the risk of a financial asset can be hedged with options. The price of both the underlying asset and the option changes over time, so the hedge ratio is in fact dynamic, requiring that adjustments to the portfolio be made in order to maintain a target level of hedging. The hedge ratio of a call is between 0 and 1, and the delta of a put option is between −1 and 0.

For example, imagine that the delta of a call option that is slightly out of the money is 0.5, meaning that if the price of the underlying stock increases (decreases) by $1, the value of the call increases (decreases) by $0.50. This implies that if we want to neutralize, over a short time horizon, the risk of a long position in a call contract on 100 shares, we should sell short 50 shares.

The insights of the model introduced by Black and Scholes in the 1970s have led to further applied research in finance, particularly in relation to volatility. For example, in the last two decades, in reaction to evidence that volatility in financial markets may undergo major shifts in its behavior over time (more technically, that it is "nonstationary"), researchers have begun to make use of a more dynamic approach to financial asset valuation. In particular, Robert Engle, a finance professor[8] and a leading researcher in this area, introduced the

---

[8]Previously at University of California San Diego and currently at New York University

ARCH (autoregressive conditional heteroskedasticity) volatility model during the 1980s to estimate volatility as an "auto-regressive" process. The key feature of the model is that it estimates future volatility as a function of the previous day's volatility and also introduces a correction factor for deviations from an expected volatility. Many financial institutions employ variants of the ARCH model in predicting future volatilities. (Robert Engle was the recipient of the Nobel Prize in Economics in 2003 for his work on volatility modeling.)

Modigliani and Miller (M&M)

In order to complete this brief introduction to the theoretical basis of modern risk management, we must turn to the work published by Franco Modigliani and Merton Miller in 1958 (for which they were both awarded the Nobel Prize in Economics, Modigliani in 1985 and Miller in 1990).[9] Their work does not directly involve financial markets, but rather focuses on corporate finance. Modigliani and Miller showed that in a perfect capital market, with no corporate or income taxes, the capital structure of a firm (i.e., the relative balance between equity and debt capital) has no effect on the value of the firm.

The implication of their work is that a corporation cannot increase its value by assuming greater debt, even though the expected cost of debt is lower than the expected cost of equity. Increasing the leverage of a firm (i.e., taking on more debt relative to equity) means increasing the financial risk of the firm. Hence, equity holders (whose claims on the firm's assets are subordinate to those of lenders and bondholders) will demand compensation for this risk and expect higher rates of return. Hence, under M&M assumptions, the weighted average cost of capital (WACC) for a firm will remain constant regardless of the financial leverage. This is a variation on the theme that has run through this chapter: investors look not for higher returns, but for higher risk-adjusted returns.

Modigliani and Miller's work also has important implications for discussions about capital adequacy in banks and for approaches to performance measurement such as RAROC (see Chapter 17). If we accept their propositions, then, ignoring for the moment any corporate tax effects, shareholders should be indifferent as to whether a bank has low levels of equity and high

---

F. Modigliani and M. H. Miller, "The Cost of Capital, Corporation Finance, and the Theory of Investment," *American Economic Review* 4, 1958, pp. 261–297.

levels of leverage, or vice versa. This should not adversely affect the value of the bank, nor the welfare of the shareholders. So, the Basel III intention to require much higher capital requirements from banks—i.e., more equity and lower leverage—is consistent with M&M, in cases where the tax issue is not a significant factor.

Behavioral Finance

One recent trend in the financial literature is to investigate the subjective attitude of investors to risk and return and how they react to different situations in the financial markets. Various apparent anomalies in the behavior of stock markets are then explained using theories based on psychology and human cognition.

The initial breakthrough came from the work of two psychologists, Amos Tversky and Daniel Kahneman (the latter received the Noble Prize for his work in 2002). In 1979, Kahneman and Tversky wrote *Prospect Theory: An Analysis of Decision Under Risk*, a paper that used cognitive psychology to explain various divergences of economic decision making from neoclassical theory.[10] They showed that investors misjudge opportunities with very high or very low probabilities.[11] The different cognitive biases have become known by nicknames such as "herding behavior," describing the tendency to mimic the investment behavior of large groups, and "mental accounting," which explains how investors tend to divide their investments into separate mental accounts based on criteria such as the source of the funds or the use of the funds. The "ostrich effect," meanwhile, describes how many investors do not seem to want to see risky situations and are willing to accept a lower return for an identical risk if the risky situation is not presented to them.[12]

---

[10]Daniel Kahneman and Amos Tversky, "Prospect Theory: An Analysis of Decision Under Risk," *Econometrica* 47(2), 1979, pp. 263–291.

[11]The interested reader can find basic information on the common biases in Wikipedia (http://en.wikipedia.org/wiki/Behavioral_economics) and Investopedia (http://www.investopedia.com/university/behavioral_finance).

[12]D. Galai and O. Sade, "The 'Ostrich Effect' and the Relationship between the Liquidity and the Yields of Financial Assets," *Journal of Business* 79(5), 2006, pp. 2741–2759.

The major issue with behavioral finance is whether it can help in pricing securities and, especially, in pricing risks. While it can explain some anomalies, and what to theoreticians may seem irrational investment decisions, it is not yet certain that a knowledge of behavioral theories can help organizations to manage their risks more rationally.

Conclusion

The key theoretical models help us to define risk in a consistent way and indicate which measures of risk are relevant to specific situations, pointing up the importance of:

- Elimination of arbitrage opportunities when valuing financial instruments and positions
- The critical difference between idiosyncratic (specific) risk and systematic risk
- The dependence of financial modeling on key parameters and inputs

Above all, perhaps, they help us forge a rational link between the risk management perspective of the corporation and the desires of its shareholders—something that's difficult to do in any rigorous way without reference to the CAPM and related theories.

6

INTEREST RATE
RISK AND HEDGING
WITH DERIVATIVE
INSTRUMENTS

In this chapter we look at a specific kind of market risk—namely, interest rate risk—and at how institutions can manage the risk arising from particular interest rate positions.

Interest rate risk substantially affects the values of the assets and liabilities of most corporations and is often a dominant factor affecting the values of pension funds, banks, and many other financial intermediaries. According to the Federal Reserve, the total credit market debt (public and private) in the United States at the end of 2012 amounted to $56.3 trillion, most of which was held by the financial sector.[1] Like fixed-interest government bonds, these largely fixed-interest assets fall in value when interest rates rise. Worse, mortgage loans (which amounted to approximately $10 trillion at the end of 2012) and Mortgage Back Securities (MBS) suffer from "extension risk" because consumers have the option to extend the duration of the loan when interest rates go up (making

---

[1] Some $39.2 trillion are held by the financial sector (including $9.8 trillion by U.S. depository institutions, $3.3 trillion by insurance companies, $1.2 trillion by pension funds, and $4.0 trillion by mutual funds), and $5.2 trillion of debt are held by the household sector (which at the same time owes $12.8 trillion). Board of Governors of the Federal Reserve System, "Flow of Funds Accounts of the United States, Fourth Quarter 2012," March 2013.

the value of the instruments much more sensitive to rising rates); borrowers also have the option to prepay their mortgage when interest rates decline. This need not matter if banks have carefully hedged their exposure, but it can otherwise lead to huge losses.

We'll look first at measures of interest rate risk for fixed-income instruments and then at the key derivative instruments used to manage this risk. This chapter helps set the scene for Chapter 8, which describes how the asset/liability management (ALM) function of a financial institution manages whole portfolios of instruments to control the effect of changes, or expected changes, in interest rates.

How Does Interest Rate Risk Arise?

The simplest form of interest rate risk is the risk that the value of a fixed-income security held by an institution will change as a result of a change in market interest rates.

As rates go up in the wider market, the value of owning an instrument offering a fixed rate of interest naturally falls (compared to the value of owning newly issued fixed-income securities that pay a higher coupon). To the extent that the security represents an open position—that is, to the extent that the position is not perfectly offset by changes in the value of other instruments in the institution's portfolio—the firm will suffer an economic loss. Open positions arise most often from differences in the maturities, nominal values, and rate reset dates between instruments and cash flows that are *asset*-like (i.e., longs) and those that are *liability*-like (i.e., shorts). A major mismatch between the maturities of assets and liabilities can lead to liquidity risk (Chapter 8). The degree to which such exposures threaten a firm depends not only on the amount held and each position's sensitivity to interest rate changes, but also on the degree to which these sensitivities are correlated within portfolios and, more broadly, across trading desks and business lines.

Even when instruments seem at first sight to largely offset each other's economic exposure, an imperfect correlation between offsetting instruments, both within the same maturity for different issuers and across the yield curve, can generate significant risks. The yield curve, often called the *term structure of interest rates*, measures the relationship between the discount rates—the rates which, if used to discount the expected future cash flows from the bonds, give the current market price for the bond—and the time to maturity of bonds of a given credit quality.

The most fundamental interest rate term structure is that of government bonds, spanning all maturities from three months to 30 years. It is sometimes referred to as the *riskless term structure of interest rates* or *riskless yield curve*, by which we mean that it is not exposed to default risk. Figure 6-1 shows the U.S. Treasury yield curves on August 27, 2013, when short-term rates were near zero, and on April 20, 2007, before the start of the subprime crisis, when rates were much higher (see comments below on how monetary policy affects the shape of the Treasury yield curve).

We can also derive the term structure for high-grade bonds, say AAA–rated bonds, and then the term structure for AA+ bonds, all the way down the credit spectrum to C⁻ bonds. The degree to which each yield curve differs from the government bond yield curve represents the risk premium of the security; this largely reflects the credit risk of the bond, given its rating and duration.

Risk managers often refer to something that they call "curve risk." Curve risk arises in portfolios when long and short positions of different maturities are effectively hedged against a *parallel shift* in yields, but are not hedged against a change in the *shape of the yield curve*. Parallel shifts occur when a shock in the market has an equal effect on the yields of instruments with different maturity

FIGURE 6-1 U.S. Treasury Yield Curves

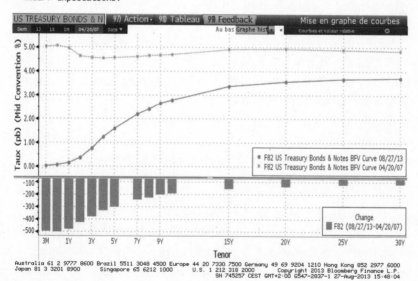

dates; conversely, the yield curve is said to "change shape," or "change slope," when a shock in the market has a stronger effect on, say, the returns of shorter-dated instruments than it has on the returns of longer-dated instruments. This may affect the slope of the yield curve and its curvature.

Figure 6-2 shows different shapes that the yield curve can assume: flat, upward-sloping, and downward-sloping. Most of the time the yield curve is upward-sloping, with short-term rates being lower than long-term rates, as was the case during August 2013 (Figure 6-1). The slope of the yield curve reflects expectations about future interest rates, as well as expectations concerning inflation rates and rates of economic growth.

The slope of the yield curve is significantly affected by monetary policy. For example, after the 9/11 terrorist attacks, Alan Greenspan, then chairman of the U.S. Federal Reserve, lowered short-term rates to 1 percent, while 10-year rates were about 5 percent. From 2004 he started raising short-term rates, a policy extended by his successor, Ben Bernanke. By April 2007, the short-term rate had reached 5 percent, while 10-year rates remained below 5 percent with an inversion of the yield curve between six months and three years (Figure 6-1). When the subprime crisis erupted at the end of July 2007, the policy changed again, this time to lowering short-term rates in order to boost the economy and to help financial institutions. Between 2009 and 2012, short-term rates remained under 0.25 percent, while the 10-year rate also remained very low (e.g., 1.72 percent at the end of 2012).

Curve risk is not the only worry. Even if offsetting positions have the same maturity, "basis" risk can arise if the rates of the positions are imperfectly correlated. For example, three-month Eurodollar instruments and three-month Treasury bills both naturally pay three-month interest rates. However, these rates are not perfectly correlated with each other, and spreads between their yields may vary over time. As a result, a three-month Treasury bill funded by three-month Eurodollar deposits represents an imperfectly hedged position.

Bond Price and Yield to Maturity

Bond portfolio managers and fixed-income derivatives traders keep a close eye on their screens for moves in the yield curve that affect the value of bonds and other fixed-income securities. They pay close attention to financial

FIGURE 6-2 Yield Curves

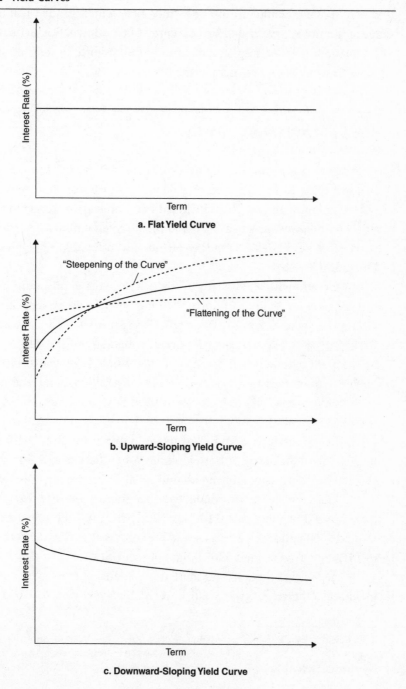

a. Flat Yield Curve

b. Upward-Sloping Yield Curve

c. Downward-Sloping Yield Curve

announcements, such as comments from the U.S. Federal Reserve Bank (FRB) that may signal a change in the Fed funds rate, which in turn will change the shape of the yield curve and drive bond prices up or down. Box 6-1 describes the FRB's Operation Twist, implemented in 2012 in order to lower long-term interest rates to stimulate investment in the U.S. economy.

BOX 6-1 OPERATION TWIST

In the years following the financial crisis of 2007–2009, the U.S. Federal Reserve used various monetary policy tools to boost the economy and reduce unemployment. These included first lowering the target for Federal funds to its lowest practical level and then implementing a series of large-scale asset purchases—including an unconventional variant nicknamed Operation Twist.

Operation Twist, officially a "maturity extension program," involved the Fed's buying billions of dollars of long-term Treasury securities while selling the same amount of shorter-dated securities. Fed Chairman Ben Bernanke said, "By reducing the average maturity of the securities held by the public, [Operation Twist] puts additional downward pressure on longer term interest rates and further eases overall financial conditions."[1]

In effect, the Fed's redeployment acted to shift money toward longer-term investment, driving up the prices of longer-term securities and lowering their yields (price and yield move in opposing directions). This in turn made it cheaper for those looking to buy homes and finance other projects, as well as signaling an accommodative Fed policy into the future.

Operation Twist was conducted on a grand scale. The first program, from around September 2011 to June 2012, involved the sale/purchase of around $400 billion of securities, and the second, from July 2012 to the end of 2012, involved around $267 billion of securities.

The Federal Reserve said there was evidence that its asset purchases, including Operation Twist, had lowered the yield on 10-year Treasury

---

[1] Chairman Ben Bernanke, "Monetary Policy Since the Onset of the Crisis," speech, August 31, 2012, available at http://www.federalreserve.gov/newsevents/speech/bernanke20120831a.htm.

FIGURE 6B-1 Impact of Operation Twist on the U.S. Government Yield Curve (July 28, 2011 vs. February 10, 2012)

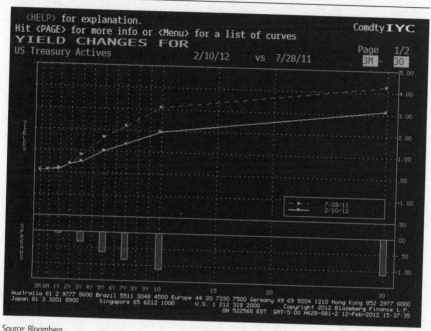

Source: Bloomberg

bonds, perhaps by around 100 basis points. Figure 6B-1 shows the U.S. government yield curve in July 2011 (dashed line), before Operation Twist, and as of February 2012 (solid line) following the Fed programs.

While Operation Twist seems to have achieved its objective in the short term, it is difficult to be sure what would have happened if it had not been put in place. Economists will continue to debate its longer-term benefits and whether similar tools might be applied to flatten the yield curve in the future, e.g., to reduce the attraction of risky maturity transformation by banks.[2]

---

[2]Governor Jeremy Stein, "Overheating in Credit Markets: Origins, Measurement, and Policy Response," speech, February 7, 2013, available at http://www.federalreserve.gov/newsevents/speech/stein20130207a.htm.

In fact, the price of a bond, as discussed in this section, can be derived directly from the term structure of interest rates for any given class of credit risk: government bonds, corporate bonds rated AAA, those rated AA, and so on. (Conversely, the yield curve can be implied from the term structure of bond prices, where this is known.)

The pricing of bonds is based on the present value concept—i.e., the value today of the future cash flows associated with a security. This clearly involves discounting the future cash flows to reveal their present values, but what discount rates should we use? The problem is complicated because different discount rates may apply to different kinds of bonds with different maturities. We've already covered one reason for this in our discussion of the yield curve: interest rates vary and are usually an increasing function of time to maturity (i.e., upward-sloping). Another factor that affects the relevant discount rates is the risk of the bond, especially its credit risk—i.e., the probability of default and the extent of the loss that is expected in such an event. A further factor that affects bond prices is liquidity risk—the risk that the market for the bond might not be liquid enough for the seller to receive a "fair" price at the time of sale.

Let us start with the valuation of, say, a 10-year U.S. government bond. This helps to clarify the problem because the government bonds of some particularly creditworthy nations are traditionally regarded as being almost free of credit risk.[2]

The bondholder is promised an annual fixed coupon and payment of the principal amount at the maturity of the bond. So, if the notional amount (or principal) is $1,000 and the coupon rate is 5 percent, the bondholder will receive $50 per year for the first nine years and at the end of the 10-year period the sum of the last coupon and the principal—i.e., $1,050.

The problem we face in assessing the present value of the bond is that $50 received after, say, eight years is necessarily worth less than $50 received at the end of the first year, if only because of the opportunity cost associated with obtaining cash later rather than earlier. We begin by discounting one dollar to be received a year from now to express the price today of one future dollar. For

---

[2]The number of countries regarded as largely risk-free (e.g., Germany, the United States) fell sharply after the European sovereign debt crisis unfolded during 2010. As rescue packages were extended to Portugal, Ireland, Greece, and Spain (PIGS) investors realized that the sovereign debt issued by some European countries could indeed default. Suddenly, crisis-hit countries had to pay very high spreads above the benchmark yield curve of Germany to refinance their maturing debt.

example, if the relevant discount rate is 10 percent per annum, then a dollar next year is worth $1/(1 + 0.1) = \$0.909$ today; that is, the price today of one dollar a year from now is 90.9 cents.

If the discount rate is also 10 percent between year 1 and year 2, then the price today of one dollar to be received after two years is $1/(1 + 0.1)^2 = \$0.826$, or 82.6 cents. It is worth 90.9 cents in terms of year 1 dollars, and $90.9/1.01 = 82.6$ cents in terms of present dollars. In Box 6-2 we give the formula for the bond price and a numerical example.

BOX 6-2 VALUATION OF A BOND AND YIELD TO MATURITY

The present value of a bond is determined by:

- Its stream of future cash flows, which consist of the n annual coupon payments cF during the life of the bond and the repayment of principal F at the maturity date n, with c being the coupon rate
- Its discount curve, or zero-coupon curve, which specifies the annualized spot rates $R_1, R_2, \ldots, R_n$ at which each cash flow should be discounted to produce its present value

The first coupon, payable in one year, has a present value of $\dfrac{cF}{1+R_1}$.

Similarly, the coupon payable in two years has a present value of $\dfrac{cF}{(1+R_2)^2}$.

The bond has a present value that is the sum of the present values of its future cash flows:

$$P = \frac{cF}{1+R_1} + \frac{cF}{(1+R_2)^2} + \ldots + \frac{cF}{(1+R_{n-1})^{n-1}} + \frac{cF+F}{(1+R_n)^n} \qquad (6\text{-}1)$$

By definition, the yield to maturity y satisfies the relation

$$P = \frac{cF}{1+y} + \frac{cF}{(1+y)^2} + \ldots + \frac{cF}{(1+y)^{n-1}} + \frac{cF+F}{(1+y)^n} \qquad (6\text{-}2)$$

The yield to maturity of a bond, y, is the single rate of interest that makes the present value of the future cash flows equal to the price of the bond. This single rate is used to discount all the cash flows. It is only when the spot zero-coupon curve is flat (i.e., when all the spot zero-coupon rates are the same across all maturities and equal to R) that the yield to maturity y is equal to the interest rate R.

NUMERICAL EXAMPLE

The following term structure of interest rates applies to a three-year bond that pays an annual coupon of 4 percent and has a nominal value of $100:

t	1	2	3
R_t (%)	3	3.75	4.25

Then, according to Equation (6-1), the price of the bond is

$$p = \frac{4}{1.03} + \frac{4}{1.0375^2} + \frac{104}{1.0425^3} = 99.39 \qquad (6\text{-}3)$$

The yield to maturity y is the solution of Equation (6-2), i.e.,

$$p = \frac{4}{1+y} + \frac{4}{(1+y)^2} + \frac{104}{(1+y)^3} = 99.39 \qquad (6\text{-}4)$$

which gives $y = 4.22$ percent.

The value of the bond can therefore be found by discounting all the expected future payments by the relevant discount factors. (These discount factors are also referred to as "zero-coupon rates," referring to zero-coupon bonds, which have only a single bullet payment at maturity.) If all yearly discounted interest rates are known, then our job is rather simple. In practice, however, we can't observe interest rates directly; dealers report only bond prices. The yield curves that traders and fund managers observe on their screens are calculated—i.e., derived implicitly—from these bond prices so that the discounted value of the scheduled coupons and redemption value of the bonds is equal to the actual observed bond prices.

Now we can ask the following question: For a given current bond price and cash-flow stream from the bond, what is the single discount yield across all coupon dates that, if applied to the cash-flow stream, will result exactly in the price of the bond? This is the *yield to maturity* (YTM) of a bond, and it measures the average annual yield of the bond over its lifetime, given its present price. The yield to maturity is actually the internal rate of return (IRR) of the bond. There is a one-to-one relationship between the YTM of a bond and its price: given the stream of coupon payments, together with the redemption value and the bond price, one can derive the bond yield; conversely, given the stream of coupon payments, the redemption value, and the bond yield, one can calculate the price of the bond. In fact, many bonds are quoted not in dollars but in terms of yield (YTM). In Box 6-2 we show how to calculate the yield to maturity.

When reading the financial press or observing a quotation screen, one needs to be careful, as the term *yield curve* is sometimes used loosely; it can refer in practice to either the term structure of zero-coupon discount rates or the term structure of yields to maturity.

There are many theories and empirical studies concerning the structure and behavior of the yield curve for government bonds. We mentioned before that yield usually increases with time to maturity, a shape known as the *normal yield curve*, as shown in Figure 6-1. At the end of March 2013, the one-year Treasury bill rate was 0.15 percent, while the 10-year bond yielded approximately 2 percent and a 30-year government bond yielded 3.16 percent per annum.

Different yield curves, or, equivalently, different spread curves (the spread curve is the difference between the corporate yield curve and the risk-free government yield curve, or alternatively the swap curve when it is more liquid than the government curve[3]), can be estimated for corporate bonds with different credit ratings. The rating agencies—Standard & Poor's, Moody's, Fitch and others—periodically publish the yield curves for corporate bonds based on their

---

[3]The swaps market for very long government debt can be more liquid than the underlying market in government debt. Where this is the case, traders use the swaps market to observe the yield curve across the relevant maturities.

ratings. These curves represent the average yields of the bonds belonging to a given credit-rating category.

Traders and fund managers often base their decisions on the "forward curve," or the term structure of forward rates. A forward rate tells us, for example, the expected interest rate for a three-month bond, six months from now, for a given risk category of bonds. The forward rates can be derived directly from the spot (current) term structure of interest rates. When the spot yield curve is upward-sloping, the forward curve is above the spot curve; conversely, when the spot curve is downward-sloping, the forward curve is below the spot curve.

For example, we can estimate the one-year forward interest rate for government bonds between one and two years from now from the yields to maturity of one- and two-year government T-notes. If the one- and two-year T-notes have a yield to maturity of 2 percent and 2.5 percent, respectively, then the expected future interest rate between the end of year 1 and the end of year 2 is estimated as $(1 + 0.025)^2/(1 + 0.020) - 1 = 0.030$ or 3.0 percent. The forward rate of 3 percent, in this case, is the rate of interest that, when compounded with the one-year rate of 2 percent, will generate a yield to maturity of 2.5 percent for a two-year bond.

The forward rate is a key building block of interest rate risk management and of the interest rate derivatives used by investors, financial institutions, and corporations to hedge interest rate risk. The forward rate can be locked in by arbitrage. For example, the 3 percent forward rate between year 1 and year 2 can be achieved with certainty by buying a two-year T-note and shorting a one-year note (or, equivalently, borrowing the price of the two-year T-note for one year at the one-year rate of 2 percent). For this trade, there is no initial cash outflow. At the end of year 1, closing out the short position will necessitate cashing out $100(1.02) = 102. At the end of year 2, the two-year T-note will mature and pay $100(1.025)^2 = 105.06, generating a return of $(1.025)^2/1.02 - 1 = 3$ percent during the investment period between year 1 and year 2.

This practice of financing the purchase of long-dated securities by borrowing short-term is commonly known as a *repurchase agreement* or "repo." When an investor enters into a repo agreement, he sells a security to another party and simultaneously agrees to buy it back at a later date at a prearranged price. In the example just given, the investor buys a two-year T-note and finances the purchase by means of a repo. That is, the investor sells the two-year T-note to the dealer for $100 and makes a commitment to buy the note back from the dealer one year later for $102.

In practice, dealers require a protective cushion against credit risk because the value of the bond will fluctuate over time, and it may depreciate in value if interest rates increase. For example, if interest rates increase such that the T-note is worth $98 and the investor defaults, then the dealer has lost $2 (since the dealer provided $100 at the inception of the repo and now holds a T-note worth only $98). So dealers demand a haircut—i.e., they lend less than the full amount of the bond (say, $98). The difference ($2) can be thought of as collateral against the loan.

Repos allow investors to finance a significant portion of their investment with borrowed money. But these borrowings, or *leverage*, mean that the profit or loss on any position is multiplied; even a small change in market prices can have a significant financial effect on the investor.

Leverage through the use of repos was part of the undoing of California's Orange County in December 1994 after the Federal Reserve had boosted the Fed funds rate six times during the previous year for a total of 250 basis points. Mr. Citron, the Orange County treasurer, had managed to borrow $12.9 billion through the repo market. This enabled him to accumulate around $20 billion of securities even though the fund he managed had only $7.7 billion invested in it. In the favorable upward-sloping-curve environment in the years before 1994, Mr. Citron was able to increase the return of the fund by 2 percent compared to similar pools of assets. When interest rates started to rise, however, the market value of his positions dropped substantially, generating a loss of $1.5 billion by December 1994 (7 percent of the total investment in the fund). At the same time, some of the lenders to the fund stopped rolling over their repo agreements. Ultimately, Orange County filed for bankruptcy. More recently, repo financing also played a part in the fall of the investment bank Lehman Brothers during the 2007–2009 financial crisis (Chapter 8, Box 8-3).

The Risk Factor Sensitivity Approach

At the trading desk level and for specific financial markets, traders long ago developed specialized measures of the sensitivity of an instrument to changes in the value of primary risk factors. Depending on the market, such primary risk factors might take the form of interest rates, yield to maturity, volatility, stock price, and so on. In the case of fixed-income products, a popular risk measure among traders is "DV01," also known as "value of an 01." DV01 is a trader's abbreviation for the change (delta) in the value of a security after a change in yield or a change in interest rate of 1 basis point—i.e., 1 percent of a percentage point, or 0.0001 in decimal form.

The DV01 measure is consistent with the conventional "duration" analysis of a bond, which is often thought of as the average life of a bond. More formally, it is the weighted average of the dates (expressed in years) of each cash flow, where the weights are the present value of the cash payments divided by the sum of the weights—i.e., the price of the bond itself.

The "modified duration" of a bond, a measure often used in bond calculations, is the duration divided by 1 plus the yield to maturity of the bond. Box 6-3 offers a more technical explanation of the relationship between bond price, bond duration, and modified duration.

For small and parallel shifts of the yield curve, the price sensitivity of a fixed-income product can be approximated by a simple (linear) function of the

---

BOX 6-3 DURATION OF A BOND

Given the pricing equation for a bond—i.e., Equation (6-2) in Box 6-2—the duration of the bond can be defined as the weighted average of the dates (expressed in years) of each cash flow, where the weights are the present value of the cash payment divided by the sum of the weights—i.e., the price of the bond itself:

$$D = \frac{\dfrac{1 \cdot cF}{1+y} + \dfrac{2 \cdot cF}{(1+y)^2} + \ldots + \dfrac{(n-1) \cdot cF}{(1+y)^{n-1}} + \dfrac{n \cdot (cF+F)}{(1+y)^n}}{P} \qquad (6\text{-}5)$$

Note that the sum of the weights in Equation (6-5) is equal to 1:

$$\frac{\dfrac{cF}{1+y}}{P} + \frac{\dfrac{cF}{(1+y)^2}}{P} + \ldots + \frac{\dfrac{cF}{(1+y)^{n-1}}}{P} + \frac{\dfrac{(cF+F)}{(1+y)^n}}{P} = 1 \qquad (6\text{-}6)$$

since the numerator of Equation (6-6) is, according to Equation (6-2), the price of the bond.

NUMERICAL EXAMPLE (CONTINUATION OF BOX 6-2 EXAMPLE)

Consider the three-year bond presented in Equation (6-3) in Box 6-2. Its duration is

$$D = \frac{\dfrac{1 \cdot 4}{1.0422} + \dfrac{2 \cdot 4}{1.0422^2} + \dfrac{3 \cdot 104}{1.0422^3}}{99.39} = 2.89$$

D is referred to as Macaulay duration. Note that the duration of this three-year bond is less than three years, its maturity. The duration would be exactly three years only for a three-year zero-coupon bond.

DURATION AS A MEASURE OF INTEREST-RATE SENSITIVITY

The differentiation of Equation (6-2), which relates the bond price P to its yield to maturity y, offers

$$\Delta P \cong -P \frac{D}{1+y} \Delta y = -PD^* \Delta y \qquad (6\text{-}7)$$

where ΔP is the change in price corresponding to a change in yield Δy and

$$D^* = \frac{D}{1+y} \qquad (6\text{-}8)$$

D* as defined in Equation (6-8) is called *modified duration.*

There is a linear relationship between the change in price of a bond and the change in yield. The higher the duration, the higher the price volatility. However, as the price/yield relationship for a bond is nonlinear, duration is only a first-order approximation of the impact of a change in yield on the price of a bond. This means that it only offers a good approximation for small variations in yield (see Figure 6B-2).

FIGURE 6B-2 Duration as a Measure of Interest Rate Sensitivity

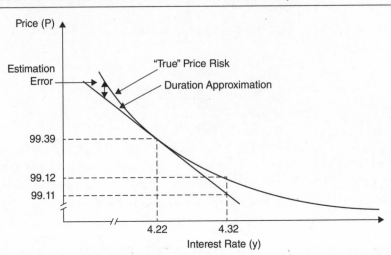

NUMERICAL EXAMPLE (CONTINUATION)

Assume a change of 10 basis points in the yield of the three-year bond defined by Equations (6-3) and (6-4) in Box 6-2, with a price $P = 99.39$, a duration $D = 2.89$, and a yield $y = 4.22$ percent. Then, according to Equation (6-7),

$$\Delta y = 0.001$$

$$\Delta P \cong -99.39 \frac{2.89}{1.0422} 0.001 = -0.28$$

while the actual price change is -0.27.

change in yield. That is, the percentage change in the price of a bond is the negative of the product of the change in yield to maturity and the modified duration of the bond. The modified duration is actually the measure of the elasticity of the bond price with respect to the yield or, in simple terms, the percentage change in the value of the bond as a result of a 1 percent change in the market yield.

Consider, for example, a bond trading at $90 with a yield to maturity of 5 percent and a modified duration of eight years. According to this approximation, a 5-basis-point increase in yield results in a price decline of 0.05% × 8 = 0.4% or $0.36.

Figure 6-3 offers an example of the price sensitivity of par bonds of different maturities, expressed in dollars per million of notional value, for a change

FIGURE 6-3 Interest Rate Sensitivity Measures: Value of an "01"

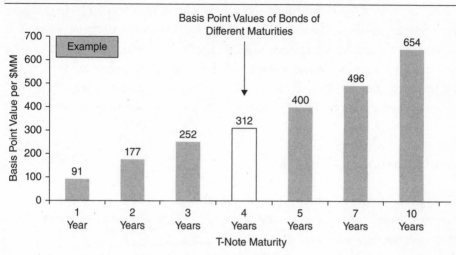

in yield of 1 basis point. This example illustrates that the longer the maturity of the bond, the higher its duration and the more sensitive the price of the bond to a change in yield.

But duration and related measures offer only a first-order approximation of the impact of a change in yield on the price of a bond. A more accurate approximation of the price change requires a second-order adjustment known as the convexity adjustment (Figure 6-4), which attempts to capture the *sensitivity* of a

FIGURE 6-4 Convexity Adjustment to Interest Rate Sensitivity

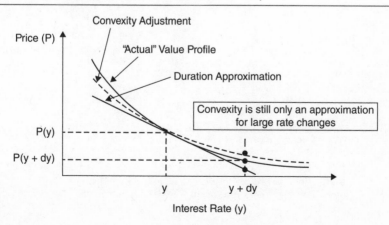

bond's duration to a change in interest rates. The straight line in Figure 6-4 represents the value of the bond around its current value when the changes in value are adjusted for duration. The dotted curve represents the value of the bond around its current value after it has been adjusted for both duration and convexity. The value of the bond adjusted for convexity follows very closely the exact price of the bond, represented by the continuous black curved line, although it is not perfect and is still only an approximation when there are large variations in yields.

Portfolios of Instruments

For a portfolio of instruments priced from the same yield curve, price sensitivities can be easily aggregated by calculating the weighted-average-modified duration of the instruments held in the portfolio.

Alternatively, price sensitivities can be expressed in terms of a benchmark representative instrument—e.g., the four-year Treasury note (T-note) in Figure 6-4. In this case, each position is converted into the DV01 equivalent of the reference instrument—i.e., the four-year T-note. For instance, the 10-year T-note has a DV01 that is 2.1 times greater than the DV01 of a four-year T-note, so a $1 million 10-year T-note is said to be equivalent to $2.1 million of the reference four-year T-note (Figure 6-5). The risk of the portfolio is then evaluated as if it were a single position in the reference asset.

FIGURE 6-5 Interest Rate Sensitivity Measures: Relative Value of an "01"

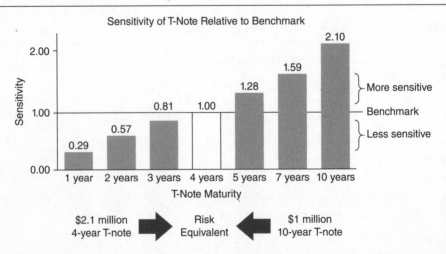

In the next chapter, we propose a more encompassing risk measure for fixed-income portfolios: value-at-risk, or VaR. This measure allows risk managers to aggregate both the duration effect and the convexity adjustment into a single number (as well as to compare and aggregate financial risks arising from many other sources).

Instruments for Hedging Interest Rate Risk

We've discussed how interest rate risk arises and some specific ways of measuring this risk. But what kind of instruments and strategies can be used to manage the risks that we have measured (beyond simply selling the instruments or assets that give rise to the exposure)?

The answer, of course, lies in the world of derivatives contracts, such as swaps, forwards, futures, and options, whose values are derived from various underlying assets or rates. In this section, we describe how derivatives can be used to manage interest rate risk. But the same basic principles apply to derivatives based on other asset types, such as equities, stock indices, currencies, and commodities.

Over the years, and especially since the 1970s, many different kinds of derivative instruments with varying levels of complexity and customization have been invented to hedge (or assume) financial risk. Some instruments are traded on formal exchanges around the world, such as the Treasury bond futures traded on the Chicago Board of Trade (CBOT) or the Eurodollar futures traded on the Chicago Mercantile Exchange (CME). These exchange-traded derivatives are fairly simple and standardized contracts, backed by a clearinghouse to ensure contract integrity and to eliminate counterparty risk.

Many derivatives are not traded on exchanges but instead are private bilateral contracts between a dealer and a customer known as over-the-counter (OTC) derivatives. Such OTC derivative contracts can be highly customized to the needs of a customer; the drawback is that they are less liquid than exchange-traded futures, and their execution is backed only by the capital of the provider or dealer. This is why the key players in the OTC derivatives market are expected to be financial institutions with a good credit standing. Interest rate swaps, swaptions, forward rate agreements, caps, floors, and collars—the key derivative instruments used by investors, corporations, and financial institutions to manage interest rate risk—have all traditionally been traded over-the-counter. However, the failure of Lehman Brothers in September 2008 created such chaos in the financial markets, as OTC-traded instruments failed to deliver, that regulators are pushing the financial industry to standardize derivatives as much as possible and to clear trades through well-capitalized clearinghouses (see Chapters 3 and 13).

While press headlines tend to concentrate on risk management failures and speculation in the derivative markets, there's no doubt that interest rate derivatives are an essential tool for managing risk. The size of government debt, on a worldwide basis, is enormous. Coupled with corporate bonds and bank loan portfolios, it gives rise to a huge pool of assets and liabilities that are sensitive to changes in interest rates. So it is not surprising to find that the OTC market for interest rate derivatives is also very sizable, having reached $490 trillion ($490,000,000,000,000) in notional value at year-end 2012.[4]

Let's now look at some particular types of instrument.

Forward and Futures Contracts

A forward contract allows its buyer to lock in today the future price of an asset such as an interest-rate-linked security, a currency, a stock, or a commodity. The buyer has to pay the agreed-upon price on the settlement date, whether or not the rate or the price of the underlying asset has moved in his or her favor. The seller is generally required to deliver the asset on the settlement date, whatever the asset's price on the spot market. However, some contracts, such as interest rate forwards, are "cash settled"—i.e., one party has to pay the other the difference between the contract value of the forward and its spot value at the maturity date. In the case of forward transactions, there is no up-front fee to pay and no cash changes hands before the settlement date. Forward contracts are essentially OTC instruments and therefore can be highly customized.

A futures contract is simply a forward contract that is traded on an exchange. Unlike forwards, futures have standardized terms, such as the underlying cash instrument or rate, the notional amount, and maturities. (This standardization is essential if the market for the contract is to be liquid.) At its initiation, a futures contract has zero value. However, anyone buying a futures contract must deposit an initial payment, called *initial margin*, with the clearinghouse of the exchange. Then, every day, the contract is "marked-to-market" and daily cash payments

---

[4]Bank for International Settlements, "Statistical Release: OTC Derivatives Statistics at year-end 2012," May 2013. According to this report, the total notional amount outstanding of OTC derivatives year-to-year 2012 was $633 trillion, while the amount for credit default swaps was $25 trillion.

(*variation margin*) are executed that correspond to daily changes in the futures price (determined in the marketplace)—i.e., the party with a position that has lost value pays the difference to the gaining party. The total of the daily installments and the payment at maturity equals the futures price set when the contract was initiated.

Both forwards and futures allow investors to protect open positions from adverse price movements: any losses and gains on the open positions are offset by the payoff of the derivatives contracts. In the case of interest rate forwards or futures, if the actual interest rate at the maturity of the contract is different from the predetermined rate, money is paid or received, depending on whether the difference is positive or negative.

In practice, there's a slight wrinkle in the definition of contracts on short-term interest rates. For example, a futures contract on a one-year T-bill rate is defined as 100 minus the promised interest rate. Thus, if the predetermined futures rate is 2.5 percent, then the contract is on a predetermined price of 97.5 (= 100 − 2.5). If, at the end of the year, the actual rate on a one-year T-bill is 3.2 percent, the realized value is then 100 − 3.2 = 96.8. In such a case, the holder of the long position will be paid by the seller of the contract the sum of 97.5 − 96.8 = 0.7 per unit of the contract.

Such a contract allows a company to hedge a "one-period" rate change and is similar to the forward rate agreement (FRA) contracts that are traded on the OTC markets. FRA contracts are very popular with short-term borrowers who are trying to fix today the effective interest rate they will have to pay at a future date.

The contracts just described are all "cash settled" at maturity; however, some futures contracts on long-term rates are settled by delivering specific long-term bonds (usually from a list of government bonds). Futures, forwards, and FRA contracts are traded in very competitive markets, and the bid/offer spread for these contracts is usually very narrow.

Swaps

Another simple instrument for hedging interest rate risk, and possibly the most frequently used, is the interest rate swap. A swap is an OTC agreement between two parties to exchange the cash flows of two different securities throughout the life of the contract. It can be viewed as a series of forwards and, as with forwards, the contract is binding on both sides of the transaction (whether or not the contract has evolved in one party's favor).

Interest rate swaps are very flexible hedging instruments. They are used by treasurers in asset and liability management and by bond portfolio managers to reduce or extend the duration of an open position.

The most common form of interest rate swap is the fixed/floating interest rate swap, in which the "fixed" side pays a fixed interest rate on a notional amount—e.g., $1 million, quarterly or semiannually—and the "floating" side pays a floating rate on the same notional amount. The reference rate on the floating side, usually the rate on short-term instrument, might be LIBOR, the rate in the commercial paper markets, the T-bill rate, or any other reference agreed upon by the parties to the contract. There is no exchange of principal, as the principals on both sides of the swap cancel out both at the inception and at the maturity of the contract.

In a currency swap, on the contrary, both sides of the transaction exchange the principal amounts, denominated in different currencies, both at the start and at the maturity of the transaction. The exchange rate for the two currencies is decided when the swap is initiated, so that both sides are locked into the future exchange rate. At intervals (monthly, quarterly, semiannually, and so on) throughout the life of the currency swap, both sides exchange interest rate payments, either fixed or floating, denominated in the relevant currencies.

As is the case with forwards and futures, no up-front fee is payable when a swap is initiated, as all swap transactions are priced initially so that the net present value (NPV) of both legs of the swap is the same. As time goes on and interest rates vary, the NPVs of both legs of the swap vary and the difference between the NPVs can become negative or positive. If interest rates rise, the cash flows on the floating leg increase, as does the contract's NPV; conversely, the NPV of the fixed leg declines.[5]

---

[5]In Chapter 13 we discuss the choice of the discount curve, value adjustments for counterparty risk, and the impact of these on the pricing of interest rate swaps and, more generally, derivative products. Most derivatives dealers now use the "overnight indexed swap" (OIS) rates for discounting when derivative securities are collateralized. In mid-2010, LCH.Clearnet, a major central clearinghouse for swap products, switched from discounting at LIBOR to discounting at the OIS rate for interest rate swaps. The reason for using the OIS rate as the discount rate for collateralized transactions is that this rate is derived from the Federal funds rate, which in turn is the interest rate generally earned on the collateral held against the trade. In U.S. dollars, the index rate is the effective Federal funds rate. In euros, it is the Euro Overnight Index Average (EONIA); in sterling, it is the Sterling Overnight Index Average (SONIA).

Interest rate swaps are used by corporations or financial institutions to change the nature of their payments on loans either from fixed to variable rates or from variable to fixed rates, depending on the nature of the corporation's income stream. Swaps are a convenient tool for managing the interest rate risks implied by the company's forecasts of interest rate behavior: if interest rates are expected to rise sharply, the company will try to fix interest payments; in a declining interest rate environment, the company will tend to convert fixed rates into variable rates.

For example, imagine that parties A and B enter into a five-year interest rate swap with a notional value of $100 million. Party A will pay party B each year, at year-end, a sum equal to $100 million times a fixed interest rate, say 4 percent, and will receive from party B a sum equal to $100 million times the one-year T-bill rate plus a spread of, say, 1 percent. So, each year party A pays a fixed amount of $4 million to party B, while party B pays an amount determined by the variable rate (the T-bill rate at the beginning of the period plus 1 percent).

In practice, there is a netting procedure, and only the difference is paid. So, if the T-bill rate at the beginning of the year is less than 3 percent, party A pays party B the difference between 4 percent and the T-bill rate plus 1 percent times $100 million. For example, if the one-year T-bill rate is 2.5 percent, party A will pay party B $[0.04 - (0.025 + 0.01)] \times \$100,000,000 = \$500,000$. If the one-year T-bill rate is 3.8 percent, then party B will pay party A the sum of $[(0.038 + 0.010) - 0.040] \times \$100,000,000 = \$800,000$.

Swap transactions are often used by corporate treasurers as a way of bridging the gap that tends to exist between the particular needs of a company and the needs of the market. For example, a treasurer may for practical reasons issue a five-year bond denominated in Swiss francs, paying a fixed coupon also in Swiss francs, although his preferred exposure might be in U.S. dollars floating with a LIBOR reference. His preferred exposure can be achieved by means of a currency swap: on one side of the transaction, the treasurer receives the cash flows of the bond issued in Swiss francs; on the other side of the transaction, he pays floating LIBOR.

Interest rate and currency swaps are the major components of the OTC derivatives market. But the basic principle of swapping has been applied to all asset classes, such as equities and commodities. Asset swaps have become very popular, as they allow investors to transfer the cash flows and the risk associated with various kinds of assets to other market players in exchange for floating interest payments, usually based on LIBOR.

Options: Calls, Puts, and Exotics

Call options are contracts that allow the buyer to purchase the underlying instrument (say, a particular bond) at a predetermined price (the striking or exercise price) during a given period or at the maturity date. An option that can be exercised only at the maturity of the contract is termed a "European" option, while one that can be exercised at any time, up to and including the maturity date, is termed an "American" option. Call options give the buyer the right to exercise the option when the future price movement of the underlying bond or rate is favorable to the buyer—i.e., when the price of the underlying instrument at the exercise time is above the predetermined exercise price. But the purchaser of an option, unlike the counterparty to a forward, future, or swap, may allow the contract to expire without exercise. For this one-sided right, the buyer must pay a premium.

It is important to emphasize the difference between purchasing a call option and purchasing a futures or forward contract. The futures must be executed at maturity at the agreed-upon terms, whereas the call may end unexercised if the price goes against the buyer. Another important difference is that while the buyer of a call pays the seller of the contract a price that reflects the value of the right, futures and forward contracts have zero value at initiation; the futures price for the futures transaction is set at such a level that the contract has a zero present value.

A put option is the opposite of a call option; it gives the holder the right to *sell* the underlying bond at a predetermined price, at any time up to (American put) or exactly and only at (European put) the maturity date. A stand-alone put option on a bond is therefore a bet on the decline in the value of the bond (or, equivalently, a bet on an increase in interest rates). Put options also allow the holder of an open position to insure against a loss of value: the open position and the option "hedge" offset each other. In this case, we can view the exercise price of the option contract, relative to the current value of the bond, as the insurance "deductible"—that is, the amount of value that the bond must lose before the option insurance takes effect.

Put-call parity describes the relationship between the price of a European call option and put option with identical strike price and expiration date. It can be shown, through put-call parity, that buying a futures contract is similar to simultaneously buying a call option and selling a put option on the same underlying bond, where the exercise price of the call and the put are equal to the forward price of the bond. In the same way, one can create a synthetic call option by buying a forward contract and a put option on the same underlying instrument.

A huge number of strategies for hedging interest rate risks can be put in place by buying and selling call and put options at different exercise prices for different maturities. In effect, "slices" of the future probability distributions of the prices of the underlying instruments can be priced via options and can be traded. The different strategies are characterized by various risk/return trade-offs, hopefully in line with the risk appetite of the investor.

Buying a put and a call with the same exercise price is called a *straddle* and represents a bet on increased volatility—that is, sharp moves up or down in the price of the underlying asset. An investor can therefore "sell volatility" in interest rates by selling a straddle—i.e., by selling a put and a call contract simultaneously that have the same exercise price and maturity. Traders often use straddles when an announcement about a change in interest rates is expected and the outcome of the announcement is uncertain, or before some other major macroeconomic decision by a government or central bank. On the other side of the deal, an investor who purchases a straddle is really insuring against a major increase or a major decrease in the price of the underlying asset during the life of the option.

Volatility can be purchased more cheaply by buying a put and a call option at different exercise prices, with both options out of the money. For example, if the bond price is 100, one might buy a put option with an exercise price of 95 and a call with an exercise price of 105. Such a "strangle" will be much cheaper than an at-the-money straddle with an exercise price of 100.

Caps, Floors, and Collars

Let's use the market in the United States for adjustable rate mortgages (ARMs) as an intuitive way to explore caps, floors, and collars.

The adjustable interest rate on an ARM might be based on the rate of the six-month Treasury bill; over the next six months, the borrower will pay that rate plus a spread of, say, 2 percent per annum. Often, adjustable rate borrowers are offered a "cap" on the interest rate of their long-term loans, so that when short-term interest rates rise above a predetermined rate, say 5 percent, the borrower does not pay more than the 5 percent cap plus the add-on (for a total of 7 percent, in our example).

This cap is clearly an attractive feature for the borrower, and it costs money to put it in place. In order to reduce the cost of the cap, the borrower might also be offered a "floor." A floor sets a minimum interest payment per period: even when short-term interest rates decline substantially, the borrower won't benefit from the reduction in rates below this floor. In our numerical example, if the floor is set at a T-bill rate of 2 percent, the borrower will pay a minimum of 4 percent (i.e., the 2 percent floor plus the 2 percent add-on).

Now, the floor and the cap can be set at such levels that their premiums exactly offset each other. Such an arrangement is often termed a "zero-cost collar" or "zero-cost cylinder."

We can see caps and floors and their combinations used in many different risk management markets. For example, the collar, or cylinder, as a combination of a ceiling and floor agreement on periodic payments, is a very popular way to hedge foreign currency positions.

Swaptions

Options on a swap, referred to as "swaptions," represent the right to enter into a swap on or before a specified date at currently determined terms. Such options may be either European or American in style. If the buyer of the swaption has the right to pay a fixed rate in the swap upon exercise, it is called a payer's swaption. If the buyer of the swaption has the right to receive a fixed rate, it is called a receiver's swaption. Such options may be structured with fixed and floating legs in different currencies. A swaption clearly offers more flexibility than a straight swap, but the purchaser must pay an option premium for that added benefit.

Exotic Options

So far, we've considered straightforward or "plain vanilla" options. Options with more complicated terms are known as *exotic options*. One of the most popular is an option that has as its reference the *average* price of the underlying instrument over some agreed-upon period of time. For example, one might purchase a call contract from a major bank that entitles the owner to receive the difference, if positive, between the average price of a 30-year bond, say one month before its maturity date, and an exercise price agreed upon in advance (say, 100). The volatility of an average rate option is lower than the volatility of the corresponding vanilla option.

Knock-in and knock-out options are also quite common. These options may be exercised or expire during an agreed-upon time period before the formal maturity date of the option contract if the price of the underlying instruments "hits" a certain predetermined price level. These options, like most exotic options, are "path dependent": their value is dependent on certain paths that the price of the underlying instrument may take. There is an endless list of exotic options that were popular before the 2007–2009 financial crisis, with names such as Himalayan, octopus, ratchet, chooser, lookback, and barrier options. The financial crisis has reduced the appetite of investors for excessively complex structures, at least for a time. However, in the low interest rate environment that has characterized the post-crisis years, asset managers searching for yield can still find structured products attractive—e.g., hybrid equity/credit notes that pay a higher coupon than market rates with capital at risk depending on the change in the price of an asset or a credit spread.

Pricing and hedging exotic options relies on complex mathematical models that are prone to model risk (see Chapter 15). In addition, some of these exotic structures, such as barrier options, can expose the seller of the option to significant risks, as there is no perfect hedge for them.

Financial Engineering

Forwards, swaps, and options are the main building blocks of financial engineering. They can be used separately to hedge specific risks or combined to form complex structures that meet the needs of customers.

In particular, derivatives allow investors and institutions to break apart or "segment" risks (or, conversely, to bundle them together). Take, for example, a U.S. fund manager who holds a bond denominated in euros. The fund manager is exposed to interest rate risk in the euro fixed-income market and to changes in the dollar/euro exchange rate. The manager can hedge both risks by means of a currency swap. Alternatively, she can hedge the foreign exchange exposure through a currency forward or currency option. The fund manager could also avoid the trouble of hedging only the currency exposure by entering into a so-called quanto swap. Under this structure, she would receive the coupon of the bond in dollars at a prearranged exchange rate and pay U.S. LIBOR floating.

There is almost no limit to the imagination of the structurers in banks who are responsible for devising complex instruments intended to match the risk/return appetite of their clients. But financial engineering is not by itself risk management, and in the world of derivatives there is often a fine line between hedging and speculation. Firms can be tempted to enter into complex transactions that enhance portfolio returns. Enhancing returns always means taking on more risk, in some form or other. Often it means marginally increasing returns in the present in exchange for assuming an unlikely but potentially very severe loss in the future, as we discussed in Chapter 1. Too often, the risk embedded in complex structures is not fully understood by corporations entering into complex derivative transactions (Box 6-4) or is not fully communicated to senior managers or other stakeholders.

Earlier we mentioned the story of Orange County and its financial collapse in 1994, due in part to excessive leverage. The other reason for the failure of Orange County was that the fund purchased complex inverse floating rate notes whose coupon payments decline when interest rates rise (as opposed to

---

BOX 6-4 THE RISKS OF COMPLEX DERIVATIVES

Back in the 1990s, before the bond market crash of 1994, Bankers Trust (BT) proposed to clients such as Procter & Gamble (P&G) and Gibson Greetings that they enter into complex leveraged swaps to achieve a lower funding cost. In the swap with P&G, BT would pay a fixed rate to P&G for five years, and P&G would pay a floating rate, which was the commercial paper rate minus 75 basis points if rates remained stable. But, through a complex formula, the floating rate would increase considerably if rates rose during the period—for example, an increase of 100 basis points in rates produced a spread over the commercial paper rate of 1,035 basis points! Each basis point move in the yield curve was magnified about 30 times.

The Fed increased the Fed funds rate by 250 basis points in 1994, causing colossal losses for both P&G and Gibson Greetings. Both companies sued BT for misrepresenting the risk embedded in these complex swap transactions. BT never quite recovered from the damaging impact of these events on its reputation and, much later, was acquired by Deutsche Bank.

conventional floaters whose payments increase in such a circumstance). It was the combination of excessive leverage and a risky, and eventually wrong, interest rate bet embedded in the securities bought by the fund that led to the Orange County debacle.

The board and senior management of a corporation need to understand the risks that are inherent in the firm's business model. Senior management then needs to deploy robust policies and risk measures that tie the firm's risk management strategy, and particularly its use of derivatives, to the firm's risk appetite and to the business strategy it has communicated to stakeholders. Our next chapter explores the value-at-risk (VaR) framework that is widely used by financial institutions and major corporations to measure and communicate risk across their various activities—and assesses the strengths and weaknesses of this approach.

7

MEASURING MARKET RISK: VALUE-AT-RISK, EXPECTED SHORTFALL, AND SIMILAR METRICS

The measurement of market risk has evolved from simple naïve indicators, such as the face value or "notional" amount of an individual security, through more complex measures of price sensitivities, such as the basis point value or duration approach of a bond (Chapter 6) and various specific measures of risk for derivatives ("the Greeks"), to relatively sophisticated risk measures such as the latest value-at-risk (VaR) methodology for whole portfolios of securities and new risk metrics such as stress-VaR, expected shortfall, and scenario analysis.

In this chapter we'll chart this evolutionary trajectory and spend some time examining the principles that lie behind VaR and associated techniques to make clear the strengths and weaknesses of the approaches in nonmathematical language.

The limitations of VaR as a risk metric have been understood for years, but they played a significant role in obfuscating the risks run by the banking industry in the buildup to the 2007–2009 financial crisis. The result has been a series of attempts by regulators and the industry both to improve VaR analysis[1]

Particularly by making the right design choices when setting up a VaR model. A post-crisis survey of bank practice summed this up as "probing for the right balance between sophistication and accuracy, on the one hand, and simplicity, transparency and speed, on the other." Amit Mehta et al., "Managing Market Risk: Today and Tomorrow," McKinsey Working Papers on Risk, No. 32, May 2012.

and to reduce the financial industry's reliance on VaR numbers. In this chapter we therefore also look at "expected shortfall" approaches that attempt to look beyond the VaR number to summarize the risk in the tail of any loss distribution, and we discuss how VaR fits with the many other risk methodologies that make up a best-practice approach to risk measurement, including stress testing and scenario analysis—approaches we deal with in depth in Chapter 16.

The VaR Controversy: A Quick Primer

Since the late 1990s, VaR has become the standard way to measure and report market risk, and the methodology has also been extended to credit risk (Chapter 11). VaR is a very useful risk measure during normal market conditions—i.e., much of the time—and offers a powerful way of assessing the overall market risk of trading positions over a short horizon, such as a two-week (i.e., 10 trading days) period. In effect, the methodology allows us to capture in a single number the multiple components of market risk, such as curve risk, basis risk, and volatility risk.

However, each time there is turmoil in the world's markets, the limitations of VaR and other sophisticated measures of market risk are revealed. The reason is simple: VaR models are based on the assumption that key parameters such as volatilities and correlations are stationary—i.e., that they do not change in value during the period in which the risk is measured. This assumption is often proven to be wrong during extreme market conditions, making VaR an unreliable measure of risk at exactly the moment that robust risk analytics are most required.

Exceptional market shocks, such as the crisis in the world markets in 1998 that capsized the giant U.S. hedge fund Long-Term Capital Management (LTCM) or the more recent financial crisis of 2007–2009 that led to several bank failures such as Lehman Brothers in September 2008, are usually accompanied by a drying up of market liquidity and huge trading losses.[2] The risk these events pose can be captured only by means of supplemental methodologies, so each crisis reemphasizes the importance of using multiple risk measurement tools, including stress tests and scenario analyses, and of achieving the right blend of quantitative rigor and qualitative assessment. Using a wide range of risk

---

[2]When liquidity disappears, trading desks cannot rebalance their hedging positions as markets move against them and, as a consequence, losses start to accumulate.

measures helps because each approach has particular limitations and particular strengths.

Just as VaR cannot easily capture the impact of disruptions in liquidity, prices, volatility, and correlations, it also struggles to capture strong nonlinearities in risk of the kind seen in complex structured products—e.g., subprime CDOs (Chapter 15). Again, using different kinds of risk analysis is essential.

There is another reason why firms should not overrely on their VaR models or, indeed, any single type of risk model. If too many firms rely on a single view of risk, then this industry-standard risk measure can exacerbate market volatility and, ironically, make markets less stable and more prone to crisis. When financial institutions sell assets in volatile markets in order to keep within the limits set by senior management (e.g., VaR limits), this tends to depress market prices even further and increase the volatility and correlation of the risk factors for these assets. This, in turn, can cause another set of financial institutions to exceed their VaR limits, forcing the institutions to reduce their exposure by selling still more of the same assets—perpetuating a vicious circle. If this happens at the turn of the economic cycle, it can potentially transform the industry reliance on VaR models into a powerful procyclical mechanism.[3]

Like any complex model, VaR also suffers from the model risks that we discuss in detail in Chapter 15. Mistakes in applying and interpreting the model can be made by accident and, given VaR's importance in terms of risk reporting, they may also be made intentionally in order to suppress reported risk numbers. It's not unknown for institutions to tweak VaR models so that they give the "right" numbers or to replace a model that seems to indicate that a business practice is uncomfortably risky with an "improved" model that happens to offer lower risk numbers.

This litany of problems makes one wonder why institutions use VaR in the first place.[4] The answer is simple: applied in the right way, it is a useful summary statistic that can help overcome many of the issues associated with measuring risk and, especially, aggregating risks. Let's take a quick look at the evolution of measures of market risk in the derivative markets before the advent of VaR to

---

[3] The phenomenon of "procyclicality" is further discussed in Chapter 3.

[4] Indeed, for many years some critics have argued that VaR is so flawed and so open to misuse and abuse that it should be abandoned. See, for example, N. Taleb, "Against Value-at-Risk: Nassim Taleb Replies to Philippe Jorion," http://fooledbyrandomness.com, 1997.

see why the VaR approach has proved so attractive. Then we'll explore how VaR is calculated, its resulting strengths and weaknesses, and the new approaches to mending some of the weaknesses we have identified.

The Notional Amount Approach

Until relatively recently, major banks often assessed the amount of market risk generated by their trading desks in terms of the notional or nominal amounts of the portfolio held by the desk. For example, the risk of a portfolio might be assessed with reference to the fact that it contained $30 million of government debt or $30 million of options on the equity of, say, a telecom company. These flawed nominal measures were often routinely presented to senior management and the board as measures of market risk. This is an appealingly simple approach, but it is fatally flawed because it does not:

- Reflect the fact that different assets have vastly different price volatilities (e.g., high-quality government bonds are less likely to fluctuate violently in price than are telecom stocks)
- Take into account the tendency for the value of different assets in the portfolio to rise and fall at the same time (i.e., the correlation of the assets in the portfolio)
- Differentiate between short and long positions that might cancel one another out or partially hedge one another (e.g., a long position in a forward contract on the euro with notional value of $100 million maturing in June and a short position in a forward contract on the euro with a notional value of $50 million maturing in July)

In the case of derivative positions, there are often very large discrepancies between the notional amount, which may be huge, and the true amount of market exposure, which is often small. For example, two call options on the same underlying instrument with the same notional value and the same time to expiration may have very different market values if their strike prices are different—the first option may be deep in the money, and the other one may be deep out of the money. The first option might be very valuable, while the second might be almost worthless, meaning that they represent very different risk exposures.

As another example, imagine a situation in which interest rate swaps are written with many different counterparties and some of these swaps are being used to hedge the market risk exposure created by the other swaps. In this instance, the deals are designed to cancel each other out in terms of their effect on the aggregate market risk in the portfolio. Adding up the notional amounts of the deals will generate an entirely misleading picture of the market risk of the portfolio (although it will offer some indication of overall credit risk exposure).

Price Sensitivity Measures for Derivatives

In Chapter 6 we looked at some of the specific measures of market risk in the interest rate and bond markets. But bond market traders are not the only practitioners who depend on market-specific risk measures. Practitioners in the derivative markets have developed their own specialized risk measures to describe the sensitivities of derivative instruments to various risk factors. The risk measures are named after letters in the Greek alphabet, and are therefore known collectively as the Greeks. How do these measures relate to the risk measures that we discussed in Chapter 6?

First, consider a European call option on an individual stock that does not pay any dividend. According to the classic Black-Scholes formula for option pricing, the price of this option is a function of the stock price, the risk-free rate of interest, the instantaneous volatility of the stock return, the strike price, and the option's maturity.

In the option price equation, the stock price plays the same role as the yield in the bond price relationship that we described in Chapter 6. The sensitivities of the call option price with respect to the stock price are known as the delta and gamma, so we can think of the delta and gamma price risks of a derivative as analogous to the duration and convexity of a bond, respectively. Table 7-1 gives the definitions of the Greeks in more detail.

The list of sensitivities for derivatives in Table 7-1 is longer than a similar list for a standard bond. This is because the value of a derivative is affected by additional risk factors, such as volatility, the discount rate, the passage of time, and when several risk factors are involved, the correlation between the risk factors.

TABLE 7-1 The Greek Alphabet for a European Equity Call Option

Delta, or price risk	Delta measures the degree to which an option's value is affected by a small change in the price of the underlying instrument.
Gamma, or convexity risk	Gamma measures the degree to which the option's delta changes as the reference price underlying the option changes. The higher the gamma, the more valuable the option is to its holder. For a high-gamma option, when the underlying price increases, the delta also increases, so the option appreciates more in value than a gamma-neutral position. Conversely, when the underlying price falls, the delta also falls, and the option loses less in value than if the position were gamma neutral. The reverse is true for short positions in options: high-gamma positions expose their holders to more risk than gamma-neutral positions.
Vega, or volatility risk	Vega measures the sensitivity of the option value to changes in the volatility of the underlying instrument. A higher vega typically increases the value of the option to its holder.
Theta, or time decay risk	Theta measures the time decay of an option. That is, it reflects how much the value of the option changes as the option moves closer to its expiration date. Positive gamma is usually associated with negative time decay—i.e., a natural price attrition of the option as its maturity declines.
Rho, or discount rate risk	Rho measures the change in value of an option in response to a change in interest rate—more specifically, a change in the zero-coupon rate of the same maturity as the option. Typically, the higher the value of rho, the lower the value of the option to its holder.

Weaknesses of the Greek Measures

Traders on options desks use the Greeks to monitor the sensitivities of their market positions and to discuss risk with trading desk risk managers. But each of the sensitivities measured by the Greeks provides only a partial measure of financial risk. The measurements of delta, gamma, and vega complement one another, but they cannot be aggregated to produce an overall measure of the risk generated by a position or a portfolio. In particular:

- Sensitivities cannot be added up across risk types—e.g., the delta and gamma risk of the same position cannot be summed.

- Sensitivities cannot be added up across markets—e.g., one cannot sum the delta of a euro/U.S. dollar call and the delta of a call on a stock index.

Since the sensitivities cannot be aggregated, they cannot be used to assess the magnitude of the overall loss that might arise from a change in the risk factors. As a consequence:

- Sensitivities cannot be used directly to measure the amount of capital that the bank is putting at risk.
- Sensitivities do not facilitate financial risk control. Position limits expressed in terms of delta, gamma, and vega are often ineffective because they do not translate easily into a "maximum loss acceptable" for the position.

This explains the desire for a comprehensive measure of market risk for individual securities and for portfolios. Value-at-risk is one answer to this quest for a consistent measure of market risk.

Defining Value-at-Risk

Value-at-risk (VaR) can be defined as the worst loss that might be expected from holding a security or portfolio over a given period of time (say, a single day, or 10 days for the purpose of regulatory capital reporting), given a specified level of probability (known as the *confidence level*).

For example, if we say that a position has a daily VaR of $10 million at the 99 percent confidence level, we mean that the realized daily losses from the position will on average be higher than $10 million on only 1 day in every 100 trading days (i.e., two to three days each year).

This means that VaR is *not* the answer to the simple question "How much can I lose on my portfolio over a given period of time?" The answer to this question is "everything," or almost the entire value of the portfolio! Such an answer is not very helpful in practice: it is the correct answer to the wrong question. If all markets collapse at the same time, then naturally prices may plunge and, at least in theory, the value of the portfolio may drop to near zero.

Instead, VaR offers a probability statement about the potential change in the value of a portfolio resulting from a change in market factors over a specified period of time. Crucially, the VaR measure also does not state by *how much* actual losses are likely to exceed the VaR figure; it simply states how likely (or unlikely) it is that the VaR measure will be exceeded. We look at supplemental approaches that help address this critical problem later in this chapter.

Most VaR models are designed to measure risk over a short period of time, such as one day, or 10 days in the case of the market risk measurements required by the regulators for regulatory capital. The confidence level for the calculation of market risk introduced by the Basel Committee in 1998 is set at 99 percent (Chapter 3). However, for the purposes of allocating internal capital, VaR may be derived at a higher confidence level, say 99.96 percent; this level of confidence is consistent with the level of confidence inherent in an AA credit rating awarded by a public ratings agency.

There are two key steps in calculating VaR. First, derive the forward distribution of the portfolio, or the money returns on the portfolio, at the chosen horizon (in this case, one day). We describe later how this distribution can be derived using three different approaches: historical price distributions (nonparametric VaR); assumptions about normal distributions (parametric VaR); and Monte Carlo analysis.

This distribution is then plotted out as the curve shown in Figure 7-1. This figure shows us how likely it is (vertical axis) that losses of a particular dollar value (horizontal axis) will occur.

Second, identify the required percentile of this distribution so that a particular loss number can be read off. We've selected the first percentile of the distribution in Figure 7-1 because, in this example, we assumed that management has asked for a VaR number measured at the 99 percent confidence level. In Figure 7-1, we also assume that the distribution is a normal, bell-shaped curve rather than a distribution that is skewed toward particularly light or heavy losses. Thus, a confidence level of 99 percent corresponds to a VaR of 2.33 standard deviations.

If the confidence level had been set at 99.96 percent, then we would have calculated the 4-basis-point (bp) quantile, and we would have ended up with a larger number for the VaR. (Note that the extent to which the VaR number rises as confidence levels are set more stringently depends on the shape of the distribution.)

The VaR of the position or portfolio is simply the maximum loss at this 99 percent confidence level, measured relative to the expected value of the portfolio at the target horizon. That is, VaR is the distance of the first percentile from the mean of the distribution.

FIGURE 7-1 Defining Value-at-Risk

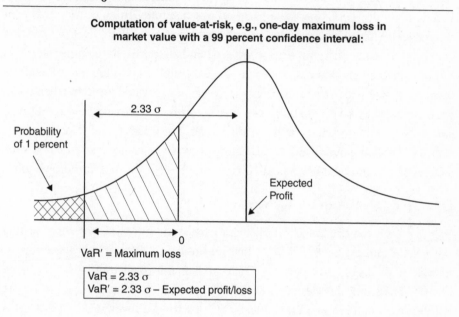

Computation of value-at-risk, e.g., one-day maximum loss in market value with a 99 percent confidence interval:

2.33 σ

Probability of 1 percent

Expected Profit

0

VaR' = Maximum loss

VaR = 2.33 σ
VaR' = 2.33 σ – Expected profit/loss

VaR = expected profit/loss – worst-case loss at the 99 percent confidence level

An alternative and even simpler definition of VaR is that it represents the worst-case loss at the 99 percent confidence level:

VaR' = worst-case loss at the 99 percent confidence level

VaR' is also known as *absolute VaR*. However, only our first definition of VaR is consistent with economic capital attribution and the kind of risk-adjusted return on capital (RAROC) calculations we describe in Chapter 17. (Essentially, this is because capital needs to be provided only as a cushion against unexpected losses; in VaR the expected profit or loss is already priced in and accounted for in the return calculation.)

So, how exactly does the VaR number relate to economic capital and to regulatory capital? VaR represents the economic capital that shareholders should invest in the firm (or set aside against a particular position or portfolio) to limit the probability of default to a given predetermined level of confidence. Regulatory capital, on the other hand, is the minimum amount of capital imposed by the regulator, as described in Chapter 3. Even when regulatory capital measures are based on a VaR calculation rather than on much simpler rules, economic capital differs from regulatory capital because the confidence level and the time horizon chosen are usually different. For example, when banks are determining their economic capital for market risk, they may choose a higher confidence level than the 99 percent set by the regulator. They may also vary the time horizon when making economic capital calculations, perhaps using one day for very liquid positions, such as government bonds, and as much as several weeks for illiquid positions, such as long-dated over-the-counter equity derivatives. By contrast, the regulator arbitrarily sets the time horizon at 10 days for any position in the trading book.

From One-Day VaR to 10-Day VaR

VaR is often used to manage market risk over a one-day time horizon. For this purpose, it's necessary to derive VaR from the daily distribution of the portfolio values. However, we mentioned earlier that the regulators have set a time horizon of 10 days for the purpose of VaR calculations that are used to report regulatory capital requirements. Ideally, this 10-day VaR would be derived from a corresponding distribution of results over a 10-day horizon. This is problematic, however, as it implies that the time series of data used for the analysis must be much longer—indeed, 10 times longer—than that employed in any one-day VaR analysis. As a result, many banks employ a work-around that allows them to derive an approximation of 10-day VaR from daily VaR data by multiplying the daily VaR by the square root of time (here, 10 days). The "square root of time" rule is endorsed by the regulators; it should be noted, however, that it is not really a sound approach and remains something of a rule of thumb.

How Is VaR Used to Limit Risk in Practice?

VaR is an aggregate measure of risk across all risk factors. A special attraction is that it can be calculated at each level of activity in the business hierarchy of a company. For example, it can be calculated for each activity (e.g., trading desk) at both the business unit level (e.g., equity trading) and the level of the firm as a whole.

At the level of the firm, VaR offers a good way of representing the (short-term) "risk appetite" of the firm, since it measures the maximum loss that the firm might incur, under normal market conditions, over a short period of time (in effect, 1 to 10 days). The risk appetite of the firm over a longer period of time, say a quarter, is usually set in terms of a worst-case scenario analysis. For example, the board of the bank can set a limit on the maximum loss that it is prepared to tolerate over a quarter if the worst-case crisis that the bank's risk managers think plausible in that period should, in fact, occur.

At many financial institutions, the board of directors sets an overall VaR limit whose control is delegated to the chief executive officer (CEO). In practice, this control is often delegated, in turn, to a risk management committee chaired by the CEO. In many banks, the risk management committee appoints a chief risk officer (CRO) or similar risk executive to report on firmwide risk and therefore help maintain effective control of this limit. We discuss this cascade of accountability in more detail in Chapter 4. Box 7-1 reviews the strengths of VaR, not only as a measurement tool but also as a managerial instrument.

Figures 7-2a and 7-2b help us to visualize what VaR measures mean in practice, and how they are used to manage risk on a trading desk. (For this example, we'll stick with the nonparametric, or historical VaR, approach to calculating VaR, one of a set of calculation approaches that we explain in more detail later on.) In this illustrative example, the average daily revenue for our example bank's trading portfolio during 1998 was C\$0.451 million; we've chosen

---

BOX 7-1   VAR IS FOR MANAGING AS WELL AS MEASURING RISK

In the main text, we highlight the problems inherent in the simplifying assumptions that must be made whenever a VaR number is calculated. In this box, let's remind ourselves of the great strengths of VaR and its wide range of uses:

- *VaR provides a common, consistent, and integrated measure of risk across risk factors, instruments, and asset classes.* For example, it allows managers to measure the risk of a fixed-income position in a way that is comparable and consistent with their risk assessment of an equity derivative position. VaR also takes into account the correlations between the various risk factors, somewhat in the spirit of portfolio theory.
- *VaR can provide an aggregate measure of risk and risk-adjusted performance.* This single number can then be easily translated into

a capital requirement. VaR can also be used to reward employees on the basis of the risk-adjusted return on capital generated by their activities. In other words, it can be used to measure risk-adjusted performance (see Chapter 17).

- *Business line risk limits can be set in terms of VaR.* These limits can be used to ensure that individuals do not take more risk than they are allowed to take. Risk limits expressed in VaR units can easily be aggregated up through the firm, from the business line at trading desk level to the very top of the corporation. The drill-down capability of a VaR system allows risk managers to detect which unit is taking the most risk and also to identify the type of risk to which the whole bank is most exposed—e.g., equity, interest rate, currency, or equity vega.

- *VaR provides senior management, the board of directors, and regulators with a risk measure that they can understand.* Managers and shareholders, as well as regulators, can decide whether they feel comfortable with the level of risk taken on by the bank in terms of VaR units. VaR also provides a framework for assessing, *ex ante*, investments and projects on the basis of their expected risk-adjusted return on capital.

- *A VaR system allows a firm to assess the benefits of portfolio diversification within a line of activity and across businesses.* VaR allows managers to assess the daily revenue volatility they might expect from any given trading area, but it also allows them to compare the volatilities of different business areas, such as equity and fixed-income businesses, so that they can understand better how each business line offsets, or contributes to, the revenue volatility of the whole firm.

- *VaR has become an industry-standard internal and external reporting tool.* VaR reports are produced daily for managers of business lines and are then aggregated for senior management. VaR is also communicated to the regulators and has become the basis for calculating regulatory capital in some areas of risk measurement. The rating agencies take VaR calculations into account in establishing their ratings of banks. Increasingly, VaR and the results of the back testing of VaR are published in banks' annual reports as a key indicator of risk.

FIGURE 7-2A Net Daily Trading Revenues for 1998 (C$ Millions)

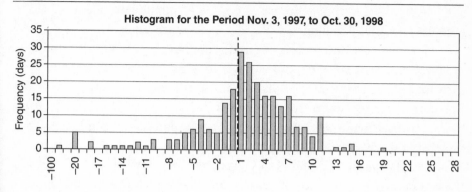

to look back to 1998 because it proved to be an interesting year for the purpose of analyzing risk management decisions. But what we are immediately interested in is the distribution of the bank's gains and losses, represented in Figure 7-2a, which tells us how frequently the bank incurred each loss amount. The first percentile of the historical distribution represented in Figure 7-2a—i.e., the cutoff point on this distribution such that only 1 percent of the daily revenues lies on the distribution's left-hand side—is C$25.919 million. This represents VAR', or the absolute VaR to a 99 percent level of confidence. From our earlier discussion, we know that to work out the true one-day historical VaR for the portfolio,

FIGURE 7-2B Net Daily Trading Revenues During 1998 Versus One-Day VaR at the 99 Percent Confidence Level

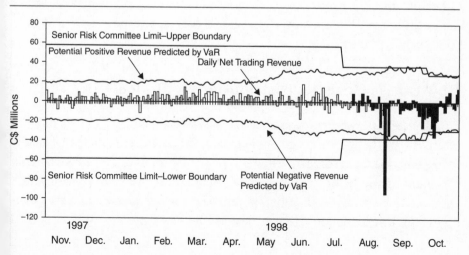

we need to take the expected profit or loss into account. So our VaR number to a 99 percent level of confidence based on this 12-month set of data is 0.451 − (−25.919) = C$26.37 million.

Now let's turn to Figure 7-2b to discuss how VaR limits are used as a practical tool for managing market risk. In 1998, market participants were surprised by the severe market disruptions in the month of August, after the Russian government defaulted on its debt. Liquidity suddenly evaporated from many financial markets, causing asset prices to plunge and producing large losses for many financial institutions (and the near-collapse of the U.S. hedge fund LTCM). Figure 7-2b shows the aggregate VaR creeping up slowly during the first part of the year, then increasing substantially during May and June as market volatility edged higher. During that period, the Senior Risk Committee limit at our example bank remained at $58 million, well above the daily VaR. As risk kept increasing during the summer, the Senior Risk Committee prophetically lowered the limit to $38 million in July before the August market crisis. At the peak of the market disruption during the month of August, the new VaR limit became binding, putting pressure on the bank's trading businesses to lower their risks. We can see from the figure that the bank experienced substantial trading losses during the month of August, and after this the VaR limit was further reduced in order to force the trading businesses to reduce their risk exposure still further.

As a general point, VaR limits for individual business lines such as trading desks must be set at a level consistent with the firm's overall VaR limit. Otherwise the risk exposures of all the business units might remain within their own limits while the firm's aggregate risk breached the overall VaR limit set at the top of the firm.

How Do We Generate Distributions for Calculating VaR?

To calculate VaR, we first need to select the factors that drive the volatility of returns in the trading or investment portfolio. We can then use these risk factors to generate the forward distribution of the portfolio values at the risk horizon (or, equivalently, the distribution of the changes in the value of the portfolio). Only after generating the distribution can we calculate the mean and the quantiles of this distribution to arrive at the portfolio VaR.

Selection of the Risk Factors

The change in the value of the portfolio is driven by changes in the market factors that influence the price of each instrument. The relevant risk factors depend on the composition of the portfolio. The selection of risk factors is straightforward for a simple security, but it requires judgment for more complex products.

In the case of a simple security, such as a US$/€ forward, the value of the position is affected only by the US$/€ forward rate. In the case of a US$/€ call option, the value of the position depends not only on the US$/€ exchange rate but also on the dollar and euro interest rates over the maturity of the option and on the US$/€ volatility (Table 7-2).

In the case of a stock portfolio, the risk factors are the prices of the individual stocks that make up the portfolio, or, to make calculations more practical, the risk factors may be the market index and possibly some additional industrial indexes that are believed to explain the rates of return of individual securities. For a bond portfolio, the choice of the risk factors depends on the degree of "granularity" required to understand the risk in hand. For example, the risk factor for each bond might simply be its yield to maturity, as described in Chapter 6. Alternatively, it might be a selection of zero-coupon rates on the risk-free term structure of interest rates for each currency. The selection might comprise the overnight, 1-month, 3-month, 6-month, 1-year, 3-year, 5-year, 10-year, and 30-year zero-coupon rates, as well as the spread in yields between different risk ratings or issuers for the same terms (so that the calculation captures ratings or issuer risk).

TABLE 7-2 Example of a Selection of Risk Factors

US$/€ Forward	US$/€ Option
• US$/€ forward rate	• US$/€ exchange rate
	• US$ interest rates
	• € interest rates
	• US$/€ volatility

Choice of a Methodology for Modeling Changes in Market Risk Factors

Having identified the risk factors that generate the volatility in the portfolio's returns, the risk analyst must choose an appropriate methodology for deriving the distribution. There are three alternatives:

- The analytic variance/covariance approach
- The historical simulation approach
- The Monte Carlo simulation approach

Analytic Variance/Covariance Approach (CoVaR): Case of a Portfolio Linear in Risks

To simplify the derivation of VaR, we can choose to make certain assumptions. Under the analytic variance/covariance or "delta normal" approach, we assume that all the risk factors and the portfolio values are log normally distributed or, equivalently, that the natural log of the returns are normally distributed. This makes the calculation much simpler because the normal distribution is completely characterized by its first two moments, the mean and the variance, and the analyst can analytically derive the mean and the variance of the portfolio return distribution from:

- The multivariate distribution of the risk factors
- The composition of the portfolio

A simple example should help make the process clear. Suppose our example portfolio is composed of two stocks, Microsoft and Exxon. In this example, the risk factors that generate the returns in the portfolio are straightforward: the stock prices for each of the companies, the volatility of both stocks, and the correlation coefficient that describes the extent to which the stock prices of Microsoft and Exxon go up and down together.

From historical data on the behavior of the two stocks, we can estimate the simple historical mean and standard deviation of the daily returns for each of the two stocks for each day over a one-year trading period. We could obtain this stock price information from any of the major market information providers, such as Reuters or Bloomberg.

The historical data also allow us to estimate a correlation risk factor for the price relationship between the two stocks. The correlation risk factor is quite important: when the stocks are perfectly correlated, the VaR will be the sum of the VaRs of the individual stocks. Most stocks are not strongly correlated, however, so the VaR tends to be considerably less than the sum of the VaRs of the individual stocks.

Under this approach, remember that we assume that the rates of return on the stocks follow a multivariate normal distribution. This assumption means that we can apply our risk factor analysis to the present portfolio to generate a distribution of returns of the portfolio into the future. Of course, we must take into account the present price of the portfolio and the percentage of each stock that the portfolio contains.

Having generated the distribution using our five risk factors, we can plot the distribution so that it looks rather like the curve in Figure 7-1, referred to earlier in our discussion. It is now a simple enough matter to read off the VaR number that is relevant to our selected confidence level (e.g., 99 percent), as described earlier for Figure 7-1.

Our discussion of this approach to calculating VaR begs a major question: how dangerous is our simplifying assumption that returns are normally distributed? In fact, there is a large amount of evidence that many individual return distributions are not normally distributed, but rather exhibit what are known as "fat tails." The term *fat tails* arises out of the shape of certain distributions when plotted on a graph. In these distributions, there are more observations far away from the mean than is the case in a normal or bell-shaped distribution. So whereas a normal distribution tails off quickly (to reflect the rarity of unlikely events), the tail of a fat-tailed distribution remains relatively thick. We can see the difference in Figure 7-3, where the dotted line represents a normal distribution and the solid line a fatter-tailed distribution.

Fat tails in distributions should worry risk managers because they imply that extraordinary losses occur more frequently than a normal distribution would lead us to believe.

We would expect the VaR derived from a fat-tailed distribution to be higher than that derived from a normal distribution—perhaps much higher. It follows that if we assume that a distribution is normal in our VaR calculation when in fact it has a fat tail, we are likely to underestimate the VaR number associated with the financial portfolio.

Luckily, even if the returns of an individual risk factor do not perfectly follow a normal distribution, we can reasonably expect that the returns of a well-diversified

FIGURE 7-3 Comparison of the Normal and a Fat-Tailed Distribution

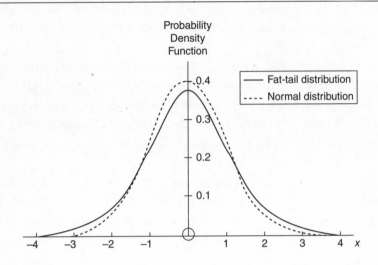

portfolio (i.e., a portfolio subject to many different risk factors) will still exhibit a normal distribution. This effect is explained by the central limit theorem, which tells us that the independent random variables of a well-behaved distribution will have a mean that converges, in large samples, to a normal distribution.

In practice, this result implies that a risk manager can assume that a portfolio has a normal distribution of returns, provided that the portfolio is fairly well diversified and the risk factor returns are sufficiently independent of one another (even when they are not themselves normally distributed).

However, the potential effect on VaR calculations of fat tails, lumpy portfolios, and correlated risk factor returns should send a warning signal to support staff and senior managers who use VaR numbers to gain comfort about risk levels.

Historical Simulation Approach

The historical simulation approach to VaR calculation is conceptually simple and does not oblige the user to make any assumptions about the distributions. However, at least one to three years of historical data are necessary to produce meaningful results. We've already applied the principles of this approach in our earlier example of the VaR number associated with trading revenues in 1998. In this special case, there was only one risk factor: the daily trading revenue of the firm. In the following, we consider the more usual case: analyzing the VaR of a whole portfolio of securities.

First, the changes in relevant market prices and rates (the risk factors) are analyzed over a specified historical period—say, two years. The portfolio under examination is then revalued, using changes in the risk factors derived from the historical data, to create the distribution of the portfolio returns from which the VaR of the portfolio can be derived. Each daily simulated change in the value of the portfolio is considered as an observation in the distribution.

Three steps are involved:

1. Select a sample of actual daily risk factor changes over a given period of time—say, 500 days (i.e., two years' worth of trading days)—using the same period of time for all the factors.
2. Apply those daily changes to the current value of the risk factors, revaluing the current portfolio as many times as the number of days in the historical sample. Sum these changes across all positions, keeping the days synchronized—i.e., each day of historical changes in the factors is applied to today's factors to yield a simulated observation for the distribution for the specific portfolio.
3. Construct the histogram of portfolio values and identify the VaR that isolates the first percentile of the distribution in the left-hand tail (assuming VaR is derived at the 99 percent confidence level).

Let's illustrate the approach using an example. Assume that the current portfolio is composed of a three-month US\$/€ call option. The market risk factors for this position are:

- US\$/€ exchange rate
- US\$ three-month interest rate
- € three-month interest rate
- Three-month implied volatility of the US\$/€ exchange rate

In the following, we neglect the impact of interest rate risk factors and consider only the level of the exchange rate and its volatility. The first step is to report daily observations of the risk factors we've selected over the past 100 days, as shown in abbreviated form in columns 2 and 3 of Table 7-3.

Historical simulation, like Monte Carlo simulation, requires the repricing of the position in question using the historical distribution of the risk factors. In

TABLE 7-3 Historical Market Values for the Risk Factors over the Last 100 Days

Day (t)	US$/€ (FX_t)	FX Volatility (σ_t)
−100	1.3970	0.149
−99	1.3960	0.149
−98	1.3973	0.151
. . .	. . .	. . .
−2	1.4015	0.163
−1	1.4024	0.164

TABLE 7-4 Simulating Portfolio Values Using Historical Data (Current Value of the Portfolio: $1.80)

				Change from Current Value ($1.80)
Alternative price	100	$= C(FX_{100}; \sigma_{100})$	= $1.75	−$0.05
Alternative price	99	$= C(FX_{99}; \sigma_{99})$	= $1.73	−$0.07
Alternative price	98	$= C(FX_{98}; \sigma_{98})$	= $1.69	−$0.11
. . . .				
Alternative price	2	$= C(FX_2; \sigma_2)$	= $1.87	+$0.07
Alternative price	1	$= C(FX_1; \sigma_1)$	= $1.88	+$0.08

this example, we use the Black-Scholes model adapted by Garman and Kholhagen (1983) to currency options. The results of this step are reported in Table 7-4.[5]

The last step consists of constructing the histogram of the portfolio returns based on the last 100 days of history or, equivalently, sorting the changes in portfolio values to identify the first percentile of the distribution. Table 7-5

---

[5] F. Black and M. Scholes, "The Pricing of Options and Corporate Liabilities," *Journal of Political Economy* 81, 1973, pp. 637–654; M. B. Garman and S. Kohlhagen, "Foreign Currency Option Values," *Journal of International Money and Finance* 2, December 1983, pp. 231–237.

TABLE 7-5 Identifying the First Percentile of the Historical Distribution of the Portfolio Return

Rank	Change from Current Value
100	−$0.05
99	−$0.07
98	−$0.11
. . .	. . .
2	+$0.07
1	+$0.08

shows the ranking of the changes in the value of the portfolio. Using this, we identify the first percentile as −$0.07.

Figure 7-4 shows the histogram of these values. VaR (1; 99) at the 99 percent confidence level is simply the distance to the mean ($0.01) of the first percentile—i.e., VaR (1; 99) = $0.08, while absolute VaR is the first percentile itself—i.e., VaR' (1; 99) = $0.07. Note that this histogram is similar to the histogram that we derived for daily trading revenues in Figure 7-2a.

This three-step procedure can easily be generalized to any portfolio of securities.

The major attraction of historical simulation is that the method is completely nonparametric (i.e., we don't need to worry about setting parameters) and does not depend on any assumptions about the distribution of the risk factors.

FIGURE 7-4 VaR from Historical Simulations

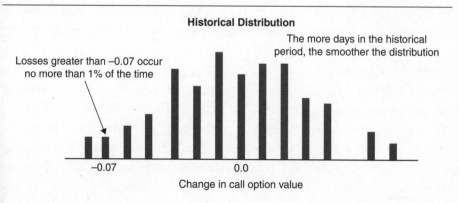

Historical Distribution

The more days in the historical period, the smoother the distribution

Losses greater than −0.07 occur no more than 1% of the time

−0.07   0.0

Change in call option value

In particular, we do not need to assume that the returns of the risk factors are normally distributed and independent over time.

The nonparametric nature of historical simulation also obviates the need to estimate volatilities and correlations. Historical volatilities and correlations are already reflected in the data set, so all we need to calculate are the synchronous risk factor returns over a given historical period. Historical simulation has also no problem accommodating fat tails in distributions because the historical returns already reflect actual synchronous moves in the market across all risk factors. Another advantage of historical simulation over the variance/covariance approach is that it allows the analyst to calculate confidence intervals for VaR.

The main drawback of historical simulation is its complete dependence on a particular set of historical data and thus on the idiosyncrasies of this data set. The underlying assumption is that the past, as captured in this historical data set, is a reliable representation of the future (i.e., the past is prologue). This implicitly presumes that the market events embedded in the historical data set will be reproduced in the months to come. However, the historical period may cover events, such as a market crash or, conversely, a period of exceptionally low price volatility, that are unlikely to be repeated in the future. Historical simulation may also lead to a distorted assessment of the risk if we employ the technique regardless of any structural changes anticipated in the market, such as the introduction of the euro in the foreign exchange markets at the beginning of 1999.

Another practical limitation of historical simulation is data availability. One year of data corresponds to only 250 data points (trading days) on average—i.e., 250 scenarios. By contrast, Monte Carlo simulations usually involve at least 10,000 simulations (i.e., scenarios). Employing small samples of historical data inevitably leaves gaps in the distributions of the risk factors and tends to underrepresent the tails of the distributions—i.e., the occurrence of unlikely but extreme events.

Monte Carlo Approach

Monte Carlo simulation consists of repeatedly simulating the random processes that govern market prices and rates. Each simulation (scenario) generates a possible value for the portfolio at the target horizon (e.g., 10 days). If we generate enough of these scenarios, the simulated distribution of the portfolio's values will converge toward the true, although unknown, distribution. The VaR can be easily inferred from the distribution, as we described earlier.

Monte Carlo simulation involves three steps:

1. *Specify all the relevant risk factors.* As in the other approaches, we need to select all the relevant risk factors. In addition, we have to specify the dynamics of these factors—i.e., their stochastic processes—and we need to estimate their parameters (volatilities, correlations, mean reversion factors for interest rate processes, and so on).

2. *Construct price paths.* Price paths are constructed using random numbers produced by a random number generator. For a simple portfolio without complex exotic options, the forward distribution of portfolio returns at a 10-day horizon can be generated in one step. Alternatively, if the simulation is performed on a daily basis, a random distribution is drawn for each day to calculate the 10-day cumulative impact.

   When several correlated risk factors are involved, we need to simulate multivariate distributions. Only in the case where the distributions are independent can the randomization be performed independently for each variable.

3. *Value the portfolio for each path (scenario).* Each path generates a set of values for the risk factors for each security in the portfolio that are used as inputs into the pricing models. The process is repeated a large number of times, say 10,000 times, to generate the distribution, at the risk horizon, of the portfolio return. This step is equivalent to the corresponding procedure for historical simulation, except that Monte Carlo simulation can generate many more scenarios than historical simulation.

VaR at the 99 percent confidence level is then simply derived as the distance to the mean of the first percentile of the distribution, as for our other calculation methods.

Monte Carlo simulation is a powerful and flexible approach to VaR. It can accommodate any distribution of risk factors to allow for fat-tailed distributions, where extreme events are expected to occur more commonly than in normal distributions, and "jumps" or discontinuities in price processes. For example, a process can be described as a mixture of two normal distributions or as a jump diffusion process where the number of jumps in any time interval is governed by, say, a Poisson process (both processes are consistent with fat tails).[6]

In a jump-diffusion process the underlying asset exhibits jumps in addition to having continuous diffusion paths.

Monte Carlo simulation, like historical simulation, allows the analyst to calculate the confidence interval of VaR—i.e., the range of likely values that VaR might take if we repeated the simulation many times. The narrower this confidence interval, the more precise the estimate of VaR. Monte Carlo simulation has a particular advantage here: it is easy to carry out sensitivity analyses by changing the market parameters used in the analysis, such as the term structure of interest rates.

One disadvantage of the Monte Carlo approach is that the analyst must be able to estimate the parameters of the distributions, such as the means, the variances, and the covariances. The major limitation of the approach, however, is more pragmatic: the amount of computer resources it consumes. Variance reduction techniques can be used to reduce the computational time, but Monte Carlo simulation remains very computer intensive and cannot be used to calculate the VaR of very large and complex portfolios.

Pros and Cons of the Different Approaches

Each of the approaches we have described has advantages and limitations; no single technique is "perfect," and no technique should be regarded as dominating the others.

For this reason, it is important that financial professionals and managers who rely on VaR numbers to measure risk—or to gain comfort about the risks that an institution is taking—be familiar with the basic principles of the VaR calculation. Increasingly, equity analysts and investors also need to understand these numbers if they are to assess the information that a bank makes public about its risk profile.

Tables 7-6a, 7-6b, and 7-6c summarize the pros and cons of the different approaches. Together with the information contained in this chapter, they can be used to frame questions about how any particular VaR number has been produced.

Above all, professionals using VaR numbers must remember that they are not a "magic bullet" for measuring and managing risk. In the right hands, VaR techniques help to offer risk analysts a rational and comparable snapshot of the risk of a particular position or portfolio. But like every financial measure, VaR numbers in the wrong hands can be used to mislead and obfuscate. Their reliability as a decision-making tool depends on the skill and experience of the analyst, the nature of the problem that is being explored, and the ability of decision makers to ask intelligent questions about meaning and provenance.

TABLE 7-6A Pros and Cons of the Variance/Covariance Approach

Pros	Cons
Computationally efficient; it takes only a few minutes to run the position of the entire bank.	Assumes normality of the return portfolio.
Because of central limit theorem, the methodology can be applied even if the risk factors are not normal, provided the factors are numerous and relatively independent.	Assumes that the risk factors follow a multivariate log normal distribution, and thus does not cope very well with "fat-tailed" distributions.
No pricing model is required; only the Greeks are necessary, and these can be provided directly by most of the systems that already exist within banks (i.e., the legacy systems).	Requires estimation of the volatilities of the risk factors as well as the correlations of their returns.
It is easy to handle incremental VaR.	Security returns can be approximated by means of a Taylor expansion. In some instances, however, a second-order expansion may not be sufficient to capture option risk (especially in the case of exotic options).
	Cannot be used to derive the confidence interval for VaR.

How Is VaR Used in Practice?

Given the different methodologies that can be applied to calculate VaR and the many different ways in which the results can be used, how is VaR used in practice by banks and other firms around the world?

As far as methodology is concerned, in practice banks are using all three methods. However, the historical simulation approach is by far the most popular.[7]

VaR is reported at the firm level but also in terms of individual risk categories, businesses, and geographic regions (see Figure 7-5).

---

[7]See the survey and discussion of industry practice regarding VaR in Amit Mehta et al., "Managing Market Risk: Today and Tomorrow," McKinsey Working Papers on Risk, No. 32, May 2012. According to this report, some 75 percent of the banks that participated in the survey use historical simulation and only 15 percent use Monte Carlo simulation. While Monte Carlo simulation is recognized as a better theoretical approach, it is viewed as too computationally intensive.

TABLE 7-6B Pros and Cons of the Historical Simulation Approach

Pros	Cons
No need to make any assumption about the distribution of the risk factors.	Complete dependence on a particular historical data set and its idiosyncrasies (past in prologue). For example, extreme events such as market crashes either lie outside the data set and are ignored or lie within the data set and (for some purposes) act to distort it.
No need to estimate volatilities and correlations; they are implicitly captured by the actual (synchronous) daily realizations of the market factors.	Cannot accommodate changes in the market structure, such as the introduction of the euro in January 1999.
Fat tails of distributions and other extreme events are captured so long as they are contained in the data set.	Short data set may lead to biased and imprecise estimation of VaR.
Aggregation across markets is straightforward.	Cannot be used to conduct sensitivity analyses.
Allows the calculation of confidence intervals for VaR.	Not always computationally efficient when the portfolio contains complex securities.

Firms use the VaR numbers for reporting purposes—e.g., to report exposure to market risk in their trading book (complying with Pillar III of Basel II). The numbers are also often used to calculate the regulatory capital the bank needs to hold against the trading book (complying with Pillar I).

TABLE 7-6C Pros and Cons of the Monte Carlo Simulation Approach

Pros	Cons
Can accommodate any distribution of risk factors.	Outliers are not incorporated into the distribution.
Can be used to model any complex portfolio.	Computer intensive.
Allows the calculation of confidence intervals for VaR.	
Allows the user to perform sensitivity analyses and stress testing.	

FIGURE 7-5 Examples of Detailed VaR Reporting

As of or for the year ended December 31, (in millions)	2012			2011			At December 31	
	Avg.	Min	Max	Avg.	Min	Max	2012	2011
CIB trading VaR by risk type								
Fixed income	$ 83 (a)	$ 47	$ 131	$ 50	$ 31	$ 68	$ 69	$ 49
Foreign exchange	10	6	22	11	6	19	8	19
Equities	21	12	35	23	15	42	22	19
Commodities and other	15	11	27	16	8	24	15	22
Diversification benefit to CIB trading VaR	(45) (b)	NM (c)	NM (c)	(42) (b)	NM (c)	NM (c)	(39) (b)	(55) (b)
CIB trading VaR	84	50	128	58	34	80	75	54
Credit portfolio VaR	25	16	42	33	19	55	18	42
Diversification benefit to CIB trading and credit portfolio VaR	(13) (b)	NM (c)	NM (c)	(15) (b)	NM (c)	NM (c)	(9) (b)	(20) (b)
Total CIB trading and credit portfolio VaR	96 (a)(c)	58	142	76	42	102	84 (a)(c)	76
Other VaR								
Mortgage Production and Mortgage Servicing VaR	17	8	43	30	6	98	24	16
Chief Investment Office ("CIO") VaR	92 (a)(d)	5	196	57	30	80	6	77
Diversification benefit to total other VaR	(8) (b)	NM (c)	NM (c)	(17) (b)	NM (c)	NM (c)	(5) (b)	(10) (b)
Total other VaR	101	18	204	70	46	110	25	83
Diversification benefit to total CIB and other VaR	(45) (b)	NM (c)	NM (c)	(45) (b)	NM (c)	NM (c)	(11) (b)	(46) (b)
Total VaR	$ 152	$ 93	$ 254	$ 101	$ 67	$ 147	$ 98	$ 113

(a) JP Morgan Chase: 2012 Annual Report (VaR based on historical simulation at the 95 percent confidence level using 12 months of daily data)

In millions	Year Ended December		
Risk Categories	2012	2011	2010
Interest rates	$78	$94	$93
Equity prices	26	33	68
Currency rates	14	20	32
Commodity prices	22	32	33
Diversification effect	(54)	(66)	(92)
Total	$86	$113	$134

(b) Goldman Sachs: 2012 Annual Report (VaR based on historical simulation at the 95 percent confidence level using five years of data with full valuation of approximately 70,000 market factors)

FIGURE 7-5 (Continued)

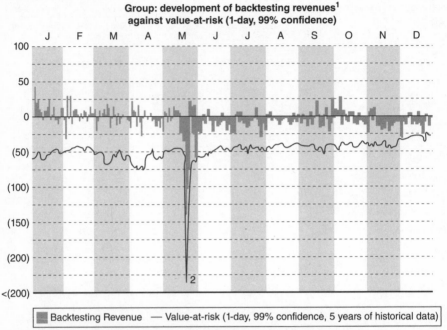

**Group: development of backtesting revenues[1]
against value-at-risk (1-day, 99% confidence)**

■ Backtesting Revenue — Value-at-risk (1-day, 99% confidence, 5 years of historical data)

1 Excludes non-trading revenues, such as commissions and fees, and revenues from intraday trading.
2 Due to previously disclosed incident related to the Facebook initial public offering.

(c) UBS: 2012 Annual Report (VaR calculated based on historical simulation using five years of data)

The daily average, maximum and minimum values of DVaR, Expected Shortfall and 3W (audited)

For the year ended 31 December	2012			2011		
DVaR (95%)	Average £m	High £m	Low £m	Average £m	High £m	Low £m
Interest rate risk	14	23	7	17	48	8
Inflation risk	3	7	2	4	9	2
Spread risk	23	31	17	25	40	17
Credit risk	26	44	18	29	48	17
Basis risk	11	21	5	6	6	6
Foreign exchange risk	6	10	2	5	8	2
Equity risk	9	19	4	18	34	9
Commodity risk	6	9	4	12	18	7
Diversification effect	(60)	na	na	(54)	na	na
Total DVaR	38	75	27	57	88	33
Expected Shortfall	47	91	30	71	113	43
3W[c]	77	138	44	121	202	67

(d) Barclays: 2012 Annual Report (Daily VaR (DVaR) based on historical simulation at the 95 percent confidence level using two years of data). Note that Barclays shows the expected shortfall (ES) and an additional measure of tail risk, 3W, which is the average of the worst three losses during the year.

Supplementing VaR: The Expected Shortfall Approach

One of the biggest criticisms of VaR is inherent in the methodology. VaR does not attempt to offer any indication of how large or frequent a loss might be once the loss exceeds the VaR number—i.e., VaR fails to capture what is known as "tail risk."[8]

For example, we might hope that a portfolio with a VaR of $100 million at the 99 percent confidence level is unlikely to experience losses above $100 million more often than once every 100 days (i.e., 1 percent of the time), or two to three times in one year. Even supposing the VaR is accurately estimated, we can therefore *expect* losses of over $100 million on around three trading days for any particular year. "Expected shortfall" (ES), also called "conditional VaR" (CVaR), is an alternative risk measure that gives an indication of the magnitude of the potential losses in the tail:

$$ES = \text{Expected loss beyond VaR (i.e., the expected loss } given \text{ that the loss exceeds the VaR)}[9]$$

ES then measures the downside risk beyond VaR at a given confidence level.

Taking account of tail risk using ES is likely to become a critical capability in many institutions. In its "Fundamental Review of the Trading Book," published in 2012, the Basel Committee even went so far as to propose adopting this risk metric in lieu of VaR.

Measuring ES

Different approaches can be applied to estimate VaR and ES simultaneously.

- For a normal distribution, VaR and ES can be derived directly from the volatility of the portfolio return distribution. For example, assuming zero expected profit/loss and confidence levels of 95 and 99 percent, then VaR can be found directly from the statistical table for the normal

---

[8]For a discussion of stress VaR, see Chapter 3.

[9]Expected shortfall is a conditional expectation. It is obtained by dividing the probability-weighted average of the losses beyond VaR by the probability of the losses beyond VaR—i.e., $1-\alpha$, where α is the confidence level. See C. Alexander, *Market Risk Analysis: Vol. IV. Value-at-Risk Models*, Wiley, 2009.

distribution, which shows quantile values of 1.65 and 2.33, respectively. The corresponding ES are 2.06 and 2.67, respectively. These values will be higher than the corresponding VaR at the same confidence levels.

- When VaR is derived from a Monte Carlo simulation with 100,000 runs (scenarios), then ES at the 99 percent confidence level is simply the average value of the 1,000 worst-case scenarios.
- A more sophisticated approach, known as "Extreme Value Theory," consists of fitting the tail of the historical distribution of the portfolio returns to a fat-tail distribution called a Generalized Pareto Distribution (GPD). Once the GPD has been calibrated, VaR and ES can be derived analytically.

Conclusion: Embedding VaR in a Wider Risk Management Framework

VaR is far from being a perfect or complete measure of risk—no such thing exists. The use and reliability of VaR is often dictated by the availability of data—for instance, on volatilities and correlations.[10] And to facilitate the implementation of a VaR model, especially in the case of the analytic variance/covariance and Monte Carlo approaches, it is common to assume that market conditions will remain stationary. Prices and values are assumed to have a "smooth" behavior that excludes the possibility of jumps and other extreme events.

This makes VaR an unreliable risk metric at times of crisis and disruption. For example, in the third quarter of 2007 after the subprime crisis erupted, major banks reported a number of VaR exceptions way beyond what might be expected under normal conditions (i.e., two or three each year on average at the 99 percent confidence level). Credit Suisse declared 11 exceptions, Bear Stearns 10, and UBS 16; Lehman Brothers declared 3, Goldman Sachs 5, and Morgan Stanley 6, with the VaR of the three last banks being calculated at the 95 confidence level.[11]

---

[10]We should separate out issues with VaR as a conceptual model and as an implemented risk metric. In essence, VaR is a conceptual approach telling the user to look at the left-hand tail of the distribution of returns. As such, it does not specify that any particular statistical procedure should be applied to derive the distribution. If the wrong statistical procedure is applied, the VaR number can be wrong and misleading.

[11]"VaR Counts," *Risk Magazine*, January 2008, pp. 68–71.

We don't yet know how to construct a VaR model that would combine, in a meaningful way, periods of normal market conditions with periods of market crises characterized by large price changes, high volatility, and a breakdown in the correlations among the risk factors. Another problem is that VaR is usually calculated within a static framework and is therefore appropriate only for relatively short time horizons, which in turn means that we can't include dynamic liquidity risks in the VaR analysis.

This does not mean that VaR is of little use as a risk metric; its critics are sometimes in danger of throwing the baby out with the bath water. It does mean that VaR needs to be carefully applied and the results interpreted by decision makers who understand the necessary limitations of VaR numbers. It also means that gaining a fuller picture of risk requires supplemental risk measures, such as stress testing and scenario analysis, to analyze the possible effects of extreme events that lie outside normal market conditions. The many different dimensions of risk require a range of complementary risk metrics, and always have done.

8

ASSET/LIABILITY MANAGEMENT

Asset/liability management (ALM) is the structured decision-making process for matching, and deliberately mismatching, the mix of assets (e.g., loans) and liabilities (e.g., deposits) on a firm's balance sheet.

ALM is particularly critical for financial institutions, such as commercial banks, savings and loans, insurance companies, and pension funds. Banks, for example, are involved in collecting deposits and extending loans to retail and corporate clients. This financial intermediation activity generates two types of imbalances: first, an imbalance between the amount of funds collected and lent, and second, an imbalance between the maturities as well as the interest rate sensitivities of the sources of funding and the loans extended to clients.

These imbalances drive the net worth of the bank—and its risk profile. For example, deposits generally have a shorter maturity than loans, so the net worth of many banks benefits from a fall in interest rates: the bank pays *less* interest to its depositors but continues for a period to receive the *higher* rate from its borrowers. Conversely, the net worth of the same bank will tend to deteriorate if interest rates go up. If this downside risk is not managed, it can lead to insolvency in individual institutions or even in whole banking industries. Likewise, the mismatching of assets and liabilities almost inevitably leads to a degree of liquidity risk—the greater the mismatch, the more difficult it is to ensure the institution has cash on hand to fulfill all of its commitments immediately in any conceivable circumstance (e.g., the return of on-demand deposits).

It is this last point that has made ALM, and specifically liquidity risk management, such a key risk topic over the last few years, following the 2007–2009 financial crisis. As we'll describe later in this chapter, many of the institutions that were at the epicenter of the crisis combined high leverage with severe maturity mismatches, while failing to compensate for this with robust funding liquidity risk management. As a result, Basel III seeks to restrict bank leverage and also introduces two significant mechanisms to enforce improvements in bank liquidity. Box 8-1 looks at these reforms and highlights some strategic implications for the financial industry and the practice of ALM. In some countries, such as the United Kingdom, proposals to ring-fence retail banks from riskier activities, such as investment banking, may also have implications for the practice of ALM.

BOX 8-1   BASEL III'S LIQUIDITY RISK MECHANISMS: STRATEGIC IMPLICATIONS

Basel III introduces an entirely new framework for managing bank liquidity risk by means of two key mechanisms:

- The *liquidity coverage ratio (LCR)* requires that banks maintain high-quality liquid assets sufficient to withstand a 30-day stressed funding scenario specified by supervisors. The stress scenario will include a number of shocks, such as the run-off of a proportion of retail deposits, the partial loss of unsecured short-term financing, rating downgrade, and so on.
- The *net stable funding ratio (NSFR)* is a longer-term (one-year) structural ratio designed to address liquidity mismatches and reduce reliance on wholesale funding.

These mechanisms, described in more detail in Chapter 3, are being phased in over a number of years, and their exact nature is still under discussion. One problem is that the new liquidity standards will affect the profitability of banks and reduce their capacity to finance the economy. To mitigate this, the Basel Committee decided in January 2013 to revise its original conception of the LCR (expanding the range of assets classified as high-quality liquid assets, modifying the calculation of net cash outflows, and phasing in the new standard more gradually, from January 1, 2015).

The next priority of the Basel Committee will be to reexamine the NSFR before it is applied in 2018, not least because European banks are more involved in maturity intermediation than their U.S. counterparts, so meeting the NSFR rule will increase funding costs and may oblige them to reduce the maturity and size of loans that they offer.

The difficulty the regulators are finding in reaching the right balance between bank lending capacity and bank risk management mirrors, in larger form, the kind of strategic trade-off faced every day by ALM committees in banks around the world. However, while some of the details of the Basel III mechanisms may change, the regulators learned painful lessons during the 2007–2009 financial crisis.

Going forward, the banking industry will have to take seriously the need to hold significant emergency liquidity reserves and to address structural funding weaknesses. Certain bank business models will, in effect, be ruled out.

Banks' earnings are particularly sensitive to changes in interest rates and the cost of funds. But many ALM principles apply equally to corporations outside the financial sector whose assets and liabilities are sensitive to market risk factors. In this chapter, we first look briefly at the goals and scope of ALM and at the nature of the two main focuses of ALM, interest rate and liquidity risk management. We then explain in more detail the role of the ALCO (asset/liability management committee) responsible for coordinating the management of the firm's balance sheet and look at the techniques applied to assess interest rate risk in the balance sheet—i.e., gap analysis, duration gap/duration of equity, and long-term VaR. Finally, we discuss funds transfer pricing and liquidity debits and credits.

ALM Goals, Scope, Techniques, and Responsibilities

In the banking industry, the three key goals of ALM are to:

- Stabilize net interest income (NII)—that is, the difference between the amount the bank pays out in interest for funding and the amount it receives from holding assets such as loans (as measured by accounting earnings).

- Maximize shareholder value or net worth (NW), as reflected in long-term economic earnings.
- Make sure the bank doesn't assume too much risk from the mismatching of maturities and amounts between assets and liabilities and from funding liquidity risk (the danger that the bank won't be able to raise funds quickly and cheaply enough to fulfill its obligations and remain solvent).

These three key objectives give ALM a very wide scope, which can include managing market risk (i.e., interest rate risk, foreign exchange risk, commodity price risk, and equity price risk), liquidity risk, trading risk, funding and capital planning, taxation, and regulatory constraints, as well as profitability and growth. ALM also involves off-balance-sheet activity, such as the use of hedges designed to offset interest rate exposures. The scope and importance of ALM explain why the ALM committee has often evolved into the senior risk committee of each bank.

While value-at-risk (VaR) is the technique adopted by most financial institutions to control market and credit risk in the trading book, ALM involves a distinct set of techniques used to control risk in the banking book, such as gap analysis, duration gap analysis, and long-term VaR. The difference in techniques is driven by the fact that most of the assets and liabilities in the banking book have long maturities and are much less liquid than are traded financial instruments. Liquidity risk management is an important discipline within ALM that has many of its own tools, including specialized cash flow analysis and liquidity stress testing.

ALM strategy is the responsibility of the treasurer of the company, but the control of the *risk* in the balance sheet is typically a part of the mandate of the risk management function—and should remain independent of the risk takers. ALM management typically operates under the assumption that there is no credit risk (e.g., loans do not default), leaving credit risk under the purview of the groups within risk management who are responsible for managing corporate and retail credit risk.

Interest Rate Risk

Interest rate risk is a critical focus for financial institutions because it has a direct impact on:

- *Net interest income (NII):* i.e., interest earned less interest paid on interest-bearing assets and liabilities. NII, traditionally a key indicator of bank profitability, is affected by the pricing mismatches of assets and liabilities (on- and off-balance-sheet). The impact of interest rate volatility on NII is usually analyzed over a short time horizon, such as one quarter or one year, and is referred to as earnings-at-risk (EaR). It relies essentially on accounting data.

- *Net worth (NW):* i.e., the net present value of assets minus the net present value of liabilities, plus or minus the net present value of off-balance-sheet items. Net worth analysis is meant to provide an economic measure of shareholders' wealth, and it should also provide an institution with early warning of potential solvency problems. The impact of interest rates on NW is considered over a relatively long time horizon.

- *Noninterest income:* The income from servicing loans and other fee-based income is known in the financial industries as "noninterest income," but it, too, can be affected by interest rate fluctuations. For example, a change in interest rates might affect mutual fund sales fees, fees from securities lending, mortgage and loan application fees, refinancing fees, securitization fees, and so on.

Although, over the last few years, a lot of regulatory attention has been focused on funding liquidity risk, interest rate risk has precipitated the failure of banks and even whole industries (Box 8-2). The effectiveness of the banking industry's interest rate risk management is likely to be tested again when developed economies begin to recover and central banks reduce their strategies of monetary easing—leading to a rise in both absolute interest rates and, perhaps, to interest rate volatility.

To mitigate interest rate risk, the structure of the balance sheet has to be managed in such a way that the effect on assets of any movement of interest rates remains highly correlated with its effect on liabilities, even in a volatile interest rate environment. The amount of earnings volatility that is acceptable will depend on the risk appetite of the institution; the board may well approve risk limits to constrain earnings volatility resulting from interest rate volatility. These limits are generally based on worst-case scenarios, such as a 200-basis-point (bp) parallel shift in interest rates across all maturities (up and down); each scenario can be considered in relation to its impact on NII (accounting profit), NW, and capital-to-asset ratio. To take a rather

---

BOX 8-2 THE SAVINGS AND LOAN CRISIS

The savings and loan (S&L) industry in the United States prospered through most of the twentieth century thanks to the upward-sloping shape of the yield curve. The upward-sloping curve meant that the interest rate on a 10-year residential mortgage (a typical product offered by S&Ls) exceeded rates on the short-maturity savings and time deposits that were the S&L's main source of funding. In the banking industry's vocabulary, S&Ls simply had to "ride the curve" to make money.

However, during the period October 1979 to October 1982, the Fed's restrictive monetary policy led to a sudden and dramatic surge in interest rates, with the yield from Treasury bills rising as high as 16 percent. The increase in short-term rates pushed up the cost of funds for S&Ls, sweeping away the interest rate margin they depended on. Indeed, in this period, the spike in their cost of funding meant that S&Ls generated *negative* net interest margins on many of their long-term residential mortgage portfolios.

The failure of the S&Ls to manage their interest rate risk helped to spark the long-running S&L crisis in the United States, which gathered force through the 1980s as S&Ls desperately sought to repair their balance sheets with new business activities and risky lending—only to find themselves losing even more money through poorly controlled credit and business risk. Ultimately, a large number of S&Ls failed or were taken over, especially in 1988 and 1989. The number of S&Ls fell from 4,000 to 2,600 between 1980 and 1989, and the crisis necessitated one of the world's most expensive banking system bailouts—courtesy of the American taxpayer.

Over the 1986–1995 period, 1,043 thrifts with total assets of more than $500 billion failed. The thrift crises cost taxpayers $124 billion and the thrift industry another $24 billion, for an estimated total loss of $153 billion.

---

simple and static example, the board might approve a limit for a plausible worst-case scenario at a maximum negative impact of $1 billion on the NW of the institution, $100 million on NII for the quarter, and $300 million on NII for the year.

As we'll see later in this chapter, some banks use sophisticated computer simulations that determine the impact on NII and NW of numerous interest rate scenarios, balance sheet trends, and strategies over various time horizons. These more complex simulations may specify strategies for originating funds through retail products (e.g., through attracting more deposits) and for the refinancing of maturing liabilities.

Foreign exchange risk and commodity risk can also be important components of balance sheet risk management, depending on the institution's activities.

Funding Liquidity Risk

Funding liquidity risks can stem from external market conditions or structural problems within the bank's balance sheet—most often a combination of both. The collapse of Bear Stearns and Lehman Brothers in 2008 at the height of the 2007–2009 financial crisis (Box 8-3) and the near collapse of the giant hedge fund Long-Term Capital Management (LTCM) a decade earlier in 1998 (see Chapter 15) offer examples of funding liquidity crises that were prompted by unexpected external conditions, but which also exposed vulnerabilities inherent in the institutions' business models.

BOX 8-3   LIQUIDITY CRISIS AT LEHMAN BROTHERS

On September 15, 2008, Lehman Brothers, one of the top U.S. investment banks, filed for bankruptcy in the largest such proceedings ever seen.[1] Over the previous decade, the 150-year-old institution had become heavily invested in the U.S. real estate market, helping to pioneer an integrated business model in which it sold mortgages to residential customers,[2] turned these into highly rated securities using financial engineering, and then sold the securities to investors.

---

[1]Report of Anton Valukas, Examiner, to the United States Bankruptcy Court, RE Lehman Brothers Holdings Inc., March 11, 2010.

[2]To this end, in the early years of the millennium, Lehman had acquired a number of mortgage lenders, including BNC Mortgage (subprime) and Aurora Loan Services (an Alt-A loans provider).

As the U.S. real estate markets began to turn sour in 2006 and 2007, after years of a booming economy and rising house prices, Lehman continued to build its real-estate-linked businesses and to increase the amount of mortgage-related assets it held as longer-term investments (rather than simply acting as a middle man).[3]

As part of this change of business model and its aggressive growth strategy, the bank had also begun to make outsized bets on U.S. commercial real estate. But if Lehman's business model looked like a risky bet on the U.S. economy and housing market, it was the firm's leverage ratio and funding strategy that threatened to turn it into a disaster.

Banks are naturally highly leveraged entities—i.e., they take on a large amount of debt rather than equity to fund their activities. However, in the run-up to the 2007–2009 crisis, Lehman, like other investment banks in the boom years, pursued this to excess, with a ratio of assets to equity of around 31:1 in 2007.

Meanwhile, the bank's funding strategy—the way it borrowed money to grow its operations—introduced a fatal element of fragility. The bank was borrowing huge amounts of money in the short-term markets—e.g., borrowing daily from the repo markets—to fund potentially illiquid long-term real estate assets. This meant that Lehman depended on maintaining the confidence of its funders and bank counterparties if it was to continue to borrow and stay in business.[4]

During 2007 it became evident that the U.S. housing bubble had burst and that the subprime market was in deep trouble. Confidence began to erode in firms depending on subprime securitization as a business model or investment strategy. In March 2008, Bear Stearns, another highly leveraged subprime-linked firm, collapsed after a loss of confidence by its repo lenders and bank counterparties and had to be acquired by JP Morgan.

---

[3]"Mortgage-related assets on Lehman's books increased from $67 billion in 2006 to $111 billion in 2007," Financial Crisis Inquiry Commission, *The Financial Crisis Inquiry Report*, January 2011, p. 177.

[4]When investment banks came under close scrutiny in 2007–2008, it was tempting for them to play down their leverage: "According to the bankruptcy examiner, Lehman understated its leverage through "Repo 105" transactions—an accounting maneuver to temporarily remove assets from the balance sheet before each reporting period." Financial Crisis Inquiry Commission, *The Financial Crisis Inquiry Report*, January 2011, p. 177.

In the months following, investors began to doubt Lehman's ability to survive and to question how it valued its real estate assets. The confidence so critical to the firm's funding strategy, and therefore its liquidity, was ebbing fast.

As the crisis mounted, the firm's major counterparties began to demand more collateral for funding transactions, others began reducing their exposure, and some institutions simply refused to deal with the firm.

Attempts to organize an industry rescue or sell the firm to another large bank failed: at 1:45 a.m. on September 15, 2008, Lehman Brothers filed for bankruptcy, presaging months of panic and uncertainty in the world's financial markets.

The case of Continental Illinois Bank (Box 8-4), which had to be rescued in 1984 after investors began to worry about the condition of the bank's credit portfolio and cut off short-term funding, is an example of how internal credit portfolio problems can precipitate a funding liquidity crisis. This was then exacerbated by weaknesses in the institution's funding strategy.

BOX 8-4   LIQUIDITY CRISIS AT CONTINENTAL ILLINOIS

Continental Illinois was the largest bank in Chicago, and one of the largest in the United States, before it had to be rescued by regulatory agencies in May 1984 after a massive liquidity crisis.

The bank had been pursuing a growth strategy since the late 1970s, and in the five years prior to 1981 its commercial and industrial lending jumped from approximately $5 billion to more than $14 billion (and total assets grew from $21.5 billion to $45 billion).

The first sign of Continental's problems surfaced with the closing of Penn Square Bank in Oklahoma. This smaller bank had been issuing loans to oil and natural gas companies in Oklahoma during the oil and natural gas boom of the late 1970s. It passed large loans that it could not service through to substantial institutions such as Continental Illinois. But as prices for oil and gas dropped from 1981 onward, some of the oil and natural gas companies began to default on their debt, and in 1982 U.S. regulators stepped in to close Penn Square.

Continental was the largest participant in Penn Square's oil and gas loans (more than $1 billion) and suffered heavy losses on those loans, as well as on loans in its own loan portfolio. Many other banks also suffered credit losses in this period, but Continental was unusual in that it had only a small retail banking operation and a relatively small amount of core deposits. It relied primarily on federal funds and on issuing large certificates of deposit to fund its lending business.

When Penn Square failed, Continental found itself increasingly unable to fund its operations from the U.S. markets and turned to raising money in foreign wholesale money markets, such as Japan, at much higher rates.

But when rumors about Continental's still worsening financial condition spooked the international markets in May 1984, the bank's foreign investors quickly began to withdraw the funds deposited in the bank ($6 billion in 10 days). In a matter of a few days, Continental Illinois was confronted with a full-blown liquidity crisis, obliging the U.S. regulatory authorities to step in to avoid the danger of a domino effect on other banks—which they feared might put the entire U.S. banking system at risk.

More recently, the failure of Northern Rock, a U.K. mortgage bank, in September 2007, soon after the start of the subprime crisis, is another illustration of liquidity risk related to structural weaknesses in the bank's business model (Box 8-5). The combination of excessive short-term financing of long-term assets and the sudden loss of market confidence in the financial strength of the institution triggered a funding liquidity crisis that rapidly led to disaster.[1]

---

[1] In the summer of 2008, California's IndyMac also suffered a bank run. IndyMac's weakness was more conventional: poor underwriting and increasing difficulties in selling on the mortgages that the bank had originated.

BOX 8-5   NORTHERN ROCK: LIQUIDITY AND BUSINESS MODELS

Northern Rock, a fast-growing medium-sized mortgage bank based in Newcastle upon Tyne in the northeast of England, was brought down by a bank run in mid-September 2007—at the very start of the 2007–2009 financial crisis.

The bank had been growing assets at around 20 percent a year for a number of years, specializing in residential mortgages, and it continued to expand aggressively in the marketplace into the first quarter of 2007.

The bank's rate of growth was supported by a business model and funding strategy that was unusual among U.K. banks. From around 2000, the bank developed an "originate to distribute" approach, under which it raised money through securitizing mortgages, selling covered bonds, and making use of the wholesale funding markets. Northern Rock soon relied much more heavily on investors and wholesale markets (and less on retail deposits) for its funding than many of its U.K. peers.

To mitigate possible weaknesses in this funding strategy, the bank tried to diversify its funding markets geographically. For example, it tapped markets in Europe and America as well as the United Kingdom.[1]

However, the bank had miscalculated. After years of strong economies and rising house prices, widespread doubts began to surface about mortgage-related assets among investors during early 2007. The doubts were triggered initially by rising default rates in the U.S. subprime market, but soon spread to asset-backed securities as an investment class, to institutions that invested in or depended on securitizations, and eventually to the interbank markets.

When the funding market freeze arrived in early August 2007, all of Northern Rock's global funding channels seized up simultaneously in a scenario that the bank's executives later claimed was "unforeseeable."

Ironically, earlier in the summer of 2007, the bank had announced increased interim dividends after a Basel II waiver had been approved by U.K. regulators, allowing the bank to adopt advanced approaches to

---

[1]See comments by Adam Applegarth, ex-CEO of Northern Rock, to the House of Commons, Treasury Committee, *The Run on the Rock*, January 2008, p. 15.

calculating credit risk that looked likely to reduce its minimum required regulatory capital.[2]

After the funding markets froze, the U.K. authorities discussed various strategies to relieve the bank's difficulties. However, news of the Bank of England's planned support operation for Northern Rock leaked and was reported by the BBC, setting the scene for a run on deposits between 14 and 17 September. The panic was exacerbated by the tight rules then in place for compensating depositors,[3] and calm only slowly returned after a public promise from the U.K. authorities that deposits would be repaid. Northern Rock accepted emergency government support and then public ownership.

---

[2]Though the timing of the waiver later embarrassed the bank and its regulators, it was not a significant factor in the loss of confidence in the bank.

[3]At the time, deposits were fully guaranteed only up to £2,000, with a further guarantee of 90 percent of sums up to a ceiling of £33,000.

Box 8-6 sets out some sound practices put forward by the U.S. regulatory agencies in an attempt to counter the pre-crisis weaknesses of bank liquidity management. The U.S. Federal Reserve has also begun to run liquidity stress testing programs for the largest banks in order to make sure the banks have liquidity and funding strategies that will survive systemwide stressful scenarios.[2]

In essence, the challenge of managing funding liquidity risk lies in optimizing the borrowing capacity of the firm and in coordinating contractual maturities of assets and liabilities (either directly or synthetically through the use of derivatives, primarily interest rate swaps). However, like most complicated decisions, asset/liability management decisions are driven by trade-offs. For example:

---

[2]The so-called "C-Lar" program. See Shahien Nasiripour, "Fed Begins Stress Tests on Bank Liquidity," *Financial Times*, December 13, 2012.

BOX 8-6   SOUND PRACTICES OF LIQUIDITY RISK MANAGEMENT: U.S. INTERAGENCY POLICY STATEMENT

- Effective corporate governance consisting of oversight by the board of directors and active involvement by management in an institution's control of liquidity risk
- Appropriate strategies, policies, procedures, and limits used to manage and mitigate liquidity risk
- Comprehensive liquidity risk measurement and monitoring systems (including assessments of the current and prospective cash flows or sources and uses of funds) that are commensurate with the complexity and business activities of the institution
- Active management of intraday liquidity and collateral
- An appropriately diverse mix of existing and potential future funding sources
- Adequate levels of highly liquid marketable securities free of legal, regulatory, or operational impediments, that can be used to meet liquidity needs in stressful situations
- Comprehensive contingency funding plans (CFPs) that sufficiently address potential adverse liquidity events and emergency cash flow requirements
- Internal controls and internal audit processes sufficient to determine the adequacy of the institution's liquidity risk management process

Source: U.S. Interagency Policy Statement on Funding and Liquidity Risk Management, March 17, 2010, pp. 2–3.

- There is a trade-off between funding liquidity and interest rate risk: short-term liabilities (assets) carry less interest rate risk and higher funding liquidity risk than longer-term liabilities (assets).
- There is also a trade-off between cost and risk. For example, in order to mitigate funding liquidity risk in a positively sloped yield curve environment, institutions can increase the maturity of their funding liabilities, but this will clearly cost them more than will cheaper shorter-term funding.

Banks might also mitigate funding liquidity risk by reducing the maturity of their assets (such as their commercial loans), but this is not always possible because asset maturity is often driven by the nature of the bank's business and its competitive environment.

As it is not possible to optimize and coordinate with perfection, firms also need emergency funding liquidity cushions to make sure they can meet their commitments. The larger and the better the quality of the funding liquidity cushion, the lower the risk; however, this comes at a cost because highly liquid and marketable assets yield lower returns than less liquid assets. Again, therefore, there is a significant trade-off to be made between pursuing a risky strategy (in funding liquidity terms) and the cost (in terms of funding strategies and funding liquidity reserves). Box 8-7 sets out some of the key components of funding liquidity risk monitoring and management. It makes clear the range of activities that are necessary if a bank is to achieve the right balance in its strategic decisions on liquidity risk management.

BOX 8-7 LIQUIDITY RISK MANAGEMENT AND MONITORING: KEY ACTIVITIES AND CONSIDERATIONS

Cash flow and contractual maturity mismatch analysis: Banks need to analyze how cash flow develops across various time periods to examine their liquidity requirements. The analysis should be extended to include a series of stressed scenarios.

Funding concentration and diversification: Banks need to look at where their funding comes from (e.g., on-demand deposits), at the "stickiness" of these funds, and at the diversity of that funding across various dimensions (e.g., number of names, but more important, product type, counterparty type, and nature of funding market).

Monitoring liquidity ratios: Banks can keep a close eye on a series of key ratios such as wholesale funding to total liabilities, particular types of short-term borrowings, and so on.

Monitoring asset concentrations: Banks need to monitor at the enterprise level for too much investment in particularly illiquid (e.g., complex, structured) and unsalable assets and act to limit concentrations even when this threatens business models (e.g., of bank divisions or the bank as a whole).

Monitoring contingent liabilities: For example, lines of credit and similar liabilities can represent a threat to liquidity (i.e., if they cannot be canceled).

Liquidity reserves or cushions: Banks should draw up a list of unencumbered assets that, crucially, would remain salable in a series of stressed scenarios, together with the relevant haircuts to the value of each asset.

Currency considerations: Foreign currency exchange risk can contribute to liquidity risk in stressed conditions.

Behavioral and structural assumptions: Banks must be wary about assuming that behaviors in normal markets, or even during historical crises, will determine all future behaviors (e.g., degree of depositor stickiness in a crisis), especially where markets have changed in size, structure, or participant profile.

Early warning mechanisms: Banks can monitor for potential liquidity difficulties in funding markets and in markets where they might need to sell assets to raise cash during a crisis.

Sources: Various, including Basel III: A Global Regulatory Framework for More Resilient Banks and Banking Systems, December 2010 (rev. June 2011), pp. 9–10; U.S. Interagency Policy Statement on Funding and Liquidity Risk Management, March 17, 2010, pp. 4–5.

It follows from our discussion that all the components of an ALM policy are linked together—interest rate risk management, funding liquidity risk management, profit planning, product pricing, capital management, and fundamental business strategies—and must be part of a holistic and integrated approach to balance sheet management.

ALCO

The asset/liability management committee (ALCO) is the traditional name in the banking industry for what is often known today as the senior risk committee. ALCO is typically chaired by the CEO and composed of the senior executive team of the bank along with key executives in the risk management and treasury groups. This key corporate governance committee might meet once a week to review the risk positions of the bank, discuss specific risk-related issues, and endorse policy decisions proposed by the chief risk officer (CRO), such as trading and lending limits. (Chapter 4 discusses risk committee organization in more detail.)

While the senior risk committee is the structure through which coordination of the institution's risk management takes place, ALCO, in its more restrictive definition, is a subcommittee, cochaired by the CRO and the treasurer, that gives a strategic direction in terms of product mix, pricing, and risk profile.

Each operating entity in the bank assesses the structural interest rate risks that arise in its business and transfers such risks to its local treasury unit for management, or transfers the risks to separate books managed by the local ALCO. The risks can then be managed through:

- On-balance-sheet business strategies that involve changes in the product mix and pricing of loans, deposits, and other borrowings. These are *core* business decisions.
- On-balance-sheet investment or funding strategies that involve changes in the maturity mix and rate characteristics of investment securities and of wholesale funding. These are *discretionary* business decisions.
- Off-balance-sheet strategies that involve the use of off-balance-sheet items, such as derivatives, to manage balance sheet risks.

As an example, let us suppose that a bank has a balance sheet composed of floating-rate deposits and fixed-rate loans. This exposes the bank to interest rate risk—namely, if rates increase, it will have to pay out more to attract depositors, and its profitability will decline.

To achieve the right product mix, it may be necessary for the institution to restructure its assets or liabilities (or possibly both). It may also have to reprice its retail products to make them more or less attractive to customers:

- Asset restructuring involves reducing the proportion of fixed-rate assets and increasing the proportion of floating-rate assets. This can be achieved by increasing the interest rate the bank charges on fixed-rate assets and reducing the rate the bank charges on floating-rate assets.

- Liability restructuring involves increasing the proportion of fixed-rate liabilities and reducing the proportion of floating-rate liabilities. This can be achieved by offering a higher rate on fixed-rate liabilities and a reduced rate on floating-rate liabilities.
- The institution can also enter into an interest rate swap that pays a fixed rate and receives floating rates; this swap has the effect of converting a portion of the bank's floating-rate debt to a fixed-rate resource to reduce the potential impact of an increase in interest rates.

It's easier to implement a hedging strategy than it is to change the firm's business strategy, but a number of factors affect the decision on how to manage a bank's interest rate risk profile.

Entering into derivatives transactions such as swaps, options, or futures is simple, easy, and fast. However, it requires the proper back- and front-office infrastructures to monitor those transactions and assess their risks.

Likewise, some firms have policies that limit the use of derivatives, or operate in countries where derivatives markets are not yet developed. These firms have to manage their interest rate risk by changing the product mix and pricing in their business strategy, in a way that is consistent with customer needs.

We can see from our discussion so far that ALM involves answering three critical risk-related questions:

- *How much risk do we want to take?* Answering this question is a function of the risk appetite of the firm.
- *How much risk do we have now?* Answering this question means developing tools to measure the risks of the firm's assets and liabilities.
- *How do we move from where we are now to where we want to be?* Answering this question involves the execution of cost-effective risk management strategies of the kind we outlined earlier.

In the next sections we describe some tools used by financial institutions to measure their balance sheet sensitivity to interest rate changes. The first tools we'll look at are simple approaches; they provide partial, though useful, answers to complicated questions.

Gap Analysis

Most banks use gap analysis to measure interest rate risk in their balance sheets. The *gap* is defined as the difference between the amounts of rate-sensitive assets and rate-sensitive liabilities maturing or repricing within a specific time period. In other words:

$$\text{Gap} = \text{rate-sensitive assets (RSA)} - \text{rate-sensitive liabilities (RSL)}$$

A firm is said to have a *positive gap* within a specific time period when its rate-sensitive assets exceed its rate-sensitive liabilities—i.e., "assets reprice before liabilities," in the professional jargon. It describes the case in which an institution's short-term assets are funded by long-term liabilities. An increase (decrease) in interest rates leads to an increase (decrease) in NII.

When the gap is negative, we refer to it as "liabilities reprice before assets." It describes the case in which the institution's long-term assets are funded with short-term liabilities. An increase (decrease) in interest rates leads to a decrease (increase) in NII. This is typically the case for financial intermediaries operating in an interest rate environment where the yield curve has a positive slope. Financial institutions are then said to "ride the yield curve" by borrowing on short maturities and lending long-term: the positive spread between short-term and long-term rates generates a profit margin as long as rates remain stable. This profit margin is, however, at risk when rates start to move up (Box 8-2).

In Table 8-1 and Figure 8-1 we show the values at maturity, or at repricing time, of assets and liabilities for each time period, and the gap between them. Traditionally, banks put numbers around their positive and negative gap risk by means of a detailed gap analysis. Table 8-1 illustrates the concept of gap and "cumulative gap" in such an analysis.

TABLE 8-1 Gap Analysis

Maturity Period	1	2	3	4	5	6	7	8	Total
Assets	100	120	150	200	50	60	70	50	800
Liabilities	20	30	40	50	100	200	150	210	800
Gap	80	90	110	150	−50	−140	−80	−160	
Cumulative gap	80	170	280	430	380	240	160	0	

The bar chart in Figure 8-1 depicts assets with positive bars and liabilities with negative bars, and also tracks the cumulative gap. The positive cumulative gap bars in Figure 8-1 indicate that the institution has borrowed long-term and lent short-term. Negative cumulative gap bars would indicate the reverse— i.e., that the institution has funded long-term assets with short-term liabilities. Observe that the cumulative gap at the end of the eighth period equals zero since the assets must equal liabilities across the sum of all the buckets.

Putting this kind of gap analysis into practice involves:

- *Slotting on- and off-balance-sheet items into different time buckets.* The length of the time buckets depends on the composition of the balance sheet and the maturity mix of assets and liabilities. Generally, narrow buckets are used for short-term items and wide buckets are used for long-term items. The length of the buckets varies according to the type of institution. For example, a commercial bank typically uses the following gap structure: up to one month, over one month and up to three months, over three months and up to six months, over six months and up to one year, over one year and up to three years, and beyond three years. More granularity can be introduced in both the short-term and the long-term end of the maturity spectrum in order to achieve a smoother distribution of assets and liabilities across buckets. Box 8-8 discusses how different instruments are slotted into the right buckets.

FIGURE 8-1 Gap Analysis: Asset/Liability Position

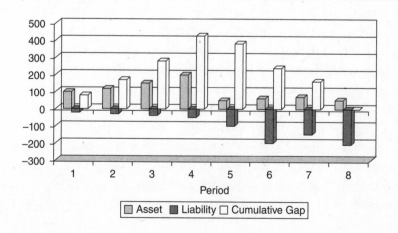

BOX 8-8 SLOTTING INSTRUMENTS INTO THE RIGHT GAP ANALYSIS TIME BUCKETS

In general, an instrument must be slotted into a time bucket that corresponds to the shorter of the repricing maturity and the remaining contractual maturity. Floating-rate instruments should be slotted into the time bucket corresponding to their repricing maturity. For example, a five-year floating-rate bond with a coupon of six-month LIBOR should be slotted into the six-month bucket, because the bond reprices according to movements of the six-month LIBOR interest rate. A three-year floating-rate bond with six-month repricing maturity and only two months remaining maturity will be slotted into the two-month bucket.

Only the principal amount is placed into the bucket. All future cash flows should be ignored so that the total amount on the balance sheet matches the total in the gap report. However, the accrued interest should be slotted into the bucket corresponding to the period in which it will be received (if it is shown on the balance sheet). For example, in the case of an amortizing loan, where the borrower makes equal annual payments over the loan period, only the principal amount repaid in each period should be slotted into the corresponding time bucket. In the case of a zero-coupon bond, the carrying value—i.e., the purchase price plus accrued interest—is slotted into the bucket corresponding to the remaining maturity. (The balance sheet will also reflect the carrying value.)

Liabilities with contractual maturity are straightforward: they can be slotted into the bucket corresponding to their maturity. In the case of liabilities with noncontractual maturities, such as deposits in checking accounts, it is necessary to perform a statistical analysis based on the bank's past experience. For example, 40 percent of the items might be slotted into the first bucket because they are viewed as short-term or subject to flight; the balance might be viewed as long-term core deposits and would therefore be slotted into the last bucket.

Home mortgages, mortgage-backed securities, and asset-backed securities are subject to prepayment. To work out how to slot these into time buckets, the bank may have to perform a statistical analysis of the amount that's likely to be prepaid in the future, based on the institution's experience (the problem becomes more complex when prepayment depends on the level of interest rates, as for home mortgages). The same applies to deposit redemption: historical data can provide information on the speed and the extent of depositors' response to higher-yielding deposit accounts.

See Box 8-9 for a discussion of off-balance-sheet items.

- *Producing a cumulative gap report.* The cumulative gap in one period is the cumulative gap in the previous period plus the gap in the current period (Figure 8-1).
- *Setting gap limits.* Gap limits are defined as the maximum permitted difference between assets and liabilities within a specific time bucket. Gap limits can be defined in terms of dollar value or as a percentage of interest-rate-sensitive assets. For long maturities, gap limits can be formulated in terms of a percentage of shareholders' equity (NW).
- *Formulating gap management strategies.*

In order to use the gap report to control the volatility of the NII, it is necessary to define the relationship between NII and the gap position. In other words, it is necessary to estimate the impact of the gap position on the income statement (Table 8-2).

TABLE 8-2 Examples of the Relationship Between NII and the Gap Position

	Interest Rate	Gap	Impact on NII
Scenario 1:	Up	+	+
Net assets will benefit from an increase in rates			
Scenario 2:	Up	−	−
Net liabilities will cost more if rates go up			
Scenario 3:	Down	+	−
Net assets will earn less from a decline in rates			
Scenario 4:	Down	−	+
Net liabilities will cost less as a result of a decrease in rates			

Table 8-2 assumes that there will be a straightforward "parallel shift" in the yield curves for all the firm's interest-rate-sensitive assets and liabilities, rather than a more complex shift in yield curve relationships. It omits other risks, such as:

- *Basis risk.* Consider, for example, a situation in which rates have gone up and the gap is positive. Assume, however, that the rate increase on the asset side is smaller than the rate increase on the liability side. As a result, the increase in the cash inflows might be less than the increase in the cash outflows, resulting in a fall in the NII.

- *Mismatches within each bucket.* Within a bucket, assets may reprice toward the end of the time zone and liabilities may reprice towards the beginning. For example, assets may have a five-month maturity and liabilities may have only a three-month maturity. Therefore, for an increase in rates, the increase in cash outflows starts earlier than the increase in cash inflows. Despite a positive gap and rising rates, the impact on NII might be negative.

- *Timing of rate changes.* The timing of interest rate changes may be different for the asset side and the liability side. The increase in rates on the liability side may be immediate, whereas the rate change on the asset side may come later. This may be due to lags in the repricing of assets: such a repricing decision needs the agreement of the ALCO, and competitive pressures may not allow the bank to pass on to the customer any increase in funding cost. Here again, the impact on NII of an increase in rates might be negative even when the gap analysis suggests that the impact should be positive.

- *Embedded options risk.* Retail products offer customers different types of "free" options, such as a prepayment option on mortgages and personal loans, and mortgage commitment options (i.e., the bank is committed to the best rate for a period of time before the customer signs the mortgage contract). In a sense, deposit withdrawal is another option risk as depositors have, at any instant, the option to walk away and invest their funds in higher-yield short-term instruments, such as money market funds, if interest rates move up. These options are interest-rate-dependent, and they are hard to incorporate into the gap framework.

- *Maturing of items with off-market interest rates.* As maturity shrinks, all items on the balance sheet will eventually end up in the first bucket of any gap analysis. It is likely that several of these items have off-market coupons. For example, a 10-year bond with a 10 percent coupon that matures in less than three months will fall into the first bucket. The current interest rate may be 5 percent, low compared with the coupon on the asset when it was purchased 10 years ago. Even if rates go up by 1 percent, an item with a 10 percent coupon will be replaced by an item with, say, a 6 percent coupon. This will have a negative impact on NII, even though the gap was positive and rates went up.
- *Average versus beginning-of-the-period balances.* The balances during the period differ from the balances at the beginning of the period. After all, financial institutions are dynamically managed; thus, their positions change all the time. This issue can be addressed by reducing the length of the time buckets.

Pros and Cons of Gap Analysis

Gap analysis is attractive because it is simple. It relies on accounting data and does not involve complex mathematics (such as duration and convexity) and statistics (such as volatilities and correlations). It is a very effective tool for balance sheets that are dominated by instruments that do not have options embedded in them.

However, the approach is prone to inaccuracies for several reasons:

- Gap reports identify only repricing risks. As we outlined earlier, various kinds of risk are not captured in the gap analysis framework. In particular, gap analyses do not consider basis risk and yield curve risk, such as a steepening of the yield curve. Gap reports also cannot capture foreign exchange risk or the correlation risk between interest rate changes in two currencies.
- Gap analysis does not consider the impact of offsetting positions in different buckets. For example, mismatches in the 1- to 3-month bucket may partially offset the mismatches in the 6- to 12-month bucket. It may be necessary to hedge only the net mismatch.
- Gap analysis ignores interest flows and the associated reinvestment risk of coupons and interest payments.

- Gap analysis uses only accounting data—i.e., book values—which may differ significantly from market value and therefore may bias the measurement of risk.
- Gap analysis may result in large discontinuities in reported positions when positions switch buckets. For example, a 194-day asset, which is in the 7- to 12-month bucket today, will move to the 3- to 6-month bucket after two weeks. This may cause a huge reported mismatch in both buckets.

Gap analysis is static in nature; it cannot take into account the impact of new volumes on gap positions. However, *dynamic gap* reporting addresses this issue. Dynamic gap reporting accounts for the rollover strategy of the institution—i.e., its origination strategy and its funding policy. It deals with how maturing assets are replaced by new products, such as the incentives a bank might offer to new customers to take variable rate mortgages in a declining-interest-rate environment (while maturing mortgages are mostly fixed-rate).

Earnings at Risk

On a periodic basis, the potential impact of the firm's various gap positions (and current gap limit policies) on the income statement for the current quarter and the full year must be calculated. These calculations offer the bank an earnings-at-risk (EaR) measure.

Consider the gap table shown in Box 8-9. Here we suppose that all the bank's assets and liabilities are linear instruments without embedded options, such as loans, bonds, forward rate agreements (FRAs), and swaps. For simplicity, we'll also assume that all these items are evenly spread across the gap analysis time buckets and that the rate changes are the same across all maturities (i.e., there is a parallel shift of the yield curve). Let us next consider the impact of a 100-bp increase in rates for the quarter and the full year.

Impact for the Quarter

The gap report in Box 8-9 (before hedging) shows negative gaps for both the first (0–1 month) and the second (1–3 months) buckets—i.e., -$50,000 and -$250,000, respectively. As assets and liabilities are spread evenly across each bucket, the change in interest rates will affect the first-quarter NII for 2.5 months

BOX 8-9   HOW DO WE SLOT DERIVATIVE INSTRUMENTS INTO TIME BUCKETS?

Off-balance-sheet items such as interest rate swaps, futures, forwards, options, caps, and floors represent both assets and liabilities to the bank, so how they are slotted into time buckets depends on the structure of each instrument.

Consider a five-year, $10 million interest rate swap paying a fixed 10 percent and receiving a floating six-month LIBOR. This swap can be viewed as the sum of a five-year fixed-rate asset, which can be slotted into the corresponding maturity bucket, and a five-year floating-rate liability repricing every six months, which can be slotted into the bucket containing the six-month term. The cumulative gap for the swap is zero.

Consider now a long position in a three-month futures contract six months from now. This futures position is equivalent to borrowing for three months and then investing for nine months, so we can treat it like a nine-month asset and a three-month liability. As for the swap, the cumulative gap for the futures position is zero. Forward instruments, such as forward rate agreements, are treated in a similar fashion.

The table shows how a gap report for Bank XYZ treats a five-year $200 million swap hedge. The swap means that the bank pays a five-year fixed rate of 5 percent and receives a floating rate of three-month LIBOR.

Gap Report for Bank XYZ (in millions of dollars)							
	0–1 Month	1–3 Months	3–6 Months	6–12 Months	1–3 Years	Beyond 3 Years	Total
Assets	50	60	130	180	150	320	890
Liabilities	100	310	100	150	130	100	890
Gap before hedging	–50	–250	30	30	20	220	
Swap (hedge)	0	200	0	0	0	–200	
Net gap after hedging	–50	–50	30	30	20	20	

for the first bucket and for 1 month for the second bucket (Figure 8-2). Since the average maturity of the gap for the first bucket is 0.5 month, there is an excess of liabilities over assets of $50,000; hence, an increase in interest rate of 1 percent will cost the institution an additional 1 percent for the remaining 2.5 months until the end of the quarter, or $50,000 × 2.5/12 × 1/100 = $104.17.

For each bucket, the impact of the interest rate shock on NII is equal to the gap times the repricing gap (in terms of years) times the size of the interest rate change. Similarly, we can derive the impact of an interest rate shock of 100 bp on the NII for the year.

The negative $312.50 EaR impact depends solely on the size of the gap. For example, if we reduce offsetting assets and liabilities of say $40,000 in each bucket during the first quarter, then it will not change the EaR. On the other hand, if the size of the negative gap in our example doubled in both the first and second buckets, then the impact on EaR would also double to a negative $625.

We can also calculate the impact of an increase or decrease in the slope of the yield curve on the NII. For example, if the yield curve increased 1 percent in the first bucket and 2 percent in the second bucket, then the impact on EaR would be the same as before in the first bucket (−$50,000 × 2.5/12 × 1/100 = −$104.17) but would result in an increase in EaR from the gap in the second bucket

FIGURE 8-2 Impact of Gap on NII for the Quarter

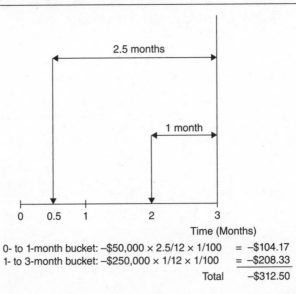

0- to 1-month bucket: −$50,000 × 2.5/12 × 1/100 = −$104.17
1- to 3-month bucket: −$250,000 × 1/12 × 1/100 = −$208.33
Total −$312.50

of –$416.66 (–$250,000 × 1/12 × 2/100 = –$416.66) for a total negative impact on EaR of $510.83 across the two buckets.

Impact for the Year

With a one-year horizon, the average repricing gap for the 0- to 1-month bucket is 11.5 (=12 – 0.5) months; it is 10 months for the 1- to 3-month bucket, 7.5 months for the 3- to 6-month bucket, and 3 months for the 6- to 12-month bucket (Figure 8-3). Then, again with reference to the gap table in Box 8-9, the full impact for the year, before hedging with the swap, is

0- to 1-month bucket: –$50,000 × 11.5/12 × 1/100 = –$479.17

1- to 3-month bucket: –$250,000 × 10/12 × 1/100 = –$2,083.33

3- to 6-month bucket: $30,000 × 7.5/12 × 1/100 = $187.50

6- to 12-month bucket: $30,000 × 3/12 × 1/100 = $75.00

Total = –$2,300.00

FIGURE 8-3 Impact of Gap on NII for the Year

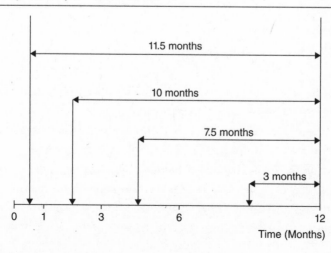

11.5 months

10 months

7.5 months

3 months

0 1 3 6 12

Time (Months)

Now, what is the impact of the hedge described in the gap table in Box 8-9? If we assume that the repricing of the floating-rate leg of the swap hedge is exactly three months from now, the hedge reduces the impact on NII by

$$\$200,000 \times 9/12 \times 1/100 = \$1,500$$

Thus, the net impact on NII after hedging is −$800 (= −$2,300 + $1,500).

The Multicurrency Balance Sheet Issue

Firms with multicurrency balance sheets are exposed to mismatches in the currency position of assets and liabilities in addition to interest rate risk. There are two approaches to dealing with multicurrency balance sheets:

- Consolidated gap reporting, which consists of converting all foreign currency positions into the home currency. This approach implicitly assumes that all foreign exchange risks have been hedged. Moreover, consolidated gap analysis is likely to overstate interest rate risk, as rates in different currencies are not perfectly correlated—i.e., they are unlikely to all move in the same direction at the same time.
- Separate currency gap reporting, which consists of preparing a gap report for each currency. This approach can be confusing if too many reports are produced, as it becomes difficult to figure out the aggregate interest rate risk in the firm's balance sheet.

Duration Gap Approach

The approaches we've looked at so far should be viewed as "back of the envelope" calculations. The gaps measured by gap analysis offer some sense of the interest rate exposure of the balance sheet, but they are not a very precise measure of interest rate exposure for reasons that we've already mentioned.

Duration, as introduced in Chapter 6, is a measure of the interest rate sensitivity of any cash flow series. The duration concept is useful as a complement to gap and EaR analysis because it summarizes cash flow characteristics, taking into account both the size and timing of these cash flows. It does not hide cash flow timing mismatches within the maturity buckets, as gap analysis does.

So, how do we use the duration concept to improve our estimate of changes in NII? Box 8-10 offers a more technical explanation, but basically we need to calculate the duration gap for NII. This calculation depends on the durations and market values of the rate-sensitive assets and liabilities. The calculation is quite straightforward because durations are additive.

If an asset (or liability) does not generate any cash flow during the accounting period, then it influences NII only in an accrual sense and should be excluded from the calculation.

The duration gap approach is very easy to implement as long as the accounting information is available. However, the same limitations that apply to the duration concept as a measure of interest rate risk also apply here.

BOX 8-10   DURATION AND NET INTEREST INCOME

In this box, we supply some of the mathematical notation for our main text discussion of duration and net interest income. The dollar change in NII (ΔNII) approximately equals the duration gap for NII (DG_{NII}) multiplied by the change in interest rates (Δi):

$$\Delta NII = DG_{NII} \times \Delta i$$

where the duration gap DG_{NII} is the difference between the market value of the rate-sensitive assets MV_{RSA} times 1 minus the duration of the rate-sensitive assets D_{RSA} and the market value of the rate-sensitive liabilities MV_{RSL} times 1 minus the duration of the rate-sensitive liabilities D_{RSL}:

$$DG_{NII} = MV_{RSA} \times (1 - D_{RSA}) - MV_{RSL} \times (1 - D_{RSL})$$

To be precise, here NII is the book value amount expected at the end of the accounting period—say, one quarter or one year. If an asset (or liability) does not generate any cash flow during the accounting period, then it influences NII only in an accrual sense and should be excluded from the calculation.

- The term structure of interest rates is assumed to be flat, only parallel shifts in the yield curves are considered, and the rate change is assumed to be small. That is, the calculation assumes that there is no risk from changes in the shape of the yield curve and that there is no convexity risk (though this last can be corrected by a convexity adjustment, as explained in Chapter 6).
- The same rate change affects both the assets and the liabilities (there is no basis risk, no correlation risk, and no volatility risk).
- Deposit withdrawals and loan prepayments are not interest rate sensitive (there is no embedded options risk).

Duration of Equity

EaR is an accounting concept. It cannot fully convey the impact of a rate change on net wealth from a shareholder's perspective. To capture this impact, we need the *duration of equity* measure, described in technical terms in Box 8-11. As we note in the box, the duration of equity is quite long, much longer than the duration of the assets or the liabilities. Equity can be viewed as a highly leveraged purchase of an asset with high price volatility, funded by a less price-volatile liability.

BOX 8-11 DURATION OF EQUITY

How do we calculate the duration of equity? The market value of equity, net worth or NW, is simply the difference between the market value of assets MV_A and the market value of liabilities MV_L:

$$NW = MV_A - MV_L$$

From this economic identity and the definition of the duration of a fixed-income position (Chapter 6), it follows that the duration of equity D_{NW} is:

$$D_{NW} = \frac{(MV_A \times D_A - MV_L \times D_L)}{NW}$$

where D_A and D_L denote the duration of the assets and liabilities, respectively.

For example, suppose we have $100 in assets with a duration of 7.5 years and $90 in liabilities with a duration of 2.3 years; then the duration of equity is:

$$D_{NW} = \frac{(100 \times 7.5 - 90 \times 2.3)}{10} = 54.3$$

The duration of equity is quite long, much longer than the duration of the assets or the liabilities. Equity can be viewed as a highly levered purchase of an asset with high price volatility funded by a less price-volatile liability. In this example, assuming a yield of 5 percent on both assets and liabilities, a 10 bp (= 0.1 percent = 1/1000) increase in rates would lead to a change in NW of:

$$\Delta NW = -NW \times D_{NW} \times \frac{\Delta i}{1+i} = -10 \times 54.3 \times \frac{1/1000}{1.05} = -\$0.52$$

One cannot hedge both NII and NW simultaneously, as the hedge position that would reduce the duration of NII to zero differs from the hedge position that would reduce the duration of equity to zero. It is therefore critical to articulate clearly the objectives of any hedging program.

Beyond Duration Analysis: Long-Term VaR

Duration gap analysis allows a more accurate assessment of interest rate risk in the balance sheet than simple gap analysis. However, both frameworks are static in nature and do not capture the stochastic nature of interest rates and foreign exchange rates and the fact that the balance sheet evolves over time. New retail products are originated, and maturing assets and liabilities are rolled over as they mature—not necessarily into instruments with similar characteristics.

Long-term VaR (LT-VaR) is an extension of the classic VaR framework presented in Chapter 7 in the context of the trading book. The time horizon in a classic VaR framework is very short: one day for market risk management purposes and 10 days for regulatory capital reporting. For the banking book, the risk horizon is much longer, at least one year. The objective of LT-VaR is to generate the statistical distributions of EaR and NW at different horizons, say next quarter and end of year for EaR and one and two years for NW, in order to produce the worst-case EaR and NW at a given confidence level, say 99 percent.

This ambitious procedure can be achieved only by means of powerful Monte Carlo simulations of:

- The correlated term structure of interest rates, such as swap rates, cost-of-funds rates, and mortgage rates, over very long horizons
- Implied volatilities for various types of instruments
- Interest-rate-sensitive prepayment of mortgages and other loans, as well as changes in deposits and savings balances, including seasonal variations in demand for loans and deposits
- Loan defaults
- Renewals (retention rates) and new volume (new origination) for retail products such as mortgages and other consumer loans, on the asset side of the balance sheet, and funding products on the liability side

At each step of the simulation, pricing models must be used to assess the value of assets and liabilities at that point in time. The simulation should also trigger hedges, when required along a simulation path, in order to comply with any ALCO policy regarding maximum risk exposures (e.g., gap limits).

Pros and Cons of LT-VaR

LT-VaR is a dynamic and forward-looking VaR framework that helps firms manage risk over a long-term horizon. However, it is complex, and modelers must have access to the firm's detailed balance sheet positions.

Bank businesses that focus on lending to corporate clients are characterized by a limited number of relatively large loans, but retail banks authorize thousands and thousands of small loans, credit cards, mortgages, and so on. Retail products must be aggregated into homogeneous pools so that LT-VaR simulation can be conducted at the pool level.

The quality of any simulation depends on the assumptions that drive the dynamics of interest rates and the changes in the balance sheet structure. Inconsistent assumptions can distort the results, potentially misleading the ALCO in some very important decisions.

Funding Liquidity Risk: Credits and Debits

One should not confuse interest rate sensitivity with funding liquidity risk. Interest rate sensitivity is determined by the frequency of the repricing of assets and liabilities. In contrast, the contractual maturity of an item determines whether it contributes to a funding liquidity gap.

For example, a three-year fixed-rate loan has an interest rate sensitivity of three years and a liquidity maturity of three years. A variable-rate three-year loan priced off six-month LIBOR has an interest rate sensitivity of six months and a liquidity maturity of three years.

A business unit's impact on institutional liquidity can be characterized by means of a liquidity measurement system. This must at least be directionally correct; a liability-gathering unit should be credited for supplying liquidity, and an asset-generating unit should be charged for using liquidity. As discussed earlier, funding liquidity risk can stem from both the *external* (e.g., funding or asset market) and *internal* (e.g., poor risk management) environment.

Table 8-3 illustrates a spectrum of funding sources and indicates that a bank might assign a higher liquidity credit for stable funds than for hot funds. *Hot funds* are funds supplied by depositors that could be quickly removed from the bank in the event of a crisis (e.g., funds from dealers). Table 8-3 ranks the sources of funds in terms of their liquidity.

One can illustrate the key features of a best-practice liquidity quantification scheme through a simplified version of this liquidity ranking process. The liquidity ranking process should enable the bank to quantify credits and charges depending on the degree to which a business unit is a net supplier or net user of liquidity.

Liquidity can be quantified using a symmetrical scale. Such scales help managers to compute a business unit's liquidity score more objectively, through

TABLE 8-3 Funds Source Spectrum

Open Market	Direct	Unconventional	Core Funds	Capital Market Funds
HOT ◄─────────────────────────────────►				STABLE
Brokers/Dealers (e.g., Negotiable CDs)	Wholesale Placements (e.g., Large CDs, BAs, Repos, Fed Funds)	Customized Term Placements (e.g., Special 5-Year CDs)	• DDAs • MMAs • Savings • CDs	• Common Equity • Preferred Equity • Term Notes/Bonds

a ranking and weighting process. A quantification scheme such as this also helps the bank to determine the amount of liquidity in the system and to set targets in terms of a desirable and quantifiable level of liquidity.

The liquidity rank (LR) attributed to a product is determined by multiplying the dollar amount of the product by its rank. For example, if business unit XYZ is both a supplier and a user of liquidity, then a net liquidity calculation needs to be made. Looking at Table 8-4, if we assume that business unit XYZ supplied $10 million of the most stable liquidity, $3 million of the next most stable, and so on, then a total credit of 94 ($5 \times 10 + 4 \times 3 + 3 \times 6 + 2 \times 5 + 1 \times 4 = 94$) would be assigned.

TABLE 8-4 Liquidity Rank Measurement Units for Business Unit XYZ

Liquidity Suppliers		Liquidity Users	
Rank Score	**Amount ($MM)**	**Rank Score**	**Amount ($MM)**
+5	$10	−1	$4
+4	$3	−2	$8
+3	$6	−3	$6
+2	$5	−4	$3
+1	$4	−5	$10
Total	94	Total	−100
Net		−6 (= 94 − 100)	

Similarly, if we assume in our example that business unit XYZ used $10 million of the most expensive liquidity, $3 million of the next most expensive, and so on, then a total charge of 100 ($4 \times 1 + 8 \times 2 + 6 \times 3 + 3 \times 4 + 10 \times 5 = 100$) would be assigned. The net result of the two calculations is a liquidity rank of minus $6 million ($94 - 100 = -6$). If the balance sheet of XYZ doubles across all maturities, then the net result is a liquidity rank of minus $12 million since the liquidity rank measure is linear.

The LR approach is simply a heuristic tool that helps managers to control the liquidity profile of their institution. The next step is to charge each business unit for the liquidity risk that it generates.

Funds Transfer Pricing

Funds transfer pricing is always a controversial issue in organizations, as it affects the measured profitability of the various business lines.

The rationale for funds transfer pricing is that there are economies of scale and scope in centralizing the management of interest rate risk. Business units have no control over the dynamics of yield curves and other market indices such as the prime rate. So the objective of funds transfer pricing is to remove the noncontrollable interest rate risk from business results. The funds transfer pricing system is used to charge each business unit that requires funds the cost of funding its activity (such as the funding cost to make loans) and hedging its interest rate risk. The funds transfer pricing system is also used to credit each business unit for its activity to supply funds (such as a branch that raises deposits).

Each business unit will then be able to secure its profit margin at the time of origination of its products (say, mortgages) and can focus on developing and managing the business side of its activity as well as the credit quality of its portfolio (i.e., credit risk remains with the business unit). The transfer pricing system needs to spell out if certain interest rate risks, such as basis risk (e.g., the spread between the prime rate and LIBOR for variable-rate loans indexed on the prime rate) and options risk (e.g., commitment risk for mortgages), will remain with the business unit.

The issue remains: what is the appropriate cost of funds to charge to the business units? We recommend *matched-maturity funds transfer pricing*, an approach illustrated by the following example. Consider a financial institution with the following assets and liabilities:

	Unit	Balance	Maturity (years)	Rate	Interest Income (Expense)
Assets					
Corporate loan	Corporate	$100	1	8%	$8.00
Liabilities					
Savings account	Retail	$100	0.25	3%	($3.00)
			Net	**5%**	**$5.00**

Assume for illustrative purposes that the interest rate sensitivity of all assets and liabilities is at a fixed rate and therefore their interest rate sensitivity matches their maturity. At first glance, one might consider charging the corporate unit only 3 percent as its cost of funds, leading to a healthy profit margin of 5 percent for the unit. But this would be unfair. The corporate unit would be benefiting from the bank's retail franchise, which allows the retail unit to raise funds at a cost that is well below the market funding rate otherwise applied to the institution. Charging the corporate unit only 3 percent also fails to account for gap risk—after all, the bank is funding a one-year asset by means of a three-month liability.

The correct approach consists of charging both business units—i.e., the corporate and retail units—the firm's cost of funds, say LIBOR if the firm has a credit rating of AA, so that both business units are rewarded (penalized) for their ability to lend (raise funds) above (below) the funding cost.

Assume that the three-month and one-year LIBOR rates are 4 percent and 6 percent, respectively; then the matched-maturity transfer pricing is:

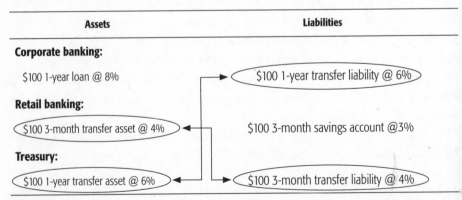

Assets	Liabilities
Corporate banking:	
$100 1-year loan @ 8%	$100 1-year transfer liability @ 6%
Retail banking:	
$100 3-month transfer asset @ 4%	$100 3-month savings account @3%
Treasury:	
$100 1-year transfer asset @ 6%	$100 3-month transfer liability @ 4%

It follows that the profit margins are:

- 2 percent (8% – 6%) for the corporate banking unit (not 5 percent)
- 1 percent (4% – 3%) for the retail banking unit (not 0 percent)
- 2 percent (6% – 4%) for the treasury unit as a compensation for the cost of rolling over the three-month liability over one year and for hedging the gap risk

The total corresponds to the net margin of 5 percent in the previous table.

We think that banks would be wise to set out a consistent framework for constructing transfer prices, based on a consistent set of rules or principles. Below we put forward a draft of these principles, which we preface with a discussion of one key issue: determining the interest rate sensitivity of the assets and liabilities in order to decide into which time periods (or buckets) the assets and liabilities should be placed, so that they can be matched up to facilitate the process of "match funding."

Placing Assets and Liabilities into Buckets

To conduct ALM and accurate FTP, banks need to place assets, liabilities, and off-balance-sheet items into buckets in terms of their known interest rate sensitivities (for match funding purposes) and maturities (for funding liquidity purposes).

The two activities are distinct. For example, as we discussed earlier in the funding liquidity risk measurement section, a three-year floating-rate loan that has a one-year floating-rate coupon would be perfectly matched up against a one-year fixed-rate certificate of deposit for matched funding interest rate sensitivity purposes; however, it would have a funding liquidity maturity mismatch (of two years).

Here we focus on creating buckets according to interest rate sensitivities, which allows the firm to match-fund assets and liabilities—e.g., to relate the price of funding a one-year loan to the price of securing one-year funds. A key task for ALM is to define the maturity of the interest rate sensitivity of assets in both normal and stressed markets. This task includes estimating the time it would take the firm to dispose of assets in an enforced (or "fire sale") situation, such as a period in which the bank suffered a large withdrawal of deposits.

It is not always obvious into which bucket an asset or liability should be placed. For example, the maturity of the asset or liability is a question of judgment in the case of demand deposits and market-driven maturities such as option-based instruments (e.g., mortgages). Many retail and commercial banking operations generate assets that do not have an explicit maturity date—e.g., current account overdrafts and credit card balances. These can be balanced against undated liabilities, such as current or checking accounts and instant-access deposit accounts.

Typically, practitioners split the bank's total liabilities into *core* and *unstable* balances. Core balances are placed in the long-dated bucket, and unstable balances are placed in the shortest dated bucket. The core balance needs to be reanalyzed periodically over time to make sure that it remains accurate.

ALM needs to make projections based on observable variables that are correlated with outstanding balances of deposits. For instance, such variables could be based on the level of economic growth. ALM needs to deal also with contingencies built into the nature of its business. For example, a bank will have committed lines of credit, the utilization of which will depend on customer demand.

Transfer Pricing Rules: An Example Framework

A framework of transfer pricing rules needs to be accepted in the firm as a practical guide toward constructing transfer prices for all products. For example:

1. The transfer pricing (TP) rules for match-funding a unit shall be determined by interest rate sensitivity. For example, a three-year floating-rate loan that pays interest on a periodic annual basis has a one-year interest rate sensitivity and, therefore, has the same interest rate sensitivity as a one-year fixed-rate certificate of deposit (CD).
2. Units shall be protected from directional risk, such as an increase in interest rates. For example, a wholesale business unit that made a three-year floating-rate loan to a corporation would be protected against a decline in interest rates but would still bear the credit risk associated with the loan.
3. Units shall be protected from significant options risk. For example, a retail business unit that offers a mortgage would be protected against the mortgage holder's prepaying her mortgage due to, say, declining interest rates but would still bear the credit risk associated with the mortgage holder's defaulting on her debt.
4. Units shall not be protected from basis (spread) risk unless the risk is hedgeable and the units pay for the hedge based on current market

rates and for an agreed volume. For example, basis risk occurs when a business unit makes a prime rate loan that is funded by a LIBOR-based liability. If the basis risk could be effectively hedged, then the business would be protected against this basis risk for an agreed volume of loans. The business unit would still bear the basis risk for any transaction that could not be effectively hedged or where the volume of loans turned out to be different from the amount initially agreed.

5. The transfer pricing rate (TPR) will be based on minimizing spread volatility while striving to price at the margin. For example, if a six-month $100 prime rate loan were hedged with a mix of LIBOR-based liabilities, then the TPR would be based on the optimal mix of LIBOR-based liabilities necessary to minimize the spread volatility (say, a combination of $48 of five-month and $52 of seven-month maturities).

6. The transfer pricing system (TPS) shall be impervious to arbitrage. For example, the TPR in the United States for making a one-year U.S. dollar loan should not be able to arbitrage the TPS by first borrowing in Canadian dollars for the same maturity and immediately converting the loan into U.S. dollars and lending this amount to a U.S. borrower with the certitude of realizing a profit by converting the repaid loan plus interest back into Canadian dollars.

7. The TPS shall be global in scope.

8. The TPS shall be institution and country specific. For example, the TPR for a three-year floating-rate Canadian dollar loan that pays interest on an annual basis would be different from the TPR for a three-year floating-rate U.S. dollar loan that also pays interest on an annual basis.

9. The TPS shall reflect the profitability that can be achieved by the institution. For example, the TPR for a three-year floating-rate loan that pays interest on an annual basis should reflect the actual cost of funding of the institution given its rating (say, A), not the cost of funding for a target rating (say, AA).

10. The TPR shall be explicit, consistent, goal congruent, and determined solely by the true economics of the transaction. For example, the TPR should not be set differently from the economic value of the cost of funding an asset.

The final point deserves some explanation. Bank managements sometimes award business lines a funding cost that is out of line with the funding markets, with the intention of encouraging (or discouraging) the growth of a particular business activity or asset portfolio. This simply confuses the issue. It is better to determine the cost of funds on an objective basis and keep any strategic subsidies fully transparent.

9

CREDIT SCORING AND RETAIL CREDIT RISK MANAGEMENT[1]

This chapter examines credit risk in retail banking, an industry that is familiar to almost everyone at some level. Once seen as unglamorous compared to the big-ticket lending of corporate banking and trading, retail banking has been transformed over the last few years by innovations in products, marketing, and risk management.

Retail banking has proved particularly important to the financial industry in the postmillennium years. On the positive side, retail businesses provided growing, relatively stable earnings in the early years of the millennium. However, poorly controlled subprime lending in the U.S. mortgage market provided the fuel for the disastrous failures of the U.S. securitization industry in the run-up to the financial crisis of 2007–2009—a topic we address in detail in Chapter 12.

In this chapter, we'll first take a look at the different nature of retail credit risk and commercial credit risk, including the "darker side" of risk in the retail credit businesses. Then we'll take a more detailed look at the process of credit scoring. Credit scoring is now a widespread technique, not only in banking but also in many other sectors where there is a need to check the credit standing of a customer (e.g., a telephone company) or estimate the likelihood that a client will file a claim (e.g., an insurance company).

---

[1]We acknowledge the coauthorship of Rob Jameson for sections of this chapter.

Retail banking, as defined in Box 9-1, serves both small businesses and consumers and includes the business of accepting consumer deposits as well as the main consumer lending businesses.

- *Home mortgages.* Fixed-rate mortgages and adjustable-rate mortgages (ARMs) are secured by the residential properties financed by the loan. The loan-to-value ratio (LTV) represents the proportion of the property value financed by the loan and is a key risk variable.
- *Home equity loans.* Sometimes called home equity line of credit (HELOC) loans, these can be considered a hybrid between a consumer loan and a mortgage loan. They are secured by residential properties.
- *Installment loans.* These include revolving loans, such as personal lines of credit that may be used repeatedly up to a specified limit. They also include credit cards, automobile and similar loans, and all other loans

---

BOX 9-1   BASEL'S DEFINITION OF RETAIL EXPOSURES

The Basel Committee, the banking industry's international regulatory body, defines retail exposures as homogeneous portfolios that consist of:

- A large number of small, low-value loans
- With either a consumer or business focus
- Where the incremental risk of any single exposure is small

Examples are:

- Credit cards
- Installment loans (e.g., personal finance, educational loans, auto loans, leasing)
- Revolving credits (e.g., overdrafts, home equity lines of credit)
- Residential mortgages

Small business loans can be managed as retail exposures, provided that the total exposure to a small business borrower is less than 1 million euros.

---

not included in automobile loans and revolving credit. Such things as residential property, personal property, or financial assets usually secure ordinary installment loans.

- *Credit card revolving loans.* These are unsecured loans.
- *Small business loans (SBL).* These are secured by the assets of the business or by the personal guarantees of the owners. Business loans of up to $100,000 to $200,000 are usually considered as part of the retail portfolio.

The Nature of Retail Credit Risk

The credit risks generated by retail banking are significant, but they are traditionally regarded as having a different dynamic from the credit risk of commercial and investment banking businesses. The defining feature of retail credit exposures is that they arrive in bite-sized pieces, so that default by a single customer is never expensive enough to threaten a bank. Corporate and commercial credit portfolios, by contrast, often contain large exposures to single names and also concentrations of exposures to corporations that are economically intertwined in particular geographical areas or industry sectors.

The tendency for retail credit portfolios to behave like well-diversified portfolios in normal markets makes it easier to estimate the percentage of the portfolio the bank "expects" to default in the future and the losses that this might cause. This expected loss number can then be treated much like other costs of doing business, such as the cost of maintaining branches or processing checks. The relative predictability of retail credit losses means that the expected loss rate can be built into the price charged to the customer. By contrast, the risk of loss from many commercial credit portfolios is dominated by the risk that credit losses will rise to some unexpected level.

Of course, this distinction between retail and corporate lending can be overstated, and sometimes diversification can prove to be a fickle friend. The 2007–2009 financial crisis demonstrated that, at the end of a long credit boom, housing prices could fall at about the same time right across even a large economy such as the United States. Diversification turned out to offer less than perfect protection to large portfolios of mortgage risk, though the extent of the house price fall varied considerably from region to region. Likewise, a systematic change in behavior in consumer lending industries—e.g., advancing money to consumers without checking their incomes—can introduce a hidden systematic risk into credit portfolios, and even whole credit industries. In the event of economic trouble, this can lead to sudden lurches upward in the default rate and to unexpected falls in key asset and collateral values (e.g., house prices). This is the "dark side" of retail credit risk, described in Box 9-2, and it played a significant role in sparking the 2007–2009 crisis.

BOX 9-2   DOES RETAIL CREDIT RISK HAVE A DARK SIDE?

In the main text, we deal mainly with how credit scoring helps put a number to the expected level of credit risk in a retail transaction. But there is a dark side to retail credit, too. This is the danger that losses will suddenly rise to unexpected levels because of some unforeseen but systematic risk factor that influences the behavior of many of the credits in a bank's retail portfolio.

The dark side of retail risk management has four prime causes:

- Not all innovative retail credit products can be associated with enough historical loss data to make their risk assessments reliable.
- Even well-understood retail credit products might begin to behave in an unexpected fashion under the influence of a sharp change in the economic environment, particularly if risk factors all get worse at the same time (the so-called perfect storm scenario). For example, in the mortgage industry, one ever-present worry is that a deep recession combined with higher interest rates might lead to a rise in mortgage defaults at the same time that house prices, and therefore collateral values, fall very sharply.
- The tendency of consumers to default (or not) is a product of a complex social and legal system that continually changes. For example, the social and legal acceptability of personal bankruptcy, especially in the United States, is one factor that seemed to influence a rising trend in personal default during the 1990s.
- Any operational issue that affects the credit assessment of customers can have a systematic effect on the whole consumer portfolio. Because consumer credit is run as a semiautomated decision-making process

rather than as a series of tailored decisions, it's vital that the credit process be designed and operated correctly.

Almost by definition, it's difficult to put a risk number to these kinds of wild-card risk. Instead, banks have to try to make sure that only a limited number of their retail credit portfolios are especially vulnerable to new kinds of risk, such as subprime lending. A *little* exposure to uncertainty might open up a lucrative business line and allow the bank to gather enough information to measure the risk better in the future; a *lot* makes the bank a hostage to fortune.

Where large conventional portfolios such as mortgage portfolios are vulnerable to sharp changes in multiple risk factors, banks must use stress tests to gauge how devastating each plausible worst-case scenario might be.

It would, however, be a mistake to think that the potential for this kind of mishap became apparent only *following* the 2007–2009 crisis: Box 9-2 is reproduced word for word from the pre-crisis 2006 edition of this book. In the same edition, we included a box on subprime lending in the United States that pointed out that subprime was:

> . . . *a risky business for the unwary bank. If subprime customers turn out to be much more prone to default than the bank has calculated, or if their behavior changes as part of a social trend, then the associated costs can cut through even the fat interest margins and fees associated with the sector. Subprime lending is a new sector for most retail banks. That means that banks lack the historical data to predict the default rate of their subprime customers reliably.*[2]

---

[2] *The Essentials of Risk Management*, 2006, p. 216. While we also dwelt on the degree to which regulatory arbitrage motivated the securitization of consumer portfolios (p. 226) and mentioned the problem of valuing risky residual tranches from a securitization (p. 227). The fragility of AAA-rated securitizations posed an extraordinary threat to financial system stability. We concluded our discussion of the transfer of consumer risk (p. 227) with an explicit warning: "Banks need to watch out for the effect [securitization strategies] can have on liquidity. Can the bank be certain that the option of funding through securitization will remain open if circumstances change (such as deterioration in the institution's credit rating)?"

Since the crisis, various industry reforms and regulations, such as the Consumer Financial Protection Bureau (CFPB) have evolved out of the Dodd-Frank Act (DFA) to help deal with the dark side of retail credit risk. For example, the CFPA requires originators of credit to determine if the consumer has the ability to repay the mortgage. If a mortgage is labeled a "qualified mortgage" (QM), then a creditor can assume the borrower has met this requirement. The CFPA also introduced an "ability to repay" consideration that asks the lender to consider underwriting standards (Box 9-3).

BOX 9-3 QUALIFIED MORTGAGES AND ABILITY TO REPAY

"Qualified mortgages" features include:

- No excess upfront points and fees
- No toxic loan features (e.g., negative amortization loans, terms >30 years, interest-only loans for a specified period of time)
- Cap on how much income can go toward debt (e.g., debt to income (DTI) < 43%)[1]
- No loans with balloon payments

"Ability to repay" calls for a lender to consider eight underwriting standards:

- Current employer status
- Current income or assets
- Credit history
- Monthly payment for mortgage
- Monthly payments on any other loans associated with the property
- Monthly payments on any mortgage-related obligations (such as property taxes)
- Other debt obligations
- The monthly DTI ratio (or residual income) the borrower would be taking on with the mortgage

---

[1]DTI = Total monthly debt divided by total monthly gross income.

A more benign feature of many retail portfolios is that a rise in defaults is often signaled in advance by a change in customer behavior—e.g., customers who are under financial pressure might fail to make a minimum payback on a credit card account. Warning signals like this are carefully monitored by well-run retail banks (and their regulators) because they allow the bank to take preemptive action to reduce credit risk. The bank can:

- Alter the rules governing the amount of money it lends to existing customers to reduce its exposures.
- Alter its marketing strategies and customer acceptance rules to attract less risky customers.
- Price in the risk by raising interest rates for certain kinds of customers to take into account the higher likelihood of default.

By contrast, a commercial credit portfolio is something of a supertanker. By the time it is obvious that something is going wrong, it's often too late to do much about it.

Of course, the warning signals sometimes apparent in consumer credit markets are not always heeded. Too often, retail banks are tempted to ignore early warnings signs because they would steer the bank away from fast-growing, apparently lucrative business lines. Instead, banks compete for even more business volume by lowering standards: the U.S. subprime mortgage industry in the run-up to the 2007–2009 crisis provided a dramatic example of this (Box 9-4).

BOX 9-4 SLIPPING STANDARDS IN SUBPRIME LENDING

In the period between 2002 and the onset of the 2007 subprime crisis, consumers and the industry allowed themselves to believe that real estate prices would continue to escalate.

Combined with low interest rates, poorly structured incentives for brokers, and an increasingly competitive environment, this led to a lowering of underwriting standards. Banks and brokers began to offer products to borrowers who often could not afford the loans or could not bear the associated risks.

Many of the subprime mortgage loans underwritten during this time had multiple weaknesses: less creditworthy borrowers, high cumulative loan-to-value ratios, and limited or no verification of the borrower's income.

Some loans took the hybrid form of 2/28 or 3/27 adjustable rate mortgages (ARMs). That is, they offered a fixed low "teaser" rate for the first two or three years and adjustable rates thereafter. The jump in rates this implied meant the mortgages were designed to be refinanced—feasible only under the assumption of an increase in the collateral value (i.e., a rise in house prices)—or risked falling into default. Because many of these mortgages were set around the same time, lenders had inadvertently created an environment that would lead to a systemic wave of either refinancing or default.

In addition, consumer behavior with respect to default on mortgage debt changed in ways that were not anticipated by banks (or rating agencies).

When the subprime crisis broke in 2007, many commentators called it a "perfect storm" in that everything possible seemed to go wrong. But it was a perfect storm that had, to a large degree, been created by the banking industry itself.

Regulators accept the idea that retail credit risk is *relatively* predictable, and also that mortgage loans are safer due to the specific real estate asset that is backing the loan. As a result, retail banks are asked to set aside a relatively small amount of risk capital under Basel II and III compared with regulatory capital for corporate loans. But banks will have to provide regulators with probability of default (PD), loss given default (LGD), and exposure at default (EAD) statistics for clearly differentiated segments of their portfolios. The regulators say that segmentation should be based on credit scores or some equivalent measure and on vintage of exposures—that is, the time the transaction has been on the bank's books.

Credit risk is not the only risk faced by retail banking, as Box 9-5 makes clear, but it is the major financial risk across most lines of retail business. We'll now take a close look at the principal tool for measuring retail credit risk: credit scoring.

BOX 9–5   THE OTHER RISKS OF RETAIL BANKING

In the main text, we focus on credit risk as the principal risk of retail credit businesses. But just as in commercial banking, retail banking is subject to a whole range of market, operational, business, and reputation risks.

- *Interest-rate risk* is generated on both the asset and liability side whenever the bank offers specific rates to both borrowers and depositors. This risk is generally transferred from the retail business line to the treasury of a retail bank, where it is managed as part of the bank's asset/liability and liquidity risk management (see Chapter 8).
- *Asset valuation risks* are really a special form of market risk, where the profitability of a retail business line depends on the accurate valuation of a particular asset, liability, or class of collateral. Perhaps the most important is prepayment risk in mortgage banking, which describes the risk that a portfolio of mortgages might lose its value when interest rates fall because consumers intent on remortgaging pay down their existing mortgage unexpectedly quickly, removing its value. The valuation and the hedging of retail assets that are subject to prepayment risk is complex because it relies on assumptions about customer behavior that are hard to validate. Another example of a valuation risk is the estimation of the residual value of automobiles in auto leasing business lines. Where this kind of risk is explicitly recognized, it tends to be managed centrally by the treasury unit of the retail bank.
- *Operational risks* in retail banking are generally managed as part of the business in which they arise. For example, fraud by customers is closely monitored and new processes, such as fraud detection mechanisms, are put in place when they are economically justified. Under Basel II and III, banks allocate regulatory capital against operational risk in both retail and wholesale banking. A subdiscipline of retail operational risk management is emerging that makes use of many of the same concepts as bank operational risk at a firmwide level (see Chapter 14).

- *Business risks* are one of the primary concerns of senior management. These include business volume risks (e.g., the rise and fall of mortgage business volumes when interest rates go up and down), strategic risks (such as the growth of Internet banking or new payments systems), and decisions about mergers and acquisitions.
- *Reputation risks* are particularly important in retail banking. The bank has to preserve a reputation for delivering on its promises to customers. But it also has to preserve its reputation with regulators, who can remove its business franchise if it is seen to act unfairly or unlawfully.

Credit Scoring: Cost, Consistency, and Better Credit Decisions

Every time you apply for a credit card, open an account with a telephone company, submit a medical claim, or apply for auto insurance, it is almost certain that a *credit scoring* model—or, more precisely, a *credit risk scoring* model—is ticking away behind the scenes.[3]

The model uses a statistical procedure to convert information about a credit applicant or an existing account holder into numbers that are then combined (usually added) to form a score. This score is then regarded as an indicator of the credit risk of the individual concerned—that is, the probability of repayment. The higher the score, the lower the risk.

Credit scoring is important because it allows banks to avoid the most risky customers. It can also help them to assess whether certain kinds of businesses are likely to be profitable by comparing the profit margin that remains

---

[3]Good general references to credit scoring include Edward M. Lewis, *An Introduction to Credit Scoring* (San Raphael, CA: Fair Isaac Corporation, 1992); L. C. Thomas, J. N. Crook, and D. B. Edelman, eds., *Credit Scoring and Credit Control* (Oxford: Oxford University Press, 1992); and V. Srinivasan and Y. H. Kim, "Credit Granting: A Comparative Analysis of Classification Procedures," *Journal of Finance* 42, 1987, pp. 665–683. More recent references include E. Mays and Niall Lynas, *Credit Scoring for Risk Managers: The Handbook for Lenders*, 2011, and N. Siddiqi, *Credit Risk Scorecards: Developing and Implementing Intelligent Credit Scoring*, Wiley, 2005.

once operating and estimated default expenses are subtracted from gross revenues.

But credit scoring is also important for reasons of cost and consistency. Major banks typically have millions of customers and carry out billions of transactions each year. By using a credit scoring model, banks can automate as much as possible the adjudication process for small credits and credit cards. Before credit scoring was widely adopted, a credit officer would have to review a credit application and use a combination of experience, industry knowledge, and personal know-how to reach a credit decision based on the large amount of information in a typical credit application. Each application might typically contain about 50 bits of information, although some applications may call for as many as 150 items. The number of possible combinations of information is staggering, and, as a result, it is almost impossible for a human analyst to treat credit decisions in identical ways over time.

By contrast, credit risk scorecards consistently weight and treat the information items that they extract from applications and/or credit bureau reports. The credit industry calls these items *characteristics*, and they correspond to the questions on a credit application or the entries in a credit bureau report. The answers given to the questions in an application or the entries of a credit bureau report are known as *attributes*. For example, "four years" is an attribute of the characteristic "time at address." Similarly, "rents" is an attribute of the characteristic "residential status."

Credit scoring models assess not only whether an attribute is positive or negative but also by how much. The weighting of the values associated with each answer (or attribute) is derived using statistical techniques that look at the odds of repayment based on past performance. ("Odds" is the term the retail banking industry uses to mean "probability.") Population odds are defined as the ratio of the probability of a good event to the probability of a bad event in the population. For example, an applicant drawn randomly from the population with 15:1 odds has a probability of 1 in 16—i.e., 6.25 percent—of being a bad customer (by which we mean delinquent or the subject of a charge-off).

The statistical techniques employed to weight the information in a credit report include linear or logistic regression, mathematical programming or classification trees, neural nets, and genetic algorithms (with logistic regression being the most common).

Figure 9-1 shows what a credit scoring table might look like—in this case, one used to differentiate between credit applications.

FIGURE 9-1 Example of an Application Scoring Table

Years on job	Less than 6 months	6 months to 1 year	1 yr 7 months to 6 yrs 8 months	6 yrs 9 months to 10 yrs 5 months	10 yrs 6 months or more	
	5	14	20	27	39	
Own or rent	Own or buying	Rent	All others			
	40	19	26			
Banking	Checking account	Savings account	Checking and savings account	None		
	22	17	31	0		
Major credit cards	Yes	No				
	27	11				
Occupation	Retired	Professional	Clerical	Sales	Service	All others
	41	36	27	18	12	27
Age of applicant	18–25	26–31	32–34	35–51	52–61	62 and over
	19	14	22	26	34	40
Worst credit reference	Major derogatory	Minor derogatory	No record	One satisfactory	Two or more satisfactory	No investigation
	–15	–4	–2	9	18	0

Source: Lewis, 1992, p. xv.

What Kind of Credit Scoring Models Are There?

For the purpose of scoring consumer credit applications, there are really three types of models:

- *Credit bureau scores.* These are often known as FICO scores, because the methodology for producing them was developed by Fair Isaac Corporation (the leader in credit risk analytics for retail businesses). In the United States and Canada, bureau scores are also maintained and supplied by companies such as Equifax and TransUnion. From the bank's point of view, this kind of generic credit score has a low cost, is quickly installed, and offers a broad overview of an applicant's overall creditworthiness (regardless of the type of credit for which the applicant is applying). For example, Fair Isaac credit bureau risk scores can be tailored to the preferences of a financial institution (they usually range from 300 to 850; subprime lending typically targets customers with scores below 660).
- *Pooled models.* These models are built by outside vendors, such as Fair Isaac, using data collected from a wide range of lenders with similar credit portfolios. For example, a revolving credit pooled model might

be developed from credit card data collected from several banks. Pooled models cost more than generic scores, but not as much as custom models. They can be tailored to an industry, but they are not company specific.

- *Custom models.* These models are usually developed in-house using data collected from the lender's own unique population of credit applications. They are tailored to screen for a specific applicant profile for a specific lender's product. Custom models have allowed some banks to become expert in particular credit segments, such as credit cards and mortgages. They can give a bank a strong competitive edge in selecting the best customers and offering the best risk-adjusted pricing.

Let's take a closer look at the generic information offered by credit bureaus. Credit bureau data consist of numerous "credit files" for each individual who has a credit history. Each credit file contains five major types of information:

- *Identifying information.* This is personal information; it is not considered credit information as such and is not used in scoring models. The rules governing the nature of the identifying information that can be collected are set by local jurisdictions. In the United States, for example, the U.S. Equal Opportunity Acts prohibits the use of information such as gender, race, or religion in credit scoring models.
- *Public records (legal items).* This information comes from civil court records and includes bankruptcies, judgments, and tax liens.
- *Collection information.* This is reported by debt collection agencies or by entities that grant credit.
- *Trade line/account information.* This is compiled from the monthly "receivables" data that credit grantors send to the credit bureaus. The tapes contain reports of new accounts as well as updates to existing account information.
- *Inquiries.* Every time a credit file is accessed, an inquiry must be placed on the file. Credit grantors only see the inquiries that are placed for the extension of new credit.

Some credit bureaus, such as Equifax, allow individuals to obtain their own score, together with an explanation of how to improve their current score (and what-if analyses, such as the impact on the score of reducing the balance on the customer's credit cards).

A bureau score can be used to derive a more all-encompassing credit score, taking into account a series of key variables including loan-to-value and the quality of the loan documentation. For example:

$$Risk\ Score = f(Doc\ Type,\ Transaction\ Type,\ FICO,\ LTV,\ DTI,\ Occup\ Type,\ Prop\ Type,\ Pmt,\ Economic\ Cycle)$$

Box 9-6 gives the definition of the key variables that require more explanation. One of the problems in the run-up to the financial crisis of 2007–2009 was that some originators were relying too heavily on bureau credit scores and not taking into proper account the wider set of risk variables.

BOX 9-6   DEFINITIONS OF SOME KEY VARIABLES IN MORTGAGE CREDIT ASSESSMENT

- Documentation (doc) type:
  - Full doc: A mortgage loan that requires proof of income and assets. Debt-to-income ratios are calculated.
  - Stated income: Specialized mortgage loan in which the mortgage lender verifies employment but not income.
  - No income / No asset: Reduced documentation mortgage that allows the borrower to state income and assets on the loan application without verification by the lender; however, the source of the income is still verified.
  - No ratio: A mortgage loan that documents employment but not income. Income is not listed on the application, and no debt-to-income ratios are calculated.
  - No doc: A mortgage loan that requires no income or asset documentation. Neither is stated on the application, and fields for such information are left blank.
- FICO: Number score of the default risk associated with a borrower's credit history.
- DTI: Debt-to-income ratio is used to qualify mortgage payment and other monthly debt payments versus income.

- LTV: The ratio expresses the amount of a first mortgage lien as a percentage of the total appraised value of the property—i.e., the loan-to-value ratio.
- Payment type (Pmt)—e.g., adjustable rate mortgage, monthly treasury average.

After years of very poor underwriting standards and irresponsible lending, mortgage products returned to more traditional standards following the financial crisis—e.g., full documentation loans, with borrowers obliged to have credit scores above 680, and significantly larger down payments. The industry has moved away from loans featuring negative amortization, stated income, no income/no assets, no documentation, or 100 percent financing.

From Cutoff Scores to Default Rates and Loss Rates

In the early stages of the industry's development of credit scoring models, the actual probability of default assigned to a credit applicant did not much matter. The models were designed to put applicants *in ranked order* in relation to their *relative* risk. This was because lenders used the models not to generate an absolute measure of default probability but to choose an appropriate cutoff score—i.e., the point at which applicants were accepted, based on subjective criteria.

We can see how cutoff scores work if we look at Figure 9-2, which shows the distribution of "good" and "bad" accounts by credit score. Suppose we set the minimum acceptable score at 680 points. If only applications scoring that value or higher were accepted, the firm using the scoring system would avoid lending money to the body of bad customers to the left of the vertical line, but would forgo the smaller body of good accounts to the left of the line. Moving the minimum score line to the right will cut off an even higher fraction of bad accounts but forgo a larger fraction of good accounts, and so on. The score at which the minimum score line is set—the cutoff score—is clearly an important decision for the business in terms of both its likely profitability and the risk that the bank is taking on.

FIGURE 9-2 Distributions of "Goods" and "Bads"

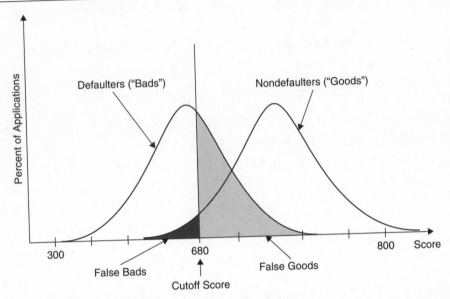

Given the cutoff score, the bank can determine, based on its actual experience, the loss rate and profitability for the retail product. Over time, the bank can adjust the cutoff score in order to optimize the profit margin for each product as well as to reduce the false goods and the false bads. In retail banking, unlike wholesale banking, banks have lots of customers, and it doesn't take too much time to accumulate enough data to assess the performance of a scorecard. However, only by using longer time series can the bank hope to capture behavior through a normal economic cycle. Usually, the statistics on loss rates and profitability are updated on a quarterly basis.

The Basel Capital Accord requires that banks segment their retail portfolios into subportfolios with similar loss characteristics, especially similar prepayment risk. Banks will have to estimate both the PD and the LGD for these portfolios. This can be achieved by segmenting each retail portfolio by score band, with each score band corresponding to a risk level. For each score band, the bank can estimate the loss rate using historical data; then, given an estimate of the LGD, the bank can infer the implied PD. For example, if the actual historical loss rate is 2 percent with a 50 percent LGD, then the implied PD is 4 percent.

The bank should adopt similar risk management policies with respect to all borrowers and transactions in a particular segment. These policies should include

derwriting and structuring of the loans, economic capital allocations, pricing
l other terms of the lending agreement, monitoring, and internal reporting.

easuring and Monitoring the Performance of a Scorecard

: purpose of credit scoring is to predict which applications will prove to be
od or bad risks into the future. To do this, the scorecard must be able to differ-
iate between the two by assigning high scores to good credits and low scores
oor ones. The goal of the scorecard, therefore, is to minimize the overlapping
a of the distribution of the good and bad credits, as we saw in Figure 9-2.

This leads to a number of practical problems that are of interest to risk
nagers. How can we measure a scorecard's performance? How do we know
en to adjust and rebuild scorecards or to change the operating policy?

The validation technique traditionally employed is the cumulative accu-
y profile (CAP) and its summary statistic, the accuracy ratio (AR), illustrated
Figure 9-3. On the horizontal axis are the population sorted by score from
highest risk score to the lowest risk score. On the vertical axis are the actual
aults in percentage terms taken from the bank's records. For example, assume
t the scoring model predicts that 10 percent of the accounts will default in the
t 12 months. If our model were perfect, the actual number of accounts that
aulted over that time period would correspond to the first decile of the score
ribution—the perfect model line in the figure. Conversely, the 45-degree line
responds to a random model that cannot differentiate between good and bad
tomers.

Clearly, the bank hopes that its scoring model results are relatively close to
perfect model line. The area under the perfect model is denoted A_P, while
area under the actual rating model is denoted A_R. The accuracy ratio is
$= A_R/A_P$, and the closer this ratio is to 1, the more accurate is the model.

The performance of a scoring model can be monitored—say, every quar-
-by means of a CAP curve, and the model replaced when its performance
eriorates. The performance of scoring systems tends not to change abruptly,
it can deteriorate for several reasons: the characteristics of the underlying
ulation may change over time, and/or the behavior of the population may
lve so as to change the variables associated with a high likelihood of default.

Another reason for replacing a scoring model is that the bank has changed
nature of the products that it is offering to customers. If a financial institution

FIGURE 9-3 Cumulative Accuracy Profile (CAP) and Accuracy Ratio (AR)

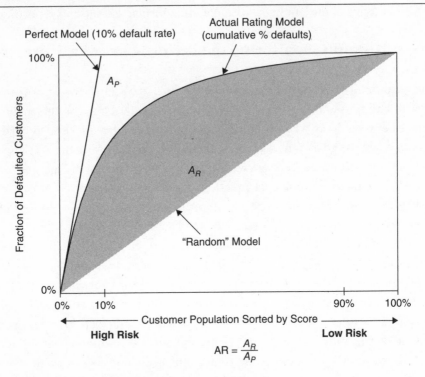

$$AR = \frac{A_R}{A_P}$$

that offers auto loans decides to sell this business and issue credit cards instead, it is highly probable that the target customer population will be different enough to justify the development of a new custom scorecard.

From Default Risk to Customer Value

As the technology of scorecards has developed, banks have progressed from scoring applications at one point in time to periodic "behavior scoring." Here the bank uses information on the behavior of a current customer, such as usage of the credit line and social demographic information, to determine the risk of default over a fixed period of time. The approach is similar to application scoring, but it uses many more variables that describe the past performance of customers.

This kind of risk modeling is no longer restricted to default estimation. Some time ago, lenders began to shift from simply assessing default risk to making more subtle assessments that are directly linked to the value of customers to the bank. Credit scoring techniques have been applied to new areas, such as response scorecards that predict whether the consumer is likely to respond to a direct marketing offer, usage scorecards that predict how likely it is that the customer will make use of the credit product, and attrition scorecards that estimate how long the customer will remain loyal to the lender. Each customer may now be described by a number of different scores (Box 9-7).

There is often a trade-off to be made between the creditworthiness of customers and their profitability. After all, there's not much point in issuing costly credit cards to creditworthy customers who never use them. Conversely, customers who are marginally more likely to default might be still be more profitable than customers with higher scores—e.g., if they tend to borrow money often or are prepared to pay a higher rate of interest. (The key risk management

---

BOX 9-7   SOME DIFFERENT KINDS OF SCORECARDS

- *Credit bureau scores* are the classic FICO credit scores available from the main credit bureaus in the United States and Canada.
- *Application scores* support the initial decision as to whether to accept a new applicant for credit.
- *Behavior scores* are risk estimators similar to application scores, but they use information on the behavior of existing credit account holders—e.g., usage of credit and delinquency history.
- *Revenue scores* aim at predicting the profitability of existing customers.
- *Response scores* predict the likelihood that a customer will respond to an offer.
- *Attrition scores* estimate the likelihood that existing customers will close their accounts, won't renew a credit such as a mortgage, or will reduce their balance on existing credits.
- *Insurance scores* predict the likelihood of claims from insured parties.
- *Tax authority scores* predict whom the tax inspector should audit in order to collect additional revenues.

question here is whether the additional profitability really does offset the risks run by the business line over the longer term—i.e., will the default rate for the marginally less creditworthy customer shoot up if the economy turns sour?)

Leading banks are therefore experimenting with ways to take into account the complex interplay of risk and reward. They are moving away from traditional credit default scoring toward product profit scoring (which seeks to estimate the profit the lender makes on a specific product from the customer) and to customer profit scoring (which tries to estimate the total profitability of the customer to the lender). Using this kind of advanced information, lenders can select credit limits, interest margins, and other product features to maximize the profitability of the customer. And they can adjust these risk, operating, and marketing parameters during their relationship with the customer.

In particular, the market is becoming accustomed to "risk-based pricing" for credit products—the idea that customers with different risk profiles should pay different amounts for the same product. Increasingly, banks understand that a "one price fits all" policy in a competitive market leads to *adverse selection*—i.e., the bank will primarily attract high-risk customers, to whom the product is attractive, and discourage low-risk customers (for the opposite reason). The degree of adverse selection suffered by a bank may only become apparent when the economic climate deteriorates.

Figure 9-4 summarizes the customer relationship cycle that best-practice banks have been developing for some years. *Marketing initiatives* include targeting new and existing customers for a new product or tailoring an existing

FIGURE 9-4 The Customer Relationship Cycle

Marketing Initiatives	Screening Applications	Managing Accounts
Target prospect/existing customer?	Accept/reject?	Increase/decrease credit line?
	Tier pricing?	Tier pricing?
Tailor product offering/ message?	Initial credit line?	Collect?
Mail/don't mail?		Authorize?
How frequently?		Reissue?
		Customer service level?

Cross-Sell

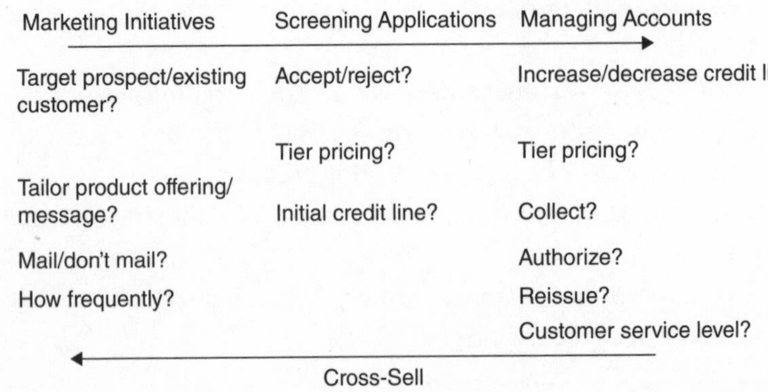

product and/or offer to the specific needs of a customer; these initiatives are the result of detailed marketing studies that analyze the most likely response of various client segments. *Screening applicants* consists of deciding which applications to accept or reject on the basis of scorecards, in terms of both granting the initial credit line and setting the appropriate pricing for the risk level of the client. *Managing the account* is a dynamic process that involves a series of decisions based on observed past behavior and activity. These include modifying a credit line and/or the pricing of a product, authorizing a temporary excess in the use of a credit line, renewing a credit line, and collecting past due interest and/or principal on a delinquent account. *Cross-selling* initiatives close the loop on the customer relationship cycle. Based on a detailed knowledge of existing customers, the bank can initiate actions to induce existing customers to buy additional retail products. For example, for a certain category of customers who already have checking and savings accounts, the bank can offer a mortgage, a credit card, insurance products, and so on. In this retail relationship cycle, risk management has become an integral part of the broader business decision-making process.

Since the 2007–2009 financial crisis, a couple of significant trends have emerged to improve this classic approach to credit scoring and its application.[4] First, there has been a bigger push to understand how changes in macroeconomic factors (e.g., house prices, unemployment) might affect the behavior of given score bands so that predicted default rates can be adjusted to account for the current stage of the economic cycle. This effort ties in with the efforts to stress test how retail credit risk portfolios might perform in stressful macroeconomic scenarios. The hope is that business decisions can be made more forward-looking if they are adjusted to account for baseline projections for the economy (i.e., consensus macroeconomic expectations) and also take into account the capital costs and potential losses implied by the raised default rates of adverse scenarios. This kind of forward-looking economic calibration can be augmented with other kinds of adjustment for potential social and behavioral changes—e.g., changes in the laws surrounding personal finance.

Second, firms have begun to look more closely at how they can test responses to variations in product offerings and then monitor the early performance of those taking up retail offers (e.g., credit cards). Lessons from this

---

[4]For example, see discussion in Andrew Jennings, "A 'New Normal' Is Emerging—But Not Where Most Banks Expect," *FICO Insights*, No. 53, July 2011.

market and performance "tasting" exercise can then be fed back into the wider marketing campaign, after the implications have been filtered through a sophisticated understanding of how any strategy adjustments will affect capital costs and risk-adjusted profitability.

Both of these trends can be seen as part of the broader attempt to make risk-adjusted decision making in retail banking more forward-looking, granular, and responsive to social and economic change (as opposed to a more static, less focused view based on historical data).

The Basel Regulatory Approach

Traditionally, consumer credit evaluation has modeled each loan or customer in isolation—a natural outcome of the development of application scoring. But lenders are really interested in the characteristics of whole *portfolios* of retail loans. This interest has been reinforced by the emphasis on internal ratings-based modeling in Basel II and III.

As we discussed in Chapter 3, the Basel III regulatory framework allows banks to use either a Standardized Approach or an Advanced Approach to calculate the required amount of regulatory capital. Under the Advanced Approach, the bank itself estimates parameters for probability of default and loss given default and applies these to its consumer credit risk model in order to estimate the distribution of default loss for various consumer segments.

The Accord considers three retail subsectors—residential mortgages, revolving credit, and other retail exposures such as installment loans—and applies three different formulas to capture the risk of the risk-weighted assets. It's an approach that has highlighted the need for banks to develop accurate estimates of default probability (rather than simply rely on relative credit scores) and to be able to segment their loan portfolios. Provided banks can convince regulators that their risk estimates are accurate, they will be able to minimize the amount of capital required to cover expected and unexpected retail default losses.

Securitization and Market Reforms

We discuss securitization and the transfer of consumer credit risk in Chapter 12, with a quick recap here because securitization has been such an important feature of the consumer lending markets.

Before the start of the subprime crisis in 2007, around 50 percent of all home mortgages were securitized in the United States. Though the crisis halted almost all private label mortgage securitizations (i.e., those not backed by the guarantees of government-sponsored entities), the private label market was reformed in the post-crisis years and is slowly reviving. Meanwhile, certain securitization markets based on consumer lending, including those for auto lending, credit card receivables, and student loans, continued to perform in relatively good health.

The phenomenon of securitization initially took hold in the U.S. home mortgage markets. By the late 1970s, a substantial proportion of home mortgages were being securitized, and the trend intensified in the 1980s. A catalyst for the development of mortgage securitization in the United States was the federal government's sponsorship of some key financial agencies—namely, the Federal National Mortgage Association (FNMA, or Fannie Mae), the Federal Home Loan Mortgage Corporation (FHLMC, or Freddie Mac), and the Government National Mortgage Association (GNMA, or Ginnie Mae). These agencies issue securities that pay out to investors using income derived from pools of home mortgages originated by banks and other financial intermediaries. In order to qualify for inclusion in these pools, mortgages must meet various requirements in terms of structure and amount. However, from the 1990s, the market for private label securitization began to grow quickly and to develop various different kinds of mortgage-backed and other securitization products.

Collateralized Mortgage Obligation (CMO) payments are divided into tranches (such as mortgage-backed securities or MBS), with the first tranche receiving the first set of payments and other tranches taking their turn. Asset-backed securities (ABSs) is a term that applies to instruments based on a much broader array of assets than MBSs, including, for example, credit card receivables, auto loans, home equity loans, and leasing receivables.

Selling the cash flows from these loans to investors through some kind of securitization means that the bank gains a principal payment up front, rather than having the money trickle in over the life of the retail product. The securities might be sold to third parties or issued as tranched bonds in the public marketplace—i.e., classes of senior and subordinated bonds awarded ratings by a rating agency.

Securitizations can take many forms in terms of their legal structure, the reliability of the underlying cash flows, and the degree to which the bank sells off or retains the riskier tranches of cash flows. In some instances, the bank substantially shifts the risk of the portfolio to the investors and through this process reduces the economic risk (and the economic capital) associated with the portfolio. The bank gives up part of its income from the borrowers and is left with a profit margin that should compensate it for the initiation of the loans and for servicing them.

In other instances, the securitization is structured with regulatory rules in mind to reduce the amount of risk capital that regulators will require the bank to set aside for the particular consumer portfolio in question. Sometimes, this means that only a much smaller amount of the economic risk of the portfolio is transferred to investors, a practice motivated by *regulatory arbitrage*—i.e., reduction in the capital charges attracted by different kinds of asset.

In the run-up to the 2007–2009 financial crisis, three key trends undermined the health of the mortgage (and other) securitization markets:

- Subprime and similarly risky lending began to be originated specifically for securitization, often by firms (e.g., brokers) that were lightly capitalized and regulated and that had no long-term interest in controlling the quality of the underlying loans (Box 9-4).
- Subprime credit was wrapped up into complex securities, which were given high ratings that turned out to be based on fragile assumptions.
- Banks failed to distribute the securitized risk and instead held large amounts of the securitized risk themselves, either directly or through investment vehicles of various kinds.

We discuss the crisis and the securitization reforms it led to in more detail in Chapter 12. From the perspective of originators of consumer credit, the key effect of these reforms will be to:

- Improve disclosure and transparency by providing investors with more detailed and accurate information about the assets underlying the securitization
- Make originators more accountable by obliging them to retain a portion (e.g., 5%) of the economic interest
- Make rating methodologies and assumptions public, and rating agencies more accountable

- Set capital requirements to a level that better reflects the risks of securitizations

In addition, the crisis led to a series of reforms aimed at preventing financial institutions from abusing customers. These are likely to have a significant effect on behavior in the U.S. retail markets over the long term.

Risk-Based Pricing

We mentioned earlier that risk-based pricing (RBP) is increasingly popular in retail financial services, encouraged by both competitive and regulatory trends. By risk-based pricing for financial services we mean explicitly incorporating risk-driven account economics into the annualized interest rate that is charged to the customer at the account level. The key economic factors here include operating expenses, the probability of take-up (i.e., the probability that the customer will accept a product offering), the probability of default, the loss given default, the exposure at default, the amount of capital allocated to the transaction, and the cost of equity capital to the institution.

Many leading financial institutions have already adopted some form of RBP for acquisitions in their auto loan, credit card, and home mortgage business lines. Since the 2007–2009 financial crisis, banks have recognized the need to factor into RBP some longer-term considerations. Still, RBP in the financial retail area remains in its infancy. A bank's key business objectives are seldom adequately reflected in its pricing strategy. For example, the ability to properly price low-balance accounts versus high-balance revolvers is often inadequate. Further, setting cutoff scores in concert with *tiered pricing*[5] is often based on ad hoc heuristics rather than deep pragmatic analytics. A tiered pricing policy that sets price as an increasing function of riskier score bands can make risk-based pricing easier and more effective. A well-designed RBP strategy allows the bank to map alternative pricing strategies at the credit score level to key corporate metrics (e.g., revenue, profit, loss, risk-adjusted return, market share, and portfolio value) and is a critical component of best-practice retail management.

---

[5]By tiered pricing, we mean pricing differentiated by score bands above the cutoff score—the higher the score, the lower the price.

RBP incorporates key factors from both the external market data (such as the probability of take-up, which in turn is a function of price and credit limit) and internal data (such as the cost of capital).

RBP enables retail bank managers to raise shareholder value by achieving management objectives while taking multiple constraints into consideration, including trade-offs among profit, market share, and risk. Mathematical programming algorithms (such as integer programming solutions) have been developed to efficiently achieve these management objectives, subject to the aforementioned constraints. Pricing is a key tool for retail bankers as they balance the goal of increasing market share against the goal of reducing the rate of bad accounts.

To increase market share in a risk-adjusted manner, a retail bank might examine the rate of bad accounts as a function of the percentage of the overall population acceptance rate (strategy curve). Traditional retail pricing leaves a considerable amount of money on the table; better pricing can improve key corporate performance metrics by 10 to 20 percent or more.

RBP should also be used, in our view, when nonbanks offer credit to customers and small businesses. However, it requires a logistical and operational infrastructure that many retailers lack. Hence they tend to rely more on credit card payments as well as payments backed by financial institutions.

Tactical and Strategic Retail Customer Considerations

There are various tactical applications for scoring technologies, such as determining which customers are more likely to stay (or to leave) and finding approaches to reduce attrition (or increase loyalty) among the right customers. The technologies might also help banks decide on the best product to offer a particular customer, help them work out how to interest customers in new types of services such as retirement planning, and help them determine how aggressively they should be approaching customers.

There are also many strategic considerations. For example, is the bank extracting enough "lifetime value" from an individual account? How much future value can the bank expect from its customer portfolio, and what are the real sources of this value? Ideally, the bank should be able to compare its performance relative to its peers (e.g., in terms of market share) as it strives to win and keep the right kind of customer portfolios.

Conclusion

In this chapter, we've seen that many quantitative advances have emerged in the retail credit risk area to help shape business strategies throughout the customer life cycle.

At credit origination, analytical models can now help to identify customers who are likely to be profitable, predict their propensity to respond to an offering, align consumer preferences with products, assess borrowers' creditworthiness, determine line/loan authorization, apply risk-based pricing, and evaluate the relationship value of the customer.

Throughout loan servicing, analytical methods are used to anticipate consumer behavior or payment patterns, determine opportunities for cross-selling, assess prepayment risk, identify any fraudulent transactions, optimize customer relationship management, and prioritize the collection effort (to maximize recoveries in the event of delinquency). Increasingly, risk-based pricing can be used to analyze trade-offs and to determine the "optimal" multitier, risk-based pricing strategy.

However, in applying the quantitative methodologies to measure expected loss, banks have to be sure they are not overlooking the darker side of retail risk. Every new product or marketing technology introduces the danger that a systematic risk will be introduced into the credit portfolio—i.e., a common risk factor that causes losses to rise unexpectedly high once the economy or consumer behavior moves into a new configuration. The new scoring models are a tool that must be applied with a considerable dose of judgment, based on a deep understanding of each consumer product and the role it plays in the relevant customer segment.

10

COMMERCIAL CREDIT
RISK AND THE RATING
OF INDIVIDUAL CREDITS

Commercial credit risk is the largest and most elementary risk faced by many banks, and it is a major risk for many other kinds of financial institution and corporation as well. Assessing commercial credit risk is a complicated task because many uncertain elements are involved in determining both how likely it is that an event of default will happen and how costly default will turn out to be if it does occur. It's therefore no surprise to find that there are many different approaches to the problem.

Some of the newest approaches employ equity market data to track the likelihood of default by public companies; others assess credit risk at the portfolio level using mathematical and statistical modeling. We'll take a look at these modern quantitative approaches to the problem in the next chapter. More traditional approaches to the credit risk conundrum are based on credit risk assessments within an overall framework known as a *credit rating system*—the subject of the present chapter.

To make a credit assessment, analysts must take into consideration many complex attributes of a firm—financial and managerial, quantitative and qualitative. They must ascertain the financial health of the firm, determine whether earnings and cash flows are sufficient to cover any debt obligations, analyze the quality of the firm's assets, and examine its liquidity position. In addition, analysts must take into account the nature of the industry to which the potential client belongs, the status of the new client within that industry, and the potential effect of macroeconomic events on the firm (including any country risks, such as a political upheaval or currency crisis).

A credit rating system is simply a way of organizing and systematizing all these procedures so that credit analysts—across a firm and through time—can arrive at ratings that are rational, coherent, and comparable.

We'll look first at how credit rating agencies (key players in the development of modern ratings) arrive at their public credit ratings of large corporations. Then we'll take a look at how banks arrive at their own private internal ratings of firms, large and small, that lack a public credit rating.

Internal risk rating systems are one of the banking industry's oldest and most widely used credit risk measurement tools, but practices are changing fast as a result of both regulatory and competitive pressures. Internal rating systems allow the analysis of thousands of borrowers within a consistent framework and permit comparisons across the entire loan portfolio. Large banks use these internal ratings in several critical aspects of credit risk management, such as loan origination, loan pricing, loan trading, credit portfolio monitoring, capital allocation and reserve determination, profitability analysis, and management reporting (Box 10-1).

BOX 10-1 PURPOSE OF INTERNAL RISK RATING SYSTEMS (IRRS)

Traditionally IRRS are used by financial institutions for a variety of purposes:

- *Setting of limits and acceptance or rejection of new transactions.* The strength of the rating awarded to an entity or transaction is likely to play a key role in the decision to accept or reject a particular transaction. Credit risk limits are often set in terms of rating categories. Also, concentration limits by name, industry, and country are established and revised annually by the senior risk committee of the bank.
- *Monitoring of credit quality.* Ratings should be reviewed periodically—at least once a year or if a specific event justifies the revision of the credit assessment of a borrower. Credit migration is a critical component in monitoring the credit quality of the loan portfolios of banks.

- *Attribution of economic capital.* Best-practice institutions will have a risk-adjusted return on capital (RAROC) system in place to assess the contribution to shareholder value of the firm's activities and portfolios (see Chapter 17). Internal ratings are a key input when determining the amount of economic capital that should be allocated to each credit portfolio.
- *Adequacy of loan loss reserves.* Both regulators and management use the distribution of portfolio quality, as measured by internal ratings, to judge the adequacy of the financial accounting-based reserve for loan losses and the provision for losses in the current accounting period.
- *Adequacy of capital.* Again, both regulators and management, and also rating agencies, use the portfolio risk profile, as measured by internal ratings, to judge the fundamental creditworthiness of the institution as a whole. More specifically, internal ratings are a key input when calculating capital adequacy using Basel II/III's Internal Ratings Based approaches to capital requirements.
- *Pricing and trading of loans.* Internal ratings are key inputs for credit portfolio models (see Chapter 11), from which the risk contribution of each facility in a credit portfolio can be derived. In turn, these risk contributions help determine the minimum spread that an institution should charge on a credit facility in order to factor in the cost of credit risk. Failing to take account of the relative cost of extending credit destroys shareholder value.

Since these internal risk rating systems are such a key element of the credit risk management systems of financial institutions, it is not surprising that they are at the center of the Basel II and Basel III regulatory capital attribution process. A bank's internal risk rating system and the associated probability of default (PD) and loss given default (LGD) statistics are potentially key inputs into the bank's regulatory capital calculations. However, banks can use their own internal risk rating systems to set credit risk capital requirements only if they can show that those systems meet certain criteria (Box 10-2).

BOX 10-2   CRITERIA TO BE MET BY IRRS TO BE ELIGIBLE FOR BASEL II/III

To be eligible for the Internal Ratings Based (IRB) approach proposed under Basel II/III (described in Chapter 3), a bank must demonstrate that it meets certain minimum criteria both at its adoption of the IRB approach and on an ongoing basis. Most of these criteria focus on the ability of the internal risk rating system to rank-order and quantify risk in a consistent, reliable, and verifiable fashion. The main criteria are:

- *Meaningful differentiation of risk.* The Basel rules suggest a minimum of six to nine rating categories for nondefaulted borrowers as well one category for defaulted borrowers. A borrower's grade must be defined as an assessment of borrower risk on the basis of a specified and distinct set of rating criteria. The grade definition should include an estimated probability of default range and the criteria used to distinguish that level of credit risk. If a bank has a loan concentration within a particular range of default risk, it must offer a minimum grade differentiation within this range.
- *Reliable estimation of risk components.* A bank's rating definitions must be sufficiently detailed to allow those charged with assigning ratings to consistently assign the same grade to borrowers or facilities posing similar risks. Rating consistency must be satisfied across business lines and geographical locations. The rating process should also be independent of the staff in the bank who originate the deals (to prevent any conflict of interest).
- *Clarity of the documentation of rating systems and decisions.* To maintain consistency and integrity in the rating process, banks must ensure that the process is applied uniformly across the institution. Therefore, the risk rating assignment process must be well documented. Organizational controls to ensure the independence of the grade assignment and its validation must be in place.
- *Risk quantification and back testing.* The IRB approach requires banks to translate internal borrower and facility ratings into firm probability of default (PD) and loss given default (LGD) estimates,

respectively. Banks will be allowed to use a range of data sources (internal, external, and pooled) and quantification methodologies to make these estimates. But the estimates must be back-tested using historical data to verify that they are accurate estimates of actual default rates and credit losses going forward. The relative scarcity of credit and default data compared to, say, market risk data makes back testing a daunting task. Banks are required to collect data on borrower and facility ratings histories, including key data that are used to derive ratings. Banks must also collect default histories, including cause, timing, and components of loss. In addition, banks must capture predicted and realized default rates, LGDs, and exposures at default by rating category.

Rating Agencies

The External Agency Rating Process

The issuance of bonds by corporations is a twentieth-century phenomenon. Soon after bonds began to be issued, companies such as Moody's (1909), Standard & Poor's (1916), and other agencies started to offer independent assessments of how likely it was that particular bonds would repay investors in the way they were intended to do. Over the last 30 years, the introduction of new financial products has led to the development of new methodologies and criteria for credit rating: Standard & Poor's (S&P) was the first rating company to rate mortgage-backed bonds (1975), mutual funds (1983), and asset-backed securities (1985).

A credit rating is not, in general, an investment recommendation for a given security.[1] In the words of S&P, "A credit rating is S&P's opinion of the general creditworthiness of an obligor, or the creditworthiness of an obligor with respect to a particular debt security or other financial obligation, based on relevant risk factors."[2] When rating a security, a rating agency focuses more on

---

[1] In the United States, agency ratings have generally been considered as "opinions," so long as the ratings are widely disseminated. This has allowed the agencies to benefit from the freedoms established under the First Amendment of the U.S. Constitution and to gain many of the legal protections afforded to journalism.

[2] S&P Corporate Ratings Criteria, 1998, p. 3

the potential downside loss than on the potential upside gain. In Moody's words, a rating is "an opinion on the future ability and legal obligation of an issuer to make timely payments of principal and interest on a specific fixed income security."[3] S&P and Moody's have access to a corporation's internal information, and since they are considered to have expertise in credit rating and are generally regarded as unbiased evaluators (with some caveats discussed in Box 10-3), their ratings are widely accepted by market participants and regulatory agencies. Financial institutions, when required by their regulators to hold investment-grade bonds, use the ratings of credit agencies such as S&P and Moody's to determine which bonds are of investment grade.

BOX 10-3   ARE THE RATING AGENCIES UP TO THE JOB AND SHOULD WE RESTRICT THEIR ROLE?

Over the last few years, there has been mounting criticism of the *role* and *performance* of rating agencies.

The main criticism of the role that agencies play centers on their dominance of the credit rating market and their source of income. The demand for ratings has been artificially encouraged by a growing reliance on ratings as a tool of regulation. Since 1975, U.S. Securities and Exchange Commission regulations have relied on ratings from "nationally recognized statistical rating organizations" (NRSROs) to distinguish between the risks of various credit risky securities. Other regulators have required that many institutional investors hold only investment-grade instruments with ratings from one of the 10 firms registered with the SEC.

The intention behind this is to protect investors. But the importance of complying with the SEC and other government regulations that refer to officially recognized credit ratings has given NRSOs a semiofficial status.

More recently, the Basel II Accord explicitly refers to the rating grades of the major rating agencies for the calculation of risk-weighted assets (RWAs) and regulatory capital. Meanwhile, the European Central Bank is required to sell all non-investment-grade bonds in its portfolio.

---

[3]Moody's Credit Ratings and Research, 1998, p. 4

The semiofficial status of the rating agencies is compounded by the fact that they are in a quasi-monopolistic position. As of 2011, there were 10 U.S.-approved credit rating firms.[1] However, the three main rating agencies (Moody's, S&P, and Fitch) have a combined U.S. market share of about 95 percent.

Critics also point to a long-standing conflict of interest in the way that ratings are funded. Ideally, users of the ratings, such as investors, would pay agencies to rate companies; the company under the microscope would not make any payments at all to the rating agency. In reality, the largest rating agencies rely on issuer fees for the majority of their income, leading to fears that in certain circumstances they might lose their objectivity.

The potential for conflicts of interest might become worse in the future if the main agencies further develop risk consultancy and advisory services that take additional fees from the corporations that they rate.

The agencies respond by saying that they have put many processes in place to prevent any conflict of interest affecting a rating, and that they have a good track record of making accurate ratings.

Even so, rating agencies have been criticized for their performance. The main recent criticisms concern their rating of complex securitizations and the role this played in the 2007–2009 financial crisis. In Chapter 12 we discuss in detail why the methodology for rating structured credit products should be different from the approach used for corporate and municipal bonds (see Appendix 12.1).

However, there are also some long-standing concerns about the agencies' performance when rating corporations and corporate bonds. Some commentators said that the rating industry performed poorly in "calling" the 1997 crisis in the Asian markets. Many companies in the region were downgraded only after the crisis was well under way.

---

[1]The 10 are as follows, with the year each rating agency started: A.M. Best (1907), Moody's (1909), S&P (1923), Fitch (1927), Dominion Bond Rating Service (1976), Kroll Bond Rating Agency (1984), Japan Credit Rating Agency (1985), Rating and Investment Information (1986), Egan-Jones Ratings (1995), and Morningstar Credit Ratings (2001). As of 2011, according to securities filings, the three major rating agencies have about 2.5 million ratings on corporate, municipal, sovereign, and other types of debt, while the other seven ratings firms overseen by the SEC have just 84,000 ratings.

They also seemed to perform poorly in spotting very highly leveraged or poorly managed companies (such as the failed energy giant Enron) at the tail end of the millennial stock boom. The agencies themselves admitted that there were an unusually high number of "fallen angels"—that is, sudden downgrades from investment-grade status—after this boom turned to bust. But they pointed to their long-term record and said that many of the investors who use credit ratings in their investment decisions want relatively stable credit ratings, not ratings that jump up and down along with market perceptions.[2]

Another controversy surfaced in August 2011 when S&P downgraded the United States from AAA to AA+. Together with downgrades of sovereigns in Europe, particularly the sudden downgrades of Greece, Portugal, and Spain in April 2010, this fueled a debate on whether sovereigns should be rated by rating agencies. Politicians openly questioned the validity of the rating methodology for sovereigns and asked for an audit of the approach followed by the rating agencies.[3]

Ironically, the problem has arisen at least partly because of the semi-official status awarded to ratings by regulators. Ideally, rating agency grades should not have any more value than the opinions of other analysts or economic experts.[4] In reality, when a sovereign loses its AAA rating or a

---

[2]As a result of criticisms following the millennial stock boom and bust, regulatory authorities such as the U.S. Securities and Exchange Commission conducted a series of long-running investigations into the way the rating industry works—e.g., U.S. Securities and Exchange Commission, *Report on the Role and Function of Credit Rating Agencies in the Operation of the Securities Markets*, January 2003, available at http://www.sec.gov/news/studies/credratingreport0103.pdf. In the years following the 2007–2009 financial crisis, other reports examined rating agency practices, though often with a focus on structured finance—e.g., U.S. Securities and Exchange Commission, *Report to Congress on Assigned Credit Ratings*, December 2012, available at http://www.sec.gov/news/studies/2012/assigned-credit-ratings-study.pdf.

[3]The Treasury said that the S&P analysis that led to the U.S. downgrade revealed "a basic math error of significant consequence," while S&P argued that it was not an error but simply a change in assumptions that did not affect its final decision to cut the rating. The proposed SEC rules would require rating agencies to submit regular self-assessments of their internal controls to regulators. Also, rating agencies would be required to notify the public of "significant errors" that they find in their methodologies.

[4]Credit opinions are not the only avenue. CDS spreads provide a market measure of default risk that can be used to complement the rating assessment.

corporation loses its investment-grade rating, then institutional investors are required to sell the downgraded securities. This leads to a fall in the price of the relevant security and to an increase in the financing cost of the issuer, worsening the issuer's economic condition.[5] This perverse feedback played a significant role in the crises affecting Ireland and more recently Greece, Portugal, and Spain.[6]

How to reform the current system? One solution proposed by the Dodd-Frank Act in the United States is to suppress references to ratings in legislation and securities regulation,[7] starting with Basel II/III. The thinking behind this is that assessing the credit quality of borrowers is the core competency of banks, so banks should use their own internal rating system provided it has been validated by the regulators. It is also the responsibility of investors to perform their own due diligence and base their investment decisions on their own judgment and the opinion of a *range* of experts.

An alternative proposal by the European Commission involves the creation of an official rating agency under the control of a new single regulatory authority, the European Securities and Market Authority. This solution may not be ideal as it is difficult to believe that such an agency would remain free from political interference.

---

[5]When S&P downgraded Greek debt from A– to BBB+, then to BB+, the yield on the new Greek bonds went up from 5.5 percent to 10.7 percent.

[6]So far, U.S. debt has been less affected because it continues to be viewed as a safe haven by most international investors. There is currently no alternative to U.S. Treasuries for countries such as China, given the sheer size of their currency reserves.

[7]The SEC and other U.S. agencies are reviewing and changing their rules in accordance with the Dodd-Frank Act—e.g., SEC, *Report on Review of Reliance on Credit Ratings*, July 2011.

There are two main classes of ratings. With *issuer credit ratings*, the rating is an opinion on the obligor's overall capacity to meet its financial obligations. In the issuer credit rating category are counterparty ratings, corporate credit ratings, and sovereign credit ratings. Another class of rating is *issue-specific credit ratings*. In this case, the rating agency makes a distinction, in its rating system and symbols, between long-term and short-term credits. The short-term ratings

FIGURE 10-1 Moody's Rating Analysis of an Industrial Company

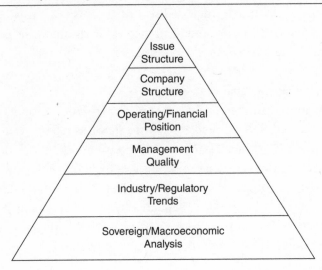

Issue
Structure

Company
Structure

Operating/Financial
Position

Management
Quality

Industry/Regulatory
Trends

Sovereign/Macroeconomic
Analysis

Source: Moody's.

apply to commercial paper (CP), certificates of deposit (CD), and put bonds.[4] In rating a specific issue, the attributes of the issuer, the specific terms of the issue, the quality of the collateral, and the creditworthiness of the guarantors are taken into account.

The rating process includes quantitative, qualitative, and legal analyses. The quantitative analysis is mainly financial analysis and is based on the firm's financial reports. The qualitative analysis is concerned with the quality of management; it includes a thorough review of the firm's competitiveness within its industry as well as the expected growth of the industry and its vulnerability to business cycles, technological changes, regulatory changes, and labor relations.

Figure 10-1 illustrates the process of rating an industrial company. The process allows the analyst to work through sovereign and macroeconomic issues, industry outlook, and regulatory trends to specific attributes (including quality

---

[4]A put bond is a bond stipulation that allows the holder to redeem the bond at face value at a specific, predetermined time, so that if interest rates go up, the holder can avoid losing money (so long as the stipulation remains in operation).

of management, operating position, and financial position) and eventually to the issue-specific structure of the financial instrument.

The assessment of management, which is subjective in nature, investigates how likely it is that management will achieve operational success in light of its tolerance for risk. The rating process includes meetings with the management of the issuer to review operating and financial plans, policies, and strategies. All the information is reviewed and discussed by a rating committee with appropriate expertise in the relevant industry, which then votes on the recommendation. The issuer can appeal the rating before it is made public by supplying new information. The rating decision is usually issued four to six weeks after the agency is asked to rate a debt issue.

Usually the ratings are reviewed once a year based on new financial reports, new business information, and review meetings with management. A "credit watch" or "rating review" notice is issued if there is reason to believe that the review may lead to a credit rating change. A change of rating has to be approved by the rating committee.

Credit Ratings by S&P and Moody's

Standard & Poor's (S&P) is one of the world's major rating agencies, operating in more than 50 countries. Moody's operates mainly in the United States but has many branches internationally. Tables 10-1 and 10-2 provide the definitions of the ratings categories used by S&P and Moody's for long-term credit. Issues rated in the four highest categories (i.e., AAA, AA, A, and BBB for S&P and Aaa, Aa, A, and Baa for Moody's) are generally considered to be of investment grade. Some financial institutions, for special or approved investment programs, are required to invest only in bonds or debt instruments that are of investment grade. Obligations rated BB, B, CCC, CC, and C by S&P (Ba, B, Caa, Ca, and C by Moody's) are regarded as having significant speculative characteristics. BB (Ba in Moody's) is the least risky, and C is the riskiest.

S&P uses plus or minus signs to modify its AA to CCC ratings to indicate the relative standing of a credit within the major rating categories. Similarly, Moody's applies numerical modifiers 1, 2, and 3 in each generic rating classification from Aa through Caa. The modifier 1, for example, indicates that the obligation ranks at the higher end of its generic rating category; thus B1 in Moody's rating system is a ranking equivalent to B+ in S&P's rating system.

FIGURE 10-2 Average Cumulative Default Rates for Corporate Bond Issuers (1981–2012)

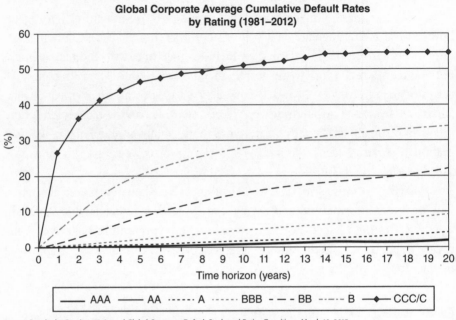

Source: Standard & Poor's 2012 Annual Global Corporate Default Study and Rating Transitions, March 18, 2013.

How accurate are agency ratings for corporations? The answer is provided in Figure 10-2, which shows the average cumulative default rates for corporate bond issuers for each rating category over bond holding periods of 1 year up to 20 years after bond issuance. The figure is based on data from the period 1981 to 2012. It can be seen that the lower the rating, the higher the cumulative default rates. The AAA and AA bonds experienced very low default rates; after 10 years, less than 1 percent of the issues had defaulted. Almost 30 percent of the B-rated issues, however, had defaulted after 10 years.

Historical data as presented in Figure 10-2 and Table 10-1 seem to offer a general validation of agency ratings of corporations, despite the failure of some high-rated banks during the 2007–2009 financial crisis.[5] But the data are useful for another reason: they allow risk analysts to attach an objective likelihood of default to any company that has been rated by an agency or that has been rated by banks in a manner thought to be equivalent to an agency rating.

---

[5]Agency ratings of structured products, especially those backed by subprime loans, have fared less well, for reasons we discuss in Chapter 12.

Global Corporate Average Cumulative Default Rates (1981-2012) (%)

Rating	-Time horizon (years)-														
	1	2	3	4	5	6	7	8	9	10	11	12	13	14	15
AAA	0.00	0.03	0.14	0.25	0.36	0.48	0.54	0.63	0.69	0.76	0.79	0.83	0.86	0.94	1.02
	(0.00)	(0.01)	(0.07)	(0.13)	(0.19)	(0.25)	(0.28)	(0.27)	(0.24)	(0.21)	(0.20)	(0.19)	(0.18)	(0.18)	(0.19)
AA	0.02	0.07	0.14	0.25	0.37	0.49	0.60	0.70	0.78	0.88	0.96	1.05	1.13	1.21	1.30
	(0.01)	(0.03)	(0.04)	(0.09)	(0.15)	(0.22)	(0.28)	(0.36)	(0.37)	(0.40)	(0.42)	(0.46)	(0.43)	(0.41)	(0.39)
A	0.07	0.17	0.29	0.45	0.62	0.81	1.03	1.23	1.43	1.65	1.84	2.02	2.19	2.35	2.55
	(0.02)	(0.03)	(0.05)	(0.08)	(0.09)	(0.10)	(0.13)	(0.17)	(0.25)	(0.39)	(0.52)	(0.56)	(0.57)	(0.55)	(0.55)
BBB	0.22	0.63	1.08	1.62	2.18	2.72	3.19	3.66	4.12	4.59	5.08	5.49	5.89	6.31	6.73
	(0.06)	(0.14)	(0.17)	(0.24)	(0.31)	(0.42)	(0.53)	(0.64)	(0.78)	(0.91)	(1.00)	(0.91)	(0.78)	(0.67)	(0.60)
BB	0.86	2.60	4.63	6.59	8.37	10.06	11.52	12.82	14.03	15.09	15.95	16.70	17.34	17.88	18.52
	(0.31)	(0.58)	(0.87)	(1.26)	(1.75)	(2.37)	(2.39)	(2.54)	(2.90)	(3.17)	(3.63)	(3.69)	(3.70)	(3.53)	(3.41)
B	4.28	9.58	14.07	17.56	20.18	22.30	24.03	25.42	26.64	27.84	28.84	29.65	30.40	31.10	31.82
	(0.93)	(1.96)	(2.20)	(2.43)	(2.89)	(2.85)	(2.98)	(3.16)	(3.10)	(2.77)	(2.24)	(2.16)	(2.04)	(2.17)	(2.33)
CCC/C	26.85	35.94	41.17	44.19	46.64	47.71	48.67	49.44	50.39	51.13	51.80	52.58	53.45	54.26	54.26
	(6.93)	(7.13)	(8.23)	(9.08)	(9.19)	(7.79)	(8.01)	(8.01)	(7.67)	(6.32)	(6.47)	(6.57)	(6.38)	(5.07)	(5.07)
Investment grade	0.11	0.31	0.54	0.82	1.12	1.41	1.68	1.94	2.19	2.45	2.70	2.91	3.11	3.32	3.54
	(0.03)	(0.06)	(0.09)	(0.13)	(0.15)	(0.16)	(0.18)	(0.22)	(0.30)	(0.41)	(0.50)	(0.50)	(0.46)	(0.41)	(0.36)
Specultive grade	4.11	8.05	11.46	14.22	16.44	18.30	19.85	21.16	22.36	23.46	24.38	25.15	25.85	26.48	27.12
	(0.96)	(1.39)	(1.72)	(1.84)	(1.87)	(1.65)	(1.73)	(1.75)	(1.64)	(1.53)	(1.51)	(1.52)	(1.53)	(1.50)	(1.47)
All rated	1.55	3.06	4.40	5.53	6.48	7.29	7.98	8.58	9.12	9.63	10.08	10.45	10.80	11.12	11.45
	(0.37)	(0.59)	(0.81)	(0.93)	(0.98)	(0.92)	(0.93)	(0.86)	(0.76)	(0.60)	(0.45)	(0.44)	(0.46)	(0.51)	(0.56)

Note: Numbers in parentheses are standard deviations. Sources: Standard & Poor's Global Fixed Income Research and Standard & Poor's CreditPro®.

Source: Standard & Poor's 2012 Annual Global Corporate Default Study and Rating Transitions, March 18, 2013.

TABLE 10-1 S&P Ratings Category Definitions

AAA   An obligation rated AAA has the highest rating assigned by Standard & Poor's. The obligor's capacity to meet its financial commitment on the obligation is extremely strong.

AA   An obligation rated AA differs from the highest rated obligations only in small degree. The obligor's capacity to meet its financial commitment on the obligation is very strong.

A   An obligation rated A is somewhat more susceptible to the adverse effects of changes in circumstances and economic conditions than obligations in higher rated categories. However, the obligor's capacity to meet its financial commitment on the obligation is still strong.

BBB   An obligation rated BBB exhibits adequate protection parameters. However, adverse economic conditions or changing circumstances are more likely to lead to a weakened capacity of the obligor to meet its financial commitment on the obligation.

BB   An obligation rated BB is less vulnerable to nonpayment than other speculative issues. However, it faces major ongoing uncertainties or exposure to adverse business, financial, or economic conditions which could lead to the obligor's inadequate capacity to meet its financial commitment on the obligation.

B   An obligation rated B is more vulnerable to nonpayment than obligations rated BB, but the obligor currently has the capacity to meet its financial commitment on the obligation. Adverse business, financial, or economic conditions will likely impair the obligor's capacity or willingness to meet its financial commitment on the obligation.

CCC   An obligation rated CCC is currently vulnerable to nonpayment and is dependent upon favorable business, financial, and economic conditions for the obligor to meet its financial commitment on the obligation. In the event of adverse business, financial, or economic conditions, the obligor is not likely to have the capacity to meet its financial commitment on the obligation.

CC   An obligation rated CC is currently highly vulnerable to nonpayment.

C   The C rating may be used to cover a situation where a bankruptcy petition has been filed or similar action has been taken, but payments on this obligation are being continued.

D   The D rating, unlike other ratings, is not prospective; rather, it is used only where a default has actually occurred—and not where a default is only expected. Standard & Poor's changes ratings to D either:
- On the day an interest and/or principal payment is due and is not paid. An exception is made if there is a grace period and S&P believes that a payment will be made, in which case the rating can be maintained; or
- Upon voluntary bankruptcy filing or similar action. An exception is made if S&P expects that debt service payments will continue to be made on a specific issue. In the absence of a payment default or bankruptcy filing, a technical default (i.e., covenant violation) is not sufficient for assigning a D rating.

+ or −   The ratings from AA to CCC may be modified by the addition of a plus or minus sign to show relative standing within the major rating categories.

R   The symbol is attached to the ratings of instruments with significant noncredit risks. It highlights risks to principal or volatility of expected returns which are not addressed in the credit rating. Examples include obligations linked or indexed to equities, currencies, or commodities; obligations exposed to severe prepayment risk—such as interest-only or principal-only mortgage securities; and obligations with unusually risky interest terms, such as inverse floaters.

Source: S&P's Corporate Ratings Criteria for 1998.

TABLE 10-2 Moody's Rating Category Definition

Aaa	Bonds that are rated Aaa are judged to be of the best quality. They carry the smallest degree of investment risk and are generally referred to as "gilt edged." Interest payments are protected by a large or an exceptionally stable margin, and principal is secure. While the various protective elements are likely to change, such changes as can be visualized are most unlikely to impair the fundamentally strong position of such issues.
Aa	Bonds that are rated Aa are judged to be of high quality by all standards. Together with the Aaa group, they comprise what are generally known as high-grade bonds. They are rated lower than the best bonds because margins of protection may not be as large as in Aaa securities, fluctuation of protective elements may be of greater amplitude, or there may be other elements present that make the long-term risk appear somewhat larger than with the Aaa securities.
A	Bonds that are rated A possess many favorable investment attributes and are to be considered as upper medium-grade obligations. Factors giving security to principal and interest are considered adequate, but elements may be present that suggest a susceptibility to impairment sometime in the future.
Baa	Bonds that are rated Baa are considered as medium-grade obligations (i.e., they are neither highly protected nor poorly secured). Interest payments and principal security appear adequate for the present, but certain protective elements may be lacking or may be characteristically unreliable over any great length of time. Such bonds lack outstanding investment characteristics and have speculative characteristics as well.
Ba	Bonds that are rated Ba are judged to have speculative elements; their future cannot be considered as well assured. Often the protection of interest and principal payments may be very moderate, and thereby not well safeguarded during both good and bad times over the future. Uncertainty of position characterizes bonds in this class.
B	Bonds that are rated B generally lack characteristics of the desirable investment. Assurance of interest and principal payments or of maintenance of other terms of the contract over any long period of time may be small.
Caa	Bonds that are rated Caa are of poor standing. Such issues may be in default, or there may be present elements of danger with respect to principal or interest.
Ca	Bonds that are rated Ca represent obligations that are speculative in a high degree. Such issues are often in default or have other marked shortcomings.
C	Bonds that are rated C are the lowest rated class of bonds, and issues so rated can be regarded as having extremely poor prospects of ever attaining any real investment standing.

Source: Moody's Credit Ratings and Research, 1995.

While the major rating agencies use similar methods and approaches to rate debt, they sometimes come up with different ratings for the same debt investment. Academic studies of the credit rating industry have shown that only a little over half of the firms rated AA or Aa and AAA or Aaa in a large sample were rated the same by the two top agencies. The same study found that smaller agencies tend to rate debt issues higher than or the same as S&P and Moody's; only rarely do they award a lower rating.[6]

Debt Rating and Migration

Bankruptcy, whether defined as a legal or an economic event, usually marks the end of a corporation in its current form. It is a discrete event, yet it is also the end point in what can be a long-running process—the moment when it is finally recognized that a firm cannot meet its financial obligations. Analysts who focus solely on the event of bankruptcy disregard a lot of useful information about the status of a firm, its total value, and the value of its liabilities.

Of course, credit agencies do not focus simply on default. At discrete points in time, they revise their credit ratings of corporate bonds. This evolution of credit quality is very important for an investor holding a portfolio of corporate bonds.

Using transition matrices, we can see how different rating categories have changed over time. Table 10-3 is based on S&P's experience from 1981 to 2012; it contains the empirical results for the migration from one credit risk category to all other credit risk categories within one year. The values on the diagonals of the transition matrix show the percentage of bonds that remained in the same risk category at the end of the specified time period as at the beginning.

For example, we see that 87.17 percent of the bonds rated AAA remained in the same rating category a year later. Observe that 8.69 percent were downgraded to AA, 0.54 percent downgraded to A, and so on. Similar multiyear transition matrices can also be produced (for reasons of space, these are not shown in this chapter). For example, on average, a firm rated BBB remained in

---

[6]R. Cantor and F. Packer, "Sovereign Credit Ratings," Federal Reserve Bank of New York, *Current Issues in Economics and Finance* 1(3), 1995.

TABLE 10-3 Average Transition Rates, (1981–2012)

From/To	AAA	AA	A	BBB	BB	B	CCC/C	D	NR
Global Corporate Average Transition Rates (1981-2012) (%)									
One-year									
AAA	87.17	8.69	0.54	0.05	0.08	0.03	0.05	0.00	3.38
	(9.11)	(9.13)	(0.86)	(0.31)	(0.25)	(0.20)	(0.40)	(0.00)	(2.66)
AA	0.54	86.29	8.36	0.57	0.06	0.08	0.02	0.02	4.05
	(0.55)	(4.90)	(3.99)	(0.75)	(0.25)	(0.24)	(0.07)	(0.07)	(1.91)
A	0.03	1.86	87.26	5.53	0.36	0.15	0.02	0.07	4.71
	(0.13)	(1.15)	(3.47)	(2.10)	(0.49)	(0.35)	(0.07)	(0.11)	(1.91)
BBB	0.01	0.12	3.54	85.09	3.88	0.61	0.14	0.22	6.39
	(0.06)	(0.23)	(2.31)	(4.62)	(1.82)	(1.02)	(0.24)	(0.26)	(1.79)
BB	0.02	0.04	0.15	5.18	76.12	7.20	0.72	0.86	9.71
	(0.06)	(0.16)	(0.39)	(2.35)	(5.02)	(4.63)	(0.92)	(1.04)	(2.84)
B	0.00	0.03	0.11	0.23	5.42	73.84	4.40	4.28	11.68
	(0.00)	(0.13)	(0.37)	(0.33)	(2.50)	(5.30)	(2.52)	(3.32)	(2.98)
CCC/C	0.00	0.00	0.16	0.24	0.73	13.69	43.89	26.85	14.43
	(0.00)	(0.00)	(0.70)	(1.01)	(1.29)	(8.42)	(12.62)	(12.48)	(7.19)

Note: Numbers in parentheses are standard deviations. NR denotes ratings withdrawn.

Source: Standard & Poor's 2012 Annual Global Corporate Default Study and Rating Transitions, March 21, 2012.

the same risk category after five years in 48.20 percent of the cases, while there was a 10.60 percent chance of that firm being upgraded to a rating of A. Bonds rated BBB had a 2.39 percent chance of defaulting within five years.

Such transition matrices highlight the differences between the higher and the lower ratings grades. For example, bonds with an initial rating of CCC defaulted in 26.82 percent of cases within one year, in 42.69 percent of cases within three years, and in 45.93 percent of cases within five years. For bonds rated AAA, the percentages were 0 percent for one year, 0.14 percent for three years, and 0.35 percent for five years, respectively. After five years, however, only 52.33 percent of the AAA-rated bonds had maintained their initial rating, while about 17 percent had had their ratings withdrawn (these data are not shown in Table 10-3).[7]

Clearly, issuers that are rated AAA can't be upgraded; they either maintain their rating or are downgraded. CCC-rated bonds can maintain their rating, be upgraded, or go into default. But what of BBB-rated bonds? Based on their history, they seem to have an equal chance of being upgraded or downgraded within a period of one or two years. However, over periods of five and ten years, they seem more likely to be upgraded than downgraded.

Transition matrices play a major role in CreditMetrics, an approach to portfolio credit risk measurement that we examine in the next chapter. Transition matrices are important to CreditMetrics because the approach uses the past (i.e., historical data) as the basis for estimating probabilities for future migration among risk categories.

Introduction to Internal Risk Rating

Banks are in the business of lending money to a very wide spectrum of companies, not just those that issue public debt and that therefore find it useful to invest in gaining a credit rating. Many smaller and private companies are not even listed on a public stock exchange and the available financial data may be of unproven quality.

In this section we look at the internal risk rating system (IRRS) of a typical bank. A robust IRRS should offer a carefully designed, structured, and documented series of steps for the assessment of each rating. The goal is to generate accurate and consistent risk ratings for many different types of company, yet also to allow professional judgment to significantly influence a rating where this is appropriate.

---

[7]Rating agencies typically rate the obligor from a longer-term through the (credit) cycle (TTC) perspective; however, many analytic modelers typically rate the obligor from a point in time (PIT) perspective. Analytic modelers' ratings more appropriately reflect the probability of default in the short term. The realized transition and default probabilities vary substantially over the years, depending on whether the economy is in recession or is expanding. Some practitioners adjust their average historical transition probabilities to reflect assessment of the current economic environment. Transition matrices for ratings based on a TTC approach show a lower volatility of expected losses and economic capital calculations compared to transition matrices based on a PIT approach. The probability of staying in the same PIT rating grade is smaller than when the rating is TTC, and PIT ratings are generally more volatile.

To be reliable, any such classification method must be consistent over time and must be based on sound economic principles. The IRRS we describe here is based on the authors' extensive experience as, in one case, a bank chief risk officer, and also as money managers at major commercial banks dealing with counterparty credit risk. The approach presented here is also consistent with the directives in Basel II and III, which oblige banks to put in place a systematic procedure for credit risk assessment.

Typically, a bank IRRS assigns two kinds of ratings. First, it assigns an obligor default rating (ODR) to each borrower (or group of borrowers) that identifies the borrower's probability of default. Second, it assigns a loss given default rating (LGDR) to each available facility, independently of the ODR, that identifies the risk of loss from that facility in the event of default on the obligation.

To understand the fundamental difference between these two kinds of ratings, let's consider the key concept of *expected loss*. The expected loss of a particular transaction or portfolio is the product of the amount of credit *exposure at default* (EAD) (say, $100) multiplied by the *probability of default* (PD) (say, 2 percent) for an obligor (or borrower) and the *loss rate given default* (LGD) (say, 50 percent) in any specific credit facility. In this example, the expected loss (EL) is

$$EL = EAD \times PD \times LGD = \$100 \times 0.02 \times 0.50 = \$1$$

The ODR represents simply the probability of default by a borrower in repaying its obligation in the normal course of business. The LGDR, on the other hand, assesses the conditional severity of the loss, should default occur. The severity of the loss on any facility is considerably influenced by whether the bank has put in place risk mitigation tools such as guarantees, collateral, and so on.

As well as identifying the risks associated with a borrower and a credit facility, an IRRS also provides a key input for the capital charges used in various pricing models and for risk-adjusted return on capital (RAROC) systems of the kind we describe in Chapter 17. It can also assist in establishing loan loss reserves—i.e., the accounting provisions that the bank sets aside to cover the expected cost of default. The IRRS can be used to rate credit risks in most of the major corporate and commercial sectors, but it is unlikely to cover all business sectors. Typically, a bank's principal IRRS excludes real estate credits, banks, agriculture, public finance, and other groups of credits identified as having special factors that need to be considered in their credit assessments, such as sovereigns.

TABLE 10-4 Risk Rating Continuum (Prototype Risk Rating System)

Risk	IRR	S&P Equivalent	Moody's Equivalent	
Sovereign	0	Not applicable		
Low	1	AAA	Aaa	
	2	AA	Aa2	Investment Grade
	3	A	A2	
Average	4	BBB⁺/BBB	Baa1/Baa2	
	5	BBB⁻	Baa3	
	6	BB⁺/BB	Ba1/Ba2	
	7	BB⁻	Ba3	
	8	B⁺/B	B1/B2	Below Investment Grade
	9	B⁻	B3	
High	10	CCC⁺/CCC	Caa1/Caa2	
	11	CC	Ca	
	12	In default		

A typical IRRS, as shown in Table 10-4, includes a category 0 to capture the government debt of developed economies (say, Canadian or U.S. federal government debt), as this is generally regarded as being without risk. Category 1 is reserved for corporate debt with the highest credit quality. The risk grades in the middle of the rating scheme (e.g., BBB and BB) are often split to obtain greater differentiation in risk assessment, as they often correspond to the range of risk where most of the credits are concentrated.

The steps in the IRRS (eight in our illustrative system: seven for the ODR and one for the LGDR) typically start with a financial assessment of the borrower (initial obligor rating) that sets a ceiling on the obligor rating. A series of further steps (six) leads to a final obligor rating. Each one of Steps 2 to 7 may result in a downgrade of the initial rating attributed at Step 1. These steps include analyzing the managerial capability of the borrower (Step 2), examining the borrower's absolute and relative position within the industry (Step 3), reviewing the quality of the financial information (Step 4), analyzing country risk (Step 5), comparing the preliminary ODR reached in Step 5 to default ratings provided by external rating agencies and by consulting and software firms such as KMV Corporation (Step 6; see Chapter 11), and considering the impact of the loan structure on the default probability (Step 7). The process ensures that all credits are objectively rated using a consistent process to arrive at accurate ratings.

The LGDR is derived in a final phase (Step 8) independent of the ODR.

Our eight steps are really the "factory floor" of any credit rating system. The usefulness of any internal rating, and the integrity of the bank's risk management system as a whole, relies upon each step being executed in a robust fashion. So let's take a closer look at each of the steps.

Financial Assessment (Step 1)

Introduction

This step formalizes the thinking process of a good credit analyst (or good equity analyst), whose goal is to ascertain the financial health of an institution. The credit analyst might begin by studying the institution's financial reports to determine whether the earnings and cash flows are sufficient to cover the debt repayments. The credit analyst will study the degree to which the trends associated with these "financials" are stable and positive. The credit analyst will also want to analyze the company's assets to determine whether they are of high quality and to make sure that the obligor has substantial cash reserves (e.g., substantial working capital[8]). The analyst will also want to examine the firm's leverage. Similarly, the credit analyst will want to analyze the extent to which the firm has access to the capital markets and whether it can borrow the money it will need to carry out its business plans. The rating should reflect the company's financial position and performance and its ability to withstand any financial setbacks.

Procedure

A prototype financial assessment table encompassing the risk rating 4 is shown in Table 10-5. The three main assessment areas, as illustrated in the column heads of Table 10-5, are (1) earnings and cash flow; (2) asset values, liquidity, and leverage; and (3) financial size, flexibility, and debt capacity.

A measure for earnings and cash flow in column 1 would take into account interest coverage expressed in terms of key accounting ratios—for example, the ratio of earnings before interest and taxes (EBIT) to interest expense and the ratio of earnings before interest, taxes, depreciation, and amortization (EBITDA) to interest expense.[9] The analysis would emphasize the current year's

---

Working capital is defined as the difference between current assets and current liabilities.

For definitions of key accounting ratios, see the appendix to this chapter.

TABLE 10-5 Step 1: Financial Assessment

	Asset Values (AV)	Financial Size (FS)
Earnings (E)	**Liquidity (LIQ)**	**Flexibility (F)**
RR **Cash Flow (CF)**	**Leverage (LEV)**	**Debt Capacity (DC)**
4 • Very satisfactory earnings and cash flow with substantial extra coverage • Positive and quite consistent/stable trends	• Assets of above average quality • Good liquidity/working capital • Better than average leverage • Appropriate matching of tenor of liabilities to assets	• General access (rated BBB+/ BBB) to capital markets; may experience some barriers because of difficult market or economic conditions • Ready access to alternative financing through banks or other financial institutions, if sought • Bank debt modest with large unused capacity

performance, with some recognition of the previous few years as appropriate. When assessing companies in cyclical industries, the analyst should adjust the financial results and key ratios so that the cyclical effect is incorporated.

A measure for leverage in column 2 might be ratios of debt to net worth, such as total liabilities to equity or (total liabilities minus short-term debt) to equity.

When assessing the financial size, flexibility, and debt capacity category, the size of the market capitalization will be an important factor. The "access to capital markets" bullet point in this third assessment area refers to the demonstrated ability (or potential in the near term) to issue public securities (equities or medium- to long-term debt instruments).

The analyst would calculate a risk rating for each of the three assessment areas and then arrive at an assessment of the best overall risk rating.[10] This is the initial obligor rating.

---

[10] As an appropriate control, the average might first be compared to the worst of the three risk levels. The rating should not be more than 1.0 better than the worst rating. In other words, if it exceeds this control, then it must be adjusted downward. For example, if the three assessment areas were respectively rated 2, 2, and 5 then the average is 3, but the rating should be adjusted to 4 (which is 1.0 better than the 5 risk level). If the worst of the three risk levels is not an integer (say 4.5), then reducing it by 1 would leave a rating of 3.5. One typically uses judgment and sets the rating at either 3 or 4.

TABLE 10-6 Some Key Financial Ratios

1.	EBIT interest coverage (%)
2.	EBITDA interest coverage (%)
3.	Funds from operations/total debt (%)
4.	Free operating cash flow/total debt (%)
5.	Pretax return on capital (%)
6.	Operating income/sales (%)
7.	Long-term debt/capital (%)
8.	Total debt/capitalization (%)

Industry Benchmarks

The analysis of a firm's competitive position and operating environment helps in assessing the firm's general business risk profile. This profile can be used to calibrate quantitative information drawn from the financial ratios for the firm, shown in Table 10-6. For example, the credit quality of a counterparty rises as an increasing function of the ratio of EBITDA to the amount of interest owed (i.e., EBITDA interest coverage).

A company with an excellent business in a growing or stable sector can assume more debt than a company with less glowing prospects.[11]

Adjustment Factors for Obligor Default Rating (ODR)

Management and Other Qualitative Factors (Step 2)

This second step considers the impact on an obligor rating of a variety of qualitative factors, such as discovering unfavorable aspects of a borrower's management. Step 2 analysis may bring about a downgrade if standards are not acceptable.

---

[11]Business risk is defined as the risk associated with the level and stability of operating cash flows over time.

A typical Step 2 approach would require such activities as examining day-to-day account operations, assessing management, performing an environmental assessment, and examining contingent liabilities.

For example, in the case of day-to-day account operations, is the firm's financial reporting on a timely basis and of good quality? Does the firm satisfactorily explain any significant variations from projections? Are credit limits and terms respected? Does the company honor its obligations to creditors?

In the case of a management assessment, the analyst might check that management skills are sufficient for the size and scope of the business. Does management have a record of success and appropriate industry experience? Does management have adequate depth (for example, are succession plans in place)? Is there an informed approach to identifying, accepting, and managing risks? Does management address problems promptly, exhibiting the will to take hard decisions as necessary, with an appropriate balance of short- to long-term concerns? Is management remuneration prudent and appropriate to the size, financial strength, and progress of the company?

Industry Ratings Summary (Step 3a)

This portion of the third step explicitly recognizes the importance of the interaction between an industry rating and the relative position of the borrower within its industry. Experience has shown that poorer-tier performers in weak, vulnerable industries are major contributors to credit losses.

To take this into account, the analyst needs to rate each type of industry on, say, a scale of 1 to 5 using an industry assessment (IA) ratings scheme for each industry. To calculate the industry assessment, the analyst first assigns a score of 1 (minimal risk) to 5 (very high risk) for each of a set of, say, eight criteria established by the bank. For example, each industry might be described in terms of its competitiveness, trade environment, regulatory framework, restructuring, technological change, financial performance, long-term trends affecting demand, and vulnerability to the macroeconomic environment.

Tier Assessment (Step 3b)

The criteria and process used to assess industry risk can often be reapplied to determine a company's relative position (say, on a scale of tiers 1 to 4) within an industry. A business should be ranked against its appropriate competition. That is, if the company supplies a product or service that is subject to global competition, then it should be ranked on a global basis. If the company's competitors are by nature local or regional, as is the case for many retail businesses, then it should be ranked on that basis (while recognizing that competition may increase).

In a four-tier system, tier 1 players are major players with a dominant share of the relevant market (local, regional, domestic, international, or niche). They have a diversified and growing customer base and have low production costs that are based on sustainable factors (such as a diversified supplier base, economies of scale, location and resource availability, continuous upgrading of technology, and so on). Such companies respond quickly and effectively to changes in the regulatory framework, trading environment, technology, demand patterns, and macroeconomic environment.

Tier 2 players are important or above-average industry players with a meaningful share of the relevant market (local, regional, domestic, international, or niche).

Tier 3 players are average (or modestly below average) industry players, with a moderate share of the relevant market (local, regional, domestic, international, or niche).

Tier 4 players are weak industry players with a declining customer base. They have a high cost of production as a result of factors such as low leverage with suppliers, obsolete technologies, and so on.

Industry/Tier Position (Step 3c)

This final part of the third step (Step 3c) combines the assessments of the nature and health of the industry (i.e., the industry rating) and the position of a business within its industry (i.e., the tier rating). While the tier rating can be lowered if the industry/tier assessment is weak, it will not be raised if this position is strong. The process reveals the vulnerability of a company, particularly during recessions. Low-quartile competitors within an industry class almost always have higher risk (modified by the relative health of the industry).

Financial Statement Quality (Step 4)

This fourth step recognizes the importance of the quality of the financial information provided to the analyst. This includes consideration of the size and capabilities of the accounting firm compared to the size and complexities of the borrower and its financial statements. Again, the rating should not be raised even if the result is good; the point of this step is to define the highest *possible* rating that can be obtained.

Country Risk (Step 5)

This fifth step adjusts for the effect of any country risk. Country risk is the risk that a counterparty or obligor will not be able to pay its obligations because of cross-border restrictions on the convertibility or availability of a given currency. It is also an assessment of the political and economic risk of a country. Country risk exists when more than a prescribed percentage (say 25 percent) of the obligor's (gross) cash flow (or assets) is located outside of the local market. Country risk may be mitigated by hard currency cash flow received or earned by the counterparty. Hard currency cash flow refers to revenue in a major (i.e., readily exchanged) international currency (primarily U.S. and Canadian dollars, sterling, euro, and Japanese yen).

Again, Step 5 limits the best possible rating. For example, if the client's operation has a country rating in the "fair" category, then the best possible obligor rating might be limited to 5.

Comparison to External Ratings (Step 6)

When the obligor is rated by an external rating agency or when it is included in the database of an external service providing default probability estimates, such as Moody's KMV, the preliminary ODR produced in Step 5 is compared to these external ratings. The intent is not to align the internal rating with that of an external agency but to ensure that all appropriate risk issues have been factored into the final ODR.

When the ODR differs substantially from the external rating, then the rater should review the assessment on which the rating process is based (Steps 1 to 5). If the comparison suggests that important risk factors were overlooked or underestimated in the preliminary analysis, then these factors should be incorporated in the final ODR by revising Steps 1 through 5.

This step can be viewed as a sanity check to validate the internally derived ODR and ensure the completeness of the analysis followed in Steps 1 through 5. The PD can vary significantly in periods of downturn, and therefore it is important to cross-check an internal rating with data from external sources in order to capture any broad trends in the migration of the PD.

Loan Structure (Step 7)

The risk rating process (Steps 1 through 6) assumes that most credits have an appropriate loan structure in place. If so, Step 7 has no impact on the ODR. However, if the loan structure is not sufficiently strong and is viewed as having a negative impact on the risk of default of the obligor, then a downgrade is required. As a general rule, the weaker the preliminary ODR concluded in Step 6, the more stringent the loan structure should be to be regarded as appropriate.

The components of the loan structure that may affect default risk are the financial covenants, the term of the debt, its amortization scheme, and change-of-control restrictions. For example, in the case of high-risk companies, financial ratio requirements should be progressive and should fit tightly with the company's own forecasts. In addition, significant amortization of debt over the tenure of the facilities should be imposed, and nonmerger restrictions should be put in place.

Loss Given Default Rating (LGDR)

Step 8 assigns a loss given default rating to each facility. This rating is determined independently of default probabilities. The probability of default and the loss experienced in the event of default are separate risk issues and therefore should be looked at independently. Typically, each LGDR is mapped to an LGD factor—i.e., a number between 0 and 100 percent, with 0 percent corresponding to the case of total recovery and 100 percent to the situation where the creditor loses all the amount due. The LGD should be calculated net of the recovery cost.

Different evaluation methods are used depending on whether the credit is unsecured or is secured by third-party support or collateral.

The presence of security should mitigate the severity of the loss given default for any facility. The quality and depth of security varies widely and will determine the extent of the benefit in reducing any loss.

When the credit is secured by a guarantor, the analyst must be convinced that the third party/owner is committed to ongoing support of the obligor.

When a facility is protected by collateral, the collateral category should reflect only the security held for the facility that is being rated. (Exceptions are where all security is held for all facilities, and where all facilities are being rated as one total.) Documentation risk (the proper completion of security) is always a concern and should be considered when assessing the level of protection.

Collateral can have a major effect on the final LGDR, but the value of collateral is often far from straightforward. The value of securities used as collateral is often a function of movements in market rates. In the most worrying situation, collateral values tend to move down as the risk of obligor default rises. For example, real estate used as collateral for a loan to a property developer has a strong tendency to lose its value during a property downturn—the moment in the sector cycle when a property developer is most likely to default.

Many banks continue to apply relatively simplistic industry averages or judgment-based numbers as their LGD factors; Table 11-3 in Chapter 11 is based on averages as estimated by the rating agencies. However, the perceived importance of LGD calculations has grown in recent years, particularly since the financial crisis of 2007–2009.[12] Three issues are particularly worthy of note:

- Banks using advanced internal ratings-based approaches for calculating regulatory capital adequacy are required to calculate LGD rates in such a way that they take into account the rates likely in any economic downturn, and they must base their calculations on data covering at least one economic cycle.
- Banks are making efforts to systematize the collection of LGD data in their internal records and in specialized LGD databases. The challenge here is that the historical information must be as comprehensive as possible across a number of dimensions, including not only the amount of the eventual loss but also the bank's exact exposure at default, covenants, collateral values, recovery costs, appropriate discount rates, and so on. In addition, various industry databases have been constructed to pool

---

[12]It should be noted that under Basel II and III, for regulatory capital calculation, the credit risk assessment is executed on a per obligor basis and then a simple summation is applied. To calculate LGD for a portfolio of loans, the correlations of LGDs must be taken into account, but this is not required so far for calculating regulatory capital.

information on the losses associated with different kinds of collateral and loan facility.

- More sophisticated methodologies are being designed to help banks use the improved data to calculate the LGD rates associated with different kinds of facility and collateral. The key challenge here is how to apply a mix of internal and external LGD information in a granular way that is sensitive to the variety of secured and unsecured facilities across a range of business lines. A degree of business judgment also needs to be factored in because business line experts often understand the nuances of collateral and facility risk better than groupwide risk functions.

Conclusion

We've seen how credit analysts can systematically employ a series of quantitative and judgmental tools to arrive at an ODR and LGDR.

As we discuss in Chapter 3, the Basel II and Basel III Capital Accord places a special emphasis on the internal rating–based approach for credit risk attribution. Banks can use their internal ratings to calculate the amount of regulatory risk capital they must put aside for key credit risks. But to do so, banks have to prove that their internal rating system meets certain standards.

Most of the world's larger banks are adopting a system of rigorous internal ratings that meet the quality standards outlined in the Accord, in pursuit of compliance or to protect their reputation in the face of raised industry standards. In doing so, they will also improve their ability to differentiate and price risk in pursuit of some key business goals. These include improved risk selection, risk-adjusted pricing, risk-adjusted profitability analysis, improved investor communication, and more efficient risk transfer.

Nonfinancial corporations can also use the credit rating system we've described to assess any credit granted to major customers. Also, financial institutions such as insurance companies can use similar systems to evaluate loans to corporations and the credit risk associated with any private bond issues that they purchase for their portfolios.

APPENDIX 10.1

DEFINITIONS OF KEY FINANCIAL RATIOS

1. EBIT interest coverage = (times interest earned)

$$\frac{\text{Earnings from continuing operations before interest and taxes}}{\text{Gross interest incurred before subtracting (1) capitalized interest and (2) interest income}}$$

2. EBITDA interest coverage = (cash interest coverage)

$$\frac{\text{Earnings from continuing operations before interest, taxes, depreciation, and amortization}}{\text{Gross interest incurred before subtracting (1) capitalized interest and (2) interest income}}$$

3. Funds from operations/total debt =

$$\frac{\text{Net income from continuing operations plus depreciation, amortization, deferred income taxes, and other noncash items}}{\text{Long-term debt plus current maturities, commercial paper, and other short-term borrowings}}$$

4. Free operating cash flow/total debt =

$$\frac{\text{Funds from operations minus capital expenditures, minus (plus) the increase (decrease) in working capital (excluding changes in cash, marketable securities, and short-term debt)}}{\text{Long-term debt plus current maturities, commercial paper, and other short-term borrowings}}$$

5. Pretax return on capital =

$$\frac{\text{Pretax income from continuing operations plus interest expense}}{\begin{array}{c}\text{Sum of (1) average of beginning of year and end of year current maturities, long-term debt,}\\ \text{noncurrent deferred taxes, and equity and (2) average short-term borrowings during year}\\ \text{as disclosed in footnotes}\end{array}}$$

6. Operating income/sales =

$$\frac{\begin{array}{c}\text{Sales minus cost of goods manufactured (before depreciation and amortization),}\\ \text{selling, general and administrative, and research and development costs}\end{array}}{\text{Sales}}$$

7. Long-term debt/capital =

$$\frac{\text{Long-term debt}}{\text{Long-term debt plus shareholders' equity (including preferred stock) plus minority interest}}$$

8. Total debt/capital =

$$\frac{\text{Long-term debt plus current maturities, commercial paper, and other short-term borrowings}}{\begin{array}{c}\text{Long-term debt plus current maturities, commercial paper, and other short-term}\\ \text{borrowings plus shareholders' equity (including preferred stock) plus minority interest}\end{array}}$$

Source: S&P's Corporate Ratings Criteria, 1998.

11

QUANTITATIVE APPROACHES TO CREDIT PORTFOLIO RISK AND CREDIT MODELING

In Chapter 10 we described the traditional way in which rating agencies and large financial institutions rate the credit risk of bonds and corporate loans using a judgmental approach supported by certain key financial numbers. In this chapter we describe efforts to model and measure credit risk in whole portfolios using statistical and economic tools, including the Merton model, the actuarial approach, reduced-form models, and hybrid models. We also briefly review scoring models that can be applied to measure the risk of individual private firms as opposed to publicly traded companies. These models complement, and to a degree compete with, the traditional approaches to measuring credit risk described in Chapter 10.

The new ways to measure and monitor credit risk, though developed in the financial industries, can also be applied by large nonfinancial corporations that need to both monitor customer credit risk and track supplier risk in today's globalized economy.

We can think of these more quantitative approaches to measuring individual and portfolio risk as an attempt by institutions to apply to credit risk the kind of "rocket science" that has made such a difference to their management of market risk and derivatives trading.

It's an exciting industry project, but one with potential pitfalls. As the financial industry develops better ways to estimate credit risk, it is becoming more and more dependent on these techniques. It's important that a wide range of support staff and senior managers understand in principle the strengths and the limitations of these approaches to credit risk modeling.

Why Is Credit Risk Modeling So Important—and So Difficult?

There are many reasons why lending institutions want to attach objective numbers to the credit risks that they run. One of the most fundamental reasons is so they can accurately attribute credit risk (regulatory or economic) capital, either to a transaction or a whole portfolio, as described in Box 11-1. This is important for risk management purposes, but it also allows the bank to price the transaction accurately—for example, by adjusting the interest rate charged to the customer in line with the customer's risk of default. Objective estimates of default also offer an independent check on traditional "judgment" ratings.

BOX 11-1   CREDIT VAR AND CALCULATION OF AN ECONOMIC CAPITAL CHARGE

Economic capital is the financial cushion that a bank employs to absorb unexpected losses—e.g., those related to credit events such as default and/or credit migration. It's clearly important that a bank reserve the right amount of economic capital if it is to remain solvent to any degree of confidence (see Chapter 17). But economic capital is also increasingly important for helping banks to price risk and to set sophisticated risk limits for individual businesses.

The modeling approaches we describe in the main text allow a bank to model the distribution of values of its portfolio of obligors and derive an economic capital number, or VaR number, in the same way that we described for market risk in Chapter 7.

Figure 11B-1 illustrates how a capital charge related to credit risk can be derived from the distribution of values of a credit portfolio. In this figure,

$P(c)$ = value of the portfolio in the worst-case scenario at the $(1 - c)$ percent confidence level, say 99 percent if c is equal to 1 percent
FV = forward value of the portfolio = $V_0(1 + PR)$
V_0 = current marked-to-market value of the portfolio
PR = promised return on the portfolio
EV = expected value of the portfolio = $V_0(1 + ER)$
ER = expected return on the portfolio
EL = expected loss = FV − EV

The expected loss is not part of required economic capital, precisely because it is expected and is therefore priced into the interest charge that the customer pays on each loan. The capital charge is instead a function of the portfolio's unexpected losses. That is,

$$\text{Capital} = \text{EV} - P(c)$$

FIGURE 11B-1 Credit VaR and Calculation of Economic Capital

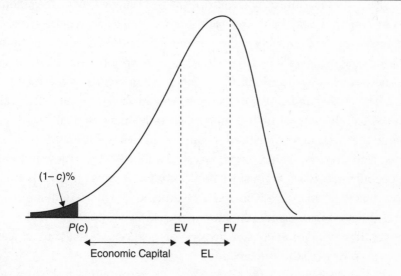

As with market risk, the confidence level is set in line with the bank's risk appetite or solvency standard—often its target credit rating. For example, if the confidence level is 1 percent, then the bank would be able to reassure itself that 99 times out of 100, it would not incur losses above the economic capital level over the period corresponding to the credit risk horizon (say, one year).

Banks, in particular, need to assess the credit quality of loan portfolios as a whole, because the stability of each bank depends to a large extent on the number and extent of credit-related losses across its entire credit portfolio in any given period. But accurately estimating the risk of loans or bonds and modeling portfoliowide credit risk is a complicated task that must take into account multiple factors. Some factors are economywide, such as the level of interest rates, sector performance, and the growth rate of the economy. Other factors are specific to the individual credit, such as the business risk of the firm or its capital structure.

Regulation is also helping to promote the formal quantification of credit risk and the use of credit portfolio models in the banking and insurance industries. We've already discussed in this book how current bank regulation is encouraging better differentiation among individual obligors based on their credit ratings. Analytical approaches to estimating credit risk are increasingly driving the amount of regulatory capital a bank has to set aside. Bank capital aside, regulators tell bank examiners to look at the quality of the loan portfolio and the level of concentration by industry and region (Pillar II of the Basel II regulation, described in Chapter 3).

There are many decisions to be made when selecting the appropriate approach to credit modeling. For example, should the credit modeler evaluate credit risk as a discrete event and concentrate only on a potential default event, or should the modeler analyze the dynamics of the debt value and the associated credit spread over the whole time interval to maturity? For risk management, it is generally necessary to consider both. Another important issue is the data sources that are available to help assess credit risk. To what extent are relevant internal transactions related and external market data available, and to what extent are the available data of sufficiently high quality? Are markets sufficiently efficient to convey reliable information?

An even more fundamental problem is determining what we mean by default and how this might relate to notions of credit risk, bankruptcy, and

FIGURE 11-1 Quarterly Defaults/Bankruptcies, North American Public Companies, 1973–March 2013

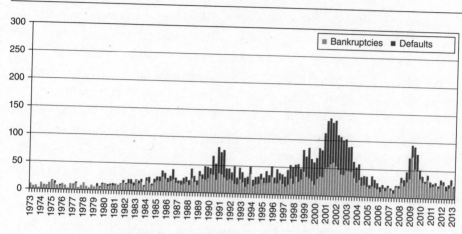

loss from default. In practice, default is distinct from bankruptcy. Bankruptcy describes the situation in which the firm is liquidated and the proceeds from the asset sale distributed to the various claim holders according to prespecified priority rules. Default, on the other hand, is usually defined as the event when a firm misses a payment on a coupon and/or the reimbursement of principal at debt maturity. Cross-default clauses in debt contracts are such that when the firm misses a single payment on a debt, it is declared in default on all its obligations.[1]

The relationship between default and bankruptcy is far from constant over time. Since the early 1980s, Chapter 11 regulation in the United States has protected firms in default and helped to maintain them as going concerns during a period in which they attempt to restructure their activities and their financial structure. Figure 11-1 compares the number of bankruptcies to the number of defaults during the period 1973 to March 2013 for North American public companies.

---

[1] In the case of bank loans to corporations, the situation is generally more complex. Bank loans typically have financial covenants that, when broken, serve to create a technical default even if there has not been a payment default. Technical defaults result in either debt restructuring or acceleration—i.e., paying back the debt faster than originally scheduled. Also, regulatory rules may stipulate that an asset has to be treated as impaired if it is unlikely that the loan will perform in accordance with the original terms and conditions, even though no payment has yet been missed.

What Drives Credit Risk at the Portfolio Level?

The first factor affecting the amount of credit risk in a portfolio is clearly the credit standing of specific obligors. One bank might concentrate on prime or investment-grade obligors, so that there is a very low probability of default for any individual obligor in its portfolio. Another bank might choose to concentrate on riskier, speculative-grade obligors who pay a much higher coupon rate on their debt. The critical issues for both types of institution are to charge the appropriate interest rate, or spread, to each borrower so that the lender is compensated for the risk it undertakes and to set aside the right amount of risk capital. Only by setting aside the right amount of capital can the bank limit the chance of itself defaulting to the level of confidence approved by its board.

The second factor is *concentration risk*, or the extent to which the obligors are diversified in terms of number, geography, and industry. A bank with only a few big-ticket corporate clients, most of which are in commercial real estate, is rightly considered to be riskier than a bank that has made many corporate loans to borrowers that are distributed over many industries. Also, a bank serving only a narrow geographical area is likely to be hit hard by a slowdown in the economic activity of that particular region (and see a subsequent rise in defaults). However, apparent diversification across industry sectors can be misleading if different industries are exposed to common macro-risk factors—e.g., oil price.[2]

This leads us to the third important factor that affects the risk of the portfolio: the state of the economy. During the good times of economic growth, the frequency of default falls sharply compared to periods of recession. Conversely, the default rate rises again as the economy enters a downturn. To make things worse, periods of high default rates, such as 2001–2002 and 2008–2009, are characterized by a low rate of recovery on defaulted loans—that is, banks tend to find that the various assurances and collateral that they use to secure the loans are less valuable during a recession. Put another way, the recovery rate is negatively correlated with the frequency of default.

Recovery risk is a major determinant of credit risk. To understand the risk in a portfolio, it is therefore necessary to consider default probabilities, default correlations, recovery rates, and the state dependent nature of recovery rates.

---

[2]The reduced-form approach to modeling credit portfolio risk, discussed later, models default correlations through risk factors common to companies.

In Figure 11-2 we present the record of defaults from 1981 to 2012. In 1990–1991, in 2001–2002, and more recently in 2008–2009, when the world economies were in recession, the frequency of defaults increased substantially. But recessions are not created equal in terms of the defaults they precipitate. In 2002, the total amount of debt that defaulted reached the unprecedented level at the time of $191 billion, compared with the earlier peak of $24 billion in 1991. But a new record was achieved in 2008–2009 during the subprime crisis, especially in 2009 after Lehman's bankruptcy, when the amount of debt that defaulted reached the new highs of $430 and $628 billion, respectively.

Downturns in the credit cycle often uncover the hidden tendency of customers to default together, with banks being affected to the degree that they have allowed their portfolios to become concentrated in various ways (e.g., customer,

FIGURE 11-2 Corporate Defaults Worldwide: Number of Firms and Amount Defaulted, 1981–2012

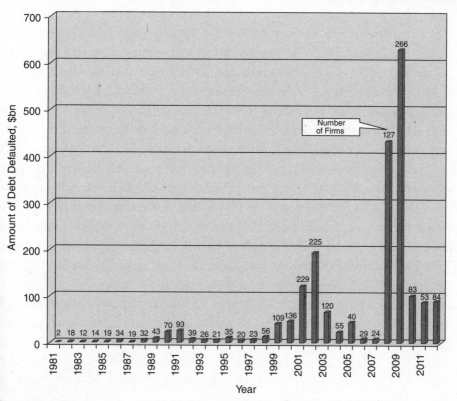

Source: Standard and Poor's.

region, and industry concentrations). The CreditMetrics, Moody's KMV, and Kamakura (KRIS) models we discuss later in this chapter are an attempt to discover the degree of correlation and concentration risk in a bank portfolio; the CreditRisk+ approach attempts much the same thing, only with an emphasis on uncovering the macroeconomic factors that cause default correlations.

The creditworthiness of the portfolio can also be affected by the maturities of the loans, as longer loans are generally considered riskier than short-term loans. Lending institutions that build portfolios that are not concentrated in particular maturities—*time diversification*—can reduce this kind of portfolio maturity risk. This also helps to reduce liquidity risk, or the risk that the bank will run into difficulties when it tries to refinance large amounts of its assets at the same time (see Chapter 8).

Estimating Portfolio Credit Risk: Overview

We can make a *qualitative* assessment of the risk in a bank portfolio by examining the portfolio in relation to the risk factors we have just discussed. For example, do the risk policies and risk limits used by the bank put an appropriate upper limit on the amount lent to any one borrower or any one industry? But in order to put an *objective number* on the credit risk in a portfolio that can support the kind of calculation we see in Box 11-1, we must estimate the future distribution of the values of the loan portfolio while taking credit risk into account.

Estimating the future value of a credit portfolio is much more complicated than estimating the value of a portfolio of market-traded instruments such as stocks and bonds. The main reason for this is that only small amounts of data about defaults are available. Whereas market prices move every day, helping financial institutions to make their market value-at-risk estimations, large companies fall into default only very rarely. The relative rarity of default events also makes it difficult to estimate potential correlations among potential default events. While there is a lot of data available on market prices of market-traded debt instruments (bonds and so on) and their cross correlations, many debt instruments are traded only rarely, and the majority of bank loans are never traded at all. The problem becomes even more complicated once we consider that default correlations are not fixed and stationary; instead, they change as a result of industrywide or economywide factors.

To overcome some of the estimation problems, credit portfolio models such as MSCI's CreditMetrics and Moody's KMV derive default correlations (which are not directly observable) from equity correlations.[3] That is, they assume that correlations in company share price returns that are computed using equity prices can be used to infer default correlations. Still, the estimation problem remains huge, since many pairs of cross correlations must be estimated for any portfolio of obligors.

For example, even a small portfolio of 1,000 obligors requires the estimation of 499,500 correlations (1,000 multiplied by 999 and divided by 2). The problem can really be circumvented only by using a multifactor approach. Under a multifactor approach, we make the assumption that the rate of return for each firm, or stock, can be generated by a linear combination of a few country- or industry-based indexes. This approach reduces the calculation requirement to that of estimating the correlations among pairs of indexes—a much simpler exercise. But it also introduces a simplifying assumption that is a potential source of error.

For other approaches, such as Kamakura (KRIS), default correlations are induced by common macro risk factors (such as commodity prices, real estate prices, and so on) that affect, with various intensity levels, the default risk of many companies.

CreditMetrics and the Credit Migration Approach

The CreditMetrics approach—initiated by JP Morgan, the leading U.S. bank, in 1997, subsequently spun off to RiskMetrics Inc., and acquired by MSCI in 2010—is based on the analysis of credit migration. That is, the approach is underpinned by estimates of how likely it is that a borrower will move from one credit quality to another, including default, within a given time horizon (usually one year).

This approach allows a bank using CreditMetrics to estimate the full one-year forward distribution of the values of any bond or loan portfolio, where the changes in values are related to credit migration only. (The forward values and exposures of the debt instruments in the portfolio are derived from deterministic forward curves of interest rates.) A key assumption of the approach

---

[3]KMV derives default correlations from asset returns correlations. Historical asset values are reconstituted from the market value of equity and the value of the various debt financing instruments on the balance sheet of the firm.

is that the past migration history of thousands of rated bonds accurately describes the probability of migration in the next period. Such an assumption is problematic, especially in times of financial turbulence.

The CreditMetrics risk measurement framework can be thought of in terms of two main building blocks:

1. Credit value-at-risk (Credit VaR) due to credit for a single financial instrument
2. Credit VaR at the portfolio level, which accounts for portfolio diversification effects

These building blocks are implemented by means of a four-step process. The first step of this approach is to specify a rating system, with rating grades, together with the probabilities of migrating from one credit quality to another over the credit risk horizon.

The second step is to specify a risk horizon, usually taken to be one year.

The third step is to specify the forward discount curve at the risk horizon for each credit category. This will allow us to value the bond using the zero curve corresponding to the potential future credit ratings of the issuer. In the case of default, the value of the instrument should be estimated in terms of the recovery rate. This is instrument specific and could be expressed, for example, as a percentage of face value or par, or alternatively as a percentage of the value of the security just before the issuer defaulted.

In the fourth and final step, the information from the first three steps is combined to calculate the forward distribution of the changes in the portfolio value consequent on credit migration.

The key problem in all this is the estimation of the rating transition probabilities, or rating transition matrix, using historical default data from either an external or an internal rating system (Tables 10-3 and 11-1).

Let's take the case of an approach based on the Standard & Poor's rating system and data. S&P employs seven principal rating categories. The highest credit rating is AAA; the lowest, CCC. (The rating agencies also supply more finely graded statistics, with each rating category from AA to CC being split into three subcategories; for example, S&P's rating category A is split into A+, A, and A−; see Chapter 10.) Default is defined as a situation in which the obligor cannot make a payment related to a bond or a loan obligation, whether the payment is a coupon payment or the redemption of principal.

TABLE 11-1 Transition Matrix: Probabilities of Credit Rating Migrating from One Rating Quality to Another, Within One Year

Initial Rating	Rating at Year-End (%)							
	AAA	AA	A	BBB	BB	B	CCC	Default
AAA	90.81	8.33	0.68	0.06	0.12	0	0	0
AA	0.70	90.65	7.79	0.64	0.06	0.14	0.02	0
A	0.09	2.27	91.05	5.52	0.74	0.26	0.01	0.06
BBB	0.02	0.33	5.95	86.93	5.30	1.17	0.12	0.18
BB	0.03	0.14	0.67	7.73	80.53	8.84	1.00	1.06
B	0	0.11	0.24	0.43	6.48	83.46	4.07	5.20
CCC	0.22	0	0.22	1.30	2.38	11.24	64.86	19.79

Source: Standard & Poor's *CreditWeek*, April. 15, 1996 (CreditMetrics, JP Morgan).

Let's take as an example a bond issuer that currently has a BBB rating. The shaded line in Table 11-1 shows the probability, as estimated by Standard & Poor's, that the credit rating of this BBB issuer will migrate, over a period of one year, to any one of eight possible states, including default. The most probable situation is that the obligor will remain in the same rating category, BBB; this has a probability of 86.93 percent. The probability of the issuer's defaulting within one year is only 0.18 percent, while the probability of the issuer's being upgraded to AAA is also very small—i.e., 0.02 percent.

Ratings agencies produce a transition matrix like this for all their initial ratings based on the history of credit events that have occurred in the firms rated by those agencies (Moody's publishes similar information). The probabilities published by the agencies are based on more than 20 years of data across all industries and disregarding firms' size. Obviously, these data should be interpreted with care, since they represent average statistics across a heterogeneous sample of firms and over several business cycles. For this reason, many banks prefer to rely on their own statistics, which are more closely related to the composition of their loan and bond portfolios.[4]

---

[4]When banks use their internal rating system, the available statistics on default and credit migration tend to be concentrated in the middle of the rating range, say A to BB, reflecting the credit quality of most bank corporate clients. Therefore, internal statistics need to be complemented with statistics from rating agencies for the high and low rating grades.

The rating agencies typically rate the obligor from a "through-the-cycle" perspective. In other words, the rating agencies discount the normal effects of the business cycle on an obligor as long as they believe that the structural estimation of the obligor's credit risk over the cycle hasn't changed. Conversely, analytic modelers (such as the Moody's KMV approach described later) typically rate the obligor from a "point-in-time" perspective, and therefore their ratings more appropriately reflect the probability of default in the short term. A bank that sets up an internal risk rating system needs to decide whether it wants the rating and any associated probability of default statistic to be based on a through-the-cycle or a point-in-time approach. If the bank decides to use a point-in-time approach, then the volatility of ratings, and therefore of credit VaR and economic capital, will clearly be greater than if it uses a through-the-cycle approach.

The realized transition and default probabilities vary quite substantially over the years, depending on whether the economy is in recession or is expanding, as we saw in Figure 11-2. When implementing a model that relies on transition probabilities, the bank may have to adjust the average historical values—those shown in Table 11-1—to make them consistent with its assessment of the current and anticipated economic environments. The probabilities on the diagonal of the transition matrix for a point-in-time approach are smaller than those for the through-the-cycle approach, since with a point-in-time approach there is less likelihood that the rating will remain the same in the subsequent periods.

The next step in creating our distribution of values for a single bond is to value the bond in each of its possible seven credit qualities. This requires us to specify seven possible one-year forward zero curves so that the bond can be priced in all of its possible states. These curves can be generated from market data, using bond prices, as depicted in Table 11-2. (Forward zero curves depict the implied discount rates for future cash flows, as reflected in current bond prices for given credit ratings and different maturities; see Chapter 6.) If the issuer defaults then we cannot assume that the bond is worth nothing at the end of the year. Depending on the seniority of the instrument, a recovery rate of a percentage of par value is realized by the investor. These recovery rates are again estimated from historical data provided by the rating agencies. Table 11-3 shows the expected recovery rates for bonds of different seniority classes as estimated by Moody's. Therefore, in simulations performed to assess the portfolio distribution, the recovery rates are not taken as fixed, but rather drawn from a distribution of possible recovery rates. (As a rule, bank loan recovery rates tend

TABLE 11-2 One-Year Forward Zero Curves for Each Credit Rating (%)*

Category	Year 1	Year 2	Year 3	Year 4
AAA	3.60	4.17	4.73	5.12
AA	3.65	4.22	4.78	5.17
A	3.72	4.32	4.93	5.32
BBB	4.10	4.67	5.25	5.63
BB	5.55	6.02	6.78	7.27
B	6.05	7.02	8.03	8.52
CCC	15.05	15.02	14.03	13.52

Source: CreditMetrics, JP Morgan.

*See Chapter 6 for the derivation of forward rates.

to be much higher than bond recovery rates.)[5] For many financial instruments, such as credit default swaps, the recovery rate is defined in terms of the market price of the underlying asset postdefault.

We are now in a position to calculate the distribution of the changes in the bond value, at the one-year horizon, resulting from an eventual change in credit quality. Table 11-4 and Figure 11-3 show these changes for our example BBB bond.

TABLE 11-3 Recovery Rates by Seniority Class (Percent of Face Value, or Par)

Seniority Class	Mean (%)	Standard Deviation (%)
Senior secured	53.80	26.86
Senior unsecured	51.13	25.45
Senior subordinated	38.52	23.81
Subordinated	32.74	20.18
Junior subordinated	17.09	10.90

Source: Carty and Lieberman, 1996 (CreditMetrics, JP Morgan).

---

[5]As we mentioned earlier, each debt instrument exhibits a specific recovery rate. In this example we use Moody's historical statistics by debt seniority for the sake of illustration.

TABLE 11-4 Distribution of the Bond Values, and Changes in Value of a BBB Bond, in One Year

Year-End Rating	Probability of State p (%)	Forward Price V ($)	Change in Value ΔV ($)
AAA	0.02	109.35	1.82
AA	0.33	109.17	1.64
A	5.95	108.64	1.11
BBB	86.93	107.53	0
BB	5.30	102.00	−5.53
B	1.17	98.08	−9.45
CCC	0.12	83.62	−23.91
Default	0.18	51.11	−56.42

Source: CreditMetrics, JP Morgan.

The first percentile of the distribution, which corresponds to the credit value-at-risk or credit VaR of the credit instrument at a confidence level of 99 percent, is 23.91 (Figure 11-3). That is, we can say that if we have a portfolio of 100 independent obligors, all rated BBB, each with face value of 100 dollars, then in a year we can expect one obligor to suffer a loss greater than 23.91.

However, we should also note the small but significant chance of a very large loss in the event of default. Any distribution curve fitted around the bars on this figure would exhibit what risk modelers call a long "downside tail," often referred to as a "fat tail"—a common feature of credit distributions.

Credit VaR for a Loan or Bond Portfolio

So far we have shown how to derive the future distribution of values for a given bond (or loan). In what follows, we focus on how to estimate potential changes in the value of a whole portfolio of creditors. We assume that the changes are due to credit risk only (i.e., there is no market risk) and that credit risk is expressed as potential rating changes during the year.

An important complicating factor in the portfolio assessment is the degree of correlation between any two obligors in terms of changes in credit ratings or default. The overall credit VaR is quite sensitive to these correlations, and their accurate estimation is therefore one of the key determinants of portfolio optimization.

FIGURE 11-3 Histogram of the One-year Forward Prices and Changes in Value of a BBB Bond

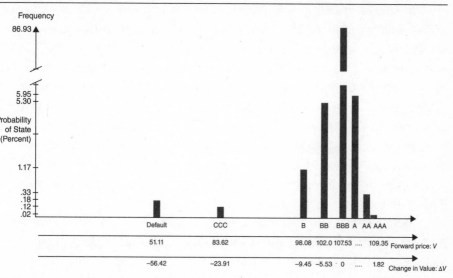

As we explained in our general discussion, default correlations might be expected to be higher for firms within the same industry or in the same region and to vary with the relative state of the economy throughout the business cycle. If there is a slowdown in the economy or a recession, most of the assets of the obligors will decline in value and quality, and the likelihood of multiple defaults increases substantially. Thus, we cannot expect default and migration probabilities to stay stationary (i.e., stable) over time, and we need some kind of model that relates changes in default probabilities to fundamental variables.

CreditMetrics derives the default and migration probabilities from a correlation model of the firm's asset value. As the firm's true asset value is not directly observable, CreditMetrics makes use of a firm's stock price as a proxy for its asset value. (This is another simplifying assumption made by CreditMetrics that may affect the accuracy of the approach.) CreditMetrics estimates the correlations between the equity returns of various obligors. Then it infers the correlations between changes in credit quality directly from the joint distribution of these equity returns.

We can illustrate how these correlation estimates affect the joint probability of default of two creditors in the portfolio with a very simple numerical example. If the probabilities of default for obligors rated A and BB are $p_A = 0.06$ percent and $p_{BB} = 1.06$ percent, respectively, and the correlation coefficient between the rates of return on the two assets is taken from stock price analysis to be $\rho = 20$ percent, it can be shown that the joint probability of default is only 0.0054 percent and that the correlation coefficient between the two default events is 1.9 percent. (If the default events were independent, then the joint probability of default would be simply the product of the two default probabilities, i.e., 0.06 × 1.06 = 0.0064 percent.) Asset return correlations are approximately 10 times larger than default correlations for asset correlations in the range from 20 percent to 60 percent (i.e., in our example, for an asset return correlation of 20 percent, the estimated default correlation is 1.9 percent). This shows that the joint probability of default is in fact quite sensitive to pairwise asset return correlations, and it illustrates how important it is to estimate these data correctly if one is to assess the diversification effect within a portfolio.

It can be shown that the impact of correlations on credit VaR is quite large. And it is larger for portfolios with relatively low-grade credit quality than it is for high-grade portfolios. Indeed, as the credit quality of the portfolio deteriorates and the expected number of defaults increases, this rise in defaults is magnified by an increase in default correlations.

The analytic approach to assessing a portfolio is not practicable for large portfolios. The number of paired correlations can become excessive. Instead, CreditMetrics makes use of numerical approximations by applying a Monte Carlo simulation approach to generate the full distribution of the portfolio values at the credit horizon of one year.

Estimation of Asset Correlations

As we discussed earlier, default correlations are derived from asset return correlations, for which equity return correlations are in turn a proxy. For a large portfolio of bonds and loans, with thousands of obligors, this still requires the computation of a huge correlation matrix to include the correlation for each pair of obligors.

To reduce the dimensionality of this estimation problem, CreditMetrics uses multifactor analysis. This approach maps each obligor to the countries and industries that are most likely to determine the obligor's performance. Equity returns are correlated to the extent that firms are exposed to the same industries and countries. To implement CreditMetrics, the user specifies the industry and country weights for each obligor, as well as the firm-specific risk, which is not correlated with any other obligor or to any index.

Estimation of Loss Given Default

The estimation of the loss given default (LGD), which can also be defined as one minus the recovery rate (RR), is facility specific. It depends on the seniority of the facility, the nature of the collateral, and other covenants and securities attached to the debt instrument. Statistics reported by rating agencies, such as those used earlier to illustrate how CreditMetrics works, are of little practical use as they are averages over a large spectrum of instruments with different types of collateral and covenants. The huge standard deviation around the mean value shows that for the same seniority of the debt instrument there is a wide dispersion of recovery rates.

Recovery rates are also time dependent and are somewhat driven by the state of the economy. We mentioned earlier that empirical evidence shows a strong negative correlation between PDs and RRs: during recessionary periods with high default rates—e.g., 2001–2002 and 2008–2009—recovery rates tend to be lower than in periods of normal activity. Collateral, including other securities, tends to be less valuable during difficult times. When PDs decline, recovery rates tend to improve.[6] (See Chapter 10 for further discussion about LGD.)

Applications of CreditMetrics

One of the keys to controlling the kind of "model risk" that we discuss in Chapter 15 is to make sure that models are applied only to the appropriate kind of problem. The CreditMetrics approach is designed primarily for bonds and loans, which are both treated in the same manner. It can also be easily extended to financial claims (such as receivables or financial letters of credit) for which we can derive the forward value at the risk horizon for all credit ratings. However, for derivatives such as swaps or forwards, the model needs to be somewhat adjusted or "twisted," because there is no satisfactory way to derive the exposure and the loss distribution within the proposed framework (since it assumes deterministic interest rates). This is why we must turn to structural or reduced-form modeling approaches for a more reliable way to price credit derivatives.

---

[6] See E. Altman, A. Resti, and A. Sironi (eds.), *Recovery Risk* (London: Risk Books, 2005) and C. Chava, C. Stefanescu, and S. M. Turnbull, "Modeling Expected Loss," *Management Science,* 57(7), July 2011, 1267–1287.

The Contingent Claim or Structural Approach to Measuring Credit Risk

The CreditMetrics approach to measuring credit risk, as described in the previous section, is rather appealing as a methodology. Unfortunately, it has a major weakness: it relies on rating transition probabilities based on average historical frequencies of defaults and credit migration.

The approach therefore implies that all firms within the same rating class have the same default rate and the same spread curve, even when recovery rates differ among obligors, and that the actual default rate is equal to the historical average default rate. Credit ratings and default rates are taken to be synonymous—that is, the rating changes when the default rate is adjusted, and vice versa.

This view was strongly challenged during the 1990s by researchers working for the consulting and software corporation KMV, a firm that specialized in credit risk analysis. (The name KMV comes from the first letter of the last names of Stephen Kealhofer, John McQuown, and Oldrich Vasicek, the academics who founded KMV Corporation in 1989; KMV has since become a division of rating agency Moody's, but for clarity we continue to refer to the "KMV approach.") Indeed, the CreditMetrics assumption cannot be true because we know that default rates evolve continuously whereas ratings are adjusted only periodically. This lag occurs because rating agencies necessarily take time to upgrade or downgrade companies whose default risk has changed. They also adopt a largely "through-the-cycle" approach—i.e., a long- rather than short-term perspective on credit risk—and tend not to change ratings due to changes in the environment or in the firm that the ratings agencies perceive as temporary.

Instead, the KMV researchers proposed a "structural" approach, based on an option pricing model approach first introduced in 1974 by Nobel Prize winner Robert Merton.[7] Let's look first at the underlying logic of the Merton model and then, in the next section, at KMV's adaptation of it into an analytical credit tool.

The Merton model is based on the limited liability rule, which allows shareholders to default on their obligations while surrendering the firm's assets to its various stakeholders—such as bondholders and banks—according to pre-specified priority rules. The firm's liabilities are thus viewed as contingent claims

---

[7]Robert C. Merton, "On the Pricing of Corporate Debt: The Risk Structure of Interest Rates," *Journal of Finance* 29, 1974, 449–470.

ssued against the firm's assets, with the payoffs to the various debt holders being completely specified by seniority and safety covenants. According to this logic, the firm will default at debt maturity whenever its asset value falls short of its debt value (at that time). Under this model, the default likelihood and the loss at default depend on the firm's asset value, the firm's liabilities, the asset volatility, and the default-free interest rate for the debt maturity.

To determine the value of the credit risk arising from a bank loan using this theoretical approach, we must first make two assumptions: that the zero coupon loan is the only debt instrument of the firm, and that the only other source of financing is equity. In this case, the present value of credit risk is equal to the value of a put option on the value of the assets of the firm at a strike price that is equal to the face value of the debt (including accrued interest) and at a time to expiration corresponding to the maturity of the debt. If the bank purchased such a put option, it would completely eliminate the credit risk associated with the loan.

This implies that by purchasing the put on the assets of the firm for the term of the debt, with a strike price equal to the face value of the loan, a bank could, in theory, convert any risky corporate loan into a riskless loan. Thus, the value of the put option is the cost of eliminating the credit risk associated with providing a loan to the firm—that is, the cost of providing credit insurance.

It follows that if we make the various assumptions that are needed to apply the Black-Scholes (BS) model to equity and debt instruments, we can express the value of the credit risk of a firm in an option-like formula.

The Merton model illustrates that one can quantify the cost of credit risk, and hence also credit spreads, as a function of the riskiness of the assets of the firm and the time interval until debt is paid back. The cost is an increasing function of the leverage or debt burden of the firm. The cost is also affected by the risk-free interest rate: the higher the risk-free interest rate, the less costly it is to reduce credit risk. The numerical examples in Table 11-5 show the default spread for various levels of asset volatility and different leverage ratios.

The structural approach offered by the Merton model seems to offer a way of assessing the likelihood of default of an individual firm, and also an alternative to the credit migration approach to the estimation of portfolio credit risk. The merit of this approach is that each firm can be analyzed individually, based on its unique features, to arrive at an estimated likelihood of default. But this is also the principal drawback of the approach, because the information required for such an analysis is often not available to the bank or the investor.

TABLE 11-5 Default Spread for Corporate Debt (for $V_0 = 100$, $T = 1$, and $r = 10\%$[1])

	Volatility of Underlying Asset			
Leverage Ratio LR	0.05	0.10	0.20	0.40
0.5	0	0	0	1.0%
0.6	0	0	0.1%	2.7%
0.7	0	0	0.4%	5.6%
0.8	0	0.1%	1.7%	9.6%
0.9	0.1%	0.9%	4.6%	14.6%
1.0	2.2%	4.6%	9.5%	20.7%

[1]10% is the annualized interest rate discretely compounded, which is equivalent to 9.5% continuously compounded.

Moody's KMV Approach

During the 1990s, KMV used the Merton model to develop a radically new approach to calculating default probabilities. KMV's methodology differs from CreditMetrics in that it derives an objective "expected default frequency," or EDF™, for each issuer using equity market information, rather than relying on judgmental credit ratings and the average historical transition frequencies produced by the rating agencies for each credit class. KMV also expanded its methodology from calculating the EDF for individual firms to measuring portfolio credit risk.

EDF can be viewed as a "cardinal ranking" of obligors in terms of their default risk, as opposed to the more conventional "ordinal ranking" proposed by rating agencies (which relies on letters such as AAA, AA, and so on). An EDF can easily be mapped onto any rating system to derive the equivalent rating of the obligor. Thus, with some careful interpretation, it can be used as an independent check on traditional internal bank rating systems and as an indication of the appropriate price for the credit risk of an individual firm (Table 11-6).[8]

---

[8]Moody's maps the EDF to Moody's credit ratings using both a spot approach based on current month data and a long-term approach based on five years of data.

TABLE 11-6 Mapping of EDF to Credit Ratings for Nonfinancial Companies in North America, 2013

Rating from Moody's	Median EDF	Min EDF	Max EDF
Investment Grade			
Aaa	0.01%	0.01%	0.013%
Aa1	0.016%	0.013%	0.018%
Aa2	0.02%	0.018%	0.021%
Aa3	0.023%	0.021%	0.024%
A1	0.026%	0.024%	0.028%
A2	0.03%	0.028%	0.034%
A3	0.040%	0.034%	0.045%
Baa1	0.052%	0.045%	0.060%
Baa2	0.069%	0.060%	0.077%
Baa3	0.085%	0.077%	0.095%
Sub-Investment Grade			
Ba1	0.106%	0.095%	0.118%
Ba2	0.131%	0.118%	0.157%
Ba3	0.189%	0.157%	0.226%
B1	0.271%	0.226%	0.324%
B2	0.389%	0.324%	0.575%
B3	0.852%	0.575%	1.262%
Caa1	1.868%	1.262%	2.766%
Caa2	4.096%	2.766%	4.898%
Caa3	5.857%	4.898%	8.374%
Ca	11.974%	8.374%	35%
C	35%	35%	35%

Source: Moody's Analytics.

In Table 11-6, the cutoff EDF between investment-grade and non-investment-grade companies in 2013 was 9.5 basis points (0.095 percent), reflecting an improvement in the creditworthiness of North American nonfinancial companies compared to a cutoff score of 0.74 percent year-end 2008.[9]

Because it relies on the insights of the Merton model, the EDF for each firm is a function of the firm's capital structure, the current asset value, and—importantly—the volatility of the asset returns. The value of the firm's assets is inferred from the market value of equity, meaning that the KMV approach is best applied to publicly traded companies, where the value of the equity is determined and made transparent by the stock market.

The KMV approach translates the information contained in the firm's stock price and balance sheet into an implied risk of default by means of a three-stage process:

1. Estimation of the market value and volatility of the firm's assets as revealed in the stock markets
2. Calculation of the "distance to default," which is an index measure of default risk
3. The scaling of the distance to default to actual probabilities of default, using a default database

Let's take a look at the two latter stages in more detail.

Calculation of the Distance to Default and the Probabilities of Default

In order to make the model tractable, the KMV approach assumes that the capital structure of a corporation is composed solely of equity, short-term debt (considered equivalent to cash), long-term debt (in perpetuity), and convertible preferred shares. In Merton's option pricing framework for credit risk, default occurs when the firm's asset value falls below the value of the firm's liabilities. In practice, however, for most public firms, only the price of equity is directly observable (in some cases, part of the debt is also actively traded). Using a sample of several hundred companies, KMV observed that, in the real world, firms default when their asset value reaches a level that is somewhere *between* the value of total liabilities and the value of short-term debt. Therefore, the tail of the distribution of asset values below total debt value may not be an accurate measure of the actual probability of default.

---

[9] The cutoff EDF at the end of 2006 before the start of the financial crisis was around 0.1 percent.

The model may also suffer a loss of accuracy from factors such as the non-normality of the asset return distribution, and from practical assumptions made during the model's implementation, such as the simplifying assumptions that the KMV analysts made about the capital structure of the firm. This may be further aggravated if a company can draw on (otherwise unobservable) lines of credit. If the company is in distress, using these lines might (unexpectedly) increase its liabilities while providing the necessary cash to honor promised payments.

For all these reasons, before computing the probabilities of default, the KMV approach implements an intermediate phase involving the computation of an index called the *distance to default* (DD). DD is the number of standard deviations between the mean of the distribution of the asset value and a critical threshold, the *default point* (DPT). The DPT is set at the par value of current liabilities, including short-term debt, to be serviced over the time horizon plus half the long-term debt (Figure 11-4).

FIGURE 11-4 Distance to Default (DD)

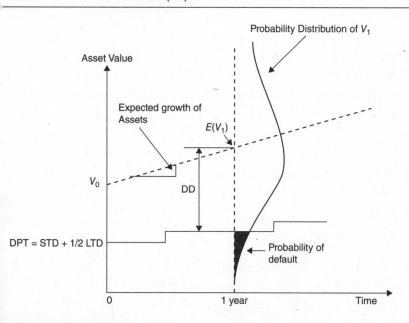

STD = short-term debt
LTD = long-term debt
DPT = default point = STD + 1/2 LTD
DPT = Distance to default, which is the distance between the expected asset value in one year, $E(V_1)$, and the default point, DPT. It is expressed in terms of standard deviation of asset returns:

$$DD = \frac{E(V_1) - DPT}{\sigma}$$

FIGURE 11-5 Mapping of the Distance to Default into EDF for a Given Time Horizon

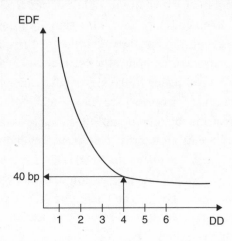

The calculation of DD allowed KMV's modelers to map the DD to the actual probabilities of default for a given time horizon (see Figure 11-5). KMV calls these probabilities expected default frequencies, or EDF. These procedures are based on KMV's own empirical studies.

Using historical information about a large sample of firms, including firms that have defaulted, one can track, for each time horizon, the proportion of firms of a given ranking, say DD = 4, that actually defaulted after one year. This proportion, say 40 basis points (bp), or 0.4 percent for DD = 4, is the EDF, as shown in Figure 11-5.

The Federal Express example offered in Box 11-2 illustrates the main causes of change in an EDF—i.e., variations in the stock price, the debt level (leverage ratio), and asset volatility.

How Useful Is the EDF?

KMV's Credit Monitor service began publishing estimated EDF back in 1993. Many banks have found the EDF to be a useful leading indicator of default, or at least of the degradation of the creditworthiness of issuers. Also, KMV analyzed more than 2,000 U.S. companies that have defaulted or entered into bankruptcy over the last 30 years; in all cases, KMV was able to show a sharp increase in the slope of the EDF a year or two prior to default.

When the financial situation of a company starts to deteriorate, the EDF tends to rise quickly until default occurs, as shown in Figure 11-6.

FIGURE 11-6 EDF of a Firm That Defaulted (Eastman Kodak) vs. Firms in U.S. Printing Group in Various Quantiles

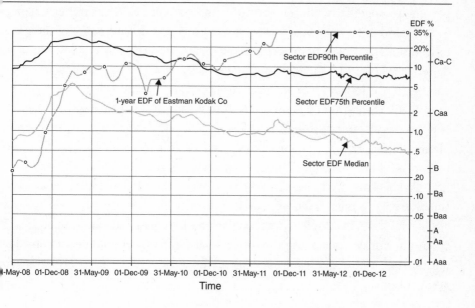

BOX 11-2   NUMERICAL EXAMPLE FOR CALCULATING THE DISTANCE TO DEFAULT AND ITS IMPLEMENTATION

This example, provided by KMV, relates to Federal Express on two different dates: June 2012 and June 2013.

Federal Express ($ figures are in billions of $US)		
	June 2012	**June 2013**
Market capitalization (price × shares outstanding)	$ 28.1	$ 31.4
Book liabilities	$ 10.2	$ 14.6
Market value of assets	$ 38.2	$ 46.4
Asset volatility	19.1%	16.6%
Default point	$ 7.7	$ 10.2
Distance to default (DD)	$\dfrac{38.2-7.7}{0.191\times38.2}=4.2$	$\dfrac{46.4-10.2}{0.166\times46.4}=4.7$
EDF	0.06% (6bp) ≡ Baa1	0.045% (4.5bp) ≡ A3

Such increases in EDF are usually in response to sharp declines in the value of the firm's equity. On the vertical axis of Figure 11-7, the EDF is shown as a percentage, together with the corresponding Standard & Poor's rating. Changes in EDF tend to anticipate—by at least one year—the downgrading of the issuer in traditional rating schemes run by agencies such as Moody's and Standard & Poor's (Figure 11-7). KMV's approach is clearly a point-in time approach, in contrast to the longer term perspective adopted by the rating agencies.

Unlike Moody's and Standard & Poor's historical default statistics, the EDF is not biased by periods of high or low defaults. The distance to default can be observed to shorten during periods of recession, when default rates are high, and to increase during periods of prosperity, characterized by low default rates.

At the same time, we should not think of the EDF as replacing conventional credit ratings. Each approach has its own strengths and weaknesses, and each is most suitable for particular credit risk management purposes. It should be emphasized again that in calculating the EDF, qualitative considerations, such as the quality of management or the quality of control systems, are ignored.

FIGURE 11-7 EDF of a Firm That Defaulted (Eastman Kodak) vs. Standard & Poor's and Moody's Ratings

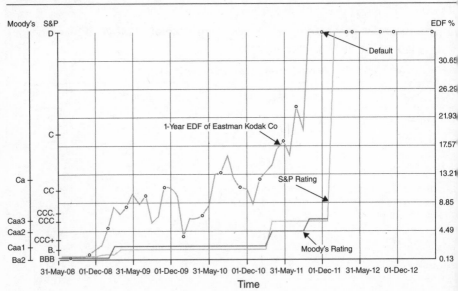

The Evaluation of Credit Portfolios

As we discussed earlier, the key risk measurement concern when individual obligors are combined into a portfolio is estimating the relevant credit risk correlations. How likely is it that companies will default together? Moody's KMV has proposed a model for evaluating credit correlations that, like CreditMetrics, derives asset return correlations by means of an economic model that links correlations to fundamental factors. By imposing a structure on the return correlations, the model achieves improved accuracy in forecasting correlations—and, as we mentioned earlier, such multifactor models reduce dramatically the number of correlations that need to be calculated.

It is assumed that the firm's asset returns are generated by a set of common, or systematic, risk factors and specific factors. To derive the asset return correlation between any number of firms, we therefore need to estimate the systematic factors and the covariance matrix for the common factors. How do we specify the structure of the factors?

CreditMetrics and Moody's KMV proposed relatively similar models, so here we will present only the KMV model (which is more comprehensive and elaborate). The KMV approach constructs a three-layer factor structure model, as shown in Figure 11-8.

- First level: a composite company-specific factor, constructed individually for each firm based on the firm's exposure to each country and industry
- Second level: country and industry factors
- Third level: global, regional, and industrial sector factors

The process for determining country and industry returns can be illustrated as follows:

$$
\begin{bmatrix} Country \\ return \end{bmatrix} = \begin{bmatrix} Global \\ economic \\ effect \end{bmatrix} + \begin{bmatrix} Regional \\ factor \\ effect \end{bmatrix} + \begin{bmatrix} Sector \\ factor \\ effect \end{bmatrix} + \begin{bmatrix} Country\text{-} \\ specific \\ risk \end{bmatrix}
$$

$$
\begin{bmatrix} Industry \\ return \end{bmatrix} = \begin{bmatrix} Global \\ economic \\ effect \end{bmatrix} + \begin{bmatrix} Regional \\ factor \\ effect \end{bmatrix} + \begin{bmatrix} Sector \\ factor \\ effect \end{bmatrix} + \begin{bmatrix} Industry\text{-} \\ specific \\ risk \end{bmatrix}
$$

FIGURE 11-8 Factor Model for Asset Return Correlations

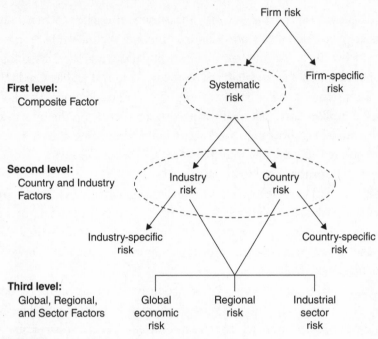

Source: KMV Corporation.

The Actuarial and Reduced-Form Approaches to Measuring Credit Risk

Two other approaches to estimating portfolio credit risk have been proposed. These are the actuarial approach, based on statistical models used by the insurance industry, and the reduced-form approach.

The structural model of default (e.g., the Merton 1974 framework) is based on information extracted from equity prices and the fundamental analysis of the balance sheet of the firm; it models the way in which firms default when their asset value falls below a certain boundary. By contrast, the actuarial model and the reduced-form models treat the firm's road to bankruptcy, including recovery, as factors external to the modeling process—i.e., they make assumptions about the number and timing of default events rather than attempting to derive them internally. The actuarial approach uses historical data on defaults to calibrate default probabilities while the reduced-form approach uses the information from the market credit spreads in bonds or CDSs.

The Actuarial Approach

CreditRisk+, released in late 1997 by the investment bank Credit Suisse Financial Products (CSFP), is a purely actuarial model based on mortality models developed by insurance companies. The probabilities of default that the model employs are based on historical statistical data on default experience. Unlike the KMV approach, there is no attempt to relate default to a firm's capital structure or balance sheet.

CreditRisk+ makes a number of assumptions:

- For a loan, the probability of default in a given period, say one month, is the same as in any other period of the same length, say another month.
- For a large number of obligors, the probability of default by any particular obligor is small, and the number of defaults that occur in any given period is independent of the number of defaults that occur in any other period.

Under these assumptions, and based on empirical observation, the probability distribution for the number of defaults during a given period of time (say, one year) is well represented by a certain shape of statistical distribution known as a Poisson distribution. We expect the mean default rate to change over time depending on the business cycle. This suggests that the distribution can be used to represent the default process only if, as CreditRisk+ suggests, we make the additional assumption that the mean default rate is itself changing, following a certain distribution.

In CreditRisk+, obligors are divided into bands, or subportfolios, and all obligors in a band are characterized by approximately the same average exposure, net of the recovery adjustments. If we know the distribution of defaults in each band, then we can find the distribution of defaults over all bands for the whole portfolio. CreditRisk+ derives a closed-form solution for the loss distribution of the loan portfolio.

CreditRisk+ has the advantage that it is relatively easy to implement. First, as we just mentioned, closed-form expressions—i.e., explicit formulas—can be derived for the probability of portfolio bond or loan losses, and this makes CreditRisk+ very attractive from a computational point of view. In addition, marginal risk contributions by obligor can be computed. Second, CreditRisk+ focuses on default, and therefore it requires relatively few estimates and inputs.

For each instrument, only the probability of default and the loss given default statistics are required.

One disadvantage of CreditRisk+ is that it ignores migration risk: the exposure for each obligor is fixed and is not sensitive to possible future changes in the credit quality of the issuer. (Indeed, this is the major difference between the approaches of CreditRisk+ and CreditMetrics.)

Default correlations between obligors only arise through dependence on a common set of risk factors—e.g., macroeconomic indexes for the areas of capital markets, consumption, employment, foreign investments, income, and prices. These risk factors are incorporated into the specification of the default rates, allowing the default rate itself to have a probability distribution. When the default rate volatilities are set to zero, the default events become independent.

Even in its most general form, where the probability of default depends on several stochastic risk factors, the credit exposures in the portfolio under examination are taken to be constant and are not related to changes in these factors. In reality, credit exposure is often linked quite closely to risk factors such as interest rates and the probability of default. For example, in the case of a loan commitment, a corporate borrower has the option of drawing on its credit line—and is more likely to exercise this option when its credit standing is deteriorating.

Finally, like CreditMetrics and Moody's KMV, CreditRisk+ is not able to cope satisfactorily with nonlinear products such as options and foreign currency swaps.

The Reduced-Form Approach

Structural models imply that default events are predictable, since the evolution of the value of the firm follows a continuous process without jumps.[10] However, in reality, default may happen at any time—a phenomenon that is known as "jump to default." For example, at the time of the millennial stock boom and bust, certain large firms such as Enron and Parmalat surprised investors by suddenly defaulting because of accounting frauds.[11] Also, a firm may be solvent

---

[10]This is true for the standard Merton model. However, more sophisticated models now incorporate random default barriers, and models have been developed under which the value of the firm follows a process with jumps.

[11]However, KMV has shown that both companies' EDF had gradually deteriorated over the two or three years preceding the defaults.

from the perspective of its long-term economics but simply run out of cash and become unable to pay salaries and make other critical payments; if the firm is unable to borrow additional money from the bank, it is likely to be pushed into default. In addition to these issues, it has proved difficult to reproduce the credit spreads observed in the real world using structural models.

Reduced-form models, also called intensity-based models, were introduced to address some of these shortcomings.[12] One of the fundamental advantages of the reduced-form approach is that it produces explicit formulas for the value of risky debt and credit derivative products, and provides a bridge between default probabilities and the credit spreads seen in the financial markets.

These advantages arise from the nature of reduced-form models. Unlike structural model approaches, such as Moody's KMV, reduced-form models don't attempt to predict default by looking at its underlying causes; they are essentially statistical (like CreditRisk+) and are calibrated using credit spreads that are observable in the world's financial markets. The reduced-form approach is therefore less intuitive than a structural model from an economic point of view, and it does not necessarily require balance sheet information. Instead, the data used to feed the models are principally credit instrument prices derived from markets such as the corporate bond, corporate loan, and credit derivatives markets (in contrast to the equity price data from stock markets employed by the KMV approach).

Although this distinction is important in principle, it is not absolute. Reduced-form models depend principally on credit market spreads, but they may also use other input factors—including equity prices and balance sheet information—to better disentangle the estimation of default probabilities from loss given default.[13]

---

[12]This approach models default as an exogenous event whose instantaneous rate of occurrence, the hazard rate, is the key parameter to calibrate.

[13]In the model introduced by Jarrow and Turnbull, the loss given default and the determinants of default can be empirically estimated. Duffie and Singleton (1999) describe an extension of the model. However, their extension suffers from the fact that the loss given default and the determinants of default cannot be separately identified. This is known as the "indetermination problem"— i.e., the calibration of the model produces one number, the expected loss by unit of exposure (PD × LGD). The estimation of PD requires making an assumption about the LGD.

In theory, by looking at the price of credit risky securities over time and subtracting the price of similar securities that do not incur credit risk (such as U.S. government bonds), the "price of credit" can be made transparent. Unfortunately, there are many complications and other real-world problems. The reduced-form modelers' task is to overcome these problems and derive the term structure of risk-adjusted implied default probabilities from the term structure of credit spreads apparent in the market—and then to find the most valid way to reapply this information to a particular bank loan or portfolio in the pursuit of better risk analysis.

Another, more challenging problem is that the world's credit markets are very imperfect as sources of data. Unfortunately, credit risk is not the only determinant of price for credit risky securities—various other risk factors and market inefficiencies interfere with the credit price signals. In particular, although the corporate bond markets are large, the market for each individual bond tends to be quite illiquid and much less transparent than share prices in an equity market (not least because many bond transactions are conducted over the counter rather than on a formal exchange). The heterogeneous nature of bonds as financial instruments is also tricky: many are structured with embedded options (e.g., convertible bonds, callable bonds, and so on), and bond prices may be affected by various regulations and taxes in local markets. (Jarrow's generalization of the reduced-form model proposes a general formulation for the impact of liquidity on bond market prices, as discussed in Appendix 11.1.)

These are empirical challenges, but there are also more fundamental analytical challenges. For example, how do the various credit risk factors interact over a period of time to produce the credit spread visible in bond market data? The relative contribution of default probability and loss given default (or recovery rate) is not at all clear in the market data, yet distinguishing between the effects of these factors in the historical market data is important if the modeling results are to be applied to predict the future default and loss given default rates of loan portfolios.[14]

---

[14]The problem is important because the default probability and the loss given default associated with an instrument vary over time and also depend on the nature of the credit portfolio. At the top of their business cycle, for example, airlines tend not to default, and if they do, any collateral to a bank loan can be sold for a top price. Five years later, the story on both counts will be very different.

Appendix 11.1 offers a more technical introduction to the basic ideas underlying reduced-form models, as pioneered by Jarrow and Turnbull in 1995.[15]

KRIS (Kamakura Risk Information Services) Credit Portfolio Model

Kamakura's credit portfolio model (KRIS) is based on Jarrow's generalization of the reduced-form model sketched in Appendix A11.1. The approach proposed by Kamakura is quite general and can be applied to the construction of default models for all types of borrowers: retail, small business, large unlisted, municipal, and sovereign. Jarrow's model can be fitted to bond prices alone, bond prices and equity prices simultaneously, credit derivatives prices, and historical data on defaults.

The fitting process involves hazard rate modeling, known as logistic regression, an extension of credit scoring technology that has been used for retail and small business default probability estimation for many years. The logistic regression formula which predicts the default hazard rate—i.e., the probability of default P(t) for a given time period t, provided the firm has survived until that time—is a function of explanatory variables that take the following form:

$$P(t) = 1 \: / \: [1 + \exp{(- \alpha - \Sigma \beta_i \, X_i)}]$$

where the explanatory variables, X_i, i = 1, ..., n, include accounting financial ratios such as return on assets and leverage ratio; macroeconomic factors such as the unemployment rate; multiple inputs from the stock price, such as the monthly excess return over a stock market index, monthly equity volatility, and their history for each company; multiple inputs from the comprehensive stock market index for the relevant country; the company's size relative to the total market capitalization of the relevant country; industry variables; seasonality; and so on. KRIS uses historical default data from the KRIS proprietary default database to calibrate the model. Jarrow's specification of the reduced-form model, which incorporates a liquidity premium, allows the endogenous estimation of the LGD.

---

[15]R.A. Jarrow and S. M. Turnbull, "Pricing Derivatives on Financial Securities Subject to Credit Risk," *Journal of Finance* 50(1), March 1995, 53–85.

KRIS provides monthly default probabilities for a full 10-year horizon: P(1) is the probability of default for the first month; P(2) is the probability of default for the second month, conditional on surviving the first month; and so on. P(120) is the probability of default for the last month of the forecasting period, conditional on surviving the 119 previous months.[16]

Empirical studies show that the reduced-form approach has been better able to predict U.S. corporate defaults than other approaches. For example, adding KMV's EDF or distance to default makes only a marginal contribution to the predictive accuracy of the model.[17]

Figure 11-9 shows the annualized KRIS term structure of default for Bank of America on February 27, 2009, during the financial crisis—a period of heightened uncertainty for banks. The upper part shows the annualized monthly probability of default over a 10-year horizon. For example, the annualized three-month default rate for Bank of America on this date is 24.27 percent. The lower part of Figure 11-9 shows the same default risk for Bank of America, this time displayed on a cumulative basis. For example, the 10-year cumulative default risk of the bank was 37.89 percent.[18]

Hybrid Structural Models

While the structural model approach is theoretically appealing, the predicted default probabilities and credit spreads calculated from the Merton model and some of its later extensions are too low compared to those observed

---

[16]These default probabilities can be combined to produce a term structure of cumulative default probabilities (Appendix A11.1).

[17]J. Y. Campbell, J. Hilscher, and J. Szilagyi, "In Search of Distress Risk," *The Journal of Finance*, 63(6), December 2008, 2899–2939; J. Y. Campbell, J. Hilscher, and J. Szilagyi, "Predicting Financial Distress and the Performance of Distressed Stocks," *Journal of Investment Management* 9(2), 2011, 1–21; S. Bharath and T. Shumway, "Forecasting Default with the KMV-Merton Model," *Review of Financial Studies* 21(3), May 2008, 1339–1369.

[18]These calculations were performed after an injection of $45 billion into the bank under the U.S. government's Troubled Asset Relief Program.

FIGURE 11-9 Term Structure of KRIS Default Probabilities for Bank of America on February 27, 2009[19]

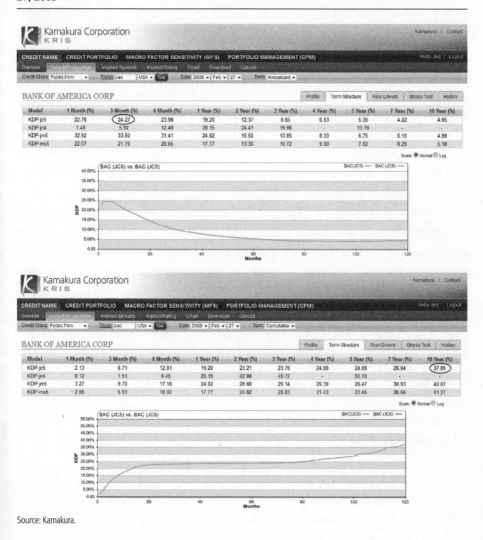

Source: Kamakura.

---

[19]The first line, JC5, corresponds to the version of the KRIS model recommended by Kamakura.

empirically.[20] The KMV proprietary model represented one attempt to circumvent this limitation. More recently, researchers have proposed hybrid structural models that combine the structural model approach with additional accounting and credit information.

The underlying reason for this effort is that default is a complex process and cannot be described simply in terms of an asset value crossing a particular default point. Instead, we must try to take into account the firm's behavior as it approaches the default point. For example, firms that are solvent according to the Merton model can still default on their obligations as a result of severe liquidity problems. Also, as the credit quality of a firm deteriorates, its capacity to borrow and to refinance its debt can determine whether or not it actually defaults.

The firm's borrowing capacity is the result of the borrower's ability to generate revenues for servicing its debt and the value of any assets it can employ as collateral. Both are clearly related to accounting information, such as the borrower's profitability, liquidity, and capital structure, as well as information about the business environment and the borrower's competitiveness (see Chapter 10).

For this reason, proponents of a hybrid approach are attempting to bring together various accounting and market variables to describe the value of the firm's assets and its borrowing capacity. In one such recent approach, for example, the variables are the firm's market equity, stock volatility, stock return, book value of total assets, current liabilities, long-term debt, and net income.[21]

Scoring Models

Credit scoring models are statistical models that weight key factors, such as accounting financial ratios, into a quantitative score. The credit scores are then scaled in order to be interpreted in terms of percentage probabilities of default (PDs).

---

[20]See D. Galai, A. Raviv, and Z. Wiener, "Liquidation Triggers and the Valuation of Equity and Debt," *Journal of Banking and Finance* 31(12), 2007, pp. 3604–3620, for extensions of Merton's economic model of the firm taking into account various legal structures regarding bankruptcy laws.

[21]J. Sobehart and S. Keenan, "Hybrid Probability of Default Models: A Practical Approach to Modeling Default Risk," working paper, Citigroup Global Markets, October 2003.

In Chapter 9 we discussed retail scoring techniques: ordinal systems that rank borrowers into a good and a bad group, based on a cutoff score. In this section we review two of the most popular corporate credit scoring models: Moody's KMV RiskCalc™ and the Altman Z-score model.

Moody's KMV RiskCalc

In the KMV approach described earlier, estimates of EDF are derived from stock prices. Therefore, KMV's approach can only be applied to public companies whose equity is traded in a liquid market. For private firms, Moody's KMV proposes an alternative approach, RiskCalc, which estimates default probabilities known as RiskCalc EDF.

The RiskCalc developers identified a range of firm-specific financial ratios and macro risk factors that are taken to explain the default risk of private companies (Table 11-7). The model also makes adjustments for each firm's industry and for the current stage of the credit cycle.

The most important categories of risk factors are "Leverage" and "Liquidity." But the relative importance of these variables varies among industries.

Moody's KMV RiskCalc has developed country-specific models for the large Western European countries, as well as for Japan, Korea, Singapore, Australia, Russia, and China. For the United States, RiskCalc is composed of four separate submodels for corporations, not-for-profit, real estate operators, and dealerships.

Altman Z-Score[22]

Altman Z-score model is a classification model for corporations that uses linear discriminant analysis built on the value of financial ratios. This approach generates a credit score that best discriminates between firms that default and those that do not. The rationale behind this approach is that companies that default exhibit financial ratios and financial trends that are very different from those of financially healthy firms.

---

[22]J. B. Caouette, E. I. Altman, P. Narayanan, and R. W. J. Nimmo, *Managing Credit Risk*, 2nd edition, Wiley, 2008.

TABLE 11-7 Financial Statement Variables in RiskCalc U.S. 4.0 and Their Weights in the EDF

RiskCalc U.S. 4.0	Weight
Activity	15%
Inventory/Sales	
Current Liabilities/Sales	
Change in Working Capital over Sales	
Growth	7%
Sales Growth	
Leverage (Capital Structure)	26%
Long-term debt (LTD)/LTD + Net worth	
Retained earnings/Current liabilities	
Liquidity	20%
Cash and Marketable Securities/Assets	
Profitability	13%
Return on Assets (ROA) (Net Income/Assets)	
Change in ROA	
Debt Coverage	13%
EBITDA/Interest Expense	
Size	6%
Total Assets	

The discriminant function in the Z-score model for industrial firms is

$$Z = 1.2\,X_1 + 1.4\,X_2 + 2.3\,X_3 + 0.6\,X_4 + 0.999\,X_5$$

where the financial ratios are

X_1 = Working capital / Total assets
X_2 = Retained earnings / Total assets
X_3 = Earnings before interest and taxes (EBIT) / Total assets
X_4 = Market value of equity / Book value of liabilities
X_5 = Sales / Total assets

Altman found that a lower boundary Z-score value of 1.81 (failed) and an upper boundary of 2.99 (nonfail) represented the optimal cutoff points. Any score falling in the range 1.81–2.99 is treated as occupying the "zone of ignorance"—i.e., where it is impossible to discriminate with precision between "bad" and "good" credits.[23]

The Altman Z-score model can be applied to assign a "bond rating equivalent" to each score.

Altman has developed a number of variants of his original Z-score: Z'-score (Z prime) model for privately held manufacturing companies; Z"-score (Z double prime) for nonmanufacturers; and Z-score for emerging market companies.[24] All these models employ different weighting schemes and explanatory financial ratios to best estimate the Z-score for the various classes of companies.

Conclusion

There is no single solution to the problem of how we measure credit risk—no Holy Grail of credit modeling. Instead, there are a variety of approaches, all of which must be regarded as works in progress. The industry is still trying to understand the pros and cons of the various assumptions underlying the various proposed approaches and how they can be best applied alongside the more traditional approaches to credit rating described in Chapter 10.

So far, risk modelers have not found any easy way to integrate market risk and credit risk. The next generation of credit models should remedy this important weakness.

Table 11-8 summarizes the key features of the principal existing credit portfolio models as we've discussed them in this chapter. The table may look complicated, but it again makes clear the great diversity of approaches in this field. Each approach is based on a somewhat different set of assumptions; even

---

[23]The major drawback of the Z-score is its Type II error. While it classified all defaulting firms in the right cell, it also classified in the same cell many firms that eventually did not default (false "bads"). This Type II error of the model is often too high to be useful for banks because they would have to reject too many good clients.

[24]A second-generation model named ZETA makes several enhancements to the original Z-score to reflect changes in accounting and financial reporting.

TABLE 11-8 Key Features of Credit Models

	Credit Migration Approach		Contingent Claim Approach	Actuarial Approach	Reduced-Form Approach
Software	CreditMetrics	CreditPortfolio-View	KMV	Credit Risk+	Kamakura
Definition of risk	Δ Market value	Δ Market value	Δ Market value	Default losses	Default losses
Credit events	Downgrade/default	Downgrade/default	Δ Continuous default probabilities (EDFs)	Δ Actuarial default rate	Δ Default intensity
Risk drivers	Correlated asset values	Macro factors	Correlated asset values	Expected default rates	Hazard rate
Transition probabilities	Constant	Driven by macro factors	Driven by • Individual term structure of EDF • Asset value process	N/A	N/A
Correlation of credit events	Standard multivariate normal distribution (equity factor model)	Conditional default probabilities function of macro factors	Standard multivariate normal asset returns (asset factor model)	Conditional default probabilities function of common risk factors	Conditional default probabilities function of macro factors

Recovery rates	Random (beta distribution)	Random (empirical distribution)	Random (beta distribution)	Loss given default deterministic	Loss given default deterministic
Interest rates	Constant	Constant	Constant	Constant	Stochastic
Numerical approach	Simulation/analytic Econometric	Simulation Econometric	Analytic/simulation Econometric	Analytic	Tree-based/ simulation Econometric

the definition of credit risk may not be the same. The input parameters common to all are credit exposures, recovery rates (or, equivalently, the loss given default), and default correlations.

As we've explained in this chapter, default correlations are captured in a variety of ways. The KMV approach derives default correlations from asset return correlations; CreditMetrics relies on a similar model but employs equity return correlations as a proxy for asset returns. In the other models, the default probabilities are conditional on common systemic or macro factors. Any change in these factors affects all the probabilities of default, but to a different degree, depending on the sensitivity of each obligor to each risk factor.

Appendix 11.1

THE BASIC IDEA OF THE REDUCED FORM MODEL

Consider a defaultable zero-coupon debt instrument issued by a corporation with a promised payment at maturity, say one year, of $100.

Notations:

RR: recovery rate as a percentage of the promised payment = 1 – LGD (loss given default)

PD: one-year risk-neutral probability of default[1]

---

[1]This cumulative probability of default, PD, over the time horizon of one year for the purpose of this illustration, is derived from the term structure of "hazard rates"—i.e., the probabilities of default over small time intervals. Denote by $\lambda(t)$ the hazard rate (or intensity), then the probability of default in the time interval $[t, t+\Delta t]$ is, by definition, $P(t) = \lambda(t)\Delta t$, having not defaulted before time t.

Then, the probability of survival—i.e., the absence of default in the time interval $[t, t+\Delta t]$—is: $1 - \lambda(t)\Delta t$.

Now, consider the time interval $[0,T]$ and assume that there are n time intervals $[t_{k-1},t_k]$ of length Δt, with k = 1 to n, with a constant hazard rate $\lambda(k)$ in each time interval $[t_{k-1},t_k]$. Then, the survival probability over the period $[0,T]$—i.e., the probability of no default between 0 and T—is:

$$S(T) = [1- \lambda(1)\Delta t] \, [1- \lambda(2)\Delta t] \ldots [1- \lambda(n)\Delta t] = [1 - P(1)] \, [1 - P(2)] \ldots [1 - P(n)]$$

And the probability of default between time T and T+ Δt, as seen at time 0, is:

$$q(T) \, \Delta t = \lambda(T) \, \Delta t \times S(T)$$

i: one-year risk-free interest rate
y: one-year risk-adjusted yield

P: zero-coupon bond price

There are two approaches to value this defaultable zero-coupon bond:

- The risk-neutral valuation where expected cash flows (using risk-neutral probabilities) are discounted at the risk-free rate:

$$P = [100 (1 - PD) + 100 \times PD \times RR] / (1 + i) \qquad (A11\text{-}1)$$

- The risk-adjusted valuation where promised payments are discounted at a risk-adjusted rate of return, y:

$$P = 100 / (1 + y) \qquad (A11\text{-}2)$$

From these two expressions for the price of this defaultable zero-coupon bond, it follows:

$$1 + i = [1 - PD \times LGD] (1 + y) \qquad (A11\text{-}3)$$

Numerical example:

$$P = 95, i = 5\% \text{ and } RR = 50\%$$

then, from (A11-2) y = 5.26% and from (A11-3) it follows that PD = 0.5%

If we assume a constant hazard rate, λ, over the period [0,T], then the risk-neutral survival probability, S(T), and the risk-neutral default probability, PD(T), over the time interval [0,T] are, respectively:

$$S(T) = \exp(-\lambda T) \text{ and } PD(T) = 1 - \exp(-\lambda T)$$

This formula tells us that survival probabilities have the same structure as discount factors, with the default intensity, or hazard rate, playing the role of interest rates. Thus, hazard rates can be viewed as credit spreads.

Assuming for simplicity that the hazard rate and interest rates are constant, then it can be shown that the fair value of the CDS spread is:

$$S = \lambda (1 - RR)$$

The continuous time equivalent of (A11-3) is:

$$y = i + PD \times LGD \tag{A11-4}$$

This one-period example can be generalized to a multiperiod setting. In Chapter 6 we showed how to derive forward interest rates given a term structure of zero-coupon interest rates. Applying the reasoning that led to (A11-3) to forward rates allows to derive the forward default probabilities (hazard rates). In a two-period setting:

P(1) denotes the probability of default during the first period, say one year.

P(2) denotes the probability of default during the second period, say year 2, conditional on no default occurring during the first year. Then, the two-year cumulative probability of default, PD(2), is: 1 – the survival probability over the first two years—i.e.,

$$PD(2) = 1 - [1 - P(1)][1 - P(2)]$$

Numerical example:

Given P(1) = 0.2% and assuming that P(2) = 0.3%, then PD(2) = 0.5%

Simple reduced-form models are confronted with the identification problem expressed in formula A11-4. The credit spread is the expected loss—i.e., the product of the probability of default and the loss given default. Jarrow and Turnbull (1995) assume a constant LGD and an independent default intensity process with a Poisson distribution that determines the time to default. Default probabilities are nonrandom time-dependent functions. The default and interest rates are not correlated.

Jarrow has generalized the Jarrow-Turnbull model in several directions.[2] First, default probabilities are assumed to be stochastic with an explicit dependence on stochastic interest rates and an arbitrary number of risk factors. Some of the risk factors are firm specific, while the others are macro factors driving default correlations, such as commodity prices and real estate prices.

---

[2] R. Jarrow, "Default Parameter Estimation Using Market Prices," *Financial Analysts Journal* 57(5), 2001.

Jarrow also incorporates a liquidity factor that affects the prices of bonds but not equities. This liquidity factor can be random and different for each issuer, and it can be a function of the same macro risk factors that determine the default intensity.

Jarrow's generalization of the Jarrow-Turnbull model has two key features: it examines both debt and equity prices with the assumption that, in the event of default, the equity value is zero; and it incorporates liquidity risk and illiquid spreads. These features allow the model to resolve the indetermination problem mentioned earlier by permitting the calculation of an implied recovery parameter expressed as a fraction of the market value of the risky debt an instant prior to bankruptcy—rather than as a fraction of the principal of the bond, as assumed earlier in our illustration. This model is the analytical framework implemented in the Kamakura-KRIS credit portfolio model.

The term structure of hazard rates can be fitted to bond prices (as well as bond prices and equity prices simultaneously), to credit derivatives prices (CDS spreads), and to historical data on defaults. The reduced form model can be used to improve portfolio hedging.[3]

---

[3]H. Doshi, J. Ericsson, K. Jacobs, and S. M. Turnbull, "Pricing Credit Default Swaps with Observable Covariates," *Review of Financial Studies*, forthcoming.

12

THE CREDIT TRANSFER MARKETS—AND THEIR IMPLICATIONS

A number of years ago, Alan Greenspan, then chairman of the U.S. Federal Reserve, talked of a "new paradigm of active credit management." He and other commentators argued that the U.S. banking system weathered the credit downturn of 2001–2002 partly because banks had transferred and dispersed their credit exposures using novel credit instruments such as credit default swaps (CDSs) and securitization such as collateralized debt obligations (CDOs).[1] This looked plain wrong in the immediate aftermath of the 2007–2009 financial crisis, with credit transfer instruments deeply implicated in the catastrophic buildup of risk in the banking system.

Yet, as the dust has settled in the years after the crisis, a more measured view has taken hold. First, it became evident that in certain respects the CDS market had performed quite robustly during and after the crisis and had indeed helped to manage and transfer credit risk, though at the cost of some major systemic and counterparty concerns that needed to be addressed. Second, many commentators came around to the view that although the crisis was precipitated in part by complex credit securitization such as CDOs, this may have had more to do with the inadequacies of the pre-crisis securitization process than with the underlying principle of credit risk transfer. Some parts of the securitization industry, such as

---

[1] Alan Greenspan, "The Continued Strength of the U.S. Banking System," speech, October 7, 2002.

securitizing credit card receivables, remained viable through much of the crisis and beyond—perhaps because risk remained relatively transparent to investors.

Going forward, the picture for credit transfer markets and strategies is mixed (Table 12-1). Some pre-crisis markets and instruments were killed off by the turmoil and seem likely never to reappear, at least in the shape and size they once assumed. Others remained moribund for a couple of years after the crisis but then began to recover and reform: they may grow quickly again once the economy picks up and interest rates rise high enough to support expensive securitization processes. Still others were relatively unhurt in the crisis.

Meanwhile, new credit risk transfer strategies are appearing, including a trend for insurance companies to purchase loans from banks to build asset portfolios that match their long-term liabilities. Indeed, the high capital costs

TABLE 12-1 Credit Transfer Markets: Will They Survive and Revive?

Under scrutiny, but relatively robust	• Credit default swaps. • Consumer asset-backed securities (non–real estate)–e.g., auto loans, credit card receivables, leases, student loans. • Government entity sponsored MBS. • Asset-backed commercial paper programs (traditional model).
Low-state convalescence, but reforming with potentially fast revival	• Private label mortgage backed securities (MBS): U.S. market gradually picking up but suffering from uncertainty about regulatory proposals. • CLO: Despite some mild downgrades, CLO credit quality was relatively robust during and after the crisis. The market was largely dormant for a few years, but volumes of new CLOs began to grow quite quickly through 2011 and 2012 into 2013.
Moribund, with limited chance of revival	• CDO-squared. • Other forms of overly complex securitization (single-tranche CDOs). • Asset-backed commercial paper nontraditional programs (including complex securitizations).
New and revived post-crisis markets	• Partnerships with insurance companies: Banks originate and structure loans—e.g., long-term infrastructure loans—which are funded by insurance companies. Risk is transferred in total or partially to the insurance company. • Covered bonds: These are funding instruments, as no credit risk is transferred. Covered bond markets were well established in some countries—e.g., Germany (Pfandbriefe)—before the crisis and have spread and grown since the crisis as a funding technique trusted by investors. • Resecuritization of downgraded AAA products (Re-Remics, etc.).

associated with post-crisis reforms (e.g., Basel III) suggest that the "buy and hold" model of banking will remain a relatively inefficient way for banks to manage the credit risk that lending and other banking activities generate. Regulators as well as industry participants are keen to support the reemergence of reformed securitization markets in order to help banks obtain funding and encourage economic growth. In the longer term, the 2007–2009 crisis is likely to be seen as a constructive test by fire for the credit transfer market rather than a test to destruction.

It is another episode in a longer process, observable since the 1970s, in which developing and maturing credit markets have driven changes in the business models of banks. Each crisis, each new regulation, eventually drives banks further away from the buy-and-hold traditional intermediation model toward adopting the originate-to-distribute (OTD) business model that surfaces throughout this chapter and that is introduced in Box 12-1.

BOX 12-1 CREDIT MARKETS ARE DRIVING LONG-TERM CHANGES IN BANKS

New technologies aren't the only thing that's driving change in the banking industry. Over the last two decades or so, the portfolios of loans and other credit assets held by banks have become increasingly more concentrated in less creditworthy obligors. This situation has made some banks more vulnerable during economic downturns, such as in 2001–2002 and 2008–2009, when some banks experienced huge credit-related losses in sectors such as telecommunications, cable, energy, and utilities (2001–2002) or real estate, financial institutions and insurance, and automobiles (2008–2009).

Defaults have reached new levels during each successive credit crisis since the early 1990s. Default rates for speculative-grade corporate bonds were 9.2 percent and 9.5 percent in 2001 and 2002, respectively, versus 8 percent and 11 percent in 1990 and 1991, respectively, and 3.6 percent and 9.5 percent in 2008 and 2009, respectively. However, in terms of volume, the default record was much worse in later crises than in the early 1990s: it reached the unprecedented peak of $628 billion in 2009, according to Standard & Poor's, compared with approximately $20 billion in 1990 and 1991 and $190 billion in 2002.[1]

At the same time that default rates were high, recovery rates were also abnormally low, producing large credit-related losses at most major banks.

---

[1]Standard & Poor's, *Annual Global Corporate Default Study*, March 2012.

Two forces have combined to lead to a concentration of low-quality credits in loan portfolios:

- First, there is the "disintermediation" of banks that started in the 1970s and continues today. This trend means that large investment-grade firms are more likely to borrow from investors by issuing bonds in the efficient capital markets, rather than borrowing from individual banks.
- Second, current regulatory capital rules make it more economical for banks on a risk-adjusted return basis to extend credit to lower-credit-quality obligors.

As a consequence, and due to enhanced competition, banks have found it increasingly difficult to earn adequate economic returns on credit extensions, particularly those to investment-grade borrowers. Lending institutions, primarily commercial banks, have determined that it is no longer profitable to simply make loans and then hold them until they mature.

But we can put a positive spin on this story, too. Banks are finding it more and more profitable to concentrate on the origination and servicing of loans because they have a number of natural advantages in these activities. Banks have built solid business relationships with clients over the years through lending and other banking services. Banks also have hugely complex back offices that facilitate the efficient servicing of loans. In addition, despite setbacks from the 2007–2009 financial crisis, the major banks have a distribution network that allows them to dispose of financial assets to retail and institutional investors, either directly or through structured products. Finally, some banks have developed a strong expertise in analyzing and structuring credits (see Chapter 10).

Banks are better able to leverage these advantages as they move away from the traditional "buy and hold" business model toward an "originate to distribute" (OTD) business model. Under this model, banks service the loans, but the funding of the loans is outsourced to investors and, to some extent, the risk of default is shared with outside parties. Much of this chapter discusses the problems with the execution of the OTD model that helped provoke the 2007–2009 financial crisis—a mode of execution that required reform. However, the OTD model itself has not gone away and is likely to continue to help shape the future of banking.

The first section of this chapter discusses what went wrong with the securitization of subprime mortgages and the important lessons to be learned. The rest of the chapter takes a look at how leading global banks and major financial institutions continue to manage their credit portfolios using credit risk transfer instruments and strategies, including traditional strategies such as loan sales. We explore how these techniques affect the way in which banks organize their credit function, and we examine the different kinds of credit derivatives and securitization. Although the following discussion is framed in terms of the banking industry, much of it is relevant to the management of credit risks borne by leasing companies and large nonfinancial corporations in the form of account receivables and so on. This is particularly true for manufacturers of capital goods, which very often provide their customers with long-term credits.

What Went Wrong with the Securitization of Subprime Mortgages?

Securitization involves the repackaging of loans and other assets into securities that can then be sold to investors. Potentially, this removes considerable liquidity, interest rate, and credit risk from the originating bank's balance sheet compared to a traditional "buy and hold" banking business model.

Over a number of years, certain banking markets shifted quite significantly to this new "originate to distribute" (OTD) business model, and the move gathered pace in the years after the millennium. Credit risk that would once have been retained by banks on their own books was sold, along with the associated cash flows, to investors in the form of mortgage-backed securities and similar investment products. In part, the banking industry's enthusiasm for the OTD model was driven by Basel capital adequacy requirements: banks sought to optimize their use of capital by moving capital-hungry assets off their books. Accounting and regulatory standards also tended to encourage banks to focus on generating the upfront fee revenues associated with the securitization process.

For many years, the shift toward the OTD business model seemed to offer many benefits to the financial industry, not least by facilitating portfolio optimization through diversification and risk management through hedging.

- Originators benefited from greater capital efficiency, enhanced funding availability, and, at least in the short term, lower earnings volatility (since the OTD model seemed to disperse credit and interest rate risk across many participants in the capital markets).

- Investors benefited from a greater choice of investments, allowing them to diversify and to match their investment profile more closely to their preferences.
- Borrowers benefited from the expansion in credit availability and product choice, as well as lower borrowing costs.

However, the benefits of the OTD model were progressively weakened in the years preceding the financial crisis, and risks began to accumulate. The fundamental reasons for this remain somewhat controversial, at least in terms of their relative importance. However, everyone agrees that one problem was that the OTD model of securitization reduced the incentives for the originator of the loan to monitor the creditworthiness of the borrower—and that too few safeguards had been in place to offset the effects of this.

For example, in the securitization food chain for U.S. mortgages, every intermediary in the chain charged a fee: the mortgage broker, the home appraiser, the bank originating the mortgages and repackaging them into mortgage-backed securities (MBS), the investment bank repackaging the MBS into collateralized debt obligations, and the credit rating agencies giving their AAA blessing to such instruments. But the intermediaries did not necessarily retain any of the risk associated with the securitization, and the intermediary's income, as well as any bonuses paid, was tied to deal completion and deal volume rather than quality.

Eventually the credit risk was transferred to a structure that was so complex and opaque that even the most sophisticated investors had no real idea what they were holding. Instead, investors relied heavily on rating agency opinions and on the credit enhancements made to the securities by financial guarantors (monolines and insurance companies such as AIG). The lack of transparency of the securitized structures made it difficult to monitor the quality of the underlying loans and added to the fragility of the system.

The growth of the credit default swap market and related credit index markets made credit risk easier to trade and to hedge. This greatly increased the perceived liquidity of credit instruments. In the broader market, the low credit risk premiums and rising asset prices contributed to low default rates, which again reinforced the perception of low levels of risk.

Nevertheless, although the flawed securitization process and the failures of the rating agencies (see Appendix 12.1) were clearly important factors, the financial crisis occurred largely because banks did *not* follow the OTD business model. Rather than acting as intermediaries by transferring the risk from mortgage lenders to capital market investors, many banks themselves took on the role of investors.[2] For example, relatively little credit transfer took place in the mortgage market; instead, banks retained or bought a large amount of securitized mortgage credit risk.

In particular, risks that should have been broadly dispersed under a classic OTD model turned out to have been concentrated in entities set up to get around regulatory capital requirements. Banks and other financial institutions achieved this by establishing highly leveraged off-balance-sheet asset-backed commercial paper (ABCP) conduits and structured investment vehicles (SIVs). These vehicles allowed the banks to move assets off their balance sheets; it cost a lot less capital[3] to hold a AAA-rated CDO tranche at arm's length in an investment vehicle than it did to hold a loan on the balance sheet.

While the capital charges fell, the risks mounted up. The conduits and SIVs were backed by small amounts of equity and were funded by rolling over short-term debt in the asset-backed commercial paper markets, mainly bought by highly risk-averse money market funds. If things went wrong, the investment vehicles had immediate recourse to their sponsor bank's balance sheet through various pre-agreed liquidity lines and credit enhancements (and because bank sponsors did not want to incur the reputational damage of a vehicle failure).[4]

In many cases, banks set up their investment vehicles to warehouse undistributed CDO tranches for which they could not find any buyers. In other cases, banks set up the vehicles to hold senior tranches of CDOs and similar, rated AAA or AA, because the yield was much higher than the yield on corporate bonds with the same rating. There was a reason for this higher yield, of course. In Boxes 12-2 and 12-3 we discuss why banks bought so many subprime securities and how the involvement of European banks helped to transfer a crisis in U.S. subprime lending across the Atlantic.

---

[2]According to the *Financial Times* (July 1, 2008), 50 percent of AA-rated asset-backed securities were held by banks, conduits, and SIVs. As much as 30 percent was simply parceled out by banks to each other, while 20 percent sat in conduits and SIVs.

[3]Capital requirements for such off-balance-sheet entities were roughly one-tenth of the requirement had the assets been held on the balance sheet.

[4]These enhancements implied that investors in conduits and SIVs had recourse to the banks if the quality of the assets deteriorated—i.e., investors had the right to return assets to the bank if they suffered a loss. There was very little in the way of a capital charge for these liquidity lines and credit enhancements.

BOX 12-2 WHY DID BANKS BUY SO MANY SUBPRIME SECURITIES?

In mid-2007, at the start of the financial crisis, U.S. financial institutions such as banks and thrifts, government sponsored enterprises (GSEs), broker-dealers, and insurance companies, were holding more than $900 billion of tranches of subprime MBS. Why did they hold so much?

At the peak of the housing bubble, spreads on AAA-rated tranches of subprime MBSs (based on the ABX index) were 18 bps versus 11 bps for similarly rated bonds. The yields were 32 bps versus 16 bps for AA-rated securities, 54 bps versus 24 bps for A-rated securities, and 154 bps versus 48 bps for BBB-rated securities.

Taking a position in highly rated subprime securities therefore seemed to promise an outsized return, most of the time. Investing institutions would face losses only in the seemingly unlikely event that, say, the AAA-rated tranches of the CDOs were obliged to absorb losses. If this rare event occurred, however, it would surely be in the form of a systemic shock affecting all markets. Financial firms were, in essence, writing a very deep out-of-the-money put option on the market.

Of course, the problem with writing a huge amount of systemic insurance like this is that in the middle of any general crisis, firms would be unlikely to easily absorb the losses and the financial system would be destabilized. Put simply, firms took a huge asymmetric bet on the U.S. real estate market—and the financial system lost.

BOX 12-3 SACHSEN AND SUBPRIME SECURITIES

It is striking that some of the biggest buyers of U.S. subprime securities were European banks, including publicly owned banks in Germany: the Landesbanken.

One of the most notorious examples was the Sachsen Landesbank located in Leipzig in the State of Saxony, deep within the boundaries of the old East Germany. Landesbanks traditionally specialize in lending to regional small- and medium-sized companies, but during the boom years some began to open overseas branches and develop investment banking businesses.

Sachsen opened a unit in Dublin, Ireland, which focused on establishing off-balance-sheet vehicles to hold very large volumes of mainly highly rated U.S. mortgage-backed securities. However, in effect, the vehicles benefited from the guarantee of the parent bank, Sachsen itself.

The operation was highly profitable until 2007, contributing 90 percent of the group's total profit in 2006.[1] However, the operation was too large relative to the size of the balance sheet and capital of the parent bank. When the subprime crisis struck in 2007, the rescue operation wiped out the capital of the parent bank, and Sachsen had to be sold to another German state bank.

---

[1]See P. Honohan, "Bank Failures: The Limitations of Risk Modelling," Working Paper, 2008, for a discussion of this and other bank failures. Honohan (p. 24) says that reading Sachsen's 2007 Annual Report suggests, "The risk management systems of the bank did not consider this [funding liquidity commitment] as a credit or liquidity risk, but merely as an operational risk, on the argument that only some operational failure could lead to the loan facility being drawn down. As such it was assigned a very low risk weight attracting little or no capital."

While the banks' investment vehicles benefited from regulatory and accounting incentives, they operated without real capital buffers and were running considerable risks in the event of a fall in market confidence.

- Some leveraged SIVs incurred significant liquidity and maturity mismatches, making them vulnerable to a classic bank run (or, in this case, shadow bank run).
- The banks and those that rated the bank vehicles misjudged the liquidity and credit concentration risks that would be posed by any deterioration in economic conditions.
- Investors often misunderstood the composition of the assets in the vehicles; this made it even more difficult to maintain confidence once markets began to panic.
- Banks also misjudged the risks created by their explicit and implicit commitments to the vehicles, including reputational risks arising from the sponsorship of the vehicles.

- Financial institutions adopted a business model that assumed substantial ongoing access to funding liquidity and asset market liquidity to support the securitization process.
- Firms that pursued a strategy of actively packaging and selling their original credit exposures retained increasingly large pipelines of these exposures without adequately measuring and managing the risks that would materialize if markets were disrupted and the assets could not be sold.

These problems, and the underlying weaknesses that gave rise to them, show that the underpinnings of the OTD model need to be strengthened. Bank leverage, poor origination practices, and the fact that financial firms chose not to transfer the credit risk they originated—while pretending to do so—were major contributors to the crisis. Among the issues that need to be addressed are:[5]

- Misaligned incentives along the securitization chain, driven by the search for short-term profits. This was the case at many originators, arrangers, managers, and distributors, while investor oversight of these participants was weakened by complacency and the complexity of the instruments.
- Lack of transparency about the risks underlying securitized products, in particular the quality and potential correlations of underlying assets

---

[5]Currently, regulations under the Dodd-Frank Wall Street Reform and Consumer Protection Act propose that banks keep 5 percent of each CDO structure they issue. The regulations shall, according to the Dodd-Frank Act, "prohibit a securitizer from directly or indirectly hedging or otherwise transferring the credit risk that the securitizer is required to retain with respect to an asset." However, as discussed in Acharya et al. (2010), an important missing element in the Dodd-Frank Act is a precise discussion of how the 5 percent allocation should be spread across the tranches and how this will affect capital requirements. In particular, regulators should decree that first-loss positions be included in the retained risks.

As proposed by Acharya et al. (2010), it may be necessary to enforce rigorous underwriting standards—e.g., a maximum loan-to-value (LTV) ratio, a maximum loan to income that varies with the credit history of the borrower, and so on. More generally, the answer might be found in some careful combination of underwriting standards and skin-in-the-game risk retentions.

V. Acharya, T. Cooley, M. Richardson, and I. Walter, eds., *Regulating Wall Street: The Dodd-Frank Act and the New Architecture of Global Finance*, Wiley, 2010.

- Poor management of the risks associated with the securitization business, such as market, liquidity, concentration, and pipeline risks, including insufficient stress testing of these risks.
- Overreliance on the accuracy and transparency of credit ratings. Despite their central role in the OTD model, CRAs did not adequately review the data underlying securitized transactions and also underestimated the risks of subprime CDO structuring. We discuss this further in Appendix 12.1.

Later in the chapter, we summarize some of the practical industry reforms that have been taken, or are in development, to address these issues. For the moment, though, let's remind ourselves of why various forms of credit transfer are so important to the future of the banking industry.

Why Credit Risk Transfer Is Revolutionary . . . If Correctly Implemented

Over the years, banks have developed various "traditional" techniques to mitigate credit risk, such as bond insurance, netting, marking to market, collateralization, termination, or reassignment (see Box 12-4). Banks also typically syndicate loans to spread the credit risk of a big deal (as we describe in Box 12-5) or sell off a portion of the loans that they have originated in the secondary loan market.

BOX 12-4 "TRADITIONAL" CREDIT RISK ENHANCEMENT TECHNIQUES

In the main text, we talk about the newer generation of instruments for managing or insuring against credit risk. Here, let's remind ourselves about the many traditional approaches to credit protection:

- *Bond insurance.* In the U.S. municipal bond market, the issuer purchases insurance to protect the purchaser of the bond (in the corporate debt market, it is usually the lender who buys default protection). Approximately one-third of new municipal bond issues are insured, helping municipalities to reduce their cost of financing.

- *Guarantees.* Guarantees and letters of credit are really also a type of insurance. A guarantee or letter of credit from a third party of a higher credit quality than the counterparty reduces the credit risk exposure of any transaction.
- *Collateral.* A pledge of collateral is perhaps the most ancient way to protect a lender from loss. The degree to which a bank suffers a loss following a default event is often driven largely by the liquidity and value of any collateral securing the loan; collateral values can be quite volatile, and in some markets they fall at the same time that the probability of a default event rises (e.g., the collateral value of real estate can be quite closely tied to the default probability of real estate developers).
- *Early termination.* Lenders and borrowers sometimes agree to terminate a transaction by means of a mid-market quote on the occurrence of an agreed-upon event, such as a credit downgrade.
- *Reassignment.* A reassignment clause conveys the right to assign one's position as a counterparty to a third party in the event of a ratings downgrade.
- *Netting.* A legally enforceable process called netting is an important risk mitigation mechanism in the derivative markets. When a counterparty has entered into several transactions with the same institution, some with positive and others with negative replacement values, then, under a valid netting agreement, the net replacement value represents the true credit risk exposure.
- *Marking to market.* Counterparties sometimes agree to periodically make the market value of a transaction transparent and then transfer any change in value from the losing side to the winning side of the transaction. This is one of the most efficient credit enhancement techniques, and in many circumstances it can practically eliminate credit risk. However, it requires sophisticated monitoring and back-office systems.
- *Put options.* Many of the put options traditionally embedded in corporate debt securities also provide investors with default protection, in the sense that the investor holds the right to force early redemption at a prespecified price—e.g., par value.

BOX 12-5 PRIMARY SYNDICATION

Loan syndication is the traditional way for banks to share the credit risk of making very large loans to borrowers. The loan is sold to third-party investors (usually other banks or institutional investors) so that the originating or lead banks reach their desired holding level for the deal (usually set at around 20 percent by the bank's senior credit committee) at the time the initial loan deal is closed. Lead banks in the syndicate carry the largest share of the risk and also take the largest share of the fees.

Syndicates operate in one of two ways: firm commitment (underwritten) deals, under which the borrower is guaranteed the full face value of the loan, and "best efforts" deals.

Each syndicated loan deal is structured to accommodate both the risk/return appetite of the banks and investors that are involved in the deal and the needs of the borrower. Syndicated loans are often called leveraged loans when they are issued at LIBOR plus 150 basis points or more.

As a rule, loans that are traded by banks on the secondary loan market begin life as syndicated loans. The pricing of syndicated loans is becoming more transparent as the syndicated market grows in volume and as the secondary loans market and the market for credit derivatives become more liquid.

Under the active portfolio management approach that we describe in the main text, the retained part of syndicated bank loans is generally transfer-priced at par to the credit portfolio management group.

These traditional mechanisms reduce credit risk by mutual agreement between the transacting parties, but they lack flexibility. Most important, they do not separate or "unbundle" the credit risk from the underlying positions so that it can be redistributed among a broader class of financial institutions and investors.

Credit derivatives, such as credit default swaps (CDS), are specifically designed to deal with this problem. They are off-balance-sheet arrangements that allow one party (the beneficiary) to transfer the credit risk of a reference asset to another party (the guarantor) without actually selling the asset. They allow users to strip credit risk away from market risk and to transfer credit risk independently of funding and relationship management concerns. (In the same way, the development of interest rate and foreign exchange derivatives in the 1980s allowed banks to manage market risk independently of liquidity risk.)

Nevertheless, the credit derivative revolution arrives with its own unique set of risks. Counterparties must make sure that they understand the amount and nature of risk that is transferred by the derivative contract, and that the contract is enforceable. Even before the 2007–2009 financial crisis, regulators were concerned about the relatively small number of institutions—mainly large banks such as JP Morgan Chase and Deutsche Bank—that currently create liquidity in the credit derivatives market. They feared that this immature market might be disrupted if one or more of these players ran into trouble. We address the important topic of counterparty credit risk in detail in Chapter 13. However, it is interesting to note that even at the height of the credit crisis, the single-name and index CDS market operated relatively smoothly—given the extreme severity of the crisis—under the leadership of ISDA (International Swaps and Derivatives Association).[6]

As we've already discussed, securitization gives institutions the chance to extract and segment a variety of potential risks from a pool of portfolio credit risk exposures and to sell these risks to investors. Securitization is also a key funding source for consumer and corporate lending. According to the IMF, securitization issuance soared from almost nothing in the early 1990s to reach a peak of almost $5 trillion in 2006. Then, with the advent of the subprime crisis in 2007, volumes collapsed, especially for mortgage CDOs as well as collateralized loan obligations (CLOs). Only the securitization of credit card receivables, auto loans, and leases remained relatively unaffected. Since 2012, the market for the securitization of corporate loans (CLOs) has begun to revive, as these structures are transparent for investors and the collateral is reasonably easy to value.

When properly executed in a robust and transparent market, credit derivatives should contribute to the "price discovery" of credit. That is, they make clear how much economic value the market attaches to a particular type of credit risk. As well as putting a number against the default risk associated with many large

---

[6]As mentioned in Box 12-6, some 103 CDS credit events have triggered settlements of CDS between June 2005 and April 2013 without disrupting the CDS market, partly thanks to ISDA's Credit Derivatives Determinations Committees (DCs). These DCs were established in 2009 to make binding decisions as to whether a credit event triggering the settlement of a CDS has occurred, whether an auction should be held to determine the final price for CDS settlement, and which obligations should be delivered or valued in the auction.

corporations, CDS market prices also offer a means to monitor the default risk attached to large corporations in real time (as opposed to periodic credit rating assessments).

Over time, the hope is that improvements in price discovery will lead to improved liquidity, more efficient market pricing, and more rational credit spreads (i.e., the different margins over the bank's cost of funds charged to customers of different credit quality) for *all* credit-related instruments.

The traditional corporate bond markets perform a somewhat similar price discovery function, but corporate bonds are an asset that blends together interest rate and credit risk, and corporate bonds offer a limited lens on credit risk because only the largest public companies tend to be bond issuers. Credit derivatives can, potentially at least, reveal a pure market price for the credit risk of high-yield loans that are not publicly traded, and for whole portfolios of loans.

In a mature credit market, credit risk is not simply the risk of potential default. It is the risk that credit premiums will change minute by minute, affecting the relative market value of the underlying corporate bonds, loans, and other derivative instruments. In such a market, the "credit risk" of traditional banking evolves into the "market risk of credit risk" for certain liquid credits.

The concept of credit risk as a variable with a value that fluctuates over time is apparent, to a degree, in the traditional bond markets. For example, if a bank hedges a corporate bond with a Treasury bond, then the spread between the two bonds will rise as the credit quality of the corporate bond declines. But this is a concept that will become increasingly critical in bank risk management as the new credit technologies and markets make the price of credit more transparent across the credit spectrum.

How Exactly Is All This Changing the Bank Credit Function?

In the traditional model, the bank lending business unit holds and "owns" credit assets such as loans until they mature or until the borrowers' creditworthiness deteriorates to unacceptable levels. The business unit manages the quality of the loans that enter the portfolio, but after the lending decision is made, the credit portfolio remains basically unmanaged.

Let's remind ourselves here of some credit terminology and work out how it relates to the evolution of bank functions.

In modern banking, exposure is measured in terms of the notional value of a loan, or exposure at default (EAD) for loan commitments. The risk of a facility is characterized by:

- The external and/or internal rating attributed to each obligor, usually mapped to a probability of default (PD)
- The loss given default (LGD) and EAD of the facilities

The expected loss (EL) for each credit facility is a straightforward multiplicative function of these variables:

$$EL = PD \times EAD \times LGD$$

Expected loss, as defined here, is the basis for the calculation of the institution's allowance for loan losses, which should be sufficient to absorb both specific (i.e., identified) and more general credit-related losses.[7] EL can be viewed as the cost of doing business. That is, on average, over a long period of time and for a well-diversified portfolio, the bank will incur a credit loss amounting to EL. However, actual credit losses may differ substantially from EL for a given period of time, depending on the variability of the bank's actual default experience. The potential for variability of credit losses beyond EL is called unexpected loss (UL) and is the basis for the calculation of economic and regulatory capital using credit portfolio models (as discussed in Chapter 11).

In the traditional business model, risk assessment is mostly limited to EL and ignores UL. EL, meanwhile, is usually priced into the loan in the form of a spread charged to the borrower above the funding cost of the bank. To limit the risk of default resulting from unexpected credit losses—i.e., actual losses beyond EL—banks hold capital, although traditionally they did not employ rigorous quantitative techniques to link their capital to the size of UL. (This is in contrast to more modern techniques, which use UL for capital attribution and also for

---

[7]When a loan has defaulted and the bank has decided that it won't be able to recover any additional amount, the actual loss is written off and the EL is adjusted accordingly—i.e., the written-off loan is excluded from the EL calculation. Once a loan is in default, special provisions come into effect, in addition to the general provisions, in anticipation of the loss given default (LGD) that will be incurred by the bank once the recovery process undertaken by the workout group of the bank is complete.

the risk-sensitive pricing of loans; the topic of new techniques of economic capital attribution is addressed in Chapter 17.)

Under the traditional business model, risk management is limited to a binary approval process at origination. The business unit compensation for loan origination is based, in many cases, more on volume than on a pure risk-adjusted economic rationale. Likewise, the pricing of the loans by the business unit is driven by the strength of competition in the local banking market rather than by risk-based calculations. To the extent that traditional loan pricing reflects risk at all, this is generally in accordance with a simple grid that relates the price of the loan to its credit rating and to the maturity of the facilities.

By contrast, under the originate-to-distribute business model, loans are divided into core loans that the bank holds over the long term (often for relationship reasons) and noncore loans that the bank would like to sell or hedge. Core loans are managed by the business unit, while noncore loans are transfer-priced to the credit portfolio management group. For noncore loans, the credit portfolio management unit is the vital link between the bank's origination activities (making loans) and the increasingly liquid global markets in credit risk, as we can see in Figure 12-1.

FIGURE 12-1 Originate-to-Distribute Model

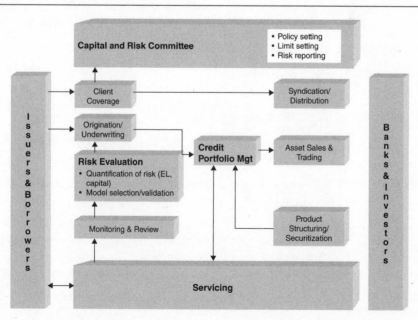

Economic capital is the key to assessing the performance of a bank under this new model. Economic capital is allocated to each loan based on the loan's contribution to the risk of the portfolio. At origination, the spread charged to a loan should produce a risk-adjusted return on capital that is greater than the bank's hurdle rate. Table 12-2 notes how all this changes the activities of a traditional credit function, and helps to make clear how the move to active portfolio management is linked to improved credit-market pricing and the kind of risk-adjusted performance measures we discuss in Chapter 17.

In part, the credit portfolio management group must work alongside traditional teams within the bank such as the loan workout group. The workout group is responsible for "working out" any loan that runs into problems after the credit standing of the borrower deteriorates below levels set by bank policy. The workout process typically involves either restructuring the loan or arranging for compensation in lieu of the value of the loan (e.g., receiving equity or some of the assets of the defaulted company).

But managing risk at the portfolio level also means monitoring the kind of risk concentrations that can threaten bank solvency—and that help to determine

TABLE 12-2 Changes in the Approach to Credit Risk Management

	Traditional Credit Function	Portfolio-Based Approach
Investment strategy	Buy and hold	Originate to distribute
Ownership of the credit assets	Business unit	Portfolio management or business unit/portfolio management
Risk measurement	Use notional value of the loan	Use risk-based capital
	Model losses due only to default	Model losses due to default and risk migration
Risk management	Use a binary approval process at origination	Apply risk/return decision-making process
Basis for compensation for loan origination	Volume	Risk-adjusted performance
Pricing	Grid	Risk contribution
Valuation	Held at book value	Marked-to market (MTM)

the amount of expensive risk capital the bank must set aside. Banks commonly have strong lending relationships with a number of large companies, which can create significant concentrations of risk in the form of overlending to single names. Banks are also prone to concentration as a function of their geography and industry expertise. In Canada, for example, banks are naturally heavily exposed to the oil and gas, mining, and forest products sectors.

Some credit portfolio strategies are therefore based on defensive actions. Loan sales, credit derivatives, and loan securitization are the primary tools banks use to deal with local, regional, country, and industry risk concentrations. Increasingly, however, banks are interested in reducing concentration risk not only for its own sake, but also as a means of managing earnings volatility—the ups and downs in their reported earnings caused by their exposure to the credit cycle.

The credit portfolio management group also has another important mandate: to increase the velocity of capital—that is, to free capital that is tied up in low-return credits and reallocate it to more profitable opportunities. Nevertheless, the credit portfolio management group should not be a profit center but should instead be run on a budget that allows it to meet its objectives.

Trading in the credit markets could potentially lead to accusations of insider trading if the bank trades credits of firms with which it also has some sort of confidential banking relationship. For this reason, the credit portfolio management group must be subject to specific trading restrictions monitored by the compliance group. In particular, the bank has to establish a "Chinese wall" that separates credit portfolio management, the "public side," from the "private side" or insider functions of the bank (where the credit officers belong). The issue is somewhat blurred in the case of the loan workout group, but here, too, separation must be maintained. This requires new policies and extensive reeducation of the compliance and insider functions to develop sensitivity to the handling of material nonpublic information. The credit portfolio management team may also require an independent research function.

The counterparty risk that arises from trading OTC derivatives has become a major component of credit risk in some banks (see Chapter 13) and a major concern since the fall of Lehman Brothers in September 2008. In some institutions, both credit risk related to the extension of loans and counterparty credit risk arising from trading activities are managed centrally by new credit portfolio management groups. The credit portfolio management group also advises deal originators on how best to structure deals and mitigate credit risks. In addition,

FIGURE 12-2 Credit Portfolio Management

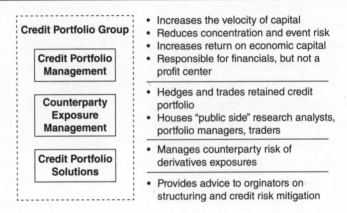

the bank personnel managing credit risk transfers have to deal with the new transparency, disclosure, and fiduciary duties that post-crisis regulation is imposing on banks. Figure 12-2 summarizes the various functions of the credit portfolio management group.

Loan Portfolio Management

There are really two main ways for the bank credit portfolio team to manage a bank credit portfolio:

- Distribute large loans to other banks by means of primary syndication at the outset of the deal so that the bank retains only the desired "hold level" (see Box 12-5).
- Reduce loan exposure by selling down or hedging loans (e.g., by means of credit derivatives or loan securitization).

In turn, these lend themselves to two key strategies:

- Focus first on high-risk obligors, particularly those that are leveraged in market value terms and that experience a high volatility of returns.
- Simultaneously sell or hedge low-risk, low-return loan assets to free up bank capital.

In pursuit of these ends, the credit portfolio management group can combine traditional and modern tools to optimize the risk/return profile of the portfolio. At the traditional end of the spectrum, banks can manage an exit from a loan through negotiation with their customer. This is potentially the cheapest and simplest way to reduce risk and free up capital, but it requires the borrower's cooperation.

The bank can also simply sell the loan directly to another institution in the secondary loan market. This requires the consent of the borrower and/or the agent, but in many cases modern loan documentation is designed to facilitate the transfer of loans. (In the secondary loan market, *distressed loans* are those trading at 90 percent or less of their nominal value.)

As we've discussed, the bank may also use securitization and credit derivatives to transfer credit risk to other financial institutions and to investors. In the rest of this chapter, we'll take a more detailed look at the techniques of securitization and credit derivative markets and the range of instruments that are available.

Credit Derivatives: Overview

Credit derivatives such as credit default swaps (CDS), spread options, and credit-linked notes are over-the-counter financial contracts with payoffs contingent on changes in the credit performance or credit quality of a specified entity.

Both the pace of innovation and the volume of activity in the credit derivative markets were quite spectacular until the beginning of the subprime crisis in 2007. Post-crisis, as of 2013, most of the activity remains concentrated on single-name CDS and index CDS. The Bank for International Settlements reports that the outstanding notional amount for CDS (including single names, multinames, and tranches) was almost nil in 1997 and reached its highest level of $62.2 trillion in 2007. This number dropped to $41.9 trillion in 2008 and has fallen further since to reach $25 trillion at year-end 2012; this includes $14.3 trillion of single-name CDS notionals (including the notionals of $2.9 trillion of sovereign single-name CDS) and $10.8 trillion of multiname CDS notionals (mostly index products).[8] However, we should be careful about assuming these

---

[8]According to the Bank for International Settlements (OTC Derivatives Statistics at year-end 2012), these numbers pale before the aggregate notional amount outstanding for interest rate contracts (FRAs, swaps, and options) of $490 trillion. The amount for foreign exchange contracts is $67.4 trillion.

numbers fully capture CDS market trends as there are a number of challenges in accurately assessing CDS volumes; notably, compression techniques designed to remove offsetting and redundant positions have grown fast since 2008, significantly reducing gross notional values.[9] The general picture of the post-crisis CDS market is of a relatively stable market that is in a downward trend in terms of volume. Sovereign CDS (SCDS) is the exception (Box 12-6).

In line with this, there have been a number of significant improvements in market infrastructure over the last few years, notably the introduction of the "Big Bang Protocol"—i.e., the revised Master Confirmation Agreement published by ISDA in 2009. Alongside changes intended to improve the standardization of contracts, the protocol set in place Determination Committees, to determine when a credit event has taken place, and established auctions as the standard way to fix an agreed price for distressed bonds. Fixing this price is a key task for the cash settlement of CDS after a credit event has occurred because the market for a distressed bond soon after a credit event tends to be very thin.

BOX 12-6 THE SPECIAL CASE OF SOVEREIGN CDS (SCDS)

SCDS are still a small part of the CDS market with, year-end 2012, an amount outstanding of $2.9 trillion versus $25 trillion in CDS as a whole. They also represent a small part of the sovereign debt market when compared to the total government debt outstanding (roughly $50 trillion).

However, the market for SCDS has been growing since the early 2000s and has increased in size noticeably since 2008, while other CDS markets have declined. The post-2008 surge corresponded with a perceived increase in sovereign debt risk, culminating in the European sovereign debt crisis in 2010 and the restructuring of Greek sovereign debt in March 2012.

Although SCDS can provide useful insurance against governments defaulting, their role has been controversial during the European debt crisis. After accusations that speculative trading was exacerbating the crisis, the European Union decided in November 2012 to ban buying

---

[9]International Organization of Securities Commissions, *The Credit Default Swap Market*, Report, June 2012, pp. 6–7.

naked sovereign credit default swap protection—i.e., where the investor does not own the underlying government bond. The ban had already negatively affected the liquidity and trading volumes of SCDS that referenced the debt of eurozone countries because of the fear of less efficient hedging.

The measure was criticized by the International Monetary Fund (IMF), which said that it found no evidence that SCDS spreads had been out of line with government bond spreads and that, for the most part, premiums reflected the underlying country's fundamentals, even if they reflected them faster than the bond market.[1]

The measure was also criticized on the grounds that sovereign debt holders are not the only ones affected when a country defaults. Every sector is affected except possibly the domestic export sector and the tourism industry. Domestic importers and foreign exporters suffer when the default is followed by a devaluation; financial institutions and investors in domestic corporate debt suffer depreciation in the value of their assets; and domestic companies suffer as their credit risk increases.[2]

According to the IMF report, between June 2005 and April 2013 there were 103 CDS credit events, but only two SCDS credit events with publicly documented settlements (Ecuador in 2008 and Greece in 2012). The most recent SCDS credit event was the March 2012 Greek debt exchange, which was the largest sovereign restructuring event in history. About €200 billion of Greek government bonds were exchanged for new bonds. Holders of the old bonds who had SCDS protection ultimately recovered roughly the par value of their holdings. However, there was uncertainty about the payout of the SCDS contracts in this particular situation, caused by the exchange of new bonds for old bonds. The International Swaps and Derivatives Association (ISDA) is looking at modifying the CDS documentation to deal with such situations.

---

[1]International Monetary Fund, *Global Financial Stability Report*, April 2013.

[2]L. M. Wakeman and S. Turnbull, "Why Markets Need 'Naked' Credit Default Swaps," *Wall Street Journal*, September 12, 2012.

More generally, the CDS market has been moving toward increased transparency,[10] standardization of contracts, and the use of electronic platforms. Even so, the market remains relatively opaque compared to some other investment markets—e.g., in terms of posttrade information and information about deals outside the interdealer community.

Furthermore, the CDS market remains dominated by a relatively small number of large banks, leading to continuing fears about the collapse of a major market participant and the effect of this on the CDS and wider financial markets. The proportion of CDS cleared through central counterparties is low but increasing,[11] in line with the regulatory push for all standardized OTC derivative contracts to move to central clearing. Collateralization has also tended to increase, though it varies considerably from market to market in terms of both frequency and adequacy.[12]

Today, the risks in the corporate universe that can be protected by using credit derivative swaps are largely limited to investment-grade names. In the shorter term, using credit derivative swaps might therefore have the effect of shifting the remaining risks in the banking system further toward the riskier, non-investment-grade end of the spectrum. For the market to become a significant force in moving risk away from banks, the non-investment-grade market in credit derivatives needs to become much deeper and more liquid than it is today. There is some evidence that this is occurring, at least in the United States.

---

[10]For example, since 2006 the Depository Trust & Clearing Corporation has run a Trade Information Warehouse to serve as a centralized global electronic data repository containing detailed trade information for the CDS market. From January 2011, this has included a Regulators Portal to give regulators better access to more granular trade data. Larry Thompson (Managing Director, DTCC), "Derivatives Trading in the Era of Dodd-Frank's Title VII," Speech, September 6, 2012.

[11]The Bank of England Financial Stability Report of June 2012 remarked that "around 50% of IRS contracts are centrally cleared compared with around 10% of CDS contracts." (Bank of England, *Financial Stability Report*, June 2012, Box 5, p. 38). Other accounts put the number of *new* trades that are centrally cleared rather higher, at around a third (International Organization of Securities Commissions, *The Credit Default Swap Market*, Report, June 2012, p. 26). The proportion of cleared trades may increase quite rapidly.

[12]For estimates, see International Organization of Securities Commissions, *The Credit Default Swap Market*, Report, June 2012, p. 24.

End User Applications of Credit Derivatives

Like any flexible financial instrument, credit derivatives can be put to many purposes. Table 12-3 summarizes some of these applications from an end user's perspective.

Let's develop a simple example to explain why banks might want to use credit derivatives to reduce their credit concentrations. Imagine two banks, one of which has developed a special expertise in lending to the airline industry and has made $100 million worth of AA-rated loans to airline companies, while the other is based in an oil-producing region and has made $100 million worth of AA-rated loans to energy companies.

In our example, the banks' airline and energy portfolios make up the bulk of their lending, so both banks are very vulnerable to a downturn in the fortunes of their favored industry segment. It's easy to see that, all else equal, both banks would be better off if they were to swap $50 million of each other's loans. Because airline companies generally benefit from declining energy prices, and energy companies benefit from rising energy prices, it is relatively

TABLE 12-3 End User Applications of Credit Derivatives

Investors	• Access to previously unavailable markets (e.g., loans, foreign credits, and emerging markets)
	• Unbundling of credit and market risks
	• Ability to borrow the bank's balance sheet, as the investor does not have to fund the position and also avoids the cost of servicing the loans
	• Yield enhancement with or without leverage
	• Reduction in sovereign risk of asset portfolios
Banks	• Reduce credit concentrations
	• Manage the risk profile of the loan portfolio
Corporations	• Hedging trade receivables
	• Reducing overexposure to customer/supplier credit risk
	• Hedging sovereign credit-related project risk

unlikely that the airline and energy industries would run into difficulties at the same time. After swapping the risk, each bank's portfolio would be much better diversified.

Having swapped the risk, both banks would be in a better position to exploit their proprietary information, economies of scale, and existing business relationships with corporate customers by extending more loans to their natural customer base.

Let's also look more closely at another end user application noted in Table 12-3 with regard to investors: yield enhancement. In an economic environment characterized by low (if potentially rising) interest rates, many investors have been looking for ways to enhance their yields. One option is to consider high-yield instruments or emerging market debt and asset-backed vehicles. However, this means accepting lower credit quality and longer maturities, and most institutional investors are subject to regulatory or charter restrictions that limit both their use of non-investment-grade instruments and the maturities they can deal in for certain kinds of issuer. Credit derivatives provide investors with ready, if indirect, access to these high-yield markets by combining traditional investment products with credit derivatives. Structured products can be customized to the client's individual specifications regarding maturity and the degree of leverage. For example, as we discuss later, a total return swap can be used to create a seven-year structure from a portfolio of high-yield bonds with an average maturity of 15 years.

This said, users must remember the lessons of the 2007–2009 financial crisis: these tools can be very effective in the right quantity so long as they are priced properly and counterparty credit risk is not ignored.

Even when institutional investors can access high-yield markets directly, credit derivatives may offer a cheaper way for them to invest. This is because, in effect, such instruments allow unsophisticated institutions to piggyback on the massive investments in back-office and administrative operations made by banks.

Credit derivatives may also be used to exploit inconsistent pricing between the loan and the bond market for the same issuer or to take advantage of any particular view that an investor has about the pricing (or mispricing) of corporate credit spreads. However, users of credit derivatives must remember that as well as transferring credit risk, these contracts create an exposure to the creditworthiness of the counterparty of the credit derivative itself—particularly with leveraged transactions.

Types of Credit Derivatives

Credit derivatives are mostly structured or embedded in swap, option, or note forms and normally have tenures that are shorter than the maturity of the underlying instruments. For example, a credit default swap may specify that a payment be made if a 10-year corporate bond defaults at any time during the next two years.

Single-name CDS remain the most popular instrument type of credit derivative, commanding more than 50 percent of the market in terms of their notional outstanding value. The demand for single-name CDSs has been driven in recent years by the demand for hedges of pre-crisis legacy positions such as synthetic single-tranche collateralized debt obligations—we discuss the mechanics of these instruments later—and by hedge funds that use credit derivatives as a way to exploit capital structure arbitrage opportunities. The next most popular instruments are portfolio/correlation products, mostly index CDS.

Credit Default Swaps

Credit default swaps can be thought of as insurance against the default of some underlying instrument or as a put option on the underlying instrument.

In a typical CDS, as shown in Figure 12-3, the party selling the credit risk (or the "protection buyer") makes periodic payments to the "protection seller" of a negotiated number of basis points times the notional amount of the underlying bond or loan.[13] The party buying the credit risk (or the protection seller) makes no payment unless the issuer of the underlying bond or loan defaults or there is an equivalent credit event. Under these circumstances, the protection seller pays the protection buyer a default payment equal to the notional amount minus a prespecified recovery factor.

Since a credit event, usually a default, triggers the payment, this event should be clearly defined in the contract to avoid any litigation when the contract is settled. Default swaps normally contain a "materiality clause" requiring that the

---

[13]Before 2009, the "par spread," or premium, was paid monthly by the protection buyer and was calculated so that the spread discounted back to the origination date was equal to the expected discounted value of the settlement amount in case of a credit event. Starting in 2009, the protection buyer pays an annual premium paid in quarterly installments that has been set at one of several standardized levels—i.e., 25, 100, 300, 500, or 1,000 basis points plus or minus an upfront payment to compensate for the difference between the par spread and the fixed premium. This convention already applied to index CDS and was generalized to single-name CDS in 2009.

FIGURE 12-3 Typical Credit Default Swap

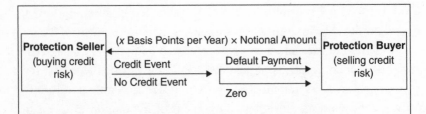

Credit Events

- Bankruptcy, insolvency, or payment default.
- Obligation acceleration, which refers to the situation where debt becomes due and repayable prior to maturity. This event is subject to a materiality threshold of $10 million unless otherwise stated.
- Stipulated fall in the price of the underlying asset.
- Downgrade in the rating of the issuer of the underlying asset.
- Restructuring: this is probably the most controversial credit event (see the Conseco case in Box 12-7).
- Repudiation/moratorium: this can occur in two situations. First, the reference entity (the obligor of the underlying bond or loan issue) refuses to honor its obligations. Second, a company could be prevented from making a payment because of a sovereign debt moratorium (City of Moscow in 1998).

Default Payment

- Par minus postdefault price of the underlying asset as determined by a dealer poll.
- Par minus stipulated recovery factor, equivalent to a predetermined amount (digital swap).
- Payment of par by seller in exchange for physical delivery of the defaulted underlying asset.

change in credit status be validated by third-party evidence. However, Box 12-7 explores the difficulty the CDS market has had in defining appropriate credit events. For this reason, the Determination Committees we mentioned earlier have been on hand since 2009 to settle whether a credit event has occurred or not.

The payment made following a legitimate credit event is sometimes fixed by agreement, but a more common practice is to set it at par minus the recovery rate. (For a bond, the recovery rate is determined by the market price of the bond after the default.[14]) For most standardized CDS the recovery is contractually

---

[14]For a discussion of the contract liquidation procedures and other aspects of how the CDS market functions, see International Organization of Securities Commissions, *The Credit Default Swap Market*, Report, June 2012.

BOX 12-7   CONTROVERSIES AROUND THE "RESTRUCTURING" CREDIT EVENT

"CHEAPEST TO DELIVER": THE CONSECO CASE

In its early years, the credit derivatives market struggled to define the kind of credit events that should trigger a payout under a credit derivative contract. One of the most controversial aspects was whether the restructuring of a loan—which can include changes such as an agreed-upon reduction in interest and principal, postponement of payments, or changes in the currencies of payment—should count as a credit event.

The Conseco case famously highlighted the problems that restructuring can cause. Conseco is an insurance company, headquartered in suburban Indianapolis, that provides supplemental health insurance, life insurance, and annuities. In October 2000, a group of banks led by Bank of America and Chase granted to Conseco a three-month extension of the maturity of approximately $2.8 billion of short-term loans, while simultaneously increasing the coupon and enhancing the covenant protection. The extension of credit might have helped prevent an immediate bankruptcy,[1] but as a significant credit event, it also triggered potential payouts on as much as $2 billion of CDSs.

The original sellers of the CDSs were not happy, and they were annoyed further when the CDS buyers seemed to be playing the "cheapest to deliver" game by delivering long-dated bonds instead of the restructured loans; at the time, these bonds were trading significantly lower than the restructured bank loans. (The restructured loans traded at a higher price in the secondary market because of the new credit mitigation features.)

In May 2001, following this episode, the International Swaps and Derivatives Association (ISDA) amended its definition of a restructuring credit event and imposed limitations on deliverables.

---

[1]Conseco filed a voluntary petition to reorganize under Chapter 11 in 2002 and emerged from Chapter 11 bankruptcy in September 2003.

THE "BAIL-IN" TYPE EVENT

The new resolution regimes in the United States (Dodd-Frank Act) and Europe (European Banking Law) will give supervisory authorities the power to "bail in" the debt of failing financial institutions. Regulatory authorities will have the power to write down debt to avoid bankruptcies and to ensure that bondholders, rather than taxpayers, absorb bank losses.

Although these resolution measures are not yet effective, the European sovereign debt crisis provides a preview of how these regimes may play out in practice. For example, the Irish bank restructuring in 2011 meant that subordinated debt was written down by 80 percent, while the Dutch government later nationalized SNS, a mid-tier lender (wiping out subordinated bondholders). The Cyprus bailout wrote down senior debt and forced a haircut on uninsured depositors.

These bank restructurings raise the concern that the current CDS definitions may not properly cover future reorganizations, such as nationalizations. ISDA is working on a proposal for the specific credit event of a government's using a restructuring resolution law to write down, expropriate, convert, exchange, or transfer a financial institution's debt obligations.

At the same time, the rules governing CDS auctions are being altered to ensure that the payout on the contracts will adequately compensate protection buyers for losses incurred on their bond holdings. In particular, the rules would allow written-down bonds to be delivered into a CDS auction based on the outstanding principal balance before the bail-in happened. In other words, if $100 of bonds were written down to 40 percent of face value, then to satisfy $100 of CDS protection it would only be necessary to deliver into the auction the $40 of the newly written down bonds. This should apply also to sovereign debt (see Box 12-6).

---

set at 60 percent for a bank loan and 40 percent for a bond. The protection buyer stops paying the regular premium following the credit event. CDSs provide major benefits for both buyers and sellers of credit protection (see Box 12-8) and are very effective tools for the active management of credit risk in a loan portfolio.

Since single-name CDSs are natural credit risk hedges for bonds issued by corporations or sovereigns, it is also natural to arbitrage pricing differences between CDS and underlying reference bonds by taking offsetting positions. This

BOX 12-8 BENEFITS OF USING CDSs

- CDSs act to divorce funding decisions from credit risk-taking decisions. The purchase of insurance, letters of credit, guarantees, and so on are relatively inefficient credit risk transfer strategies, largely because they do not separate the management of credit risk from the asset associated with the risk.
- CDSs are unfunded, so it's easy to make leveraged transactions (some collateral might be required), though this may also increase the risk of using CDSs. The fact that CDSs are unfunded is an advantage for institutions with a high funding cost. CDSs also offer considerable *flexibility* in terms of leverage; the user can define the required degree of leverage, if any, in a credit transaction. This makes credit an appealing asset class for hedge funds and other nonbank institutional investors. In addition, investors can avoid the administrative cost of assigning and servicing loans.
- CDSs are customizable—e.g., their maturity may differ from the term of the loan.
- CDSs improve flexibility in risk management, as banks can shed credit risk more easily than by selling loans. There is no need to remove the loans from the balance sheet.
- CDSs are an efficient vehicle for banks to reduce risk and thereby free up capital.
- CDSs can be used to take a spread view on a credit. They offer the first mechanism by which short sales of credit instruments can be executed with any reasonable liquidity and without the risk of a "short squeeze."
- Dislocations between the cash and CDS markets present new "relative value" opportunities (e.g., trading the default swap basis).
- CDSs divorce the client relationship from the risk decision. The reference entity whose credit risk is being transferred does not need to be aware of the CDS transaction. This contrasts with any reassignment of loans through the secondary loan market, which generally requires borrower/agent notification.
- CDSs bring liquidity to the credit market, as they have attracted nonbank players into the syndicated lending and credit arena.

is the purpose of "basis trading." To give some sense of the intuition underlying this kind of trade, consider a 10-year par bond with a 6 percent coupon that could be funded over the life of the bond at 5 percent.[15] This would produce a positive annual cash flow of 1 percent, or 100 basis points. The CDS referencing that bond should also be trading at a "par spread" of 100 basis points. Also, if a credit event occurs, the loss on the bond would be covered by the gain on the CDS.

First-to-Default CDS

A variant of the credit default swap is the *first-to-default* put, as illustrated in the example in Figure 12-4. Here, the bank holds a portfolio of four high-yield loans rated B, each with a nominal value of $100 million, a maturity of five years, and an annual coupon of LIBOR plus 200 basis points (bp). In such deals, the loans are often chosen such that their default correlations are very small—i.e., there is a very low probability at the time the deal is struck that more than one loan will default over the time until the expiration of the put in, say, two years. A first-to-default put gives the bank the opportunity to reduce its credit risk exposure: it will automatically be compensated if one of the loans in the pool of four loans defaults at any time during the two-year period. If more than one loan defaults during this period, the bank is compensated only for the first loan that defaults.

If default events are assumed to be uncorrelated, the probability that the dealer (protection seller) will have to compensate the bank by paying it par— that is, $100 million—and receiving the defaulted loan is the sum of the default probabilities, or 4 percent. This is approximately, at the time, the probability of default of a loan rated B for which the default spread was 400 bp, or a cost of 100 bp per loan—i.e., half the cost of the protection for each individual name.

Note that, in such a deal, a bank may choose to protect itself over a two-year period even though the loans might have a maturity of five years. First-to-default structures are, in essence, pairwise correlation plays. The yield on such structures is primarily a function of:

- The number of names in the basket
- The degree of correlation between the names

---

[15]In order to obtain fixed-rate funding, the bonds are typically funded in the repo market on a floating-rate basis and swapped into fixed rates over the full term using interest rate swaps. In practice, the trade is more complex since, if the bond defaults, the swap should be canceled.

FIGURE 12-4 First-to-Default Put

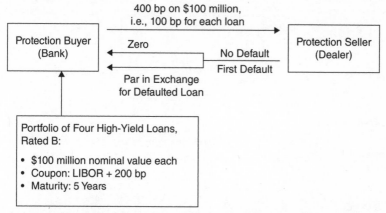

Probability of Experiencing Two Defaults = $(1\%)^2$ 4 × 3/2 = 0.0006 = 0.06%[1]

[1] The probability that more than one loan will default is the sum of the probabilities that two, three, or four loans will default. The probability that three loans or four loans will default during the same period is infinitesimal and has been neglected in the calculation. Moreover, there are six possible ways of pairing loans in a portfolio of four loans.

The first-to-default spread will lie between the spread of the worst individual credit and the sum of the spreads of all the credits—closer to the latter if correlation is low and closer to the former if correlation is high.

A generalization of the first-to-default structure is the *nth-to-default* credit swap, where protection is given only to the *nth* facility to default as the trigger credit event.

Total Return Swaps

Total return swaps (TRSs) mirror the return on some underlying instrument, such as a bond, a loan, or a portfolio of bonds and/or loans. The benefits of TRSs are similar to those of CDSs, except that for a TRS, in contrast to a CDS, both market and credit risk are transferred from the seller to the buyer.

TRSs can be applied to any type of security—for example, floating-rate notes, coupon bonds, stocks, or baskets of stocks. For most TRSs, the maturity of the swap is much shorter than the maturity of the underlying assets—e.g., 3 to 5 years as opposed to a maturity of 10 to 15 years.

The purchaser of a TRS (the total return receiver) receives the cash flows and benefits (pays the losses) if the value of the reference asset rises (falls). The purchaser is synthetically long the underlying asset during the life of the swap.

FIGURE 12-5 Generic Total Return Swap (TRS)

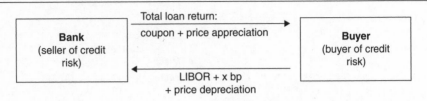

Cash flows for a TRS

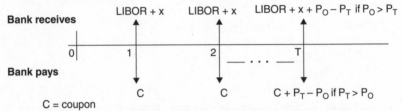

C = coupon
P_O = market value of asset (e.g., loan portfolio) at inception (time 0)
P_T = market value of asset (e.g., loan portfolio) at the maturity of the TRS (time T)

Both market risk and credit risk are transferred in a TRS

In a typical deal, shown in Figure 12-5, the purchaser of the TRS makes periodic floating payments, often tied to LIBOR. The party selling the risk makes periodic payments to the purchaser, and these are tied to the total return of some underlying asset (including both coupon payments and the change in value of the instruments). We've annotated these periodic payments in detail in the figure.

Since in most cases it is difficult to mark-to-market the underlying loans, the change in value is passed through at the maturity of the TRS. Even at this point, it may be difficult to estimate the economic value of the loans, which may still not be close to maturity. This is why in many deals the buyer is required to take delivery of the underlying loans at a price P_0, which is the initial value.

At time T, the buyer should receive $P_T - P_0$ if this amount is positive and pay $P_0 - P_T$ otherwise. By taking delivery of the loans at their market value P_T, the buyer makes a net payment to the bank of P_0 in exchange for the loans.

In some leveraged TRSs, the buyer holds the explicit option to default on its obligation if the loss in value $P_0 - P_T$ exceeds the collateral accumulated at the expiration of the TRS. In that case, the buyer can simply walk away from the deal, abandon the collateral to the counterparty, and leave the counterparty to bear any loss beyond the value of the collateral (Figure 12-6).

FIGURE 12-6 Leveraged Total Return Swap (TRS)

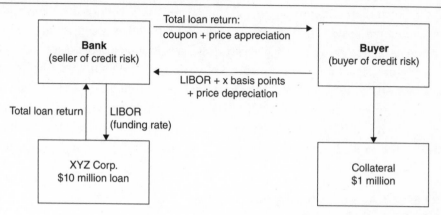

A total return swap is equivalent to a synthetic long position in the underlying asset for the buyer. It allows for any degree of leverage, and therefore it offers unlimited upside and downside potential. It involves no exchange of principal, no legal change of ownership, and no voting rights.

In order to hedge both the market risk and the credit risk of the underlying assets of the TRS, a bank that sells a TRS typically buys the underlying assets. The bank is then exposed only to the risk of default of the buyer in the total return swap transaction. This risk will itself depend on the degree of leverage adopted in the transaction. If the buyer fully collateralizes the underlying instrument, then there is no risk of default and the floating payment should correspond to the bank's funding cost. If, on the contrary, the buyer leverages its position, say, 10 times by putting aside 10 percent of the initial value of the underlying instrument as collateral, then the floating payment is the sum of the funding cost and a spread. This corresponds to the default premium and compensates the bank for its credit exposure with regard to the TRS purchaser.

Asset-Backed Credit-Linked Notes

An asset-backed credit-linked note (CLN) embeds a default swap in a security such as a medium-term note (MTN). Therefore, a CLN is a debt obligation with a coupon and redemption that are tied to the performance of a bond or loan, or to the performance of government debt. It is an on-balance-sheet instrument, with exchange of principal; there is no legal change of ownership of the underlying assets.

Unlike a TRS, a CLN is a tangible asset and may be leveraged by a multiple of 10. Since there are no margin calls, it offers its investors limited downside and unlimited upside. Some CLNs can obtain a rating that is consistent with an investment-grade rating from agencies such as Fitch, Moody's, or Standard & Poor's.

Figure 12-7 presents a typical CLN structure. The bank buys the assets and locks them into a trust. In the example, we assume that $105 million of non-investment-grade loans with an average rating of B, yielding an aggregate LIBOR + 250 bp, are purchased at a cost of LIBOR, which is the funding rate for the bank. The trust issues an asset-backed note for $15 million, which

FIGURE 12-7 Asset-Backed Credit-Linked Note (CLN)

Structure:

- Investor seeks $105 million of exposure with a leverage ratio of 7, i.e., while investing only $15 million in collateral.
- Investor purchases $15 million of CLN issued by a trust.
- Trust receives $105 million of non-investment-grade loans that are assumed to yield LIBOR + 250 bps on average.
- $15 million CLN proceeds are invested in U.S. Treasury notes that yield 6.5%.
- Bank finances the $105 million loans at LIBOR and receives from the trust LIBOR + 100 bps on $105 million to cover default risk beyond $15 million.

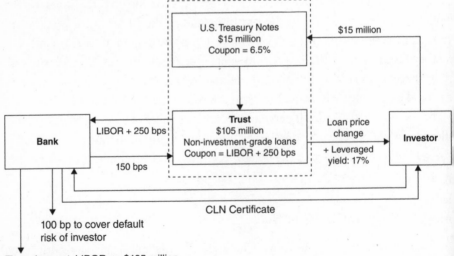

- Coupon spread on non-investment-grade loans: 250 bp
- Leveraged yield: 6.5% (U.S. T-notes) + 150 bp × 7 (leverage multiple) = 17%
- Option premium (default risk of investor) = 100 bp
- Leverage: 7

is bought by the investor. The proceeds are invested in U.S. government securities, which are assumed to yield 6.5 percent and are used to collateralize the basket of loans. The collateral in our example is 15/105 = 14.3 percent of the initial value of the loan portfolio. This represents a leverage multiple of 7 (105/15 = 7).

The net cash flow for the bank is 100 bp—that is, LIBOR + 250 bp (produced by the assets in the trust) minus the LIBOR cost of funding the assets minus the 150 bp paid out by the bank to the trust. This 100 bp applies to a notional amount of $105 million and is the bank's compensation for retaining the risk of default of the asset portfolio above and beyond $15 million.

The investor receives a yield of 17 percent (i.e., 6.5 percent yield from the collateral of $15 million, plus 150 bp paid out by the bank on a notional amount of $105 million) on a notional amount of $15 million, in addition to any change in the value of the loan portfolio that is eventually passed through to the investor.

In this structure there are no margin calls, and the maximum downside for the investor is the initial investment of $15 million. If the fall in the value of the loan portfolio is greater than $15 million, then the investor defaults and the bank absorbs any additional loss beyond that limit. For the investor, this is the equivalent of being long a credit default swap written by the bank.

A CLN may constitute a natural hedge to a TRS in which the bank receives the total return on a loan portfolio. Different variations on the same theme can be proposed, such as compound credit-linked notes where the investor is exposed only to the first default in a loan portfolio.

Spread Options

Spread options are not pure credit derivatives, but they do have creditlike features. The underlying asset of a spread option is the yield spread between a specified corporate bond and a government bond of the same maturity. The striking price is the forward spread at the maturity of the option, and the payoff is the greater of zero or the difference between the spread at maturity and the striking price, times a multiplier that is usually the product of the duration of the underlying bond and the notional amount.

Investors use spread options to hedge price risk on specific bonds or bond portfolios. As credit spreads widen, bond prices decline (and vice versa).

Credit Risk Securitization

In this section, we offer a quick introduction to the basics of securitization and a recap on key themes in the ongoing attempts to reform and revitalize the securitization markets (Box 12-9).[16] Then we describe the different types of instruments, including some that are not used for securitizing at the present but that are still "in play" in the portfolios of financial institutions (and that remain of historical interest because of their role in provoking the 2007–2009 crisis).

BOX 12-9   KEY SECURITIZATION MARKET REFORMS: AN ONGOING PROCESS

Mending the failings of the securitization industry that helped provoke the 2007–2009 crisis is seen as crucial by both the industry and its regulators if key securitization markets are to be revived in a healthier form.[1]

Securitization markets are highly varied in terms of their jurisdiction, regulatory authorities, and underlying assets, and one of the challenges of the reform process has been to produce a reasonably consistent response (e.g., in Europe versus the United States) rather than a patchwork of local rules. The reform process has also been slow, beginning in 2009 and continuing through 2013 and beyond.

However, in the years since the crisis, both the industry and its regulators have begun changing industry practices in the following key areas:

- *Risk retention.* There is general agreement that originators (e.g., banks) need to retain an interest in each of their securitizations, to

---

[1]For example, see Basel Committee, *Report on Asset Securitization Incentives*, July 2011.

---

[16]The market for securitization is recovering faster in the United States than in Europe, where it is still depressed. According to a report by IOSCO (International Organization of Securities Commissions), in the United States, new issuance totaled $124 billion in 2011 and increased to reach $100 billion in the first half of 2012, down from a peak in 2006 of $753 billion. Half of these new issuances are backed by auto loans, while credit cards receivables account for almost 20 percent. In Europe, new issuance totaled €228 billion in 2011, down from a peak of €700 billion in 2008. More than half of the new issuances are RMBS (residential mortgage-backed securities). See IOSCO *Global Developments in Securitization Regulation*, November 16, 2012, pp. 11–12.

make sure they have some "skin in the game." Examples of reforms include rules in Europe preventing credit institutions from investing unless an originating party keeps 5 percent or more of the economic interest. The U.S. agencies require a similar level of retention, though the rules focus on the sponsor rather than the investor and there are important exemptions for securitizations based on assets of apparently higher credit quality.

- *Disclosure and transparency.* Disclosure requirements and proposed disclosures vary across regions and markets, but they cover issues such as the cash flow or "waterfall" structuring of the securitization, trigger events, collateral support, key risk factors, and so on. Two key post-crisis issues are the granularity (or level of detail) of information given to investors about the assets that underlie the securitization and the amount and kind of information that should be given to investors to allow them to understand (or independently analyze) what might happen in a stressed scenario.[2]
- *Rating agency role.* The main worries here are that investors rely too heavily on rating agencies, that agencies suffer from conflicts of interest, and also that securitizing banks "shop around" among the competing rating agencies to find the agency that offers the highest rating. A number of measures are being considered to reduce these issues, including obliging or pushing agencies to:

    - Publish details of their rating methodologies, procedures, and assumptions
    - Distinguish clearly between securitization ratings and other kinds of ratings
    - Make rating agencies more accountable (e.g., to the SEC in the United States)
    - Adopt mechanisms that discourage ratings shopping
    - Reduce the chance that conflicts of interest will affect rating decisions (e.g., keeping rating analysts away from fee discussions)

---

[2]In the United States, the securitization industry has launched Project Restart to agree and promote improved standards of reporting on the composition of underlying asset pools and their ongoing performance.

- *Capital and liquidity requirements.* Various aspects of Basel III reforms are intended to tighten up the treatment of securitization, and proposed revisions will substantially increase capital requirements. Resecuritizations, in particular, attract much higher capital charges, and securitization liquidity facilities are charged a higher credit conversion factor (CCF)—i.e., 50 percent instead of 20 percent in Basel II Standardized Approach.[3]

Sources: IOSCO, *Global Developments in Securitization Regulation*, Final Report, November 16, 2012; IMF, *Global Financial Stability Report*, October 2009, Chapter 2: "Restarting Securitization Markets: Policy Proposals and Pitfalls."

---

[3]In December 2012, the Basel Committee launched a consultative paper that proposed a major overhaul of the regulatory treatment of securitization. (Basel Committee on Banking Supervision, *Revisions to the Basel Securitization Framework*, Consultative Document, BIS, December 2012.)

Basics of Securitization

Securitization is a financing technique whereby a company, the *originator*, arranges for the issuance of securities whose cash flows are based on the revenues of a segregated pool of assets—e.g., corporate investment-grade loans, leveraged loans, mortgages, and other asset-backed securities (ABS) such as auto loans and credit card receivables.[17]

Assets are originated by the originator(s) and funded on the originator's balance sheet. Once a suitably large portfolio of assets has been originated, the assets are analyzed as a portfolio and then sold or assigned to a bankruptcy-remote company—i.e., a special purpose vehicle (SPV) company formed for the specific purpose of funding the assets.[18] The pool of loans is therefore taken *off* the originator's balance sheet. Alternatively, loans can be bought from other financial institutions.

---

[17]The borrower may be unaware of this, as the lender normally continues to be the loan servicer.

[18]The SPVs are also known as SIVs (special investment vehicles).

The SPV issues tradable "securities" to fund the purchase of the assets. These securities are claims against the underlying pool of assets. The performance of these securities is directly linked to the performance of the assets and, in principle, there is no recourse back to the originator.

Tranching is the process of creating notes of various seniorities and risk profiles, including senior and mezzanine tranches and an equity (or first loss) piece. As a result of the prioritization scheme, also known as the "waterfall," used in the distribution of cash flows to the tranche holders, the most senior tranches are far safer than the average asset in the underlying pool. Senior tranches are insulated from default risk up to the point where credit losses deplete the more junior tranches. Losses on the mortgage loan pool are first applied to the most junior tranche until the principal balance of that tranche is completely exhausted. Then losses are allocated to the most junior tranche remaining, and so on.

This ability to repackage risks and create apparently "safe" assets from otherwise risky collateral led to a dramatic expansion in the issuance of structured securities, most of which were regarded by investors as virtually free of risk and certified as such by the rating agencies. Figure 12-8 gives a graphical representation of the securitization process.

FIGURE 12-8 Securitization of Financial Assets

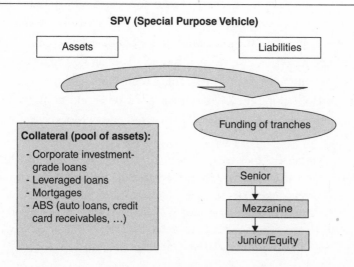

SPV (Special Purpose Vehicle)

Assets   Liabilities

Funding of tranches

Collateral (pool of assets):
- Corporate investment-
  grade loans
- Leveraged loans
- Mortgages
- ABS (auto loans, credit
  card receivables, ...)

Senior

Mezzanine

Junior/Equity

Securitization of Corporate Loans and High-Yield Bonds

Collateralized loan obligations (CLOs) and collateralized bond obligations (CBOs) are simply securities that are collateralized by means of high-yield bank loans and corporate bonds. (CLOs and CBOs are also sometimes referred to generically as collateralized debt obligations, or CDOs.) Banks that use these instruments can free up regulatory capital and thus leverage their intermediation business.

A CLO (CBO) is potentially an efficient securitization structure because it allows the cash flows from a pool of loans (or bonds) rated at below investment grade to be pooled together and prioritized, so that some of the resulting securities can achieve an investment-grade rating. This is a big advantage because a wider range of investors, including insurance companies and pension funds, are able to invest in such a "senior class" of notes. The main differences between CLOs and CBOs are the assumed recovery values for, and the average life of, the underlying assets. Rating agencies generally assume a recovery rate of 30 to 40 percent for unsecured corporate bonds, while the rate is around 70 percent for well-secured bank loans. Also, since loans amortize, they have a shorter duration and thus present a lower risk than their high-yield bond counterparts. It is therefore easier to produce notes with investment-grade ratings from CLOs than it is from CBOs.[19]

Figure 12-9 illustrates the basic structure of a CLO. A special purpose vehicle (SPV) or trust is set up, which issues, say, three types of securities: senior secured class A notes, senior secured class B notes, and subordinated notes or an "equity tranche." The proceeds are used to buy high-yield notes that constitute the collateral. In practice, the asset pool for a CLO may also contain a small percentage of high-yield bonds (usually less than 10 percent). The reverse is true for CBOs: they may include up to 10 percent of high-yield loans.

A typical CLO might consist of a pool of assets containing, say, 50 loans with an average rating of, say, B1 (by reference to Moody's rating system).

---

[19]Despite some rating downgrades (then upgrades), CLO credit quality was relatively robust during and after the financial crisis of 2007–2009. The market was largely dormant immediately after the crisis, but volumes of new CLOs began to grow quite quickly through 2011 and 2012. Post-crisis CLOs tend to protect their senior tranches with higher levels of subordination and with generally stricter terms. See Standard & Poor's Rating Services, "CLO Issuance Is Surging, Even Though the Credit Crisis Has Changed Some of the Rules," *CDO Spotlight*, August 2012.

FIGURE 12-9 Typical Collateralized Loan Obligation (CLO) Structure

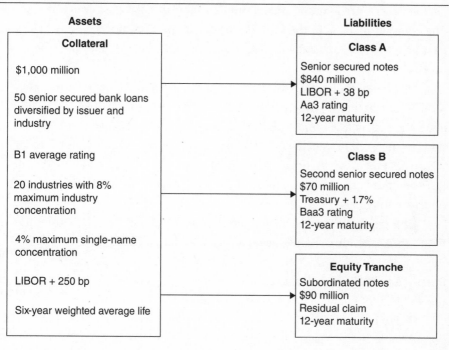

Assets	Liabilities
Collateral	**Class A**
$1,000 million	Senior secured notes $840 million LIBOR + 38 bp Aa3 rating 12-year maturity
50 senior secured bank loans diversified by issuer and industry	
B1 average rating	**Class B**
	Second senior secured notes $70 million Treasury + 1.7% Baa3 rating 12-year maturity
20 industries with 8% maximum industry concentration	
4% maximum single-name concentration	**Equity Tranche**
LIBOR + 250 bp	Subordinated notes $90 million Residual claim 12-year maturity
Six-year weighted average life	

These might have exposure to, say, 20 industries, with no industry concentration exceeding, say, 8 percent. The largest concentration by issuer might be kept to, say, under 4 percent of the portfolio's value. In our example, the weighted-average life of the loans is assumed to be six years, while the issued notes have a stated maturity of 12 years. The average yield on these floating-rate loans is assumed to be LIBOR + 250 bp.

The gap in maturities between the loans and the CLO structure requires active management of the loan portfolio. A qualified high-yield loan portfolio manager must be hired to actively manage the portfolio within constraints specified in the legal document. During the first six years, which is called the reinvestment or lockout period, the cash flows from loan amortization and the proceeds from maturing or defaulting loans are reinvested in new loans. (As the bank originating the loans typically remains responsible for servicing the loans, the investor in loan packages should be aware of the dangers of moral hazard and adverse selection for the performance of the underlying loans.) Thereafter, the three classes of notes are progressively redeemed as cash flows materialize.

The issued notes consist of three tranches: two senior secured classes with an investment-grade rating and an unrated subordinated class or equity tranche. The equity tranche is in the first-loss position and does not have any promised payment; the idea is that it will absorb default losses before they reach the senior investors.

In our example, the senior class A note is rated Aa3 and pays a coupon of LIBOR + 38 bp, which is more attractive than the sub-LIBOR coupon on an equivalent corporate bond with the same rating. The second senior secured class note, or mezzanine tranche, is rated Baa3 and pays a fixed coupon of Treasury + 1.7 percent for 12 years. Since the original loans pay LIBOR + 250 bp, the equity tranche offers an attractive return as long as most of the loans underlying the notes are fully paid.

The rating enhancement for the two senior classes is obtained by prioritizing the cash flows. Rating agencies such as Fitch, Moody's, and Standard & Poor's have developed their own methodologies for rating these senior class notes. (Appendix 12.1 discusses why agency ratings of CDOs in the run up to the 2007–2009 financial crisis were misleading.)

There is no such thing as a free lunch in the financial markets, and this has considerable risk management implications for banks issuing CLOs and CBOs. The credit enhancement of the senior secured class notes is obtained by simply shifting the default risk to the equity tranche. According to simulation results, the returns from investing in this equity tranche can vary widely: from –100 percent, with the investor losing everything, to more than 30 percent, depending on the actual rate of default on the loan portfolio. Sometimes the equity tranche is bought by investors with a strong appetite for risk, such as hedge funds, either outright or more often by means of a total return swap with a leverage multiple of 7 to 10. But most of the time, the bank issuing a CLO retains this risky first-loss equity tranche.

The main motivation for banks that issued CLOs in the period before the 2007–2009 crisis was thus to arbitrage regulatory capital: it was less costly in regulatory capital terms to hold the equity tranche than to hold the underlying loans. However, while the amount of regulatory capital the bank has to put aside might fall, the economic risk borne by the bank was not necessarily reduced at all. Paradoxically, credit derivatives, which offer a more effective form of economic hedge, received little regulatory capital relief. This form of regulatory arbitrage won't be allowed under the new Basel Accord.

The Special Case of Subprime CDOs

While CDO collateral pools can consist of various forms of debt, such as bonds, loans, or synthetic exposures through CDS (credit default swaps), subprime CDOs were based on structured credit products such as tranches of subprime residential mortgage-backed securities (RMBS) or of other CDOs.[20]

A typical subprime trust is composed of several thousand individual subprime mortgages, typically around 3,000 to 5,000 mortgages, for a total amount of approximately $1 billion.[21] The distribution of losses in the mortgage pool

---

[20] Issuance of these credit products increased dramatically after 2004, leading up to the financial crisis of 2007–2009. They represented 49 percent of the $560 billion worth of CDO issuance in 2006, up from 40 percent in 2004.

[21] "Subprime" mortgages are mortgages to less creditworthy borrowers. A rule of thumb is that a subprime mortgage is a home loan to someone with a credit FICO score of less than 620. Subprime borrowers have limited credit history or some other form of credit impairment. Some lenders classify a mortgage as subprime when the borrower has a credit score as high as 680 if the down payment is less than 5 percent. Alt-A borrowers fall between subprime and prime borrowers. They have credit scores sufficient to qualify for a conforming mortgage but do not have the necessary documentation to substantiate that their assets and income can support the requested loan amount.

Prior to 2005, subprime mortgage loans accounted for approximately 10 percent of outstanding mortgage loans. By 2006, subprime mortgages represented 13 percent of all outstanding mortgage loans, with origination of subprime mortgages totaling $420 billion (according to Standard & Poor's). This represented 20 percent of new residential mortgages, compared to the historical average of 8 percent. By July 2007, there was an estimated $1.4 trillion of subprime mortgages outstanding.

Subprime mortgages that required little or no down payment, as well as no documentation of the borrower's income, were known as "liar loans" because people could safely lie on their mortgage application, knowing there was little chance their statements would be checked. They accounted for 40 percent of the subprime mortgage issuance in 2006, up from 25 percent in 2001. (These loans were also called NINJA, with reference to applicants who had No Income, No Job, and no Assets.)

This phenomenon was aggravated by the incentive compensation system for mortgage brokers, which was based on the volume of loans originated rather than their performance, with few consequences for the broker if a loan defaulted within a short period. Originating brokers had little incentive to perform due diligence and monitor borrowers' creditworthiness, as most of the subprime loans originated by brokers were subsequently securitized. Fraud was also identified among some brokers—e.g., inflating the declarations of some applicants to make it possible for the applicant to obtain a loan. See M. Crouhy, "Risk Management Failures During the Financial Crisis," in D. Evanoff, P. Hartmann, and G. Kaufman, eds., *The First Credit Market Turmoil of the 21st Century: Implications for Public Policy*, World Scientific Publishing, 2009, pp. 241–266.

FIGURE 12-10 Securitization of Asset-Backed Securities Such as Mortgages vs. Securitization of Corporate Loans

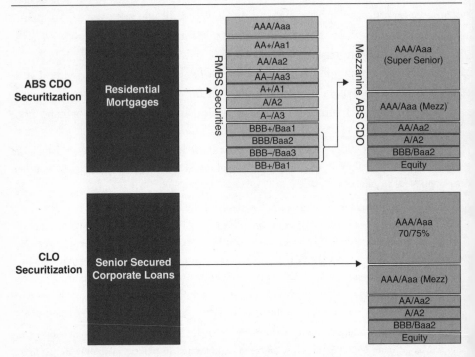

is tranched into different classes of residential mortgage-backed securities (RMBS) from the equity tranche, typically created through overcollateralization, to the most senior tranche, rated triple-A. A subprime CDO is therefore a CDO-squared, with a pool of assets composed of RMBS bonds rated double-B to double-A, with an average rating of triple-B.[22] Figure 12-10 illustrates the difference between the securitization of asset-backed securities such as mortgages, taking the form of a CDO-squared, and the more straightforward securitization of corporate loans in the form of a CLO.

---

[22] As discussed earlier, there was a huge demand for AAA-rated senior and super-senior tranches of CDOs from institutional investors because these tranches offered a higher yield than traditional securities with equivalent ratings—e.g., corporate and Treasury bonds. Hedge funds were the main buyers of the equity tranches. The high interest rate paid on these tranches meant they would pay a good return so long as defaults in the underlying asset pool occurred late in the life of the CDO. Mezzanine tranches, with an average rating of BBB, were harder to distribute, so banks securitized these tranches in new CDOs, referred to as "CDO-squareds."

In a typical subprime CDO, approximately 75 percent of the tranches benefit from a triple-A rating. On average, the mezzanine part of the capital structure accounts for 20 percent of the securities issued by the SPV and is rated investment grade; the remaining 5 percent is the equity tranche (first loss) and remains unrated.

Re-Remics

Re-Remics are a by-product of the crisis. Many AAA-rated CDO tranches were downgraded during the subprime crisis; however, some investors can only retain these securities if the securities maintain their AAA rating. In addition, maintaining a AAA rating can save a substantial amount of regulatory capital. For example, the Basel 2.5 risk weighting of a BB-rated tranche is 350 percent under the standardized approach, while it is only 40 percent for a AAA-rated resecuritization.[23]

Re-Remics consist of resecuritizing senior mortgage-backed securities (MBS) tranches that have been downgraded from their initial AAA rating. Only two tranches are issued: a senior AAA tranche for approximately 70 percent of the nominal and an unrated mezzanine tranche for around 30 percent of the nominal.

Given the new regulatory capital regime, the total risk weight would decline from 350 percent (assuming the collateral is rated BB) to

$$70\% \times 40 + 30\% \times 650 = 223 \text{ percent}$$

where 70 percent and 30 percent are the size of the AAA and mezzanine tranches, respectively, and 40 and 650 are the risk weights for the resecuritization exposures rated AAA and unrated, respectively.

Synthetic CDOs

In a traditional CDO, also called a "cash-CDO," the credit assets are fully cash funded using the proceeds of the debt and equity issued by the SPV; the repayment of obligations is tied directly to the cash flows arising from the assets. Figure 12-9 offers an example of this kind of structure—in this case the example

---

[23]Basel Committee on Banking Supervision, *Enhancements to the Basel II Framework*, Bank for International Settlements, July 2009.

FIGURE 12-11 Capital Structure of a Synthetic CDO

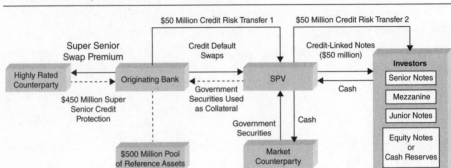

of a CLO, one of the main types of CDO. A synthetic CDO, by contrast, transfers risk without affecting the legal ownership of the credit assets. This is accomplished through a series of CDSs.

The sponsoring institution transfers the credit risk of the portfolio of credit assets to the SPV by means of the CDSs, while the assets themselves remain on the balance sheet of the sponsor. In the example in Figure 12-11, the right-hand side is equivalent to the cash CDO structure presented in Figure 12-9, except that it applies to only 10 percent of the pool of reference assets. The left-hand side shows the credit protection in the form of a "super senior swap" provided by a highly rated institution (a role that used to be performed by monoline insurance companies before the subprime crisis).

The SPV typically provides credit protection for 10 percent or less of the losses on the reference portfolio. The SPV, in turn, issues notes in the capital markets to cash collateralize the portfolio default swap with the originating entity. The notes issued can include a nonrated equity piece, mezzanine debt, and senior debt, creating cash liabilities. Most of the default risk is borne by the investors in these notes, with the same risk hierarchy as for cash CDOs—i.e., the equity tranche holders retain the risk of the first set of losses, and the mezzanine tranche holders are exposed to credit losses once the equity tranche has been wiped out. The remainder of the risk, 90 percent, is usually distributed to a highly rated counterparty via a senior swap.

Before the 2007–2009 financial crisis, reinsurers and insurance monoline companies, which typically had AAA credit ratings, exhibited a strong appetite for this type of senior risk, often referred to as super-senior AAAs. The initial proceeds of the equity and notes are invested in highly rated liquid assets.

FIGURE 12-12 Single-Tranche CDO

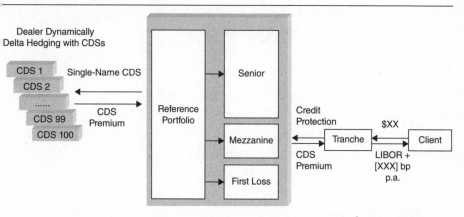

If an obligor in the reference pool defaults, the trust liquidates investments in the trust and makes payments to the originating entity to cover the default losses. This payment is offset by a successive reduction in the equity tranche and then the mezzanine tranche; finally, the super-senior tranches are called on to make up the losses.

Single-Tranche CDOs

The terms of a single-tranche CDO are similar to those of a tranche of a traditional CDO. However, in a traditional CDO, the entire portfolio may be ramped up, and the entire capital structure may be distributed to multiple investors. In a single-tranche CDO, only a particular tranche, tailored to the client's needs,[24] is issued, and there is no need to build the actual portfolio, as the bank will hedge its exposure by buying or selling the underlying reference assets according to hedge ratios produced by its proprietary pricing model.

In the structure described in Figure 12-12, for example, the client has gained credit protection for a mezzanine or middle-ranking tranche of credit risk in its reference portfolio but continues to assume both the first-loss (equity) risk tranche and the most senior risk tranche. The biggest advantage of this kind of instrument is that it allows the client to tailor most of the terms of the transaction.

---

[24]The client can be a buyer or a seller of credit protection. The bank is on the other side of the transaction.

The biggest disadvantage tends to be the limited liquidity of tailored deals. Dealers who create single-tranche CDOs have to dynamically hedge the tranche they have purchased or sold as the quality and correlation of the portfolio change.

Credit Derivatives on Credit Indices

Credit trading based on indices ("index trades") had become popular before the crisis and is still active, although there is less activity for index tranches. The indices are based on a large number of underlying credits, and portfolio managers can therefore use index trades to hedge the credit risk exposure of a diversified portfolio. Index trades are also popular with holders of CDO tranches and CLNs who need to hedge their credit risk exposure.

There are several families of credit default swap indices that cover loans as well as corporate, municipal, and sovereign debt across Europe, Asia, North America, and emerging markets. Markit, a financial information services company, owns and manages these credit indices, which are the only credit indices supported by all major dealer banks and buy-side investment firms (Figure 12-13).

The two major families of credit indices are CDX for North America and emerging markets and iTraxx for Europe and Asia. CDX indices are a family of indices covering multiple sectors. The main indices are CDX North American Investment Grade (CDX.NA.IG), with 125 equally weighted North American names; CDX North America Investment Grade High Volatility (30 names from CDX.NA.IG); and CDX North America High Yield (100 names). Similarly, for Europe there is an iTraxx Investment Grade index, which comprises 125 equally weighted European names. The iTraxx Crossover index comprises the 40 most liquid sub-investment-grade European names.

These indices trade 3-, 5-, 7- and 10-year maturities, and a new series is launched every six months on the basis of liquidity.

Like CDOs, iTraxx and CDX are tranched, with each tranche absorbing losses in a predesignated order of priority. The tranching is influenced by the nature of the respective geographic markets. For example, CDX.NA.IG tranches have been broken down according to the following loss attachment points: 0–3 percent (equity tranche), 3–7 percent, 7–10 percent, 10–15 percent, 15–30 percent, and 30–100 percent (the most senior tranche), as illustrated in Figure 12-14. For iTraxx, the corresponding tranches are 0–3 percent, 3–6 percent, 6–9 percent, 9–12 percent, 12–22 percent, and 22–100 percent. The tranching of the European and U.S indices is adjusted so that tranches of the same seniority

FIGURE 12-13 Markit Credit Indices and Their Key Features

Structured Finance		US	Markit ABX, CMBX, PrimeX, IOS, PO, MBX, TRX	
Synthetic Credit	Loans	US	Markit LCDX	
		Europe	MarkitiTraxx LevX	
	Sovereigns	Global	Markit CDX EM	Emerging Markets
				EM Diversified
			MarkitiTraxx SovX	Western Europe
				CEEMEA
				Asia Pacific
				Latin America
				G7
				Global Liquid Investment Grade
				BRIC
	Corporate Bonds	North America	Markit CDX NA	Investment Grade (IG, HVol)
				Crossover
				High Yield (HY, HY.B, HY.BB)
				Sectors
		Europe	MarkitiTraxx Europe	Europe (Investment Grade)
				HiVol
				Non-Financials
				Financials (Senior, Sub)
				Crossover
		Asia	MarkitiTraxx Asia	Japan
				Asia ex-Japan (IG, HY)
				Australia
	Municipal Bonds	US	Markit MCDX	

Key features of the indices

	Index	# Entities (1)	Roll Dates	Maturity in years (2)	Credit Events
CDX	IG	125	3/20–9/20	1,2,3,5,7,10	Bankruptcy, Failure to Pay
	HVOL	30	3/20–9/20	1,2,3,5,7,10	
	HY	100	3/27–9/27	3,5,7,10	
	XO	35	3/20–9/20	3,5,7,10	
	EM	15 (variable)	3/20–9/20	5	Bankruptcy, Failure to Pay,
	EM Diversified	40	3/20–9/20	5	Restructuring,
iTraxx Europe	Europe	125	3/20–9/20	3,5,7,10	Bankruptcy, Failure to Pay,
	– Non financials	100	3/20–9/20	5,10	Restructuring
	– Senior financials	25	3/20–9/20	5,10	
	– Sub financials	25	3/20–9/20	5,10	
	– High volatility	30	3/20–9/20	3,5,7,10	
	Crossover	40	3/20–9/20	3,5,7,10	
iTraxx Asia	Japan	50	3/20–9/20	5	Bankruptcy, Failure to Pay,
	Asia ex-Japan IG	50	3/20–9/20	5	Restructuring
	Asia ex-Japan HY	20	3/20–9/20	5	
	Australia	25	3/20–9/20	5	
iTraxx SovX	Western Europe	15	3/20–9/20	5,10	Failure to Pay, Restructuring,
	CEEMEA	15	3/20–9/20	5,10	Repudiation/Moratorium
	Asia Pacific	10	3/20–9/20	5,10	
	Latin America*	8	3/20–9/20	5,10	
	G7*	Up to 7	3/20–9/20	5,10	
	Global Liquid IG*	11 to 27	3/20–9/20	5,10	
	BRIC*	Up to 4	3/20–9/20	5,10	
MCDX	MCDX	50 credits	4/3–10/3	3,5,10	Failure to Pay, Restructuring
LCDX	LCDX	100	4/3–10/3	5	Bankruptcy, Failure to Pay
iTraxx LevX	LevX Senior	40	3/20–9/20	5	Bankruptcy, Failure to Pay, Restructuring

1. All indices are equally weighted, except for CDX.EM. and Traxx SovXCEEMEA.
2. Exact maturity is June 20th for the indices rolling on March 20th, March 27th and April 3rd and December 20th for indices rolling on September 20th, September 27th and October 3rd to coincide with IMM roll dates.
3. *Theoretical Indices.

Source: Markit.

FIGURE 12-14 Tranched U.S. Index of Investment-Grade Names: CDX.NA.IG

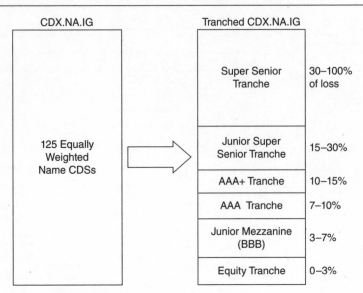

in both indices receive the same rating. The tranches of the U.S. index are thicker because the names that compose the U.S. index are on average slightly more risky than the names in the European index.

There is currently a limited active broker market in tranches of both the iTraxx and the CDX.NA.IG, with 3- and 5-year tranches quoted on both indices. There is also activity in the 3- and 5-year tranches of the HY CDX.

The quotation of each tranche is made of two components: the "upfront" payment and a fixed "coupon" paid on a quarterly basis. These quotes are also converted in an equivalent "spread." At the end of August 2013, for example, the junior mezzanine tranche for the iTraxx index (tenor 5 years, Series 19, issued in March 2013) was quoted at an equivalent spread of 521 bp. The annualized cost for an investor who bought the junior mezzanine tranche of a $1 billion iTraxx portfolio at 521 bp would be 521 bp annually on $30 million (3 percent of $1 billion); in return, the investor would receive from the seller for any and all losses between $30 and $60 million of the $1 billion underlying iTraxx portfolio (representing the 3–6 percent tranche).

Options have been traded on iTraxx and CDX to meet the demand from hedge funds and proprietary trading desks looking to trade credit volatility and take views on the direction of credit using options.

Securitization for Funding Purposes Only

For some years after the 2007–2009 financial crisis—triggered by problems in the subprime lending markets—investors remained wary about credit-linked investments. In the same period, funding became a major issue for banks because confidence in the financial system, and bank soundness, had also been severely damaged.

As securitization with credit risk transfer ground to a halt, banks began to use different kinds of funding vehicles in which all, or virtually all, of the credit risk remains with the bank. Below are two examples of such funding structures.

Covered Bonds

Covered bonds are debt obligations secured by a specific reference portfolio of assets. However, covered bonds are not true securitization instruments, as issuers are fully liable for all interest and principal payments; thus, investors have "double" protection against default, as they have recourse to both the issuer and the underlying loans. The "cover pool" of loans is legally ring-fenced on the issuer's balance sheet. Covered bonds are essentially a funding instrument, as no risk is transferred from the issuer to the investor.

In Europe, financial institutions have used covered bonds extensively to finance their mortgage lending activity—e.g., the "German Pfandbriefe," examined below, and the French "Obligations Foncières." According to the IMF, the covered mortgage bond market in Europe in 2009 constituted a $3 trillion market—i.e., 40 percent of European GDP.

While these instruments are not new, the 2007–2009 financial crisis reignited interest in this alternative source of capital market funding. In addition, the European Central Bank (ECB) launched a €60 billion covered bond purchase program in May 2009 (effective from July 2009 to July 2010), which had a strong positive impact on the volume of issuance and also led to narrower spreads.

Pfandbriefe[25]

A Pfandbrief bank is a German bank that issues covered bonds under the German Pfandbrief Act. These bonds, or Pfandbriefe, are AAA– or AA-rated bonds

---

[25]The origins of Pfandbrief banks lie in eighteenth-century Prussia; they now constitute the largest covered-bond market in the world.

backed by a cover pool that includes long-term assets such as residential and commercial mortgages, ship loans, aircraft loans, and public sector loans.

Loans are reported in the Pfandbrief bank's balance sheet as assets in specific cover pools. Cover assets remain on the balance sheet and are supervised by an independent administrator. Pfandbriefe are collateralized by the cover assets and are subject to strict quality requirements—e.g., regional restrictions, senior loan tranches, and low loan-to-value ratios. The Pfandbrief Act ensures that the cover pools are available only to the relevant Pfandbrief creditor in the event of the bank's insolvency.

Several European banks have elected to create a German Pfandbrief subsidiary rather than a domestic covered bond program because the German Pfandbrief market is highly liquid and benefits from lower funding spreads than other covered bond markets in Europe.

Funding CLOs

Funding CLOs are balance sheet cash flow CLO transactions with only two tranches. The senior tranche, or funding tranche, is issued to investors. This tranche is rated by a rating agency and is structured so that it is given a AAA rating. The junior tranche, or subordinated note, is unrated, bears the first loss, and is kept by the bank.

Conclusion

Credit derivatives and securitization are key tools for the transfer and management of credit risk and for the provision of bank funding. However, for some years following the financial crisis, some of the key securitization markets were effectively closed for new issuance though others (e.g., auto loans) remained active. The process of agreeing how to reform and revitalize the markets has been slow, but there are signs that credit transfer markets, such as the CLO market, are once again reviving.

This may be timely. Basel III and the Dodd-Frank Act are likely to raise the cost of capital for banks. Banks may, in the longer term, have no alternative other than to adopt the originate-to-distribute business model and use credit derivatives and other risk transfer techniques to redistribute and repackage credit risk outside the banking system (notably to the insurance sector, investment funds, and hedge funds).

Up until recently, one of the main reasons for using the new credit instruments was regulatory arbitrage; it was this that led to the setting up of conduits and SIVs. Basel III should align regulatory capital requirements more closely to economic risk and provide more incentives to use credit instruments to manage the "real" underlying credit quality of a bank's portfolio.

Nevertheless, opportunities for regulatory arbitrage will remain. In the case of retail products such as mortgages, the very different regulatory capital treatment for Basel III compliant banks, compared to the treatment of banks that remain compliant with the current Basel I rules, will itself give rise to an arbitrage opportunity.

There is another kind of downside. The final paragraph of this chapter in the 2006 edition of this book, written well before the 2007–2009 financial crisis erupted, warned:

> *Risks assumed by means of credit derivatives are largely unfunded and undisclosed, which could allow players to become leveraged in a way that is difficult for outsiders (or even senior management) to spot. So far, we've yet to see a major financial disaster caused by the complexities of credit derivatives and the new opportunities they bring for both transferring and assuming credit risk. But such a disaster will surely come, particularly if the boards and senior managers of banks do not invest the time to understand exactly how these new markets and instruments work—and how each major transaction affects their institution's risk profile.*[26]

Despite attempts by regulators and the market to improve disclosure, this surely remains significantly true. Credit risk transfer is an enormously powerful tool for managing risk and for distributing risk to those most able to assume it. However, used without due care and attention, it can also devastate institutions and whole economies.

---

[26]See pages 323–324 of the 2006 edition.

Appendix 12.1

WHY THE RATING OF CDOs BY RATING AGENCIES WAS MISLEADING[1]

Investors in complex credit products were particularly reliant on rating agencies because they often had little information at their disposal to assess the underlying credit quality of the assets held in their portfolios.

In particular, investors tended to assume that the ratings for structured products were stable: no one expected triple-A assets to be downgraded to junk status within a few weeks or even a few days.[2] (However, the higher yields on these instruments, compared to the bonds of equivalently rated corporations, suggests that the market understood to some degree that the investments were not equivalent in terms of credit and/or liquidity risk.)

The sheer volume of downgrades of structured credit products focused attention on the nature of their ratings and how they might differ from the longer

---

[1] This appendix relies in part on an earlier work published by one of the authors. See M. Crouhy, "Risk Management Failures During the Financial Crisis," in D. Evanoff, P. Hartmann, and G. Kaufman, eds., *The First Credit Market Turmoil of the 21st Century: Implications for Public Policy*, World Scientific Publishing, 2009, pp. 241–266.

[2] Moody's first took rating action on 2006 vintage subprime loans in November 2006. In 2007, Moody's downgraded 31 percent of all tranches for CDOs of ABS that it had rated, including 14 percent of those initially rated AAA.

established ratings—e.g., those for corporate debt. Perhaps the most fundamental difference is that corporate bond ratings are largely based on firm-specific risk, whereas CDO tranches represent claims on cash flows from a portfolio of correlated assets. Thus, rating CDO tranches relies heavily on quantitative models, whereas corporate debt ratings rely essentially on the judgment of an analyst.

While the rating of a CDO tranche should exhibit the same expected loss as a corporate bond of the same rating, the volatility of loss—i.e., the unexpected loss—is quite different. It strongly depends on the correlation structure of the underlying assets in the pool of the CDO. This in itself warrants the use of different rating scales for corporate bonds and structured credit products.

For structured credit products, such as ABS collateralized debt obligations, it is necessary to model the cash flows and the loss distribution generated by the asset portfolio over the life of the CDO. This implies that it is necessary to model *prepayments* and *default dependence* (correlation) among the assets in the CDO and to estimate the parameters describing this dependence over time. In turn, this means modeling the evolution of the different factors that affect the default process and how these factors evolve together. It is critical to assess the sensitivity of tranche ratings to a significant deterioration in credit conditions that might drive default clustering. This relationship depends on the magnitude of the shocks and tends to be nonlinear.

If default occurs, it is necessary to estimate the resulting loss. Recovery rates depend on the state of the economy, the condition of the obligor, and the value of its assets. Loss rates and the frequency of default are dependent on each other: if the economy goes into recession, both the frequency of default and the loss rates increase. It is a major challenge to model this joint dependence.

Subprime lending on any scale is a relatively new industry, and the limited set of historical data available increased the model risk inherent in the rating process. In particular, historical data on the performance of U.S. subprime loans were largely drawn from a benign economic period with constantly rising house prices, making it difficult to estimate the correlation in defaults that would occur during a broad market downturn.

Many industry players misunderstood the nature of the risk involved in holding a AAA-rated super-senior tranche of a subprime CDO. Subprime CDOs are really CDO-squared because the underlying pool of assets of the CDO is not made up of individual mortgages. Instead, it is composed of subprime RMBS, or mortgage bonds, that are themselves tranches of individual subprime mortgages.

After the crisis, many commentators questioned whether the CRAs' poor ratings performance in structured credit products might be related to conflicts of interest. The CRAs were paid to rate the instruments by the issuer (not the investor), and these fees constituted a fast growing income stream for CRAs in the run-up to the crisis.

Another worry was the quality of the due diligence concerning the nature of the collateral pools underlying rated securities. Due diligence about the quality of the underlying data and the quality of the originators, issuers, or servicers could have helped to identify fraud in the loan files.

In addition, CRAs did not take into account the substantial weakening of underwriting standards for products associated with certain originators.

Commentators also questioned the degree of transparency about the assumptions, criteria, and methodologies used in rating structured credit products.

Since the crisis, regulators have tried to address the role that ratings played in the crisis in a variety of ways. For example, the Dodd-Frank Act explicitly calls for replacing the language of "investment-grade" and "non-investment-grade" and proposes that federal agencies undertake a review of their reliance on credit ratings and develop different standards of creditworthiness.[3] The aim is to encourage investors to perform their own due diligence and assess the risk of their investments, reducing the systemic risk that arises when too many investors rely too heavily on external risk assessment.

This might require a review of the very foundations of the Standardized Approach in Basel II (see Chapter 3), which relies explicitly on the ratings awarded by rating agencies and other nationally recognized statistical rating organizations (NRSRO).

13

COUNTERPARTY CREDIT RISK: CVA, DVA, AND FVA

Counterparty credit risk (CCR) is the risk that a counterparty to a financial contract, such as a derivative, will default prior to the expiration of the contract and fail to make the required payments.

Before about 2006, financial institutions managed CCR mainly by measuring their potential future exposures—i.e., the likely maximum credit losses they might suffer—and then imposing limits on exposures to given counterparties and classes of counterparties. Firms also applied a range of collateralization and netting procedures to try to minimize their counterparty exposures.

Over time, some larger institutions began to calculate the expected losses associated with a counterparty exposure—effectively, the value or price associated with CCR. This became a more important and widely adopted procedure from 2006 when new "fair value" accounting regulations obliged firms to adjust the value of derivative positions to reflect counterparty risk, a process termed a credit value adjustment, or CVA. Soon after this, the 2007–2009 financial crisis drove home the importance of counterparty credit risk through the failure and near-failure of major firms such as Lehman Brothers.[1]

In the years following the crisis, CCR emerged as a key focus for regulators, who were worried that a cascade of counterparty failures could lead to major disruptions in financial markets. They set in train a series of reforms to try to

---

[1] Lehman Brothers had entered into a notional $800 billion of OTC derivatives at the time it was declared bankrupt in September 2008. This represented a complex web of transactions, collateral positions, and SPVs (special purpose vehicles) that all needed to be unwound.

reduce CCR and its systemic effects (Box 13-1). At the level of the firm, too, the costs and risks associated with counterparty exposures became one of the hottest topics in the financial industry.

In this chapter we will define CCR and look briefly at the building block strategies for risk-managing CCR before examining CVA and related measures, as well as how banks calculate minimum capital requirements for counterparty credit risk. There are many contentious debates surrounding the correct treatment

---

BOX 13-1 CCR MITIGATION IN THE WORLD FINANCIAL SYSTEM

Basel III and the Dodd-Frank Act in the United States propose several measures to reduce CCR and the systemic risk it poses. Here are the key points:

- OTC markets that grow sufficiently large should trade through a centralized clearinghouse that also acts as counterparty to all trades, ensuring minimal, near-zero counterparty risk.
- Relatively standardized products such as credit default swaps (CDS) and credit indexes should ideally move to exchange-based trading where well-capitalized market makers provide liquidity, the exchange clearinghouse acts as counterparty to all trades, and there is significant transparency in terms of aggregate and trade-level price and volume information.
- OTC markets that are not large enough to support a centralized clearinghouse, but where deals are deemed to have important counterparty risk, should be subject to a centralized registry of transaction data.
- Collateral and margining should be marked-to-market daily and carefully designed to ensure that centralized counterparties in credit derivatives face minimal counterparty risk.
- Regardless of market structure (centralized registry, centralized clearinghouse, or exchange), regulators should have expedient access to information on bilateral positions in significant OTC markets.

of CVA and its capital treatment, but one thing is for sure: CCR is now recognized as one of the foremost risks in the financial industry and a major driver of profit and loss at firms.[2]

Defining Counterparty Credit Risk

CCR is typically defined as arising from two broad classes of financial products:

- Over the counter (OTC) derivatives such as interest rate swaps, FX forwards and credit default swaps[3]
- Securities financing transactions, such as repos and reverse repos as well as securities lending and borrowing

The former category is by far the most significant due to the size of the market[4] and the diversity and complexity of OTC instruments.

Two features of CCR differentiate it from traditional credit risks such as lending risk:

- The primary distinguishing feature is the uncertainty of the size of the exposure at any future date. In the case of loans, the exposure at any future date is the outstanding balance, which is known with a high degree of certainty.[5] By contrast, the exposure of a derivative at any future date is the mark-to-market (MtM) value, which depends on the future evolution

---

[2] Two books provide extensive treatments of counterparty credit risk: J. Gregory, *Counterparty Credit Risk: The New Challenge for Global Financial Markets*, Wiley, 2010; and a more technical approach by D. Brigo, M. Morini, and A. Pallavicini, *Counterparty Credit Risk, Collateral and Funding*, Wiley, 2013.

[3] By contrast, exchange-traded derivatives bear practically no CCR as they are cleared through a central clearinghouse (more on this later).

[4] As of year-end 2012, the total notional amount of OTC derivatives was $632 trillion globally. Bank for International Settlements, *Statistical Release: OTC Derivatives Statistics at end-December 2012*, May 2013.

[5] This is to set aside the issue of prepayments and lines of credit, where there is often uncertainty about the amount that might be drawn down at the time of any default.

of market factors such as the term structure of interest rates and volatility. Indeed, the value of a derivative at a potential default date—i.e., the net value of all future cash flows—can be positive or negative and generally differs substantially from the nominal amount of the transaction. For example, when a swap is initiated, the swap rate is set such that the MtM value of the swap is zero and then evolves over time, becoming either positive or negative from the perspective of each counterparty.

- Since the value of a derivative position can be positive or negative, CCR is bilateral.[6] For example, in a futures or a swap transaction, each party is exposed to the other party in the deal. The bilateral nature of counterparty credit risk was an important feature of the financial crisis of 2007–2009. If one party to the contract owes money to the other, this party has to honor the contract regardless of the default status of the other counterparty. However, if the contract value is positive for the surviving party, it will receive nothing (or only a percentage of the amount due, known as the recovery rate). In addition, it will need to pay the contract MtM value to enter into a similar contract with another creditworthy counterparty if it wishes to continue with the transaction. Therefore, the credit exposure of one counterparty to the other is potentially the maximum of the contract's risk-free value and zero.[7] Since this exposure is similar to the payoff of an option, a key aspect in assessing future exposure will be volatility of the MtM value of the position (see also Chapter 5).[8]

Building Blocks for Managing CCR

CCR exposure can be significantly reduced at the level of the firm by means of netting, collateralization, and central clearing, together with other features such as portfolio compression and termination events.

---

[6]Although the value of an option is always positive, the MtM value of an option position is positive for the buyer and negative for the seller of an option.

[7]This is the payoff of a short position on a call option with the underlying exposure following a very complex stochastic process.

[8]Note that options are complex to price relative to their underlying instruments. Hence, the quantification of credit exposure, even for a simple instrument such as a "vanilla" interest rate swap, may be quite complex.

The importance of these mechanisms, and the difficulty of assessing counterparty risk through notional contract amounts, is apparent in the following statistics. According to the BIS, the total notional outstanding for OTC derivatives at year-end 2012 was $632.6 trillion. If we set aside foreign exchange contracts and adjust for double counting of cleared transactions in a clearinghouse, this number falls to $392 trillion.[9] Portfolio compression—i.e., eliminating matched trades or trades that do not contribute risk to a dealer's portfolio—further reduced this notional amount outstanding by $48.7 trillion in 2012.[10]

However, notional amounts are not representative of the overall risk exposure in the OTC derivatives markets because the notional amount does not capture the economic value of the contracts. According to BIS, the year-end 2012 "gross

---

[9]Following ISDA, which makes two important adjustments to the BIS statistics. First, it excludes FX contracts, which typically have short maturities; other OTC derivative products have much longer maturities that can reach several years. Second, ISDA adjusts the notional outstanding of cleared transactions for double counting. For example, if two parties execute a $50 million swap on a bilateral basis, only one $50 million trade exists. However, when the transaction is booked through a clearinghouse, it will be booked as two $50 million contracts—i.e., $100 million in total. Bank for International Settlements, *Statistical Release: OTC Derivatives Statistics at end-December 2012*, May 2013; and ISDA, *OTC Derivatives Market Analysis Year-End 2012*, June 2013.

[10]Portfolio compression, also known as multilateral early termination, of OTC derivative portfolios is an exercise in which participants are able to tear up their existing trades at their own mid mark-to-market valuations, avoiding the difficult negotiation process of bilateral termination. Multilateral terminations leverage the expanded number of participants and result in increased numbers of terminated trades.

Since its introduction in 2003 by TriOptima, first for interest rate swaps (IRS), then for credit default swaps (CDS), and finally for commodity trades in energy and precious metals, portfolio compression has contributed significantly to reducing the number of transactions and the notional outstanding in the OTC derivatives markets. In 2008 alone, compression in the CDS market eliminated 50 percent of the notional outstanding globally after regulators focused on inefficiencies in the CDS market. Since then, the expansion of portfolio compression to cleared IRS trades in LCH.Clearnet's SwapClear service has dramatically reduced the IRS swaps outstanding.

Through June of 2013, $353 trillion has been eliminated from swap portfolios globally since compression was first introduced 10 years ago. ISDA recently analyzed the contribution that portfolio compression has made to controlling the growth of notional outstanding, one of the goals of global regulators. In its "OTC Derivatives Market Analysis Year End 2012", ISDA noted that over the last five years, "… portfolio compression has significantly reduced notional amounts outstanding by 25% or more."

market value,"[11] before netting, was only $24.7 trillion—i.e., 3.9 percent of the notional amounts. After netting, the "gross credit exposure" was further reduced to $3.6 trillion, or 0.6 percent of the notional amounts. ISDA estimates that after adjustment for collateral, the gross credit exposure is further reduced to $1.1 trillion, or only 0.2 percent of our original notional amounts.

A *netting agreement* is a legally binding contract between two counterparties that, in the event of default, allows the aggregation of transactions between these counterparties. The derivatives with positive values at the time of default offset the ones with negative value, and only the net value needs to be paid. Thus, the total credit exposure created by all transactions in a netting set—i.e., those under the jurisdiction of the netting agreement—is reduced to the maximum of the net portfolio value and zero.

CCR can be further reduced by *collateral agreements*. A collateral agreement limits the potential exposure of one counterparty to the other by requiring collateral if the unsecured exposure exceeds a prespecified threshold. Under a bilateral collateral agreement, both counterparties periodically, mostly daily, mark their positions to market and check their net portfolio value against the other counterparty's threshold. If the net portfolio value exceeds the threshold, the other counterparty must post collateral sufficient to cover this excess. Thus, collateral agreements attempt to limit the exposure to the unsecured portion below the threshold. The threshold value depends mainly on the credit quality of the counterparty. Collateralization can reduce counterparty risk significantly, but it generates other risks such as operational risk, liquidity risk, and legal risk.

Termination features offer protection to a surviving institution at the expense of the defaulted counterparty and its creditors. First, *close-out* permits the immediate termination of all contracts between an institution and a defaulted counterparty with netting MtM values. Close-out netting allows the surviving counterparty to immediately realize gains on transactions against losses on other transactions and effectively jump the bankruptcy queue for all but its net exposure. Second, a *walkaway* feature is a clause that allows the surviving counterparty to cancel transactions in the event that its counterparty defaults. In this

---

[11]That is, the aggregate positive market values of all outstanding contracts to in-the-money counterparties (or the absolute value of the aggregate negative market values of the contracts to out-of-the-money counterparties).

case, the asymmetry in potential losses disappears, and exposure with a walk-away feature is simply the MtM whether it is positive or negative.

CCR mitigation is a double-edged sword because it reduces the overall risks but it can also allow financial markets to develop too quickly and reach a dangerous size. Ironically, if the efficacy of risk mitigation is overstated, the overall risk in the market may actually increase due to risk mitigation. Risk mitigation is not perfect and leaves financial institutions with residual risks often referred to as basis risks.

Collateral agreements, for example, are far from being a perfect mitigant. Even with daily margin calls—i.e., the ability to call for more collateral to cover an increase in value in the position—there might be a significant delay, known as the margin period of risk (MPR), between a margin call that the counterparty does not respond to and the closing out of the portfolio. Margin calls can also be disputed, and it may take several days for the bank to realize that the counterparty is defaulting rather than disputing the call. Also, there is a grace period after the bank issues a notice of default. During this grace period, the counterparty may still post collateral. Finally, it may take time to close out and replace complex trades in the event of a default. Typically, the assumed value of the MRP for a portfolio of liquid trades with daily margin calls might be around two weeks.

In order to understand how much risk mitigation to put in place, and to understand the size of any residual risks, banks have to measure the credit exposure to any given counterparty. In the next section, we take a closer look at the various metrics that banks employ to measure credit exposure and explain how these are related to both the risk management and valuation of counterparty credit exposures.

Credit Exposure

Formal Definition of Credit Exposure

Credit exposure (CE) defines the loss conditional on a counterparty's defaulting. As we mentioned earlier, a key feature of CCR arises from the asymmetry of potential losses with respect to MtM.

If a counterparty defaults, then it will be unable to make future payments. The amount of the MtM value at the time of default, less any recovery value, represents the loss due to default to the surviving counterparty. In the case of a negative MtM, the surviving institution is still legally obliged to settle the MtM value with the defaulting counterparty—it cannot walk away from the transaction except in specially agreed cases.[12] In other words, CE is the *replacement cost*, or rehedging cost, of the defaulted transactions if they were to be replaced by equivalent positions with another counterparty, under the assumption of no transaction costs. We can then define CE as:

$$CE = Max(MtM, 0) \tag{13-1}$$

Since exposure is similar to the payoff of an option, a key aspect will be the volatility of the MtM. CE is driven by two opposing factors:

- *Future uncertainty.* Over time there will be greater uncertainty and, therefore, greater variability in the market factors, resulting in greater exposure to volatility as time progresses.
- *Roll of cash flows.* For a multitude of transactions, cash flows are paid over time so that the outstanding "notional" decreases, dropping to zero at maturity.

Metrics for Credit Exposure

Several definitions of CE fulfill different purposes since CCR is important from both a risk management and a pricing (i.e., CVA) perspective. We can define for a given time horizon:

- *Expected MtM* is the forward, or expected, value of a transaction (or a portfolio of transactions) at some time horizon in the future. The expected MtM value of a transaction can vary significantly from the current MtM, even over a short horizon, due to the specifics of the underlying cash flows.
- *Expected exposure (EE)* is the average of the positive MtM values—i.e., the situations in which there will be a loss in the case of default. By definition, the EE is greater than the expected MtM since it is the sum of only the positive MtM values.
- *Potential future exposure (PFE)* is somewhat equivalent to the traditional value-at-risk (VaR) measure as it is the worst-case exposure at a given

---

[12]See J. Gregory, *Counterparty Credit Risk: The New Challenge for Global Financial Markets*, Wiley, 2010, Section 2.3.5.

FIGURE 13-1 Illustration of EE and PFE at a Given Time Horizon

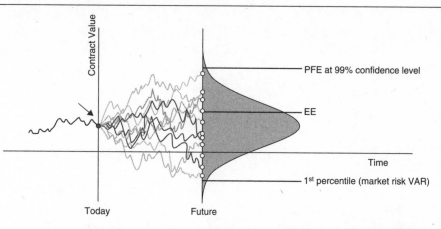

horizon and a given confidence level. For example, a PFE at a confidence level of 99 percent will define an exposure at a given time horizon that would be exceeded with a probability of 1 percent (100% – 99%). Traditional "market VaR" at the 99 percent confidence level is the lowest percentile of the distribution of MtM values. Both EE and PFE are shown in Figure 13-1 for a given time horizon and in Figure 13-2 over the life of a transaction (e.g., an interest rate swap).

FIGURE 13-2 Illustration of EE and PFE over the Life of a Transaction

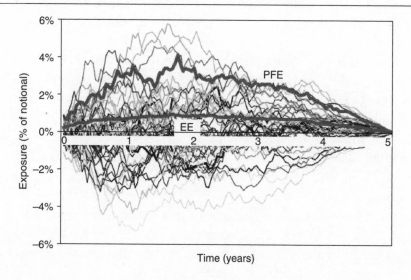

FIGURE 13-3 Illustration of EPE

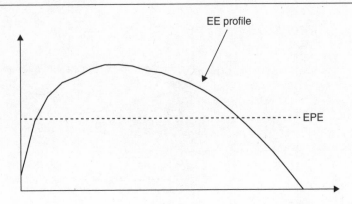

- *Expected positive exposure (EPE)* is defined as the average EE through time over the life of a transaction. Figure 13-3 illustrates EPE.

Effective EPE was introduced by the Basel Committee (BCBS 2005) because EE and EPE may underestimate exposure for short-dated transactions. Effective EE is simply a nondecreasing EE, and effective EPE is the average of the effective EE.

Credit Exposure Limits

In the introduction to this chapter we mentioned that, traditionally, financial institutions have managed CCR by setting credit exposure limits at the counterparty level.

The idea is to estimate the potential future exposure (PFE)—as defined above—to a counterparty over time and to ensure that this does not exceed the credit limit (after netting and other mitigants). Before a new transaction is executed, the total credit exposure to the counterparty is recalculated with the new transaction included. If the new transaction brings total exposure to that counterparty above the limit, the transaction is not executed. The limit value usually depends on the credit quality of the counterparty and the risk appetite of the financial institution.

Credit limits act to control exposure in a rather binary way without reference to the factors that characterize the dynamic of future exposure—i.e., changes in the default probability of a counterparty, the expected recovery rate on a transaction, the downgrade probability of a counterparty, and the correlation between counterparties.

Since the limits are set for each counterparty individually, the credit limits do not take into account the dependence between the credit quality of the counterparties. To account for this dependence, the financial institution would need to calculate the distribution of losses for its entire portfolio, taking into account default correlations. It would then need to quantify the portfolio risk from this distribution and allocate this risk to individual counterparties to determine their contributions to the portfolio risk.

The stochastic nature of credit exposures makes counterparty risk much more difficult to model than lending risk. Even a simple application of credit limits requires sophisticated modeling of counterparty exposures. The standard practice has been to apply the limits against a certain percentile (typically, in the 90–95 percent range) of the counterparty net exposure distribution at several time horizons. To generate these distributions, the firm needs to be able to generate future scenarios for all risk factors that affect the prices of all transactions with the counterparty, and price these transactions at future dates conditionally on the realization of these factors. The risk factors include foreign exchange rates, yield curves for different currencies, equity indexes, commodity prices, and so on. The scenarios for the risk factors must incorporate realistic dynamics that take into account the correlation between the risk factors. For each scenario and for each future date, the net exposure is computed from the calculated transaction values after taking netting and collateral agreements into account.

Modeling portfolio losses is even more complicated as it requires the firm to model correlated credit events in addition to modeling net exposures to all counterparties. However, the implementation of these models is vital to all market participants if they are to remain both solvent and competitive.

Unilateral CCR and CVA

A credit value adjustment (CVA) is an estimate of the cost, or price, of CCR; it allows a firm to adjust the value of a contract to account for potential future losses due to the counterparty's defaulting.

Prior to 2007, CCR was not considered to be a particularly key area, and the concept of CVA was basically ignored in favor of the risk management approaches we have just described—i.e., monitoring of potential future exposures and mitigation techniques such as netting and collateralization.[13] Until recently, therefore, CCR for OTC derivatives was treated like credit risk for the loan book and was not marked-to-market.

A key driver in the shift toward CVA was the change in accounting standards around 2006, requiring CVA, in contrast to loans, to be marked-to-market.[14] This raised the issue of how to value CVA and, by implication, how to manage CCR more dynamically. It also meant that CVA must be calculated with market-implied parameters, such as credit spreads, rather than the historical default probabilities employed when calculating credit VaR.

Bilateral CCR and DVA

The new accounting rules raised the issue of unilateral CVA, but they also forced financial institutions to consider the bilateral nature of CCR. That is, they obliged firms to evaluate CCR under the assumption that the institution itself, as well as its counterparty, may default.[15]

---

[13]The treatment of CVA developed along the following historical path: Up to 2007, CVA was practically ignored by most if not all financial institutions. Banks managed counterparty credit risk through rough and static credit limits, based on exposure measurements related to credit VaR. From mid-2007 onward, firms introduced CVA to assess the cost of counterparty credit risk. At first, CVA tended to be charged upfront and managed statically, using an insurance-based approach. Soon, however, banks began to monitor and manage CVA dynamically, using daily and even intraday CVA calculations, real-time CVA calculations, and more accurate CVA sensitivities, hedging, and management. The criticality of CVA exploded in 2008 with the default, or threatened collapse, of seven financial firms in one month (September 2008: Fannie Mae, Freddie Mac, Washington Mutual, Lehman Brothers, and three Icelandic banks), as well as the quasi-failure of Merrill Lynch (acquired by Bank of America). These events contributed to the creation of CVA desks in many institutions.

[14] In the United States, FAS 157 (Financial Accounting Standards) was introduced in 2006; the equivalent IAS 39 (International Accounting Standards) dates from 2005.

[15]Historically, the larger derivatives players had much stronger credit quality than other market participants and were considered to be virtually risk-free. A large derivatives player trading with a medium or small derivatives player would simply impose the terms on any transaction in relation to CCR, overlooking any difficulty caused by the bilateral nature of CCR. While the credit spread of large, highly rated financial institutions prior to 2007 amounted to just a few basis points per annum, this ceased to be true during and after the financial crisis of 2007–2009. The bilateral nature of CCR could no longer be ignored.

TABLE 13-1 The DVA/CVA Relationship (Illustrative Only)

Counterparty A – Deal A		Counterparty B – Deal A
$100 CVA	=	$100 DVA
$200 DVA	=	$200 CVA

When an institution itself defaults, it in some sense "gains" on any outstanding liabilities that it cannot pay in full.[16] Taking account of this theoretical gain involves what is known as a debit valuation adjustment, or DVA. We can think of DVA as the mirror image of CVA: the CVA seen from one side of the transaction is the DVA of the other side of the transaction.

As Table 13-1 helps make clear, however, this does not mean that CVA = DVA on the same side of the deal. One counterparty is likely to have a different credit standing than the other counterparty, so the CVA and DVA numbers on the same side of the deal are likely to be different. For example, in Table 13-1, Counterparty A's credit standing is worse than Counterparty B's, leading to lower CVA than DVA from Counterparty A's perspective.

DVA is required under accounting regulations (FAS 157 and IAS 39), and the concept is gradually being accepted by market participants—though not without controversy and debate. From an accounting standpoint, DVA makes sense because the market price of any security should reflect the credit risk on both sides of the transaction in order to avoid an accounting mismatch. However, the Basel Committee does not allow "profits" from DVA to be counted toward tier 1 common equity.[17]

Many institutions regard the recognition of bilateral CCR as important in order to agree on the pricing of financial transactions (see below) and the unwinding of transactions, and to minimize P&L volatility. Bilateral considerations are also important if firms are to agree on the pricing of new transactions.

---

[16] That is, if the institution itself defaults while the MtM of the position is negative (a negative exposure), there will be a shortfall because the institution will pay its counterparty only a fraction (the recovery value) of what it owes. This shortfall corresponds to the DVA.

[17] According to the Basel Committee, the main reason for not recognizing DVA as an offset is that it would be inconsistent with the overarching supervisory prudence principle under which credit cannot be given for increases in regulatory capital arising from a deterioration in the firm's own credit quality.

Equation 13-3 corresponds to the equilibrium pricing of a financial transaction that can be reached by two counterparties when each of them takes into account the risk of default of the other side of the transaction.

It may seem counterintuitive for an institution to attach a positive value to its own future risk of default. An institution that applies DVA will make a MtM gain whenever its credit standing deteriorates and its credit spread widens, and vice versa. For example, in 2009, first-quarter results of some banks were not as bad as initially feared due to gains booked on their balance sheets as a result of their own credit quality's deteriorating—e.g., Citigroup reported a profit of $2.5 billion due to its worsened credit quality. Then in August 2009, improvements in bank credit spreads led to a deterioration in financial results. The process reversed again in the third quarter of 2011, when DVA generated combined earnings of $9.35 billion at five U.S. banks. This time around, UBS reported a Sfr1.8 billion DVA gain, which almost rubbed out the Sfr1.9 billion it lost in an alleged rogue trading incident (see Chapter 14). In the same quarter, JP Morgan and Citigroup each said they made $1.9 billion gains on DVA. Morgan Stanley, whose benchmark five-year CDS spread had grown to 609 bps the month before, made a huge $3.4 billion profit.[18]

It is often argued that the MtM of an institution's own credit spread gives counterintuitive results. A more concrete objection is that the benefit of DVA is hard to monetize, except of course by going bankrupt, which most institutions are happily trying to avoid. Aside from bankruptcy, some possible ways to realize DVA include:

- *Unwinding transactions.* An institution may realize a DVA gain if a trade is unwound in the future at a price that reflects the DVA.
- *Hedging.* Hedging of CVA has become rather common over the last few years. However, DVA is much harder to hedge than CVA because a firm cannot sell CDS protection on its own name.[19] An institution might

---

[18]See Laurie Carver, "The DVA Debate," *Risk*, November 2011.

[19]Some banks, such as Goldman Sachs, have attempted to get around this problem by instead selling protection on a number of highly correlated proxies, such as a CDS on a peer or a basket of banks. This is potentially a risky strategy, however, as such a hedge might cause the bank to lose money if the bank's credit spread tightened relative to the basket or in the event of the default of one of the banks in the proxy basket. To capture the pure spread risk, it might be better to short a peer's bonds while going long a risk-free swap. Also, if a bank does manage to sell protection on other highly correlated banks, then this creates significant wrong-way risk for the protection buyer.

attempt to realize an increasing DVA by buying back its own debt, but this strategy is not sustainable.

Since DVA cannot be hedged, some institutions recommend including only CVA in the "economic" P&L of a portfolio. That is, they would apply formula 13-2, given below, corresponding to the unilateral view of CCR, instead of formula 13-3—though the latter formula has to be used to reach agreement on the price of a transaction between two counterparties.

Funding Cost and FVA

Some banks have also begun adjusting their pricing of derivatives transactions to reflect the funding costs of their trading activities using a so-called funding valuation adjustment (FVA).

When managing a trading position, firms need to obtain cash for a number of operations: hedging the position, posting collateral, paying coupons or notionals, and so on. Where are such funds obtained? Cash can be obtained from different sources: the Treasury department, the market, the payment of a coupon or notional reimbursement, a positive MtM move, receipt of collateral or interest on posted collateral, or a closeout payment. All such cash flows need to be remunerated. For example, funds obtained from the Treasury group are remunerated at the cost of funding for the bank, whereas collateral is remunerated at a different rate—i.e., the OIS (overnight index swap) rate.[20]

The industry is looking for a funding valuation adjustment that is additive, with a corrective adjustment to the risk-free price being CVA – DVA +/– FVA (pricing equation 13-4, below).

However, the practice of adjusting the price of a derivative transaction for the funding cost is controversial as it leads to subjective prices, reflecting the different rates at which banks are able to fund themselves. This seems to violate the principle of the law of one price. Indeed, just as the imposition of DVA raised the hope of realigning the symmetry of prices, funding seems again about to undermine the law of one price and make prices a matter of perspective.

---

[20]In U.S. dollars, the index rate is the effective federal funds rate. In euros, it is the Euro Overnight Index Average (EONIA), and in sterling, it is the Sterling Overnight Index Average (SONIA).

The big question is whether the FVA is a real price. Since each entity computes a different funding-adjusted price for the same product, we would argue that FVA is not really a price in conventional terms. It may be used to book a deal in the trading system or to reimburse the Treasury for funding, but not to charge a client in some more direct way. It is more a "value" than a "price." Instead, FVA should be used internally within the bank to analyze the profitability of transactions by comparing the initial margin on a trade to its funding cost over the life of the trade.[21]

Pricing and Hedging CCR: Credit Value Adjustment (CVA)

Using CVA to price counterparty risk allows us to move beyond the binary ("yes" or "no") decision-making process of credit line control. The important question is whether a transaction is profitable once the counterparty risk component has been "priced in." The value of a transaction can be thought of as the "risk-free" price (i.e., assuming no CCR) minus a component to adjust for CCR:

$$\text{Value of "risky" derivative (with CCR)} = \text{Value of "risk-free"}$$
$$\text{derivative (with no CCR)} - \text{CVA} \qquad (13\text{-}2)$$

If the profit margin after adjusting for market risk, also referred to as the "client contribution," is greater than the CVA, then the transaction is economical for the financial institution that enters that transaction.

Bilateral counterparty credit risk valuation using DVA is given by the pricing equation 13-3. When using DVA, the value of derivatives is adjusted by subtracting the CVA component, which is related to future losses due to counterparty default, and adding the DVA component, which is related to future "gains" from one's own default.

$$\text{Value of "risky" derivative (with CCR)} = \text{Value of "risk-free"}$$
$$\text{derivative (with no CCR)} - \text{CVA} + \text{DVA} \qquad (13\text{-}3)$$

Note that when pricing a transaction, the institution adds the CVA to the risk-free value and deducts the DVA. The difference (CVA − DVA) is what the institution needs to charge the counterparty on the transaction as a credit charge.

---

[21]It is in the spirit of the RAROC approach described in Chapter 17.

When the counterparty is riskier than the institution, the credit charge by the institution is positive. From the counterparty's point of view, DVA is greater than CVA, because it is more likely to default than the institution—a benefit that explains why it needs to pay the institution a counterparty risk charge to enter the transaction.

There are some attractive, and some counterintuitive, implications of pricing with DVA:

- The overall counterparty risk adjustment may be beneficial if the DVA is greater in magnitude than the CVA. This would imply that the risky value of a derivative is greater than the risk-free value.
- If two counterparties agree on the approach and parameters for the calculation of CVA and DVA, then they will agree on a price by symmetry: one party's CVA is the other party's DVA, and vice versa.
- Risk mitigants such as netting and collateral tend to reduce *both* the CVA and DVA associated with a deal, so there may be no clear accounting signals about the benefits of risk mitigation.

If all the parties in the marketplace agree on the approach and the parameters for the calculation of CVA and DVA, then the total valuation of counterparty risk in the market (as represented by the sum of all CVAs less the sum of all DVAs) will be zero. Again, this follows from the symmetry of each deal, in that every CVA will have an equal and opposite DVA on the other side of the deal. Finally, adjusting for CVA, DVA, and FVA leads to the following pricing equation:

$$\text{Value of "risky" derivative (with CCR)} = \text{Value of "risk-free"}$$
$$\text{derivative (with no CCR)} - \text{CVA} + \text{DVA} +/- \text{FVA} \qquad (13\text{-}4)$$

Note that CVA and DVA are not obtained simply by adding a spread to the discount factor of asset cash flows. Similarly, FVA cannot be arrived at by simply applying a spread to the discounting of borrowing and lending cash flows. Simple spreads only really apply to very simple deals and under simplifying assumptions (no correlations, unidirectional cash flows, and so on).[22] Instead, firms have to carefully and properly analyze and price the real cash flows.

---

[2]The industry is looking for a simple pricing equation such as equation 13-4. However, funding, credit, and market risk interact in a nonlinear and recursive way, and, at least in theory, they cannot be decomposed additively.

Some people in the financial industry have argued that DVA is a component of FVA. DVA is indeed related to funding costs when the payout is unidirectional—e.g., issuing a bond, borrowing by issuing a loan, or writing a call option. If an institution is short simple products that are unidirectional in cash flows, it is basically borrowing. As the credit quality of the institution deteriorates, its funding cost will increase. At the same time, its DVA also goes up—i.e., in relation to its exposure and the deteriorating credit quality of the institution. This has brought a number of practitioners to identify DVA as a component of FVA for such simple unidirectional trades.

As discussed earlier, the funding-adjusted "price" is not really a price but instead a "value" that can be used to book a deal in the bank's system and measure the profitability of a trade.[23]

CVA Desk

Most banks have a dedicated central CCR risk management unit, often referred to as the CVA desk, in charge of pricing and managing all the CCR within an institution. In most best-practice banks, the CVA desk is located within the capital markets/trading floor division, since it is a trading desk. Occasionally it may sit in the Treasury department. Since the Treasury controls collateral flows and the funding policy of the bank, this can help the various teams coordinate CVA and FVA calculations and collateral charges. In a few cases, the desk is a stand-alone entity—i.e., sitting outside the standard departmental classifications.

The CVA desk charges a premium to each business unit for assuming responsibility for the CCR of a new trade, after taking advantage of portfolio-level risk mitigants such as netting and collateralization. The trader's P&L (profit and loss) is reduced by the CVA amount. Hence, the trader is forced to factor in the cost of CCR when pricing a new transaction. The advantage for the traders is that they can then concentrate on hedging market risk and ignore counterparty credit risk. This frees most traders from the need to develop advanced credit models, which in turn would need to be coupled to models for the classical asset classes (FX, equity, rates, commodities, and so on). It also frees them from the need to understand the netting sets within the bank's trading portfolios. Instead,

---

[23]See D. Brigo, M. Morini, and A. Pallavicini, *Counterparty Credit Risk, Collateral and Funding*, Wiley, 2013.

the CVA desk takes care of the "options on whole portfolios" embedded in counterparty risk pricing and hedging.

In addition to exposure, the calculation of CVA should account for the default probability of the counterparty; the default probability of the institution, in the case of bilateral pricing; netting and collateral agreements; and hedging costs.

Assuming no wrong-way risk—i.e., assuming independence among default probabilities, exposures, and recovery values—CVA is the expected loss, defined as:[24]

$$\mathrm{CVA} \approx \mathrm{LGD} \sum_{j=1}^{m} B(t_j) EE(t_j) q(t_{j-1}, t_j) \qquad (13\text{-}5)$$

where:

- LGD is loss given default—i.e., the percentage amount of the exposure expected to be lost if the counterparty defaults.
- $B(t_j)$ is the risk-free discount factor at time t_j.
- $EE(t_j)$ is the expected exposure for the time slot $(t_{j-1} - t_j)$ for $j = 1$ to m, with t_0 the time at which the valuation is made and t_m the maturity of the transaction.
- $q(t_{j-1}, t_j)$ is the marginal probability of default in the time interval $(t_{j-1} - t_j)$, assuming there was no default prior to time t_{j-1}.

In Equation 13-5, default enters the calculation only as default probabilities at future dates. This means that while we need a simulation framework in order to compute the exposures at different dates over the life of a transaction, it is not necessary to simulate default events.

In the case where EPE and default probabilities are reasonably constant over the life of the deal, then the CVA can be expressed as a running credit spread (CS) approximated by:

$$\mathrm{CVA} \approx \mathrm{CS} \times \mathrm{EPE} \qquad (13\text{-}6)$$

---

[24]See J. Gregory, *Counterparty Credit Risk: The New Challenge for Global Financial Markets*, Wiley, 2010, Chapter 7.

As an illustration, assuming that the EPE for a derivative position is 4 percent and the credit spread of the counterparty is 400 bps per annum, then a "back of the envelope" calculation of the CVA, as a running spread, is:

$$4\% \times 400 = 16 \text{ bps per annum}$$

The total CVA book (after netting and collateral arrangements) may represent a very large component in the P&L of an institution. Hence, it is important to hedge the overall CVA to market moves in case CVA translates into a negative impact on profitability.[25] Hedging CVA poses many challenges because of the number of market variables involved and the linkages between them.

Hedging the market risk exposure component of CCR is relatively straightforward because of the underlying liquidity and the offset of sensitivities across counterparties. However, hedging the credit component of CVA is more problematic because the credit default swap (CDS) and contingent CDS (CCDS) markets are not liquid enough to allow complete protection.[26] In addition, credit hedges are far from perfect and single-name protection is often unavailable, in which case most of the hedging must be executed using a credit index. It follows that there are significant benefits to hedging residual CVA exposure at the aggregate counterparty level rather than hedging individual transactions.

That said, a central CVA desk raises political challenges over pricing and P&L. Institutions that have tried both configurations have usually concluded that credit risk belongs in a support-oriented risk management unit that has the ability to execute hedges but that does not have a P&L mandate. A CVA desk can also act as a catalyst for bringing together different bank functions that influence

---

[25]Recall that during the crisis, mark-to-market losses due to CVA represented around two-thirds of the losses from counterparty credit risk; only one-third was due to actual defaults.

[26]The reference obligation for a CCDS is a derivative—e.g., an interest rate swap—and the notional amount is the fluctuating MtM value of that derivative at each payment date. While CCDS are tailor-made to transfer CCR within a given contract, extending them to cover many netted contracts and include collateral agreements would be extremely complex, not least in terms of the required documentation. For these reasons, the market for CCDS products has not developed very far and is not very liquid despite increasing focus on CCR.

The potential systemic impact of hedging CVA with illiquid sovereign CDS instruments during the Greek crisis in May 2010 raised concerns among regulators. There is a fear that a massive increase in demand from CVA desks might bid up the cost of sovereign CDS protection during a sovereign crisis and trigger market dislocations.

CCR, such as collateral management, market and credit risk management, and credit derivatives trading.

A key element in relation to quantifying CCR is incremental or "pre-deal" CVA. Since risk mitigants such as netting and collateral cover many trades, and often all trades with a given counterparty across several asset classes, the CVA of a new deal must consider all existing deals that are covered by the same risk mitigants. Considering a deal in isolation (stand-alone CVA) leads to very conservative estimates and may lead to lost opportunities due to an overstatement of the underlying risk. However, the proper calculation of predeal CVA is complex because it requires repricing all existing deals with a counterparty and then incorporating the impact of the proposed transaction. A framework and system that can make timely computations of predeal CVA is increasingly regarded as a standard requirement in large banks, as this is the only way to properly account for risk mitigants and therefore charge appropriately for new business as well as capture the impact of unwinding or canceling a trade and the various kinds of optionality embedded in transactions.

Wrong-Way Risk

Wrong-way risk is a term used to describe an unfavorable correlation between exposure and counterparty credit quality—i.e., exposure tends to be high when the counterparty is more likely to default, and vice versa.[27] Long protection credit derivatives trades are inherently wrong-way risk products because of the unfavorable relationship between the value of the contract and the chance that the protection seller will default—e.g., the counterparty risk posed by monolines and AIG during the subprime crisis.

---

[27] As an example of right-way risk, consider an airline that enters into an oil receiver swap with a financial institution (the latter receiving the fixed rate on the swap) in a bid to hedge its exposure to rising oil prices. The financial institution will be exposed to the airline when the price of oil is low—i.e., when the airline's cash flows benefit from reduced fuel costs. When the price of oil is high, and the airline may be in a weaker financial situation, the cash flows are in the other direction—i.e., there is no CCR exposure for the financial institution.

That said, some subtleties can complicate any assumptions over whether a risk is right-way or wrong-way. In our example, if an economic recession leads to a large drop in the price of oil, the right-way risk can shift into wrong-way risk because the low cost of oil is unlikely to compensate for the airline's loss of revenue from dramatically falling seat sales.

CVA desks must be able to address wrong-way risk in its two forms—i.e., general and specific. General wrong-way risk derives from macroeconomic effects, such as the fact that corporate defaults are generally higher when interest rates are low. Such effects should be incorporated into models so that the impact on CVA and its hedges is known across all relevant products (in this case, all interest rate products with corporate counterparties).

In addition, desks must be able to capture the specific wrong-way risk that occurs at the transaction level due to trade-specific linkages between market factors—e.g., FX or commodity prices—and counterparty credit quality. Specific wrong-way risk may lead to very high CVA charges and large MtM losses even if the counterparty does not default.

Regulatory Capital Under Basel II and Basel III for CCR

The Basel II and III framework applies a loan equivalent approach to derivatives and structured finance, under which the exposures are translated into their loan equivalents and the relevant Basel rules for loans are then applied. Under the Basel rules, one of three different approaches can be selected to translate exposures into loan equivalents: the current exposure method (CEM), the standardized method (SM), and the internal model method (IMM).

Current Exposure Method (CEM)

The current exposure method follows the approach of Basel I regulatory capital requirements for derivatives OTC instruments:

$$EAD = CE + \text{add-on} \qquad (13\text{-}7)$$

where EAD is the exposure at default, CE is the current exposure, and add-on is the estimated amount of potential exposure over the remaining life of the transaction. The current exposure, or current replacement cost, is the MtM value of the transaction when positive, or zero otherwise. The add-on is calculated for each transaction as the product of the notional amount and the add-on factor, which varies with the type of instrument and the remaining time to maturity of the deal, according to Table 13-2.

The EAD, or credit equivalent of the transaction, can be interpreted as the on-balance-sheet loan equivalent amount for regulatory capital purposes. Then, Basel I rules apply to calculate the amount of regulatory capital.

TABLE 13-2 Add-on Factors of the Current Exposure Method (CEM) by Remaining Maturity and Type of Underlying Asset

Remaining Maturity	Interest Rates	FX and Gold	Equities	Precious Metals (except gold)	Other Commodities
<1 year	0%	1%	6%	7%	10%
1–5 years	0.5%	5%	8%	7%	12%
>5 years	1.5%	7.5%	10%	8%	15%

Source: Basel Committee on Banking Supervision, *The Application of Basel II to Trading Activities and the Treatment of Double Default Effects*, July 2005, p. 39.

Banks using the CEM are allowed to net fully the transactions covered by a legally enforceable bilateral netting agreement when they calculate the CE. In addition, for a collateralized counterparty, unlike Basel I, the CE can be reduced by the current market value of the collateral, subject to a haircut.

Standardized Method (SM)

The SM approach in Basel II was designed for banks that do not qualify for modeling counterparty exposure via their internal model but would like to adopt a more risk-sensitive approach than the CEM. Under the SM, the EAD for derivatives transactions within a netting set is:

$$EAD = \beta * \max\left[MtM - C, \sum_i | RPE_i - RPC_i | * CCF_i \right] \qquad (13\text{-}8)$$

where $MtM = \sum_i MtM_i$ and $C = \sum_i C_j$ represent the current marked-to-market value of the trades in the netting set and the current market value of all the collateral positions assigned against the netting set, respectively. The terms $|RPE_i - RPC_i|$ represent a net risk position within a "hedging set" i, which forms an exposure add-on then multiplied by a conversion factor CCF_i determined by the regulators according to the type of position. Finally, β is the supervisory scaling factor, set at 1.4, which can be considered similar to the α-factor discussed below.

Internal Model Method (IMM)

Banks that are eligible for the internal model approach for market risk are allowed to compute the distribution of exposure at future dates using their own models. The IMM approach then prescribes a way of calculating EAD and effective maturity M from the EE profile.

Not only does the IMM allow a realistic treatment of netting and collateral, it permits netting across asset classes and cross-product netting between OTC derivatives and SFTs—i.e., repo-style transactions.

Under the IMM, EAD is calculated at the netting set level as a loan equivalent exposure:

$$EAD = \alpha \times EEPE \qquad (13\text{-}9)$$

where EEPE (effective expected positive exposure) is calculated within a netting set from the EE profile and α is a multiplier fixed by the Basel Committee at a level of 1.4.

While this number may be appropriate for banks with small derivative portfolios, it may be conservative when applied to large OTC derivatives dealers (assuming there is no significant wrong-way risk). Banks using the IMM have the option to compute their own estimate of α, subject to the supervisor approval, although this estimate is subject to a floor of 1.2.

Double Default

The credit risk of an exposure can be hedged with a product such as a CDS or otherwise guaranteed by a third party. This should give rise to some capital relief, since the risk has been reduced to the hopefully remote chance of a default by *both* the original counterparty and the party providing the guarantee.

Under Basel II, there are two possible ways in which to account for hedged or guaranteed exposures: *substitution*, where the default probability of the guarantor (provider of protection) may be substituted for the default probability of the original counterparty; and *double default*, which is recognized in Basel II via a formula to account for the fact that risk only arises from joint default. A key consideration in this formula is the correlation between the original counterparty and the guarantor.

Central Counterparty Clearinghouses (CCPs)

The Dodd-Frank Act in the United States and EMIR in Europe push financial institutions to conduct their derivatives trading through central counterparty clearinghouses (CCPs).[28] Basel III will also be a major driver for the increased use of CCPs, as the proposed regulation reduces the risk weighting for cleared

---

[28]CCP is the acronym for central counterparty in a central counterparty clearinghouse.

exposures to near zero.[29] In addition, legislation in the United States and European Union mandates clearing as broadly as possible.

CCPs are commercial entities that interpose themselves between the two parties in a trade:

- Each party posts collateral margins, say daily, every time the MtM value of the trade goes against that party.
- Collateral is held by the CCP as a guarantee for the other party.
- If a party in the deal defaults and the MtM is in favor of the other party, then the surviving party obtains the collateral from the CCP and consequently should not be affected by counterparty risk.
- Moreover, parties are also obliged to pay an initial margin at the outset of the deal that covers additional risks such as any deterioration in the quality of the collateral, gap risk, wrong-way risk, and so on.

CCPs act to centralize counterparty credit risk and to mutualize any losses. They seem to offer a way to defuse the "domino effects" and systemic risks caused by counterparty risk. But it remains to be seen how effective clearing will be. If there are many clearinghouses competing within certain product areas, and not all products can be cleared, then net counterparty risk could even increase. The increased dependence on central counterparties might not prove to be a panacea and raises issues concerning:

- The appropriateness of the initial margins and overcollateralization buffers that are supposed to account for wrong-way risk and collateral gap risk
- The default risk of the CCPs themselves, as concentrating such a large amount of risk under one roof could lead to CCPs becoming "too big to fail"[30]

---

[29]Basel Committee on Banking Supervision, *Capitalisation of Bank Exposures to Central Counterparties*, Consultative Paper, June 2010.

[30]CCPs can and have defaulted: in 1974, the Caisse de Liquidation des Affaires en Marchandises (France); in 1983, Kuala Lumpur Commodity Clearing House; in 1987, Hong Kong Futures Exchange. Others have been close to default: in 1987, the CME and OCC in the United States; in 1999, the BM&F in Brazil. J. M. Schwab, *Central Clearing: A New Headache for Credit Risk Managers*, White Paper, SunGard, 2012. Given that CCPs may default, there is clearly a degree of counterparty risk even when dealing with a CCP, and a CVA charge should apply.

- The moral hazard and asymmetric information problems created by eliminating the incentive for market participants to monitor carefully the counterparty risk of one another[31]

CVA VaR

Modeling CCR has become increasingly significant from a regulatory perspective, and the Basel Committee has come up with a number of proposals to improve the capitalization of CCR. These proposals were motivated by the realization that the major component of CCR-related losses (around two-thirds) during the financial crisis of 2007–2009 arose not from actual defaults but from MtM losses. Basel III therefore proposes measuring the "CVA VaR" arising from the activities of the CVA desk and charging capital against the desk's potential MtM losses.

The volatility of credit spreads and potential magnitude of CVA VaR means that large dealers will have a big incentive to actively hedge CVA to reduce this capital charge, particularly as the CVA charge comes on top of Basel III's general increase in capital requirements and additional charges for systemically important institutions.

However, the idea of quantifying CVA VaR remains highly controversial and seems somewhat optimistic on methodological grounds. CVA VaR is not simply a spin on traditional credit VaR, but something much more sophisticated. It represents a percentile of future possible losses due to future adverse movements of the pricing of counterparty risk. Many in the financial industry think it would be better to focus on undercapitalization as a function of the underestimation of default probabilities and correlation parameters, rather than adding new and complex CVA VaR capital charges.[32]

---

[31]Cf. D. Duffie, A. Li, and T. Lubke, *Policy Perspectives on OTC Derivatives Market Infrastructure*, Federal Reserve Bank of New York, Staff Report No. 424, March 2010; C. Pirrong, *Mutualization of Default Risk, Fungibility and Moral Hazard: The Economics of Default Risk Sharing in Cleared and Bilateral Markets*, Working Paper, University of Houston, June 2010; and C. Pirrong, *The Inefficiency of Clearing Mandates, Policy Analysis 665*, Cato Institute, June 2010.

[32]See J. Gregory, *Counterparty Casino: The Need to Address a Systemic Risk*, European Policy Forum, September 2010.

Conclusion

Better management of CCR and CVA is driving many firms to fundamentally reevaluate their risk management systems. Firms have found that the proper calculation of CVA is not a trivial task, and this is driving internal and academic researchers to come up with improved models for CVA on a stand-alone and portfolio basis.

Trading systems have not been designed to deal appropriately with CCR and CVA measurement. Most systems are compartmentalized and process only a subset of all the trades with a given counterparty. They often do not have the ability to model netting and collateral agreements, and most systems do not have the horsepower to calculate the Greeks (sensitivities) required to manage CVA.

The key to running a successful CVA desk is to find the right balance between risk taking and active hedging. While CVA must be partially hedged to avoid dramatic P&L swings, any hedges that can be put in place will be far from perfect and the residual risks must be well understood.

14

OPERATIONAL RISK

Operational risk is both the oldest and the newest threat faced by financial and nonfinancial institutions. Banks have always had to protect themselves from key threats to their operations, such as bank robbery and white-collar fraud. But until relatively recently, the management of these threats focused on practical techniques for minimizing the chance of loss, whether this meant putting a security guard at the door, establishing the independence of the internal audit team, or building robust computer systems. Few banks attempted either to put a specific economic number on the size of the operational risks they faced or to manage these risks systematically as a risk class.

Times have changed. Over the last decade and more, banks and other financial institutions have put significant energy into wide-ranging frameworks for managing enterprisewide operational risk and have tried to relate operational risk directly to the risk capital that they set aside to cover unexpected losses—the topics that we will focus on in this chapter.

Evolution and Definition of Operational Risk Management

Attitudes toward operational risk began to evolve quickly during the late 1990s, partly because of the trend toward managing banks in terms of their risk-adjusted performance. As banks began to try to adjust the apparent profits from a business activity in line with the risks the activity generated, often using economic capital calculations, they realized that it made little sense to leave a whole class of operational risks out of the calculation. Also, as banks brought together their chief credit and market risk officers under the command of overarching risk committees and chief risk officers and attempted to build enterprise risk management frameworks, it became impossible to ignore the wide-ranging impact of operational risks.

The problem was pointed up by a series of catastrophic rogue trader scandals that began with the destruction of Barings Bank in 1995 and has carried on ever since (see Box 14-1). It was partly the advent of this kind of scandal in the 1990s that prompted the Basel Committee to require banks to actively manage their operational risks and eventually to set capital aside to cover them.

BOX 14-1 ROGUE TRADING: THE OPERATIONAL RISK THAT WON'T GO AWAY

Since February 1995, when Nick Leeson brought down Barings Bank by hiding an £830 million loss in his secret "five eights" account in Singapore, the world has become accustomed to rogue traders.

Leeson's fraud came to light soon after Joseph Jett, a trader at Kidder Peabody in New York, was accused of hiding losses of $74 million while pretending to make a profit of $264 million trading bonds. Then came Toshihide Iguchi, who accumulated losses of $1.1 billion in bond trading at Daiwa Bank in New York, confessing in September 1995. After that there was Yasuo Hamanaka, who was found in 1996 to have lost $2.6 billion trying to corner the copper market in London for Sumitomo Corporation.

A second wave broke out in 2002 with the arrest of John Rusnak, a trader for Allied Irish Banks (AIB) in Baltimore, who lost $691 million on bad currency bets that he hid with fictional trades. A group of four currency options traders at the National Australia Bank (NAB) in Melbourne lost A$360 million in 2004.

The biggest ever case emerged in 2008, when Société Générale found its trader Jérôme Kerviel had hidden €4.9 billion of losses on the bank's Delta One desk. Then in September 2011, Kweku Adoboli was accused of hiding $2.3 billion of rogue trading losses on UBS's Delta One equity derivatives desk. The list of rogue traders continues to grow. . . .

In the same period, technological change was also pushing operational risks onto the management agenda[1]—a trend that continues to the present. While technology helps banks to push down costs as well as to open up new financial markets, it is a double-edged sword. The increasing complexity of financial instruments and greater dependency on information systems increases the potential for an operational risk event. A lack of familiarity with new financial instruments may lead to their misuse and raises the chances of either mispricing or ineffective hedging. Operational errors in data feeds may also distort the bank's assessment of its risks. (In Chapter 15 we discuss model risk, which is really a special case of operational risk, in greater depth.)

But perhaps the most important force in changing attitudes to operational risk in the early years of the millennium was the Basel II Accord. This obliged many banks to set aside specific risk capital for operational risk. Regulators and the financial industry converged on a formal definition of operational risk in order to specify and quantify this capital charge within the Accord.

The regulators defined operational risk as "the risk of loss resulting from inadequate or failed internal processes, people and systems or from external events." These failures include computer breakdowns, a bug in a key piece of computer software, errors of judgment, deliberate fraud, and many other potential mishaps; Table 14-1 sets these out more formally. This definition from the Basel Committee includes legal risk (exposure to fines, penalties, and punitive damages resulting from supervisory actions as well as private settlements), but it excludes business risk, reputation risk,[2] and strategic risk.

---

[1]A prime example of a technology-oriented operational risk event from the period was the so-called Y2K event. Y2K was the acronym for the end of the millennium, when it was feared that computer programs might not function properly because of the common use of two digits to specify the calendar year. Programmers were worried that computer systems might interpret 05 as 1905 rather than 2005—or simply crash. Banks and other corporations invested many billions of dollars to avert the problem which, perhaps because of this or because the problem had been exaggerated, turned out to be something of a nonevent.

[2]Reputational concerns are right at the top of the list of problems that companies worry about. In 2011 AIG started to offer "reputation insurance." AIG, which already knows about bad publicity, offered a new type of coverage to defray the cost of bringing in outside experts when a company faces a potential public relations crisis. Companies often turn to communications firms when they need help shaping their response to events that could cause lasting damage to their brand or their business, such as product recalls, data breaches, executive scandals, or government bailouts.

TABLE 14-1 Types of Operational Failures*

1. People risk	• Incompetency
	• Fraud
2. Process risk	
A. Model risk**	• Model/methodology error
	• Mark-to-model error
B. Transaction risk	• Execution error
	• Product complexity
	• Booking error
	• Settlement error
	• Documentation/contract risk
C. Operational control risk	• Exceeding limits
	• Security risks
	• Volume risk
3. Systems and technology risk	• System failure
	• Programming error
	• Information risk
	• Telecommunications failure
4. External events	• Earthquakes

*This list is not exhaustive.
**See Chapter 15.

The definition is a practical one that helps bankers who must comply with capital regulations to detail the events that are considered as operational risk events. However, it is not a definition underpinned by logical principles. For example, one might question whether it really makes sense to include under the same umbrella external events (such as earthquakes) and the kind of internal events (e.g., failures of process) that are more obviously under the control of the board of directors or the CEO.

It is also a definition that begs many questions, especially about the relationship between operational risk and the other risk types to which banks attribute capital. Many of the failures in risk management we have discussed in this book so far, including the key failures of the financial crisis of 2007–2009—control failures, credit risk management failures, model risk failures, failures of risk communication, fraud, the overlooking of liquidity risks and risk interactions, and so on—could in some sense be attributed to operational risk.

This is why operational risk continues to present such a conundrum to the financial and other industries. Its pervasive nature makes it almost impossible to define and measure, while at the same time risk managers know that almost every catastrophe begins with an operational failure. For related reasons, some operational risk managers in financial institutions say that the real value in focusing on operational risk arises not from attempts to put an absolute number against overall operational risk but from attempts to raise awareness about how risk is generated within particular business processes (leading to a focus on the key risk indicators that we discuss later).

First, let's take a look at the key elements of operational risk management before examining operational risk measurement in more detail.

Eight Key Elements in Bank Operational Risk Management

In the authors' experience, eight key elements are necessary to successfully implement a bankwide operational risk management framework and the associated operational risk models (Figure 14-1).

They involve setting policy and identifying risk on the basis of an agreed-upon terminology, constructing business process maps, building a best-practice measurement methodology, providing exposure management, installing a timely reporting capability, performing risk analysis (inclusive of stress testing), and allocating economic capital as a function of operational risk. These key elements are consistent with the sound operational risk management principles that, according to the Basel Committee, should be adopted by all banks, regardless of their size, level of sophistication, and nature of their activities. These principles are summarized in Box 14-2.

Let's look at these elements in more detail. The first element is to develop *well-defined operational risk policies*. Banks need to establish clear guidelines

FIGURE 14-1 Eight Key Elements to Achieve Best-Practice Operational Risk Management

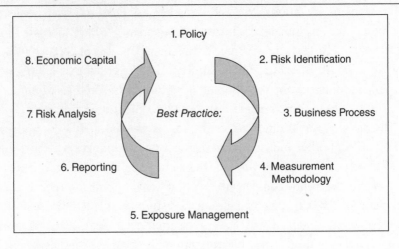

BOX 14-2 BASEL COMMITTEE PRINCIPLES FOR THE SOUND MANAGEMENT OF OPERATIONAL RISK

In June 2011, the Basel Committee set out a revised set of principles for the management of bank operational risk, presented here in an abbreviated form:

Principle 1. The board of directors should take the lead in establishing a strong risk management culture, [ensuring] that a strong operational risk management culture exists throughout the whole organization.

Principle 2. Banks should develop, implement, and maintain a framework that is fully integrated into the bank's overall risk management processes.[1]

Principle 3. The board of directors should establish, approve, and periodically review the framework [and] oversee senior management to ensure that the policies, processes, and systems are implemented effectively at all decision levels.

---

[1]The Principles document describes such a framework in some detail—e.g., that it should provide for a common taxonomy of operational risk terms and describe how limits are set.

Principle 4. The board of directors should approve and review a risk appetite and tolerance statement for operational risk that articulates the nature, types, and levels of operational risk that the bank is willing to assume.

Principle 5. Senior management should develop for approval by the board of directors a clear, effective, and robust governance structure with well-defined, transparent, and consistent lines of responsibility.

Principle 6. Senior management should ensure the identification and assessment of the operational risk inherent in all material products, activities, processes, and systems to make sure the inherent risks and incentives are well understood.[2]

Principle 7. Senior management should ensure that there is an approval process for all new products, activities, processes, and systems that fully assesses operational risk.

Principle 8. Senior management should implement a process to regularly monitor operational risk profiles and material exposures [with] reporting mechanisms at the board, senior management, and business line levels that support proactive management of operational risk.

Principle 9. Banks should have a strong control environment that utilizes policies, processes, and systems; appropriate internal controls; and appropriate risk mitigation and/or transfer strategies.

Principle 10. Banks should have business resiliency and continuity plans in place to ensure an ability to operate on an ongoing basis and limit losses in the event of severe business disruption.

Principle 11. A bank's public disclosures should allow stakeholders to assess its approach to operational risk management.

Source: Abridged from Basel Committee, *Principles for the Sound Management of Operational Risk*, June 2011.

---

[2]The Principles document lists some example tools, including internal and external loss databases, process mapping, key risk indicators and key performance indicators, scenario analysis, risk measurement, and comparative analysis.

for practices that control or reduce operational risk. For example, in the case of an investment bank that runs trading desks, the bank needs to establish policies on trader/back-office segregation, out-of-hours trading, off-premises trading, legal document vetting, the vetting of the pricing models that underpin trading decisions, and so on. Some of these practices may have been defined, and either required or encouraged, by regulators. But many others represent best-practice standards identified by tracking the findings from industry working groups, or best practices that seem to be prevalent in the bank's peer group. Other practices might have to be developed by the bank itself in response to new products and innovative business lines.

Policies should also call for initiating a variety of empirical analyses to test the links between cause and effect. The basic idea is to collect data for each operational risk and then subsequently try to fit the causes to them. The methodology for describing cause and effect is typically developed after the data have been collected.

The second element is to establish a *common language of risk identification*. For example, the term *people risk* would include a failure to deploy skilled staff, *process risk* would include execution errors, *technology risk* would include system failures, and so on. This common language can be used during either qualitative self-assessments executed by business management (and validated by the risk management function) or statistical assessment.

The third element is to develop *business process maps* for each business. For example, a risk officer might map the business process associated with the bank's dealings with a broker, so that this becomes transparent to management and auditors. The same officer might extend this description to create a full "operational risk catalogue" for all the bank's businesses. This catalogue categorizes and defines the various operational risks arising from each organizational unit in terms of people, process, and systems and technology risks (as in Table 14-1). It would include analyzing the products and services that each organizational unit offers and the actions that the bank needs to take to manage operational risk.

The fourth element is to develop a *comprehensive set of operational risk metrics*. Later in this chapter we discuss in more detail how operational risk managers should carry out risk measurement, using a quantitative methodology based on both historical loss experience and scenario analysis to derive loss frequency and loss severity distributions. These distributions can be combined to calculate the economic capital required to support the activity's operational risk.

The fifth element is to decide *how to manage operational risk exposures* and take appropriate action to hedge the operational risk. The bank should address the cost/benefit trade-offs of insuring against a given risk (for those operational risks that can be insured against, which is far from all of them).

The sixth element is to decide *how to report exposures*. The bank will have to decide which operational risk numbers are the most useful for senior management and the board when tracking the bank's firmwide operational risk profile. The bank will also have to put in place an appropriate infrastructure to support reporting to the relevant committees (e.g., the operations and administration committee as well as the capital and risk committee).

The seventh element is to develop *tools for risk analysis* and procedures for when these tools should be deployed. The bank must develop appropriate measures for exposure, up-to-date databases of internal and industrywide operational loss data, well-designed scenario analyses, and a deep knowledge of the key risk drivers in its business lines. Figure 14-2 shows how these tools feed into the calculation of operational value-at-risk, a calculation that we discuss in more detail later on. The frequency of risk assessment should be a function of the degree to which operational risks are expected to change over time as businesses undertake new initiatives or as business circumstances evolve.

FIGURE 14-2 From Tools for Risk Analysis to OpVaR

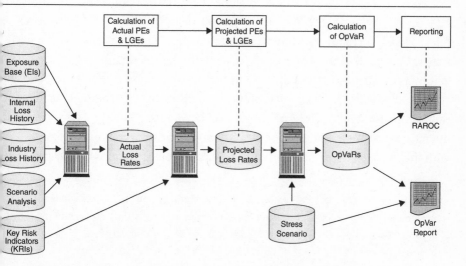

Operational risk analysis is typically performed as part of a new product process. The bank should reassess its approach whenever its operational risk profile changes significantly—e.g., after implementing a new system or offering a new service.

The eighth element is to ensure *appropriate attribution of operational risk capital* to every business.

How Can We Define and Categorize Operational Losses?

It's clear that quantifying operational risk represents one of the key challenges when implementing the framework that we've described. But before we try to attach a number to a particular operational risk, we must think through how we define and classify the operational losses that might arise from that risk. If the bank's approach to this problem is not rigorous, it will find that relating internal and external data on losses to a particular operational risk is impossible.[3]

A loss arising from an operational risk takes the form either of a direct cost or of a write-down associated with the resolution of an operational risk event, net of recoveries (mitigation benefits should be recorded separately). When the loss is deemed probable and estimable, it is likely to be recognized as a profit and loss (P&L) event for accounting purposes and can also become part of the bank's recorded internal loss history (i.e., be entered into its loss database).

The definition of operational losses should be as specific as possible. For example, an external cost should include the gross cost of compensation and/ or penalty payments made to third parties, legal liability, regulatory taxes or fines, or loss of resources. Here we can define three key terms: cost to fix, write-down, and resolution. The *cost-to-fix* statistic is best defined to include only external payments that are directly linked to the incident. For example, legal costs, consultancy costs, or costs of hiring temporary staff would be included in the cost-to-fix statistic. Internal costs associated with general management and operations are not included, as these costs are already covered in costs associated with the normal course of business. *Write-down* refers to the loss or impairment

---

[3]In this section we offer general comments on data issues. Specific regulatory guidance on the treatment of data can be found in regulatory publications, especially the Data section (pp. 20–30) of the Basel Committee's *Operational Risk – Supervisory Guidelines for the Advanced Measurement Approaches*, June 2011.

in the value of any financial or nonfinancial assets owned by the bank. *Resolution* refers to the act of correcting the individual event (including out-of-pocket costs and write-downs) and returning to a position (or standard) comparable to the bank's original state before the loss event (including restitution payments to third parties). Note that these definitions do not include lost or forgone revenue.

In sum, losses include payments to third parties, write-downs, resolutions, and cost to fix. Losses do not include the cost of controls, preventive action, and quality assurance. Losses also do not usually include investment in upgrades or new systems and processes.

In building up internal loss histories, risk managers must ensure that the boundaries between separate types of risk (e.g., market, credit, and operational risk) are clearly defined so as to avoid double counting.

One of the most frustrating problems for bankers trying to record and measure operational risks is the endless number of ways in which any particular risk might be classified in terms of both its nature and its underlying cause. For example, if a loan officer approves a loan contrary to the bank's guidelines (he or she might even have been given a bribe), any loss arising from this action should ideally be classified as an operational failure, not a credit loss. Typically, loans that default because of third-party fraud are classified as loan losses, whereas loans that default because of internal fraud are classified as operational risk losses.

A list of the sources that give rise to the main categories of operational risk exposure should be developed so that a common taxonomy of the drivers of risks can be established.

The Basel II Capital Accord helpfully considers seven level 1 loss event types.[4] These seven loss event types are further decomposed by Basel into level 2 loss event types. The bank ultimately maps their specific loss event type 3 events into the Basel defined level 2 loss event types. The Basel seven level 1 loss event types are as follows:

1. *Internal fraud.* Losses caused by acts of a type intended to defraud, misappropriate property, or circumvent regulations, the law, or company policy. For example, intentional misreporting of positions, employee theft, and insider trading on an employee's own account.

---

[4]Basel Committee on Banking Supervision, *Basel II: International Convergence of Capital Measurement and Capital Standards: A Revised Framework, Comprehensive Version,* June 2006.

2. *External fraud.* Losses caused by acts of a third party of a type intended to defraud, misappropriate property, or circumvent the law. For example, robbery, forgery, check kiting, and damage from computer hacking.

3. *Employment practices and workplace safety.* Losses arising from acts inconsistent with employment, health, or safety laws or agreements, from payment of personal injury claims, or from discrimination events. For example, violations of organized labor activities.

4. *Clients, products, and business practices.* Losses arising from an unintentional or negligent failure to meet a professional obligation to specific clients (including fiduciary and suitability requirements), or from the nature or design of a product. For example, misuse of confidential customer information.

5. *Damage to physical assets.* Losses arising from loss or damage to physical assets from natural disaster or other events. For example, terrorism, vandalism, earthquakes, fire, and floods.

6. *Business disruption and system failures.* Losses arising from disruption of business or system failures. For example, hardware and software failures, telecommunication problems, and utility outages.

7. *Execution, delivery, and process management.* Losses arising from failed transaction processing or process management, or from relations with trade counterparties and vendors. For example, data entry errors, collateral management failures, incomplete legal documentation, and unapproved access to client accounts.

What Kind of Operational Risk Should Attract Operational Risk Capital?

In most banks, the methodology for translating operational risk into capital is developed by the group responsible for making risk-adjusted return on capital (RAROC) calculations in partnership with the operational risk management group (see Chapter 17).

Mechanisms for attributing capital to operational risk should be risk-based, transparent, scalable, and fair. Specifically, capital requirements should vary directly with levels of verifiable risk and should provide incentives to manage operational risk so as to improve operational decisions and increase the risk-adjusted return on capital.

IGURE 14-3 Distribution of Operational Losses

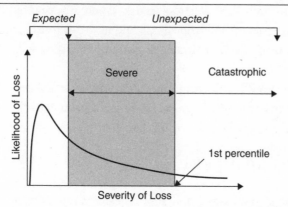

Severity of Loss

But it does not make sense to attribute risk capital to all kinds of operational loss, as Figure 14-3 makes clear. To understand this diagram, remember that operational risks can be divided into those losses that are expected and
those that are unexpected. Management knows that in the ordinary course of
business, certain operational activities will fail. There will be a "normal" amount
of operational loss (resulting from error corrections, minor fraud, and so on)
that the business is willing to absorb as a cost of doing business. These failures
are explicitly or implicitly budgeted for in the annual business plan and are
covered by the pricing of the product or service, so we should not try to allocate
risk capital against them.

Instead, risk capital makes sense only for unexpected losses, as shown in
Figure 14-3. However, as the figure suggests, unexpected failures can themselves
be further subdivided into:

- *Severe but not catastrophic losses.* Unexpected severe operational failures
  should be covered by an appropriate allocation of operational risk capital. These losses are covered by the measurement processes described in
  the following section.
- *Catastrophic losses.* These are the most extreme but also the rarest operational risk events—the kind that can destroy the bank entirely. VaR and
  RAROC models are not meant to capture catastrophic risk, since they consider potential losses only up to a certain confidence level (say 1 percent)
  and catastrophic risks are by their very nature extremely rare. Banks may

tighten procedures to protect themselves against catastrophic events or use insurance to hedge catastrophic risk. Often, it is believed that the central bank may step in and help a bank and its depositors in the event of a sudden catastrophe. But risk capital cannot protect a bank against these risks.

Given this, how can we begin to put a number to the severe but not catastrophic risk of operational loss that a bank faces through its business activities?

VaR for Operational Risk

Operational risk is notoriously difficult to measure. But, in principle at least, the classic loss distribution approach to measuring risk seen in Figure 14-3 can be deployed. This approach is one of the key sources of information employed in the Advanced Measurement Approach (AMA) proposed in the Basel II Capital Accord and is based on analytical techniques that are widely used in the insurance industry to measure the financial impact of an operational failure.

Box 14-3 reviews the three approaches proposed in the new Basel Capital Accord. Only the AMA is risk sensitive; the others are somewhat arbitrary and will not produce the right incentives to reduce operational risk.

BOX 14-3 REGULATORY APPROACHES TO OPERATIONAL RISK MODELS

The Basel regulators offer a spectrum of three increasingly risk-sensitive approaches for measuring operational risk, first set out in Basel II.

BASIC INDICATOR APPROACH

The least risk-sensitive of these approaches is the Basic Indicator Approach, in which capital is a multiple (capital factor = 15 percent) of a single indicator (base), which is the average annual gross income, where positive, over the previous three years for which gross income was positive. The regulators have postulated that gross income serves as a proxy for the scale of operational risk exposure. Gross income is defined as the sum of net interest and noninterest income.

STANDARDIZED APPROACH

The Standardized Approach divides banks' activities into eight lines of business, or LOBi (see the discussion that follows). Each line of business is then assigned an exposure indicator EIi, which is, as in the Basic Indicator Approach, the average annual gross income for that line of business, where positive, over the previous three years for which gross income was positive. Each business line is assigned a single multiplier (capital factor βi) to reflect its relative riskiness. The total capital requirement is defined as the sum of the products of the exposure and the capital factor for each of the N business lines:

$$\text{Capital requirement (OpVaR)} = \sum_{i=1}^{N} \text{EI}_i * \beta_i$$

The Basel Committee has set the betas to the following values:

i	Business Line	Beta Factor (β_i)
1	Corporate finance	18%
2	Trading and sales	18%
3	Retail banking	12%
4	Commercial banking	15%
5	Payment and settlement	18%
6	Agency services	15%
7	Asset management	12%
8	Retail brokerage	12%

ALTERNATIVE STANDARDIZED APPROACH (ASA)

The standardized approach has been criticized because it can lead to double counting for high default rate businesses. For these activities, the business is hit twice: first, on the credit side, with high regulatory capital because of the high probability of default of the borrowers, and second, on the operational risk side, with high regulatory capital because of high margins (to the extent that expected loss is priced in).

As an alternative to the standardized approach just described, national supervisors can choose to allow banks to employ an alternative standardized approach (ASA). Under the ASA, the operational risk capital framework is the same as for the standardized approach except in the case of two business lines: retail banking and commercial banking. For these business lines, the exposure indicator EI is replaced by

$$EI = m \times LA$$

where $m = 0.035$ and LA is the total outstanding retail loans and advances (non-risk-weighted and gross of provisions), averaged over the past three years.

ADVANCED MEASUREMENT APPROACH (AMA)

Under the AMA, the regulatory capital requirement is the risk measure produced by the bank's internal operational risk model. The loss distribution approach described in the main text is likely to form a core plank of any such model, but individual banks have to meet some strict qualitative standards before regulators allow them to adopt the AMA approach. The regulators say that any operational risk measurement system must have certain key features, including "the use of internal data, relevant external data, scenario analysis and factors reflecting the business environment and internal control systems." Under the AMA, the Basel II regulators have not set out exactly how these ingredients should be used. Instead, the regulators say that a bank needs to have a "credible, transparent, well-documented and verifiable approach for weighting these fundamental elements in its overall operational risk measurement system." See Box 4-5 for further discussion.

The loss distribution approach is analogous to the VaR techniques developed to measure market risk in banking, and therefore we will call it operational value-at-risk (OpVaR). Our aim is to determine the expected loss from operational failures, the worst-case loss at a desired confidence level, the required economic capital for operational risk, and the concentration of operational risk.

The firm's activities should be divided into lines of business (LOB), with each line of business being assigned an exposure indicator (EI). The primary foundation for this analysis is the historical experience of operational losses.

Since in most cases we do not have robust analytical models to evaluate operational risks, we must rely on empirical estimation procedures. Where there are no loss data, inputs have to be based on judgment and scenario analysis.

For example, a measure of EI for *legal liability* related to client exposure could be the number of clients multiplied by the average balance per client. The associated probability of an operational risk event (PE) would then be equal to the number of lawsuits per year per 1,000 clients. The loss given an event (LGE) would equal the average loss divided by the average balance per client.

A measure of EI for *employee liability* could be the number of employees multiplied by the average compensation. The PE for employee liability would then be the number of lawsuits divided by the number of employees, and the LGE would be the average loss divided by the average employee compensation.

A measure of EI for *regulatory, compliance, and taxation penalties* could be the number of accounts multiplied by the balance per account. The PE would then be the number of penalties (including cost to comply) divided by the number of accounts, and the LGE would be the average penalty divided by the average balance per account.

A measure of EI for *loss of or damage to assets* could be the number of physical assets multiplied by their average value. The associated PE would be the number of damage incidents per year divided by the number of physical assets; the LGE would be the average loss divided by the average value of physical assets.

A measure of EI for *client restitution* could be the number of accounts multiplied by the average balance per account. The PE would then be the number of restitutions per year divided by the number of accounts, and the LGE would be the average restitution divided by the average balance per account.

A measure of EI for *theft, fraud, and unauthorized activities* could be the number of accounts multiplied by the balance per account (or the number of transactions multiplied by the average value per transaction). The corresponding measures for PE would be the number of frauds in a year divided by the number of accounts or the number of frauds divided by the number of transactions. The respective LGEs would be the average loss divided by the average balance per account or the average loss divided by the average value per transaction.

A measure of EI for *transaction processing risk* could be the number of transactions multiplied by the average value per transaction. The PE would then be the number of errors divided by the number of transactions. The LGE would be the average loss divided by the average value per transaction.

If we use measures such as these, then we can begin to calculate the OpVaR for the operational risks associated with particular business lines, as we discuss in detail for credit card fraud in Box 14-4. Observe that, in this example, the expected loss per transaction in credit cards is 9.1 cents, and the statistical worst-case loss is 52 cents. The 42.9 cent difference between 52 and 9.1 cents is the severe loss; and the area beyond 52 cents is the catastrophic loss area.

The categories of operational risk cannot be viewed in isolation from one another. It will be necessary to ultimately measure the degree of interconnected risk exposures that cut across the operational risk categories in order to understand the full impact of any risk. For example, if new software is being introduced, then the implementation of that new software may generate a set of interconnected risks across people, process, and technology.

All this calls for understanding the correlations between the many different types of operational risk. The total operational risk across multiple businesses units is not simply the sum of each of the component operational risks for each business.

Internal Versus External Loss Databases

Most approaches to measuring operational risk, including the approach outlined above, depend on the analyst's having available a rich set of operational loss data across a considerable period. Over the last decade or so, some banks have built quite extensive internal loss databases to record the details of their operational losses in key categories.

The advantage of internal databases is that they can reflect the business lines and loss experience of the bank in question and also capture idiosyncrasies such as the bank's risk culture and control environment—though the bank's operational risk profile will inevitably vary over time.

The disadvantage of internal loss databases is that, by definition, they will not capture many extreme, solvency-threatening events.

The banking industry has therefore also built a number of industrywide operational loss databases—e.g., the Operational Riskdata eXchange (ORX) Association.[5] ORX is an industry association that facilitates the exchange of anonymous operational risk loss data; by 2013, it had amassed records of a total loss value of around 152 billion euros.

---

[5]For more information, see www.orx.org.

BOX 14-4 OPVAR FOR CREDIT CARD FRAUD

To work out the OpVaR number for a bank's risk of credit card fraud, the bank needs first to identify an exposure index. The exposure index (EI) chosen to measure credit card fraud might be the total dollar amount of the transactions—i.e., the product of the number of transactions and the average value of a transaction. For simplicity, let's assume that the average value of a credit card transaction is US$100.[1]

The expected probability of an operational risk event, PE, can be calculated by dividing the number of loss events due to fraud by the number of transactions. If we assume that there are 1.3 fraud loss events per 1,000 transactions, then PE is equal to 0.13 percent.

Assume that the average loss rate given a fraud event (LGE) is US$70. Accordingly, the LGE is calculated by dividing the average loss by the average value of a transaction; in our example, this comes to 70 percent.

Assume further that the statistical worst-case loss set at the appropriate loss tolerance for the industry is 52 cents (on an average transaction of US$100) and that the expected loss, or loss rate, LR, is:

$$LR = PE \times LGE = 0.13\% \times \$70 = 9.1 \text{ cents}$$

The figure below summarizes the components of our OpVaR calculation for credit card fraud losses.

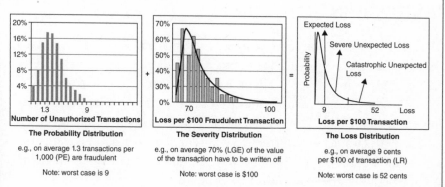

The Probability Distribution	The Severity Distribution	The Loss Distribution
e.g., on average 1.3 transactions per 1,000 (PE) are fraudulent	e.g., on average 70% (LGE) of the value of the transaction have to be written off	e.g., on average 9 cents per $100 of transaction (LR)
Note: worst case is 9	Note: worst case is $100	Note: worst case is 52 cents

---

[1]This is a generic example; the numbers do not reflect the experience of any one bank.

This kind of external database can augment internal databases. It is particularly useful for strengthening the representation of losses in the tail of the loss distribution or for applying to business lines where the bank lacks a long track record.

While helpful, external databases do not completely answer the problem of operational loss data, which to some degree may simply be intractable. Enduring issues include:

- The need to scale, filter, and adapt external data (e.g., to account for firm size) when combining these data with internal data. For example, it may not be appropriate to include multibillion-dollar losses in the case of a bank with only a few hundred million dollars of assets.
- Bias in reported losses—e.g., a bias against relatively unpublicized losses.
- Standardization and categorization issues—e.g., the selection of operational risk categories or the nature of the reference.
- Date associated with an event, or the recording of gross or net loss amounts.
- Sparse data on some rare but severe events, even in industry databases.
- The need to make the analysis more forward looking—e.g., to account for new business lines, structural changes in business lines, or changes in control environment.

Scenario, Scorecard, and Combined Approaches to Quantifying Operational Risk

The loss distribution approach, based on internal and external data, is not the only approach to quantifying operational risk. Indeed, many banks have invested heavily in developing approaches based largely on scenario generation.

These approaches take various forms but focus on the informed, forward-looking opinion of the firm's business line experts as to the likelihood and severity of particular operational risks. In addition, they may also take into account information about the condition of the relevant control environment and the status of relevant key risk drivers or indicators.

For example, the bank may run a formal poll of the firm's risk and business line experts on possible scenarios that would cause a loss in their business area. The poll might take account of their personal experience of such losses or their knowledge of their industry segment's experience of such losses. The approach also sometimes uses external loss data relevant to the particular business line as a platform for an informed discussion.

The aim is to build up a series of informed judgmental estimates of the likelihood and severity of operational loss scenarios (e.g., failure of a key banking system) in as rigorous a way as possible.

Expert opinion may also be used to select, adjust, or calibrate a particular underlying shape of loss distribution for a given business line; the shape of the loss distribution curve that is to be calibrated must be chosen carefully.

Within the scenario-building process, or as an additional stage, the bank may try to take account of the business and control environment in a particular business line. For example, it may take account of the key risk drivers we describe below, as well as information concerning the associated control environment (e.g., audit scores).

These adjustments may take the form of a balanced scorecard to try to make sure the bank retains some control over the impact of each factor on the overall risk quantification.

The advantages and disadvantages of a scenario-based approach are fairly obvious. The approach is tailored to the risk profile of an individual bank and is usefully forward looking. However, it also depends upon opinions and risk perceptions, which may not reflect the real risk of a rare event. Inevitably, the organizations that are most exposed to operational risks may not be best placed to self-assess the chance of a loss or its severity.

Many banks combine loss distribution approaches with some element of scenario analysis and scorecard analysis of the business environment. Indeed, the Basel regulators say that AMA approaches to quantifying operational risk must take account of all these different kinds of information, though the weight the bank places on each approach is left open to interpretation (see Box 14-5).

Although the financial industry has made significant efforts to improve operational risk measurement, we should not overstate the results. In truth, there is at present no satisfactory way to measure operational risk or to combine the results of the different approaches into a single operational risk metric.[6] Even banks that have worked hard to develop a sophisticated approach have been left

---

[6]See discussion, and one potential answer, in K. K. Dutta and D. Babbel, "Scenario Analysis in the Measurement of Operational Risk Capital: A Change of Measure Approach," July 5, 2012.

BOX 14-5   USE OF THE FOUR DATA ELEMENTS IN THE BASEL AMA APPROACH

In a set of supervisory guidelines on quantifying operational risk laid out in 2011, the regulators set out in more detail how each of four key data elements should be applied to the AMA approach to quantifying operational risk.

> *An AMA for calculating the operational risk capital charge of a bank requires the use of four data elements which are: (1) internal loss data (ILD); (2) external data (ED); (3) scenario analysis (SBA) and (4) business environment and internal control factors (BEICFs).*

The Basel II Framework anticipated that there would be a need for different "combinations" of the data elements depending on the behavior of the loss generating process. . . . Nevertheless, a number of key issues have been identified that are crucial to the successful implementation of an AMA:

(a) *Internal Loss Data (ILD)* The Committee expects that the inputs to the AMA model are based on data that represent or reflect the bank's business risk profile and risk management practices. It expects ILD to be used . . . to assist in the estimation of loss frequencies, to inform the severity distribution(s) to the extent possible and to serve as an input into scenario analysis.

(b) *External Data (ED)* The Committee expects ED to be used in the estimation of loss severity as such data contain valuable information to inform the tail of the loss distribution(s). ED is also an essential input into scenario analysis. Banks may choose to source ED from a public database, from a consortium where members submit their loss information, or from other means such as collecting relevant ED themselves.

(c) *Scenario Analysis* A robust scenario analysis framework is an important part of the ORMF in order to produce reliable scenario outputs which form part of the input into the AMA model. The Committee acknowledges that the scenario process is qualitative and that the output from a scenario process necessarily contains significant uncertainties. This uncertainty, together with the uncertainty from the other elements, should be reflected in the output of the model producing a range for the capital estimate. The Committee recognises that quantifying the uncertainty arising from scenario biases poses significant challenge and is an area requiring further research.

(d) *BEICFS [business environment and internal control factors]* Incorporating BEICFs directly into the capital model poses challenges given the subjectivity and structure of BEICF tools. The Committee has observed that BEICFs are widely used as an indirect input into the quantification framework and as an *ex post* adjustment to model output.

Source: Basel Committee on Banking Supervision, *Operational Risk – Supervisory Guidelines for the Advanced Measurement Approaches*, June 2011, extracted with abbreviations from points 40–42.

wondering if their operational risk numbers truly reflect their absolute level of risk, and whether these numbers can capture operational risk trends (e.g., the rise in operational risk related losses in the global financial crisis).

The Role of Key Risk Indicators[7]

The OpVaR number for a line of business or bank activity can provide an important indication of that business line's or activity's riskiness. But because quantifying operational risk remains a very inexact science, most banks make use of a number of techniques to try to understand their levels of exposure and to manage operational risk.

In any bank activity, there are likely to be a number of identifiable factors that tend to drive operational risk exposure and that are also relatively easy to track. For example, in the case of system risk, these key risk indicators (KRIs) might include the age of computer systems, the percentage of downtime as a result of system failure, and so on. Ideally, KRIs would be entirely objective

---

[7]Sometimes called key risk drivers (KRDs).

measures of some risk-related factor in a bank activity. However, we might also think of the audit score awarded to an activity or business line by the bank's internal audit team as a general example of a KRI.

Although KRIs are not a direct measure of operational risk, they are a kind of proxy for the level of risk exposure, the quality of the bank's operational performance, or the effectiveness of its controls.[8]

KRIs can be used to monitor changes in operational risk for each business and for each loss type, providing red flags that alert management to a rise in the likelihood of an operational risk event. Usually, this will mean establishing thresholds and limits for KRI values that signal an unwelcome change and that can be tied back to analysis of KRI data and operational deteriorations in the past. Unwelcome changes in KRIs can be used to prompt remedial management action, or tied to incentive schemes so that managers are given an incentive to manage their businesses in a way that is sensitive to operational risk exposures—though firms should remain aware that managing a KRI is not the same as managing the underlying risk.

KRIs are an important management information tool in themselves. But once they have been established, the bank is likely to want to map changes in an indicator to the corresponding changes in OpVaR, so that the KRI and OpVaR approaches offer consistent feedback to the bank's business lines.[9] In reality, it has proved a challenge for the financial industries to forge robust links between particular KRI levels and OpVaR, and judgment plays a significant role. However, as an illustrative example only, Table 14-2 shows that if the KRI score falls by 20 percent, OpVaR might be reduced by 15 percent.

Into the future, some firms think that using a weighted set of KRIs to produce a composite score or index may offer a metric that provides a better predictor of risk than relying on a set of individual KRIs. However, it should always be remembered that KRIs are indicators of particular changes in the risk environment, rather than true risk measures. Also, operational risk is composed of a variety of risk elements that don't have much in common: it is a challenge, for example, to combine the risk of a fire at a bank branch with the risk of fraud.

---

[8] For a longer discussion of the role of KRIs, see Institute of Operational Risk, *Key Risk Indicators*, November 2010. This is one of a series of sound practice papers published by the institute.

[9] Indeed, key risk drivers can form part of the input for the business environment and internal control factors that Basel regulators say banks must incorporate into their AMA approaches to quantifying operational risk for capital adequacy purposes.

TABLE 14-2 Example of Linkage of a Key Risk Indicator to OpVaR

	Δ KRI (%)	Δ OpVaR (%)
	+20	+25
	+10	+15
Base	0	0
	−10	−10
	−20	−15

Mitigating Operational Risk

Many banks and other financial institutions are presently struggling to rationalize how they decide which operational risks should be mitigated, and at what cost.

The process of operational risk assessment should include a review of the likelihood, or frequency, of a particular operational risk event, as well as a review of that event's possible magnitude or severity. Risk management can also integrate the distribution approach with a loss versus severity approach as described in Figure 14-4. Risk management could plot the severe amount of an operational risk (on the severity axis) and the expected frequency of an operational risk (on the likelihood axis). This diagram allows managers to visualize the trade-off between severity and likelihood. All risks along the curve exhibit the same expected loss—i.e., likelihood multiplied by severity. Point A5, for example, represents a low likelihood and a medium level of severity. Given an acceptable level of expected loss, management should take appropriate action to mitigate risks located above the curve—here, A7 and A8. A7 has a medium likelihood and medium severity, while A8 has a medium severity but a high likelihood. For both of these risks, the expected level of loss is above the acceptable level.

One major factor distinguishes operational risk from both market risk and credit risk. In making risk/reward decisions, a bank can often expect to gain a higher rate of return on its capital by assuming more market risk or credit risk—i.e., with these types of risk, there is a trade-off between risk and expected return. However, a bank cannot generally expect to gain a higher expected return by assuming more operational risk; operational risk destroys value for all claimholders.

This might suggest that banks should always try to minimize or mitigate operational risk. However, trying to reduce exposure to operational risk is costly.

FIGURE 14-4 Operational Risk Severity Versus Frequency

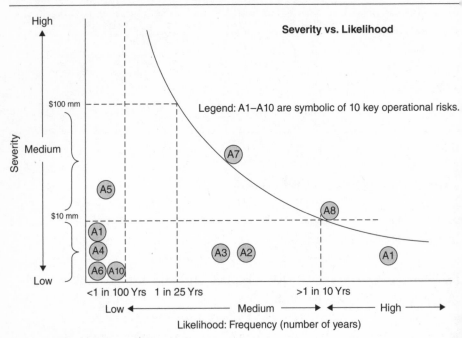

For example, a bank can install better IT systems with more security devices, and also a state-of-the-art backup system. But this investment in new technology is likely to cost the bank millions, or tens of millions, of dollars. Should the bank spend this amount of money to reduce its exposure? There is often no easy answer to this question. But banks can use the cost of risk capital (as indicated by OpVaR calculations) as one point of reference when assessing such operational risk mitigation decisions.

They can also compare the economic benefits and costs of many different kinds of risk mitigants, from system investments to risk capital to insurance. Purchasing insurance, for example, is not always an optimal policy, especially if the price for it is too high when compared to the alternative of self-insurance.

Insuring Against Operational Risk

Well before banks began to develop ways of measuring operational risks, they employed insurance contracts to mitigate the effects of key operational risk events. It is common for a bank to purchase insurance to protect itself from large single losses arising from acts of employee dishonesty (e.g., fictitious loans or unauthorized activities), robbery and theft, loans made against counterfeit securities, and various forms of computer crime.

Insurance protection for low-probability but highly severe losses such as these is available through contractually written insurance agreements, including an insurance vehicle known as the "financial institution bond and computer crime policy." Policies are also available in the insurance marketplace for catastrophic exposures associated with lawsuits (e.g., liability exposures arising from allegations of misrepresentation, breach of trust and fiduciary duty, or negligence) and for property damage resulting from major disasters such as fire or earthquake.

However, in essence, insurance is a mechanism for pooling and transferring common loss exposures within the industry or across economies. The availability of insurance for specific risks therefore depends on the ability of an insurer or group of insurers to generate sufficient premium volume and an adequate dispersion of risk to "make a market." It also depends on the insurer's being able to avoid the problem of *moral hazard*; that is, the insurer needs to make sure that the insured institution retains a strong interest in preventing any costly event. As a result, limits of up to US$500/$600 million per loss occurrence for large financial institutions are common, and banks often have to pay a "first loss" amount on operational risk insurance.

There also remains the danger that the insurance company will fail to pay out on an insurance policy that the bank is depending on for protection. The bank's overall methodology for operational risk measurement and management needs to capture, through discounts and haircuts in the amount of insurance recognition, residual risks such as the remaining life of the insurance policy (e.g., less than one year), chance of policy cancellation and nonrenewal, uncertainty of payment, and mismatches in coverage of insurance policies.

It should be noted that insuring against operational risks in a bank mainly benefits the depositors and debt holders of the bank—the stakeholders most concerned with rare but severe solvency-threatening events—while the cost of insuring is borne mainly by the shareholders. This may lead to a conflict of interest between the shareholders and debt holders of the bank.[10]

---

[10]See M. Crouhy, D. Galai, and R. Mark, "Insuring vs. Self-Insuring Operational Risk: The Viewpoint of Depositors and Shareholders," *Journal of Derivatives* 12(2), 2004, pp. 51–55.

In devising the regulatory capital charge for operational risks under Basel II, one of the most contentious points proved to be the extent to which regulators acknowledge the offsetting effects of insurance on a bank's operational risks. The most advanced methodology put forward by the regulators (AMA) recognizes the risk mitigation impact of insurance in the measures of operational risk used to calculate minimum regulatory capital requirements, but the benefit is limited to 20 percent of the total operational capital charge.

Many in the banking and insurance industry believe that the 20 percent limitation is a rather conservative reflection of the risk mitigation offered by operational risk insurance. Even so, insurance is now an important tool for banks to examine. Nevertheless, insurance cannot offer a complete answer to the problem of operational risk; it is simply one weapon in an armory that must contain a commitment to best-practice internal controls, operational risk measurement, key risk drivers, and risk capital.

Operational Risk in Nonbank Corporations

In this chapter we discuss how operational risk can be measured in banks and financial institutions. Operational risk, however, is also a critical risk in many nonbank corporations, including government agencies, nonprofit organizations, and others. Many of the terms, processes of identification, and estimation methodologies for operational risk developed in the financial industries can inform approaches in other industries. Human error can be extremely important in manufacturing industries and can cause fatal injuries. It is therefore essential for any firm to map its operational risk factors and then decide how to manage them.

Conclusion

The developments discussed in this chapter are helping institutions to select appropriate operational risk models and to manage their portfolios of operational risk more effectively. Increasingly, an institution will be able to gain a competitive advantage by monitoring and managing its operational risks on a global basis, although in order to achieve this, it is likely to have to confront some fundamental infrastructure issues.

Measuring operational risk in absolute terms is important, but it is still work in progress at an industry level. A more basic management objective is to track trends using key risk drivers, better understand how operational risk arises in business models and through failed procedures, and make operational risk increasingly transparent when the bank is taking key decisions. For example, the approaches we've described in this chapter can be used to answer the following key questions more clearly and explicitly:

- What is our largest operational risk in broad terms?
- Might the risk be large enough to threaten our solvency?
- What drives the risk in our internal and external environment?
- How is the risk changing over time?
- What risks are on the horizon?
- Will we be able to survive a selected set of plausible but extreme worst-case scenarios?
- How does our risk level compare to that of our peer group?

Another obvious objective is to provide better management of operational risk through specific action plans and rigorous implementation schedules. All too often, industry inquiries following an operational risk disaster, such as a rogue trader incident, reveal a trail of red flags leading up to the event. The trail often begins months or even years before the loss incident itself, and the red flags often include smaller losses with the same cause, "near misses" that should have alerted the bank to the risk of a large loss, or concerns raised by auditors or regulators that were not properly addressed by management.

Operational risk should be managed as a partnership between business units, business infrastructure groups, and corporate governance units such as internal audit and risk management. To this end, senior management must foster a risk-aware business culture. How the personnel of a firm behave ultimately depends on how senior management select, train, and reward them.

Arguably the greatest single challenge for senior management is to harmonize the behavior patterns of business units, infrastructure units, corporate governance units, internal audit, and risk management to create an environment in which all sides "sink or swim" together in terms of managing operational risk.

15

MODEL RISK

Models are the wonder and, on occasion, the curse of the modern financial world. They are used throughout the financial and corporate world for any number of purposes, and especially to put a number against the value, or the risk, of investments and financial positions. They have become central to many of the key corporate activities already discussed in this book, including market, credit, and asset/liability risk management.

Unfortunately, models can be wrong, in the sense of containing some internal error, and they can also be misapplied, fed the wrong input information, and their results misinterpreted. As our dependence on models to understand a complex world has grown, model risks have grown too, including within risk management. In this chapter, we explain the importance of model risk, using the example of market risk, examining:

- The extent of the problem
- Model error
- Implementation problems
- Mitigation of model risk
- A detailed case history: LTCM and model risk

Throughout the chapter, short case studies highlight the key issues, beginning with an examination of the JPMorgan Chase "London Whale" incident in 2012 (Box 15-1), which showed that model risk has no respect for the size or standing of an institution.

BOX 15-1 MODEL RISK AND GOVERNANCE: THE LONDON WHALE

During the first half of 2012, JPMorgan Chase lost billions of dollars from exposure to a massive credit derivative portfolio. We compiled this case study of the event using word-for-word extracts from the 300-page report produced by a subsequent Senate investigation.[1]

SETTING THE SCENE

"JP Morgan Chase & Company is the largest financial holding company in the United States, with $2.4 trillion in assets. It is also the largest derivatives dealer in the world and the largest single participant in world credit derivatives markets. Its principal bank subsidiary, JP Morgan Chase Bank, is the largest U.S. bank. JP Morgan Chase has consistently portrayed itself as an expert in risk management with a "fortress balance sheet" that ensures taxpayers have nothing to fear from its banking activities, including its extensive dealing in derivatives. But in early 2012, the bank's Chief Investment Office (CIO), which is charged with managing $350 billion in excess deposits, placed a massive bet on a complex set of synthetic credit derivatives that, in 2012, lost at least $6.2 billion.

The CIO's losses were the result of the so-called "London Whale" trades executed by traders in its London office—trades so large in size that they roiled world credit markets. Initially dismissed by the bank's chief executive as a "tempest in a teapot," the trading losses quickly doubled and then tripled despite a relatively benign credit environment. . . ."[2]

---

[1]United States Senate Permanent Subcommittee on Investigations, Carl Levin, Chairman, and John McCain, Ranking Minority Member, *JP Morgan Chase Whale Trades: A Case History of Derivatives Risks and Abuses*, Hearing, March 15, 2013. For the company's own account of the debacle, see *Report of JPMorgan Chase & Co Management Task Force Regarding 2012 CIO Losses*, January 16, 2013.

[2]Senate report, p. 1.

THE RISK EXPOSURE GROWS

". . . In 2006, the CIO approved a proposal to trade in synthetic derivatives, a new trading activity. In 2008, the CIO began calling its credit trading activity the Synthetic Credit Portfolio (SCP)."

"Three years later, in 2011, the SCP's net notional size jumped from $4 billion to $51 billion, a more than tenfold increase. In late 2011, the SCP bankrolled a $1 billion credit derivatives trading bet that produced a gain of approximately $400 million. In December 2011, JPMorgan Chase instructed the CIO to reduce its Risk Weighted Assets (RWA) to enable the bank, as a whole, to reduce its regulatory capital requirements. In response, in January 2012, rather than dispose of the high risk assets in the SCP – the most typical way to reduce RWA – the CIO launched a trading strategy that called for purchasing additional long credit derivatives to off-set its short derivatives positions and lower the CIO's RWA that way. That trading strategy not only ended up increasing the portfolio's size, risk, and RWA, but also, by taking the portfolio into a net long position, eliminated the hedging protections the SCP was originally supposed to provide."[3]

OPERATIONAL RISK: HIDING LOSSES

"In its first four years of operation, the SCP produced positive revenues, but in 2012, it opened the year with sustained losses. In January, February, and March, the days reporting losses far exceeded the days reporting profits, and there wasn't a single day when the SCP was in the black. To minimize its reported losses, the CIO began to deviate from the valuation practices it had used in the past to price credit derivatives. In early January, the CIO had typically established the daily value of a credit derivative by marking it at or near the midpoint price in the daily range of prices (bid-ask spread) offered in the market place. Using midpoint prices had enabled the CIO to comply with the requirement that it value its derivatives using prices that

---

[3]Senate report, pp. 3–4.

were the "most representative of fair value." But later in the first quarter of 2012, instead of marking near the midpoint, the CIO began to assign more favorable prices within the daily price range (bid-ask spread) to its credit derivatives. The more favorable prices enabled the CIO to report smaller losses in the daily profit/loss (P&L) reports that the SCP filed internally within the bank."

". . . by March 16, 2012, the SCP had reported year-to-date losses of $161 million, but if midpoint prices had been used, those losses would have swelled by at least another $432 million to a total of $593 million."[4]

". . . One result of the CIO's using more favorable valuations was that two different business lines within JPMorgan Chase, the CIO and the Investment Bank, assigned different values to identical credit derivative holdings. Beginning in March 2012, as CIO counterparties learned of the price differences, several objected to the CIO's values, resulting in collateral disputes peaking at $690 million. In May, the bank's Deputy Chief Risk Officer . . . directed the CIO to mark its books in the same manner as the Investment Bank, which used an independent pricing service to identify the midpoints in the relevant price ranges. That change in valuation methodology resolved the collateral valuation disputes in favor of the CIO's counterparties and, at the same time, put an end to the mismarking."[5]

CORPORATE GOVERNANCE: POOR RISK CULTURE

"In contrast to JPMorgan Chase's reputation for best-in-class risk management, the whale trades exposed a bank culture in which risk limit breaches were routinely disregarded, risk metrics were frequently criticized or downplayed, and risk evaluation models were targeted by bank personnel seeking to produce artificially lower capital requirements."

"The CIO used five key metrics and limits to gauge and control the risks associated with its trading activities, including the Value-at-Risk

---

[4]Senate report, p. 96.

[5]Senate report, p. 6.

(VaR) limit, Credit Spread Widening 01 (CS01) limit, Credit Spread Widening 10% (CSW10%) limit, stress loss limits, and stop loss advisories. During the first three months of 2012, as the CIO traders added billions of dollars in complex credit derivatives to the SCP, the SCP trades breached the limits on all five risk metrics. In fact, from January 1 through April 30, 2012, CIO risk limits and advisories were breached more than 330 times."

". . . The SCP's many breaches were routinely reported to JPMorgan Chase and CIO management, risk personnel, and traders. The breaches did not, however, spark an in-depth review of the SCP or require immediate remedial actions to lower risk. Instead, the breaches were largely ignored or ended by raising the relevant risk limit."[6]

MODEL RISK: FUDGING VAR MODELS

". . . CIO traders, risk personnel, and quantitative analysts frequently attacked the accuracy of the risk metrics, downplaying the riskiness of credit derivatives and proposing risk measurement and model changes to lower risk results for the SCP. In the case of the CIO VaR, after analysts concluded the existing model was too conservative and overstated risk, an alternative CIO model was hurriedly adopted in late January 2012, while the CIO was in breach of its own and the bankwide VaR limit. The bank did not obtain OCC approval as it should have to use the model for the SCP. The CIO's new model immediately lowered the SCP's VaR by 50%, enabling the CIO not only to end its breach, but to engage in substantially more risky derivatives trading. Months later, the bank determined that the model was improperly implemented, requiring error-prone manual data entry and incorporating formula and calculation errors. On May 10, the bank backtracked, revoking the new VaR model due to its inaccuracy in portraying risk, and reinstating the prior model."[7] (See Figure 15B-1.)

---

[6] Senate report, p. 7.

[7] Senate report, pp. 7–8.

FIGURE 15B-1 Value-at-Risk for the CIO: "Old" vs. "New" VaR Model

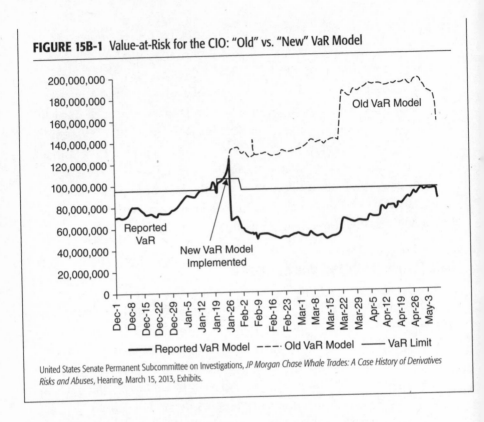

United States Senate Permanent Subcommittee on Investigations, *JP Morgan Chase Whale Trades: A Case History of Derivatives Risks and Abuses*, Hearing, March 15, 2013, Exhibits.

Why Model Risk Is Important: The Market Risk Example

For simple instruments, such as stocks and straight bonds, model risk is relatively insignificant. Market prices are normally the best indicator of the value of an asset. Model risk becomes a compelling issue, however, for institutions that trade over-the-counter (OTC) exotic derivative products and for institutions that execute complex arbitrage strategies.

In the absence of liquid markets and price discovery mechanisms, theoretical valuation models have to be used to value (or "mark-to-model") financial positions. The mark-to-model approach is accepted today both by the accounting boards (e.g., the American GAAP and the international IFRS) and by the regulatory bodies (e.g., the Basel Committee). Models are also used to assess risk exposure and to derive an appropriate hedging strategy, as we've discussed in detail in earlier chapters.

The danger of this dependence on models has been clear from early in the history of the derivatives markets. However, it became dramatically apparent during and after the 2007–2009 financial crisis, when severe losses on an entirely unexpected scale were sometimes incurred on trading positions. As a consequence, the Basel Committee required financial institutions to assess the model risk associated with their trading activities—i.e., the risk of losses due to using a wrong or misspecified model for pricing and hedging securities.[1]

Part of the challenge resides in complexity. Since 1973, with the publication of the Black-Scholes and Merton option pricing models, there has been a relentless increase in the complexity of valuation theories used to support financial innovations such as caps, floors, swaptions, spread options, credit derivatives, and other more exotic derivative instruments—and a parallel rise in the threat from model risk. Since 2004 we have seen a constant stream of new financial products based on market volatility, most notably options based on the VIX, a volatility index that we discuss below. However, product innovation has raced ahead of our ability to accurately price the new instruments or hedge the associated risks.

Technology has also played a role. Computers are now so powerful that there is a temptation to develop ever more complex models that are less and less understood by management. The technology that is available has substantially increased the chance of creating losses (as well as profits).

Today, we can liken the trader and the risk manager of a financial institution to the pilot and copilot of a plane that is almost totally dependent on instruments to land safely. Any error in the electronics on board combined with one heavy storm will be fatal to the plane.

The result is that not a single market crisis passes without several large trading losses that are the direct result of a faulty model. In the 2007–2009 crisis, model risk played a significant role in the overoptimistic rating of structured finance products (see Chapter 12), the underestimation of VaR numbers in many trading portfolios, and the poor performance of worst-case scenario analysis.

---

[1] According to the Basel Committee, "banks must explicitly assess the need for valuation adjustments to reflect two forms of model risk: the model risk associated with using a possibly incorrect valuation methodology, and the risk associated with using unobservable (and possibly incorrect) calibration parameters in the valuation model." Basel Committee on Banking Supervision, *Revisions to the Basel II Market Risk Framework, Bank for International Settlements,* February 2011.

How Widespread a Problem Is Model Risk?

The short answer is that in a modern financial system, model risk is everywhere—a fact that has been recognized for some decades. Back in 1997, the Bank of England conducted a survey highlighting the variation in models that existed among 40 major derivative trading firms based in London. Vanilla foreign exchange instruments showed a relatively low level of variation in both value and sensitivities, but some exotic derivatives displayed large variations not only in value but also in sensitivity measures: 10 to 20 percent for swaptions and up to 60 percent for exotic foreign exchange instruments. Another study in the same year showed that the different models available to calculate VaR sometimes gave very different answers when applied to the same portfolio.[2] (The authors of this book know from experience that different groups within the same financial institution can come up with significantly different valuations for similar instruments.)

It is therefore not surprising that trading firms of all kinds can experience substantial losses in stormy market environments, and sometimes even when things are calm. While most of these losses are the result of an accident or carelessness, and sometimes outright fraud, there is also the more insidious danger that a trader or other interested party might knowingly make a "mistake" that offers him or her beneficial results (in the short term, at least). Because models are used for valuation, a faulty model can make a strategy seem very profitable on paper even though the bank is incurring economic losses or unwise risk exposures—perhaps for several years. By the time the fault is corrected, a big hole may have appeared underneath the bank's accounts.

---

[2]Researchers presented an identical asset portfolio to a number of commercial vendors of software for value-at-risk (VaR) calculations. Each was asked to use the same volatility inputs, obtained from JP Morgan's Risk Metrics, and to report the aggregate VaR for the entire portfolio and the VaR figure for each type of instrument (such as swaps, caps and floors, and swaptions). The variation among vendors was striking, given that in this case they were supposed to be analyzing the same position (in relatively simple instruments), using the same methodology, and using the same market parameter values. For the whole portfolio, the estimates ranged from $3.8 million to $6.1 million, and for the portion containing options, the VaR estimates varied from $747,000 to $2,100,000. C. Marshall and M. Siegel, "Value-at-Risk: Implementing a Risk Measurement Standard," *Journal of Derivatives* 4(3), 1997, pp. 91–111.

In the next two sections of this chapter, we'll look more closely at the main causes of model risk:

- *Model error.* The model might contain mathematical errors or, more likely, be based on simplifying assumptions that are misleading or inappropriate.
- *Implementing a model wrongly.* The model might be implemented wrongly, either by accident or as part of a deliberate fraud.

Model Error

Derivatives trading depends heavily on mathematical models that make use of complex equations and advanced mathematics. In the simplest sense, a model is incorrect if there are mistakes in the analytical solution (in the set of equations or in the solution of a system of equations).

But a model is also said to be incorrect if it is based on wrong assumptions about the underlying asset price process—and this is perhaps both a more common and a more dangerous risk. The history of the financial industry is littered with examples of trading strategies based on shaky assumptions (see Box 15-2), and some model risks are really just a formalization of this kind of mistake. For example, a model of bond pricing might be based on a flat and fixed term structure at a time when the actual term structure of interest rates is steep and unstable.

BOX 15-2   WRONG ASSUMPTIONS: THE NIEDERHOFFER PUT OPTIONS EXAMPLE

A well-established hedge fund run by Victor Niederhoffer, a star trader on Wall Street, was wiped out in November 1997.[1] The fund had been writing a large quantity of naked (i.e., uncovered), deeply out-of-the-money put options on the S&P 500 stock index and collecting small amounts of option premium in return. Niederhoffer's trading strategy was based on the premise that the market would never drop by more than 5 percent

---

[1]See *Derivatives Strategy* 3(1), 1998, pp. 38–39.

on a given day. On October 27, 1997, the stock market fell by more than 7 percent in reaction to the crisis brewing in the Asian markets. (Such a fall would be virtually impossible if market returns were indeed normally distributed.) Liquidity, or rather the disappearance of liquidity after the market shock, brought the fund to its knees, and it found itself unable to meet margin calls for more than $50 million. As a consequence, Niederhoffer's brokers liquidated the positions at fire-sale prices, and the entire equity of the fund was lost.

The most frequent error in model building is to assume that the distribution of the underlying asset is stationary (i.e., unchanging) when in fact it changes over time. The case of volatility is particularly striking. For example, the volatility of the S&P 500 Index, measured by the VIX,[3] was approximately 15 percent at the beginning of July 2007, and by month-end it was over 30 percent. Later in the financial crisis, at the beginning of September 2008, the VIX was around 30 percent; within two weeks, following the collapse of Lehman Brothers, it had jumped to over 80 percent (Figure 5-5 in Chapter 5).[4] We can see how volatile the index was and how this might wrongfoot a model based on the assumption of constant volatility.

Derivatives practitioners know perfectly well that volatility is not constant and that the ideal solution would be to acknowledge that volatility is variable and to develop an option pricing model that is consistent with this. However, option valuation models become difficult computationally when any sort of stochastic volatility is included. (Moreover, introducing new unobservable parameters associated with the volatility process into the valuation model makes the estimation problem even more severe.)

Instead, derivative practitioners find themselves engaged in a continual struggle to find the best compromise between complexity (to better represent reality) and simplicity (to improve the tractability of their modeling).

While traders know that they are making simplifying assumptions about price behavior, it is not easy for them (or for risk managers) to assess the impact

---

[3] A well-known volatility index run by the Chicago Board Options Exchange (CBOE).

[4] These figures are all annualized.

of this kind of simplifying assumption on any given position or trading strategy. For example, practitioners often assume that rates of return are normally distributed—i.e., that they have a classic bell-shaped distribution. However, empirical evidence points to the existence of "fat tails" in many distributions; in these distributions, unlikely events are in fact much more common than would be the case if the distribution were normally distributed. Where possible, therefore, empirical distributions rather than theoretical distributions should be used to help alleviate the danger of an unrecognized fat tail. However, such fat tails are not accounted for in the theoretical distributions that lie behind many of the classic models reviewed in Chapter 5 (such as the CAPM or Black-Scholes option pricing model).

Another way to oversimplify a model is to underestimate the number of risk factors that it must take into account. For simple vanilla investment products, such as a callable bond, a one-factor term structure model, where the factor represents the spot short-term rate, may be enough to produce accurate prices and hedge ratios. For more complex products, such as spread options or exotic structures, not to mention a 30-year Bermudan swaption contract, a two- or three-factor model may be required, where the factors are, for example, the spot short-term and long-term rates for a two-factor model.

Another problem is that models are almost always derived under the assumption that perfect capital markets exist. In reality, many markets, especially those in less developed countries, are far from perfect. Meanwhile, even in developed markets, over-the-counter derivative products are not traded publicly and usually cannot be perfectly hedged.

As a practical example, most derivative pricing models are based on the assumption that a delta-neutral hedging strategy can be put in place for the instruments in question—i.e., that the risk of holding a derivative can be continually offset by holding the underlying asset in an appropriate proportion (hedge ratio). In practice, a delta-neutral hedge of an option against its underlying asset is far from being completely risk-free, and keeping such a position delta-neutral over time often requires a very active rebalancing strategy. Banks rarely attempt the continuous rebalancing that pricing models assume. For one thing, the theoretical strategy implies the execution of an enormous number of transactions, and trading costs are too large for this to be feasible. Nor is continuous trading possible, even disregarding transactions costs: markets close at night, on national holidays, and on weekends.

Liquidity, or rather the absence of liquidity, can also be a major source of model risk. Models assume that the underlying asset can be traded long or short at current market prices and that prices will not change dramatically when the trade is executed. During the 2007–2009 financial crisis, even some highly rated bonds that were considered very safe and liquid could not be traded for a period due to a lack of liquidity.

A model can be found to be mathematically correct and generally useful and yet be misapplied to a given situation. For example, some term structure models that are widely used to value fixed-income instruments depend upon the assumption that forward rates are "log normal"—that is, that their rates of change are normally distributed. This model seems to perform relatively well when applied to most of the world's markets—with the exception of Japan for the last 10 years and the United States and Europe in the immediate post-crisis years (because central banks implemented "quantitative easing" monetary policies and flooded the markets with huge amount of liquidity). Post-crisis markets were characterized by very low interest rates, and Japan sometimes exhibited negative rates; in these conditions, different statistical tools (e.g., Gaussian and square root models) for interest rates work much better.

In the same way, models that are safe to use for certain kinds of product might not perform well when applied to subtly different instruments. Many OTC products have options embedded within them that are ignored in the standard option pricing model. For example, using a model to value warrants may yield biased results if the warrant is also extendable. Other common errors include using the Black-Scholes option valuation model to price equity options, adjusting for dividends by subtracting their present value from the stock price. This ignores the fact that the options can be exercised early. Applying the wrong model is also easy if the researcher is not clear about whether the underlying instrument is a primary asset or is itself contingent on another underlying asset (or basket of assets).

Implementing a Model Wrongly

Even if a model is correct and is being used to tackle an appropriate problem, there remains the danger that it will be wrongly implemented. With complicated models that require extensive programming, there is always a chance that a programming "bug" may affect the output of the model. Some implementations rely on numerical techniques that exhibit inherent approximation errors and limited ranges of validity. Many programs that seem error-free have been tested only under normal conditions and so may be error-prone in extreme cases and conditions.

In models that require a Monte Carlo simulation, large inaccuracies in prices and hedge ratios can creep in if not enough simulation runs or time steps are implemented. In this case, the model might be right, and the data might be accurate, but the results might still be wrong if the computation process is not given the time it needs.

For models evaluating complex derivatives, data are collected from many different sources. The implicit assumption is that for each time period, the data for all relevant assets and rates pertain to exactly the same time instant and thus reflect simultaneous prices. Using nonsimultaneous price inputs may be necessary for practical reasons, but, again, it can lead to wrong pricing.

When implementing a pricing model, researchers use statistical tools to estimate model parameters such as volatilities and correlations. An important question, then, is, how frequently should input parameters be refreshed? Should the adjustment be made on a periodic basis, or should it be triggered by an important economic event? Similarly, should parameters be adjusted according to qualitative judgments, or should these adjustments be based purely on statistics? The statistical approach is bound to be in some sense "backward looking," whereas a human adjustment can be forward looking—that is, it can take into account a personal assessment of likely future developments in the relevant markets.

All statistical estimators are subject to estimation errors involving the inputs to the pricing model. A major problem in the estimation procedure is the treatment of "outliers," or extreme observations. Are the outliers really outliers, in the sense that they do not reflect the true distribution? Or are they important observations that should not be dismissed? The results of the estimation procedure will be vastly different depending on how such observations are treated. Each bank, or even each trading desk within a bank, may use a different estimation procedure to estimate the model parameters. Some may use daily closing prices, while others may use transaction data. Whether the researcher uses calendar time (i.e., the actual number of days elapsed), trading time (i.e., the number of days on which the underlying instrument is traded), or economic time (i.e., the number of days during which significant economic events take place) affects the calculation.

Finally, the quality of a model depends heavily on the accuracy of the inputs and parameter values that feed the model. It's easy for traders to make mistakes (Box 15-3). This is particularly true in the case of relatively new markets, where best-practice procedures and controls are still evolving. The old adage "garbage in, garbage out" should never be forgotten when implementing models that require the estimation of several parameters.

Volatilities and correlations are the hardest input parameters to judge accurately. For example, an option's strike price and maturity are fixed, and asset prices and interest rates can easily be observed directly in the market—but volatilities and correlations must be forecast.

BOX 15-3 WRONG RATE INPUT: THE MERRILL LYNCH EXAMPLE

In the mid-1970s, the Wall Street investment firm Merrill Lynch began to break down (or "strip") 30-year government bonds into their building-block components: coupon annuities and zero-coupon principal payments. It then offered these components to the market as "interest only" (IO) and "principal only" (PO) instruments.

Merrill used the 30-year par yield to price the IOs and the POs. The par yield curve was higher than the annuity yield curve, but lower than the zero-coupon curve. Therefore, by using the par rate rather than the annuity rate, the firm undervalued the IOs, and by using the par rate rather than the zero-coupon rate, it overvalued the POs, although the sum of the two valuations did add up to the bond's true value. Merrill sold $600 million of the undervalued IOs and none of the overvalued POs.

Meanwhile, the Merrill Lynch trader hedged the 30-year bonds using a duration of approximately 13 years. This was the correct decision for the bonds as long as the entire bond remained intact on the books of Merrill Lynch. However, even after all the IO components of the bonds were sold, the trader maintained the hedge at 13 years, whereas the correct duration of a 30-year PO instrument is 30 years. When interest rates rose, the firm incurred severe losses. In combination with the misvaluations, this hedging mistake resulted in the firm's booking a $70 million loss.

The subprime crisis highlighted, in a cruel way, the problem of making assumptions about correlations and assuming that return distributions are stationary.[5] At a time of financial crisis, correlations move toward the extremes, either +1 or −1, meaning that all risk factors move fully in the same direction or move fully in the opposite direction, respectively. This represents a discontinuity in correlation that can trigger a sudden jump in risk (i.e., a nonlinearity), as illustrated by the sudden default of AAA-rated tranches of subprime CDOs (Box 15-4).

BOX 15-4   MODEL RISK: STRUCTURED PRODUCTS AND CLIFF EFFECTS

Structured credit products such as collateralized debt obligations (CDOs) are highly leveraged products. The performance of each tranche depends on the position of the tranche in the capital structure of the CDO, in combination with the amount of any realized credit losses from the underlying assets.

Various structural features, such as the nature of the payment waterfalls through the tranches and any triggers that require credit enhancements or liquidation of the CDO investment vehicle, tend to create "cliff effects" (or nonlinearities) in performance. In addition, the potential loss amount depends on parameters that are hard to estimate, such as the cumulative default rate of mortgages for a particular vintage, loss given default, and default correlations. These parameters are not stable over time and strongly depend on the economic environment.

We can understand the combined effect of this better through a quick look at the investments underpinning CDO performance. In subprime CDOs, the collateral is made up of MBS—i.e., subprime bonds that are themselves tranches of pools of individual subprime mortgages.[1]

---

[1] The collateral of an MBS bond is typically composed of 3,000 to 5,000 individual mortgages.

In the first edition of this book, prepared in 2005, we warned readers that they should beware of the subprime market because it was a new market lacking in historical default data, especially downturn data (Box 9-4, p. 216).

(A subprime CDO is therefore really a kind of CDO-squared.) Typically, the collateral of a subprime CDO comprises about 100 subprime MBS series whose ratings vary between BB and AA, with an average rating of BBB.

One problem is that the initial level of subordination for a triple-B mortgage bond is relatively small, between 3 and 5 percent of the size of the CDO, and the width of the tranche is very thin at around 2.5 to 4 percent maximum (and sometimes less than 1 percent). A default rate of 20 percent on subprime mortgages and a recovery of 50 percent on foreclosed homes—realistic numbers at the peak of the subprime crisis—would be likely to hit triple-B tranches.

Moreover, the general downturn in the housing market and the sharp recession showed that the loss correlation across all the triple-B tranches was very high (in some circumstances, close to 1). With hindsight, we can see that if one triple-B tranche was hit, most were likely to be hit. And, given the thin width of the tranches, most MBS bonds would then be wiped out, in turn wiping out the super-senior tranche of the subprime CDO.

The result was that investors in CDOs unwittingly found themselves in a binary situation. Either the cumulative default rate of the subprime mortgages remained below the threshold that left underlying MBS bonds untouched, or the cumulative default rate would breach this threshold, after which it was highly likely that the super-senior tranches of subprime CDOs could all be wiped out.

To analyze the credit risk contribution of each CDO tranche at the portfolio level using standard credit VaR models, most banks used a credit proxy: a corporate bond with the same rating as the rating given by the rating agency to the tranche. However, this by no means captured the cliff effect built into CDOs and led to a massive underestimation of the risk of structured credit products in bank portfolios.

Throughout the history of the derivatives markets, the fact that model parameters such as volatility and correlation cannot be observed directly has given rise to many opportunities for both genuine mistakes and deliberate tampering that can be countered only through robust control procedures and independent vetting (see Box 15-5).

The most frequent problems in estimating values, on the one hand, and assessing the potential errors in valuation, on the other, are:

- *Inaccurate data.* Most financial institutions use internal data sources as well as external databases. The responsibility for data accuracy is often not clearly assigned. It is therefore very common to find data errors that can significantly affect the estimated parameters.
- *Inappropriate length of sampling period.* Adding more observations improves the power of statistical tests and tends to reduce the estimation errors. But the longer the sampling period, the more weight is given to potentially stale and obsolete information. Especially in dynamically changing financial markets, "old" data can become irrelevant and may introduce noise into the estimation process.
- *Problems with liquidity and the bid/ask spread.* In some markets, a robust market price does not exist. The gap between the bid and ask prices may be large enough to complicate the process of finding a single value. Choices made about the price data at the time of data selection can have a major impact on the output of the model.

BOX 15-5 IMPLEMENTATION RISK: THE NATWEST OPTION PRICING EXAMPLE

In 1997 it was discovered that certain traders at NatWest in London had been selling caps and swaptions in sterling and Deutsche marks at the wrong price since late 1994 and had been hedging their short position by buying options priced at too high a volatility vis-à-vis the volatility implied by the swaption premiums. When these discontinuities, especially for long maturities, were removed from the volatility curves in 1997, the downward revisions of NatWest's portfolio value resulted in a loss of $80 million. For risk managers around the world, verifying volatility estimates and, more generally, all the other principal inputs to a pricing model that are handed to them by a trader is a critical issue.

How Can We Mitigate Model Risk?

One important way to mitigate model risk is to invest in research to improve models and to develop better statistical tools, either internally at the bank or externally at a university (or at an analytically oriented consulting organization).

An even more vital way of reducing model risk is to establish a process for the independent vetting of how models are both selected and constructed. This should be complemented by independent oversight of the profit and loss (P&L) calculation.

The role of vetting is to offer assurance to the firm's management that any model for the valuation of a given security proposed by, say, a trading desk is reasonable. In other words, it provides assurance that the model offers a reasonable representation of how the market itself values the instrument, and that the model has been implemented correctly. Vetting should consist of the following phases:

1. *Documentation.* The vetting team should ask for full documentation of the model, including both the assumptions underlying the model and its mathematical expression. This should be independent of any particular implementation, such as a spreadsheet, R (a statistical programming language), or a C++ computer code, and should include:
   - The term sheet or, equivalently, a complete description of the transaction
   - A mathematical statement of the model, which should include:
     - An explicit statement of all the components of the model: stochastic variables and their processes, parameters, equations, and so on
     - The payoff function and/or any pricing algorithm for complex structured deals
     - The calibration procedure for the model parameters
     - The hedge ratios/sensitivities
   - Implementation features—i.e., inputs, outputs, and numerical methods employed
   - A working version of the implementation
2. *Soundness of model.* An independent model vetter needs to verify that the mathematical model is a reasonable representation of the instru-

ment that is being valued. For example, the manager might reasonably accept the use of a particular model (e.g., the Black model) for valuing a short-term option on a long-maturity bond but reject (without even looking at the computer code) the use of the same model to value a two-year option on a three-year bond. At this stage, the risk manager should concentrate on the finance aspects and not become overly focused on the mathematics.

3. *Independent access to financial rates.* The model vetter should check that the middle office has independent access to an independent market risk management financial rates database (to facilitate independent parameter estimation).

4. *Benchmark modeling.* The model vetter should develop a benchmark model based on the assumptions that are being made and on the specifications of the deal. Here the model vetter may use a different implementation from the implementation that is being proposed. A proposed analytical model can be tested against a numerical approximation technique or against a simulation approach. (For example, if the model to be vetted is based on a "tree" implementation, one may instead rely on the partial differential equation approach and use the finite-element technique to derive the numerical results.) Compare the results of the benchmark test with those of the proposed model.

5. *Health check and stress test the model.* Also, make sure that the model possesses the basic properties that all derivatives models should possess, such as put/call parity and other nonarbitrage conditions. Finally, the vetter should stress test the model. The model can be stress tested by looking at some limit scenario in order to identify the range of parameter values for which the model provides accurate pricing. This is especially important for implementations that rely on numerical techniques.

6. *Build a formal treatment of model risk into the overall risk management procedures, and periodically reevaluate models.* Also, reestimate parameters using best-practice statistical procedures. Experience shows that simple but robust models tend to work better than more ambitious but fragile models. It is essential to monitor and control model performance over time.

LTCM and Model Risk: How a Hedge Became Ineffective During a Liquidity Crisis

The failure of the hedge fund Long Term Capital Management (LTCM) in September 1998 provides the classic example of model risk in the financial industry. The failure shocked the financial community, not only because of the reputation of LTCM's principals (including two Nobel laureates along with seasoned and star traders from the legendary bond arbitrage desk at Salomon Brothers) but also because of the unprecedented amounts of capital represented by the firm's positions. LTCM's initial capital grew from $1.1 billion in March 1994 to $6.7 billion in August 1997. LTCM began 1998 with $4.8 billion in capital after having returned $2.7 billion to outside investors and employed $125 billion in total assets—that is, it had a leverage ratio of more than 25.

LTCM's crisis was triggered on August 17, 1998, when Russia devalued the ruble and declared a debt moratorium. LTCM's equity value fell 44 percent, giving it a year-to-date decline of 52 percent (a loss of almost $2 billion). The hedge fund's positions in the market were so great that the Federal Reserve Bank of New York took the unprecedented step of facilitating a bailout of the fund to avoid any risk of a meltdown in the world markets.

How could a market event, however serious, have affected LTCM so badly? LTCM's arbitrage strategy was based on "market-neutral" or "relative-value" trading, which involves buying one instrument and simultaneously selling another. These trades are designed to make money whether prices rise or fall, as long as the spread between the two positions moves in the appropriate direction.

LTCM, like other hedge funds in early 1998, had positioned its portfolios on the basis of particular bets, albeit bets that seemed pretty safe at first sight. For example, LTCM bet that the spreads between corporate bonds and government Treasuries in different countries, such as the United States and the United Kingdom, were too large and would eventually return to their normal range (as they had always done before). Such strategies are based on intensive empirical research and advanced financial modeling. A trade to capture the relative-value opportunities uncovered by such modeling might consist of buying corporate bonds and selling the relevant government bonds short. Other positions involved betting on convergence in the key European bond markets by selling German government bonds against the sovereign debt of other countries, such as Spain and Italy, which were due to sign up for European economic and monetary union (EMU). When the spread in yields narrows, such positions make money whether the price level goes up or down.

The return on such apparently low-risk strategies tends to be quite small, and it becomes smaller and smaller as more players enter the market to take advantage of the "opportunity." As a result, hedge funds are obliged to use leverage aggressively to boost their absolute performance. LTCM, for example, was trying to earn a 1 percent return on its assets, leveraged 25 times, which would yield a 25 percent return. LTCM was able to obtain huge loans, collateralized by the bonds that it had invested in, because its strategy was widely viewed as safe by the institutions that were its lenders.

LTCM failed because both its trading models and its risk management models failed to anticipate the vicious circle of losses during an extreme crisis when volatilities rose dramatically, correlations between markets and instruments became closer to 1, and liquidity dried up. Let us take a closer look at both of these aspects.

Trading Models

Price relationships that hold during normal market conditions tend to collapse during market crises such as that of August 1998. The crisis in Russia made many investors fear that other nations might follow Russia's lead and that there would be a general dislocation of the financial markets. This triggered a "flight to quality" or "flight to safety," as investors exited the emerging markets and any risky security and fled to the liquid and safe haven of the U.S. and German government bond markets.

These trends ultimately pushed the yield of U.S. 30-year government bonds to as low as 5 percent and caused the price of riskier bonds, including those of emerging markets, U.S. mortgage-backed securities, high-yield bonds, and even investment-grade corporate bonds, to sink. The same phenomena affected the relative yields of German and Italian bonds: yields started to diverge because German bonds were regarded as safer than Italian bonds. Credit spreads widened as prices for Treasury bonds increased and prices for lower-quality bonds sank—again, in an unprecedented fashion.

When spreads widened, the gains that a trader might make on short positions were not always enough to offset the losses on the long positions. Lenders therefore started to demand more collateral, forcing many hedge funds either to abandon their arbitrage plays or to raise money for the margin calls by selling other holdings at fire-sale prices. Most markets around the world, especially emerging markets, became less liquid and highly volatile.

Most of the losses incurred by LTCM were the consequence of the breakdown of the correlation and volatility patterns that had been observed in the past. Several mechanisms came into play during this market turmoil as a consequence of the "flight to quality" and the disappearance of liquidity:

1. Interest rates on Treasuries and stock prices fell in tandem, because investors deserted the stock market and purchased U.S. government bonds in a flight to quality. In normal markets, stock returns and interest rates are negatively correlated—i.e., when interest rates fall, stock prices rise.
2. When liquidity dries up in many markets simultaneously, it becomes impossible to unwind positions. Portfolios that seem to be well diversified across markets start to behave as if they were highly concentrated in a single market, and market-neutral positions become directionally exposed (usually to the wrong side of the market).

For all these reasons, LTCM found itself losing money on many of its trading positions and looked in danger of becoming insolvent. The fact that the fund was highly leveraged contributed to its problems. First, LTCM ran out of cash and was unable to meet margin calls in a timely fashion. Second, with excessive leverage amplifying its funding risk, LTCM was obliged to liquidate securities at fire-sale prices. At some point, the firm's liabilities threatened to exceed its assets; to keep the firm solvent, a number of major financial institutions were obliged to inject considerable sums.

Risk Measurement Models and Stress Testing

Risk control at LTCM relied on a VaR model. As discussed in Chapter 7, VaR represents the worst-case loss that can result from a firm's portfolio under normal market conditions, at a given confidence level, and over a given period of time. By itself, a $1 trillion notional amount, or even a figure of $125 billion in assets, does not say much about the levels of risk that the LTCM positions involved. What matters is the overall volatility of the marked-to-market value of the fund—that is, its VaR.

According to LTCM, the fund was structured so that the risk of investing in it should have been no greater than that of investing in the S&P 500. Based on the volatility of the S&P, and with equity of $4.7 billion, the expected daily volatility of LTCM should have been $44 million, and its 10-day VaR should have been approximately $320 million (at a confidence level of 99 percent). This number is calculated under the assumption that the portfolio returns are normally distributed.

However, some assumptions that are usual in regulatory VaR calculations are not realistic for a hedge fund:

1. The time horizon for economic capital should be the time it takes to raise new capital or the period of time over which a crisis scenario will unfold. Based on the experience of LTCM, 10 days is clearly too short a time horizon for the derivation of hedge fund VaR.
2. Liquidity risk is not factored into traditional static VaR models. VaR models assume that normal market conditions prevail and that these exhibit perfect liquidity.
3. Correlation and volatility risks can be captured only through stress testing. This was probably the weakest point of LTCM's VaR system.

After the crisis, William McDonough, president of the Federal Reserve Bank of New York, told the Committee on Banking and Financial Services of the U.S. House of Representatives:

> We recognize that stress testing is a developing discipline, but it is clear that adequate testing was not done with respect to the financial conditions that precipitated Long-Term Capital's problems. Effective risk management in a financial institution requires not only modeling, but models that can test the full range of financial transactions across all kinds of adverse market developments.

Instead of the envisaged $44 million daily volatility, the fund eventually experienced a $100 million and higher daily volatility. While the 10-day VaR was approximately $320 million, LTCM suffered losses of more than $1 billion from mid-August. LTCM's risk modeling had let it down.

Conclusion

Models are an inevitable feature of modern finance, and model risk is inherent in the use of models. Although our examples in this chapter have focused on market risk, many of the principles we have discussed can be applied to make model risk transparent in other spheres, including credit risk and asset/liability management.

The most important thing is to be aware of the dangers. Firms must avoid placing undue faith in the results offered by models and must hunt down all the possible sources of inaccuracy in a model. In particular, they must learn to think through situations in which the failure of a model might have a significant impact.

In this chapter, we've stressed the technical elements of model risk, but we should also be wary of the human factor in model risk losses. Large trading profits tend to lead to large bonuses for senior managers, and this creates an incentive for these managers to believe the traders who are reporting the profits (rather than the risk managers or other critics who might be questioning the reported profits). Often, traders use their expertise in formal pricing models to confound any internal critics, or they may claim to have some sort of informal but profound insight into how markets behave. The psychology of this behavior is such that we are tempted to call it the "Tinkerbell" phenomenon, after the scene in *Peter Pan* in which the children in the audience shout "I believe, I believe" in order to revive the poisoned fairy Tinkerbell (see Box 15-6). The antidote is for senior managers to approach any model that seems to record or deliver above-market returns with a healthy skepticism, to insist that models be made transparent, and to make sure that all models are independently vetted.

BOX 15-6   "TINKERBELL" RISK: BARINGS, 1995

The infamous destruction of Barings Bank by Nick Leeson in 1995 shows why large profits should act as a red flag for risk—and should prompt as much curiosity as happiness.

After moving to Singapore in June 1993 as local head of operations, Leeson started to execute trades for Barings' clients on Simex. He then received permission to implement an arbitrage strategy that was designed to exploit any differences between the prices for the Nikkei futures contract in Singapore and Osaka. Since he still controlled the Singapore back office, he was able to use a reconciliation account, #88888 (which he arranged to be excluded from the reports sent to London), to convert an actual loss of £200 million in 1994 into a sizable reported profit.

Leeson's reported profit was so large that it attracted the attention of Barings' London-based risk controllers in late 1994. However, their inquiries to his superiors were rebuffed with the comment, "Barings had a unique ability to exploit this arbitrage." After he reported a £10 million profit for one week in January 1995, risk control concerns were again summarily dismissed with the comment, "Nick is a turbo-arbitrageur." Simple calculations show that in order to make this profit, Leeson would have had to trade more than four times the total volume in the Nikkei futures contract in both Singapore and Osaka that week.

The main lesson drawn from the Barings collapse was that the front office (trading) and the middle or back office, for the purpose of control, should be separated: reporting and monitoring of positions and risks must be separated from trading. But a more general conclusion is that great success stories should always be independently checked and monitored tightly, to verify that the reported profits are for real—and continue to be for real.

16

STRESS TESTING AND SCENARIO ANALYSIS

Stress testing and scenario analysis offer a way for firms to look at the potential downside of their portfolios and businesses by thinking through the impact either of a very particular stress or of some more generalized downturn scenario.

A big advantage of the approach is that the firm is free to imagine any potentially damaging situation; it is not bound to consider only past or expected events or to limit the extent of its pessimism in other ways. It can use its imagination and business intuition. The outcome can then be analyzed at the level of product, portfolio, or enterprise.

The balance between art and science in stress testing is equally flexible, regulatory expectations aside. A stress test can vary from a simple imagining of the worst to a full-blown quantitative analysis of enterprise balance sheets (e.g., employing the credit and asset/liability systems of a major institution).

Stress testing and scenario analysis have been part of the corporate risk management armory for some decades. However, in the financial industries they have taken on a prominent role since the great financial crisis of 2007–2009 (the GFC). In this chapter we look at the reasons for this, at the types of stress and scenario testing that can be applied, the new regulatory trends that support and enforce financial institution stress testing programs, and best practice in stress testing.

Why Has Stress Testing Moved to the Fore?

The financial crisis of 2007–2009 highlighted a number of significant shortcomings in risk management and risk modeling. Models are powerful tools, but, as discussed in Chapter 15, they necessarily involve simplifications. No model can possibly capture the full extent of a risk in all its dimensions, potential interactions, and ramifications. It follows that treating the results of a risk model, a risk metric, or some similar output (such as a rating) as if it were an end in itself can be an obstacle to risk identification. Expert judgment, critical analysis, and the willingness to think a problem through and look at the bigger picture are always necessary.

In Chapter 7, we described the strengths and limitations of VaR (value-at-risk), which has been a standard risk model in the banking industry since the late 1990s. VaR serves as one useful risk measure for certain kinds of risk during normal market conditions. However, the recent crisis highlighted its limitations when either liquidity dries up or large tail events occur. Such events are a common feature of financial crises, and VaR, as a static model, does not adequately capture their impact. VaR analysis, as commonly practiced, also fails to address volatility jumps and changing correlations and can miss important nonlinearities in structured products such as subprime CDOs.

Also, most VaR models focus on hypothetical mark-to-market (MtM) changes but fail to model risk in relation to collateral calls (e.g., on a repo transaction), credit-related downgrades, operational risk events (e.g., fraud), and so on. The traditional VaR model does not easily capture exposures in trending markets over multiyear time periods (e.g., during bubbles) and the risk of instruments with nonlinear price movements—e.g., a dramatic jump in the implied volatility surface for an exotic option. We discussed many of these issues, which are part of what we refer to as "model risk," in Chapter 15.

VaR was not the only aspect of risk measurement that lost credibility during the 2007–2009 financial crisis. More generally, the financial industry's overly quantitative approach to risk, its tendency to rely on "black box" model output, and its seeming inability to understand systemic interconnections and "think the unthinkable" also came under fire.

This is where stress and scenario testing comes into its own. At their best, stress tests help make risk management more transparent by answering intuitive questions such as "How much money would we lose if the dollar fell 20 percent against sterling?" Comprehensive scenario testing tries to forge a more holistic vision of risk, helping an institution to understand the balance sheet impact of stresses on revenues, losses, and capital adequacy of a whole range of risks and risk interactions. Furthermore, focusing on a scenario encourages management to think about the risk interactions (e.g., liquidity and market risk) in a crisis situation.

The hope is that by complementing the use of risk metrics such as VaR with additional risk measurement tools such as stress tests and scenario analysis, the financial industry will add a degree of informed, qualitative judgment to quantitative rigor. It will help in highlighting some of the potential weak points of other forms of risk assessment and management.

It should be emphasized at the outset, however, that stress testing is more of an ad hoc practical approach than one entrenched in theoretical considerations. There is no economic or financial theory to support stress testing, and its usefulness depends considerably on the qualitative thought processes involved in identifying key risks and scenarios and the nature of their interactions and impacts on a firm. Nevertheless, it can be very useful in the strategic and planning process of an organization.

Types of Stress Testing and Scenario Analysis: Overview

Stress testing and scenario analysis are blanket terms that cover a wide range of methodologies, from simple sensitivity analysis to risk factor stress testing and scenario analysis.[1] Readers of the literature should be aware that, in this area of risk management, the various terms are often used loosely.

Sensitivity analysis usually indicates that the analyst changes one risk parameter only, keeping all others constant, and then measures the impact of such a change—e.g., on the value or profitability of the portfolio of assets or liabilities. The point of this is that it helps to identify the risk factors to which the portfolio is most sensitive. Traditionally, the shift in the risk parameter is not extreme.

Stress testing at the risk factor level, an activity sometimes included in the term sensitivity analysis, involves applying more extreme shocks to individual parameters or inputs. The shocks are applied without any formal reference to a wider market scenario. For example, a test might explore the impact of a drop in equity index values by 10, 20, or 30 percent; a parallel yield curve shift of plus

---

[1]See B. Schachter, "Stress Testing and Scenario Analysis," *The Encyclopedia of Quantitative Finance*, Wiley, 2010.

or minus 100 bps; a yield curve twist of plus or minus 25 bps; a currency change of plus or minus 6 percent; or a change in volatility of plus or minus 20 percent.[2]

This kind of stress testing can be particularly important for portfolios with strong nonlinearities and large negative gammas. Portfolios of this kind can incur losses whether prices rise or fall, and the magnitude of the losses accelerates as the change in price increases. Single factor stress testing ignores the existence of multiple risk factors and feedback effects, but in doing so the test gains in clarity, offering a quick assessment of portfolio sensitivity to a given risk factor and particular risk concentrations. In the next section we look at a more involved approach to risk factor stress testing that combines various tests within so-called "stress envelopes."

By contrast, *scenario analysis*, or holistic stress testing, aims to assess the impact of extreme macroeconomic as well as microeconomic events on measures such as earnings, liquidity, and economic capital. Scenario analysis often involves an extra translation stage in which the particular scenario that is to be examined is translated into a series of impacts on the risk factors that drive the portfolio in question. Scenario analysis also implies a more holistic approach in which all of the risk factors are assumed to change over the same period and the risk factors may have an effect on each other—though the degree to which this is taken into account varies considerably in practice. The macroeconomic and lower-level risk factors are also assumed to be shocked in a consistent manner,[3] according to a specific market event that is usually characterized as extreme but plausible and relevant. Scenario analyses are therefore more complex to implement, and they require a major IT investment to aggregate positions from the various bank businesses (bank systems do not necessarily communicate with one another). Later in the chapter we discuss the scenario analysis approach in more detail with examples of historical scenario replication and hypothetical one-off scenarios.

In the following we use stress testing as a generic term that includes sensitivity analysis and scenario analysis, except when specific differentiation is required in the discussion.

---

[2]These examples are loosely drawn from some specific guidelines set out back in 1995 by the Derivatives Policy Group. For the precise list, see Derivatives Policy Group, *A Framework for Voluntary Oversight*, 1995.

[3]Consistency is important in creating realistic scenario shocks because of the relationship between certain risk factors. For example, it is highly unusual to have a scenario in which U.S. stock indices fall, say, by 6 percent, and European stock indices rise sharply at the same time.

Stress Testing Envelopes

Stress testing is becoming more and more sophisticated, and one of the challenges is to work out a rigorous way of applying different kinds of stress to portfolios in a consistent manner. Here we'll consider a "stress envelope" methodology, which combines stress categories with the worst possible stress shocks across all possible markets for every business. The idea here is that after calculating the worst possible stress shocks for the relevant markets, it becomes much easier to create ad hoc scenarios by looking at combinations of these shocks at lower stress levels.

For example, as a first step, the methodology might designate seven stress categories corresponding to the various risk categories: interest rates, foreign exchange rates, equity prices, commodity prices, credit spreads, swap spreads, and volatility (vega). For each stress category, the worst possible stress shocks that might realistically occur in the market are defined. In the case of interest rates, for example, the methodology defines six stress shocks to accommodate both changes in the *level* of rates and changes in the *shape* of the yield curve (slope of the short end and the long end of the curve). In the case of credit spreads and equities, there is only one stress shock—i.e., the widening of credit spreads and the fall of equity prices, respectively. All other stress categories make use of one or two stress shocks (increases or decreases in spreads or prices), as shown in Table 16-1.

The number of markets, currencies, and businesses must be determined empirically for each institution. We can think of the stress envelope itself as the change in the market value of a portfolio position in a particular currency in response to specific stress shocks.

TABLE 16-1 Stress Categories and the Number of Stress Shocks

	Stress Category	Stress Shocks
1	Interest rates	6
2	Foreign exchange	2
3	Equity	1
4	Commodity	2
5	Credit spreads	1
6	Swap spreads	2
7	Vega (volatility)	2

FIGURE 16-1 The Seven Major Components of the Stress Envelope Approach

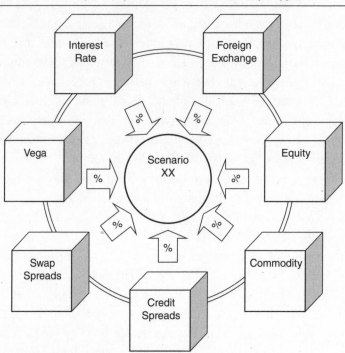

In the second stage of the process, a scenario can then be more easily created using a combination of several stress shocks (Figure 16-1) at levels somewhat lower than the worst possible case.

The following example illustrates how the stress envelope methodology works. Consider the following scenario in which three risk factors change at the same time:

1. A 10 percent fall in North American equity indices
2. A 15 percent fall in European equity indices
3. A 50 bp fall in North American short-term interest rates

The components of the scenarios are first related to the specific corresponding extreme stress shocks and their stress envelope values, modeled earlier:

1. A 25 percent fall in North American equity indices
2. A 25 percent fall in European equity indices
3. A 200 bp fall in North American short-term interest rates

TABLE 16-2 Stress Scenario

	Stress Envelope Values	Stress Envelope Shocks	Scenario Shocks	Scenario Shock Weights	Scenario Values
1	($1,000)	25%	10%	10/25 = 40%	($400)
2	($500)	25%	15%	15/25 = 60%	($300)
3	$700	200 bp	50 bp	50/200 = 25%	$175
				Total	($525)

Note: The scenario value is the product of the stress envelope value and scenario shock weight. The scenario shock weight is the ratio of the scenario shock to the stress envelope shock.

The impact of the scenario on the position is then derived by summing the appropriate percentage of the stress shock values for each of the three stress shocks (Table 16-2).

The linear interpolation in the calculation of the scenario value, with the scenario value being the worst-case stress envelope value times the scenario shock weight, is rather conservative. For nonlinear positions, the situation that concerns banks most is when gamma is negative—i.e., when the position experiences a loss whether the price of the underlying instrument moves up or down. For this situation, the scenario value derived using the methodology described above will overestimate the actual loss, since with negative gamma the magnitude of the loss accelerates with the size of the price change.

The regulators also now require that financial institutions run scenarios that capture the specific characteristics of their portfolios—i.e., scenarios that involve the particular group of risk factors to which their portfolios are most sensitive.

Regulatory Requirements for Stress Testing and Scenario Analysis

Before the 2007–2009 Financial Crisis

Stress testing and scenario analysis have been regulatory tools for a considerable period, particularly with regard to market risk. As early as 1996, the Basel Committee stated[4] that banks should subject their portfolios to a series of simulated

---

[4]Basel Committee on Banking Supervision, *Amendment to the Capital Accord to Incorporate Market Risks*, Bank for International Settlements, 1996.

TABLE 16-3 Typical Historical Scenarios Run by Banks by Type of Asset

Asset Type	Historical Scenarios
Interest rates	1994 – bond market sell-off
	1997 – Asian financial crisis
	1998 – Combined Russian debt default and LTCM failure
	2001 – 9/11 terrorist attacks in the United States
	2003 – bond market sell-off
Equities	1987 – October Black Monday
	1997 – Asian financial crisis
	2000 – bursting of the IT bubble
	2001 – 9/11 terrorist attacks in the United States
Foreign exchange	1992 – EMS (European Monetary System) crisis
	1997 – Asian financial crisis
	1998 – Russian debt default
Commodities	1973-1974 – Oil crisis
Credit	1997 – Asian financial crisis
	1998 – Combined Russian debt default and LTCM failure
	2001 – 9/11 terrorist attacks in the United States
	2007 – Subprime debt crisis
	2008 – Lehman Brothers bankruptcy and counterparty credit risk crisis
	2010 – European sovereign debt crisis

Source: Committee on the Global Financial System, *Stress Testing at Major Financial Institutions, Survey Results and Practice*, Bank for International Settlements, 2005; augmented by the authors for historical scenarios after 2004.

stress scenarios such as the 1987 equity crash, the European Exchange Rate Mechanism (ERM) crises of 1992 and 1993, or the fall in the bond markets in the first quarter of 1994.

Over the years, the list of historical scenarios gradually evolved. In 2004, the Committee on the Global Financial System (CGFS) initiated an exercise on stress tests undertaken by banks and securities firms in order to review what financial institutions perceived to be the main risk scenarios for them at that time, based on the type of enterprisewide stress test that they were running.[5] Table 16-3 provides

---

[5] See Committee on the Global Financial System, *Stress Testing at Major Financial Institutions: Survey Results and Practice*, Bank for International Settlements, January 2005. Sixty-four banks and securities firms from 16 countries participated in this survey, which was a follow-up to a similar exercise conducted by the CGFS in 2000.

a list of some of the most commonly applied historical scenarios, drawn largely from that 2004 list but brought up to date to include more recent events, such as the subprime crisis in 2007, the fall of Lehman Brothers in September 2008 and the counterparty credit risk crisis that followed, and the 2010 European sovereign debt crisis. (It is worth noting that none of the pre-2007 historical scenarios on the list would have helped institutions to anticipate the nature or effects of the subprime financial crisis.)

Pillar I of the Basel II framework required that banks choosing to employ the internal models approach to determine regulatory capital for market risk also put in place a stress testing program. Similarly, banks using the Advanced and Foundation internal ratings based (IRB) approach to credit risk regulatory capital calculations are required to conduct credit risk stress tests to assess the robustness of their capital assessment and the capital cushion above the minimum regulatory capital. Basel II also requires that banks subject their credit portfolio in the banking book to stress tests.

Weaknesses Uncovered in the 2007–2009 Financial Crisis

In light of the 2007–2009 financial crisis, it appeared that stress tests conducted by banks did not produce realistically large loss numbers. In particular, pre-crisis stress testing did not expose the inadequacy of the banking industry's capital buffers going into the crisis. Bank stress tests should have included more severe scenarios, and bank stress testing should have taken account of the way that risks interact across markets, institutions, and time to produce catastrophic levels of loss. According to the Basel Committee, the crisis highlighted several methodological weaknesses:[6]

1. At the most fundamental level, weaknesses in infrastructure limited the ability of banks to identify and aggregate risk exposures across the bank—e.g., credit risk resulting from the corporate lending activity and counterparty credit risk from derivatives businesses.
2. The crisis revealed that relying solely on historical scenarios and historical statistical relationships to assess risk is a seriously flawed approach. Historical statistics, such as correlations, proved to be

---

[6]These points are drawn from the analysis in the Basel Committee on Banking Supervision, *Principles For Sound Stress Testing Practices and Supervision*, May 2009.

unreliable once actual events started to unfold. Scenarios were too mild, and correlations between different positions, risk types, and markets were underestimated, because they did not take account of systemwide interactions and feedback effects (i.e., contagion).[7] Also, for subprime mortgages, the default rates drawn from historical analysis proved to be totally out of line with actual experience during the crisis.

3. Both trading liquidity risk and funding liquidity risk were strongly underestimated, if not totally ignored. The length of the stress period was also underestimated, which contributed to the underestimation of the level of risk, the interaction between risk, contagion effects, and liquidity problems. Most bank stress tests were thus incapable of capturing the extreme market events experienced during the financial crisis.

4. Banks did not sufficiently take qualitative expert judgment into account in order to develop innovative ad hoc stress scenarios that accounted for strong interlinkages between the lack of market liquidity and funding liquidity pressures.

5. Only a few banks had an enterprise view of their risks across all their businesses. Even those that had this view found that their stress tests were insufficient in identifying the connectedness of their activities and aggregating risks. As a result, banks did not have a comprehensive view across credit, market, and liquidity risks over various businesses.

Key Regulatory Initiatives Since the 2007–2009 Financial Crisis

After the crisis, with the banking system still in disarray, regulators in the United States, Europe, and elsewhere turned to a series of regulator-run macroeconomic scenario stress tests to examine the capital adequacy of the larger banks in national banking systems and to try to show investors that banking systems remained solvent.

Important in themselves, these regulatory initiatives were also used to probe the quality of internal bank-specified stress testing programs. Over time, they helped to set new standards in terms of identifying risks, specifying worst-case

---

[7]David Rowe notes that this systematic underestimation of risk by banks is a characteristic of corporate culture—the reluctance to contemplate failure. If financial institutions are to put a greater focus on stress testing, therefore, most of them will need to make cultural adjustments. D. Rowe, "From VaR to Stress Testing," *Risk Magazine*, September 2011.

scenarios, and modeling risk and revenue interactions over an extended period. The regulatory stress tests have also helped to shift the focus of stress testing away from a focus on market risk and toward the effect of macroeconomic downturns on a series of risks, including market, credit, business revenue, and liquidity risks.

In the United States, three distinct sets of regulatory stress tests have been conducted: first, the Supervisory Capital Assessment Program (SCAP) completed in May 2009; second, the stress tests conducted as part of the larger Comprehensive Capital Assessment Review (CCAR) in 2011 and 2012; and third, the Dodd-Frank supervisory stress tests in 2013 (DFAST 2013) and ongoing.

SCAP was a stress test in which U.S. regulators specified the common adverse scenario applied to each of the 19 largest bank holding companies (BHCs). The scenario was applied in a consistent manner across these banks to ensure the comparability of the stress results. In contrast, CCAR combines the quantitative results from the stress tests with a more qualitative assessment of the capital planning process followed by bank holding companies.[8] Regulators provided the main scenario, but the banks were required to apply the stress test in the manner they considered appropriate in assessing their capital adequacy.[9] The stress tests look not only at each bank in isolation but across all the institutions participating in the exercise so that the Federal Reserve can collect valuable systemic information—e.g., showing how a major common scenario would affect the largest banks collectively. From late 2012, U.S. regulators also began to use scenario analysis to assess the liquidity risk management process of the banks, including funding strategies during adverse situations.

The European Banking Authority (EBA) also mandated that 90 European banks in 21 countries run stress scenarios in 2010 and in 2011. The first stress test in 2010 was criticized as too soft, as several banks that passed the test—Irish banks, in particular—ran into trouble in July 2010. In 2011 the EBA came up with a new stress scenario that applied a more severe set of macroeconomic assumptions. Only eight banks failed this test, to give a capital shortfall of 8 percent of the total equity

---

[8] According to the Federal Reserve, "a capital plan describes a firm's capital planning strategies and its process for measuring potential capital needs both under expected and stressed operating environments for ensuring that it is holding adequate capital to be able to continue to function even under stress conditions." See Board of the Federal Reserve System, *Capital Plans*, 2011.

[9] Board of Governors of the Federal Reserve System, *Comprehensive Capital Analysis and Review 2012: Methodology and Results for Stress Scenario Projections*, March 2012.

capital of the European banking sector. Again, analysts criticized the test, estimating stress test losses up to 33 times larger than the official stress test results—e.g., after assuming that sovereign debt should be written down in line with market prices.[10]

From 2012, the stress testing regime in the United States began to be driven by post-crisis legislation, particularly the Dodd-Frank Act. The Act requires the Federal Reserve to conduct an annual supervisory stress test of bank holding companies (BHC) with $50 billion or more in total consolidated assets and also of nonbank financial companies designated by the Financial Stability Oversight Council (FSOC) for Federal Reserve supervision.[11] These stress tests are known under the acronym DFAST (Dodd-Frank Act stress tests).

The purpose of DFAST is to assess quantitatively how bank capital levels would fare in a stressful situation.[12] To promote transparency, Dodd-Frank also calls for the stress test results to be published—e.g., projections of post-stress capital ratios for each of 18 BHCs over a nine-quarter planning horizon.

The results reported in March 2013 projected results forward from the fourth quarter of 2012 to the end of 2014. The Federal Reserve's severely adverse scenario projections in this round of tests revealed that the 18 BHCs as a group would experience significant losses. In this scenario, losses were projected to be some $462 billion for the 18 BHCs in the aggregate over the nine quarters of the planning horizon (although, on the whole, the results were reassuring with regard to post-stress capital ratios across the industry).[13]

---

[10]*Wall Street Journal,* July 19, 2011.

[11]Although no institutions below $50 billion in assets are subject to supervisory stress testing or the requirements of CCAR, Dodd-Frank does require institutions with assets of between $10 and $50 billion to conduct and report on their own stress tests (using scenarios published by the supervisors).

[12]The post-stress capital ratios under examination include (1) tier 1 common ratio: the ratio of the common equity component of tier 1 capital to risk-weighted assets; (2) tier 1 capital ratio: the ratio of tier 1 capital to risk-weighted assets; (3) the total risk-based capital ratio: the ratio of total regulatory capital to risk-weighted assets; and (4) the tier 1 leverage ratio: the ratio of tier 1 capital to average assets. The results include projections of net income before taxes, including revenues, provisions, and losses (e.g., loan losses).

[13]Note that 19 BHCs participated in SCAP and CCAR but only 18 BHCs were part of the 2013 Dodd-Frank stress test: MetLife had participated in the earlier stress test exercises but was in the process of deregistering as a BHC when the Dodd-Frank stress test exercise began. Appendix 16.1 describes the Dodd-Frank Severely Adverse Scenario (DFAST 2013, *Supervisory Stress Test Methodology and Results*, March 2013).

Capital Adequacy and Stress Testing

The overall result of the regulatory stress testing initiatives described above is that, for some banks, stress testing has become a significant driver of regulatory capital adequacy. Large banks that fail the Dodd-Frank Act stress tests in the United States are required to submit capital plans that remedy the shortfall. Furthermore, failing a regulatory stress test has substantial reputational impact, so banks are keen to make sure their stress testing and capital planning regimes are relatively conservative.

While formal stress testing programs have been applied most rigorously to the largest U.S. banks, the expectations of regulators around the world regarding the ability of banks to withstand downturns and unexpectedly severe events has generally risen. Furthermore, even banks that are not subject to formal regulator-run stress tests may pay a capital penalty if bank examiners think that management has neglected to consider the impact of a range of adverse scenarios.

The effect on capital adequacy of efforts to take stressful periods into account has been magnified by new regulatory "stress VaR" requirements for market risk (see Box 16-1), though these are really a form of stress adjustment for VaR calculations rather than stress tests as such.

BOX 16-1   STRESS VaR AND CAPITAL REQUIREMENTS

Following the financial crisis of 2007–2009, regulators required banks to add "stress VaR" (sVaR) to their regulatory capital calculations for market risk in an amendment to the rules known as Basel 2.5 (see also Chapter 3).[1]

These new rules for deriving regulatory capital could lead to the absurd situation where the amount of regulatory capital is greater than the exposure of the portfolio. Indeed, the new rules to calculate the amount of regulatory capital in the trading book can be summarized by the formula:

$$\text{Capital} = \max\{(\text{VaR}, k^*(\text{average VaR over 60 days})\} +$$
$$\max\{\text{StressVaR}, k^*(\text{average StressVaR over 60 days})\} +$$
$$\text{IRC}$$

---

[1] Basel Committee on Banking Supervision, *Revisions to the Basel II Market Risk Framework*, July 2009.

where k is a multiplier with minimum value of 3, VaR is measured at the 99 percent confidence level over a 10-day period, StressVaR is computed using data from a stressful period such as 2007–2008, and IRC (incremental risk charge, see Chapter 3) is the CreditVaR over a one-year period at the 99.9 percent confidence level.

Assuming for illustrative purposes that volatility under stressed market conditions is three times the volatility of a normal market environment, and returns are normally distributed, StressVaR is three times NormalVaR (neglecting IRC for the purpose of the exercise).

Now suppose that the portfolio has an annualized volatility in normal market conditions of 10 percent. Then, over 10 days, the standard deviation is 2 percent. The 10-day standard deviation in stress conditions is thus 6 percent, according to our (not unreasonable) assumption. The sum of these—i.e., 8 percent, must be multiplied by the 99 percent standard normal critical value of 2.33, and then by a multiplier of at least 3. Assuming a "green zone" model—i.e., a multiplier of 3—regulatory capital under the new rules (and ignoring the IRC) is $2.33 \times 3 \times 8\% = 56\%$ of the portfolio exposure.

Note that under our simple but illustrative assumptions, the new regulatory capital charge will always be four times the capital charge without the stressed component. For instance, with a well-diversified and partially hedged portfolio having an annualized volatility of 5 percent and an "old" regulatory capital of 7 percent of the exposure, the new charge will be 28 percent. But with a partially diversified and lightly hedged portfolio having a normal volatility of 15 percent and a stress volatility of 60 percent, the new rules lead to a capital charge of 105 percent of the size of the portfolio—which, if the positions are long, is higher than the maximum loss that could be incurred on this portfolio.

Regulatory capital levels were initially described as a function of a desired confidence interval to protect the institution against default. The post-crisis incorporation of stress testing considerations to determine the required amount of capital seems logical but could lead to requirements for excessive amounts of capital—making the bank unattractive to any investor.

Best-Practice Stress Testing

So far we have focused on the program of stress tests imposed on the large banks by regulators in the post-crisis years. However, banks and their regulators are also intent on improving internal bank stress testing capabilities.

The weaknesses in bank stress testing practices prior to the crisis led the Basel Committee to produce a series of recommendations in 2009,[14] covering four broad areas: (1) use of stress testing and integration in risk governance, (2) purposes of stress testing and stress testing methodologies, (3) scenario selection, and (4) stress testing of specific risks and products. In the next four sections we explore these recommendations.

Going forward, regulators and analysts will carefully scrutinize stress test results. Banks need to put in place a planning process that ensures stress tests are credible and useful. According to William Dudley in 2011,[15] a planning process should include "description of risk appetite and capital target, robust internal controls, incorporation of stress testing and stress-test results into the decision process, good governance with respect to the role of senior management and the board of directors and well-articulated capital distribution policies that describe how decisions are made relative to expectations of future outcomes."

Use of Stress Testing and Integration in Risk Governance

Prior to the financial crisis, risk managers often found it difficult to persuade senior management and business lines to accept severe scenarios as plausible.[16]

---

[14]Basel Committee on Banking Supervision, *Principles for Sound Stress Testing Practices and Supervision*, May 2009.

[15]President and CEO of the Federal Reserve Bank of New York. See W. Dudley, *U.S. Experience with Bank Stress Tests*, Remarks at the Group of 30 Plenary Meeting in Bern, Switzerland, May 28, 2011.

[16]Prior to the crisis, stress testing in most banks tended to be performed by the risk function as an isolated exercise, with little interaction with business areas. This meant that, among other things, business areas often believed that the analysis was not credible. Many banks did not have an overarching stress testing program in place but ran separate stress tests for particular risks or portfolios with limited firm-level integration.

Board and senior management engagement and buy-in to the design of stress testing programs is critical to overcome this and to ensure:

- Consistency and control around the stress testing methodology
- Full integration of stress testing into the risk and capital management decision-making processes

In particular, the challenge includes setting clear objectives for the stress testing program, defining scenarios, and ensuring that all on- and off-balance-sheet activities are captured. The challenge also includes establishing policies and constructing methodologies that are appropriately consistent across multiple factors and business units.

Stress tests scenarios should be intuitive yet capture significant complexity in order to accurately reflect the behavior of distressed markets. The most apposite scenarios are likely to change and evolve, as well as to vary in importance, over time. It is therefore important for the stress testing methodology to facilitate frequent yet controlled review and amendment to ensure that stresses remain up to date.

Stress testing programs should feed into the decision-making process at the appropriate management level, including strategic business decisions. Stress tests should support a range of decisions and be used to:

- Set and monitor the risk appetite of the firm—e.g., define broad exposure limits consistent with the risk appetite
- Support the evaluation of strategic choices when undertaking and discussing long-term business planning
- Support the liquidity and capital planning process
- Develop "contingency action plans" to deal with catastrophic situations in advance, including written plans that connect plans to the procedures established to set stress limits

Management response is also a critical component to risk modeling. A stress test committee that collects practical views from risk takers and managers should identify "early warning signals" to be incorporated into governance responsibilities and reports. A stress test committee should also determine the required feedback, such as who acts on the results of the stress test and the appropriate follow-up with the risk-takers in case of any violations of limits (e.g., exceeding either soft stress test limits or hard stress test limits).

The board, senior management, and the risk function need to hold a periodic dialogue on stress testing, including the most relevant stresses, scenarios, and potential impacts. The board should set limits on the maximum loss acceptable, say over a quarter, under the selected set of worst-case scenarios and stresses. These limits should be viewed as an integral part of the risk appetite of the firm, defined at the board level.

Purposes and Methodologies of Stress Testing

Stress testing has many different purposes, which in turn means that stress tests take many forms and require a range of techniques. Stress testing should:

- Promote risk identification and control with a forward-looking perspective at various levels—for example, individual transaction analysis, portfolio risk management, design of business strategy.
- Provide a complementary and independent risk perspective to other risk management tools and measures such as VaR. Stress testing should include simulating shocks that have not previously occurred in the markets. In particular, appropriate stress tests should challenge the projected risk profile of new products for which limited historical data are available and which have not been subject to periods of stress in the past (e.g., stress testing should have been applied to the subprime mortgage market in the years preceding 2007).[17] Stress tests should help to detect vulnerabilities, such as unidentified concentrations or potential interactions between risk types, that could threaten the viability of the bank. If management relies purely on statistical risk management tools based on historical data, then vulnerabilities may remain undetected.

---

[17]A stress test in 2006 using a 20 to 40 percent fall in house prices, as experienced in some areas of the United States following the subprime crisis, would have raised serious concerns about the risk embedded in subprime mortgage bonds and CDOs.

- Play an important role in the communication of risk within the firm, as well as in the firm's external communication with regulators, rating agencies, and investors. A firm may want to voluntarily disclose stress test results, with their supporting assumptions and methodology, to enable the market to better understand the risk profile of the firm.
- Form an integral part of the funding liquidity and capital management of the bank. This requires banks to undertake adverse, although plausible, forward-looking stress tests that identify severe events or changes in market conditions that could impact the liquidity and solvency of the bank.

Stress Testing and Funding Liquidity Risk

Funding liquidity risk can be extremely difficult to measure. For example, stress testing the potential for large margin calls requires significant information about the firm's positions today and its likely positions in the future. Metrics such as cash flow at risk (CFaR) and liquidity at risk (LaR), while not perfect, can help capture the amount of liquidity risk in adverse markets. (See Chapter 8 for further discussion of liquidity risk management.)

Scenario Selection

The identification of relevant stress events requires the collaboration of different senior experts within the bank such as risk managers, economists, business managers, and traders. The opinions of all relevant experts must be taken into account, especially for firmwide stress tests.

Stress testing should include business cycle stresses as well as event-specific "tail risks." For example, markets with low historical volatility may experience large discrete movements; the scenario in such a case should reflect the potential interaction of market risk, trading liquidity risk, and credit risk for corporate bonds.

Stress testing should establish an integrated view of risk that stresses components on an individual as well as an aggregate basis, while modeling extreme events in significant detail. Effective scenario analysis should take into account how events unfold *over time*—for example, a quarter of limited liquidity during which it becomes impossible to hedge positions in a timely manner. They also require context. How would (did) a hypothetical (historical) stress test event unfold over time? This can be as important as the final outcome. Forward-looking stress and scenario tests must specify the length, speed, and magnitudes of events and describe the dynamics between transactions (e.g., unstable correlations that move toward 1 or −1 in stressed markets).

Scenarios should also address correlations between risk factors and distinguish between static and dynamic scenarios—i.e., one-period versus multiperiod frameworks. While trading liquidity risk is rarely factored into traditional VaR analysis, a multiperiod framework can incorporate hedging strategies to protect against losses in illiquid markets over time and incorporate management intervention as part of the picture. If the scenarios are well developed, they can form an integral part of the management culture and have a meaningful impact on business decisions.

Importantly, since each firm has different strengths and weaknesses, there is no "one size fits all" approach to scenario building. Scenarios must be "severe" but "plausible" for *that* firm. Effective stress tests should highlight specific weaknesses and surface "hot spots" visible under extreme conditions. Worst-case scenarios must measure "knock-on" risks such as the unexpected write-downs and collateral calls that devastated AIG during the 2007–2009 financial crisis. (The firm had to post about $50 billion in collateral to offset a drop of more than $400 billion in the value of securities it insured with credit default swaps.[18])

Boxes 16-2 and 16-3 present two examples of historical replication scenarios: October 19, 1987, when stock prices in the United States fell by 23 percent, or approximately 22 times their daily standard deviation; and the tightening of monetary policy by the Federal Reserve in the United States in May 1994 and the subsequent fall in bond prices.

Box 16-4 illustrates how one bank, Société Générale Group, reports its stress test program and potential losses related to both historical and hypothetical scenarios.

A stress testing program should actively seek out scenarios that could challenge the viability of the bank. One way to do this is to build "reverse

---

[18]Reportedly, no scenario was run at AIG that considered the impact of a sharp drop in housing prices on collateral calls and write-downs (*Wall Street Journal Europe*, November 3, 2008).

BOX 16-2 REPLICATION SCENARIO 1: STOCK MARKET CRASH

As an example of a historical replication scenario, consider a stock market crash reminiscent of the crisis in the global financial markets in October 1987, characterized by a combination of the following events:

- Equity markets around the globe fall by 20 percent on average, with Asian markets, such as Hong Kong, declining by 30 percent, and there is an upward shift in implied volatilities from 20 to 50 percent.
- The U.S. dollar rallies against other currencies as a consequence of a flight to quality. Asian currencies lose up to 10 percent against the dollar.
- Interest rates fall in Western markets. Hong Kong interest rates rise by 40 bps at the long end of the term structure and by 100 bps at the short end.
- Commodity prices drop as a result of fears of a recession; copper and oil prices decline by 5 percent.

BOX 16-3 REPLICATION SCENARIO 2: U.S. MONETARY TIGHTENING

In this example of a historical replication scenario, consider a U.S. inflation scare and a tightening of monetary policy by the U.S. Federal Reserve along the lines of that seen in May 1994, characterized by the following events:

- There is a 100 bp increase in the overnight interest rate and a 50 bp upward shift in the long end of the curve.
- Interest rates also increase in other G-7 countries and Switzerland, but not as much as in the United States.
- G-7 currencies depreciate against the U.S. dollar as investors chase higher rates.
- Credit spreads widen.
- Equity markets decline from 3 to 6 percent, with an upward shift in implied volatilities.

BOX 16-4 STRESS TEST ASSESSMENT BY SOCIÉTÉ GÉNÉRALE GROUP

The following are extracts from the 2012 annual report of Société Générale Group.

METHODOLOGY

Alongside the internal VaR model, Société Générale monitors its exposure using stress test simulations to take into account exceptional market occurrences.

A stress test estimates the loss resulting from an extreme change in market parameters over a period corresponding to the time required to unwind or hedge the positions affected (5 to 20 days for most trading positions).

This stress test risk assessment is applied to all of the Bank's market activities. It is based on 26 historical scenarios and 8 theoretical scenarios that include the "Société Générale Hypothetical Financial Crisis Scenario" (or "Generalised" scenario) based on the events observed in 2008.

HISTORICAL STRESS TESTS

Société Générale has defined 26 historical scenarios, including 7 new ones added in 2012:

- six of them cover the periods between Q3-2008 and Q1-2009 and are related to the subprime crisis and its consequences for all financial markets;
- the seventh corresponds to the GIIPS (Greece, Italy, Ireland, Portugal, and Spain) sovereign debt crisis in Q2-2010.

HYPOTHETICAL STRESS TESTS

The Bank's aim is to select extreme but nonetheless plausible events which would have major repercussions on all the international markets.

Société Générale has adopted eight hypothetical scenarios described below:

- **Generalized (the Société Générale Hypothetical Financial Crisis Scenario):** considerable mistrust of financial institutions after the Lehman Brothers' bankruptcy; collapse of equity markets, sharp decline in implied dividends, significant widening of credit spreads, pivoting of yield curves (rise in short-term interest rates and decline in long-term interest rates), substantial flight to quality;
- **GIIPS crisis:** mistrust in risky sovereign issuers and increased interest in higher-rated sovereign issuers such as Germany, followed by contagion of fears to other markets (equities, etc.);
- **Middle East crisis:** instability in the Middle East leading to a significant shock on oil and other energy sources, a stock market crash, and a steepening of the yield curve;
- **Terrorist attack:** major terrorist attack on the United States leading to a stock market crash, strong decline in interest rates, widening of credit spreads and sharp decline of the U.S. dollar;
- **Bond crisis:** crisis in the global bond markets inducing the delinking of bond and equity yields, strong rise in U.S. interest rates (and a more modest rise for other international rates), moderate decline on the equity markets, flight to quality with moderate widening of credit spreads, rise in the U.S. dollar;
- **U.S. dollar crisis:** collapse of the U.S. dollar against major international currencies due to the deterioration of the U.S. trade balance and budget deficit, rise of interest rates and narrowing of U.S. credit spreads;
- **Euro zone crisis:** withdrawal of some countries from the euro zone following the euro's excessive appreciation against the U.S. dollar: decline in euro exchange rates, sharp rise in euro zone interest rates, sharp fall in euro equities and rise in U.S. equities, significant widening of euro credit spreads;
- **Yen carry trade unwinding:** change in monetary policy in Japan leading to yen carry trade strategies being abandoned: significant

widening of credit spreads, decline in JPY interest rates, rise in U.S. and euro zone long-term interest rates and flight to quality.

FIGURE 16B-1 Stress Test Risk Assessment Applied to All of the Bank's Market Activities

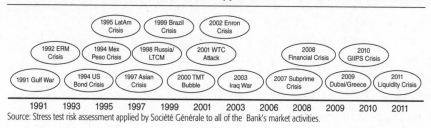

Source: Stress test risk assessment applied by Société Générale to all of the Bank's market activities.

FIGURE 16B-2 Average Stress Tests in 2012

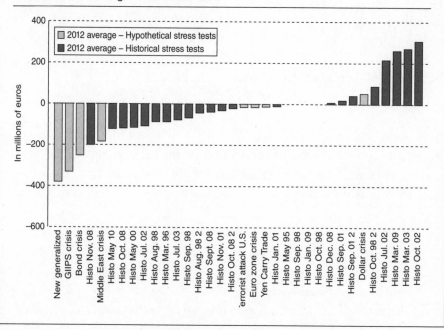

stress tests."[19] The idea here is to identify loss levels that would cause the bank to breach regulatory capital ratios or become illiquid or insolvent, and then to work backward to the kind of event that might cause this catastrophic event.

---

[19]Reverse stress testing is a requirement introduced by the U.K. Financial Services Authority (FSA) in 2008; it applies to banks, building societies, investment firms, and insurance companies. (Financial Services Authority, *Stress and Scenario Testing*, Consultation Paper, December 2008.)

Reverse stress tests look to uncover hidden weaknesses and "hot spots" in a portfolio, including under extreme negative market conditions. The approach can help firms identify and then manage, through contingency plans, the types of stresses that would cause their business model to fail.

A newer approach to stress testing is to start by simulating the major macro-economic factors and create forward-looking scenarios for the financial markets, including diffusion and jump processes. The expected trends, volatilities, and correlations of the risk drivers are calibrated to publicly available macroeconomic and market data. The diffusion process represents the stable market environment, while the jump process reflects stress events, which in turn generate spikes in volatilities and enhanced correlations and initiate potential snowball-like effects. The idea behind this approach is that the processes are internally generated, including changes in volatilities and correlations, whereas traditional approaches usually require the input of stable and constant volatilities and correlations.

Stress Testing Specific Risks and Complex Structured Products

In the past, stress tests were often based on significant historical market events. By definition, such stress tests cannot capture the risks generated by new products such as the risk of complex structured credit products in the pre-crisis years. To help counter this, stress testing programs should cover in sufficient detail:

- *The behavior of complex structured products under stress liquidity conditions.* In particular, stress tests should specifically consider the credit quality of the underlying exposures, as well as the unique characteristics of the structured product—e.g., how the cash flow "waterfall" affects the risk of specific tranches based on their subordination level. It should not be assumed that the market in structured products will remain liquid.
- *Pipeline or securitization risk.* Underestimating liquidity risk meant that banks also underestimated the risk of warehousing credit risk when issuing new structured products.
- *Counterparty credit risk.* Stress testing for counterparty risk should be improved by including wrong-way risk—i.e., the risk that a rise in exposure to a counterparty will be correlated with an increased tendency for the counterparty to default (Chapter 13).

- *Basis risk in relation to hedging strategies.* In many cases, stress tests dealt only with directional risk and did not capture basis risk—i.e., when the hedging instrument is imperfectly correlated with the position to be hedged.
- *Contingent risks.* Another weakness was that stress testing models did not capture contingent risks that arose either from legally binding credit and liquidity lines or from reputational concerns (e.g., related to bank support for off-balance-sheet vehicles).
- *Funding liquidity risk.* Stress tests did not capture the systemic nature of the crisis or the magnitude and duration of the disruption in the inter-bank markets.[20]
- *Correlation risk.* Stress testing the correlation numbers associated with structured products is particularly important, as extreme movements in correlations were the main cause of severe multinotch downgrades. The probability of moving from AAA or AA to junk status is very low for corporate bonds. But structured products can make this downward leap overnight if one seemingly unlikely event significantly increases correlations.
- *Credit rating validation.* It is also important to perform the necessary internal due diligence on the credit rating assigned to a tranche—i.e., can the agency rating be trusted? Rating agencies have a reasonably good track record of rating corporate bonds, but structured products and their downgrade transitions are a fundamentally different problem.

Stress Testing in Nonbank Corporations

At present, stress testing methodologies are being developed mainly by the banking industry, and in particular in the largest bank holding companies. Nevertheless, the concepts can be applied and used by any firm, in any industry. Nonbanking industries do not generally need to worry about allocating capital; however, stress testing can be applied to check the vulnerability of the firm to changing economic conditions, to highlight strategic issues, and to help prepare contingency plans.

---

[20]For an in-depth discussion of the shortcomings of liquidity stress tests, see Basel Committee on Banking Supervision, *Principles for Sound Liquidity Risk Management and Supervision*, September 2008.

Nonbank corporations must take into account not only financial parameters but also those parameters and scenarios that drive the demand for the firm's products or services and the stability of production inputs (e.g., critical suppliers). It is already common for business plans to include three estimates for key projections such as revenue or sales: the most likely scenario, a more optimistic scenario, and a more pessimistic scenario. The pessimistic and optimistic scenarios often differ from the expected scenario by ±20 percent. Stress testing and scenario analysis can be used to extend this thinking so that more extreme circumstances are considered, with the aim of building a robust internal planning process.

Conclusion: Stress Testing as an Evolving Practice

Stress testing is one of the fastest evolving areas of risk management. The key areas of evolution are now clear. Stress testing used to be focused largely on market risk and limited credit scenarios, but since the financial crisis of 2007–2009 it has grown in scope to include comprehensive attempts to stress credit, counterparty, and liquidity risks as well as bank revenues. Furthermore, stress testing of the whole balance sheet is now regarded as essential, and multistage scenarios stretch out a number of years into the future rather than focusing on single shocks. There is also a much more tangible link to bank strategy and capital requirements: the link between bank stress test output and bank management decisions has been strengthened.

This increase in ambitions has brought many successes, in terms of problems solved, but also many challenges. In particular, it has proved to be a major challenge to devise a best-practice way to link a change in a particular macroeconomic variable to an impact on a firm's balance sheet. It is also proving difficult to factor in risk interactions—e.g., the interaction of liquidity, market, and credit risk. While interactions can be specified, and the impacts measured to some degree, there can never be any certainty that a hypothetical scenario has captured the complex reality of risk or that replicating a complex historical scenario (e.g., events in 2007–2009) is a truly useful exercise in forward-looking risk management.

Perhaps the biggest danger, however, is that the financial industry will work hard to comply with regulators in terms of improving, and to some degree standardizing, scenario analysis only to gain an undue amount of confidence in the results. Even more than VaR and similar quantitative metrics, the success of scenario analysis depends on the knowledge, curiosity, and imagination of the analyst—as well as on the willingness of senior managers, and regulators, to think the unthinkable.

Appendix 16.1

THE 2013 DODD-FRANK SEVERELY ADVERSE SCENARIOS

The "severely adverse" scenarios designed by U.S. regulators for the 2013 round of Dodd-Frank Act stress testing included trajectories for 26 economic variables. For this round of stress tests, regulators communicated the values of the variables to banks in the fall of 2012, and the results were published in spring 2013.

The 26 variables included 14 variables that captured economic activity, asset prices, and interest rates in the U.S. economy and financial markets. The other 12 variables consisted of three variables (real GDP growth, inflation, and the U.S./foreign currency exchange rate) applied to each of four countries/country blocks. These four countries/country blocks covered the euro area, the United Kingdom, developing Asia, and Japan.

The scenario assumptions included a real GDP decline of nearly 5 percent between the third quarter of 2012 and the end of 2013; an increase in the unemployment rate of 12 percent over this period; a deceleration of the four-quarter percent change in the consumer price index (CPI) to 1 percent; a fall in equity prices of more than 50 percent over the course of the recession and, correspondingly, a jump in the equity market volatility index from about 21 in the third quarter of 2012 to more than 70 at the start of the scenario; and a decline in both housing prices and commercial real estate prices of more than 20 percent by the end of 2014. The international component of the severely adverse scenario featured recessions in the euro area, the United Kingdom, and Japan and below-trend growth in developing Asia. The severely adverse scenario was similar in severity to the 2012 CCAR supervisory stress scenario.

Among the banks subjected to the stress testing were six bank holding companies with particularly large trading, private equity, and counterparty exposures from derivatives and financing transactions. These were obliged to include a global market shock in their severely adverse scenario, specified in terms of a set of one-time hypothetical shocks to a broad range of risk factors. These shocks involved large and sudden changes in asset prices, rates, and spreads, reflecting general market stress and heightened uncertainty. The shocks were based on the price and rate movements that occurred in the second half of 2008, a period that featured severe market stress and the failure of Lehman Brothers, a major, globally active financial institution. In addition, this "global market shock" incorporated hypothetical eurozone-based shocks, including sharp increases in certain sovereign debt yields, widening corporate spreads and sovereign credit default swap (CDS) spreads, and a large depreciation of the euro against major currencies. In the scenario, the shocks were felt across the eurozone, but the severity of the shocks varied, with more pronounced effects experienced by countries on the periphery.

17

RISK CAPITAL ATTRIBUTION AND RISK-ADJUSTED PERFORMANCE MEASUREMENT

Our final chapter takes a look at the roles of risk capital and at how risk capital can be attributed to business lines as part of a risk-adjusted performance measurement (RAPM) system. This problem brings together many of the themes discussed earlier in the book. RAPM represents a key challenge for financial institutions and nonfinancial firms around the world today. Only by forging a connection between risk measurement, risk capital, risk-based pricing, and performance measurement can firms ensure that the decisions they take reflect the interests of stakeholders such as bondholders and shareholders.

What Purpose Does Risk Capital Serve?

Risk capital is the cushion that provides protection against the various risks inherent in the business of a corporation so that the firm can maintain its financial integrity and remain a going concern even in the event of a near-catastrophic worst-case scenario. Risk capital gives essential confidence to the corporation's stakeholders, such as suppliers, clients, and lenders (for an industrial firm), or claimholders, such as depositors and counterparties in financial transactions (for a financial institution).

Risk capital is often called *economic capital*, and in most instances the generally accepted convention is that risk capital and economic capital are identical (although later in this chapter we introduce a slight wrinkle by defining economic capital as risk capital plus strategic capital).

We should be careful not to confuse the concept of risk capital, which is intended to capture the economic realities of the risks a firm runs, and regulatory capital. First, regulatory capital only applies to a few regulated industries, such as banking and insurance companies, where regulators are trying to protect the interests of small depositors or policy holders. Second, while regulatory capital performs something of the same function as risk capital in the regulators' eyes, it is calculated according to a set of industrywide rules and formulas and sets only a *minimum* required level of capital adequacy. It rarely succeeds in capturing the true level of risk in a firm—the gap between a firm's regulatory capital and its risk capital can be quite wide. Furthermore, even if regulatory and risk capital are similar numbers at the level of the firm, they may not be similar for each constituent business line (i.e., regulatory capital may suggest that an activity is much riskier than management believes to be the case, or vice versa).[1]

The new regulatory capital requirements imposed by Basel III make it likely that for some activities, such as securitization, regulatory capital may end up much higher than economic capital. Still, economic capital calculation is essential for senior management as a benchmark to assess the economic viability of the activity for the financial institution. When regulatory capital is much larger than economic capital, then it is likely that over time the activity will migrate to the shadow banking sector, which can price the transactions at a more attractive level.

Risk capital measurement is based on the same concepts as the value-at-risk (VaR) calculation methodology that we discuss in Chapter 7. Indeed, risk capital numbers are often derived from, or supported by, sophisticated internal VaR models, augmented in recent years by the kind of stress testing we describe in Chapter 16. However, the choice of the confidence level and time horizon when using VaR to calculate risk capital are key policy parameters that should be set by senior management (or the senior risk management committee). Usually, these decisions should be endorsed by the board.

---

[1] This leads to various conundrums in allocating capital and capital costs to business lines. For example, some practitioners square the circle by allocating the higher of regulatory capital or economic capital to the business line.

Risk capital should be calculated in such a way that the institution can absorb unexpected losses up to a level of confidence in line with the requirements of the firm's various stakeholders. No firm can offer its stakeholders a 100 percent guarantee (or confidence level) that it holds enough risk capital to ride out any eventuality. Instead, risk capital is calculated at a confidence level set at less than 100 percent—say, 99.9 percent for a firm with conservative stakeholders. In theory, this means that there is a probability of around 1/10 of 1 percent that actual losses will exceed the amount of risk capital set aside by the firm over the given time horizon (generally one year).[2] The exact choice of confidence level is typically associated with some target credit rating from a rating agency such as Moody's, Standard & Poor's, and Fitch as these ratings are themselves explicitly associated with a probability of default. It should also be in line with the firm's stated risk appetite (see Chapter 4).

Emerging Uses of Risk Capital Numbers

Risk capital is traditionally used to answer the question, "How much capital is required for our firm to remain solvent, given our risky activities?" As soon as a firm can answer this question, it can move on to solve many other management problems. Recently, therefore, risk capital numbers have been used to answer more and more questions, particularly in banks and other financial institutions.[3] (Box 17-1 explains why risk-based calculations are so important for financial institutions.) These new uses include:

- *Performance measurement and incentive compensation at the firm, business unit, and individual levels.* Risk capital can be plugged into risk-based capital attribution systems, often grouped together under the acronym RAPM (risk-adjusted performance measurement) or RAROC

---

[2] In reality, risk capital model suffers from the model risks we discussed in Chapter 15, and the results require careful interpretation. Most firms use the output of their capital model as one key input into a wider set of judgments about the amount of capital the firm should hold.

[3] For an informal survey of how firms use economic capital and RAROC, see T. Baer et al., *The Use of Economic Capital in Performance Management for Banks: A Perspective*, McKinsey Working Papers on Risk, No. 24, January 2011.

BOX 17-1   WHY IS ECONOMIC CAPITAL SO IMPORTANT TO FINANCIAL INSTITUTIONS?

Allocating risk capital using economic capital approaches is important for financial institutions for at least four reasons.

First, capital is primarily used in a financial institution not only to provide funding for investments (as for a manufacturing corporation) but also to absorb risk. The fundamental reason for this is that financial institutions can leverage themselves to a much higher degree than other corporations at a much lower cost without raising equity, by taking retail deposits or issuing debt securities. (Their debt-to-equity ratio might be as high as 20 to 1, compared to perhaps 2 to 1 for an industrial corporation.) Moreover, many activities undertaken by financial institutions, such as derivatives trading, writing guarantees, issuing letters of credit, and other contingent commitments, do not require significant financing. Yet all these activities draw to some extent on the bank's stock of risk capital, and therefore a risk capital cost must be imputed to each activity.

This brings us to the second reason: a bank's target solvency is a vital part of the product the bank is selling. In contrast to an industrial company, the primary customers of banks and other financial institutions are also their primary liability holders—e.g., depositors, derivatives counterparties, insurance policy holders, and so on. These customers are concerned about default risk on contractually promised payments. Customers make deposits with the expectation that the safety of their deposits does not depend on the economic performance of the bank. In over-the-counter markets, institutions are concerned about counterparty risk: a bank with a poor credit rating will find itself excluded from many markets. Maintaining good creditworthiness is therefore an ongoing cost of doing business for a bank.

Third, although bank creditworthiness is critical, banks are also highly opaque institutions. Banks use proprietary technology for pricing and hedging financial instruments, especially complex financial transactions. A typical bank's balance sheet is relatively liquid and can change very quickly. Any outside assessment of the creditworthiness of a bank is therefore difficult to develop and rapidly becomes obsolete (as the risk profile of the bank keeps on changing). Maintaining enough risk capital and implementing a strong risk management culture allows the bank to reduce these "agency costs" by convincing external stakeholders, including rating agencies, of the bank's financial integrity.

Fourth, banks operate in highly competitive financial markets. Increasingly, this makes bank profitability very sensitive to the bank's cost of capital. Banks don't want to carry too much risk capital, because risk capital represents the money invested in the bank that does not have to be repaid under any fixed contractual agreement (e.g., equity capital). This flexibility, which allows risk capital to act as a safety buffer for the bank if times are hard, means that risk capital is relatively expensive to raise and hold (e.g., compared to debt capital). But banks can't carry too little risk capital, for reasons we've already made clear. So understanding the dynamic balance between the capital the bank carries and the riskiness of its activities is very important.

(risk-adjusted return on capital). These systems, a key focus of this chapter, provide both management and external stakeholders with a risk-adjusted measure of performance of various businesses. The measure can be used to compare the economic profitability, as opposed to the accounting profitability (such as return on book equity) of different activities. At the same time, RAROC numbers can be used as part of scorecards to compensate the senior management of particular business lines, as well as the infrastructure group, for their contribution to shareholder value. Since the 2007–2009 financial crisis, firms have laid a greater emphasis on compensation schemes that adjust for risk in some manner (as well as on complementary mechanisms such as deferral periods and clawbacks).

• *Active portfolio management for entry/exit decisions.* The decision to enter or exit a particular business should be based on both risk-adjusted performance measurement and the "risk diversification effect" of the business. For example, a firm that is focused on corporate lending in a particular region is likely to find that its returns fluctuate in accordance with that region's business cycle. Ideally, the firm might diversify its business geographically or in terms of business activity. Capital management decisions seek an answer to the question, "How much value will be created if the decision is taken to allocate resources to a new or existing business, or alternatively to close down an activity?"

- *Pricing transactions.* Risk capital numbers can be used to calculate risk-based pricing for individual transactions. Risk-based pricing is attractive because it ensures that a firm is compensated for the economic risk generated by a transaction. For example, common sense tells us that a loan to a non-investment-grade firm that is in relatively fragile financial condition must be priced higher than a loan to an investment-grade firm. However, the *amount* of the differential can be determined only by working out the amount of expected loss and the cost of the risk capital that has to be set aside for each transaction. Trading and corporate loan desks in many banks rely on the "marginal economic capital requirement" component in the RAROC calculation to price deals in advance—and to decide whether those deals will increase shareholder value rather than simply add to the volume of transactions.

One problem is that a single measure of risk capital cannot accommodate the four different purposes that we have just described. We'll look at the solution to this later on.

RAROC: Risk-Adjusted Return on Capital

RAROC is an approach—simple at the conceptual level—that is used to allocate risk capital to business units and individual transactions for the purpose of measuring economic performance.

Originally proposed by Bankers Trust in the late 1970s, the approach makes clear the trade-off between risk and reward for a unit of capital and, therefore, offers a uniform and comparable measure of risk-adjusted performance across all business activities. If a business unit's RAROC is higher than the cost of the bank's equity (the minimum rate of return on equity required by the shareholders), then the business unit is deemed to be adding value to shareholders. Senior management can use this measure to evaluate performance for capital budgeting purposes, and as an input to the compensation for managers of business units.

The generic RAROC equation is really a formalization of the trade-off between risk and reward. It reads:

$$\text{RAROC} = \frac{\text{after-tax expected risk-adjusted net income}}{\text{economic capital}}$$

We can see that the RAROC equation employs economic capital as a proxy for risk and after-tax expected risk-adjusted net income as a proxy for reward. Later, we elaborate on how to measure both the numerator and the denominator of the RAROC equation, and on how to tackle the "hurdle-rate" issue—that is, once we know our RAROC number, how do we know if this number is good or bad from a shareholder's perspective?

Before beginning this discussion, however, we must acknowledge that the generic RAROC equation is one of a family of approaches, all with strengths and weaknesses. The definition of RAROC that we've just offered corresponds to industry practice and can be thought of as the traditional RAROC definition. Box 17-2 presents several variants grouped under the label RAPM (risk-adjusted performance measures).

BOX 17–2 RAPM (RISK-ADJUSTED PERFORMANCE MEASUREMENT) ZOOLOGY

It's long been recognized that traditional accounting-based measures of performance at the consolidated level and for individual business units, such as return on assets (ROA) or return on book equity (ROE), fail to capture the risk of the underlying activity. The amounts of both book assets and book equity, which are accounting measures, are poor proxies for risk measures. Furthermore, accounting income misses some critical risk adjustments, such as expected loss.

RAPM (risk-adjusted performance measurement) is a generic term describing all the techniques used to adjust returns for the risk incurred in generating those returns. It encompasses many different concepts, risk adjustments, and performance measures, with RAROC being the form that is most widely used in the banking sector. These RAPM measures are not fully consistent with one another. In the main text, we propose an adjusted RAROC measure that is consistent with the capital asset pricing model (CAPM) and, therefore, with the NPV measure defined here.

- *RAROC (risk-adjusted return on capital) = risk-adjusted expected net income/economic capital.* RAROC makes the risk adjustment to the numerator by subtracting a risk factor from the return—e.g., expected loss. RAROC also makes the risk adjustment to the denominator by substituting economic capital for accounting capital.
- *RORAC (return on risk-adjusted capital) = net income/economic capital.* RORAC makes the risk adjustment solely to the denominator. In practical applications,

$$\text{RORAC} = \frac{P \,\&\, L(\text{profit and loss})}{\text{VaR}}$$

- *ROC (return on capital) = RORAC.* It is also called ROCAR (return on capital at risk).
- *RORAA (return on risk-adjusted assets) = net income/risk-adjusted assets.*
- *RAROA (risk-adjusted return on risk-adjusted assets) = risk-adjusted expected net income/risk-adjusted assets.*
- *S (Sharpe ratio) = (expected return − risk-free rate)/volatility.* The ex post Sharpe ratio—i.e., that based on actual returns rather than expected returns—can be shown to be a multiple of ROC.[1]
- *NPV (net present value) = discounted value of future expected cash flows*, using a risk-adjusted expected rate of return based on the beta derived from the CAPM, where risk is defined in terms of the covariance of changes in the market value of the business with changes in the value of the market portfolio (see Chapter 5). In the CAPM, the definition of risk is restricted to the systematic component of risk that cannot be diversified away. For RAROC calculations, the risk measure captures the full volatility of earnings, systematic and specific. NPV is particularly well suited for ventures

---

[1]See David Shimko, "See Sharpe or Be Flat," *Risk* 10(6), 1997, p. 33.

in which the expected cash flows over the life of the project can be easily identified.

- *EVA (economic value added), or NIACC (net income after capital charge)*, is the after-tax adjusted net income less a capital charge equal to the amount of economic capital attributed to the activity, times the after-tax cost of equity capital. The activity is deemed to add shareholder value, or is said to be EVA positive, when its NIACC is positive (and vice versa).[2] An activity whose RAROC is above the hurdle rate is also EVA positive.

---

[2]EVA is a registered trademark of Stern Stewart & Co.

RAROC for Capital Budgeting

The decision to invest in a new project or a new business venture, or to expand or close down an existing business line, has to be made before the true performance of the activity is known—no manager has a crystal ball. When implementing the generic after-tax RAROC equation for capital budgeting, industry practice therefore interprets it as meaning

$$RAROC = \frac{\text{expected revenues} - \text{costs} - \text{expected losses} - \text{taxes} + \text{return on risk capital} + / - \text{transfers}}{\text{economic capital}}$$

where

- *Expected revenues* are the revenues that the activity is expected to generate (assuming no losses).
- *Costs* are the direct expenses associated with running the activity (e.g., salaries, bonuses, infrastructure expenses, and so on).
- *Expected losses*, in a banking context, are primarily the expected losses from default; they correspond to the loan loss reserve that the bank must set aside as the cost of doing business. Because this cost, like other business costs, is priced into the transaction in the form of a spread over

funding cost, there is no need for risk capital as a buffer to absorb this risk. Expected losses also include the expected loss from other risks, such as market risk and operational risk.

- *Taxes* are the expected amount of taxes imputed to the activity using the effective tax rate of the company.
- *Return on risk capital* is the return on the risk capital allocated to the activity. It is generally assumed that this risk capital is invested in risk-free securities, such as government bonds.
- *Transfers* correspond to transfer pricing mechanisms, primarily between the business unit and the treasury group, such as charging the business unit for any funding cost incurred by its activities and any cost of hedging interest rate and currency risks; it also includes overhead cost allocation from the head office.
- *Economic capital* is the sum of risk capital and strategic capital where

strategic risk capital = goodwill + burned-out capital

Our last bullet point deserves some explanation. Risk capital is the capital cushion that the bank must set aside to cover the worst-case loss (minus the expected loss) from market, credit, operational, and other risks, such as business risk and reputation risk, at the required confidence threshold (e.g., 99 percent). Risk capital is directly related to the value-at-risk calculation at the one-year time horizon and at the institution's required confidence level—all topics we've covered in earlier chapters of this book.

Strategic risk capital refers to the risk of significant investments about whose success and profitability there is high uncertainty. If the venture is not successful, then the firm will usually face a major write-off, and its reputation will be damaged. Current practice is to measure strategic risk capital as the sum of burned-out capital and goodwill. Burned-out capital refers to the idea that capital is spent on, say, the initial stages of starting up a business but the business may ultimately not be kicked off due to projected inferior risk-adjusted returns. It should be viewed as an allocation of capital to account for the risk of strategic failure of recent acquisitions or other strategic initiatives built organically. This capital is amortized over time as the risk of strategic failure dissipates. The goodwill element corresponds to the investment premium—i.e., the amount paid above the replacement value of the net assets (assets – liabilities) when acquiring a company. (Usually, the acquiring company is prepared to pay a premium above the fair value of the net assets because it places a high value on intangible assets that are not recorded on the target's balance sheet.) Goodwill is also depreciated over time.

Some banks also allocate risk capital for unused risk limits, because risk capacity that can be tapped at any moment by the business units represents a potentially costly facility (in terms of the adjustments to risk capital the firm as a whole might have to make if the credit line were drawn upon).

Figure 17-1 shows the linkage between the kind of risk loss distribution that we describe in many other chapters of this book and the RAROC calculation. We show both the expected loss—in this example, 15 basis points (bps)—and the worst-case loss, 165 bps, at the desired confidence level (in this example, 99 percent) for the loss distribution derived over a given horizon, say one year. The unexpected loss is, therefore, the difference between the total loss and the expected loss—that is, 150 bps at the 99 percent confidence level—over a one-year horizon. The unexpected loss corresponds to the risk capital allocated to the activity.

Now that we understand the trickiest part of the RAROC equation, unexpected loss, we can look at a practical example of how to plug numbers into the RAROC equation.

FIGURE 17-1 The RAROC Equation

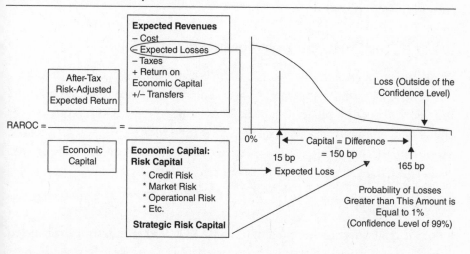

Let us assume that we want to identify the RAROC of a $1 billion corporate loan portfolio that offers a headline return of 9 percent. The bank has an operating direct cost of $9 million per annum and an effective tax rate of 30 percent. We'll assume that the portfolio is funded by $1 billion of retail deposits with a transfer priced interest charge of 6 percent. Risk analysis of the unexpected losses associated with the portfolio tells us that we need to set economic capital of around $75 million (i.e., 7.5 percent of the loan amount) against the portfolio. We know that this economic capital must be invested in risk-free securities, rather than being used to fund risky activities, and that the risk-free interest rate on government securities is 5 percent. The expected loss on this portfolio is assumed to be 1 percent per annum (i.e., $10 million).

If we ignore transfer price considerations, then the after-tax RAROC for this loan is:

$$\text{RAROC} = \frac{(90 - 9 - 60 - 10 + 3.75)(1 - 0.3)}{75} = 0.14 = 14\%$$

where $90 million is the expected revenue, $9 million is the operating cost, $60 million is the interest expense (6 percent of the $1 billion in borrowed funds), $10 million is the expected loss, and $3.75 million (= 0.05 × $75 million) is the return on economic capital.

The RAROC for this loan portfolio is 14 percent. This number can be interpreted as the annual after-tax expected rate of return on equity needed to support this loan portfolio.

RAROC for Performance Measurement

We should emphasize at this point that RAROC was first suggested as a tool for capital allocation on an anticipatory or ex ante basis. Hence, *expected* revenues and losses should be plugged into the numerator of the RAROC equation for capital budgeting purpose. When RAROC is used for ex post, or after the fact, performance evaluation, we can use realized revenues and realized losses, rather than expected revenues and losses, in our calculation.

RAROC Horizon

All of the quantities that we plug into the RAROC equation must be calculated on the basis of a particular time horizon, such as a one-year horizon or over the lifetime of a deal.[4] Box 17-3 discusses one problem that this brings up: how to harmonize the different time horizons used to measure credit, market, and operational risk. Practitioners usually adopt a one-year time horizon, as this corresponds to the business planning cycle and is also a reasonable approximation of the length of time it might take to recapitalize the company if it were to suffer a major unexpected loss.

BOX 17-3   RISK TYPES AND TIME HORIZONS

Risk capital can be characterized as the one-year value-at-risk exposure of the firm, at a confidence level consistent with the firm's target credit risk rating. But how does the time horizon in this characterization relate to the risk measurement approaches we describe in Chapter 7 for market risk, Chapter 10 for credit risk, and Chapter 14 for operational risk?

For credit risk, there is a straightforward equivalence between the one-year VaR produced by credit portfolio models, such as CreditMetrics or KMV, and risk capital. The same is also true for operational risk: most internal models used by institutions have a one-year horizon. Therefore, for both credit risk and operational risk, there is no need for any adjustment in the one-year VaR to determine risk capital.

However, this is not the case for market risk. For trading businesses, market risk is measured using only short-term horizons—one day for risk monitoring on a daily basis and 10 days for regulatory capital. So how do we translate a one-day risk measure into one-year risk capital attribution?

One approach might be to use what is commonly called the "square root of time" rule. That is, the risk analyst might approximate the one-year

---

[4] This chapter focuses on single-period RAROC models, while some large banks have moved to a multiperiod RAROC modeling approach in order to better measure RAROC over the life of long-running transactions and loans. However, major methodological issues are still unresolved when the risk of a transaction, such as a swap, or a portfolio changes substantially from one period to the next. In that case, which amount of economic capital should be allocated to the transaction or the portfolio? Allocating some average amount of capital would lead to undercapitalization and overcapitalization depending on the period.

VaR by multiplying the one-day VaR by the square root of the number of business days in one year—e.g., 252 days. If we did this, however, we'd be missing the point of risk capital. Risk capital is there to limit the risk of failure during a period of crisis, when the bank has suffered huge losses. As a worst-case scenario unfolds, the bank will naturally reduce its risk exposures in any way that it can. In the case of a proprietary trading desk, with highly liquid positions and no clients to service, this risk reduction can take place very quickly indeed. For other activities, risk can often be reduced only to a *core risk level* for the remainder of the year, defined as the minimum realistic size at which the business can be considered to be a going concern (i.e., can maintain its franchise).

Thus, to work out a meaningful one-year economic capital allocation, we need to analyze the business in question so that we can understand the *time to reduce* from the current risk position to the core risk level, which in turn reflects the relative liquidity of positions during adverse market conditions. Estimations of the time to reduce should not make the assumption that there will be a fire sale, but instead assume a relatively orderly unwinding of positions. This can take considerable time in some markets, as firms discovered to their cost in the 2007–2009 financial crisis.

Figure 17B-1 illustrates the calculation of risk capital when the core risk level is lower than the current risk position.

Across every bank, there are many other activities that must be allocated capital in a way that is sensitive to time horizons. For example, the bank should allocate capital to cover the risk of options that are embedded in many of its products. The option to prepay a mortgage is one obvious example, but there are many subtle twists on the risks generated by different types of products. For example, mortgage portfolios in Canada often incur commitment risks. These arise because the consumer automatically receives the lowest mortgage rate looking backward over a prescribed commitment period, as a function of the specific type of mortgage. In effect, the consumer has what derivatives practitioners call a "look-back option." The seriousness of the commitment risk is governed by the length of the commitment period; it represents the component that cannot be entirely eliminated by delta hedging (e.g., the basis risk between the wholesale

FIGURE 17B-1 Risk Capital Calculation for Market Risk

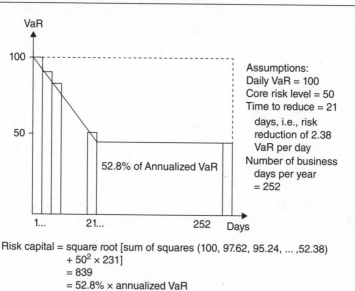

Risk capital = square root [sum of squares (100, 97.62, 95.24, ... ,52.38)
+ 50^2 × 231]
= 839
= 52.8% × annualized VaR
where annualized VaR = 100 × square root (252)

rates and the mortgage rate). All these considerations need to be taken into account in determining the risk capital needed to support a Canadian mortgage business.

However, the choice of a risk horizon for RAROC is somewhat arbitrary. One could choose to measure the volatility of risk and returns over a longer period of time, say 5 or 10 years, in order to capture the full effect of the business cycle in measuring risk. Calculating economic capital over a longer period of time does not necessarily increase capital, as the level of confidence in any firm's solvency that we require decreases as the time horizon is extended. If this seems surprising, consider the probability of default of an AA-rated firm to be around 3 basis points over a one-year period; while this probability of default naturally increases if we look at the same firm over a two-year or five-year period, this increase clearly does not affect the one-year credit rating of the firm. However, one of the practical challenges is that the risk and return data beyond one year may be of low quality.

Default Probabilities: Point-in-Time (PIT) vs. Through-the-Cycle (TTC)

A point-in-time (PIT) probability of default (PD), which is the approach of KMV and other economic/structural approaches, is reasonable for calculating near-term expected losses (EL) and for pricing financial instruments that are subject to credit risk. A through-the-cycle (TTC) PD, which is largely the approach taken by the rating agencies, is more reasonable for calculating economic capital, current profitability, and strategic decisions regarding products, geographies, and new business ventures.

The probability of a firm's staying in the same rating when it is assessed using a PIT approach is smaller than when it is assessed using a TTC approach. The TTC approach therefore reduces the volatility of economic capital, compared to PIT approaches. It is useful on a periodic basis to compare the impact of using PIT PD versus TTC PD in the RAROC calculation for both a normal part of the economic cycle and the worst part of the cycle.

Confidence Level

We mentioned earlier that the confidence level in the economic capital calculation should be consistent with the firm's target credit rating. For example, most banks today hope to obtain an AA credit rating from the agencies for their debt offerings, which implies a one-year probability of default of 3 to 5 basis points. This, in turn, corresponds to a confidence level in the range of 99.95 to 99.97 percent. We can think of this confidence level as the quantitative expression of the risk appetite of the firm.

Setting a lower confidence level may significantly reduce the amount of risk capital allocated to an activity, especially when the institution's risk profile is dominated by operational, credit, and settlement risks (for which large losses occur only with some rarity). Therefore, the choice of the confidence level can materially affect risk-adjusted performance measures and the resulting capital allocation decisions of the firm.

Hurdle Rate and Capital Budgeting Decision Rule

Most firms use a single hurdle rate for all business activities: the after-tax weighted-average cost of equity capital. Box 17-4 explains in more technical detail how this hurdle rate is calculated. The hurdle rate should be reset periodically, say every six months, or when it has changed by more than 10 percent.

BOX 17–4   TECHNICAL DISCUSSION: CALCULATING THE HURDLE RATE

Most firms use a single hurdle rate, h_{AT}, for all business activities, based on the after-tax weighted-average cost of equity capital:

$$h_{AT} = \frac{CE \times r_{CE} + PE \times r_{PE}}{CE + PE}$$

where CE and PE denote the market value of common equity and preferred equity, respectively, and r_{CE} and r_{PE} are the cost of common equity and preferred equity, respectively.

The cost of preferred equity is simply the yield on the firm's preferred shares. The cost of common equity is determined via a model such as the capital asset pricing model:

$$r_{CE} = r_f + \beta_{CE}(\overline{R}_M - r_f)$$

where r_f is the risk-free rate, $\overline{R}_M$ is the expected return on the market portfolio, and β_{CE} is the firm's common equity market beta.

When a firm is considering investing in a business or closing down an activity, it computes the after-tax RAROC for the business or activity and compares it to the firm's hurdle rate. In theory, the firm can then apply a simple decision rule:

- If the RAROC ratio is greater than the hurdle rate, the activity is deemed to add value to the firm.
- In the opposite case, the activity is deemed to destroy value for the firm and the activity should be closed down or the project rejected.

However, one can show that applying this simple rule can lead to a firm's accepting high-risk projects that will lower the value of the firm and rejecting low-risk projects that will increase the value of the firm.[5] High-risk projects,

---

[5]See Michel Crouhy, Stuart Turnbull, and Lee Wakeman, "Measuring Risk-Adjusted Performance," *Journal of Risk* 2(1), 1999, pp. 5–35.

such as oil exploration, are characterized by very volatile returns, while low-risk projects, such as properly risk-managed retail banking, produce steady revenues with low volatility.

To overcome this, we need to make an important adjustment to the RAROC calculation so that the systematic riskiness of the returns from a business activity is fully captured by the decision rule (see Box 17-5).

BOX 17-5   ADJUSTING RAROC FOR THE RISK OF RETURNS

Ideally, we would like to adjust the traditional RAROC calculation to obtain a RAROC measure that takes into account the systemic riskiness (beta risk, discussed in Chapter 5) of returns, and for which the hurdle rate (the critical benchmark above which a business adds value) is the same across all business lines. To correct the inherent limitations of the traditional RAROC measure, let's adjust the RAROC ratio as follows:

$$\text{Adjusted RAROC} \equiv \text{RAROC} - \beta_E(R_M - r_f)$$

where R_M is the expected rate of return on the market portfolio, r_f denotes the risk-free interest rate—say, the interest rate paid on three-month Treasury bills—and β_E is the beta of the equity of the firm. The new decision rule is:

Accept (reject) projects whose adjusted RAROC is greater (smaller) than r_f.

The risk adjustment, $\beta(R_M - r_f)$, is the excess return above the risk-free rate required to compensate the shareholders of the firm for the nondiversifiable systematic risk they bear when investing in the activity, assuming that the shareholders hold a well-diversified portfolio. When the returns are thus adjusted for risk, the hurdle rate becomes the risk-free rate.

Diversification and Risk Capital

The risk capital for a particular business unit within a larger firm is usually determined by viewing the business on a stand-alone basis, using the top-of-the-house hurdle rate that we discussed earlier. However, intuition suggests that the risk capital for the firm should be significantly less than the sum of the stand-alone risk capital of the individual business units, because the returns generated by the various businesses are unlikely to be perfectly correlated.[6]

Measuring the true level of this "diversification effect" is extremely problematic. As of today, there is no fully integrated VaR model that can produce the overall risk capital for a firm, taking into account all the correlation effects between market risk, credit risk, and operational risk across all the business units of a company. Instead, banks tend to adopt a bottom-up decentralized approach, under which distinct risk models are run for each portfolio or business unit.

For capital adequacy purposes, running these business-specific models at the confidence level targeted at the top of the house, for example 99.97 percent, produces an unnecessarily large amount of overall risk capital, precisely because it neglects diversification effects (across both risk types and business activities). It is therefore common practice to adjust for the diversification effects by lowering the confidence level used at the business level to, say, 99.5 percent or lower—an adjustment that is necessarily more of an educated guess than a strict risk calculation.

If this sounds unsatisfactory, we can at least put some boundaries around the problem. The aggregate VaR figure obtained by this approach should fall in between the two extreme cases of perfect correlation and zero correlation between risk types and across businesses. For example, ignoring business risk, reputation risk, and strategic risk, for illustrative purposes, suppose that we've calculated the risk capital for each type of risk as follows:

Market risk = \$200
Credit risk = \$700
Operational risk = \$300

Then aggregate risk capital at the top of the house is either

Simple summation of the three risks (perfect correlation) = \$1,200

or

Square root of the sum of squares of the three risks (zero correlation) = \$787

---

[6]It should be noted that from a purely economic point of view, disregarding strategic considerations, the decision to enter or exit a business activity should be based on the risk and return parameters of the single business activity.

We can say with some confidence, therefore, that any proposed approach for taking diversification effects into account should produce an overall VaR figure in the range of $787 to $1,200.

While the simple logic of our boundary setting makes sense, these boundaries are pretty wide! They also leave us with the reverse problem: how do we allocate any diversification benefit that we calculate for the business as a whole back to the business lines? The allocation of the diversification effect can be important for certain business decisions, such as determining the performance of each unit.

Logically, a business whose operating cash flows are strongly correlated with the earnings of the other activities in the firm should require more risk capital than a business with the same volatility whose earnings move in a countercyclical fashion. Bringing together countercyclical business lines produces stable earnings for the firm as a whole; the firm can then operate to the same target credit rating with less risk capital.

In truth, institutions continue to struggle with the problem of attributing capital back to business lines, and there are diverging views as to the appropriate approach. For the moment, as a practical solution, most institutions allocate the portfolio effect pro rata with the stand-alone risk capital.

Diversification effects also complicate matters *within* business units. Let's look at this and other issues in relation to an example business unit, BU, which comprises two activities, X and Y (Figure 17-2). When calculating the risk capital of the business unit, let's assume that the firm's risk analysts have taken into account all the diversification effects created by combining activities X and Y and that the risk capital for BU is $100. The complication starts when we try to allocate risk capital at the activity level within the business unit. There are three different measures of risk capital:

- *Stand-alone capital* is the capital used by an activity taken independently of the other activities in the same business unit—that is, risk capital calculated without any diversification benefits. In our example, the stand-alone capital for X is $60 and that for Y is $70. The sum of the stand-alone capitals of the individual constituents of the business unit is generally higher than the stand-alone risk capital of the business unit itself (it is equal only in the case of perfectly correlated activities X and Y).

FIGURE 17-2 Diversification Effect

Combination of Businesses	Economic Capital		Marginal Business	Marginal Economic Capital
X + Y	$100			
X	$60		X	$40
Y	$70		Y	$30
Diversification Effect	$30		Total	$70

- *Fully diversified capital* is the capital attributed to each activity X and Y, taking into account all diversification benefits from combining them under the same leadership. In our example, the overall portfolio effect is $30 ($60 + $70 − $100). Allocating the diversification effect is an issue here. Following our earlier discussion, we'll allocate the portfolio effect pro rata with the stand-alone risk capital, $30 × 60/130 = $14 for X and $30 × 70/130 = $16 for Y, so that the fully diversified risk capital becomes $46 for X and $54 for Y.

- *Marginal capital* is the additional capital required by an incremental deal, activity, or business. It takes into account the full benefit of diversification. In our example, the marginal risk capital for X (assuming that Y already exists) is $30 ($100 − $70), and the marginal risk capital for Y (assuming that X already exists) is $40 ($100 − $60). In the case where more than two activities are included in the business unit BU, marginal capital is calculated by subtracting the risk capital required for the BU without this business from the risk capital required for the full portfolio of businesses. Note that the summation of the marginal risk capital, $70 in our example, is less than the full risk capital of the BU.

As this example shows, the choice of capital measure depends on the desired objective. Fully diversified measures should be used for assessing the solvency of the firm and minimum risk pricing. Active portfolio management or business mix decisions, on the other hand, should be based on marginal risk capital, taking into account the benefit of full diversification. Finally, performance measurement should involve both perspectives: stand-alone risk capital for incentive compensation, and fully diversified risk capital to assess the extra performance generated by the diversification effects.

However, we must be cautious about how generous we are in attributing diversification benefits.[7] Correlations between risk factors drive the extent of the portfolio effect, and these correlations tend to vary over time. During market crises, in particular, correlations sometimes shift dramatically toward either 1 or −1, reducing or totally eliminating portfolio effects for a period of time.

RAROC in Practice

Economic capital is increasingly a key element in the assessment of business line performance, in the decision to exit or enter a business, and in the pricing of transactions. It also plays a critical role in the incentive compensation plan of the firm. Adjusting incentive compensation for risk in this way is important, because managers tend to align their performance to maximize whatever performance measures are imposed on them.

Needless to say, in firms in which RAROC has been implemented, business units often challenge the risk management function about the fairness of the amount of economic capital attributed to them. The usual complaint is that their economic capital attribution is too high (never that it is too low!). Another complaint is that economic capital attribution is sometimes too unstable—the numbers can move up and down in a way that is disconcerting for a business trying to hit a target.

The best way to defuse this debate is for the RAROC group to be transparent about the methodology used to assess risk and to institute forums where the issues related to the determination of economic capital can be debated and analyzed. From our own experience, the VaR methodologies for measuring market risk and credit risk that underpin RAROC calculations are generally well accepted by business units (although this is not yet true for operational risk). It's the setting of the parameters that feed into these models, and that drive the size of economic capital, that causes acrimony.

---

[7]For a discussion of the common economic capital aggregation techniques and how they capture diversification benefits, see *Range of Practices and Issues in Economic Capital Frameworks*, BIS, March 2009, pp. 24–31.

Here are a number of recommendations for implementing a RAROC system:

1. *Senior management commitment.* Given the strategic nature of the decisions steered by a RAROC system, the marching orders must come from the top management of the firm. Specifically, the CEO and his or her executive team should sponsor the implementation of a RAROC system and should be active in the diffusion, within the firm, of a new culture in which performance is measured in terms of contribution to shareholder value. The message to push down to the business lines is this: What counts is not how much income is generated, but how well the firm is compensated for the risks that it is taking on.

2. *Communication and education.* The RAROC group should be transparent and should explain the RAROC methodology not only to the business's heads but also to the business line managers and the CFO's office, in order to gain acceptance of the methodology throughout all the management layers of the firm.

3. *Ongoing consultation.* The firm should institute a forum such as a "parameter review group" that periodically reviews the key parameters that drive risk and economic capital. This group, composed of key representatives from the business units and the risk management function, will bring legitimacy to the capital allocation process. For credit risk, the parameters that should be reviewed include probabilities of default, credit migration frequencies, loss given default, and credit line usage given default. These parameters evolve over the business cycle and should be adjusted as more data become available. An important issue to settle is the choice of a historical period over which these parameters are calibrated—i.e., should this be the whole credit cycle (in order to produce stable risk capital numbers) or a shorter period of time to make capital more procyclical (capital goes down when the credit environment improves and goes up when it deteriorates)? For market risk, volatility and correlation parameters should be updated at least every month, using standard statistical techniques. Other key factors, such as the core risk level and "time to reduce" (see Box 17-3), should be reviewed on an annual basis. For operational risk, the risk measurement approach is currently more judgmental and, as such, more open to heated discussions!

4. *Maintaining the integrity of the process.* As with other risk calculations, the validity of RAROC numbers depends critically on the quality of the data about risk exposures and positions collected from the management systems (e.g., in a trading business, the front- and back-office systems). Only a rigorous process of data collection and centralization can ensure accurate risk and capital assessment. The same rigor should also be applied to the financial information needed to estimate the adjusted-return element of the RAROC equation. Data collection is probably the most daunting task in risk management. But the best recipe for failure in implementing a RAROC system is to base calculations on inaccurate and incomplete data. The RAROC group should be accountable for the integrity of the data collection process, the calculations, and the reporting process. The business units and the finance group should be accountable for the integrity of the specific data that they produce and feed into the RAROC system.

5. *Combine RAROC with qualitative factors.* Earlier in this chapter, we described a simple decision rule for project selection and capital attribution—i.e., accept projects where the RAROC is greater than the hurdle rate. In practice, other qualitative factors should be taken into consideration. All the business units should be assessed in the context of the two-dimensional strategic grid shown in Figure 17-3. The horizontal

FIGURE 17-3 Strategic Grid

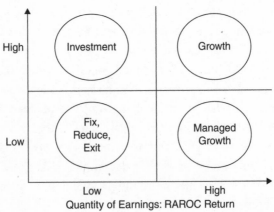

Quality of Earnings: Strategic Importance/Long-Term Growth Potential

axis of this figure corresponds to the RAROC return calculated on an ex ante basis. The vertical axis is a qualitative assessment of the quality of the earnings produced by the business units. This measure takes into consideration the strategic importance of the activity for the firm, the growth potential of the business, the sustainability and volatility of the earnings in the long run, and any synergies with other critical businesses in the firm. Priority in the allocation of balance sheet resources should be given to the businesses in the upper right quadrant. At the other extreme, the firm should try to exit, scale down, or fix the activities of businesses that fall into the lower left quadrant. The businesses in the category "managed growth," in the lower right quadrant, are high-return activities that have low strategic importance for the firm. In contrast, businesses in the category "investment," in the upper left quadrant, are currently low-return activities that have high growth potential and high strategic value for the firm.

6. *Put an active capital management process in place.* Balance sheet requests from the business units, such as economic capital, leverage ratio, liquidity ratios, and risk-weighted assets, should be channeled to the RAROC group every quarter. Limits are then set for economic capital, leverage ratio, liquidity ratios, and risk-weighted assets based on the kind of analysis we've discussed in this chapter. The treasury group often reviews limits to ensure that they are consistent with funding limits. This limit-setting process is a collaborative effort, with any disagreements about the amount of balance sheet resources attributed to a business put to arbitration by the senior executive team. Leverage ratios may restrain management from growing the bank beyond a certain level, but this in itself makes it more important that banks work every dollar of capital hard—and RAROC analysis is one way to do this.

Conclusion

RAROC systems, developed first by large financial institutions, are being implemented in smaller banks and other trading firms, such as energy trading companies. Wherever risk capital is an important concern, RAROC balances the divergent desires of the various external stakeholders, while also aligning them with the incentives of internal decision makers (Figure 17-4). When business units

FIGURE 17-4 How RAROC Balances the Desires of Various Stakeholders

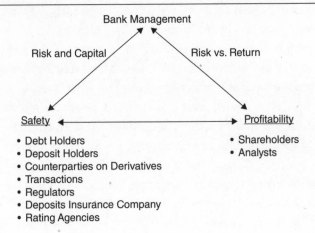

(or transactions) earn returns in excess of the hurdle rate, shareholder value is created, while the allocated risk capital indicates the amount of capital required to preserve the desired credit rating.

RAROC information allows senior managers to better understand where shareholder value is being created and where it is being destroyed. It promotes strategic planning, risk-adjusted profitability reporting and incentive compensation schemes, proactive allocation of resources, better management of concentration risk, and better product pricing.

Because RAROC is not just a common language of risk, but a quantitative technique, we can also think of a RAROC-based capital budgeting process as akin to an internal capital market in which businesses are competing with one another for scarce balance sheet resources—all with the objective of maximizing shareholder value. This makes RAROC a useful tool for capital allocation, both for banks and for nonbank corporations.

Epilogue

TRENDS IN RISK MANAGEMENT

In the first edition of *The Essentials of Risk Management*, written in 2005, we laid out 10 possible trends in risk management, ranging from "countrywide risk management" to "risk transparency." Here we offer a short discussion about the more interesting successes and failures of this piece of crystal ball gazing from the perspective of August 2013 and then, undeterred, offer five new or updated trends.

The Rights and Wrongs of Our Earlier Projections

We were nothing if not ambitious for risk management back in 2005. Our first item[1] discussed the need for countries to establish a unit to manage their own risk.[2] For example, countries with concentrations in industries might swap these exposures, or countries might issue bonds with interest rates related to that country's success in tax collection. Our concern with macro and sovereign risks proved prophetic, but we were much too optimistic. No country has yet appointed a "Country CRO" to focus on long-term risks. We would also now emphasize the need for the global regulatory community to coordinate country risk management in order to control systemic risk. We return to the country risk theme in the second part of this epilogue since the failure of

---

[1]Epilogue, p. 388.

[2]A paper by Robert Merton had prompted these thoughts.

many countries to adequately prepare for the financial crisis of 2007–2009 and the subsequent sovereign debt crises remains such a significant issue.

We were somewhat right in predicting that the insurance industry would move to a three-pillar Basel-like framework, though this proceeds slowly, led by the European Union. In addition, as we expected, the pensions industry has realized that it relies too heavily on returns from equity markets.

Since the last edition, we have been glad to see the spread of many proven risk management capabilities from the banking space into both the financial and the nonfinancial spaces, although the evolution of risk management capabilities has not moved along fast enough in the nonfinancial space. However, we have been glad to see practitioners in asset management (along with their regulators) become increasingly involved in evolving enterprise risk management (ERM) practices and techniques. We look forward to seeing risk management policies and methodologies further evolve in this segment of the financial industry, along the lines we discuss in the second part of this epilogue.

We made a hopeful plea back in 2005 for risk transparency, predicting that investors "will expect increasing disclosure of how much can be lost in extreme markets," with new techniques providing a more "objective and transparent assessment of very rare, but very extreme, forms of risk."[3] It took the expensive lessons of 2007–2009 for this to begin to come true (see Chapters 7 and 16), and, in truth, firms are still at the starting gate in terms of making extreme risks transparent to external observers.

We correctly forecast the growth in demand for "down to earth" (nonanalytic) education on the essentials of risk management, driven by a variety of stakeholders. Nevertheless, the tempo and quality of targeted training to the nonanalytic community needs to be improved and upgraded, as we argue in the second part of this epilogue. We also forecast that formal risk education would become a common component of corporate educational programs. We continue to see more and more academic courses on risk management and even specialized programs at the MBA level, training students to become risk managers.

We also noted the need for a more formalized set of generally accepted risk principles and standards,[4] and in the second part of this epilogue we make a related argument for risk management standards of practice (SOP). As we predicted,

---

[3]Epilogue, p. 392.

[4]Epilogue, p. 393.

the language and methodologies of risk are converging. Terms such as PD, LGD, and VaR are now commonly used in the fields of banking, insurance, and pension funds and also in nonbank industries and firms. The accounting standards boards are making huge efforts to expand the scope of fair values and to close the gap between accounting and economic profits. However, the problems along the way are tremendous, and hence the rules are being constantly revised and changed. Eventually, we expect that there will be a convergence between international (IFRS) and U.S. (GAAP) accounting standards and allow for a path toward a tighter convergence to economic profit.

Back in 2005, we thought that advances in risk measurement would "integrate risk management's classic statistically based approaches with nonclassic approaches such as expert judgment and structured ways to discuss plausible risk scenarios as well as causal relationships." And we hoped that volume-driven retail credit businesses would adopt new methodologies to "price their products more efficiently as a combined function of risk, cost, and behavioral factors."[5] However, on both counts, the infusion of new techniques did not occur at a sufficiently rapid pace. The financial community's risk measurement tools were too fragile and broke down in the stressed markets of 2007–2009.

The operational risk transfer techniques that we predicted also did not evolve as fast as we thought they would, though we continue to expect that the market for an operational risk transfer mechanism will eventually emerge. A prerequisite for developing these transfer techniques is introducing more successful ways to measure and price operational risk. Operational risk remains a collection of many diverse issues and events that don't have much in common, and a satisfactory advanced management approach (AMA) remains elusive.

Now for the additional five topics we think, or hope, will become key features of risk management advances over the next couple of decades.

New Trends and Old Trends Revisited

1. Country and Global Risk

In the first edition of the book, we discussed the issue of country risk and emphasized the need to manage risks on a macroeconomic and global level.

---

[5]Epilogue, pp. 394–395.

This need is even more apparent today after the global financial crisis, especially since multiple market risk and credit risk events turned out to be systemic risks. In particular, the Lehman Brothers default on September 15, 2008, had massive repercussions throughout the financial markets, not only in the United States but also on a global basis. Interbank lending froze for a few months, and credit spreads and measures of market volatility jumped to new records.

The Lehman Brothers collapse caught all market participants by surprise and showed that, in the United States, both the Federal Reserve and the Treasury were unprepared for such a massive collapse. It took time to realize that the essence of the problem is not necessarily the size of the failing institution (i.e., "too big to fail") but rather the interconnections of the failing institution with other market participants ("too connected to fail"). It is imperative that we map, at the international level, the legal interconnections among financial as well as nonfinancial corporations. As one first step, the Financial Stability Board (FSB) is initiating a standard Global Legal Entity Identifier System (GLEIS) for all financial transactions, which will also help in the construction of a tree of parent/subsidiary relationships to make organizational dependencies more transparent.

The crisis also highlighted the fact that strongly rated sovereigns can rapidly become insolvent: Iceland defaulted, while Greece hung on the verge of default until saved, for the time being, by special loans from the EU.

Another long-term aspect of country risk is the risk of shrinking economies due to the flat or negative growth rate of the population. In many developed economies, the natural growth rate of the population is below 1 percent, and in Spain, for example, it is negative. The long-run implications may be very severe, especially given that longevity is increasing. For example, in 10 to 20 years there will be fewer people working for each retired person. This may lead to the collapse of social security programs, downward pressures on productivity, and poor incentives for investing in human and physical capital—e.g., expenditure on research and development. We cannot take as given the rates of return on equities experienced in the twentieth century—often above 10 percent per annum—and defined benefit pension plans may suffer from huge deficits. Managing country risk in the long term means developing plans to cope with these fundamental risks, many of which affect the developed economies more than developing countries.

2. Capital Adequacy Requirements

Basel II and, especially, Basel III require banks to hold much more high quality capital (e.g., common equity) than the initial Accords of 1988 (for credit risk) and 1998 (for market risk), as we describe in Chapter 3. But the quantity of capital is not the only issue. Regulation has shifted its focus from ensuring the safety of small depositors or policyholders toward trying to mitigate systemic risk. Even the shadow banking system is now under increased supervision and may become as regulated as the rest of the financial system.

For example, before the global financial crisis, U.S. investment banks were not subject to Basel rules; only commercial banks held regulatory capital. This all changed after September 2008. As a result of this change in the goals of regulation, banks are now required to hold much more common equity capital than before. According to Basel III, these requirements will steadily increase and in the future may reach 15 percent of risk-weighted assets, compared to as low as 1 to 3 percent before the crisis (Chapter 3).

The Modigliani-Miller (M&M) theorems tell us that, in theory, capital structure is irrelevant to the value of a firm. One should be indifferent to common equity requirements because an increase in the equity ratio reduces the financial risk of the firm; as the risk falls, so does the expected cost of equity and debt. In theory, the effect of enhanced capital requirements should be to reduce the riskiness of all claim holders without changing the value of the enterprise. However, the M&M theorems are derived under an idealized environment of perfect capital markets and no taxation. In reality, therefore, banks are concerned that higher capital requirements will indeed hurt bank profitability. Profitability will probably fall, but, remembering M&M, there will also be a fall in the risk of equity.

Another related issue is the complexity and cost of calculating required equity when this is based on risk-weighted assets. Some argue that regulation has become unnecessarily complex and that it may be more efficient to require banks to hold regulatory capital as a function of simpler but smarter rules.[6] Others argue that it would be more transparent for banks to hold a flat percentage of their assets on their balance sheet in common equity, instead of using

---

[6]See Haldane, cited in Chapter 3, footnote 57.

risk-weighted assets as the basis for assigning regulatory capital.[7] This may save banks time and money related to IT investments and reporting, especially when compared to the advanced approaches for calculating Basel III capital requirements. In any case, the complex calculations on which Basel III is based depend on so many assumptions and approximations that they may stray some distance from the actual capital required by a bank to cover its risks (i.e., its economic capital).

3. Establishing Professional Risk Management Standards of Practice

We expect that in the near future the risk management industry will come up with drafts of professional risk management standards of practice (SOP). Most professionals, including accountants, actuaries, lawyers, and doctors, follow explicit standards of practice. However, the risk management community does not have a set of generally accepted risk management SOP for individuals working across the various risk management professions and industries.

SOP are the true sign of a profession. They would spell out "Do" and "Don't Do" commandments for those engaged in risk management. Importantly, they offer a degree of transparency and offer an easy way to say "No" for professionals who are asked to deviate from normal practices—e.g., when establishing a provision for loan losses in banking or a reserve in an insurance company. SOP also provide guidance to stakeholders (e.g., employers) and form the basis for professional opinions. They also offer a platform for any professional disciplinary process and should help to integrate regulatory requirements in most situations.

SOP also protect the professional. For example, if operational risk standards are established, ranging from vetting a mathematical model to selecting operational risk key performance indicators (KPI), then it will be much harder to successfully sue a risk manager.

If similar risk management SOP were adopted across professions and industries (e.g. banking, insurance, asset management) then the financial community would benefit. Further, risk management practitioners in one industry (such as banking) could more easily learn from the practices in another industry (such as insurance).

---

[7] See Admati and Hellwig, cited in Chapter 3, footnote 58.

A good starting point for formulating risk management SOP might be the existing actuarial SOP (ASOP),[8] which identify what the risk manager should consider, document, and disclose when performing a professional assignment.

Risk management SOP are also desirable (and doable) at a group level— e.g., risk SOP for the board, management committee, risk management unit, and business unit. However, the evolution of risk management SOP would need to proceed at a gradual pace in order to accommodate the inevitable concern among risk practitioners that adopting risk management SOP may inadvertently tie their hands.

4. Risk Control in Asset Management

New trading strategies, such as index/basket trading, and innovative traded products, such as ETFs (exchange-traded funds), have contributed to the major increase in correlations observed across equity markets—and also across different asset classes. Although correlations have declined in 2013, the average correlation in equity markets stands at about 50 to 60 percent, compared with about 25 to 30 percent some 30 years ago. As a result, traditional diversification techniques no longer provide a natural hedge to investors.

Correlation is not the only problem. The statistical literature (e.g., that focused on ARCH/GARCH) has shown that market returns and volatility are also not stationary. Many empirical studies show that periods of high and low volatility follow one another. Market events such as August 1998, or October 2008, can wipe out the cumulative returns of the most talented asset managers in a few days.

Asset managers have therefore proposed new quantitative approaches to combine asset allocation strategies with risk control techniques, and these represent one of the most interesting new frontiers of risk management.

What do these new quantitative approaches look like? One reasonable approach consists of four key steps. First, construct a risk index that includes several components, such as implied volatility (e.g., the VIX), credit spreads (e.g., the CDX Investment Grade for nonfinancials, the CDX High Yield), and

---

[8]See "Risk Evaluation in Enterprise Risk Management," Actuarial Standard of Practice No. 46, September 2012.

the yield curve dynamics of government bonds (e.g., the slope of the yield curve in the short and long end of the curve).

Second, different statistical techniques can be applied to identify various risk regimes that characterize the risk index. Over time, between two and four different risk regimes—from "high risk" to "quiet"—are likely to be identified, with some intermediate risk regimes.

Third, a selection of assets should be made that includes a risk-free asset— e.g., a money market fund. At its simplest, the portfolio allocation can be dynamically managed with only two assets—e.g., the S&P U.S. stock market index and a money market fund. However, broader worldwide asset selections may contain several equity indices (e.g., United States, Europe, and emerging markets), real estate indices, listed commodity indices, hedge fund indices, medium- and long-term bond indices, short-term bond indices, and a cash component.

Finally, for each regime, an asset allocation should be optimized—e.g., a highly aggressive allocation for the low-risk regime and a very conservative allocation, essentially cash, for the high-risk regime. The portfolio is then managed dynamically. When the statistical model indicates that a change of regime is likely to occur, with a high probability, then the allocation switches to the corresponding allocation. Highly liquid underlying assets should be selected in order to limit the cost of trading in the event of multiple regime changes.

5. Risk Education—for the Few or the Many?

In the last edition of the book, we noted the emergence of specialized risk educational programs, including dedicated graduate courses and formal certification programs, often aimed at those with the word "risk" in their job title. This has continued to snowball in the intervening years and should be applauded. However, it prompts a difficult question: "Why did the improvements in specialized risk education in the banking and risk management industries not do more to limit financial institution risk exposures during the 2007–2009 financial crisis?"

This is a slightly unfair question, partly because the initiatives we described were very young back in 2005 and the crisis was quickly upon them. It is also not possible to know whether the crisis outcome might have been even worse if some degree of risk education had not been in place.

But perhaps the real problem is that risk education is not getting to those who need it most. It is not reaching busy senior managers, or the boardroom, to anywhere near the necessary extent. It is not reaching the general public, either, who were probably taught more about the principles of risk and how financial institutions operate by the crisis itself than they ever have been in other ways.

Risk education in its broader sense is not reaching many origination staff, or those operating the infrastructure or collecting the data on which statistical risk management depends.

Furthermore, the content of existing programs has often been quite narrow—e.g., a focus on analytical methodologies and statistical techniques in a particular risk type, rather than an explanation of how risk types can interact in a given business model or the practical steps that might be taken to bring red flags to the attention of a senior manager.

If we educate only a "risk elite," then we will find that they struggle to make a difference when it really matters. In the immediate aftermath of a crisis, their opinions will be echoed and shored up by regulators and senior managers, but this will fade as the business cycle progresses and a "race to the bottom" in terms of risk standards gets under way. In the last cycle, the bullying and sidelining of those risk managers who spoke out was made easier by the fact that few others in the corporate culture were well versed in risk management concepts and attitudes.

One part of the solution must be to provide the intellectual ammunition to a large number of people without risk in their job title.

INDEX

ABOUT THE AUTHORS

Michel Crouhy, PhD

Dr. Michel Crouhy is head of Research & Development at NATIXIS Wholesale Bank, a subsidiary of Groupe BPCE. He is also the founder and chairman of the board of the NATIXIS Foundation for Quantitative Research. Formerly, Dr. Crouhy was senior vice president, in charge of Risk Analytics, Economic Capital Attribution and Operational Risk in the Risk Management Division at the Canadian Imperial Bank of Commerce.

Dr. Crouhy is a founding member of Professional Risk Managers' International Association (PRMIA) and a member of the PRMIA Blue Ribbon Panel. He is a member of the Research Advisory Council of the Global Risk Institute in Financial Services and of the Credit Committee of the International Association of Financial Engineers (IAFE). He is also associate editor of several academic journals and has been a visiting professor at the Wharton School of the University of Pennsylvania and at the University of California, Los Angeles.

He is the author and coauthor of several books, most recently *Risk Management* (McGraw-Hill, 2001) and *The Essentials of Risk Management* (McGraw-Hill, 2006), and has published extensively in academic journals in the areas of banking, options, risk management, and financial markets.

Dan Galai, PhD

Dr. Dan Galai is a principal and chairman of the board of Sigma Investment House, Ltd., and a cofounder of MutualArt Inc. He serves as a board member for several start-up companies and is a member of the Blue Ribbon Panel and regional codirector for Israel of the PRMIA.

Dr. Galai served as the dean of the School of Business Administration, the Hebrew University of Jerusalem (2009–2012) and is the Abe Gray Professor of Finance and Business Administration. He has been a visiting professor or scholar at INSEAD; the University of California, Los Angeles; IMF, Washington DC; and Melbourne Business School. He has also taught at the University of Chicago and University of California, Berkeley.

He coinvented the volatility index based on the prices of traded index options; served as a consultant for the Chicago Board Options Exchange (CBOE), the American Stock Exchange, and a number of major banks; and won the first Annual Pomeranz Prize for Excellence in options research, presented by the CBOE.

He has published numerous articles in leading business and finance journals and is a coauthor of *Risk Management* (McGraw-Hill, H 2006) and *The Essentials of Risk Management* (McGraw-Hill, 2006).

Robert Mark, PhD

Dr. Bob Mark is the founding partner of Black Diamond Risk Enterprises, which provides corporate governance, risk management consulting, risk software tools, and transaction services. He is the founding executive director of the MFE Program at the UCLA Anderson School of Management and serves on several boards (including the Milliman Risk Institute Advisory Board), as well as on Checkpoint's Investment Committee. Dr. Mark was awarded the Financial Risk Manager of the Year by GARP. He is cofounder of PRMIA, chair of PRMIA's Blue Ribbon Panel, and on the executive committee of the Board of PRMIA.

Prior to his current position, he was the CRO and corporate treasurer at CIBC; the partner in charge of the Financial Risk Management Consulting practice at C&L (now PwC); a managing director at Chemical Bank (now JPMC); and a senior officer at HSBC, where he headed the technical analysis trading group. He served on the boards of ISDA, Fields Institute for Research in Mathematical Sciences, and IBM's Deep Computing Institute, as well as chairperson of National Asset/Liability Management Association (NALMA).

Dr. Mark is an adjunct professor and coauthor of *Risk Management* (McGraw-Hill, 2000) and *The Essentials of Risk Management* (McGraw-Hill, 2006). He has published extensively in leading business and finance journals.